μC/TCP-IP™

The Embedded Protocol Stack

Christian Légaré

Micriμm
Press

Weston, FL 33326

Micriμm Press
1290 Weston Road, Suite 306
Weston, FL 33326
USA
www.micrium.com

Designations used by companies to distinguish their products are often claimed as trademarks. In all instances where Micriμm Press is aware of a trademark claim, the product name appears in initial capital letters, in all capital letters, or in accordance with the vendor's capitalization preference. Readers should contact the appropriate companies for more complete information on trademarks and trademark registrations. All trademarks and registered trademarks in this book are the property of their respective holders.

The programs and code examples in this book are presented for instructional value. The programs and examples have been carefully tested, but are not guaranteed to any particular purpose. The publisher does not offer any warranties and does not guarantee the accuracy, adequacy, or completeness of any information herein and is not responsible for any errors or omissions. The publisher assumes no liability for damages resulting from the use of the information in this book or for any infringement of the intellectual property rights of third parties that would result from the use of this information.

For bulk orders, please contact Micrium Press at: +1 954 217 2036

Micriμm
Press

ISBN: 978-1-935772-00-2

100-uC-TCPIP-TI-LM3S9B92-001

To my loving and caring wife, Nicole, our two daughters, Julie Maude and Valérie Michèle and our two grand children, Florence Sara and Olivier Alek. I have always encouraged them to follow their passion, I thank them for their support and comprehension for allowing me to follow mine.

Table of Contents

Part I: µC/TCP-IP: The Embedded Protocol Stack

Part II: TCP-IP and the Texas Instruments LM3S9B92

Table of Contents

Foreword to μC/TCP-IP by Rich Nass

Transmission Control Protocol/Internet Protocol, or more commonly known as TCP/IP. Designers take it for granted and end users have never heard of it, nor do they realize the vital role it plays in their lives. But it's the foundation of every networked device. More specifically, the Internet protocol suite is the set of communications protocols that implement the protocol stack on which the Internet and most commercial networks run. The two protocols within the TCP/IP protocol suite were also the first two networking protocols defined. Most historians will tell you that they were originally developed by the Department of Defense (DoD) in the mid 1970s.

If you follow the correct steps to implement the TCP/IP protocols, you can get past this stage of the design without any holdups. But make one wrong turn, and you could find yourself in some pretty muddy water.

There are lots of places where you can learn the ins and outs of the TCP/IP protocol. One good place is the Embedded Systems Conference (ESC). It was at an ESC quite a few years ago that I first met Christian Legare. Preceding the conference where we met, before I was involved with ESC, Christian raved about how popular his TCP/IP class was.

I decided to check it out Christian's class for myself, and truth be told, he was right, and for good reason. He held the attention of better than 50 engineers for the better part of a day. Not only that, I learned something myself. I fashioned myself as somewhat of a newbie before taking Christian's Embedding TCP/IP class, and was fairly astounded that Christian could teach the class at the differing levels of his students, almost simultaneously. Whether you were a newbie like me, or an expert like some of the other students, Christian held everyone's attention and made sure that every question was asked, answered, and understood.

I was quite pleased to see that Christian has taken a similar approach with this book. In fact, when I first saw the chapters and figures in the book, it all looked vaguely familiar. There is a definite correlation between how Christian teaches his popular class and how he has organized this book. To that I say, "Nice job." If you have a winning formula, stick with it.

It doesn't make a difference whether you're a seasoned pro (or at least think you're a pro), or you're a newbie like I was back when I first met Christian. The book starts off with the basics, explaining what TCP/IP is, why it's important, and why you need to understand it. It goes though the various elements of the protocol in a step-by-step process.

While the book explains the theory behind TCP/IP, that's not it's most useful feature—far from it. Where this book separates itself from similar books is in its ability to explain very complex concepts in a very simple manner.

In the first portion of the book, you'll learn about things like Ethernet technology and device drivers, IP connectivity, client and server architectures, and system network performance. The second portion goes into detail on a commercial product, µC/TCP-IP, which is Micrium's specific version of TCP/IP. It explains the technology through a host of sample applications.

Thank you Christian, for allowing me to precede your simple guide to embedded TCP/IP implementation. And to the readers, I hope you enjoy this book as much as I have.

Rich Nass, Director of Content/Media, EE Times Group

Preface

There are many sources that explain the TCP/IP protocol stack and how TCP/IP protocols work. These sources typically explain the protocol structure and interrelations. On occasion, authors actually provide code on the protocol stack implementation, however, these examples generally target systems with plenty of resources, which is not the case with resource-scarce embedded systems.

Semiconductor manufacturers generally produce microprocessors and microcontrollers for the embedded industry with a ROM/RAM ratio of 8:1 and, in some cases, 4:1. These systems are far from the heavyweight systems capable of running Unix, Linux or Windows since they often have access to kilobytes of code/data space as opposed to the megabytes available in larger environments.

Embedded systems often have real-time requirements that larger operating systems were not designed for. So, when used in an embedded system, a TCP/IP stack must certainly follow TCP/IP specifications, but with a watchful eye towards the resource constraints of the end product. Micrium kept these issues in mind when developing µC/TCP-IP for use in embedded systems. The µC/TCP-IP stack adheres to the same philosophy used for µC/OS-II and µC/OS-III as it pertains to the high quality of its code, its documentation, and ease of use.

It's no wonder that readers of the µC/OS-II and µC/OS-III books have been requesting an equivalent for TCP/IP.

WHAT IS DIFFERENT ABOUT THIS BOOK?

Early on, Micrium defined a set of coding standards, naming conventions and coding rules that allowed us to produce code that is clean, easy to read and maintain. These apply to all products developed at Micrium, and we thus believe that µC/TCP-IP contains the cleanest TCP/IP stack source code in the industry.

µC/TCP-IP is available in library format so you can experiment with a companion evaluation board (see Part II of this book). The full source code is provided to µC/TCP-IP licensees. With the Micrium source code, it is possible to obtain a basic understanding of how this series of complex data communications protocols work.

In this book, we take a practical approach to show you how a TCP/IP stack can be embedded in a product. The book provides multiple examples using µC/TCP-IP when specific topics are covered. Numerous illustrations are provided to help you understand the different concepts covered, as a diagram can often best represent the complexity of a network stack.

WHAT IS µC/TCP-IP?

Micrium was incorporated in 1999 to continue the development and provide support for µC/OS-II and now µC/OS-III, the Real-Time Kernel. The first version of the kernel was released in 1992. Since then, the company has received an ever-increasing number of requests for a TCP/IP stack.

In 2002, Micrium evaluated the TCP/IP stacks that were available to the embedded community. Unfortunately, we couldn't find anything that would properly complement µC/OS-II, concluding that Micrium would need to create a TCP/IP stack from the ground up. This was a huge undertaking and has taken us well over 15 man-years to develop.

The purpose of this huge undertaking was to create the best TCP/IP stack available for embedded applications. µC/TCP-IP is not an academic exercise but a world-class product which is currently used in applications worldwide.

Micrium's µC/TCP-IP assumes the use of a Real-Time Kernel, because a TCP/IP stack is highly event driven. Using a single-threaded environment would not properly satisfy most of the requirements found in resource-limited embedded systems that require TCP/IP. µC/TCP-IP was written in such a way that it would be fairly easy to adapt µC/TCP-IP to just nearly any Real-Time Kernel. Specifically, a file called **net_os.c** encapsulates the Application Programming Interface (API) calls allowing it to work equally well with μC/OS-II, μC/OS-III or other kernels.

μC/TCP-IP requires a driver for the network interface to be used in the system. Micrium provides drivers for the most popular Ethernet controllers. However, it is fairly easy to write a network interface controller driver for μC/TCP-IP if one is not available. More information on developing drivers is covered in Chapter 16, "Device Driver Implementation" on page 365.

μC/TCP-IP works best on 32-bit CPUs but may be used with high end 16-bit processors, as long as they have sufficient resources.

The footprint of μC/TCP-IP is relatively small considering that it completely implements the essential RFCs (Request For Comment, the protocol specifications) and supports private and public networks.

WHO IS THE INTENDED AUDIENCE?

Micrium's mission is to provide the best quality software to the embedded community. The use of commercial and industrial grade off-the-shelf software has proven to reduce a project development schedule by an average of three months.

Embedded software or hardware engineers developing a product and looking at using TCP/IP, will find the information they require to configure a TCP/IP stack for connectivity only and/or for performance.

μC/TCP-IP and μC/OS-III are also available as linkable object libraries to be used with the companion evaluation board available with this book.

You will need to contact Micrium to license μC/TCP-IP if you intend on using it in a commercial product. In other words, μC/TCP-IP is a licensed software. It is *not* free.

Students and teachers, however, can use the libraries and the evaluation board for academic purposes.

The embedded software version numbers used for this book are:

µC/TCP-IP	TCP-IP protocol stack	V2.10
µC/DHCPc	DHCP Client	V2.06
µC/HTTPs	HTTP Server	V1.91
µC/OS-III	Real-Time kernel	V3.01.2
µC/CPU	CPU abstraction layer	V1.31
µC/LIB	C library	V1.25

The required linkable libraries to run the examples presented in this book are downloaded from a webpage specifically dedicated to this book. This information is provided in Part II.

For licensed customers that have access to the complete µC/TCP-IP source code, it is always better to get the latest code version. If you are not currently under maintenance, please contact Micrium for update information.

ACKNOWLEDGEMENTS

First and foremost, I'd like to thank my loving and caring wife Nicole for her unconditional support, encouragement, understanding and patience. This book was a major project, and I could not have done it without her.

I also want to thank my long-term friend, colleague and partner, Jean J. Labrosse for his support and direction during this undertaking. Jean's feedback and comments improved this work immensely. It is truly a better result because of his efforts. Jean wrote a few books and often told me how exhausting such a task could be. I only have one thing to answer Jean: Now I know what you mean!

It is also very important to note that a good portion of this book builds on many chapters from the µC/TCP-IP user manual. This user manual was written by Jean J. Labrosse and the engineers who developed µC/TCP-IP. The TCP/IP team also played a huge role in reviewing the book to make sure that all the technical details were accurate.

I want to extend a special thank you to:

- Ian T Johns

- Fabiano Kovalski

- Samuel Richard

- Eric Shufro

A very special thanks to Carolyn Mathas who has done an awesome job editing and reviewing this huge project. Your patience and tenacity are greatly appreciated.

I would also like to thank the many fine people at Micrium who have tested the code, reviewed and formatted the book. In alphabetic order:

- Alexandre Portelance Autotte

- Jim Royal

- Freddy Torres

ABOUT THE AUTHOR

Christian Legare has a Master's degree in Electrical Engineering from the University of Sherbrooke, Quebec, Canada. In his 22 years in the telecom industry, he was involved as an executive in large organizations and start-ups, mainly in engineering and R&D. He was recently in charge of an Internet Protocol (IP) certification program at the International Institute of Telecom (IIT) in Montreal, Canada as their IP systems expert. Mr. Legare joined Micrium, as Vice-President in 2002, where he supervises the development of embedded communication modules, including TCP/IP. His substantial corporate and technical expertise further accelerated the company's rapid growth.

Introduction

The chapters in this book cover the theory of TCP/IP as applied to embedded systems. The topics include:

- TCP/IP technology

- How TCP/IP is applied to embedded systems via the Micrium μC/TCP-IP protocol stack

- The architecture and design of the μC/TCP-IP stack

There are many elements to consider when employing TCP/IP source code in a product design. Many of the following chapters provide the required information to use Micrium μC/TCP-IP.

HOW THE BOOK IS ORGANIZED

This book consists of two parts. Part I describes TCP/IP and its embedded implementation by Micrium, μC/TCP-IP. It is not tied to any specific CPU or network architecture. Here, you will learn about TCP/IP through μC/TCP-IP. Specifically, Ethernet technology and device drivers, IP connectivity, Client and Server architecture, system network performance, how to use μC/TCP-IP's API, how to configure μC/TCP-IP, and how to port μC/TCP-IP network driver to different network interfaces, are all topics covered.

Part II (beginning on page 1033) of this book delivers to the reader the experience of μC/TCP-IP through the use of world-class tools and step-by-step instruction. Ready-to-run μC/TCP-IP projects are provided and explained. The application examples use the evaluation board which is advertised with this book. The tools are all downloadable from the Micrium website for the code and networking tools as explained in Part II.

CONVENTIONS

There are a number of conventions in this book. First, notice that when a specific element in a figure is referenced, the element has a number next to it in parenthesis or in a circle. A description of this element follows the figure and in this case, the letter 'F' followed by the figure number, and then the number in parenthesis. For example, F3-4(2) indicates that this description refers to Figure 3-4 and the element (2) in that figure. This convention also applies to listings (starts with an 'L') and tables (starts with a 'T').

At Micrium, we pride ourselves in having the cleanest code in the industry. Examples of this are seen in this book. Jean Labrosse created and published a coding standard in 1992 that was published in the original µC/OS book. This standard has evolved over the years, but the spirit of the standard has been maintained throughout. The Micrium coding standard is available for download from the Micrium website, www.Micrium.com

One of the conventions used is that all functions, variables, macros and `#define` constants are prefixed by `Net` (which stands for Network) followed by the acronym of the module (e.g., `Buf`), and then the operation performed by the function. For example `NetBuf_Get()` indicates that the function belongs to the TCP/IP stack (µC/TCP-IP), that it is part of the Buffer Management services, and specifically that the function performs a `Get` operation. This allows all related functions to be grouped together in the reference manual, and makes those services intuitive to use.

CHAPTER CONTENTS

Figure 1-1 shows the layout and flow of Part I of the book. This diagram should be useful to understand the relationship between chapters. The first column on the left indicates chapters that should be read in order to understand µC/TCP-IP's structure. The second column relates to chapters that will help port µC/TCP-IP to different network interfaces. The third column shows chapters that are related to additional services provided by µC/TCP-IP and how to obtain valuable run-time and compile-time statistics from µC/TCP-IP. This is especially useful if developing a stack awareness plug-in for a debugger, or using µC/Probe. The top of the fourth column explains the µC/TCP-IP Application Programming Interface and configuration manuals. The middle of column four is a chapter with all the tips and tricks on configuring µC/TCP-IP. Finally, the bottom of the last column contains the Bibliography and the Licensing policy.

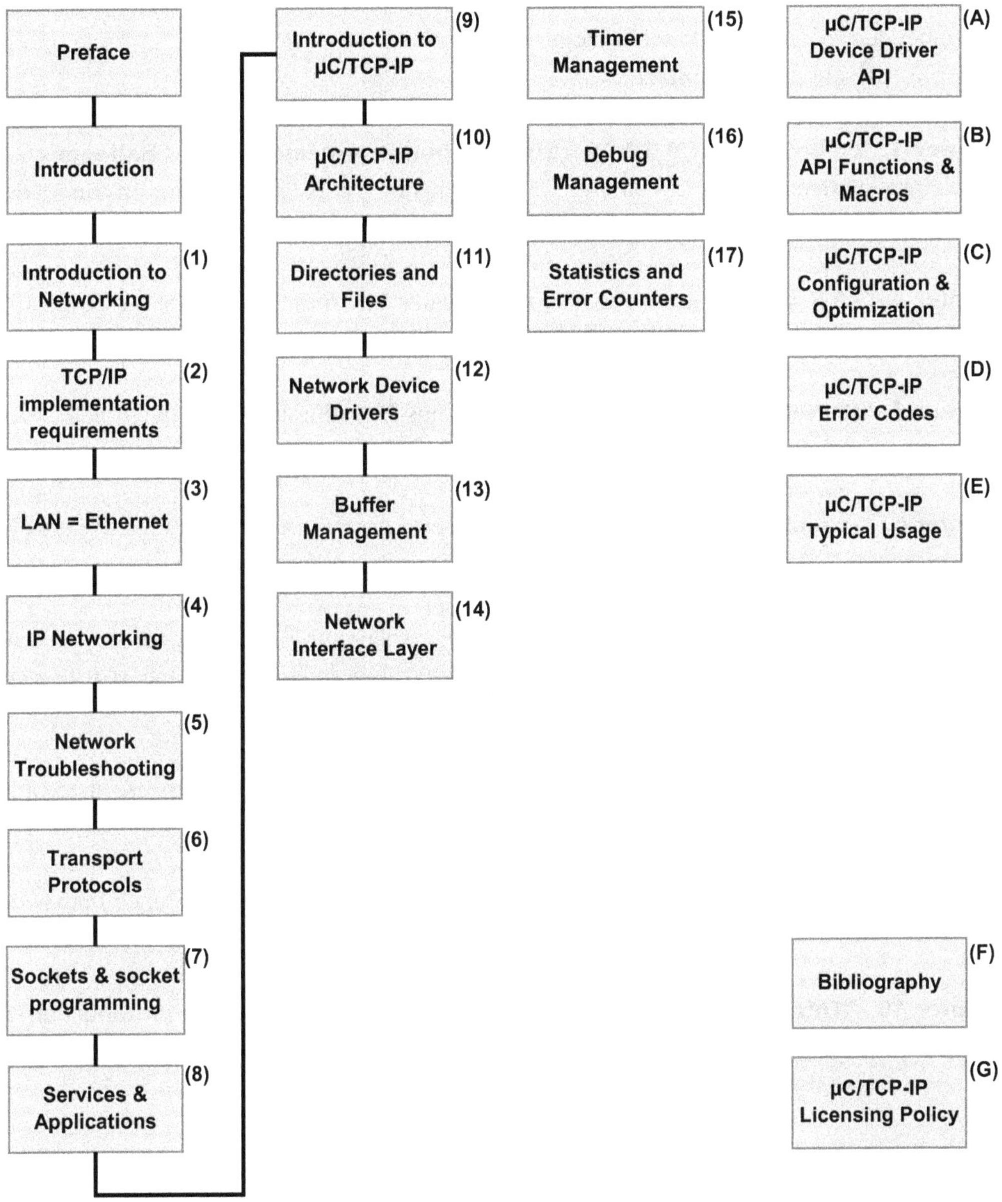

Preface	Introduction to µC/TCP-IP (9)	Timer Management (15)	µC/TCP-IP Device Driver API (A)
Introduction	µC/TCP-IP Architecture (10)	Debug Management (16)	µC/TCP-IP API Functions & Macros (B)
Introduction to Networking (1)	Directories and Files (11)	Statistics and Error Counters (17)	µC/TCP-IP Configuration & Optimization (C)
TCP/IP implementation requirements (2)	Network Device Drivers (12)		µC/TCP-IP Error Codes (D)
LAN = Ethernet (3)	Buffer Management (13)		µC/TCP-IP Typical Usage (E)
IP Networking (4)	Network Interface Layer (14)		
Network Troubleshooting (5)			
Transport Protocols (6)			
Sockets & socket programming (7)			Bibliography (F)
Services & Applications (8)			µC/TCP-IP Licensing Policy (G)

Figure 1-1 h µC/TCP-IP Book Layout

Chapter 2, "Introduction to Networking". This chapter explains networking concepts for embedded engineers. IP technology is introduced. The networking layering model concept is presented and explained.

Chapter 3, "Embedding TCP/IP: Working Through Implementation Challenges". In this chapter, understand the constraints for implementing a TCP/IP stack in an embedded system.

Chapter 4, "LAN = Ethernet". This chapter explains Ethernet, the ubiquitous Local Area Networking technology in use in most of our networks today.

Chapter 5, "IP Networking". This chapter explains IP technology, mainly IP addressing and how to configure a network interface for IP addresses.

Chapter 6, "Troubleshooting". In this chapter, learn how to troubleshoot an IP network, how to decode IP packets and how to test an IP network applications.

Chapter 7, "Transport Protocols". This chapter explains the most important protocols used in IP technology. A special attention is given to the configuration of the TCP/IP stack to optimize the embedded system networking performance.

Chapter 8, "Sockets". In this chapter, learn what a socket is and how to use it to build your application.

Chapter 9, "Services and Applications". This chapter explains the difference between a network service and a network application. The most important services are presented.

Chapter 10, "Introduction to µC/TCP-IP". This chapter is a short introduction to Micrium's TCP/IP protocol stack, µC/TCP-IP. Its attributes are covered and the application add-ons are also listed.

Chapter 11, "µC/TCP-IP Architecture". This chapter contains a simplified block diagram of the various different µC/TCP-IP modules and their relationships. The relationships are then explained.

Chapter 12, "Directories and Files". This chapter explains the directory structure and files needed to build a µC/TCP-IP-based application. Learn about the files that are needed, where they should be placed, which module does what, and more.

Chapter 13, "Getting Started with µC/TCP-IP". In this chapter, learn how to properly initialize and start a µC/TCP-IP based application for users that have access to the source code.

Chapter 14, "Network Interface Configuration". This chapter describes how to configure a network interface for µC/TCP-IP.

Chapter 15, "Network Board Support Package". This chapter describe the functions specific to a given evaluation board that are provided in a Board Support Package (BSP).

Chapter 16, "Device Driver Implementation". This chapter explains how to write a device driver for µC/TCP-IP. The configuration structure of the driver is presented.

Chapter 17, "Device Driver Validation". This chapter describes a tool called the Network Driver Integrated Tester (NDIT). The NDIT encapsulates many of the performance tests that you perform on your driver during development.

Chapter 18, "Socket Programming". This chapter discusses socket programming, data structures, and API functions calls.

Chapter 19, "Timer Management". This chapter covers the definition and usage of timers used to keep track of various network-related timeouts. Some protocols like TCP extensively use timers.

Chapter 20, "Debug Management". This chapter contains debug constants and functions that may be used by applications to determine network RAM usage, check run-time network resource usage, or check network error or fault conditions.

Chapter 21, "Statistics and Error Counters". This chapter presents how µC/TCP-IP maintains counters and statistics for a variety of expected, unexpected, and/or error conditions. The chapter also explain how to enable/disable these counters and statistics.

Appendix A, "µC/TCP-IP Ethernet Device Driver APIs". This appendix provides a reference to the µC/TCP-IP Device Driver API for Ethernet devices. Each of the user-accessible services re presented in alphabetical order.

Appendix B, "µC/TCP-IP Wireless Device Driver APIs". This appendix provides a reference to the µC/TCP-IP Device Driver API for wireless devices. Each of the user-accessible services re presented in alphabetical order.

Appendix C, "µC/TCP-IP API Reference". This appendix provides a reference to the µC/TCP-IP application programming interfaces (APIs) to functions or macros.

Appendix D, "µC/TCP-IP Configuration and Optimization". In this appendix, learn the µC/TCP-IP **#defines** found in an application's **net_cfg.h** and **app_cfg.h** files. These **#defines** allow configuration at compile time and allow the ROM and RAM footprints of µC/TCP-IP to be adjusted based the application requirements.

Appendix E, "µC/TCP-IP Error Codes". This appendix provides a brief explanation of µC/TCP-IP error codes defined in **net_err.h**.

Appendix F, "µC/TCP-IP Typical Usage". This appendix provides a brief explanation of µC/TCP-IP error codes defined in **net_err.h**.

Appendix G, "Bibliography".

Appendix H, "µC/TCP-IP Licensing Policy".

2

Introduction to Networking

Networking is a new concept for many embedded engineers. The goal of this book, therefore, is to provide a bridge that spans from basic concepts to how to add networking functionality to an embedded design. This chapter provides a quick introduction to networking protocols and then moves rapidly to a discussion on TCP/IP over Ethernet, today's preferred network technology combo with the widest usage in terms of the number of devices and applications.

Adding connectivity to an embedded system is now increasingly common, and networking options are numerous. While networking platforms include wireless (Bluetooth, ZigBee, 3G Cellular, Wi-Fi, etc...) and wired (TCP/IP over Ethernet, CAN, Modbus, Profinet, etc...), the networking technology that has revolutionized communications is the Internet Protocol (IP).

2-1 NETWORKING

The foundation of communications that we use on a daily basis is the Public Switched Telephone Network (PSTN), a global collection of interconnected public telephone networks. This circuit-switched network was the long standing fixed-line analog telephone system of the past. Today, analog has mostly given way to digital and the network includes both fixed-line telephones and mobile devices.

With PSTN, network resources are dedicated for the duration of the service, typically the length of a phone call. The same can be said for all real-time services such as voice and video. In a real-time service the data transmitted is inherently time sensitive.

In the following diagrams, elements composing the network between two connected devices are often represented as a cloud. Clouds are shown in subsequent diagrams throughout this book.

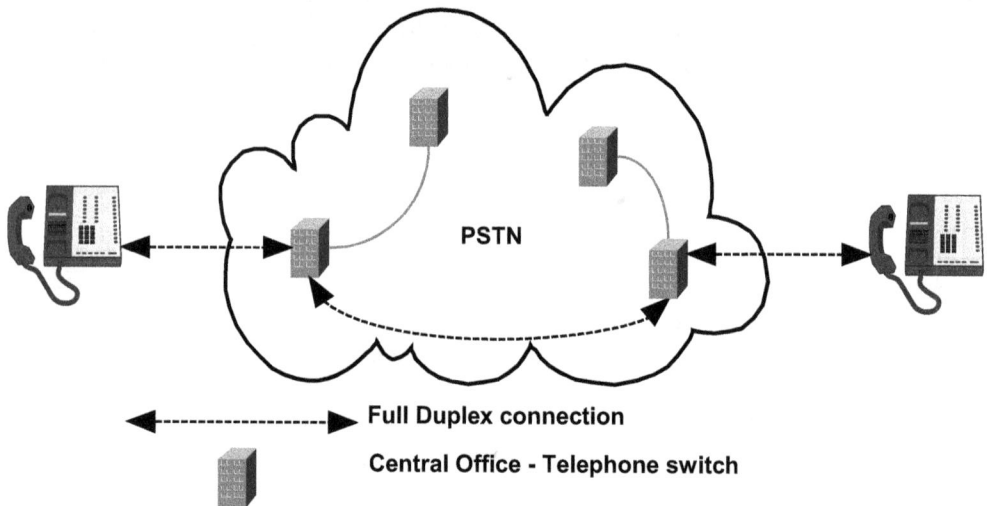

Full Duplex connection

Central Office - Telephone switch

Figure 2-1 **Public Switched Telephone Network (PSTN)**

Figure 2-1 represents a circuit-switched network such as the PSTN. In such a network, elements represented by telephone switches allocate network links between a source and destination, in both directions (full duplex), for the duration of the service. Once the circuit is established, switches do not intervene until it is time to dismantle the circuit (one of the parties hangs up). In this situation, the switches are aware of the connection, however the terminals are not.

With data services, when data is transferred, data is chopped into small entities called packets. Network resources are used only when a packet is transferred between a source and destination. This leads to improved network asset utilization as the same equipment can be used to forward packets between different sources and destinations. A permanent connection is not required since the transfer is not time sensitive. if we receive an e-mail a fraction of a second late, nobody will complain!

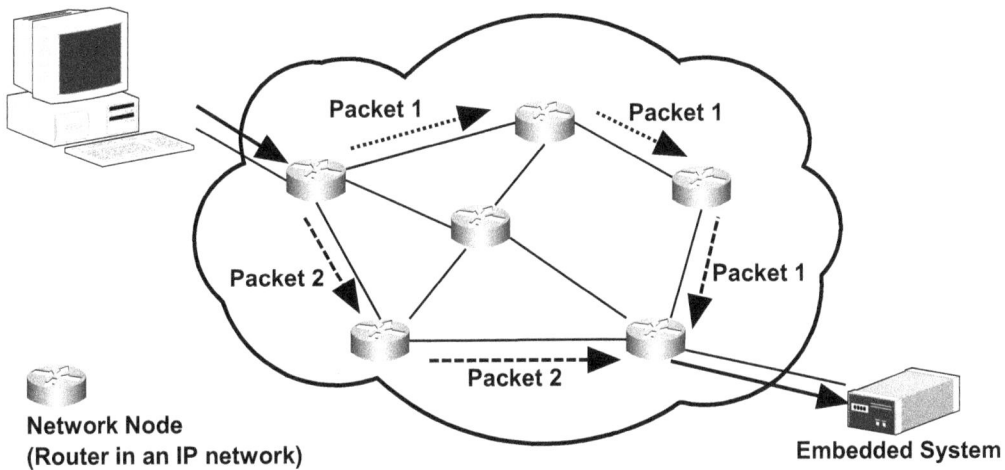

Figure 2-2 **Packet Switched Network**

Figure 2-2 represents a packet-switched network wherein terminals are the extremities of the network connections and are referred to as either hosts or devices. The network elements forwarding packets from the source to a destination are called nodes. Packets are forwarded on a node-to-node basis, one hop at a time, a hop being the path segment between two nodes. Each packet is processed by each node on the path between the source and the destination. In an IP network nodes are called routers.

IP networks are not limited to use by computers (PCs) and mainframes. In fact, increasingly more networks are formed with embedded systems: factory floor automation, household and office devices including heating systems, ovens, washing machines, fridges, drink dispensers, security alarms, Personal Digital Video Recorder, intelligent set-top-boxes, audio equipment, and more. In fact, it is easy to imagine that your refrigerator, washing machine, dryer or toaster will be Internet enabled in the not so distant future.

In Figure 2-2, packets travel in one direction, from the PC workstation to the embedded system. In a full-duplex exchange, two paths are used and processing is performed in both directions. The same processing is required for packets travelling from the embedded system to a PC workstation. An important aspect of packet switching is that packets may take different paths from a source to a destination. In this example, it is possible for packet #2 to arrive before packet #1.

In a packet-switched network, nodes are very busy since the same processing is required for every packet transmitted from the source to the destination. However, the nodes are not aware of the connection, only the terminals (hosts and devices) are.

Modern networks extensively use packet switching technology. The main characteristics of a packet-switching network include:

- Networks transfer packets using store-and-forward

- Packets have a maximum length

- Long messages are broken into multiple packets (i.e., fragmentation)

- Source and destination addresses are stored in every packet

Packet Switching technology uses packet switches (computers) and digital transmission lines. It features no per-call connections. The network resources are shared by all communications. It also uses a store-and-forward mechanism referred to as routing in IP technology.

Store-and Forward:

- Stores each arriving packet

- Reads the destination address in the packet

- Consults a routing table to determine the next hop

- Forwards the packet

At the end of the 1990's, for the first time, data service bandwidth began to exceed real-time services bandwidth. This trend created a dilemma for telecom operators. They were forced to decide whether to make capital expenditures on PSTN equipment to provide both real-time and data services when the latter represented the majority of the traffic. If not, how could they monetize their investment on the data-service side?

Today, most networking-related capital expenditure is spent on equipment supporting data services. Two technologies receiving the majority of this investment are Ethernet and Internet Protocol (IP), which are increasingly evident in embedded systems. This investment ensures that, in the near future, our phone services will run exclusively on Voice over IP (VoIP) and our television over IP networks (IPTV). Voice, video and all real-time services with time-sensitive data will depend upon IP technology.

The Internet Protocol is rapidly becoming the ubiquitous network technology. The related protocol stack used by a myriad of devices is called a *TCP/IP stack*.

2-2 WHAT IS A TCP/IP STACK?

The *Internet Protocol suite* (also referred to as network protocol suite) is the set of communication protocols upon which the Internet and most commercial networks run. Also called *TCP/IP stack*, it is named after two of the most important protocols that comprise it: the Transmission Control Protocol (TCP) and Internet Protocol (IP). While they are important networking protocols, they are certainly not the only ones.

2-3 THE OSI SEVEN-LAYER MODEL

The Internet Protocol suite can be viewed as a set of layers. Each layer solves a set of requirements involving the transmission of data, and provides a well-defined service to upper-layer protocols by implementing services provided by lower layers.

Upper-layer protocols are logically closer to the user and deal with abstract data while lower-layer protocols translate data into a form that can be physically transmitted. Each layer acts as a "black box" containing predefined inputs, outputs, and internal processes.

For clarity regarding layers, we define:

Layer: A grouping of related communications functions

- Each layer provides services to the layers above

- Layering introduces modularity and simplifies design and modification

Protocol: Rules governing how entities in a layer collaborate to deliver desired services

- There may be several protocols in each layer

Application: That which is accessed by the end user to perform a function. The application layer is built on top of a "stack" of protocols.

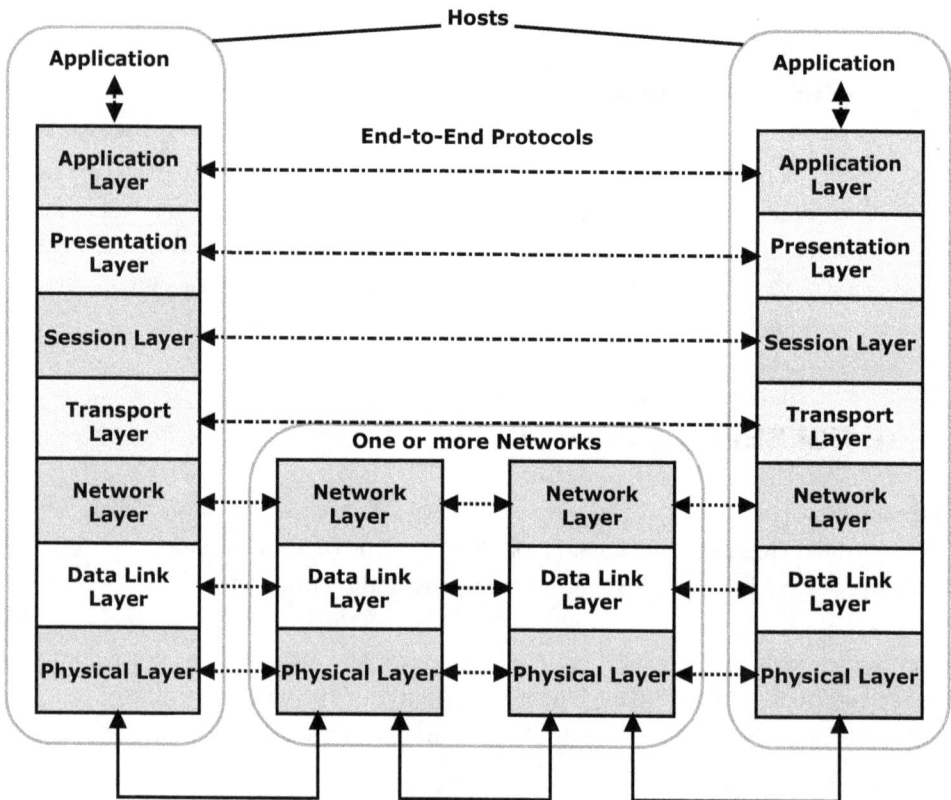

Figure 2-3 **OSI Seven-Layer Model**

The International Organization for Standardization (ISO) developed an Open Systems Interconnection (OSI) seven-layer model in 1977. In Figure 2-3, OSI Reference Model, two major components exist: an abstract model of networking, and a set of specific protocols. Hosts are separate devices connected on the same or different network, anywhere in the world. There is no notion of "distance" in the diagram. Information travels vertically in each host from top to bottom for the transmitting host and from bottom to top for the receiving host. The OSI model provides a fixed set of seven layers that can be roughly compared to the IP suite.

Conceptually, two instances at one layer are connected by a horizontal protocol connection on that layer. For example, a layer that provides data integrity supplies the mechanism needed by applications above it, while it calls the next lower layer to send and receive packets that make up the communication. This is represented by the dotted line "End-to-End Protocol."

In IP technology we group the last three layers (Session, Presentation and Application) into a single layer, and refer to this newly created single layer as the Application layer. This layer provides to various programs a means to access interconnectivity functions on lower layers, facilitating data exchange.

The Session layer controls the dialogues (sessions) between computers and establishes, manages, and terminates connections between local and remote applications. Sessions were predominant in the past with mainframe and minicomputers. However, with the arrival of IP networking, this protocol has been replaced with a new connection mechanism between the application and the TCP/IP stack. Refer to the discussion on sockets in Chapter 8, on page 209.

The Presentation layer orchestrates the handling of the data exchanged including translation, encryption, and compression, as well as data format functions. Today, there is global acceptance of the ASCII character set transferred in bytes, and such new global encoding standards as HTML or XML, simplify the Presentation layer. This layer is the main interface for the user(s) to interact first with the application and ultimately the network.

Strictly speaking, while Session and Presentation layers exist in the TCP/IP stack, they are less often used other than older protocols. For example at the Presentation Layer we find:

- Multipurpose Internet Mail Extensions (MIME) for e-mail encoding (see the section "Simple Mail Transfer Protocol (SMTP)" on page 242).

- eXternal Data Representation (XDR)

- Secure Socket Layer (SSL)

- Transport Layer Secure (TLS)

And, at the Session Layer, we find:

- Named Pipes

- Network Basic Input/Output System (NetBIOS)

- Session Announcement Protocol (SAP)

Examples of application layer protocols include Telnet, File Transfer Protocol (FTP), Simple Mail Transfer Protocol (SMTP), and Hypertext Transfer Protocol (HTTP).

2-4 APPLYING THE OSI MODEL TO TCP/IP

When working with TCP/IP, the model is simplified to four layers plus the physical layer as shown in Figure 2-4. This figure depicts the encapsulation process with protocol overhead down to Ethernet, and the proper naming for each encapsulation level throughout the layers.

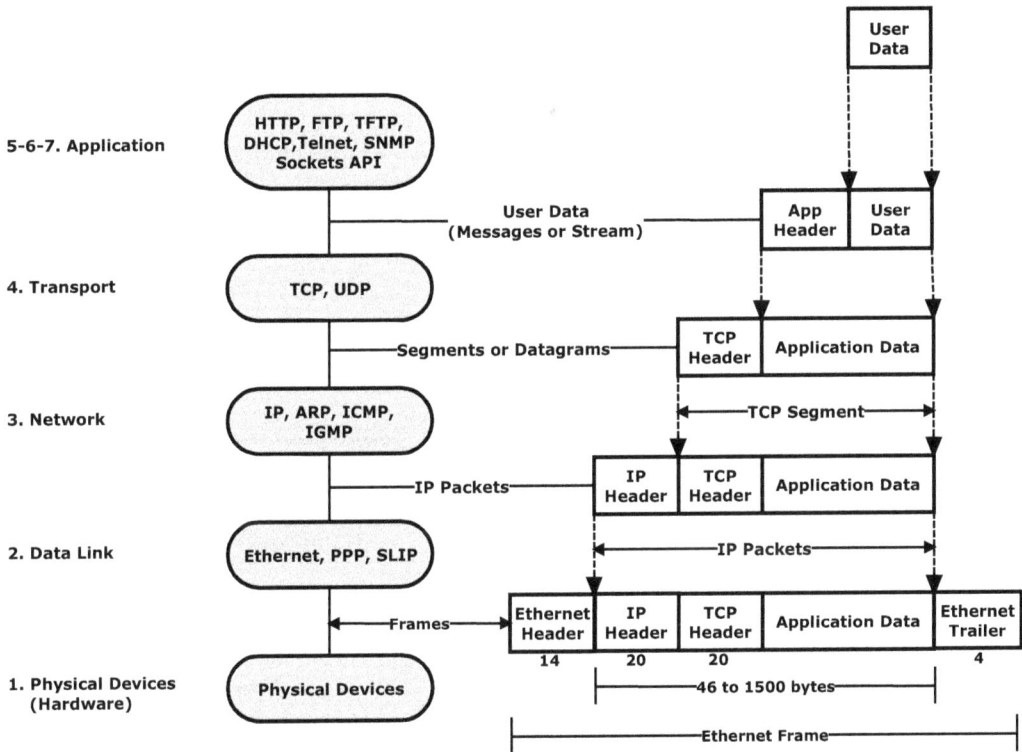

						User Data
5-6-7. Application	HTTP, FTP, TFTP, DHCP,Telnet, SNMP Sockets API					
		User Data (Messages or Stream)		App Header	User Data	
4. Transport	TCP, UDP					
		Segments or Datagrams	TCP Header	Application Data		
3. Network	IP, ARP, ICMP, IGMP			←————TCP Segment————→		
		IP Packets	IP Header	TCP Header	Application Data	
2. Data Link	Ethernet, PPP, SLIP			←————IP Packets————→		
		Frames	Ethernet Header	IP Header	TCP Header	Application Data	Ethernet Trailer
			14	20	20		4
1. Physical Devices (Hardware)	Physical Devices			←——46 to 1500 bytes——→		
			←————————Ethernet Frame————————→			

Figure 2-4 **TCP/IP Layered Model**

Ethernet is the ubiquitous Data Link layer, and will therefore be used in all of the examples provided in this book.

Protocols require that select control information be inserted into headers and trailers. Using packet-switching technology, data generated by the application is passed to the transport layer and is encapsulated with the addition of a header to the application payload, and so on, for every layer in the model.

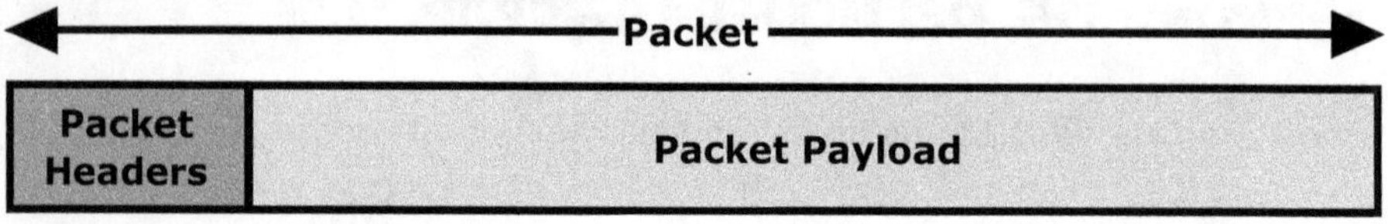

Figure 2-5 **Packet Encapsulation**

Figure 2-5 demonstrates the encapsulation mechanism when data travels from one layer to the next layer.

As information travels up and down the stack, data is encapsulated and de-capsulated in various structures (adding or removing a specific header). These structures are often referred to as packets (TCP packet, IP packet, Ethernet packet). However, there is a specific term for every type of packaging or encapsulation:

Layer Name	Layer Number	Encapsulation terminology
Data Link	2	Frame (Ethernet)
Network	3	Packet
Transport	4	TCP - Segment UDP - Datagram
Application	5-6-7	Data

Table 2-1 **Encapsulation Types**

The packet-wrapping mechanism described above is used extensively by the IP protocol suite. Every layer adds its header, and in some cases, trailer. The wrapping of information with this overhead information creates new data types (datagrams, segments, packets, frames).

Specifications for the TCP/IP protocol stack are managed by the Internet Engineering Task Force (IETF), an open standards organization. The IETF describes methods, behaviors, research, or innovations applicable to TCP/IP and Internet Protocol suite in Request for Comments (RFCs). A complete list of RFCs is available at http://www.faqs.org/rfcs/.

Micrium's µC/TCP-IP design follows the specifications contained in the RFCs.

```
/*
*********************************************************************************
*                       NetARP_CfgCacheTimeout()
*
* Description : Configure ARP cache timeout from ARP Cache List.
*
* Argument(s) : timeout_sec   Desired value for ARP cache timeout (in seconds).
*
* Return(s)   : DEF_OK,  ARP cache timeout configured.
*
*               DEF_FAIL, otherwise.
*
* Caller(s)   : Net_InitDflt(),
*               Application.
*
*               This function is a network protocol suite application interface (API)
*               function & MAY becalled by application function(s).
*
* Note(s)     : (1) RFC #1122, Section 2.3.2.1 states that "an implementation of the
*               Address Resolution Protocol (ARP) ... MUST provide a mechanism to
*               flush out-of-date cache entries. If this mechanism involves a
*               timeout, it SHOULD be possible to configure the timeout value".
*
*               (2) Timeout in seconds converted to 'NET_TMR_TICK' ticks in order to
*               pre-compute initial timeout value in 'NET_TMR_TICK' ticks.
*
*               (3) 'NetARP_CacheTimeout' variables MUST ALWAYS be accessed exclusively
*               in critical sections.
*********************************************************************************
*/
```

Listing 2-1 **RFC Reference in µC/TCP-IP Function Heading**

Every relevant RFC is implemented to the functionality provided by µC/TCP-IP. When an RFC section or the complete RFC is implemented, a note similar to Note (1) in Listing 2-1 is created. Listing 2-1 is an example from the µC/TCP-IP ARP module (**net_arp.c**).

RFCs for current IP technology are very stable. Work on newer standards continues to progress, especially involving issues of security.

When the IP protocol suite was developed, an important technical assumption was made. At the end of the 1970's, electrical transmission susceptible to electromagnetic interference was predominant, and fiber optics was only operating in R&D labs. Therefore, based on using electrical transmission systems, Layer-2 protocols were extremely complex given the amount of error checking and error corrections that needed to be performed.

The assumption made by IP designers was that the transmission network over which IP would operate would be reliable. They were correct when IP became the network protocol driving the global public Internet and later corporate networks, fiber optics were well deployed. Today, as a result, Layer-2 protocols are less complex.

In the IP protocol suite, data error detection and correction, other than simple Cyclic Redundancy Check (CRC), is the responsibility of protocols higher than Layer 2, specifically those at Layer 4 (see Chapter 7, "Transport Protocols" on page 169).

Now, however, with the rapid market penetration rate of new wireless technologies, the Layer 2 reliability assumption is no longer valid. Wireless transmission systems are highly susceptible to interference, resulting in higher bit-error rates. The IP protocol suite, especially Layer-2 protocols, must address this issue. There are a number of recommendations and improvements to the standard TCP/IP stack. For example, RFC 2018, selective acknowledgments improve performance when multiple packets are lost from one window of data (see Chapter 7, "Transport Protocols" on page 169 and other RFCs).

It seems that nearly every protocol ending in "P" is part of the IP protocol suite (a slight exaggeration, but not far from the truth). Let's look at many of these protocols as we climb from the bottom of the stack (Layer 1), the Physical layer, toward the top of the stack (Layers 5-6-7), the Application layer.

2-5 THE STARTING POINT

General literature on TCP/IP programming or usage typically explains how the stack works and how the protocol layers operate by taking the reader from the application or user data, and moving down to the physical layer. The programmer's point of view, from the application to the network interface, always assumes that the hardware is known and stable. For a programmer, that may be the case, but for an embedded engineer, the first challenge is to get the physical layer to work.

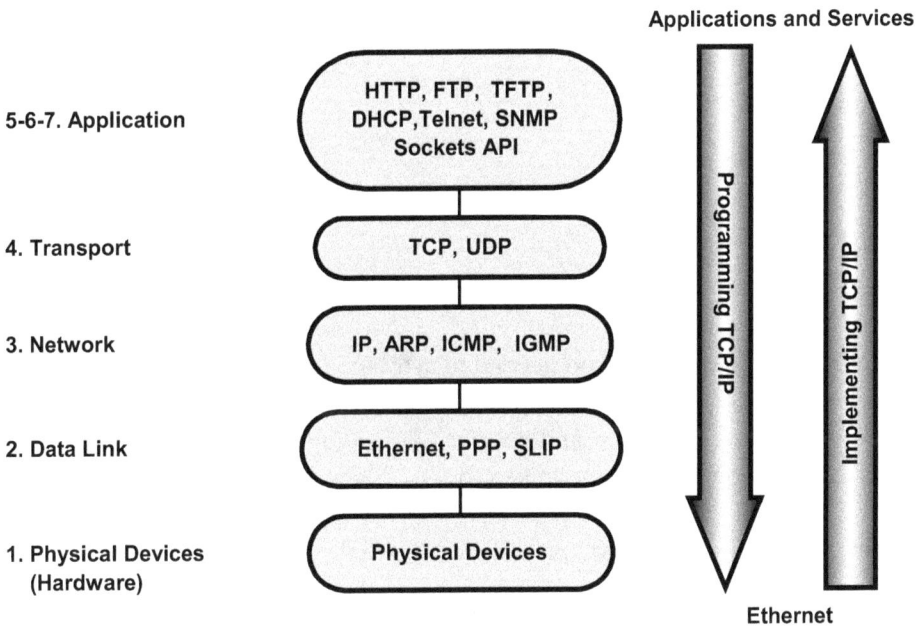

Figure 2-6 **The Starting Point**

When embedding a TCP/IP stack, the embedded engineer begins with the physical layer, since most of the time, the hardware represents a new design. First, the designer must define the Local Area Network (LAN) technology to be used. Then, the Network Interface Card (NIC) or Data Link Controller (DLC) driver must be implemented and tested.

Only when frames are transmitted and received properly by the embedded device can the embedded engineer begin to move up the stack and finally test that the data can be transmitted and received by applications. Since this book follows the point of view of the embedded engineer, the TCP/IP stack is presented from the bottom up taking an implementation point of view instead of the traditional programming top-down approach.

2-6 LAYER 1 - PHYSICAL

The Physical layer handles the transmission of bits over physical circuits. It is best described by its mechanical physical parameters, and includes such elements as:

- Cable

- Connectors

- Plugs

- Pins

And, its bit-processing techniques:

- Signaling method

- Voltage levels

- Bit times

The Physical layer defines the method needed to activate, maintain, and deactivate the link.

Technologies that use the medium and specify the method for clocking, synchronization and bit encoding include, but are not limited to:

- Ethernet: Category 5 twisted pair cable, coaxial, fiber (defined by IEEE 802 specifications)

- Wireless: frequency, modulation (Bluetooth radio, Wi-Fi IEEE 802.11, etc.)

- Digital subscriber loop (DSL) provided by the telephone operator to transport high-speed Internet on the phone line between the Central Office and the customer. This equipment is vendor specific.

- Coaxial cable (cable modem) provided by the cable operator to transport high-speed internet on the coaxial cable between the network head and the customer.

The physical layer is the hardware you can hold in your hands, the network interface card, or Data-Link controller on a board. Anything located above this layer is software.

2-7 LAYER 2 – DATA LINK

The Data-Link layer handles the packaging of bits into frames and their transmission or reception over physical circuits. It is at this layer that most error detection and correction is performed.

This layer supports various transmission protocols, including:

- Asynchronous Transfer Mode (ATM)

- Frame Relay

- Ethernet

- Token Ring

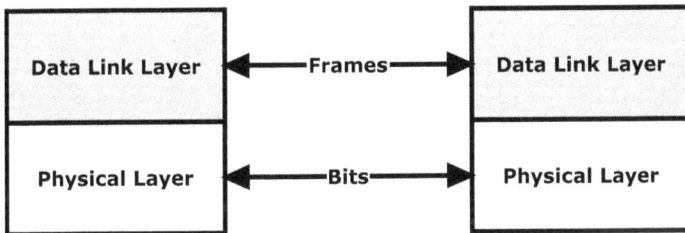

Figure 2-7 **Data Link**

The first task of the embedded engineer is to develop and test the software that drives the NIC (the network driver) used in the Data-Link Layer in Figure 2-7 (see Chapter 14, "Network Interface Configuration" on page 303 and Chapter 16, "Device Driver Implementation" on page 365).

Although a few technologies exist at this layer, Ethernet, as a Layer-2 protocol eclipses all others.

Over 95 percent of all data traffic originates and terminates on Ethernet ports according to Infonetics Research, an international market research firm specializing in data networking and telecom. Rarely has a technology proved to be so simple, flexible, cost-effective, and pervasive.

For embedded systems, Ethernet is also the most preferred Layer-2 technology (see Chapter 4, "LAN = Ethernet" on page 89). The following section on Ethernet provides a short introduction.

2-7-1 ETHERNET

Given the prevalence of Ethernet technology, there is an almost incestuous relationship between IP and Ethernet. Ethernet's meteoric rise is based on the fact that Ethernet:

- Is a simple yet robust technology

- Is a non-proprietary open standard

- Is cost effective per host

- Is well understood

- Has a range of speeds

    - 10, 100, 1000 Mbps (Megabits per second), 24 Gbps (Gigabits per second) and more…

- Runs on copper, coax, fiber, and wireless interfaces

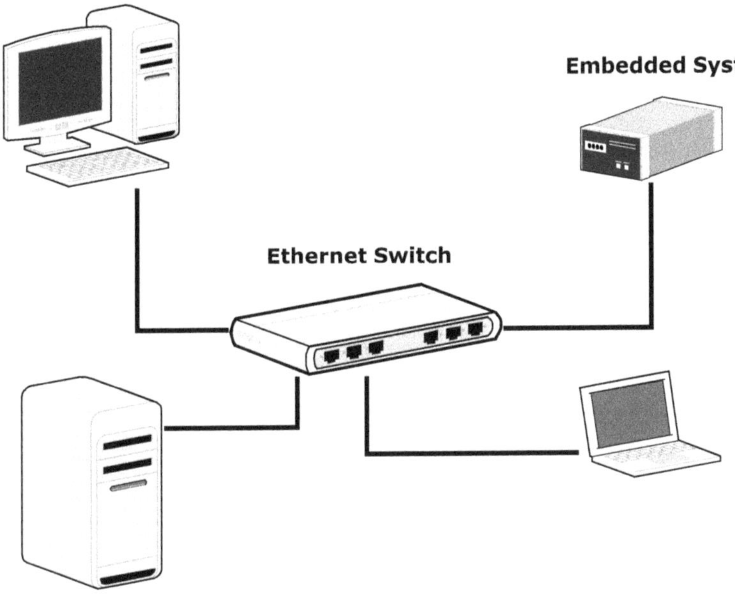

Figure 2-8 **Ethernet**

Figure 2-8 provides an example of an Ethernet-based network. The Network Interface Card (NIC) connects hosts to a Local Area Network (LAN). Each Ethernet-based NIC has a globally unique address over a "flat" address space. Given that LANs usually have a small geographic footprint, they use higher data-transfer rates than do Wide Area Networks (WANs). Ethernet and other Layer-2 protocols facilitate developers to build LANs.

Frames of data are transmitted into the physical layer medium (copper, coax, fiber, and radio interfaces). NICs listen on this physical medium for frames with unique LAN addresses, known as Media Access Control (MAC) addresses (more on this in Chapter 4, "LAN = Ethernet" on page 89).

Although the structure of data handled by Ethernet NICs is called a frame, Ethernet is a packet-switching technology. Copper wire is the predominant physical layer used by Ethernet in local areas. Its inherent star topology, as shown in Figure 2-8 and its low cost implementation are the primary reasons for Ethernet's success as a preferred LAN technology.

In the last few years, Ethernet has also emerged as a viable alternative in metro networks and Wide Area Networks (WANs) due to the rapid deployment of full-duplex, fiber optic Gigabit Ethernet technology during the now infamous techno bubble in the late 1990's. The success of the 802.11 standard (Wi-Fi) has also propelled Ethernet to predominant LAN technology status for wireless networks, as it uses and extends the Ethernet interface between Layer 3 and Layer 2.

The IEEE 802.3 standard defines Ethernet. Twisted pair Ethernet is used in the LAN, and fiber optic Ethernet is mainly used in WAN, giving rise to Ethernet as the most widespread wired networking technology. Since the end of the 1980's, Ethernet has replaced such competing LAN standards as Token Ring, Fiber Distributed Data Interface (FDDI), and Attached Resource Computer NETwork (ARCNET). In recent years, Wi-Fi has become prevalent in home and small office networks and augments Ethernet's presence. WiMAX (IEEE 802.16) will also contribute to Ethernet domination. It is used for wireless networking in much the same way as Wi-Fi but it can provide broadband wireless access up to 30 miles (50 km) for fixed stations, and 3 - 10 miles (5 - 15 km) for mobile stations.

2-8 LAYER 3 – NETWORK

To expand the reach of our hosts, internetworking protocols are necessary to enable communication between different computers attached to diverse local area networks.

Internet: a network of networks (in other words, between the networks: Inter Net)

The public Internet is a familiar example. A private network of networks is referred to as an Intranet.

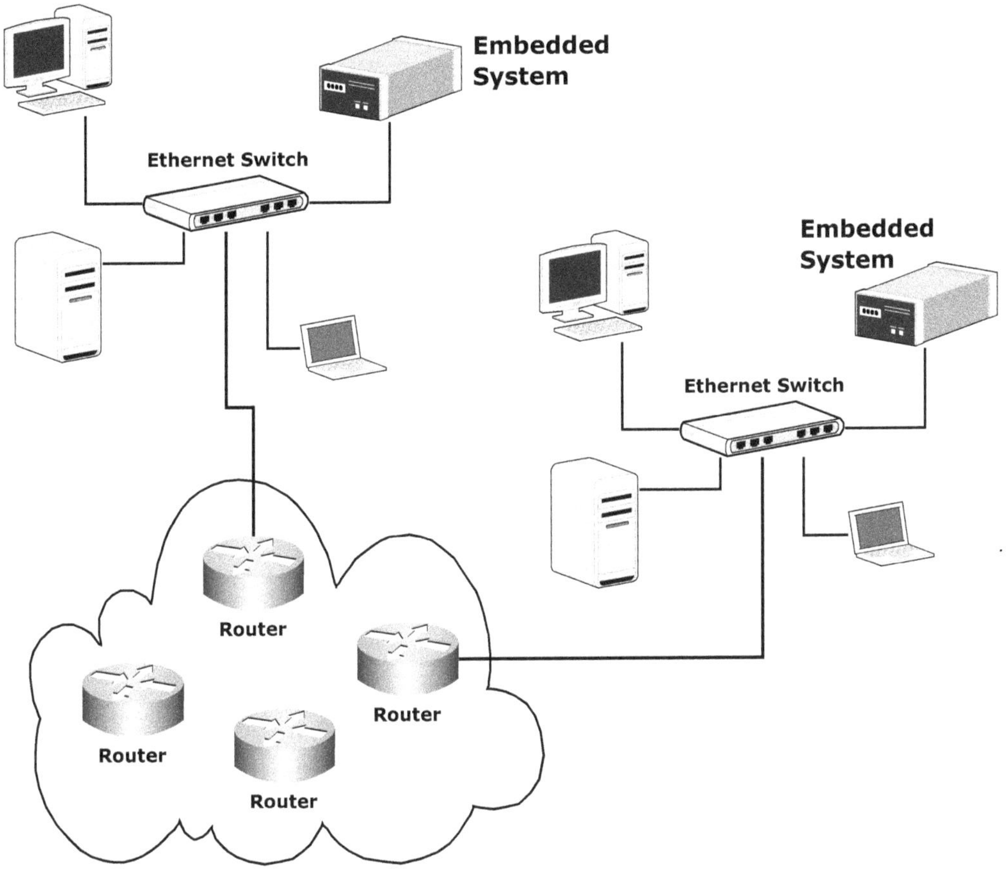

Figure 2-9 **Local Area Networking**

When it is advantageous to link together multiple LANs, Layer 3 protocols and equipment (routers) are brought into play (see Figure 2-9). Three LANs are linked together with a cloud where the Layer 3 nodes (routers), used to forward frames between the LANs, are located. The Layer 2 device, the Ethernet switch, is connected to the Layer 3 router, to participate in the larger network. The Network layer handles the packaging of frames into packets and their routing from one piece of equipment to another. It transfers packets across multiple links and/or multiple networks. What is not represented in Figure 2-9 are network connections between the nodes in the cloud.

Collectively, the nodes execute routing algorithms to determine paths across the network. Layer 3 is the unifying layer bringing together various Layer 2 technologies. Even if all of the hosts access these networks using different Layer 2 technologies, they all have a common protocol. In an IP network, this is represented by the IP packet and the well-known IP address which is used by the routing algorithm. See Chapter 5, "IP Networking" on page 117, for a complete definition of IP addresses.

We already know that a device such as an embedded system requires a MAC address to participate in the LAN. Now, we also see that in a network of networks using IP technology, each device also needs an IP address. Other configuration requirements will be covered in depth in Chapter 5, "IP Networking" on page 117.

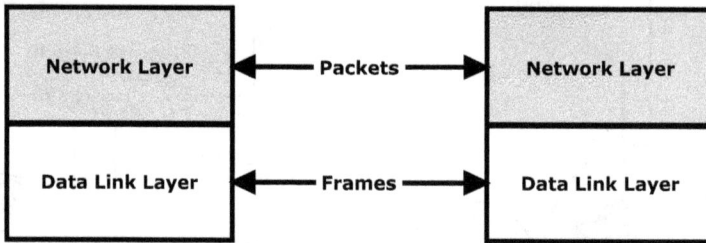

Figure 2-10 **Layer 3 – Network**

The links depicted in Figure 2-10 are not direct links, but instead represent that the information carried between the two hosts on the network is made up of structure that is relevant only to certain layers of the TCP/IP stack. The information contained in the packets encapsulated in the frames, is processed by the Network layer. When transmitting a packet, the Network layer takes the information received from the layer above and builds the packet with relevant Layer 3 information (an IP address and other data making up the Layer 3 header). The Network layer, upon receiving a packet, must examine its content and decide what do to with it. The most plausible action is to send it to the layer above.

2-9 LAYER 4 – TRANSPORT

The Transport layer ensures the reliability of point-to-point data communications. It transfers data end-to-end from a process in one device to a process in another device.

In IP technology, we have two protocols at this layer:

TRANSMISSION CONTROL PROTOCOL (TCP)

- A reliable stream transfer providing:

  - Error recovery

  - Flow control

  - Packet sequencing

USER DATAGRAM PROTOCOL (UDP)

- A quick-and-simple single-block transfer

At this stage of implementation, the embedded system engineer must evaluate which or if both of these protocols will be required for the type of embedded application at hand. Assistance to help answer these questions can be found in Chapter 7, on page 169, which describes transport layer protocols in greater detail.

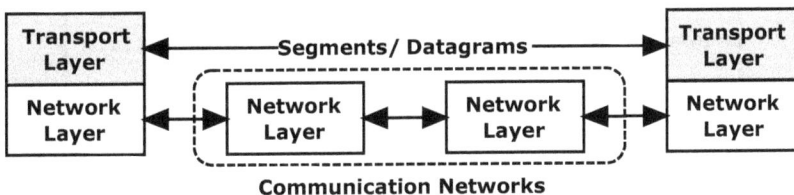

Figure 2-11 **Layers 3 and 4**

Figure 2-11 above shows that at the Network layer, the packet may have gone through different nodes between the source and destination. The information contained in the packet may be a TCP segment or a UDP datagram. The information contained in these segments or datagrams is only relevant to the transport layer.

2-10 LAYERS 5-6-7 – THE APPLICATION

It is at the Application layer that an embedded engineer implements the system's main functions. An application is the software that interfaces with the TCP/IP stack and contains either a basic network service such as file transfer, e-mail or a custom application. Chapter 9, "Services and Applications" on page 225 provides a more detailed explanation of the applications and services that can be used as add-on modules to the TCP/IP stack.

To develop a customer application, the embedded engineer must understand the interface between the application and the TCP/IP stack. This interface is referred to as the socket interface and it allows the developer to open a socket, to send data using the socket, to receive data on the socket, and so on. To use the interface and its Application Programming Interface (API), refer to Chapter 8, "Sockets" on page 209, and Chapter 18, "Socket Programming" on page 501 which contain additional information on how a socket interface works.

Micrium also provides a test application for a TCP/IP stack called µC/IPerf. This application, delivered in source code, provides examples on how to write applications using TCP/IP. Part II of this book provides many sample applications that can be customized for use.

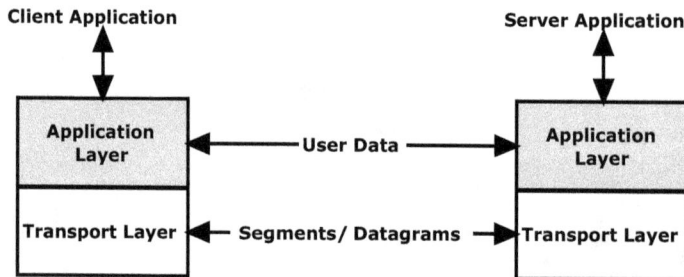

Figure 2-12 **Application Layer and Layer 4**

The interface between the Application layer and the Transport layer is often the demarcation point of the TCP/IP stack as shown in Figure 2-12. The junction of the Application Layer (5-6-7) and Layer 4 is the location of the socket interface previously discussed. The application can be a standard application such as FTP or HTTP and/or an embedded system-specific application that you would develop. As previously explained, user data going from the source host to the destination host must travel across many layers and over one or many network links.

From the concepts introduced so far, it can be deduced that the challenges for the embedded engineer reside in the driver for the Data Link Layer and in the application, assuming the project is using a commercial off the-shelf TCP/IP stack.

In fact, depending on Data Link Layer hardware, a driver is required. If the embedded engineer is lucky, the TCP/IP stack vendor already has a driver for this hardware. Otherwise, it must be developed and tested. This can be a challenge depending on the complexity of the hardware and the level of integration required with the TCP/IP stack.

The second challenge is the application itself. What does the product do? Mastering socket programming and being sufficiently knowledgeable to test the application for all possible eventualities are two important skills a developer must possess.

2-11 SUMMARY

Figure 2-13 below summarizes the concepts discussed so far.

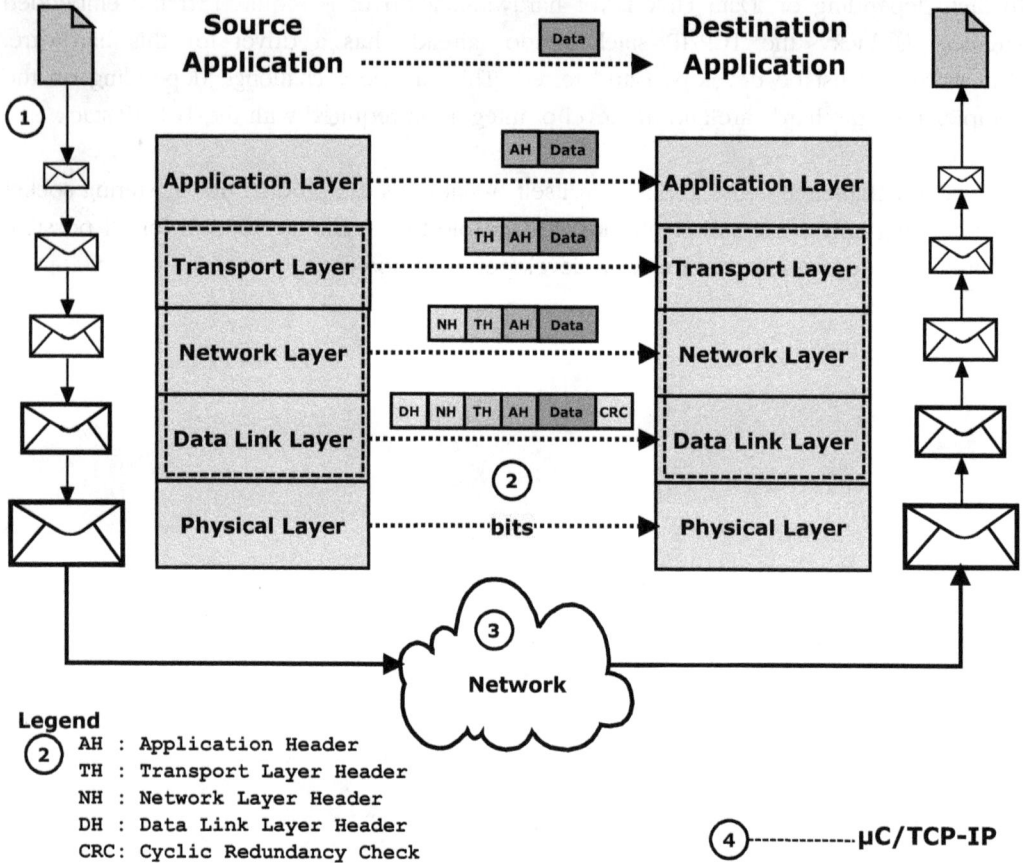

Figure 2-13 **TCP/IP process**

F2-13(1)   Data traveling through the stack from the user application down to the physical medium is encapsulated at every layer by a series of protocols. This is represented by the envelope icon, and the envelope is getting larger as user data travels toward the network interface at the physical layer. This payload inflation is referred to as protocol overhead. The overhead is a non-negligible quantity and can affect system performance, especially if user data is relatively small. The following chapters provide the size of each header so that the overhead ratio to user data payload can be calculated to estimate effective system performance.

As far as the user application is concerned, it sends data and the same data is retrieved at the other end. The application is blissfully unaware that the data went through layers and network nodes.

F2-13(2)   Each protocol adds its own header that contains control information required by this layer/protocol to perform its task. The use of protocol overhead is only relevant for the corresponding layer in the connected host. This is represented by the dotted lines in the middle of this diagram. These lines are not effective physical connections but represent logical interactions between corresponding layers in the two hosts involved in the communication.

F2-13(3)   The network is represented as a cloud. The network connection between the source and the destination can be as simple as a LAN if both hosts are on the same LAN, or as complex as the Internet if the two hosts are in different locations (anywhere in the world). Device configuration will vary depending on the reach required. Chapter 5, "IP Networking" on page 117 provides a broader discussion of these various network configurations.

F2-13(4)   The dotted line around the Transport, Network and Data Link Layers represents the software that encompasses µC/TCP-IP (or any other TCP/IP stack). The Physical Layer is the hardware used in the system. This means that when using µC/TCP-IP to develop an embedded system, the only part that is missing is the Application.

The chapters that follow provide greater detail for several important IP protocols, pointing out the advantages and possible challenges to using each in an embedded system.

Embedding TCP/IP: Working Through Implementation Challenges

Before using a TCP/IP stack in an embedded product, it is important to acknowledge and understand the reasons to do so. Obviously, the product is to be connected to an IP network. We can say the embedded system in this case requires *connectivity*. An embedded system might be called on to exchange large amounts of data over a reliable connection. In this case, we can say that the embedded system demands *performance*.

Most embedded system resources are extremely limited when compared to the resources available on a desktop or laptop PC. Product manufacturers must create products at the lowest cost possible to offer them at the best possible price to their customers, yet work within the constraints of RAM, CPU speed, and peripheral hardware performance inherent in hardware platforms used for embedded design. With limited hardware resources, how can an embedded designer meet system design requirements? They begin by asking and answering a fundamental question:

Do you need a TCP/IP stack...

- to connect to an IP network without any minimum performance requirement?

  or

- to connect to an IP network and obtain high throughput?

The answer to this question has a major impact on hardware choices that ultimately drive product cost. These hardware choices include CPU performance, NIC interface type, and RAM availability.

Connectivity, throughput and bandwidth are concepts that shape the configuration system hardware and software parameters. Let's look at an overview of each:

BANDWIDTH

As a best practice, the performance of an Ethernet connection should be measured in Megabits per second (Mbps). This allows us to easily compare system performance with respect to the Ethernet link's maximum bandwidth.

Currently, Ethernet over twisted pair is the preferred physical medium. The available bandwidth of the link is normally 10 Mbps, 100 Mbps or 1 Gbps. These numbers are used as the reference for the efficiency of an Ethernet NIC. For example, if we have an Ethernet NIC with a 100 Mbps link, we already know that our embedded system maximum bandwidth is 100 Mbps. However, there are a number of limiting factors in embedded systems that do not allow them to reach what we call the Ethernet line speed, in this case 100 Mbps. Such factors include duplex mismatch, TCP/IP stack performance based on CPU speed, RAM available for buffers, DMA vs. non-DMA Ethernet driver design, performance related to clock and peripheral power management, and the use of a true zero-copy architecture. These embedded system bandwidth-limiting factors are included in this and subsequent chapters.

CONNECTIVITY

Connectivity in this context is the exchange of information without any performance constraints. Many embedded systems requiring connectivity only may work optimally with hardware and software that provide a low-bandwidth TCP/IP connection.

For example, if an embedded system is sending or receiving a few hundreds bytes every second (let's say of sensor data), then the constraints on the system are fairly relaxed. It means that the CPU may be clocked at a lower speed. It may also mean that if the NIC is Ethernet, it can be a 10 Mpbs instead of a 100-Mbps interface and the RAM requirement is reduced since there is less data flowing in the system.

THROUGHPUT

A system that needs throughput can be one that transmits or receives streamed video, for example. Streamed video transmission can be anything from a few megabits per second (Mbps) to many Mbps depending on the signal quality and the compression rate used. This type of application requires an embedded system with sufficient resources to achieve higher bandwidth than a "connectivity-only" system. Constraints on the NIC, CPU and RAM availability are clearly higher. For the CPU and NIC, these issues are hardware dependent, but for RAM usage, the constraints are related to software and the requirements of the application.

The transport protocols at Layer 4, have a greater influence on RAM usage. It is at this layer, for example, that flow control, or how much data is in transit in the network between the hosts, is implemented. The basic premise of flow control is that the more data in transit, more RAM is required by the system to handle the data volume. Details on how these protocols work and their impact on RAM usage are located in Chapter 7, "Transport Protocols" on page 169.

Achieving high throughput in a system requires greater resources. The question becomes, how much? Each element influencing performance must be analyzed separately.

3-1 CPU

There is an inherent asymmetry in a TCP/IP stack whereby it is simpler to transmit than to receive. Substantially more processing is involved in receiving a packet as opposed to transmitting one, which is why embedded system transmit speeds are typically faster. We therefore say that most embedded targets are slow consumers.

Let's look at a personal computer by way of an example. On a PC, the CPU is clocked at approximately 3 GHz and has access to gigabytes of memory. These high-powered computers invariably have an Ethernet NIC with its own processor and dedicated memory (often megabytes worth). However, even with all of these resources, we sometimes question our machine's network performance!

Now, imagine an embedded system with a 32-bit processor clocked at 70MHz and containing a mere 64 Kilobytes of RAM which must be allocated to duties apart from networking. The Ethernet controller is capable of 100 Mbps. However, it is unrealistic to ask even a 70-MHz processor with only 64 Kbytes of RAM to be able to achieve this performance level. Standard Ethernet link bandwidths are 10, 100 Mbps and 1 Gbps and semiconductor manufacturers integrate these Ethernet controllers into their microcontrollers. The CPU may not be able to fill this link to its maximum capacity, however efficient the software.

Even when the Ethernet controller used in the system is designed to operate at 10 Mbps, 100 Mbps, or 1 Gbps, it's unlikely that the system will achieve that performance. A high-performance PC as described above will have no trouble transmitting Ethernet frames at bandwidths approaching the Ethernet line speed. However, if an embedded system is connected to such a PC, it is very possible that the embedded system will not be able to keep up with the high data rates and therefore some of the frames will be lost (dropped).

Performance is not only limited by the embedded system's CPU, but also by the limited amount of RAM available to receive packets. In the embedded system, packets are stored in buffers (called network buffers) that are processed by the CPU. A network buffer contains one Ethernet frame plus control information concerning that frame. The maximum Ethernet frame payload is 1500 bytes and therefore additional RAM is required for each network buffer. On our PC, in comparison, there is sufficient RAM to configure hundreds (possibly even thousands) of network buffers, yet this is typically not the case for an embedded target. Certain protocols will have difficulty performing their duties when the system has few buffers. Packets generated by a fast producer and received by the target will consume most or all the TCP/IP stack network buffers and, as a result, packets will be dropped. This point will be explained in greater detail when we look at Transport protocols.

Hardware features such as Direct Memory Access (DMA) and CPU speed may improve this situation. The faster the target can receive and process the packets, the faster the network buffers are freed. No matter how quickly data comes in or goes out, the CPU still must process every single byte.

3-2 ETHERNET CONTROLLER INTERFACE

Other important factors influencing the performance of an embedded system include the system's ability to receive Ethernet frames in network buffers to be later processed by upper protocol layers, and to place data into network buffers for transmission. The predominant method for moving Ethernet frames between the Ethernet controller and the system's main memory are via software (using functions such as **memcopy()** which copies every byte from one location to another), or via Direct Memory Access (DMA).

With **memcopy()**, the CPU must copy every byte from one memory location to another. As a result, it is the slower of the two methods. **memcopy()** is always slower than DMA, even when writing the **memcopy()** function in highly optimized assembly language. If the only solution is to create an optimized **memcopy()**, in µC/TCP-IP, this function is located in the µC/LIB module.

DMA support for the Ethernet controller is a means to improve packet processing. It is easy to understand that, when frames are transferred quickly to and from the TCP/IP stack, network performance improves. Rapid transfer also relieves the CPU from the transfer task, allowing the CPU to perform additional protocol processing. The most common CPU to Ethernet Controller configurations are shown in Figure 3-1.

Moving Ethernet frames between an Ethernet controller and network buffers often depends upon specific Ethernet controller and microprocessor/microcontroller capabilities.

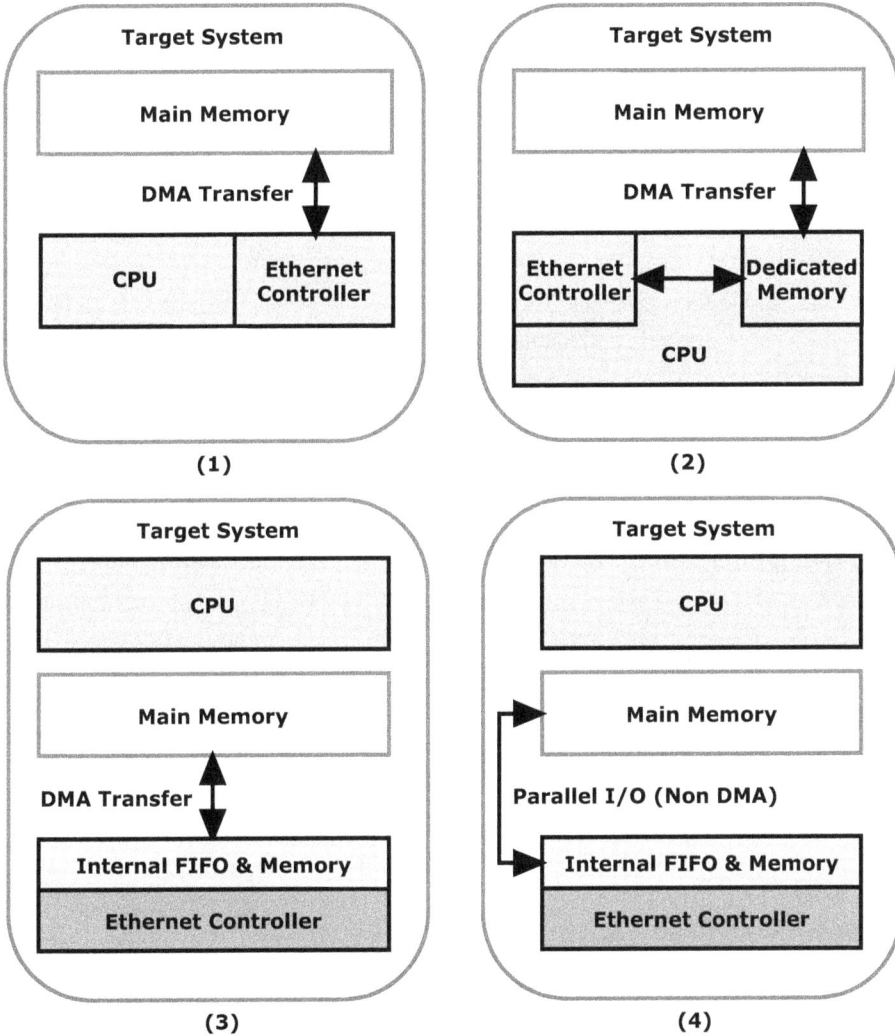

Figure 3-1 **Ethernet Controller Interface**

F3-1(1)   Illustrates a CPU with an integrated Media Access Controller (MAC). When a frame is received by the MAC, a DMA transfer from the MAC's internal buffer is initiated by the MAC into main memory. This method often enables shortened development time and excellent performance.

F3-1(2)   Represents a CPU with an integrated MAC, but with dedicated memory. When a frame is received, the MAC initiates a DMA transfer into this dedicated memory. Most configurations of type 2 allow for transmission from main memory while reserving dedicated memory for either receive or transmit operations. Both the MAC and the CPU read and write from dedicated memory, and so the TCP/IP stack can process frames directly from dedicated memory. Porting to this architecture is generally not difficult and it provides excellent performance. However, performance may be limited by the size of the dedicated memory; especially in cases where transmit and receive operations share the dedicated memory space.

F3-1(3)   Represents a cooperative DMA solution whereby both the CPU and MAC take part in the DMA operation. This configuration is generally found on external devices that are either connected directly to the processor bus or connected via the Industry Standard Architecture (ISA) or Peripheral Component Interconnect (PCI) standards. Method 3 requires that the CPU contain a DMA peripheral that can be configured to work within the architectural limitations of the external device. This method is more difficult to port, but generally offers excellent performance.

F3-1(4)   Illustrates an external device attached via the CPU's external bus. Data is moved to and from main memory and the external device's internal memory via CPU read and write cycles. This method thus requires additional CPU intervention in order to copy all of the data to and from the device when necessary. This method is generally easy to port and it offers average performance.

It is very important to understand that TCP/IP stack vendors may not use all of the Ethernet Controller capabilities, and will often implement a Memory Copy mechanism between the Ethernet Controller and the system's Main Memory. Memory Copy operations are substantially slower than DMA operations, and therefore have a major negative impact on performance.

Another important issue, especially for an embedded system design, is how the NIC driver (i.e., software) interfaces to the NIC controller. Certain TCP/IP stacks accomplish the task via polling (checking the NIC controller in a loop to see what needs to be done). This is not the best technique for an embedded system since every CPU cycle counts. The best interface mechanism is to use interrupts and have the NIC controller raise an interrupt when CPU attention is required. The µC/TCP-IP Driver Architecture is interrupt-driven. Driver development and porting are described in Chapter 16, "Device Driver Implementation" on page 365.

3-2-1 ZERO COPY

TCP/IP stack vendors may qualify their stack as a zero-copy stack. A true zero-copy architecture refers to data in the memory buffers at every layer instead of moving the data between layers. Zero copy enables the network interface card to transfer data directly to or from TCP/IP stack network buffers. The availability of zero copy greatly increases application performance. It is easy to see that using a CPU that is capable of complex operations just to make copies of data is a waste of resources and time.

Techniques for implementing zero-copy capabilities include the use of DMA-based copying and memory mapping through a Memory Management Unit (MMU). These features require specific hardware support, not always present in microprocessors or microcontrollers used in embedded systems, and they often involve memory alignment requirements.

Use care when selecting a Commercial Off-the-Shelf (COTS) TCP/IP stack. Vendors may use the zero-copy qualifier for stacks that do not copy data between layers within the stack, but perform **memcopy()** between the stack and the Ethernet controller. Optimum performance can only be achieved if zero copy is used down to the Data Link Layer. Micrium's µC/TCP-IP is an example of a zero copy stack from the Data Link layer to the Transport layer. The interface between the Transport layer and the Application layer in µC/TCP-IP is currently not a zero copy interface.

3-2-2 CHECK-SUM

Another element which combines the CPU and data moves and which is frequently used in the stack is the checksum mechanism. Providing checksum assembly routines, replacing the C equivalent functions is another optimization strategy that is effective.

3-2-3 FOOTPRINT

As we are discovering, the IP protocol family is composed of several protocols. However, when developing an embedded system, ask yourself if you need them all. The answer is, probably not.

Another important question is: Is it possible to remove certain unused protocols from the stack? If the TCP/IP stack is well written, it should be possible to exclude protocols that are not required. Because an embedded system is often used in a private network, the embedded developer may decide not to implement protocols that are required on the public Internet. At this point, understanding each protocol's capabilities, as you will see in subsequent chapters, will help in deciding if that protocol is required for the application.

For any of the protocols listed below, if the feature is not required by the system, we may want to remove it from the target's build (assuming that this is allowed by the TCP/IP stack architecture). The figures provided are only an estimate based on μC/TCP-IP. Other TCP/IP stacks may have different footprints depending on how closely they follow RFCs and how many of the specification's features are actually included in each module.

The following are candidate protocols that can be removed from a TCP/IP stack if allowed by the stack software architecture:

Protocol	Why it can be removed from the TCP/IP stack	Footprint
IGMP	Protocol allows the host to use multicasting.	1.6KB
ICMP	Protocol is used for error control and error messaging. If the system is used in a closed, private network, it may not be required.	3.3KB
IP Fragmentation	Used to reassemble IP packets travelling across networks of different Maximum Transmission Unit (MTU) size. If the system is used on networks with the same MTU, it is typically not required.	2.0KB
TCP Congestion Control	On a private network where bandwidth is known and sufficient, this TCP feature may not be required.	10.0KB
TCP Keep-alive	According to RFC 1122, TCP Keep-alive is an optional feature of the protocol and, if included, must default to off. If the system has no need to check for dead peers or prevent disconnection due to network inactivity, the feature can be removed.	1.5KB
TCP	If the system does not send substantial amounts of data and you can afford to do sequencing and data acknowledgment in the top application, the system may be happy with UDP and you can eliminate TCP. See Chapter 7, "Transport Protocols" on page 169 for more details.	35KB

Table 3-1 **Protocols that can be 'compiled out' of µC/TCP-IP**

The footprints (code size) for the protocols are approximations and can thus vary from one TCP/IP stack to another. Some of these protocols are not part of µC/TCP-IP and therefore show that a TCP/IP stack can work without them. Current µC/TCP-IP limitations include:

No IP Transmit Fragmentation	RFC #791, Section 3.2 and RFC #1122, Section 3.3.5
No IP Forwarding/Routing	RFC #1122, Sections 3.3.1, 3.3.4, 3.3.5
IP Security Options	RFC #1108
No Current PING Utility (Transmission of ICMP Echo Request)	RFC #1574, Section 3.1 Current µC/TCP-IP ICMP implementation replies with ICMP Echo Reply to ICMP Echo Request.
ICMP Address Mask Agent/Server	RFC #1122, Section 3.2.2.9
No TCP Keep Alives	RFC #1122, Section 4.2.3.6
TCP Security and Precedence	RFC #793, Section 3.6
TCP Urgent Data	RFC #793, Section 3.7

Table 3-2 **µC/TCP-IP limitations**

Without introducing all of the µC/TCP-IP modules and data structures, the following sections provide an estimate of the µC/TCP-IP code and data footprint. The complete list of files required to build µC/TCP-IP is provided in Chapter 12, "Directories and Files" on page 267.

3-2-4 µC/TCP-IP CODE FOOTPRINT

Memory footprints were obtained by compiling the code on a popular 32-bit CPU architecture. Compiler optimization was set to maximum optimization for size or speed as indicated. µC/TCP-IP options are set for most disabled or all enabled. The numbers are provided as orders of magnitude for design purposes.

The table excludes NIC, PHY, ISR and BSP layers since these are NIC and board specific.

µC/TCP-IP Protocols Layers	All Options Enabled		All Options Disabled	
	Compiler Optimized for Speed (Kbytes)	Compiler Optimized for Size (Kbytes)	Compiler Optimized for Speed (Kbytes)	Compiler Optimized for Size (Kbytes)
IF	9.3	7.3	4.2	3.9
ARP	4.3	3.8	3.3	2.6
IP	10.1	9.0	6.4	6.0
ICMP	3.3	3.0	1.7	1.7
UDP	1.9	1.9	0.4	0.4
TCP	42.7	24.4	30.2	17.3
Sockets	23.5	13.8	2.0	1.7
BSD	0.7	0.6	0.7	0.6
Utils	1.5	0.9	1.1	0.6
OS	6.3	4.7	3.4	3.1
µC/LIB V1.31	3.5	3.2	2.9	2.6
µC/CPU V1.25	0.6	0.5	0.6	0.5
µC/TCP-IP Total:	107.7	73.0	56.9	41.0

Table 3-3 µC/TCP-IP Code Footprint

To see additional information regarding options, refer to Chapter 20, "Debug Management" on page 525, Chapter 21, "Statistics and Error Counters" on page 527, and Appendix D, "µC/TCP-IP Configuration and Optimization" on page 959.

3-2-5 µC/TCP-IP ADD-ON OPTIONS CODE FOOTPRINT

As seen in Layers 5-6-7 – The Application, services and standard application software modules found at the Application layer can be used in the product design to provide certain functionalities. Such application modules are offered as options for µC/TCP-IP. Although an in-depth discussion of memory footprint is outside the scope of this book, the memory footprint for the optional modules is included below for planning purposes. Chapter 9, "Services and Applications" on page 225 describes what some of these applications and services do and how they do it.

The footprints below were obtained by compiling the code on a popular 32-bit CPU architecture. The numbers are provided as orders of magnitude for design purposes.

µC/TCP-IP Add-on Options	Compiler Optimized for Size (Kbytes)	Compiler Optimized for Speed (Kbytes)
µC/DHCPc	5.1	5.4
µC/DNSc	0.9	1.0
µC/FTPc	2.8	2.9
µC/FTPs	4.5	4.5
µC/HTTPs	2.6	2.7
µC/POP3c	1.8	2.8
µC/SMTPc	2.0	2.1
µC/SNTPc	0.5	0.5
µC/TELNETs	2.0	2.1
µC/TFTPc	1.2	1.3
µC/TFTPs	1.2	1.2

Table 3-4 **µC/TCP-IP Add-ons Code Footprint**

3-2-6 µC/TCP-IP DATA FOOTPRINT

Cutting protocols out of the code will reduce the code footprint with little impact on the data (i.e., RAM) footprint. The greatest impact on the data footprint is a result of the number of "objects" such as network buffers and connections, and most specifically from network buffers. See a detailed explanation on buffers and how to use them appropriately in Chapter 7, "Transport Protocols" on page 169 and in Chapter 9, "Buffer Management" on page 277.

Data usage estimates are provided to complement the code footprint discussion. There are multiple modules requiring data to operate as shown in Table 3-5. Many of the data sizes calculated in the following sub-sections assume 4-byte pointers. The data requirements for each of the objects must be added, as needed by the configuration of the TCP/IP stack. The configuration of the objects is represented in a formula for each. The equation variables all in upper case are **#define** configuration parameters found in Appendix D, "µC/TCP-IP Configuration and Optimization" on page 959. Calculation methods follow.

BUFFER REQUIREMENTS

µC/TCP-IP stores transmitted and received data in data structures known as network buffers. µC/TCP-IP's buffer management is designed with embedded system constraints in mind. The most important factor on the RAM footprint is the number of buffers. For this reason, three types of buffers are defined: large receive, large transmit and small transmit buffers.

The data space for EACH network interface's buffers is calculated as:

```
[(224(max) + Net IF's Cfg'd RxBufLargeSize) * Net IF's Cfg'd RxBufLargeNbr] +
[(224(max) + Net IF's Cfg'd TxBufLargeSize) * Net IF's Cfg'd TxBufLargeNbr] +
[(224(max) + Net IF's Cfg'd TxBufSmallSize) * Net IF's Cfg'd TxBufSmallNbr]
```

These calculations do not account for additional space that may be required for additional alignment requirements.

Also, the (minimum) recommended defaults for network buffer sizes:

```
RxBufLargeSize = 1518
TxBufLargeSize = 1594
TxBufSmallSize = 152
```

The data space for network buffer pools is calculated as:

384 * (NET_IF_CFG_NBR_IF + 1)

Where: **NET_IF_CFG_NBR_IF** is the (maximum) number of network interfaces configured.

NETWORK INTERFACE REQUIREMENTS

μC/TCP-IP supports multiple network interfaces if the hardware has multiple network controllers (see Chapter 16, "Network Interface Layer" on page 361). Network Interfaces are used to represent an abstract view of the device hardware and data path that connects the hardware to the higher layers of the network protocol stack. In order to communicate with hosts outside the local host, the application developer must add at least one network interface to the system. The data size for network interfaces is calculated as:

76(max) * NET_IF_CFG_NBR_IF

Where: **NET_IF_CFG_NBR_IF** is the (maximum) number of network interfaces configured.

TIMER REQUIREMENTS

μC/TCP-IP manages software timers used to keep track of various network-related timeouts. Each timer requires RAM. The data size for timers is calculated as:

28 * NET_TMR_CFG_NBR_TMR

Where: **NET_TMR_CFG_NBR_TMR** is the number of timers configured.

ADDRESS RESOLUTION PROTOCOL (ARP) CACHE REQUIREMENTS

ARP is a protocol used to cross-reference an Ethernet MAC address (see Chapter 4, "LAN = Ethernet" on page 89) and an IP address (see Chapter 5, "IP Networking" on page 117). These cross-references are stored in a table called the ARP cache. The number of entries in this table is configurable. The data size for the ARP cache is calculated as:

56 * NET_ARP_CFG_NBR_CACHE

Where: **NET_ARP_CFG_NBR_CACHE** is the number of ARP cache entries configured.

IP REQUIREMENTS

A network interface can have more than one IP address. The data size for IP address configuration is calculated as:

    [(20 * NET_IP_CFG_IF_MAX_NBR_ADDRS) + 4] * (NET_IF_CFG_NBR_IF + 1)

Where: `NET_IF_CFG_NBR_IF` is the (maximum) number of network interfaces configured, `NET_IP_CFG_IF_MAX_NBR_ADDRS` is the (maximum) number of IP addresses configured per network interface.

ICMP REQUIREMENTS

Internet Control Message Protocol (ICMP) transmits ICMP source quench messages to other hosts when network resources are low. The number of entries depends on the number of different hosts. It is recommended to start with a value of 5. The data size for ICMP source quench is calculated as:

    20 * NET_ICMP_CFG_TX_SRC_QUENCH_NBR

Where: `NET_ICMP_CFG_TX_SRC_QUENCH_NBR` is the number of ICMP transmit source quench entries configured, if enabled by `NET_ICMP_CFG_TX_SRC_QUENCH_EN`.

IGMP REQUIREMENTS

The Internet Group Management Protocol (IGMP) adds multicasting capability to the IP protocol stack (see Appendix C, "μC/TCP-IP API Reference" on page 649). The data size for IGMP host groups is calculated as:

    32 * NET_IGMP_CFG_MAX_NBR_HOST_GRP

Where: `NET_IGMP_CFG_MAX_NBR_HOST_GRP` is the (maximum) number of IGMP host groups configured, if enabled by `NET_IP_CFG_MULTICAST_SEL` configured to `NET_IP_MULTICAST_SEL_TX_RX`.

CONNECTION REQUIREMENTS

A connection is a µC/TCP-IP structure containing information regarding the IP protocol parameters required to identify two hosts communicating with each other. A connection is a structure that is used for all Layer 4 protocols (UDP and TCP). The data size for connections is calculated as:

```
56 * NET_CONN_CFG_NBR_CONN
```

Where: `NET_CONN_CFG_NBR_CONN` is the number of connections (TCP or UDP) configured.

TCP REQUIREMENTS

In addition to the connection data structure defined previously, a TCP connection requires additional state information, transmit and receive queue information as well as time-out information to be stored in a specific TCP connection data structure.

The data size for the TCP connections is calculated as:

```
280 * NET_TCP_CFG_NBR_CONN
```

Where: `NET_TCP_CFG_NBR_CONN` is the number of TCP connections configured.

SOCKETS REQUIREMENTS

As seen in section Layers 5-6-7 – The Application, the interface between the application and the TCP/IP stack is defined as a socket interface. For each socket that the application wants to open and use, a socket structure exits that contains the information about that specific socket.

The data size for sockets is calculated as:

```
48 * NET_SOCK_CFG_NBR_SOCK
```

Where: `NET_SOCK_CFG_NBR_SOCK` is the number of sockets configured.

µC/TCP-IP INTERNAL DATA USAGE

This represents the amount of data space needed for µC/TCP-IP's internal data structures and variables, and varies from about 300 to 1900 bytes depending on the options configured.

	µC/TCP-IP	Number	Bytes per	Total
1	Small transmit buffers	20	152	3,040
2	Large transmit buffers	10	1,594	15,940
3	Large receive buffers	10	1,518	15,180
4	Network interfaces	1	76	76
5	Timers	30	28	840
6	IP addresses	2 + 1	24	72
7	ICMP source quench	20	1	20
8	IGMP groups	32	1	32
9	ARP cache	10	56	560
10	Connections	20	56	1,120
11	TCP connections	10	280	2,800
12	Sockets	10	48	480
13	µC/TCP-IP fixed data usage			1,900
	Total:			42,060

Table 3-5 **µC/TCP-IP Data Footprint**

Lines 1 to 8 in Table 3-5 provide data sizes that may vary as the number of each element is determined at configuration time. You could build a spreadsheet to reproduce the table above using the equations described above. Line 9 is the fixed internal data usage for µC/TCP-IP. With such a configuration, we see that the system total RAM usage exceeds 40 K.

3-2-7 µC/TCP-IP ADD-ON OPTIONS DATA FOOTPRINT

The RAM data usage for the µC/TCP-IP add-on options is provided for planning assistance. In the following table, we use the definition of the size of **CPU_STK** as being 4 bytes.

µC/TCP-IP Add-on Options	RAM Size (Kbytes)	Based on Note
µC/DHCPc	3.4	
µC/DNSc	8.8	DNSc_MAX_HOSTNAME_SIZE * DNSc_MAX_CACHED_HOSTNAMES Where: DNSc_MAX_HOSTNAME_SIZE is the maximum DNS name size in characters DNSc_MAX_CACHED_HOSTNAMES is the maximum number of cached DNS names configured.
µC/HTTPs	17.7	sizeof(CPU_STK) * HTTP_CFG_TASK_STK_SIZE Typical configuration: HTTP_CFG_TASK_STK_SIZE = 2048
µC/FTPs	27.1	sizeof(CPU_STK) * FTP_CFG_TASK_STK_SIZE Typical configuration: FTP_CFG_TASK_STK_SIZE = 512
µC/FTPc	0.1	sizeof(CPU_STK) * FTP_CFG_TASK_STK_SIZE Typical configuration: FTP_CFG_TASK_STK_SIZE = 512
µC/TFTPs	8.6	sizeof(CPU_STK) * TFTP_CFG_TASK_STK_SIZE Typical configuration: TFTP_CFG_TASK_STK_SIZE = 1024
µC/TFTPc	2.0	sizeof(OS_STK) * TFTP_CFG_TASK_STK_SIZE Typical configuration: TFTP_CFG_TASK_STK_SIZE = 1024
µC/SNTPc	N/A	
µC/SMTPc	1.0	104 bytes + 1024 bytes (DATA memory)
µC/POP3c	1.1	128 bytes + 1004 bytes (DATA memory)
µC/TELNETs	4.1	

Table 3-6 **µC/TCP-IP Add-ons RAM Usage**

3-2-8 SUMMARY

Several considerations are necessary when adding a TCP/IP stack to an embedded system. Most of these are performance related, including:

- The CPU's ability to process all of the packets to be transmitted or received

- The Ethernet Controller type has an impact on the driver

- The transfer method between the Ethernet Controller and the TCP/IP stack has an impact on performance

  - Byte copy from one location to another via the CPU

  - DMA transfer

- The Zero-Copy architecture of the TCP/IP stack has an impact on performance

- The code and data footprints:

  - Code footprint depends on what protocols are used and this depends on what the specific goal of the application.

  - A data footprint is largely affected by the number of network buffers required. Chapter 7, "Transport Protocols" on page 169 gives the means to evaluate the number of buffers a system should configure. Sample applications provided in Part II of this book and the µC/IPerf application found in Chapter 6, "Troubleshooting" on page 139, provide additional means to evaluate a system's performance based on its configuration.

Next, we will examine Ethernet in the first layer at the bottom of the reference model to discover its importance in the product design. Ethernet driver development and test represent challenges the embedded engineer must face. We will then move up through the layers on our way to the Application layer, finding additional obstacles to overcome in order to efficiently embed a TCP/IP stack into a product.

LAN = Ethernet

With the widespread use of copper twisted pair and its star topology, Ethernet as a LAN technology offers the lowest computer or embedded target cost per node at a performance that enables a large number of applications.

Regardless of the speed (10/100/1000 Mbps) and medium (coaxial, twisted pair, fiber, radio frequencies) the following two aspects are always the same:

▣ Frame format

▣ Access method

Because these elements do not change for a specific physical medium, the interface to IP, the protocol in the layer above does not change either, which makes life a lot easier. Note that the discussion in this chapter is valid for wired Ethernet. Most of it can also be applied to Wi-Fi with minimal changes to an Ethernet frame header.

Wired Ethernet supports various speeds under the IEEE 802.3 Standard, as follows:

Speed	Standard
10 Mbps	IEEE 802.3
100 Mbps	IEEE 802.3u
1000 Mbps	IEEE 802.3z
10,000 Mbps	IEEE 802.3ae

Table 4-1 **Wired Ethernet Speeds and IEEE Standards**

4-1 TOPOLOGY

Ethernet was developed to address communication over a shared coaxial cable, as shown in Figure 4-1. The design of Ethernet had to take into account such challenges as collision detection on the coaxial cable, as it is possible for two hosts to transmit simultaneously.

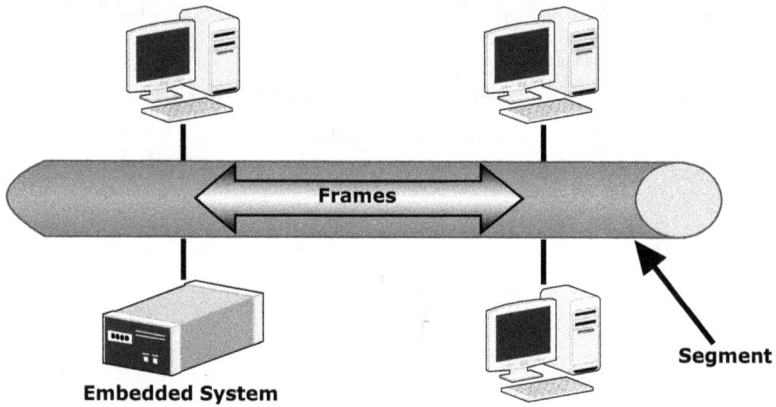

Figure 4-1 **First-Generation Ethernet – Coaxial Cable**

The sheer weight of coaxial cable made it impractical for use in high-rise buildings. Easy adaptation to telephony wiring with twisted pair cabling, hubs, and switches allows Ethernet to achieve point-to-point connectivity, and increase reliability. Twisted-pair wiring also lowers installation costs, enabling Ethernet to offer a cost per workstation that was unbeatable compared to competing technologies (i.e., ARCNET and Token Ring).

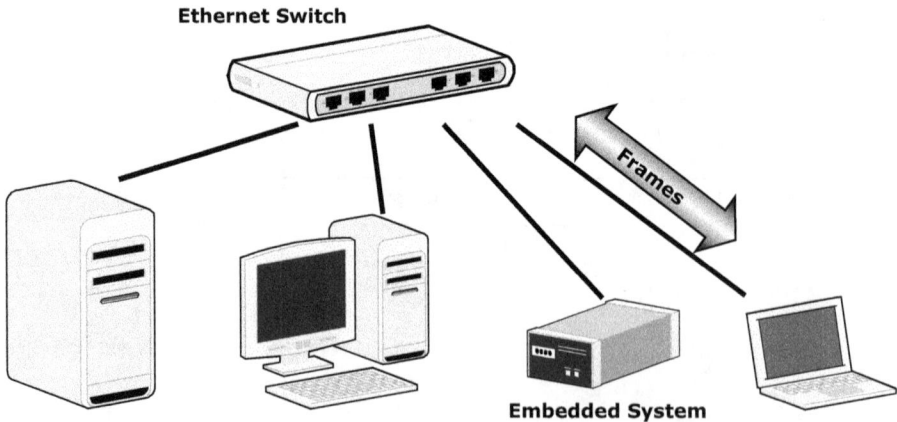

Figure 4-2 **Ethernet Today – Twisted Copper Pair and Switching**

Figure 4-2 shows an Ethernet network as we would connect it today. Between the original coaxial cable of the first generation Ethernet, and today's switch, Ethernet twisted pair cabling used hubs. A hub has the form factor of an Ethernet switch, but it acts as a coaxial cable. In a hub, all traffic from any RJ-45 port is visible on any other port, which is especially useful for troubleshooting. In that capacity, a Network protocol analyzer can be connected to any port on the hub and decode all of the traffic to and from any ports. This means that the hub is therefore the segment.

With today's Ethernet switch, each link to an RJ-45 is a segment, a concept called micro-segmentation. We will see in upcoming sections that certain traffic on an Ethernet network is undesirable. A switch allows for the removal of this traffic since the host connected to a port receives only the traffic destined to it, improving Ethernet network performance.

As with many other embedded technologies, hardware costs have constantly decreased over the past two decades. Given Ethernet's popularity, it is extremely common for a microcontroller to feature an integrated Ethernet Controller.

4-2 ETHERNET HARDWARE CONSIDERATIONS

Developing an Ethernet Driver is a fairly complex task. In addition to the Ethernet controller, often the developer must take into consideration on-chip clock and power peripheral management. If the developer is lucky, the semiconductor vendor may provide a Board Support Package (BSP) to tackle peripheral configurations. Pin multiplexing via general purpose I/O (GPIO) is required in some cases. Do not underestimate the complexity of this task.

4-3 ETHERNET CONTROLLER

In Chapter 2 we saw that there are a few Ethernet controller architectures to choose from when designing an embedded system. The main factor influencing choice is the location of the RAM used to hold received or transmitted frames.

For system design, you can use a specific chip for Ethernet or a microcontroller/ microprocessor with an integrated Ethernet controller. The Ethernet controller must cover the two bottom layers of the networking model: Data Link and Physical Layer (PHY).

IEEE-802.3 defines the Ethernet media access controller (MAC) which implements a Data Link layer. The latest MACs support operation at 10 Mbps, 100 Mbps and 1000 Mbps (1 Gbps).

The interface between the MAC and the PHY is typically implemented via the Media Independent Interface (MII), which consists of a data interface and a management interface between a MAC and a PHY (see Figure 4-3).

The PHY is the physical interface transceiver, implementing the Ethernet physical layer described in Chapter 1. IEEE 802.3 specifies several physical media standards. The most widely used are 10BASE-T, 100BASE-TX, and 1000BASE-T (Gigabit Ethernet), running at 10 Mbps, 100 Mbps and 1000 Mbps (1 Gbps), respectively.

The naming convention of 10BASE-T corresponds to the Ethernet physical media:

■ The number in the name represents the maximum line speed in megabits per second (Mbps).

■ BASE is the abbreviation for baseband. There is no frequency-division multiplexing (FDM) or other frequency shifting modulation in use; each signal (RX, TX) has full control of the wire.

■ T stands for twisted pair cable. There may be more than one twisted pair standard at the same line speed. In this case, a letter or digit is added following the T. For example, 100BASE-TX.

Typically, integrated PHY on a microcontroller use the 10/100 PHY Ethernet implementation and incorporate separate 10BASE-T (10 Mbps) and 100BASE-TX (100 Mbps) interfaces. Most recently, 1-Gbps Ethernet became available in some MACs.

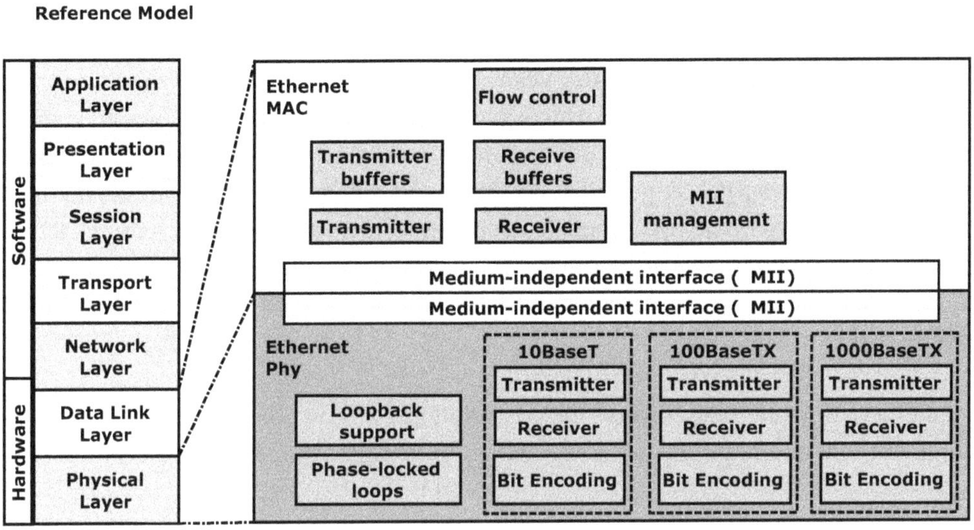

Reference Model

Figure 4-3 **10/100/1000 Ethernet MAC and PHY**

Many semiconductor vendors do not implement the PHY and MAC on the same chip since the PHY incorporates a significant amount of analog hardware. In comparison, the MAC is typically a purely digital component, and it is easier to integrate the MAC with current chip technologies. Adding the PHY adds analog signal circuits and increases the chip footprint and production costs. Semiconductor vendors sometimes leave the PHY off-chip. However, thanks to recent chip technology advances, the MAC and PHY can be effectively integrated on the same chip.

The typical PHY implementation still requires such components as an RJ-45 female jack and a local area network magnetic isolation module to protect the PHY from electrical abuse. To save space on the printed circuit board, it is possible to find dedicated Ethernet RJ-45 jacks that integrate analog components.

Single-chip Ethernet microcontrollers are popular in the embedded industry as the microcontrollers incorporating the Ethernet MAC and PHY on a single chip eliminate most external components. This reduces the overall pin count, chip footprint, and can also lower power consumption, especially if power-down mode management is available.

With the MII management interface, upper layers of the TCP/IP stack can monitor and control the PHY, for example, it can monitor the link status. Let's see how this is accomplished.

4-3-1 AUTO-NEGOTIATION

As Ethernet evolved, hubs gave way to switches, electronics improved, and the Ethernet link advanced from half duplex (alternative transmission and reception) to full duplex (simultaneous transmission and reception). Given that Ethernet offers various transmission rates (such as 10 Mbps, 100 Mbps and 1000 Mbps) and different duplex modes, a method is therefore necessary so that two Ethernet interfaces communicate together using different transmission rates (note that an Ethernet switch port is defined as an Ethernet interface). This method is called auto-negotiation, and is a feature offered in the majority of PHY interfaces used today.

For Ethernet to work with diverse link capabilities, every Ethernet device capable of multiple transmission rates uses auto-negotiation to declare its possible modes of operation.

The two devices (host and/or switch port) involved select the best possible mode of operation that can be shared by both. Higher speed (1000 Mbps) is preferred over lower speed (10 or 100 Mbps), and full duplex is preferable over half duplex at the same speed.

If one host of the two cannot perform auto-negotiation and the second one can, the host that is capable of auto-negotiation has the means to determine the speed of the facing host and set its configuration to match. This method does not, however, detect the presence of full-duplex mode. In this case, half duplex is assumed, which may create a problem called "duplex mismatch." This issue arises when one host operates in full duplex while the corresponding host operates in half duplex.

It is always a good idea to keep auto-negotiation configured, as Ethernet link capabilities are controlled via auto-negotiation.

If you believe that the PHY driver is not negotiating the link speed and duplex properly, use an oscilloscope to verify the signals on the link.

The mechanism used by auto-negotiation to communicate between two Ethernet devices is similar to the mechanism used by a 10BASE-T host to connect to another device. It uses pulses transmitted when the devices are not exchanging data.

Figure 4-4 **10BASE-T Normal Link Pulses (NLP)**

Figure 4-4 shows that the pulses are unipolar positive-only electrical pulses of 100 ns duration, generated at intervals of 16 ms (with a tolerance of 8 ms). These pulses are called link integrity test (LIT) pulses in 10BASE-T terminology, and are referred to as normal link pulses (NLP) in the auto-negotiation specification. This is usually the signal that is used to light the LED on certain RJ-45 connectors.

When a frame or two consecutive LIT pulses are received, the host will detect a valid link status. The failure of a link or a host is detected by the other host if a frame or pulses are not received for 50 to 150 ms.

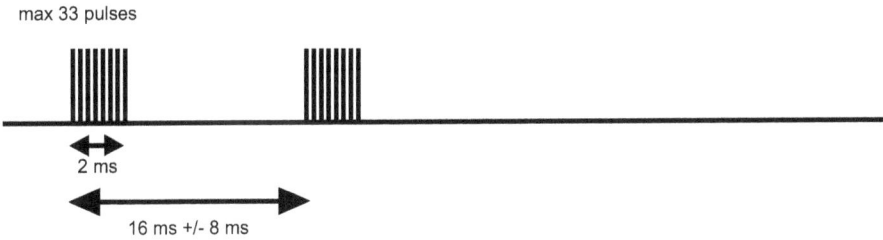

Figure 4-5 **Auto-negotiation Fast-Link Pulses (FLP)**

In Figure 4-5, auto-negotiation borrows from the pulse mechanism. The difference is that the pulse sequence is at most 33 pulses and is called a fast-link pulse (FLP) burst.

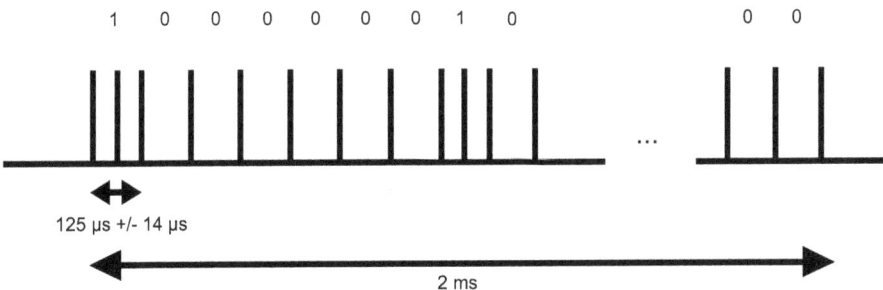

Figure 4-6 **Link code word (a 16-bit word) encoded in a fast link pulse burst**

Figure 4-6 pictures FLP made up of 17 pulses, 125 µs apart. An intermediate pulse can be inserted between each set of two pulses in the stream of the 17 pulses. The presence of a pulse represents a logical 1,and the absence a logical 0. These intermediate pulses number 16 and are called a link code word (LCW). The 17 pulses are always present and are used as a clock, while the 16 pulses represent the actual information transmitted.

The embedded software engineer can debug the PHY driver by looking at the PHY controller registers via the MII interface and make sure the values in these registers match the pulses on the link.

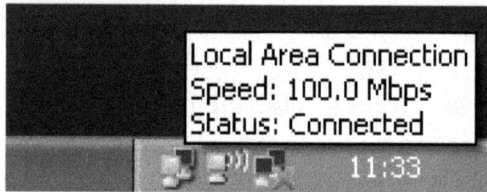

Figure 4-7 **Link status as represented in Microsoft Windows**

Figure 4-7 indicates how Ethernet PHYs and corresponding drivers can make the link status available to the stack and the stack to the application. This is how an operating system provides information on link status. µC/TCP-IP driver API allows the application to receive the link status (see Chapter 16, "Device Driver Implementation" on page 365 and Appendix A, "µC/TCP-IP Ethernet Device Driver APIs" on page 531).

The non-recognition of the FLP also can create duplex mismatch. For a 10BASE-T device, an FLP does not make an NLP. This means that when a 10BASE-T host communicates with a host at a higher speed, the 10BASE-T host detects a link failure and switches to half-duplex mode while the higher-speed host will be in full-duplex mode. The next section describes what happens in this case.

There are many possible causes for poor performance on an Ethernet/IP network. As mentioned earlier, one of them is duplex mismatch. When a system is experiencing bad performance, we are tempted to look at higher protocols to see what is wrong. Sometimes, however, the problem is with the bottom layers.

4-3-2 DUPLEX MISMATCH

When two Ethernet devices are configured in two different duplex modes, a *duplex mismatch* results. A host operation in half duplex is not expecting to receive a frame when it is transmitted. However, because the connecting host is in full duplex, frames can be transmitted to the half duplex host. The receiving host senses these frames as late collisions interpreted as a hard error rather than a normal Ethernet Carrier Sense Multiple Access/Collision Detection (CSMA/CD) collision, and will not attempt to resend the frame. At the same time, the full-duplex host does not detect a collision and thus does not resend the frame. The other host would have discarded the frame since it was corrupted by the collision. Also, the full duplex host will report frame check sequence (FCS) errors because it is not expecting incoming frames to be truncated by collision detection.

These collisions and frame errors disrupt the flow of communication. Some protocols in the Application layer or the Transport layer manage flow control and make sure packets not completed are retransmitted. This is explained in more detail when we cover Transport Protocols.

It is recommended that you avoid using older Ethernet hubs with new switches as duplex mismatch can be expected. Any duplex mismatch degrades link performance. The network runs, but at a much lower bandwidth. Never force one end of a connection to full duplex while the other end is set to auto-negotiation. Retransmission slows down data exchange. This is acceptable for a link with low traffic (connectivity needs only), but will be a real problem for a link with high-bandwidth requirements (node with throughput requirement).

Auto-negotiation in PHY driver

To avoid duplex mismatch that can be a cause for performance degradation in the Ethernet network, it is recommended that you always keep the PHY driver auto-negotiation feature enabled.

4-4 ETHERNET 802.3 FRAME STRUCTURE

4-4-1 802.3 FRAME FORMAT

This is the Ethernet frame as standardized by IEEE 802.3.

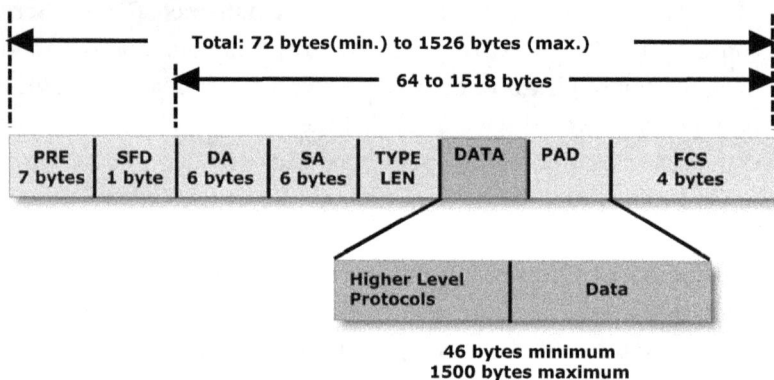

Figure 4-8 **802.3 Frame Format**

Acronym	Description
PRE	Preamble
SFD	Start Frame Delimiter
DA	Destination Address
SA	Source Address
TYPE/LEN	Length
Higher Level Protocols	Protocol code being carried in this frame
DATA	....
PAD	Padding
FCS	Frame Check Sequence

Table 4-2 **Ethernet Frame fields**

RFC 1010 EtherType (2 bytes)

0X0800	IP
0x0806	ARP

Table 4-3 **EtherTypes**

There are more protocol numbers in RFC 1010 than the two listed above. For practicality, these are the two most widely used in the type of networks we work with today.

The figure above is labeled 802.3 Frame Format, but it describes what is referred to as the Ethernet II frame or the so-called DIX (after Digital, Intel and Xerox). It is the most common frame format used and is directly used by IP.

Other Ethernet frame formats include:

▓ Novell's non-standard variation of IEEE 802.3

▓ IEEE 802.2 LLC frame

▓ IEEE 802.2 LLC/SNAP frame

With 802.3 format and the three formats listed above, depending on the types of hosts connected on the network, it is possible that on networks where the embedded system is installed there may be additional Ethernet frame formats.

A Virtual LAN (VLAN) is a network of hosts that communicate as if they were connected to the same LAN, regardless of their physical location. Ethernet frames may optionally contain an IEEE 802.1Q tag to identify what VLAN it belongs to and its IEEE 802.1p priority (class of service). The IEEE 802.3ac specification defines this encapsulation and increases the maximum frame by 4 bytes from 1518 to 1522 bytes.

This quality of service field is used by the Ethernet switches to process certain frames in priority, for example, for such real-time services as voice or video versus data. The TCP/IP stack and the Ethernet switch must be able to process 802.1Q tag and 801.1p priority if VLAN support and quality of service is required in the dedicated network.

With the evolution of Ethernet, it became necessary to eventually unify the formats. The convention is that values of the TYPE/LEN field between 64 and 1522 indicate the use of the 802.3 Ethernet format with a length field, while values of 1536 decimal (0x0600 hexadecimal) and greater indicate the use of the Ethernet II frame format with an EtherType sub-protocol identifier (see Table 4-3 above or RFC 1010). This convention allows software to determine whether a frame is an Ethernet II frame or an IEEE 802.3 frame, enabling the coexistence of both standards.

Using a Network Protocol Analyzer as explained in Chapter 6, "Troubleshooting" on page 139, it is possible to capture Ethernet frames on the network. Diagrams will often refer to frame and packet structures as decoded by the Network Protocol Analyzer. Figure 4-8, 802.3 Frame Format, is a good example. When decoding an Ethernet frame, the Network Protocol Analyzer presents the structure of the frame.

Important fields for the software are the Destination Address (DA), the Source Address (SA), the type/length of the frame (TYPE/LEN) and the payload (DATA). The Frame Check Sequence (FCS) determines the validity of the frame. If the frame is invalid, the Ethernet controller discards it.

The combination of the DA, SA and TYPE field are referred as the MAC header.

Preamble and the Start Frame Delimiter are used for clocking and synchronization. The Ethernet controller strips these out and will only transfer the remaining frame to a buffer beginning with the Destination Address and ending with the Frame Check Sequence.

Given that Ethernet was initially developed for a shared medium, Ethernet controllers transmit 12 bytes of idle characters after each frame so that interfaces detect collisions created by frames transmitted from other interfaces on the same network. For 10 Mbps interfaces this takes 9600 ns, for 100 Mbps interfaces 960 ns, and for 1 Gbps interfaces 96 ns.

4-5 MAC ADDRESS

As indicated earlier, frames of data are transmitted into the physical layer medium (copper, coax, fiber, and radio interfaces). NICs listen over the physical medium for frames with a unique LAN address called the Media Access Control (MAC) address.

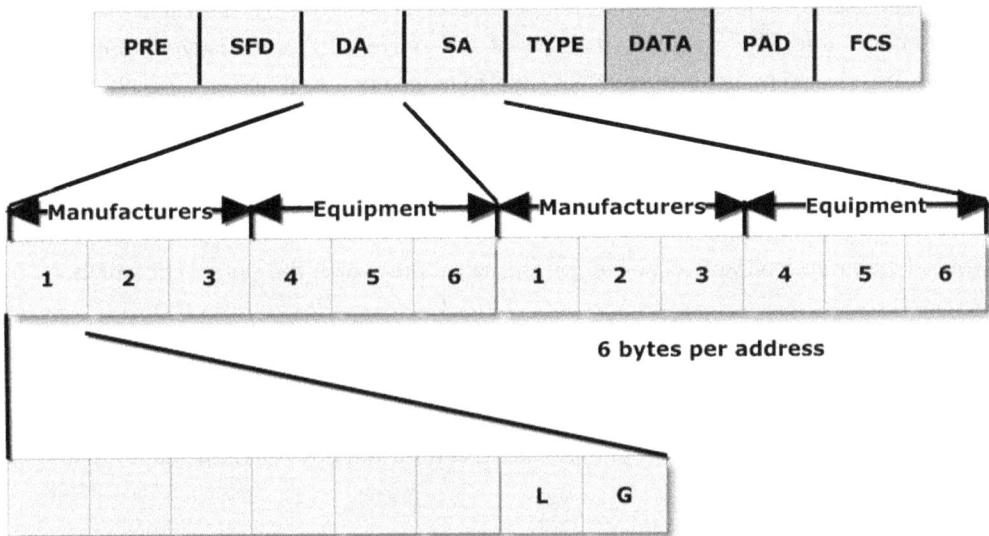

L=0 Globally administered
L=1 Locally administered
G=0 Individual address
G=1 Address group (broadcast/multicast)

Figure 4-9 **MAC Address**

Figure 4-9 Illustrates MAC addresses, Destination (DA) and Source (SA) in an Ethernet Frame. It also shows that an Ethernet MAC address is made of 6 bytes (48 bits). The first three bytes are the manufacturer ID. The last three bytes represent the serial number for the manufacturer. The MAC address is represented with each byte in hexadecimal notation separated by either a colon (:) or a hyphen (-), or a semicolon which is more common, for example: 00:00:0C:12:DE:7F. This is also referred as a universally administered individual address as per the L and G bits in Figure 4-9.

The manufacturer ID is assigned by the IEEE and is called an Organizationally Unique Identifier (OUI). The IEEE OUI Registry at http://standards.ieee.org/regauth/oui/oui.txt contains OUI that are registered. ID 00:00:0C in the previous example belongs to Cisco.

Each NIC is required to have a globally unique MAC address which is typically burned or programmed into the NIC, yet can also be overwritten via software configuration. When this happens, a locally administered address can be used. Universally administered and locally administered addresses are distinguished by setting the second least significant bit of the most significant byte of the address as depicted in Figure 4-9. The bit is 0 in all OUIs.

As its name states, a locally administered address is assigned to a host by a network administrator. Generally, however, the use of the universally administered MAC address provided by the manufacturer removes this management requirement on the network administrator.

Whichever method is used, attention should be paid to the MAC address assigned to a NIC as it could lead to duplicate MAC addresses. No two hosts can have the same MAC address. It would be akin to having two houses on the same street with the same civic number.

4-6 TRAFFIC TYPES

Network interfaces are usually programmed to listen for three types of messages that:

■ are sent to their specific address

■ qualify as a multicast for the specific interface

■ are broadcast to all NICs

There are three types of addressing:

1. Unicast: A transmission to a single interface.

2. Multicast: A transmission to a group of interfaces on the network.

3. Broadcast: A transmission to all interfaces on the network.

Figure 4-9 shows that if the least significant bit of the most significant byte of the MAC address is set to a 0, the packet is meant to reach only one receiving NIC. This is called unicast.

If the least significant bit of the most significant byte is set to a 1, the packet is meant to be sent only once but will reach several NICs. This is called multicast.

All other messages are filtered out by the interface software, unless it is programmed to operate in promiscuous mode (this is a pass-through mode that allows the driver to pass all frames decoded to an application such as a network protocol analyzer (see section 6-2-2 "Wireshark" on page 156) to perform network sniffing.

All of the above-mentioned address types are used by Ethernet; however, IP also uses the same type of addressing. The scope is evidently different as IP operates on a different layer than Ethernet.

UNICAST

Unicast is a type of frame used to send information from one host to another host when there is only one source and one destination. Unicast is the predominant form of transmission on LANs and within the Internet. You are probably quite familiar with such standard unicast applications as HTTP, SMTP, FTP, and TELNET.

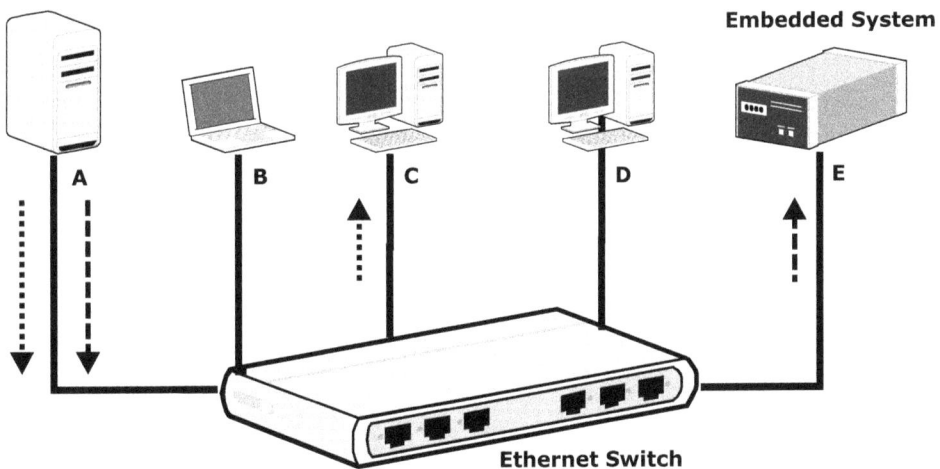

Figure 4-10 **Unicast: (host to host)**

In Figure 4-10, the dotted line represents a Unicast frame from A to C and the dashed line a Unicast frame from A to E.

BROADCAST

Broadcast is used to transmit information from one host to all other hosts. In this case there is just one source, but the information is sent to all connected destinations. Broadcast transmission is supported on Ethernet and may be used to send the same message to all computers on the LAN.

Broadcasting is very useful for such protocols as:

■ Address Resolution Protocol (ARP) on IP when looking for the MAC address of a neighboring station.

■ Dynamic Host Configuration Protocol (DHCP) on IP when a station is booting and is requesting an IP address from a DHCP server.

■ Routing table updates. Broadcasts sent by routers with routing table updates to other routers.

The Ethernet broadcast destination address in hexadecimal is FF:FF:FF:FF:FF:FF.

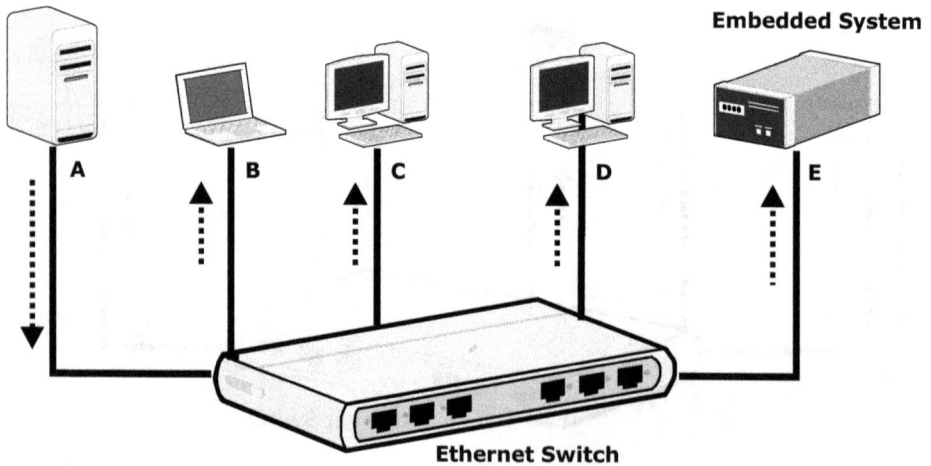

Figure 4-11 **Broadcast (one host to all hosts)**

The dotted line in Figure 4-11 is a Broadcast message from A to all other Ethernet interfaces on the LAN.

With coaxial-cable technology (shared medium), and a growing number of workstations per network, broadcast may create an undesired volume of traffic. Twisted pair physical layer and daisy-chained Ethernet switches often configured in a loop for redundancy purposes will create a broadcast storm (i.e., the broadcast message will circle forever in the loop). This is why Ethernet switches implement micro-segmentation and spanning-tree protocols. The spanning tree protocol allows Ethernet switches to determine where to break the loop to avoid a broadcast storm. It uses a Multicast address type.

MULTICAST

Multicast addressing is used to transmit data from one or more hosts to a set of other hosts. There is possibly one or multiple sources, and the information is distributed to a set of destinations. LANs using hubs/repeaters inherently support multicast since all packets reach all network interfaces connected to the LAN.

Multicasting delivers the same packet simultaneously to a group of hosts. For example, a video server application that uses multicast transmits networked TV channels. Simultaneous delivery of high-quality video to a large number of stations will exhaust the capability of even a high-bandwidth network with a powerful server. This can be a major scalability issue for applications that require sustained bandwidth. One way to optimize bandwidth usage for larger groups of clients is the use of multicast networking.

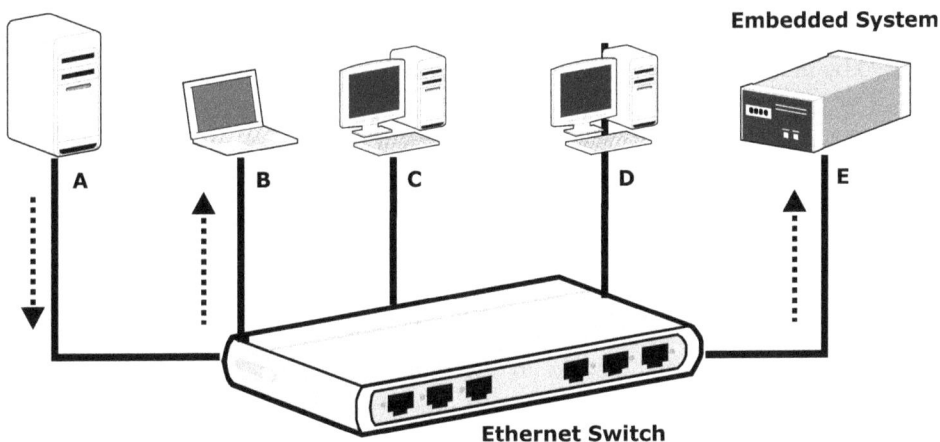

Figure 4-12 **Multicast: (from one host to a group)**

In Figure 4-12, the dotted line represents a Multicast message from A to a group of host, in this case B and E.

105

4

The Internet Assigned Numbers Authority (IANA) allocates Ethernet addresses from 01:00:5E:00:00:00 through 01:00:5E:7F:FF:FF for multicasting. This means there are 23 bits available for the multicast group ID plus reserved groups as the spanning tree group address used by Ethernet switches. The spanning tree group address is 01-80-C2-00-00-01.

4-7 ADDRESS RESOLUTION PROTOCOL (ARP)

In our discussion of Ethernet, we specified that as a Data-Link layer protocol, Ethernet employs a MAC address to identify each NIC. We also saw at the Network layer that for internetworking, we need a network address (in our case, an IP address). The IP address definition and structure is covered in the next chapter, but it is interesting to note that an IP address consists of 32 bits while a MAC address consists of 48 bits. So, the next logical question might be: "How are these addresses related to one another?"

The relationship/translation between the Data-Link address and the IP address is required so that data can follow a path between layers and this cross-reference is accomplished via the Address Resolution Protocol (ARP).

In some IP technology descriptions, ARP is placed at Layer 2 while others place it at Layer 3. In reality, we can say that ARP is a layer 2.5 protocol, as it interfaces between Network addresses and Data-Link addresses.

ARP is used by hosts on a network to find MAC addresses of neighbors when the hosts want to connect to a neighbor using an IP address.

In the figures that follow, we will track an ARP process. The result of the ARP process is a cross-reference between IP and MAC addresses. These cross-references are stored in an ARP cache, which is a data structure found in the TCP/IP stack. Each station on a network has its own ARP cache, the size of which can be configured to customize its RAM footprint. You need to know the number of stations the host will connect to on the network, since one entry per connection will be created in the ARP cache. See Appendix D, "μC/TCP-IP Configuration and Optimization" on page 959, for the μC/TCP-IP configuration parameter relating to the number of ARP cache entries.

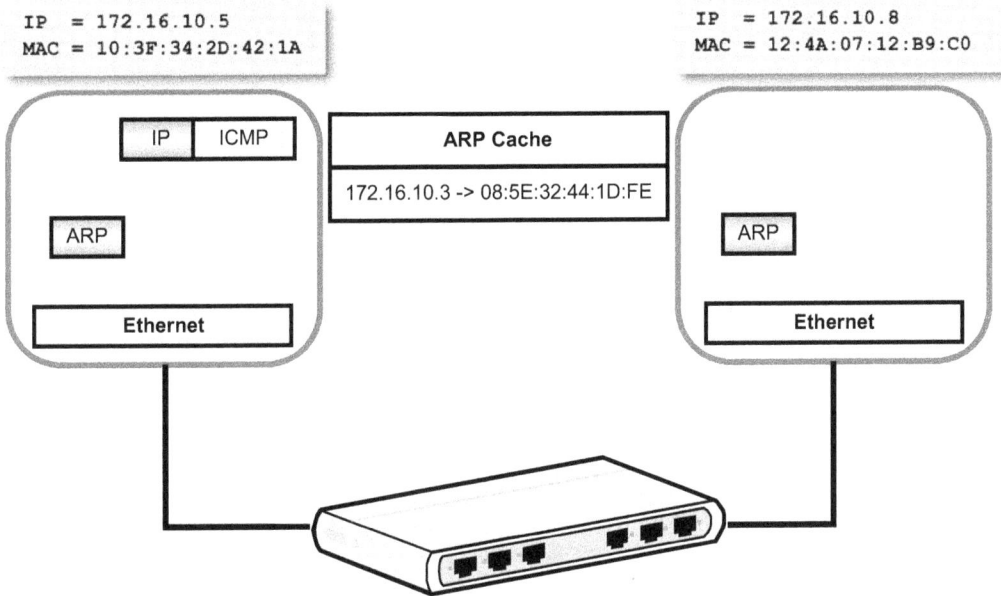

IP = 172.16.10.5
MAC = 10:3F:34:2D:42:1A

IP = 172.16.10.8
MAC = 12:4A:07:12:B9:C0

IP | ICMP

ARP

Ethernet

ARP Cache

172.16.10.3 -> 08:5E:32:44:1D:FE

ARP

Ethernet

Figure 4-13 **ARP - Step 1**

Figure 4-13 represents the network for our example. The station on the left with IP address 172.16.10.5 sends a ping request (ICMP) to station on the right with IP address 172.16.10.8.

The ICMP module of the TCP/IP stack sends the command to the IP module of the stack.

IP = 172.16.10.5
MAC = 10:3F:34:2D:42:1A

IP = 172.16.10.8
MAC = 12:4A:07:12:B9:C0

| IP | ICMP |

ARP Cache

172.16.10.3 -> 08:5E:32:44:1D:FE

ARP

ARP

Ethernet

Ethernet

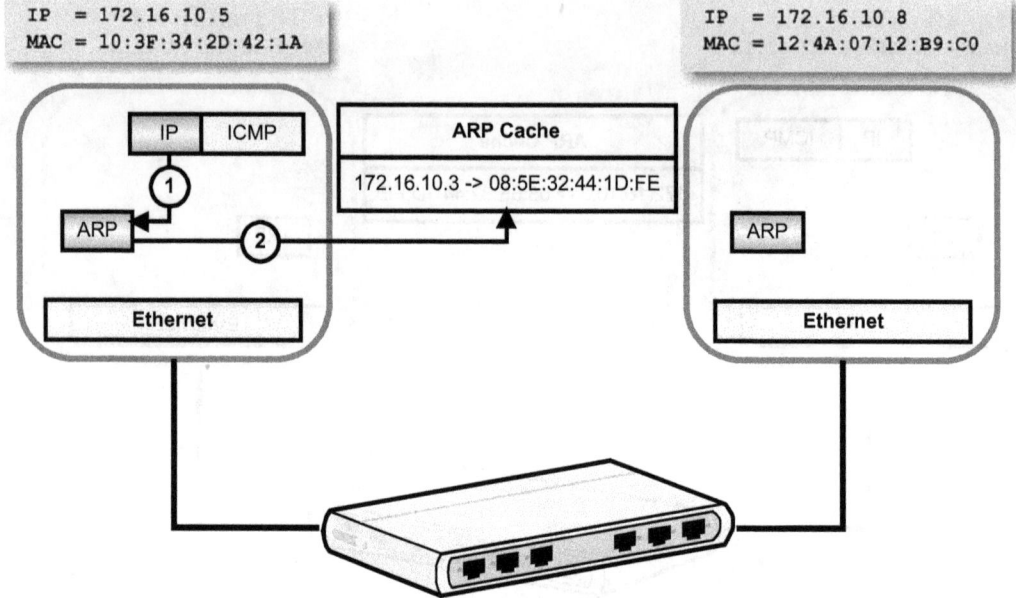

Figure 4-14 **ARP - Step 2**

F4-14(1)   The IP module asks the ARP module to supply it with the MAC address (Layer 2).

F4-14(2)   The ARP module consults its ARP cache (a table containing known IP to MAC addresses). The desired IP address is not in the table.

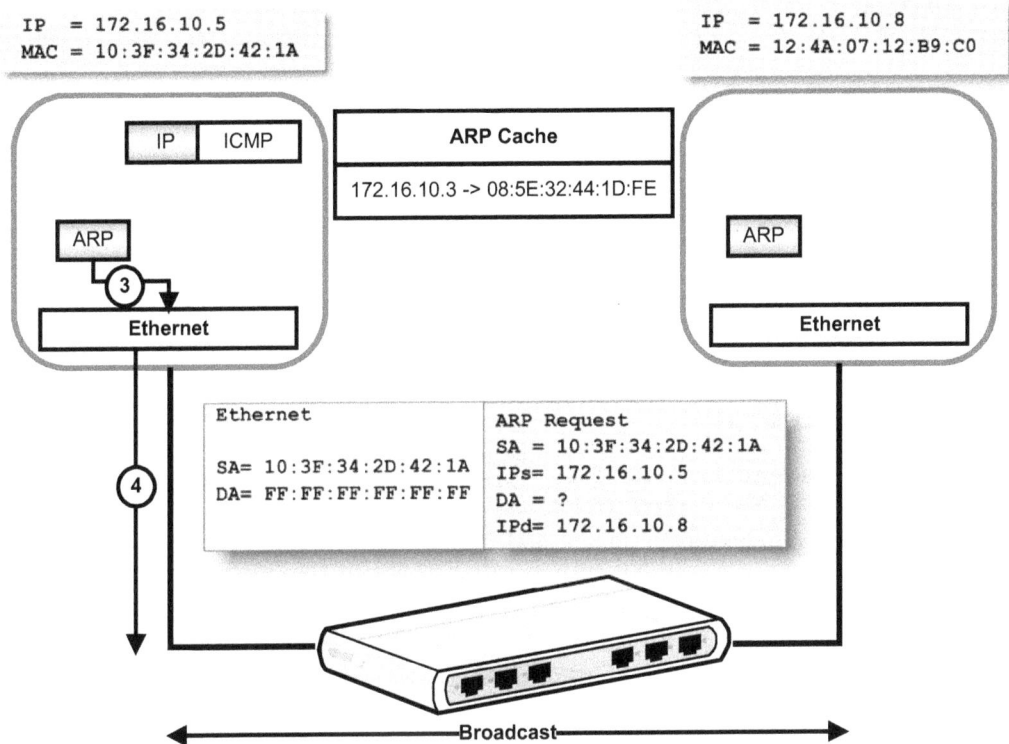

IP = 172.16.10.5
MAC = 10:3F:34:2D:42:1A

IP = 172.16.10.8
MAC = 12:4A:07:12:B9:C0

IP   ICMP

ARP Cache

172.16.10.3 -> 08:5E:32:44:1D:FE

ARP

ARP

3

Ethernet

Ethernet

Ethernet

ARP Request

SA= 10:3F:34:2D:42:1A
DA= FF:FF:FF:FF:FF:FF

SA = 10:3F:34:2D:42:1A
IPs= 172.16.10.5
DA = ?
IPd= 172.16.10.8

4

Broadcast

Figure 4-15 **ARP - Step 3**

F4-15(3)   The ARP module sends an «ARP request» packet to the Ethernet module.

F4-15(4)   The Ethernet module sends it to everyone («broadcast»). The Ethernet
            destination address (DA) in the ARP request packet is the Ethernet broadcast
            address. The source address (SA) is the MAC address of the host generating the
            request. The complete content of the ARP request is provided in the following
            section.

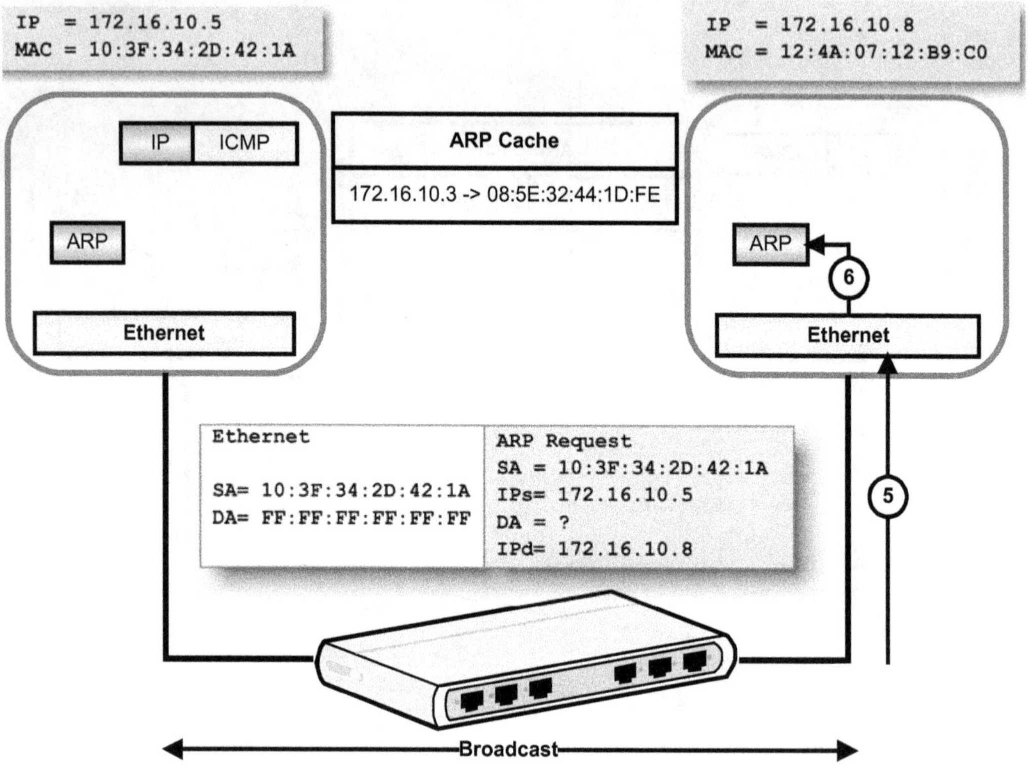

Figure 4-16 **ARP - Step 4**

F4-16(5)   All stations on this network receive and decode the Ethernet broadcast frame.

F4-16(6)   The ARP request is sent to the ARP module. Only station 172.16.10.8 realizes
that it is an «ARP request» for itself.

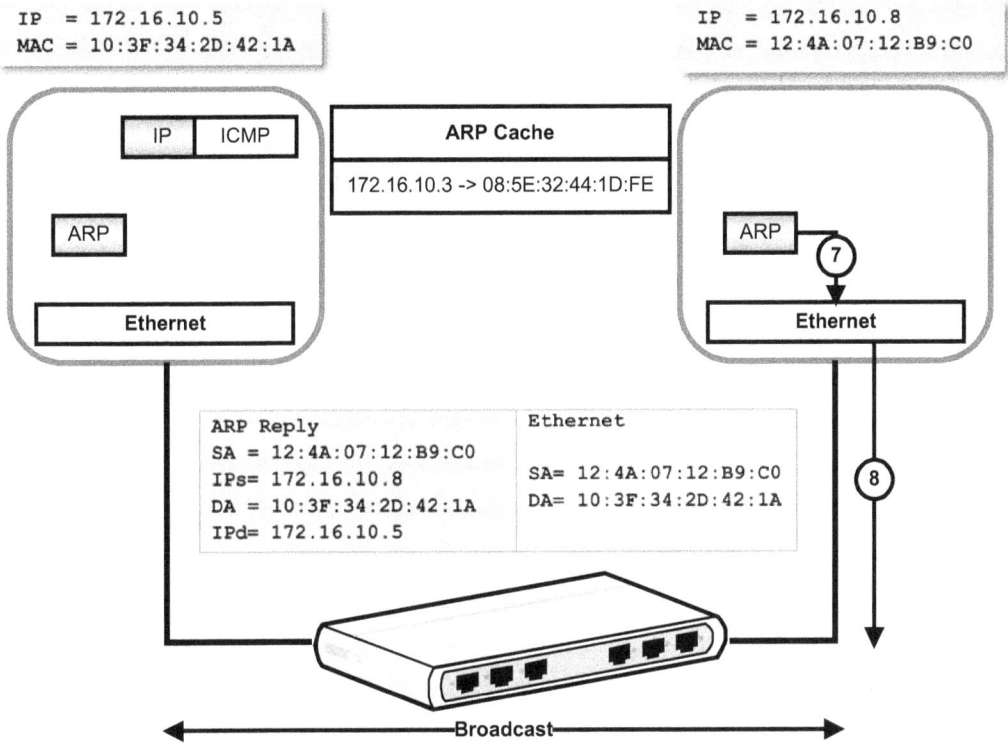

IP = 172.16.10.5
MAC = 10:3F:34:2D:42:1A

IP = 172.16.10.8
MAC = 12:4A:07:12:B9:C0

| IP | ICMP |

ARP Cache

172.16.10.3 -> 08:5E:32:44:1D:FE

ARP

ARP

7

Ethernet

Ethernet

ARP Reply
SA = 12:4A:07:12:B9:C0
IPs= 172.16.10.8
DA = 10:3F:34:2D:42:1A
IPd= 172.16.10.5

Ethernet

SA= 12:4A:07:12:B9:C0
DA= 10:3F:34:2D:42:1A

8

Broadcast

Figure 4-17 **ARP - Step 5**

F4-17(7) The ARP module in station 172.16.10.8 acknowledges the request and replies back with an answer («ARP reply») to the Ethernet module.

F4-17(8) The response is sent in an Ethernet frame to the station with the IP address 172.16.10.5. The Ethernet destination address is known because it is the source address that was part of the ARP Request. The Ethernet source address is the MAC address of station 172.16.10.8

IP = 172.16.10.5
MAC = 10:3F:34:2D:42:1A

IP = 172.16.10.8
MAC = 12:4A:07:12:B9:C0

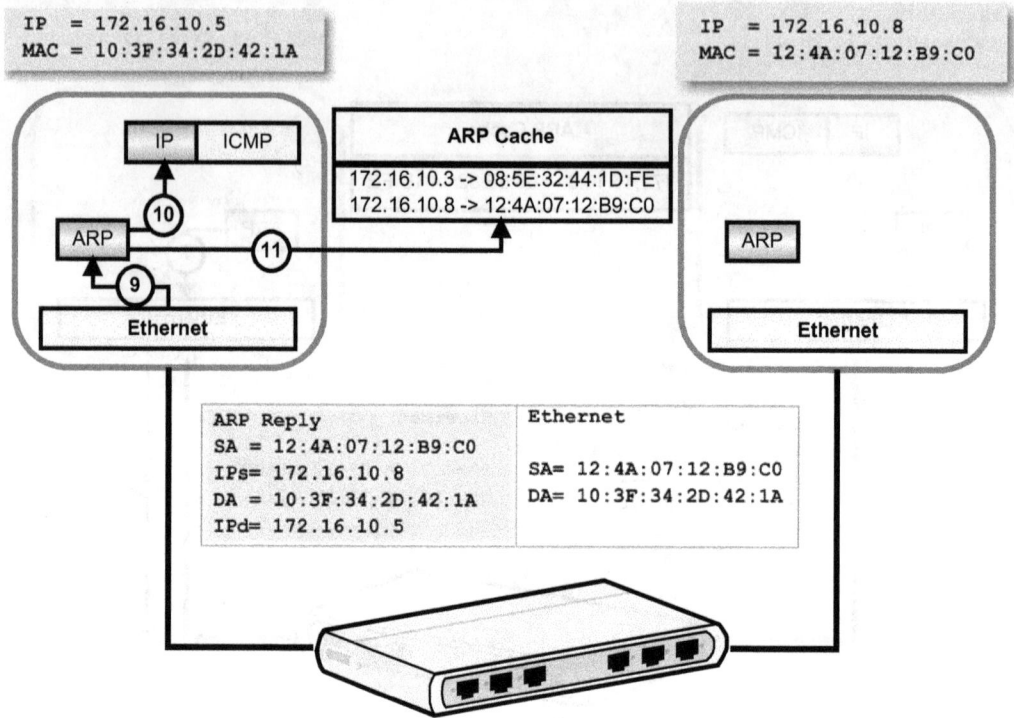

Figure 4-18 **ARP - Step 6**

F4-18(9)   The Ethernet module of the station with the MAC address corresponding to the destination address in the Ethernet frame passes the reply to the ARP module.

F4-18(10) The ARP module forwards the missing information to the IP module that requested it initially.

F4-18(11) The ARP module also stores the information in the ARP cache.

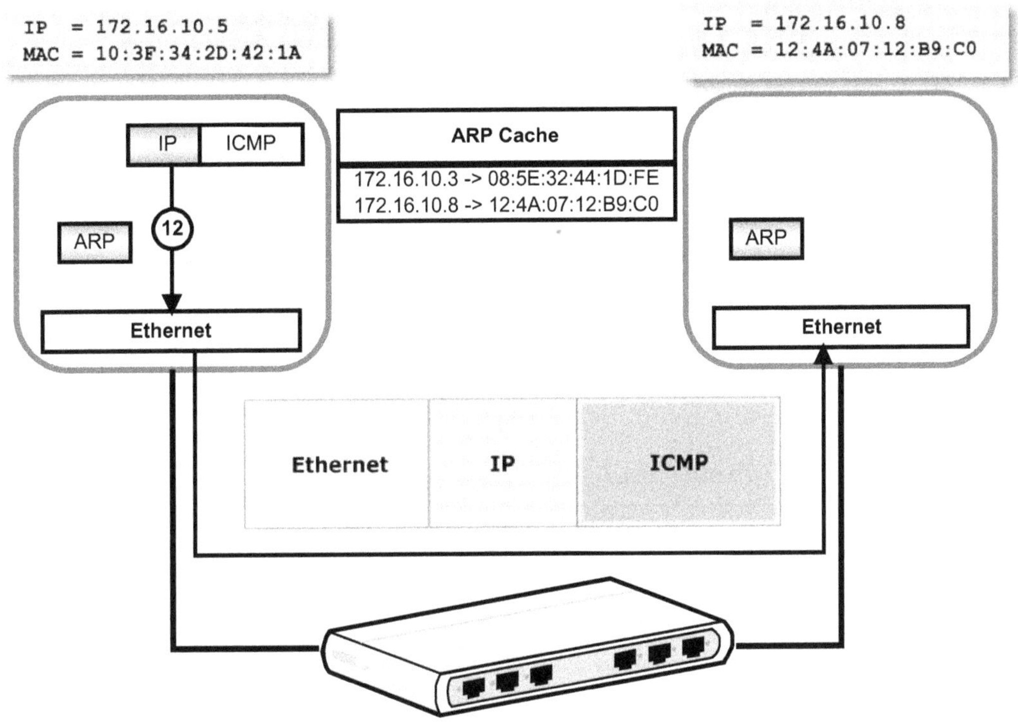

IP = 172.16.10.5
MAC = 10:3F:34:2D:42:1A

IP = 172.16.10.8
MAC = 12:4A:07:12:B9:C0

| IP | ICMP |

ARP Cache

172.16.10.3 -> 08:5E:32:44:1D:FE
172.16.10.8 -> 12:4A:07:12:B9:C0

ARP (12)

ARP

Ethernet

Ethernet

| Ethernet | IP | ICMP |

Figure 4-19 **ARP - Step 7**

F4-19(12)   The IP module now sends the initial ICMP message to the station with the IP address of 172.16.10.8 because it now knows its Ethernet address, 12:4A:07:12:B9:C0.

4-8 ARP PACKET

When a host sends a packet to another host on the LAN for the first time, the first message seen on the network will be an ARP request. The ARP header is found at the beginning of each ARP packet. The header contains fields of fixed length, and each field has a specific role to play. Figure 4-20 provides the definition of this protocol header. This representation will be use throughout this book for all protocol headers. A Network Protocol Analyzer, explained in Chapter 6, "Troubleshooting" on page 139, allows you to examine ARP requests.

0	1	2	3	4	5	6	7	8	9	1 0	1 1	1 2	1 3	1 4	1 5	1 6	1 7	1 8	1 9	2 0	2 1	2 2	2 3	2 4	2 5	2 6	2 7	2 8	2 9	3 0	3 1
Hardware																Protocol															
HLEN								PLEN								Operation															
Sender Hardware Address...																															
...Sender Hardware Address																Sender IP Address...															
...Sender IP Address																Target Hardware Address...															
...Target Hardware Address																															
Target IP Address																															

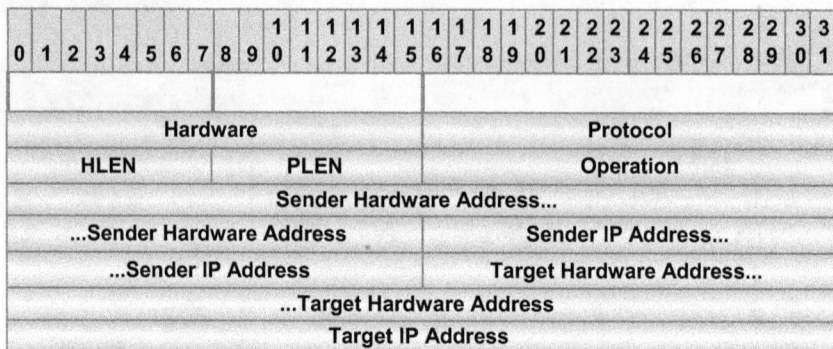

Figure 4-20 **ARP Header**

HLen	Length of the physical address in bytes, Ethernet = 6
PLen	Length of the protocol address in bytes, IP = 4
Operation	The possible values for the Operation field are: 1.ARP request 2.ARP reply 3.RARP request 4.RARP reply
Hardware	Specifies the type of hardware address (1 specifies Ethernet)
Protocol	Represents the type of protocol addressing used (IP = 0x0800)
Sender Hardware	Physical address of the sender
Target Hardware	Target hardware address (normally FF:FF:FF:FF:FF:FF)
Sender IP	IP address of the sender
Target IP	IP address of target

Table 4-4 **ARP Header Fields**

A Network Protocol Analyzer decodes the Ethernet frame and presents the frame content. In the case of ARP messages, this figure will help understand the information decoded.

4-9 SUMMARY

Ethernet is the most popular technology to use for a LAN. The driver is made of two modules: the MAC driver and the PHY driver.

MII is a simple standard for the PHY layer as this standard is very well implemented and supported by most hardware vendors. Micrium, for example, provides a generic PHY driver that can easily be adapted to most MIIs.

Getting the hardware up and running is a challenge based on the complexity of various peripherals. Ethernet controllers that are integrated inside microcontrollers are complicated to use as there are multiple configurations to take care of such as those involving clock, power and general purpose I/O pins.

When testing an Ethernet driver, the first test should be to validate that the PHY layer negotiates the link speed and duplex properly. Once this is done, the developer is ready to send a first packet to the embedded system. This is usually done using the PING utility. (see Chapter 6, "Troubleshooting" on page 139). When the Ethernet and PHY are configured properly, the first packet on the network will be an ARP request followed by an ARP reply. In this case, the ARP request will be issued from the host sending the PING and the ARP reply will come from the embedded target.

The next chapter looks deeper into the subject of IP networking and protocol possibilities.

5

IP Networking

With one or more protocols at every layer of the protocol stack, we often refer to Internet Protocol (IP) technology as the sum of all protocols. Strictly speaking, however, IP is the protocol used at the Network Layer.

For the embedded system developer, when employing IP technology in an embedded system, there is not much to actually do concerning the IP layer itself. What is important to know is how it works so that it can be used efficiently; configuring the TCP/IP stack actually requires minimal effort.

5

5-1 PROTOCOL FAMILY

The TCP/IP protocol stack is comprised of more than TCP and IP. Figure 5-1 shows that the TCP/IP stack represents a family of protocols (not all are included in this figure). The stack receives its name from the prevalent use of the TCP and IP protocols for the majority of data exchanges between two network devices.

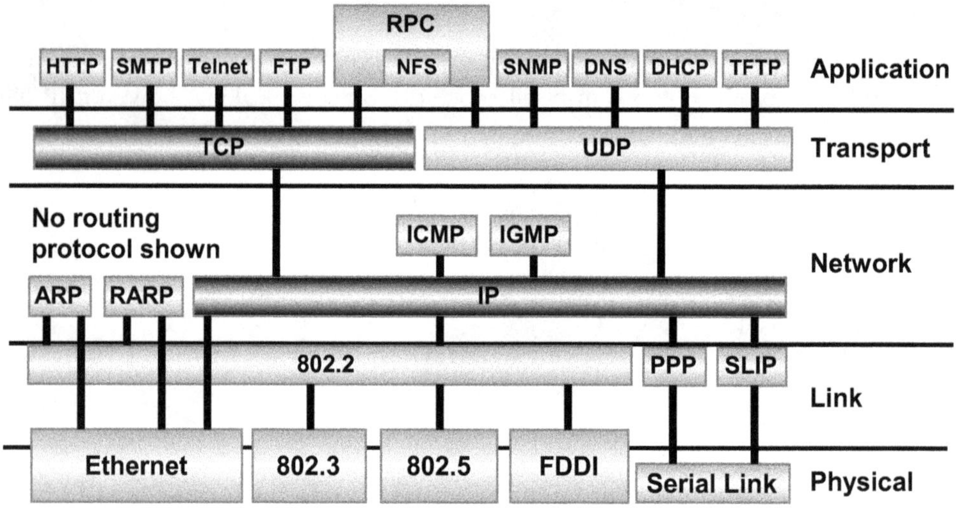

Figure 5-1 **IP Family of Protocols**

Figure 5-1 also introduces many new acronyms, and indicates which protocols are supported by Micrium's µC/TCP-IP. The important protocols used in embedded designs are covered in this book.

Protocol	Description	Micrium offer
HTTP	Hyper Text Transfer Protocol, the main web protocol	µC/HTTPs
SMTP	Simple Message Transport Protocol, used to send e-mails	µC/SMTPc
Telnet	Protocol used to provide a bidirectional interactive ASCII-based communications	µC/Telnet
FTP	File Transfer Protocol, used to exchange files	µC/FTPc and µC/FTPs

Protocol	Description	Micrium offer
RPC	Remote Procedure Call, uses Inter-Process Communication methods to create the illusion that the processes exchanging them are running in the same address space	Not Available
NFS	Network File System, file system developed by Sun Microsystems, Inc. a client/server system	Not Available
DNS	Domain Name Service, translates fully qualified domain names such as "www.mysite.com" into an IP address	µC/DNSc
DHCP	Dynamic Host Configuration Protocol, a network application protocol used by devices (DHCP clients) to obtain configuration information, primarily an IP address, subnet mask and default gateway, for operation in an IP network.	µC/DHCPc
SNMP	Simple Network Management Protocol, a set of standards for network management, including an application layer protocol, a database schema, and a set of data objects used to monitor network-attached devices.	Not available
TFTP	Trivial File Transfer Protocol, a simple file-transfer protocol, such as FTP using UDP as the transport layer.	µC/TFTPc and µC/TFTPs
TCP	Transport Control Protocol, the most widely-used transport layer protocol, developed for the Internet to guarantee the transmission of error-free data from one network device to another.	Part of µC/TCP-IP
UDP	User Datagram Protocol, the other transport layer protocol, which has no error recovery features, and is mostly used to send streamed material over the Internet.	Part of µC/TCP-IP
ARP	Address Resolution Protocol, a protocol used to map IP addresses to MAC addresses.	Part of µC/TCP-IP
RARP	Reverse Address Resolution Protocol, a protocol used by a host computer to obtain its IP address when it has its MAC address. DHCP is the current preferred method to obtain an IP address.	Not available
ICMP	Internet Control Message Protocol resides at the Network layer and is used to perform network troubleshooting and problem location.	Part of µC/TCP-IP
IGMP	Internet Group Management Protocol is used to manage the membership of IP multicast groups. IGMP is used by IP hosts and adjacent multicast routers to establish multicast group memberships.	Part of µC/TCP-IP
IP	Internet Protocol is arguably the world's single most popular network protocol	Part of µC/TCP-IP
Routing	Multiple routing protocols can be used at the IP layer.	Not available
PPP	Point-To-Point Protocol, used for the transmission of IP packets over serial lines. It is faster and more reliable than SLIP because it supports functions that SLIP does not, such as error detection, dynamic assignment of IP addresses and data compression.	Not available

Protocol	Description	Micrium offer
SLIP	Serial Line Internet Protocol is used for connection to the Internet via a dial-up connection.	Not available
FDDI	Fiber Distributed Data Interface provides a standard for data transmission in a local area network that provides a transmission range of up to 200 kilometers (124 miles). Although FDDI topology is a token ring network, it does not use the IEEE 802.5 token ring protocol as its basis;	Not available
802.2	IEEE 802.2 is the IEEE 802 standard defining Logical Link Control (LLC), which is the upper portion of the data link layer of the OSI Model.	Part of the Ethernet driver
802.3	IEEE 802.3 is a collection of IEEE standards defining the physical layer, and the media access control (MAC) sub layer of the data link layer, of wired Ethernet.	Part of the Ethernet driver
802.5	IEEE 802.5 is a collection of IEEE standards defining token ring local area network (LAN) technology. It resides at the data link layer (DLL) of the OSI model.	Not available

Table 5-1 **Short List of IP Family Protocols**

So far in this book, we've explained certain elements of a TCP/IP stack. When analyzing a network it is not surprising to open an Ethernet frame and find that the Ethernet payload is composed of an IP packet (EtherType 0x8000). Figure 5-2 shows how an IP packet is constructed. In this example, we see a Version 4 IP packet (IPv4), which is currently the Internet Protocol used in most private and public networks.

There are certain limitations in IPv4, the most important is the shortage of IP addresses for devices that can be connected globally. A new version of IP was developed at the end of the 1990's called IP Version 6 (IPv6) but is not yet widely deployed. This book, therefore, describes IPv4 since most embedded systems are devices operating in private networks that run on this protocol.

As we discussed in Chapter 1, data is encapsulated by different layers of the TCP/IP stack. As we move along the stack from the bottom to the top, every header will be described using the format shown in Figure 5-2.

The packet diagrams will become useful when analyzing network traffic using a Network Protocol Analyzer.

| | | | | | | | | | 1 | 1 | 1 | 1 | 1 | 1 | 1 | 1 | 1 | 1 | 2 | 2 | 2 | 2 | 2 | 2 | 2 | 2 | 2 | 2 | 3 | 3 |
|0|1|2|3|4|5|6|7|8|9|0|1|2|3|4|5|6|7|8|9|0|1|2|3|4|5|6|7|8|9|0|1|

Vers	**IHL**	**Type of service**	**Total length**	
Identification			**Flags**	**Fragment Offset**
Time to live		**Protocol**	**Header checksum**	
Source IP Address				
Destination Address				
Options			**Padding**	
Data				
...				

Minimum 20 bytes ← → *Maximum 60 bytes*

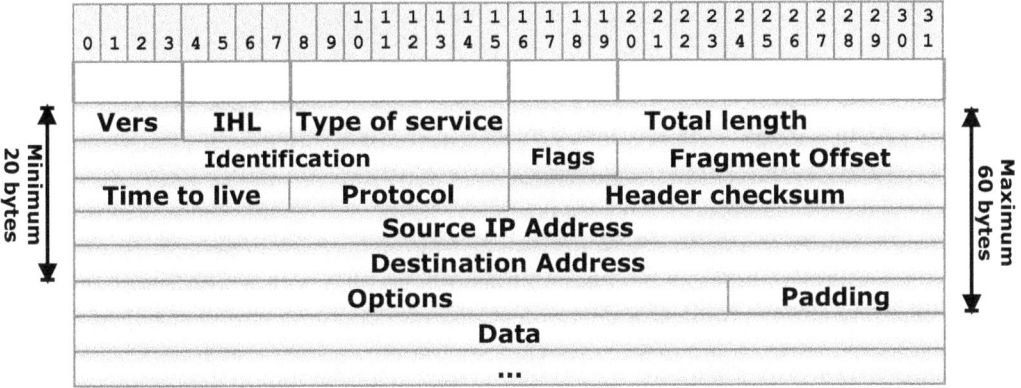

Figure 5-2 **IP version 4 Header and Packet**

5-2 INTERNET PROTOCOL (IP)

Every node on an IP network implements IP. Nodes in charge of forwarding IP packets are referred to as *routers*. Routers or gateways interconnect different networks, acting as the IP equivalent of a telephone switch.

Host computers or embedded systems prepare IP packets and transmit them over their attached network(s) using network-specific protocols (Data-Link protocols). Routers forward IP packets across networks.

IP is a best-effort protocol, since it does not provide for retransmission when the packet does not reach its final destination. Retransmission is left to protocols in the layers above IP.

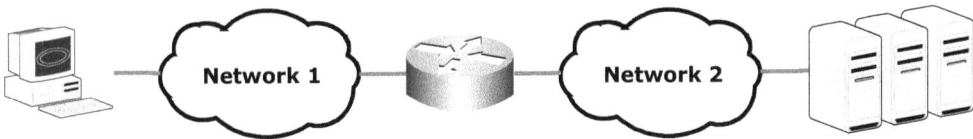

Network 1   **Network 2**

Figure 5-3 **IP Forwarding**

Figure 5-3 shows the path of IP forwarding or routing. It is the process of moving IP packets from a host on one network to a host on a different network.

IP does not offer:

■ Connections or logical circuits

■ Data-error checking

■ Flow control

■ Datagram acknowledgements

■ Retransmission of lost packets

IP's main goal, instead, is to direct packets in the networks. From the limitations listed above, it is clear that additional protocols are required to guarantee data accuracy and delivery.

A TCP/IP stack can include routing protocols. For example, a host running Microsoft Windows or Linux featuring more than one network interface may act as a router. However, a TCP/IP stack can have multiple network interfaces without necessarily performing routing. µC/TCP-IP is an example of such a stack as it does not provide routing function but can receive and transmit on more than one interface. An example using such an implementation is a gateway, a device that acts as a bridge between two networks. In this case, one interface may be in an administration network and another in a production network, with the gateway providing a level of protection and isolation between the two.

The configuration of the TCP/IP stack needs a minimum of three parameters per network interface. We already know about the MAC address. A network interface also needs an IP address. In the next sections, we'll describe how the IP address is constructed. This information will bring us to the need for the third and last parameter required to configure a network interface, the subnet mask.

5-3 ADDRESSING AND ROUTING

5-3-1 IP ADDRESS

In a network, the IP address and subnet mask are automatically provided by the network (see section 9-1-1 "Dynamic Host Configuration Protocol (DHCP)" on page 226) or configured manually by the network administrator. Even if the parameters are not chosen by the system developer it is important to understand their purpose and how to use them.

IP addresses are composed of 32 bits. An IP address is typically represented with the decimal value of 4 bytes separated by a dot (.), and is referred to as the Dotted Decimal Notation. The address is used to identify the source or destination host.

▓ Addresses are hierarchical: Net ID + Host ID (e.g., 114.35.56.130)

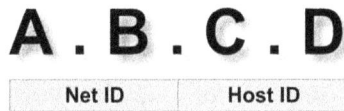

A . B . C . D

Net ID	Host ID

Figure 5-4 **IP Address**

Figure 5-4 is the graphical representation of the NetID + HostID concept. A, B, C and D are four bytes making up the IP address. IP packets are routed (forwarded) according to the Net ID. Routers automatically compute routing tables using a distributed algorithm called a routing protocol, located at the network layer.

Although IP addresses are hierarchical within their own structure, the distribution of these addresses on the surface of the Earth is not. The rapid growth of the Internet created situations where a NetID in one continent will have the preceding or following NetID in another continent. This means that the routing tables in the router must contain all the NetIDs since NetIDs may not be geographically grouped.

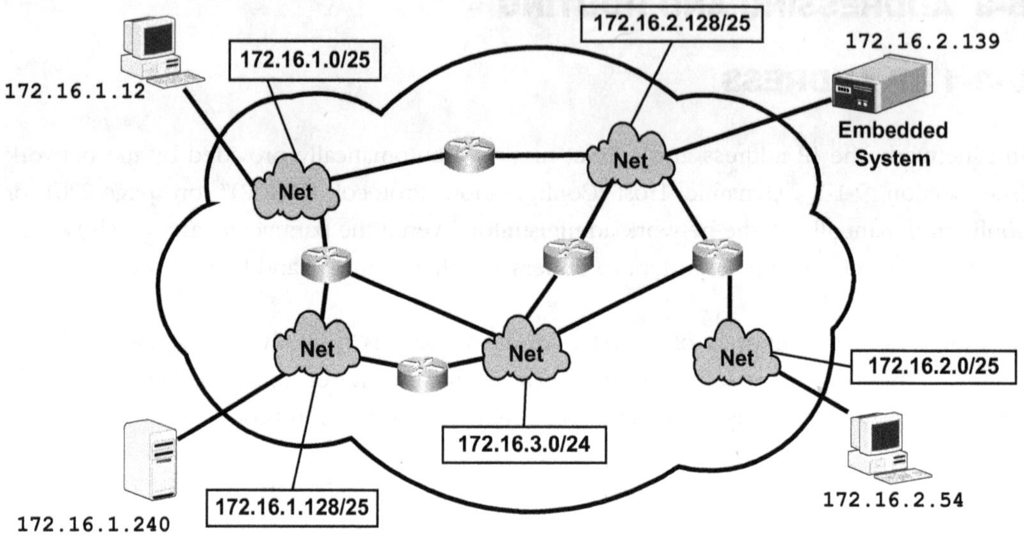

172.16.2.128/25

172.16.2.139

172.16.1.0/25

172.16.1.12

Embedded
System

Net

Net

Net

Net

Net

172.16.2.0/25

172.16.3.0/24

172.16.2.54

172.16.1.128/25

172.16.1.240

Figure 5-5 **Network of Networks**

In Figure 5-5, multiple networks are interconnected via many routers. Each router contains all of the network addresses within a routing table. The routing table identifies the interface number in order to reach the desired network.

With the current state of private and public IP networks, it is not required to have a discussion on classfull and classless networks. What is important to know now is that IP networks can be of various sizes. Network size is determined by another IP parameter, the subnet mask.

5-4 SUBNET MASK

A subnet mask is also a 32-bit element and is comprised of two sections. The first section consists of all bits set to "1" and identifies the NetID. The second section of the subnet mask consists of all bits set to "0" and identifies the HostID. The change from "1" to "0" is the limit, or frontier between the NetID and the HostID. The subnet mask is used to define network size: the larger the NetID (number of ones), the smaller the number of HostIDs available on that network.

With the rapid growth of IP networks, it became necessary to create smaller or sub-networks out of larger networks to reuse a good part of the addressing space. Today these are called classless networks.

The subnet mask is used to determine the exact values of the NetID and HostID. This also means that the frontier between NetID and HostID is not fixed to 8, 16 or 24 bits, but can be virtually anywhere within the 32-bit area.

Subnet Mask	Number Of Addresses
255.255.255.252	4
255.255.255.248	8
255.255.255.240	16
255.255.255.224	32
255.255.255.192	64
255.255.255.128	128
255.255.255.0	256
255.255.254.0	512
255.255.252.0	1024
255.255.248.0	2048
255.255.240.0	4096
255.255.224.0	8192
255.255.192.0	16384
255.255.128.0	32768
255.252.0.0	65536
255.254.0.0	131072
...	...

Table 5-2 **Variable Subnet Mask**

Table 5-2 is a quick reference to determine how many addresses can be defined in a network based on the subnet maks value. When not comfortable with binary artithmetics, software tools exist to calculate subnet mask and the number of addresses available in a network. Search for IP calculator or IPCALC on the internet.

5-5 RESERVED ADDRESSES

It is important to now note that there are restrictions for certain combinations of addresses. In fact, the following rules must be respected when the addressing plan is first developed.

In any network address range, two addresses cannot be assigned to hosts:

1   The lowest address in the range is used to define the network and is called the Network Address.

2   The highest address in the range is used to define the IP broadcast address in the same range.

Here are a few examples:

Network	Subnet Mask	Network Address	Broadcast Address
10.0.0.0	255.0.0.0	10.0.0.0	10.255.255.255
130.10.0.0	255.255.0.0	130.10.0.0	130.10.255.255
198.16.1.0	255.255.255.0	198.16.1.0	198.16.1.255
10.0.0.0	255.255.255.0	10.0.0.0	10.0.0.255
172.16.0.0	255.255.255.128	172.16.0.0	172.16.0.127
192.168.1.4	255.25.255.252	192.168.1.4	192.168.1.7

Table 5-3 **IP Addresses and Subnet Mask Examples**

The smallest network that can be defined is a network with a subnet mask of 255.255.255.252. In this type of network, there are four addresses. Two are used for devices and the remaining two are the network address and broadcast address. This network represents a point-to-point network, for example between two routers.

5-5-1 ADDITIONAL RESERVED ADDRESSES

THE 0.0.0.0 ADDRESS

The 0.0.0.0 address is used by routers to define a default route, used when no other route matches the NetID of a packet being forwarded.

THE 127.X.X.X NETWORK

When 127 appears in the first byte of the network address, it represents a network that is reserved for management functions and, more specifically, to execute loop backs (127.X.X.X). It is an address that is assigned to the TCP/IP stack itself. Any address in the 127.X.X.X range can be used as the loopback address, except for 127.0.0.0 and also 127.255.255.255. We are all familiar with the 127.0.0.1 address.

5-6 ADDRESSING TYPES

5-6-1 UNICAST ADDRESS

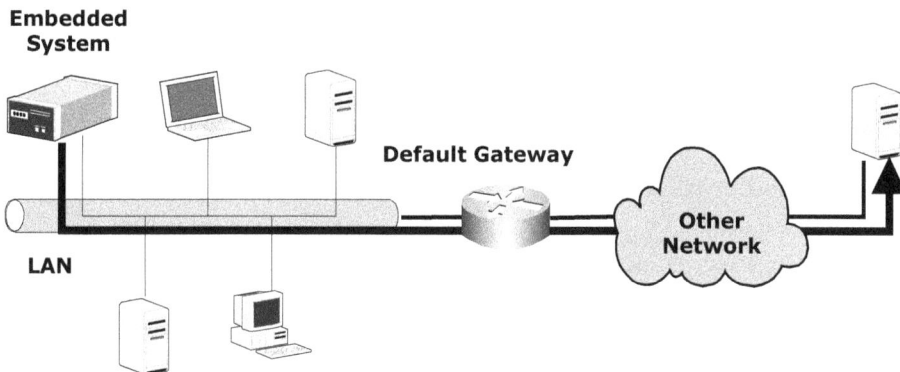

Figure 5-6 **IP Unicast Address**

Source Address	192.168. 2. 63
Source Subnet Mask	255.255.255. 0
Destination Address	207.122. 46.142

127

Figure 5-6 illustrates a host communicating with another host over an IP network using a unicast address. The embedded system is a host with IP address 192.168.2.63, and is attempting to reach a host with an IP address of 207.122.46.142.

5-6-2 MULTICAST ADDRESS

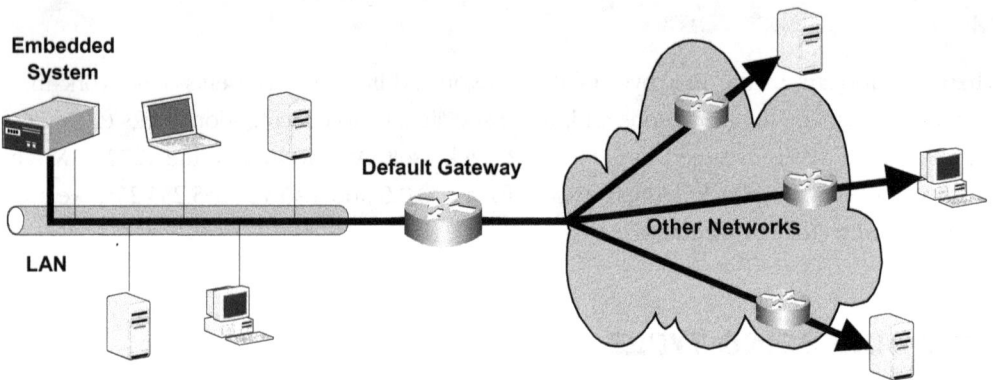

Figure 5-7 **IP Multicast Address**

Source Address	192.168. 2. 63
Destination Address	224. 65.143. 96

In Figure 5-7, a host communicating with a dedicated group of hosts over an IP network is using a multicast address. In this case, the default gateway (router) does not need the subnet mask to forward the packet (see section 5-7 "Default Gateway" on page 130 for an explanation on how to determine if a destination IP address is on its network). Multicasting forwards packets on all interfaces participating in the multicasting group.

5-6-3 BROADCAST ADDRESS

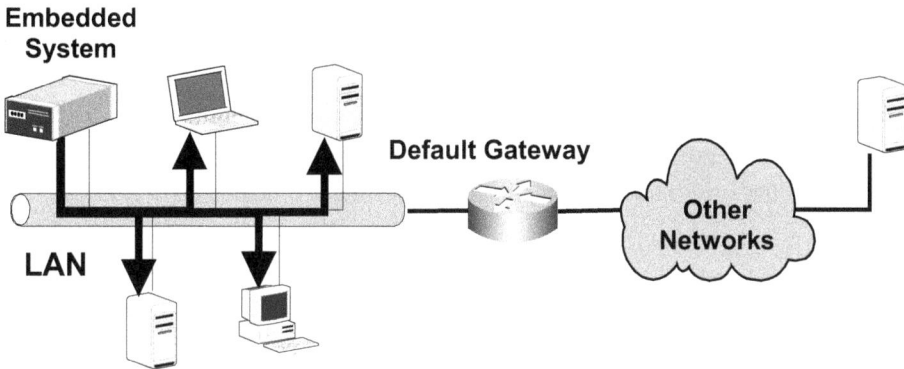

Figure 5-8 **IP Broadcast Address**

Source Address	192.168. 2. 63
Destination Address	192.168. 2. 255

In Figure 5-8, a host communicating with all the hosts on its IP network is using a broadcast address, Remember that the broadcast address is the highest address in an IP network. In this case the subnet mask is not required as the host converts the IP broadcast address into an Ethernet broadcast address to transmit the packet on the network.

On an IP network, a router will not forward broadcast messages, as these messages are dedicated to a specific network, not all networks. In certain cases, however, a router will be configured to forward certain types of IP broadcast packets. For example, proxy ARP is a method to forward ARP requests and replies in case we want to extend the network size between adjunct networks.

5

5-7 DEFAULT GATEWAY

We saw earlier how a host on a LAN communicates to neighbors on the same LAN using a physical address (MAC address in the case of an Ethernet LAN). What happens when a host wants to communicate with a host on a different network?

First, the origin host needs to know whether the receiving host is on the same network. The only information the origin host knows about the destination host is its IP address.

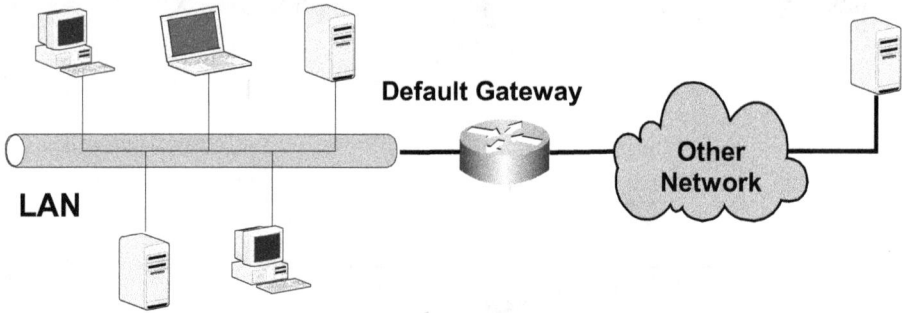

Figure 5-9 **Default Gateway**

Source Address	192.168. 2. 63
Source Host Subnet Mask	255.255.255. 0
Default Gateway	192.168. 2. 1
Destination Address	207. 65.143. 96

Figure 5-9 above indicates where the default gateway is located relative to the hosts in our network and to outside networks. Let's build an example. Figure 5-10 outlines the steps necessary to use the default gateway to forward packets outside of our network.

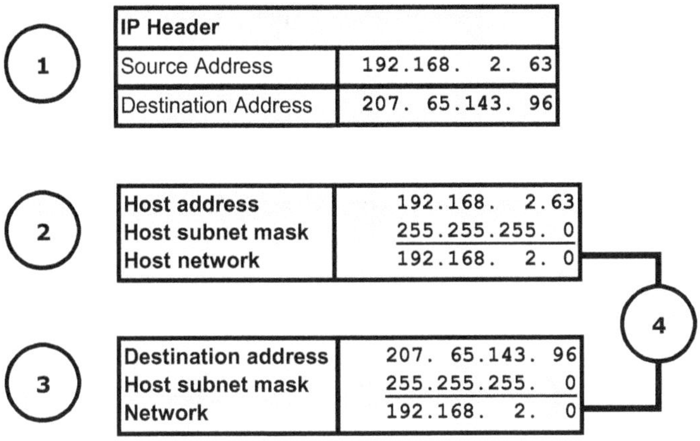

Figure 5-10 **Determining where to send an IP packet**

F5-10(1)   The IP header of the packet being sent between the source host and the destination host contains the IP address of the source host and the IP address of the destination host.

F5-10(2)   The IP layer of the TCP/IP stack calculates the network address of the source host. The TCP/IP stack applies the subnet mask of its network interface to the source IP address. The result of this logical AND operation is a network address, the host network address.

F5-10(3)   The TCP/IP stack determines if the destination host is on the same network. To achieve this, the sending host applies the subnet mask of its network to the IP address of the destination host. The result of this logical AND operation is a network address.

F5-10(4)   The question now is: Are these two network address identical? If the answer is:

YES, send the packet over the LAN using the physical address (MAC address) of the destination host.

NO, the result is not the network to which the source host is connected. The source host then needs to find a device that can forward this information. This device is the default gateway, or the router connected to this LAN.

In our example, the answer is No.

Is my default gateway on my network? YES. The default gateway is a router that has one interface in our network. This interface has an address that is part of our network. Remember that the default gateway address is one of the four mandatory parameters to configure per network interface.

The host now sends the information to the default gateway. Because the default gateway is also a host on this network, the source host will need to find the default gateway's physical address before transmitting information, using ARP in the case of Ethernet.

As a standard practice, network administrators often use the first available address in a network for the default gateway. This is a good and not-so-good practice. It is good because in this way it is possible to easily find the address of the default gateway for that network. However, it is also not the best action, since hackers also can find their way more easily into the network. To confuse hackers, use any address in the network address range other than the first available address. This is not a problem if a DHCP server is used (see Chapter 9, "Services and Applications" on page 225).

5-8 IP CONFIGURATION

A host needs four mandatory parameters for each NIC collaborating on a network (see Figure 5-11):

■ A physical address (Ethernet MAC address)

■ An IP address

■ A subnet mask

■ A default gateway IP address

There are two ways to configure these parameters in the system. They can be configured statically (hard-coded) or dynamically.

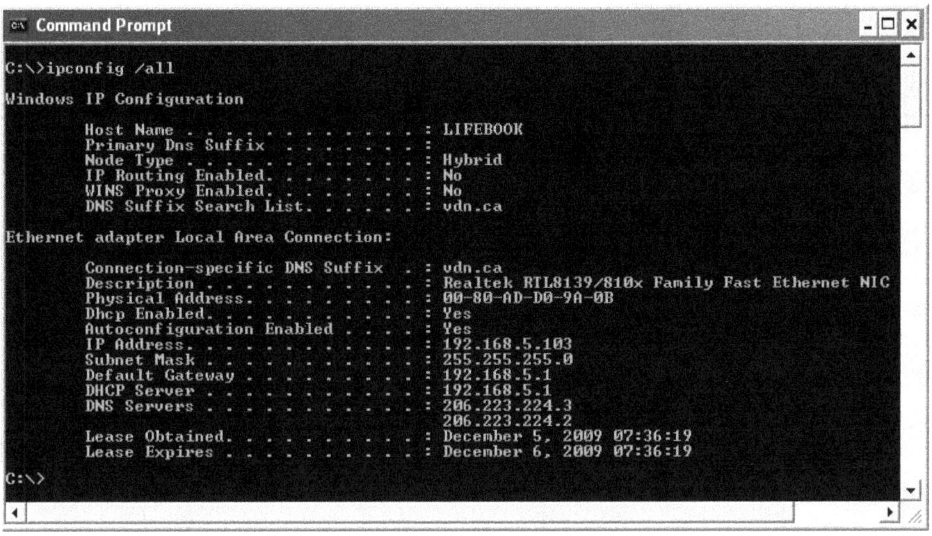

Figure 5-11 **IP Configuration**

Figure 5-11 is an example of the result of an IP configuration on a Microsoft Windows host. This configuration is a dynamic configuration as you can see from the additional DHCP server address and lease data in the list of parameters. The result of this configuration was obtained using the command: `ipconfig /all`. On a Linux host, the Terminal Window command is similar. It is `ifconfig`.

Static parameter configuration requires the knowledge of the value of these parameters and the use of certain µC/TCP-IP API functions.

```
NET_IP_ADDR    ip;
NET_IP_ADDR    msk;
NET_IP_ADDR    gateway;
CPU_BOOLEAN    cfg_success;
NET_ERR        err_net;
ip          = NetASCII_Str_to_IP((CPU_CHAR *)"192.168.0.65", &err_net);  (1)
msk         = NetASCII_Str_to_IP((CPU_CHAR *)"255.255.255.0", &err_net); (2)
gateway     = NetASCII_Str_to_IP((CPU_CHAR *)"192.168.0.1",  &err_net);  (3)
cfg_success = NetIP_CfgAddrAdd(if_nbr, ip, msk, gateway,  &err_net);      (4)
```

Listing 5-1 **Static IP Configuration**

L5-1(1)   Hard-coded IP address.

L5-1(2)   Hard-coded Subnet Mask.

L5-1(3)   Hard-coded Default Gateway IP address.

L5-1(4)   Configures the IP address, the Subnet Mask and the Default Gateway IP address.

Please refer to Appendix C, "µC/TCP-IP API Reference" on page 649, for the description of the functions in Listing 5-1.

Dynamic IP configuration is covered in Chapter 9, "Services and Applications" on page 225.

5-9 PRIVATE ADDRESSES

As IP networks evolved, the number of IP addresses became increasingly scarce. The address space of IP Version 4 is limited to approximately four billion device addresses, which is woefully inadequate to support all of the devices connected to global networks.

One way to stretch IP address availability is define private addresses and reuse them as often as possible. These private addresses include:

```
10.0.0.0/8
172.16.0.0/16 to 172.31.0.0/16
192.168.0.0/24 to 192.168.255.0/24
```

These addresses can only be used on private networks and not on the public Internet. We probably all know at least one example of a private address. The router (wired or wireless) we use at home behind our cable or DSL modem uses private addresses for home hosts.

Another group of IP addresses is also reserved in case there is no automatic IP assignment mechanism like DHCP. RFC 3927 defines the 169.254.0.0/16 range of addresses, but the first and last /24 subnet (256 addresses each) in this block are excluded from use and are reserved. This technique is also described in Chapter 9, "Services and Applications" on page 225,

The vast majority of embedded systems connected to an IP network use private addresses. When a network is built to serve a specific purpose, it does not need to be connected to the public Internet. Therefore, it makes sense to use a private addressing scheme.

However, when a host on a private network must access another host on the public network, we need to convert the private address into a public address. In our home example above, this is performed by the home gateway/router and is called Network Address Translation (NAT). Similarly in a private network where an embedded system is located, the network default gateway provides that capability for the embedded system to reach the public network.

NETWORK ADDRESS TRANSLATION - NAT

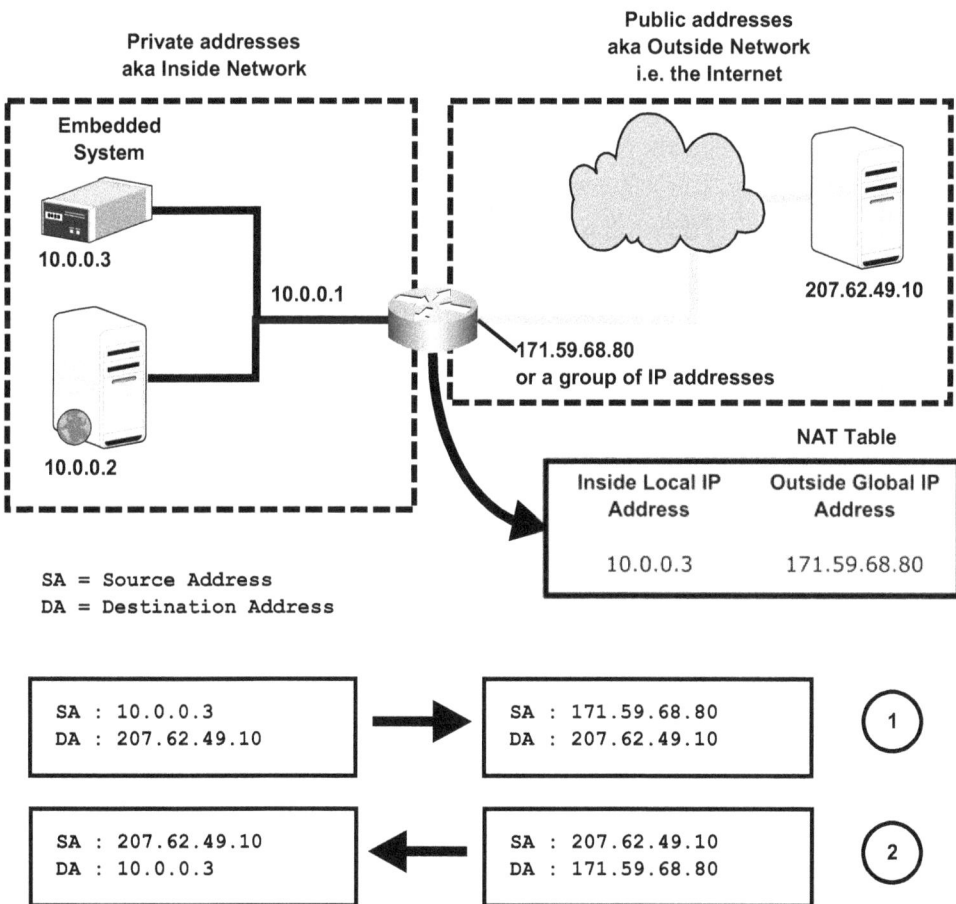

Figure 5-12 **Network Address Translation**

In Figure 5-12 above, a 10.0.0.0 private network is assigned to the network on the left. The router in the figure is the default gateway for this network. This gateway has two network interfaces: one facing the network on the left (the private network) and one facing the network on the right (the public network). We often refer to the private network as the inside network and the public network as the outside network.

F5-12(1)   In this simple case, the embedded system with IP address 10.0.0.3 on the private network wants to connect with a host at 207.62.49.10 on the Internet. The embedded system private address is translated into the public address associated with the gateway public interface of 171.59.68.80. The public address is provided by the Internet Service Provider (ISP) when the private network initially requested to connect to the Internet. In this case, the ISP provided one IP address with the contract. It is also possible to be assigned a block of IP addresses from the ISP. The cross-reference between the private address and the public address is stored in a table in the gateway. The packet sent by the embedded system now travels on the public network since all addresses are public. In this example, only one connection can be established between the private network and the Internet. One solution to access more than one connection is to have a block of public addresses. In this way, there can be as many connections as there are public addresses available, however this is a waste of IP addresses. Another method is to use one of the Transport Layer protocol fields called a port. (see section 7-3-1 "Port Address Translation (PAT)" on page 175, for more information).

F5-12(2)   When the host on the public network answers the query from the host in the private network system with IP translated to 171.59.68.80, it answers this message the same way it would answer another host request on the Internet. When the reply reaches the gateway, the gateway translates the destination address from 171.59.68.80 to 10.10.10.3 using the translation table it created on the initial outgoing packet. This works as long as the communication is established from the private network out.

Another scenario is for a host on the public network to connect to a host on the private network. In this case, the concept of nail-down public addresses must be introduced. It is possible to configure a public IP address to be always connected to a private address as in the following figure:

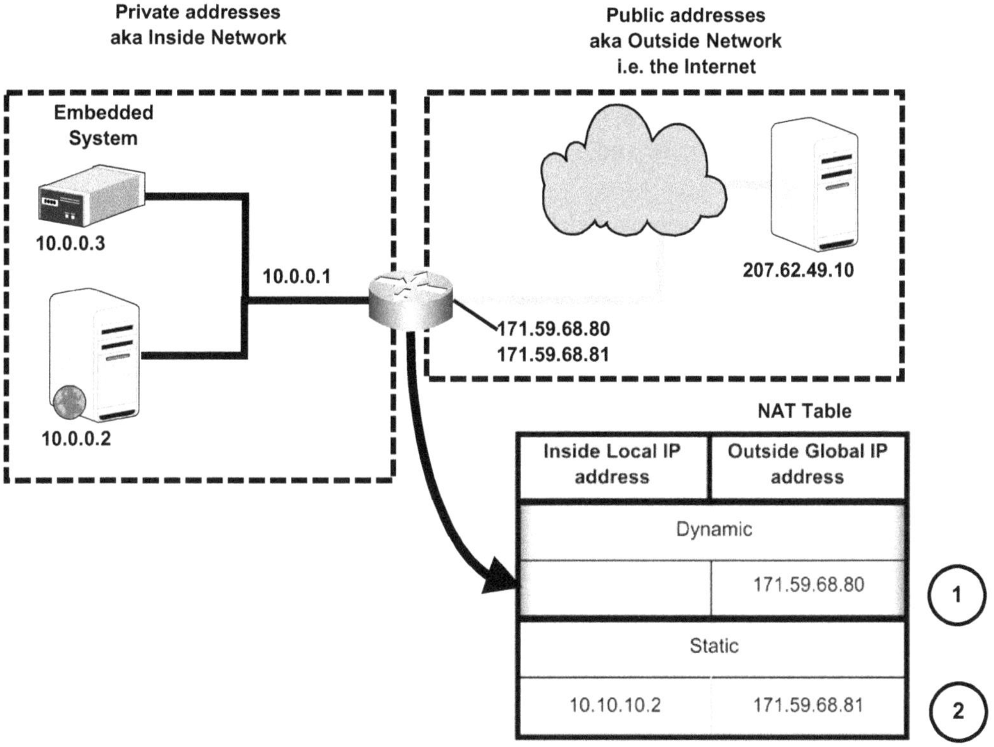

Figure 5-13 **Static Public IP Address**

F5-13(1) The Dynamic portion of the NAT table configuration in the router/gateway is similar to the previous example. It is used for private hosts that want to access public hosts.

F5-13(2) The Static portion of the NAT table configuration in the gateway ensures that a private host can always be reached from the public network. In the example, the Web server at IP address 10.10.10.3 is associated with the public IP address 171.59.69.81. The public network identifies the Web server at IP address 171.59.69.81. As long as the gateway translates 10.10.10.3 to 171.59.69.81 and vice-versa, this server will appear as any other server on the Internet. If an embedded system in this example at IP address 10.10.10.2 is offering an HTTP service, it may also be made accessible from the Internet using the exact same process. An additional Static Public IP address is required for this host.

5

5-10 SUMMARY

The IP address, subnet mask and default gateway do not directly translate to the design of the embedded system. However, it is important to know where they come from, how they are structured, which one to use and, once selected, how to configure it.

These parameters are always provided by the network administrator and are not selected randomly. The connected host must collaborate with other hosts and nodes in the network. Once these parameters are known, they need to be configured either statically or dynamically following the methods described in 5-8.

Troubleshooting

As we move up through the TCP/IP protocol stack, we'll stay at the Network layer for one more chapter. Why? Because it is at this layer that we also find a very important protocol used in the troubleshooting of IP networks.

6-1 NETWORK TROUBLESHOOTING

When a connection between two hosts is broken, it is very common for the user to attempt to reach the destination host knowing that there is a problem. Unfortunately, the problem may be located anywhere between the source host and the destination host, and the culprit is usually a failed node or link. To troubleshoot this problem, a reasonable approach is to first verify the closest links and nodes. When we are sure that the problem does not lie at this location, we move towards the destination host.

When we detect a communication problem between two hosts, the initial step is to validate that the TCP/IP stack in the source host is operational. This can be done by using the PING utility, and "pinging" the source host local host address: 127.0.0.1.

The second step is to validate that the network interface on the source host is in good working order. To achieve this on the source host, ping the IP address associated with this network interface.

The third step is to ping the IP address of the default gateway associated to the LAN to which the source host is connected.

Finally, we can ping all of the nodes on the path between the source host and destination host. The second section of this chapter demonstrates the use of another tool called "Trace Route," which will assist in identifying these nodes.

6

To recap, the sequence used to find the location of a problem on an IP network:

1   Ping the local host TCP/IP stack (127.0.0.1)

2   Ping the network interface(s)

3   Ping the default gateway

4   Ping nodes on the path between the source and destination

At this stage, it is important to understand that communications on an IP network is typically bidirectional. The path from source to destination may work, but we also have to make sure that the return path is also operational. As we learned earlier, IP is not a connection-oriented protocol. The source host and destination host are not aware of a connection between the two devices. Unlike the PSTN where a physical connection exists, with IP, a packet forwarding network, there are two paths: one from A to B and one from B to A.

The troubleshooting process therefore, must at times be able to be applied in both directions to find the cause of the network problem.

In addition to the PING Utility, let's look at the Internet Control Message Protocol (ICMP), which is used by this troubleshooting tool and others.

6-1-1 INTERNET CONTROL MESSAGE PROTOCOL (ICMP)

While the IP protocol does not guarantee datagram delivery, it does provide a means of sending alerts and diagnostic messages by way of the ICMP protocol. Such errors typically occur in intermediary routers and systems when a datagram cannot, for whatever reason, be forwarded.

There are two types of ICMP messages:

- error messages

- request/response messages

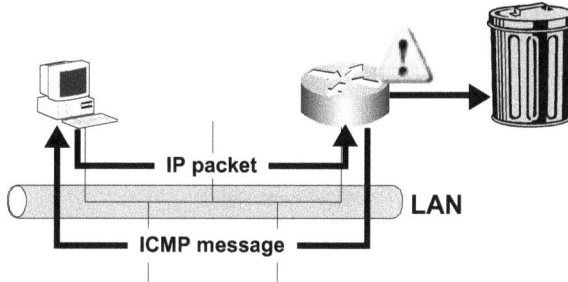

Figure 6-1 **Internet Control Message Protocol (ICMP)**

Figure 6-2 **ICMP Message Structure**

Given that the ICMP message is carried in an IP packet, the IP PROTOCOL field in the IP header is equal to 1. The ICMP message structure is as follows:

- The TYPE field is the first byte of the ICMP message. This field's value determines the contents of the rest of the data field. (see Table 6-1 for a list of TYPE-possible values).

- The CODE field depends directly on the TYPE field.

- The CHECKSUM field is the 16-bit 1's complement of the 1's complement sum of the ICMP message.

ICMP Message Type #	Function
0	Echo reply
3	Destination unreachable
4	Source quench

141

ICMP Message Type #	Function
5	Redirect
8	Echo request
9	Router advertisement
10	Router solicitation
11	Time exceed
12	Parameter problem
13	Timestamp request
14	Timestamp reply
15	Information request
16	Information reply
17	Address mask request
18	Address mask reply

Table 6-1 **ICMP Message Types**

When a datagram is transmitted on the network and the router detects an error, an error message (ICMP packet) is generated by the router back to the host that initially sent the datagram. Fields from the datagram that created the error are used in the ICMP ERROR message and include:

■ IP header (20 bytes)

■ IP options (0-40 bytes)

■ First (8) bytes of the IP packet data field (8 bytes)

The first eight (8) bytes of the data field include port numbers in the case of upper-layer TCP and UDP protocols. These ports indicate the application to which the datagram belongs, information which is very useful for troubleshooting.

0	1	2	3	4	5	6	7	8	9	1 0	1 1	1 2	1 3	1 4	1 5	1 6	1 7	1 8	1 9	2 0	2 1	2 2	2 3	2 4	2 5	2 6	2 7	2 8	2 9	3 0	3 1

TYPE	CODE	Checksum
Variable		
IP header (including options) plus first eight bytes of original datagram		

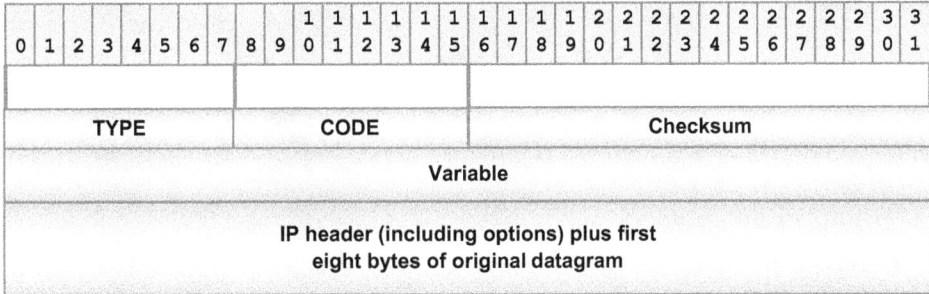

Figure 6-3 **ICMP Error Message Structure**

The next section is dedicated to troubleshooting tools. PING, as we have seen, is one of them. PING uses a form of ICMP messages, echo request and echo reply. Echo requests use type 8 and echo replies use type 0.

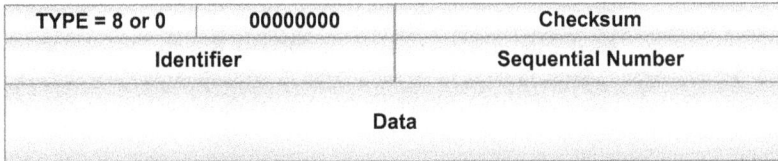

TYPE = 8 or 0	00000000	Checksum
Identifier		Sequential Number
Data		

TYPE	8 = Echo Request 0 = Echo Reply
Identifier	An arbitrary number for linking a request with a reply
Sequential Number	A counter set to 0 and incremented after a reply is received
Data	This field is used as a payload so that the Echo Reply can have something to send back. It is often the alphabet and is 32-bytes long.

Figure 6-4 **Echo Request, Echo Reply**

In the IP toolbox, there are a few tools that rely on ICMP and are quite useful. These tools are:

- PING

- Trace Route

6

6-1-2 PING

The PING utility relies on the ICMP Echo Request and Echo Reply messages. As previously indicated, PING is used when we want to know if a node is operational, or to locate a fault on the path between source and destination hosts.

Here is an example of PING:

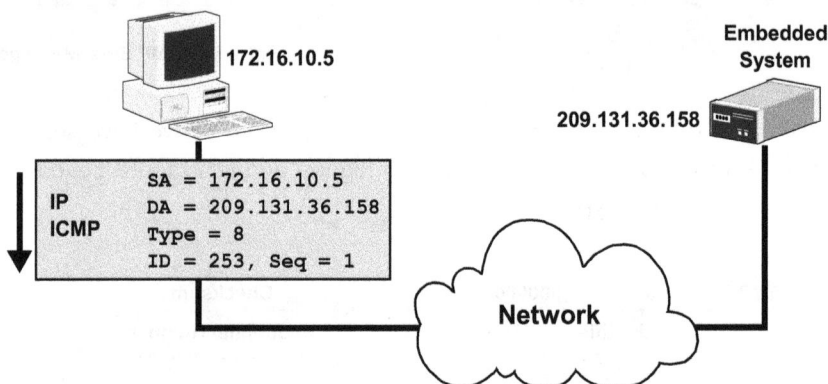

```
        SA = 172.16.10.5
IP      DA = 209.131.36.158
ICMP    Type = 8
        ID = 253, Seq = 1
```

Figure 6-5 **Echo Request**

In Figure 6-5 above, PING is used on a host with IP address 172.16.10.5. On a Windows PC, open a command prompt window and use the PING command. The format of the command is: `ping [Destination IP address or URL]`. Linux also has a PING utility that is launched from a terminal window.

If the destination IP address is known, or the name of the host you want to "PING," for example www.thecompany.com," either can be used. However, the operating system, Windows in this case, uses the Domain Name Service (DNS) to translate the name into an IP address (see Chapter 9, "Services and Applications" on page 225 for more detail).

Figure 6-6 **Ping Command in a Command Prompt Window**

In our example the host with IP address 172.16.10.5 is "pinging" the embedded system with IP address 209.131.36.158 (see Figure 6-7). The host of origin, (172.16.10.5) and the destination host (209.131.36.158) are not on the same network. In most tests, it is probable that the two hosts will be on the same network. It does not make any difference other than the reply to the PING command will have a longer RTT should the hosts be further apart.

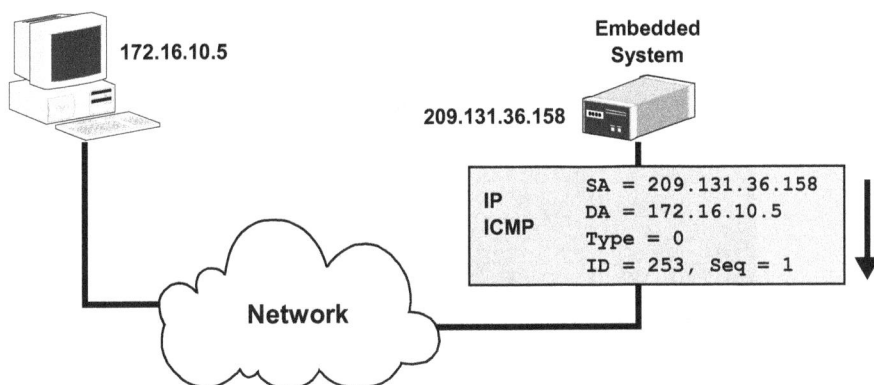

Figure 6-7 **Echo Reply**

The reply from the embedded system is shown in Figure 6-7.

Both Windows and Linux PING implementations send four echo request messages at one second intervals.

Figure 6-8 **PING Execution**

The PING utility has multiple options. To get a list of the options, simply type "ping" without any arguments.

6

The most interesting of the options include:

■ **-t** to send a Echo Request every second until the program is stopped

■ **-l** to send more than the default 32-byte standard Echo Request payload.

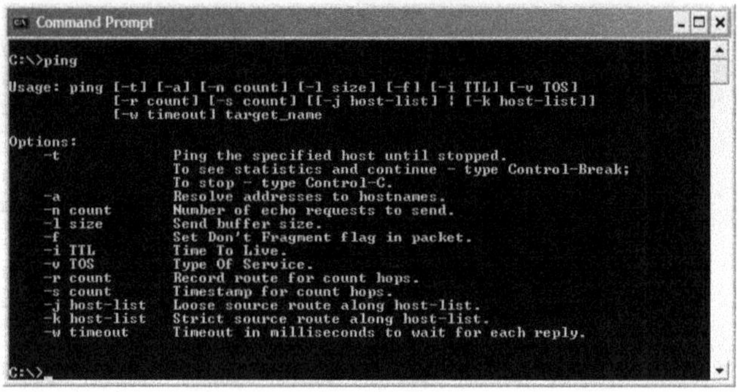

Figure 6-9 **PING Options**

The PING utility features a small default 32-byte payload. This option can be changed by issuing the '—l' argument in the command. Changing the payload, the delay, and the number of echo requests, creates an inexpensive traffic generator. However, it only tests Data Link and Network layers. In many cases, if you can ping your target, you have a good chance of having the rest of the TCP/IP stack on the target working. Arriving at this point is the most difficult part of implementing TCP/IP in an embedded system.

There are other third-party command-prompt tools that can be used for this purpose. One of them is the well-known fast PING (FPING) from www.kwakkelflap.com/downloads.html.

What is specifically important to understand is that the current version of µC/TCP-IP can reply to ICMP Echo Request, but does not initiate ICMP Echo Request messages. This means that an embedded system running µC/TCP-IP can reply to a PING command but can not initiate a PING command. In the troubleshooting scenario above, the host issuing the PING command must be a host other than the embedded system running µC/TCP-IP.

6-1-3 TRACE ROUTE

Another useful network troubleshooting tool is Trace Route ("tracert" in the command prompt). This utility uses the Time-To-Live (TTL) field of the IP packet header to retrieve the IP address of every router on the path between the source and destination. When a router processes a packet it decrements the IP packet header TTL field by 1. Initially the TTL field was designed to calculate the amount of time a packet was spent on a router, hence its name "Time-To-Live." As this example suggests, the final implementation of the TTL field is more of a hop count between the source and destination. TTL is decremented by one and when its value reaches zero, the router discards the packet and sends an error message to the host that initiated the packet. The error code of the ICMP message sent back to the source host is Type 11 (Time Exceeded).

Let's see how this works.

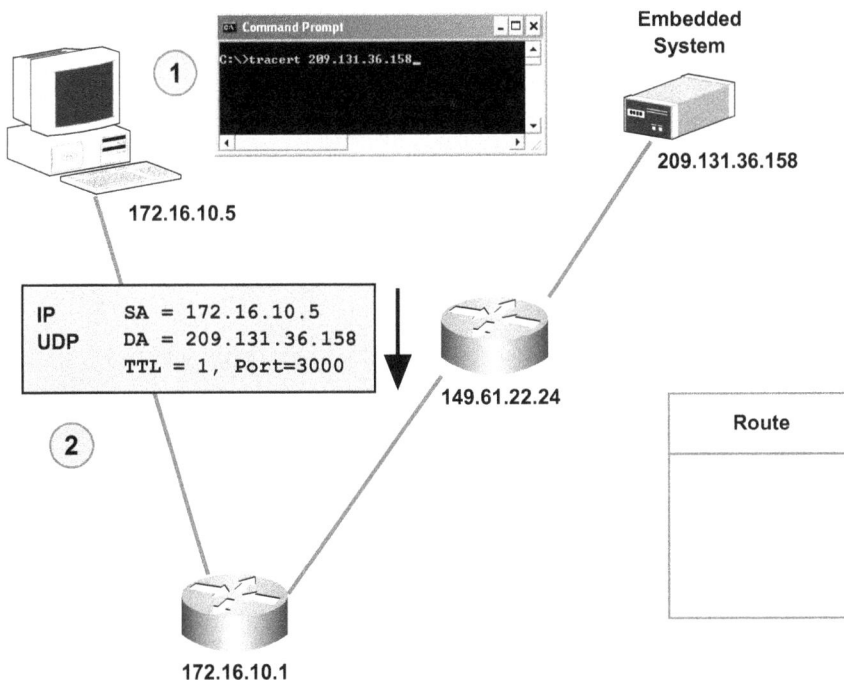

Figure 6-10 **Source Host Sends a Packet to Destination Host with TTL=1**

F6-10(1)   Host 172.16.10.5 issues a "TRACERT" command using 207.42.13.61 as the destination IP address.

6

F6-10(2)   This creates a UDP datagram to be sent to the destination address and the IP
            packet carrying this UDP datagram sees a TTL set to 1. In this example, the port
            number used is 3000, however this number is arbitrary.

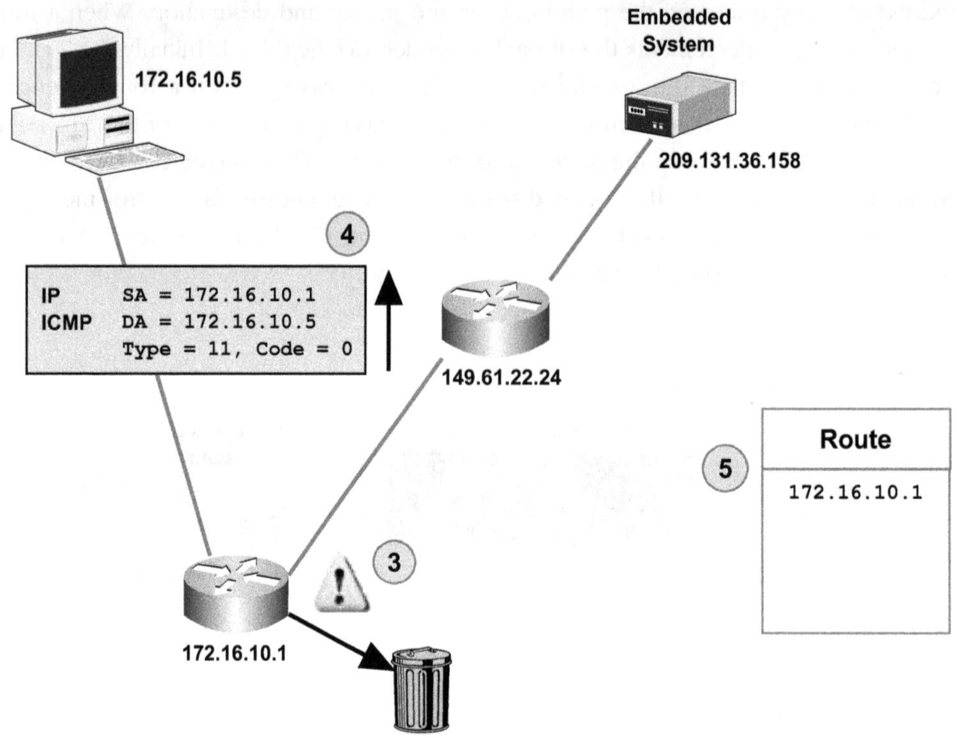

Embedded System

172.16.10.5

209.131.36.158

4

```
IP      SA = 172.16.10.1
ICMP    DA = 172.16.10.5
        Type = 11, Code = 0
```

149.61.22.24

Route
172.16.10.1

5

3

172.16.10.1

Figure 6-11 **The first node discards the packet because the "Time-To-Live" expires.**

F6-11(3)   The first node on the path between the source and the destination receives the
            packet and decrements the TTL field. Because the TTL was 1, it is now zero
            representing an error condition.

F6-11(4)   An ICMP Type 11 error message is sent back to the source host.

F6-11(5)   Because the ICMP message is from the node that detected the error, the source
            address of this node is used as the IP source address for the error message. The
            source host therefore learns the IP address of the first node on the path to the
            destination host.

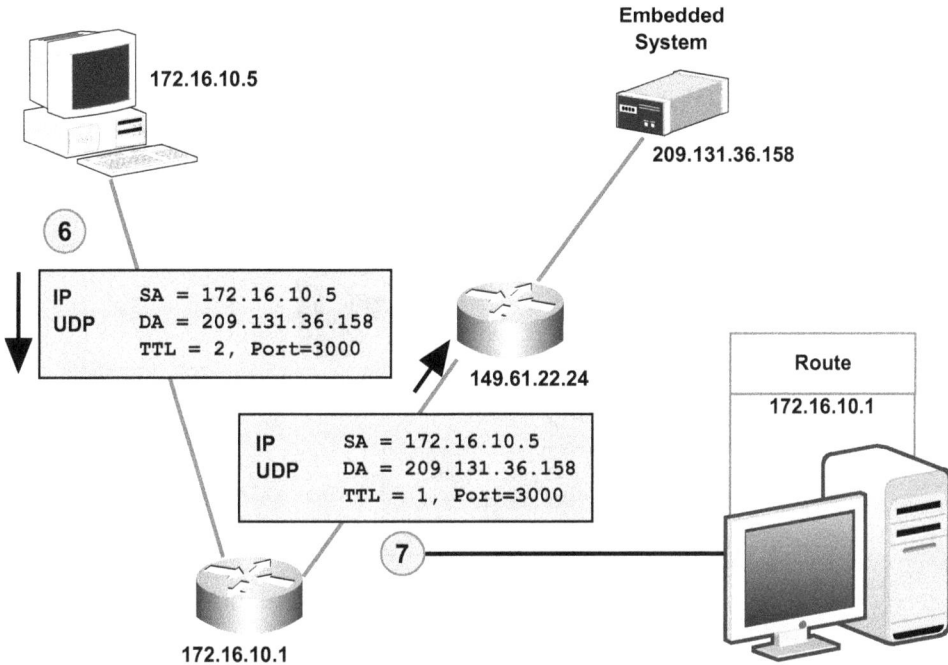

Figure 6-12 **Source Host sends a packet to Destination Host with TTL=2**

F6-12(6)   The TRACERT received the reply to the first message with TTL equal to one. The application continues. The next step is to send the same initial packet, but this time with a TTL equal to 2.

F6-12(7)   The packet processed by the first node on the path from the source to the destination will decrement the TTL from 2 to 1. The packet is then forwarded on its path to the destination.

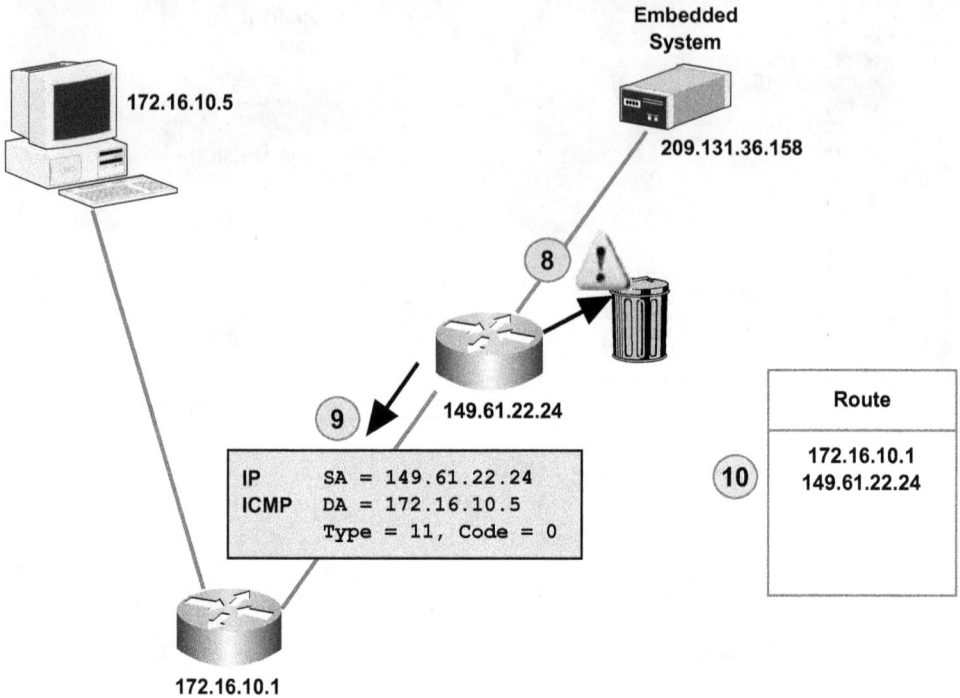

Figure 6-13 **The second node discard the packet since the "Time-To-Live" expires.**

F6-13(8)   The second node on the path from the source to the destination decrements the TLL from 1 to 0 and thus discards the packet.

F6-13(9)   An ICMP Type 11 error message is sent to the source host. Because the ICMP message is from the node that detected the error, the source address of this node is used as the IP source address for the error message.

F6-13(10)   The source host therefore learns the IP address of the second node on the path to the destination host.

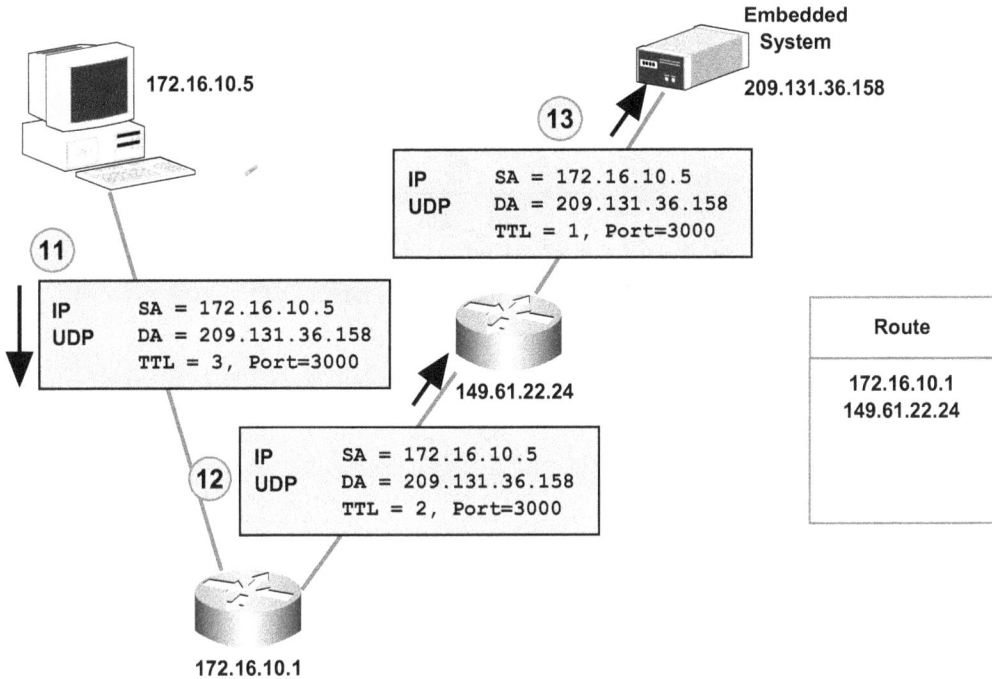

Figure 6-14 **Source Host sends a packet to Destination Host with TTL=3**

F6-14(11)   The TRACERT has received two replies so far. The application continues and the same initial packet is sent, but this time with a TTL equal to 3.

F6-14(12)   The packet processed by the first node on the path from the source to the destination decrements the TTL to 2 and forwards the packet on its path to the destination.

F6-14(13)   The second node also decrements the TTL of the packet it receives down to 1. The packet is forwarded on its path to the destination.

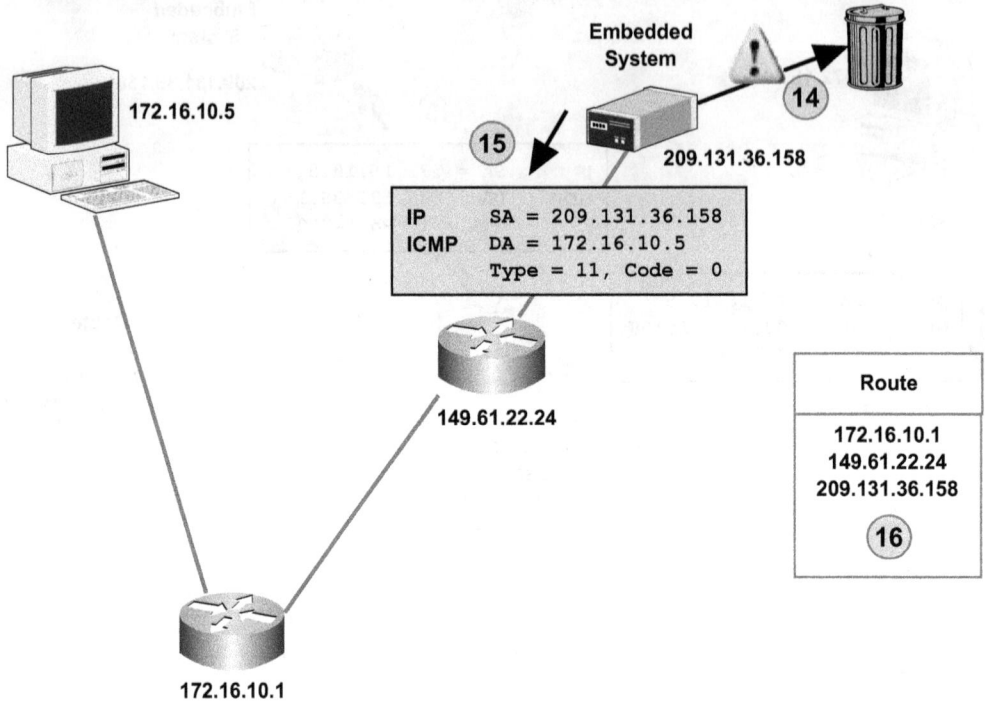

Figure 6-15 **The fourth node discards the packet since the "Time-To-Live" expires.**

F6-15(14)   The third node on the path from the source to the destination decrements the TLL. It is now zero.

F6-15(15)   An ICMP Type 11 error message is sent to the source host. Because the ICMP message is from the node that detected the error, the source address of this node is used as the IP source address for the error message.

F6-15(16)   The source host therefore learns the IP address of the third node on the path to the destination host. Because this address is the one that was used when the TRACERT utility was launched, the final destination is reached. The list of IP addresses for the nodes on the path between the source and the destination is now known.

This process can be applied to as many nodes as exist between the source and destination. The default option of the TRACERT command probes thirty nodes and then stops. If there are more than thirty nodes on the path being analyzed, the default option must be changed using the –h parameter. To display the TRACERT parameters, enter TRACERT without any parameter.

As we learned in Chapter 1, there are no dedicated circuits. It is quite possible that multiple IP packets exchanged between a source and destination take different routes. It is also possible to imagine that issuing the TRACE ROUTE command multiple times could produce different results. However, this is not the case. Current networks are stable enough and have sufficient resources to produce the same result every time.

However, if the TRACERT command fails to reach the final destination, a hint about the location of the network problem we are looking for is provided. This is likely the location of the problem.

Here is an example of the "tracert" command:

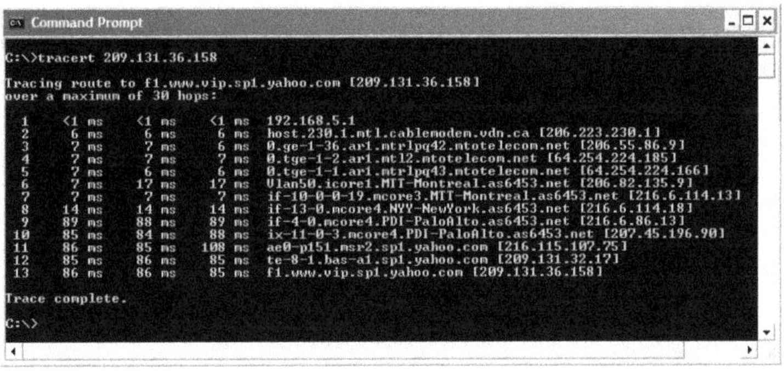

Figure 6-16 **TRACERT Execution**

There is also a graphical version of this tool called Visual TraceRoute. Search the Internet for "Visual TraceRoute," and have fun seeing geographically where all routers are located!

6-2 PROTOCOLS AND APPLICATION ANALYSIS TOOLS

The network troubleshooting tools in the first sections of this chapter are very useful to understand the workings of the network. As an embedded developer, your challenges are likely not with the network but with an ability to test to see if the system is operational. The following sections cover tools that are useful to validate TCP/IP protocol stack behavior and to test system TCP/IP performance.

6-2-1 NETWORK PROTOCOL ANALYZER

A network protocol analyzer (also known as a packet analyzer or sniffer) is software or hardware that can intercept and log traffic passing over a network. As data streams flow across the network, a network protocol analyzer captures each packet, and decodes and analyzes its content according to the appropriate RFC.

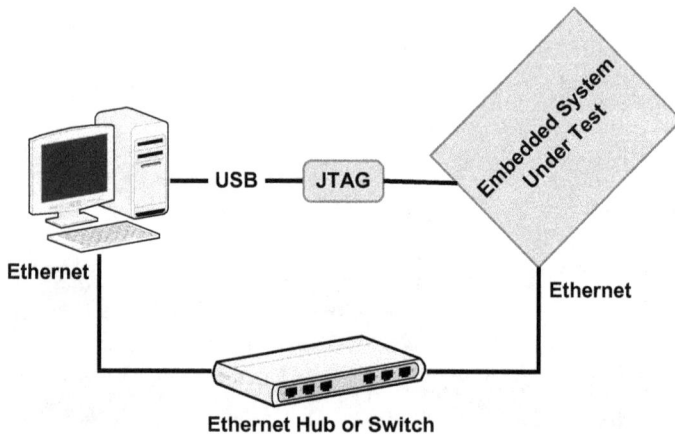

Figure 6-17 **Network Protocol Analyzer Setup**

In order to work, a network protocol analyzer must be able to capture Ethernet frames on the network. To do so, the setup requires an Ethernet hub or an Ethernet switch (see Figure 6-17).

Let's look at the various elements involved in the process. Given a hub, for example, a network protocol analyzer can connect to any port since the hub repeats all traffic from every port. In this case, the challenge is to filter the frame capture or frame display with network protocol analyzer options as the network protocol analyzer captures all network traffic, which may be more than what is needed.

An Ethernet switch is designed to reduce the traffic by micro-segmenting traffic on every port, and keeping only the traffic to and from the host connected on a specific port. To be able to monitor the traffic to and from a port on a switch, the network protocol analyzer must be connected to that port. If it is not possible to connect the network protocol analyzer to the port where the traffic needs to be monitored, a more sophisticated Ethernet switch must be used. These Ethernet switches allow the mirroring of the traffic of the port where traffic needs to be monitored to a free port where the network protocol analyzer is connected for the capture.

In the setup in Figure 6-17, the network protocol analyzer is software running in the PC. It captures all traffic to and from the PC. In this case, the PC is used for many purposes, one of them is to test the TCP/IP stack of the embedded system under test. The other use for the PC is also to load the code via a JTAG interface (or other debug interface) to test to the embedded system. The development tool chain runs on the PC and binary code is downloaded to the embedded system under test. This way, the embedded developer can also use the debugger and single step through the code as the PC tests the TCP/IP stack.

To capture traffic other than unicast traffic sent to the host running the network protocol analyzer software, multicast traffic, and broadcast traffic, the network protocol analyzer must put the NIC into "promiscuous" mode. However, not all network protocol analyzers support this. On wireless LANs, even if the adapter is in promiscuous mode, packets that are not meant for Wi-Fi services for which the NIC is configured will be ignored. To see these packets, the NIC must be in monitor mode.

For our development objectives, we want to use the network protocol analyzer to:

▪ Debug network protocol implementations

▪ Analyze network problems

▪ Debug client/server applications

▪ Capture and report network statistics

▪ Monitor network usage

There are multiple commercial network protocol analyzers. Micrium engineers typically use Wireshark, a free network protocol analyzer.

6

Wireshark uses **p**acket **cap**ture (**pcap**) and consists of an API for capturing network traffic. Unix-like systems implement pcap in the libpcap library, while Windows uses a port of libpcap known as WinPcap to configure the NIC in promiscuous mode to capture packets. Wireshark runs on Microsoft Windows and on various Unix-like operating systems including Linux, Mac OS X, BSD, and Solaris. Wireshark is released under the terms of the GNU General Public License.

6-2-2 WIRESHARK

Wireshark will be used for many of the examples provided in Part II of this book.

Wireshark, previously called Ethereal, was developed by Gerald Combs as a tool to capture and analyze packets. Today there are more than 500 contributing authors while Mr. Combs continues to maintain the overall code and releases of new versions.

Wireshark is similar to the Unix utility "tcpdump", however Wireshark features a graphical front-end, and additional data sorting and filtering options. To download and install Wireshark on a Microsoft Windows host, the WinPcap utility is installed by the installer tool. This utility enables NIC(s) to be placed in promiscuous mode so that the Wireshark software captures all Ethernet frames travelling on the Ethernet interface selected for frame capture.

WIRESHARK QUICKSTART

While Wireshark documentation is excellent, it is a very sophisticated tool with many features and options. To help the embedded developer, here are a few hints to get started quickly.

First download and install Wireshark on the PC host to be used. Wireshark is a network protocol analyzer that provides decoding for the largest number of protocols. By default all protocols are selected. To help reduce what will be captured and displayed in the Wireshark decoding window, we recommend limiting the protocols that can be decoded to only the ones that will be used for the purposes of this book.

To launch Wireshark, from the main window, select Analyze -> Enabled Protocols.

Figure 6-18 **Wireshark – Analyze, Enabled Protocols**

From this selection, the following pop-up window is displayed:

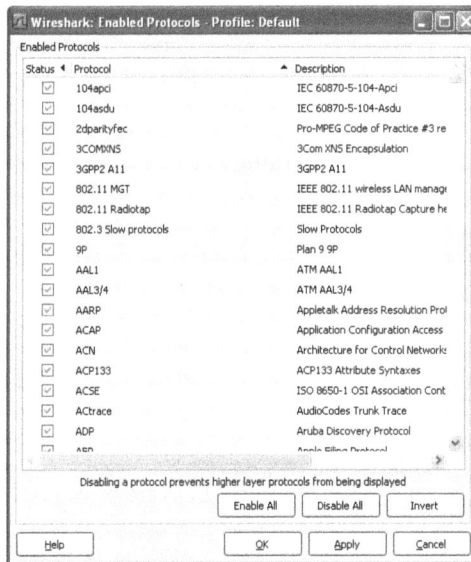

Figure 6-19 **Wireshark – Analyze, Enabled Protocols**

The protocols of interest for this book are:

- ARP

- IP

- ICMP

- TCP

- UDP

Even with these protocols, a substantial amount of data will be captured since many higher-level protocols rely on this list. When troubleshooting a HTTP service, HTTP must also be selected in the list of enabled protocols.

Before we select the interface to begin capture, there is one additional suggestion. As the Ethernet MAC address is composed of 6 bytes, where the first three bytes identify the manufacturer. By default, Wireshark will decode this address and present the manufacturer name instead of the complete MAC address. When using Wireshark for the first time, it may be confusing, therefore we suggest configuring the Name Resolution option.

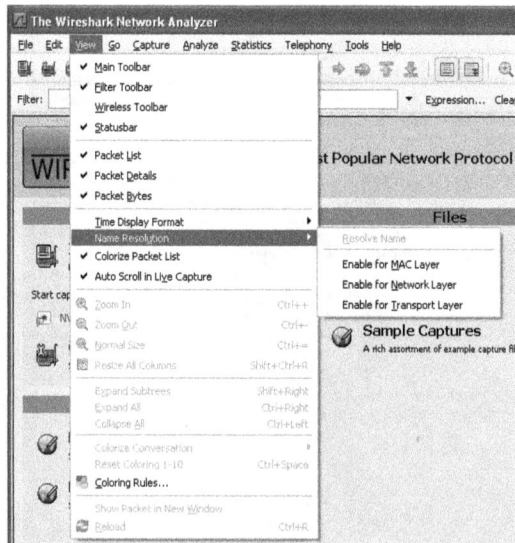

Figure 6-20 **Wireshark – Name Resolution**

From the main window drop-down menu, select View -> Name Resolution.

Name resolution can be configured for the following:

- MAC Layer (Data-Link, Ethernet in our case)

- Network Layer (IP)

- Transport Layer (TCP and UDP)

If you are new to protocol decoding, it is better to see the fields and their values rather than names. Therefore, display complete addresses and port numbers, and not aliases.

Next, configure the capture and/or display filters. The capture filter allows for a reduction in the size of the capture file by only saving the traffic of interest.

On the Wireshark main window, select Capture -> Capture Filters.

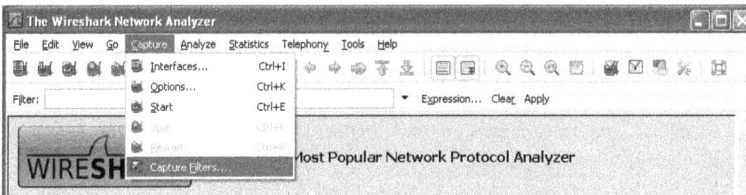

Figure 6-21 **Wireshark – Capture Filters**

This pop-up window is displayed:

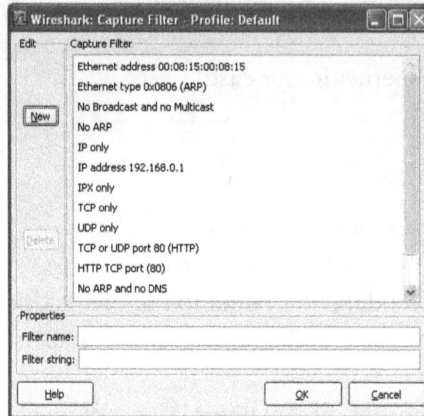

Figure 6-22 **Wireshark – Capture Filters Edition**

On the Wireshark main window toolbar, select Edit Capture Filter. Only one capture filter can be applied per capture. The capture filter is applied on the Interface Capture Options window as seen below.

A capture filter is an equation that uses protocol names, fields, and values to achieve the desired result. For an explanation on the equation syntax, please refer to Wireshark documentation or use the Help button in the bottom left corner of this window.

Capture filters allow for the reduction of the size of the capture file, but capturing everything may be required in certain cases. Capturing all the traffic on a link on a network can yield a substantial amount of data. Finding the frames of interest in a sea of frames is often difficult. However, once the data is captured, it can be displayed using different display filters to see only what is of interest.

From the main window drop-down menu, select Analyze -> Display Filters.

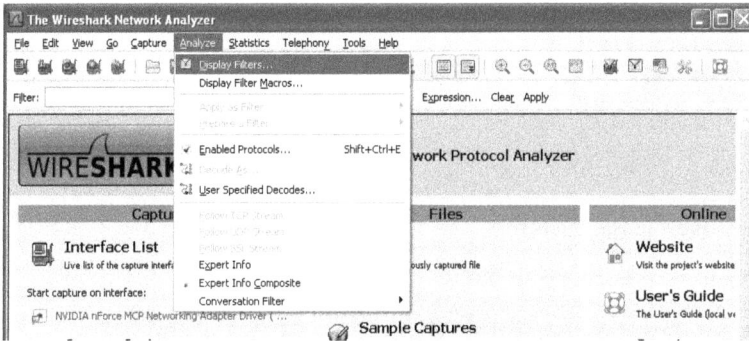

Figure 6-23 **Wireshark – Display Filters**

This pop-up window is displayed:

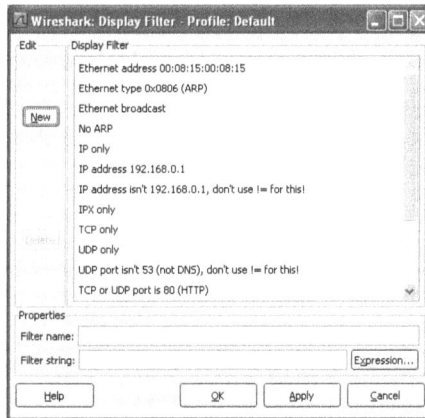

Figure 6-24 **Wireshark – Display Filters Edition**

The rules to create and edit a display filter are not the same as those used for a capture filter. Refer to the Wireshark documentation or use the Help button at the bottom left of the window.

Now, let's set the interface to be used for capturing the network traffic.

From the main window drop-down menu, select Capture -> Interfaces.

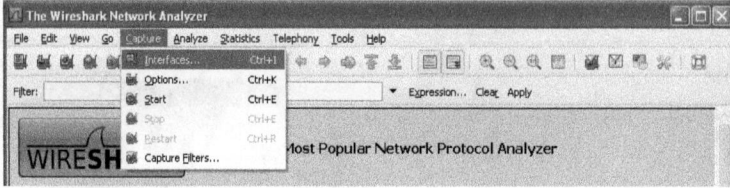

Figure 6-25 **Wireshark – Capture Interface**

This pop-up window is displayed.

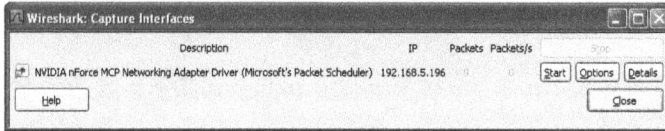

Figure 6-26 **Wireshark – Capture Interfaces**

Select the computer NIC used to connect to the network to be analyzed. Remember this is the interface that will capture the traffic to and from the embedded system.

If the name resolution is not set, do it here by clicking on the Options button associated with the interface selected.

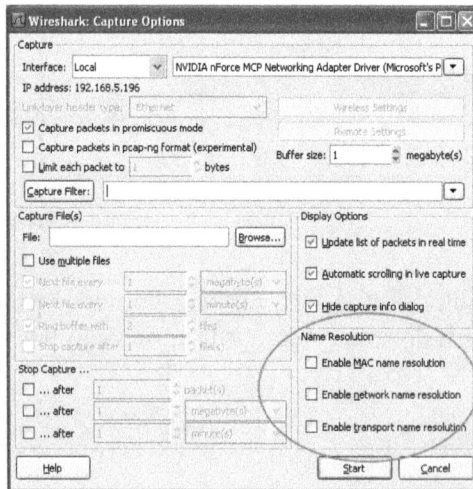

Figure 6-27 **Wireshark – Name Resolution**

Click the Start button to begin the capture. Without setting options, clicking the Start button associated to an interface of interest in the interface selection window also begins frame capturing.

The following figure provides a capture sample:

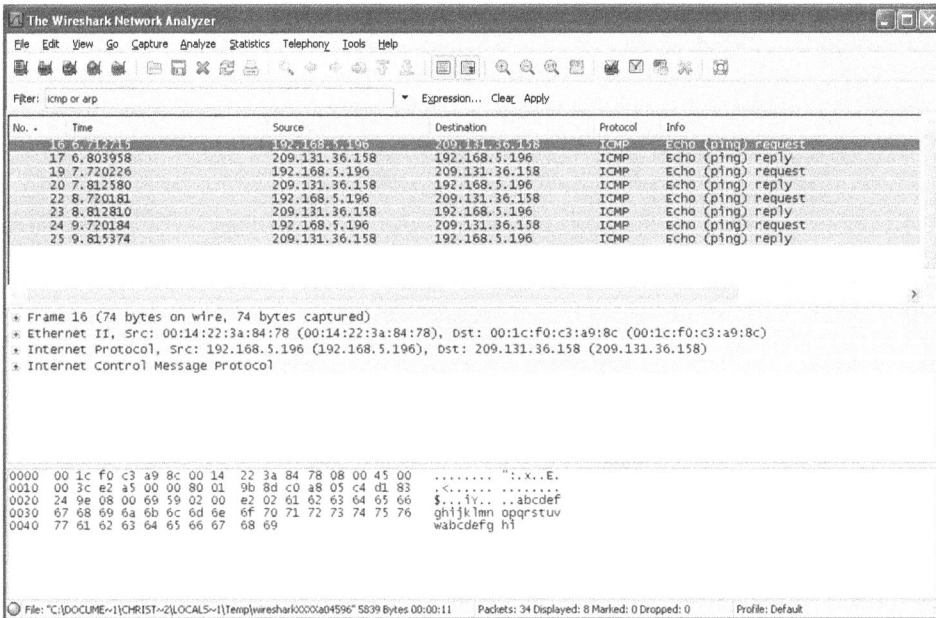

Figure 6-28 **Wireshark – Capture**

The capture shown in Figure 6-28 is a PING test from a host on a private network to a host on the Internet at IP address 209.131.36.158. For this example, the display filter is set to view ICMP traffic only. Even if what is being captured and stored are Ethernet frames, Wireshark refers to every record as a packet. The Wireshark capture window offers three different views of the captured "packets:"

- Packet List

- Packet Details

- Packet Bytes

6

The Packet list is a summary of all packets captured during the test. By default, the first packet in the list is selected. Click on any packet in the list to make it the selected packet.

Packet Details and Packet Bytes are the decoded representation of the selected packet. Packet Details is a view the can be expanded by clicking on the + expansion icons, which is a view of the encapsulation process introduced in Chapter 1.

The Packet Bytes view is often not required when analyzing a network or application problem. It is a hexadecimal and ASCII view of the packet, similar to a memory dump view. A Packet Bytes view is useful if packet construction is suspected. TCP/IP stacks are very stable software components, which mean that we can turn off this view.

From the main window drop-down menu, select View -> Packet Bytes.

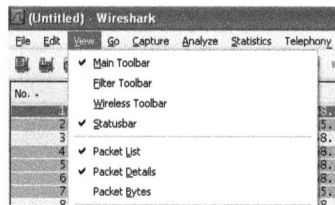

Figure 6-29 **Wireshark – Packet Bytes**

Wireshark has many more features and options including its ability to save the capture to files. In this way, when analyzing a situation, it is possible to share a problem with colleagues.

Wireshark captures are used extensively in Part II.

6-2-3 µC/IPerf

IPerf was developed by The National Laboratory for Applied Network Research (NLANR) as a means to measure maximum TCP and UDP bandwidth performance. The source code can be found on Sourceforge: http://iperf.sourceforge.net/. IPerf is open source software written in C++ that runs on various platforms including Linux, Unix and Windows. Micrium ported IPerf source code to µC/TCP-IP and created a module in C called µC/IPerf, which can be downloaded with all code and tools for this book at: http://www.micrium.com/page/downloads/uc-tcp-ip_files

IPerf is a standardized tool that can be used on any network, and outputs standardized performance measurements. It can also be used as an unbiased benchmarking tool for comparison of wired and wireless networking equipment and technologies. As the source code is available, the measurement methodology can be analyzed by anyone.

With IPerf, you can create TCP and UDP data streams and measure the throughput of a network for these streams. IPerf reports bandwidth, delay jitter, and datagram loss, and allows you to set various parameters to tune a network. IPerf has client and server functionality. Because Micrium provides the µC/IPerf source code, it is also an excellent example of how to write a client and/or server application for µC/TCP-IP. The IPerf test engine can measure the throughput between two hosts, either uni-directionally or bi-directionally. When used for testing UDP capacity, IPerf allows you to specify datagram size, and provides results for datagram throughput and packet loss. When used for testing TCP capacity, IPerf measures the throughput of the payload.

In a typical test setup with two hosts, one is the embedded system under test (see Figure 6-30). The second host is ideally a PC. A command line version of IPerf is available for PCs running Linux, Unix and Windows. There is also a graphical user interface (GUI) front end called Jperf available on sourceforge: http://iperf.sourceforge.net/. It is definitely fun to use.

The examples shown in this book use a Jperf variant called KPerf. There is no official site for KPerf and there are just a few links to download it. Micrium uses KPerf because of its ease of use. Download KPerf from the Micrium site at: www.micrium.com/page/downloads/uc-tcp-ip_files.

KPerf was originally created by the same IPerf and Jperf authors, but the source code and executables do not seem to be maintained. If you want the source code for the PC host in the test setup, Jperf is more advantageous.

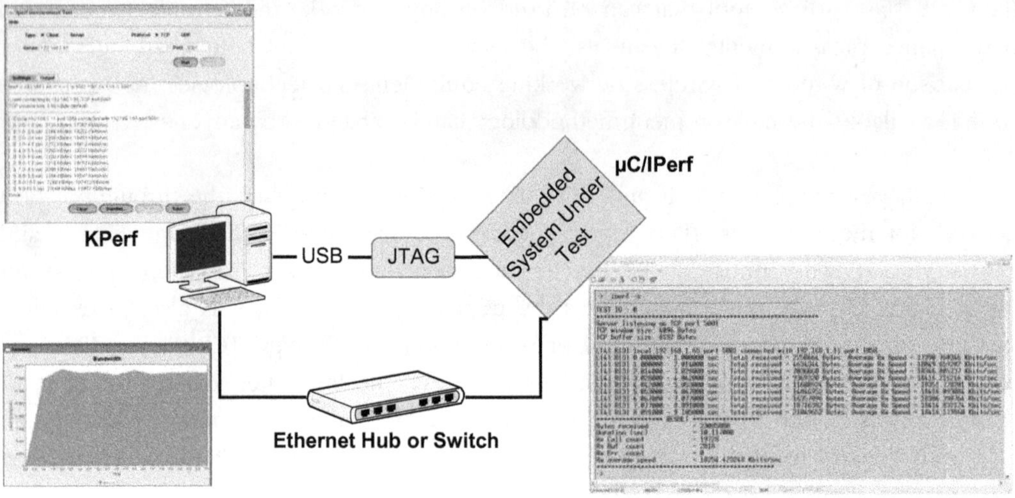

Figure 6-30 **IPerf Setup**

The µC/IPerf setup is reproduced in Figure 6-30. In this case, the Ethernet hub or switch can be replaced with a cross-over cable, an Ethernet cable where the TX wires and the RX wires are crossed so that two Ethernet devices have a face-to-face connection without the use of a hub or switch. This type of cable is very useful for troubleshooting, but must be identified carefully as using it with certain Ethernet switches may not work. More recent computer NICs and Ethernet switches detect the TX and RX wires. This is called AutoSense. With this equipment any Ethernet cable type can be used.

Typically, an IPerf report contains a time-stamped output of the amount of data transferred and the throughput measured. IPerf uses 1024*1024 for megabytes and 1000*1000 for megabits.

Here is an example of an IPerf test where the PC is configured as a client and the embedded system under test as a server.

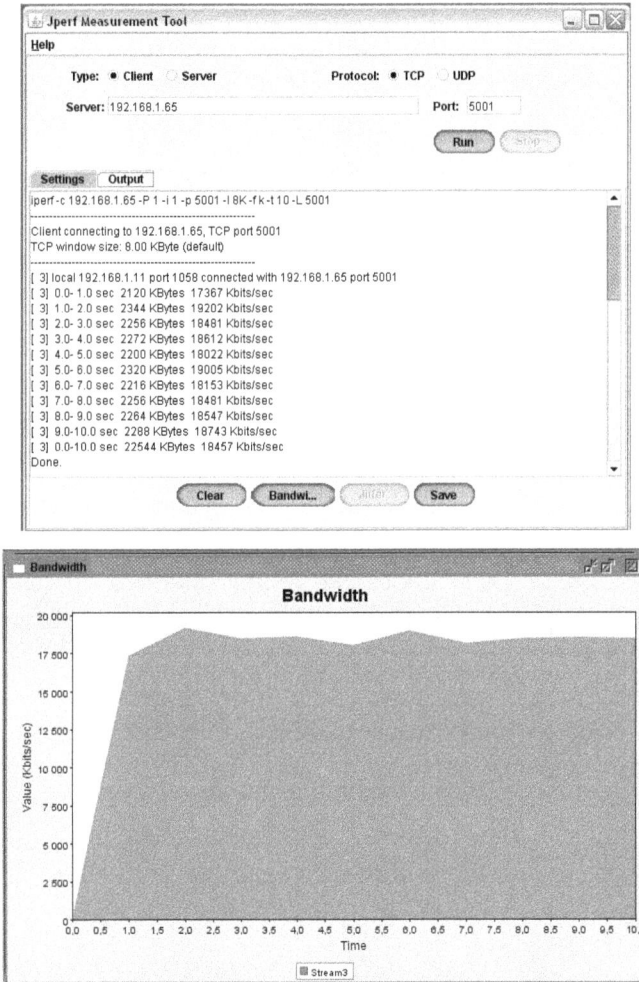

Figure 6-31 **KPerf on PC in Client mode**

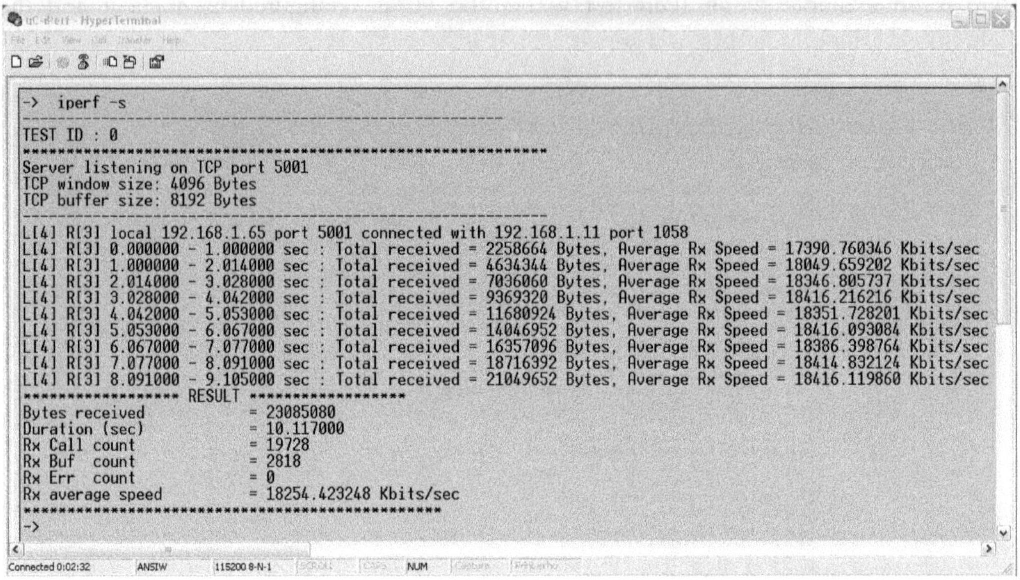

Figure 6-32 **µC/IPerf on Embedded System Under Test in Server mode**

In the Figure 6-30 setup, all possible network configurations can be tested: TCP or UDP tests in client-to-server or server-to-client mode, using different parameters settings. If necessary, refer to the IPerf or µC/IPerf user manuals.

µC/IPerf testing samples are used extensively in Part II of this book to test UDP and TCP configurations and to demonstrate concepts introduced so far, especially in the area of performance.

6-3 SUMMARY

A TCP/IP stack is a complex embedded software component and using TCP/IP can also be complicated.

In this chapter, we introduced the following network troubleshooting tools: PING, TRACEROUTE, Wireshark and IPerf. Many other network traffic analysis tools and load generators exist. It's unlikely that you will need more than the concepts presented so far when developing your TCP/IP-based embedded system.

7

Transport Protocols

Since we already know that Internet Protocol (IP) does not check data integrity, it is necessary to use protocols that have complementary characteristics to ensure that the data not only arrives at its intended destination, but is in good shape when it does. The protocols most often used with IP are Transmission Control Protocol (TCP) and User Datagram Protocol (UDP), both of which check data integrity. Although TCP and UDP have similar data-carrying capabilities, they have specific differences and characteristics that dictate their use.

7-1 TRANSPORT LAYER PROTOCOLS

The following table represents a comparison between TCP and UDP:

	TCP	UDP
Service	Connection oriented	Connectionless
Data verification	Yes	Yes
Rejection of erroneous segments/datagrams	Yes	Yes
Sequence control	Yes	No
Retransmission of erroneous and lost segments	Yes	No
Reliability	High	Low
Delay generated	High	Low
Total throughput	Lower	Higher

Table 7-1 **TCP vs. UDP at the protocol level**

Data verification is the data integrity checking capability for both protocols. If a TCP segment or UDP datagram is received and data corruption is detected, the segment or datagram is rejected.

Given that with packet networks such as IP, packets may take different paths depending on network conditions, it is possible for packets transmitted to reach their final destination out of order. With TCP, segments received out of order are re-sequenced so that the data is received in the order it was originally transmitted.

TCP also implements a flow-control mechanism which ensures that all packets transmitted are received at a pace that is based on available resources, even if the process takes longer to achieve. Flow control also prevents segments from being discarded because the receiver does not have the resources to receive it. This is why TCP is considered a high-reliability protocol in comparison to UDP. The flow-control mechanism is not part of the UDP protocol. Instead, UDP has a fire-and-forget strategy and it is also known as a best-effort protocol. TCP's reliability has a corresponding expense. All of the processing required with TCP to ensure the reliable delivery of data adds transmission delay between the source and destination. This is why in Table 7-2 it is noted that TCP has a lower total throughput than UDP.

TCP and UDP can also be differentiated by the type of applications that use them:

Protocol	Service Type	Examples
TCP	Reliable stream transfer	Non time-sensitive data transfer: File transfer, web pages (an embedded system running a web server), e-mail…
UDP	Quick-and-simple single-block transfer	Network services with short queries and short answers: DHCP and DNS Time Sensitive data that can cope with a minimal packet loss: Voice, video, repetitive sensor data

Table 7-2 **TCP vs. UDP at the Application Level**

TCP's inherent characteristics make it an appropriate protocol for transporting non real-time (data) traffic, which does not tolerate errors. The TCP Specifics section that follows this chapter provides an in-depth look at these characteristics.

Examples of standard protocols or network services that use TCP include:

■ File Transfer Protocol (FTP)

■ Hyper Text Transfer Protocol (HTTP)

■ Simple Mail Transfer Protocol (SMTP)

For an embedded system, any information exchange requiring a guarantee of delivery to the recipient benefits from TCP. A configuration application for a numerical milling machine is an example.

Delays generated by TCP's reliability have consequences on the quality of the transmission of real-time traffic, such as voice or video. Moreover, since several types of real-time traffic tolerate a certain error rate, the use of the UDP protocol is more appropriate. When the message generated by the application is short, the risk of error decreases.

Examples of standard protocols or network services that use UDP include:

■ Domain Name Service (DNS)

■ Dynamic Host Configuration Protocol (DHCP)

■ Trivial File Transfer Protocol (TFTP)

An embedded system that tolerates errors in data transmission may benefit from UDP. In fact, Micrium has many customers that use a UDP/IP configuration only. A system that collects sensor data at periodic intervals and transfers it to control a recording station is an example. If the system can suffer the infrequent loss of a report, UDP may be the best protocol option.

7-2 CLIENT/SERVER ARCHITECTURE

A very important application design feature used on IP networks is the client/server architecture, as it separates functions between service requesters (clients) and service providers (servers).

A client is a host application that executes a single task. This task is for the host alone and is not shared with any other hosts on the network. When a client requests content or a service function from a server, servers are listening to connection requests initiated by clients. Since a server shares its resources with clients, the server can execute one or more tasks.

Such familiar networked functions as email, web access, and database access, are based on the client-server model. For example, a web browser is a client application running on a host that accesses information at any web server in the world.

The client-server model is the architecture of most IP-based applications including HTTP, SMTP, Telnet, DHCP and DNS. Client software sends requests to one or many servers. The servers accept requests, process them, and return the requested information to the client.

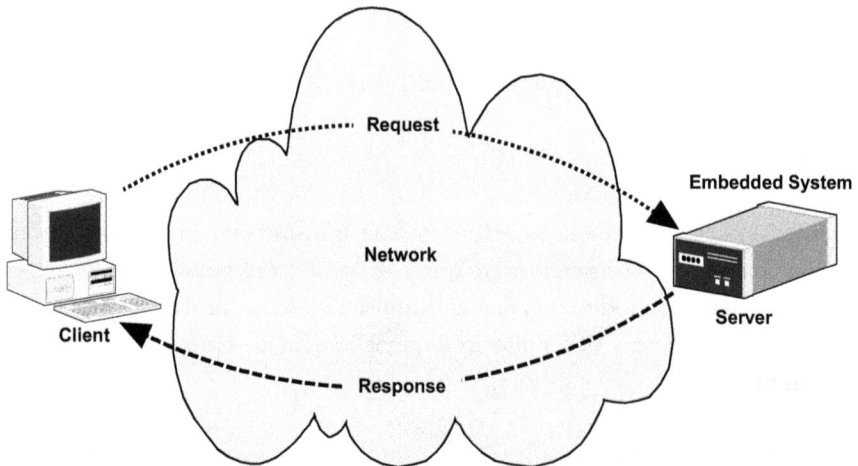

Figure 7-1 **Client/Server Architecture**

In Figure 7-1 above, note that the embedded system can also be the Client.

To implement a client/server architecture, a connection is established between the client and the server. This is where transport layer protocols come into play.

7-3 PORTS

UDP and TCP share common fields in their respective headers, two being port numbers. A port is a logical entity that allows UDP and TCP to associate a segment (datagram) with a specific application. This is how IP addresses are reused with multiple applications, or multiple instances of the same application on a single client or server Host.

The next chapter addresses socket concepts and demonstrates how a port number is used to differentiate between applications running on the same host.

For the source host, the destination port indicates to which logical entity the datagram must be sent. In a client-server environment, the destination port at the client's station normally takes on a value that is predetermined by the Internet Assigned Numbers Authority (IANA) depending on the application that is solicited. These destination ports are also identified as well-known ports and are defined in RFC 1700.

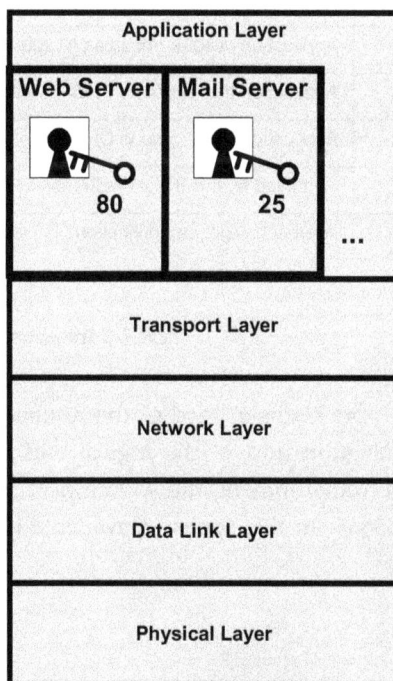

Figure 7-2 **Server application port number use**

Figure 7-2, shows two very popular services: A web server that replies to requests on port number 80 and a SMTP mail server that replies to requests on port 25.

Although UDP offers connectionless service, the station must be able to determine the application to which the information contained in the datagram will be sent. The UDP port contains this information.

Table 7-3 shows predetermined values of port numbers based on popular applications as per RFC 1700:

Port	Transport	Application	Description
20	TCP	FTP-Data	Port used by the FTP application for data transfer.
21	TCP	FTP-Control	Port used by the FTP application to transport control fields.
23	TCP	Telnet	Application providing remote access.
25	TCP	SMTP	E-mail application.
53	UDP	DNS	Application used to obtain an IP address based on a domain name.
67	UDP	BOOTPS	Application that supports DHCP (server port).
68	UDP	BOOTPC	Application that supports DHCP (client port).
69	UDP	TFTP	Port used by the Trivial File Transfer Protocol (TFTP)
80	TCP,UDP	HTTP	Internet navigation application.

Table 7-3 **Transport Layer Port Number Definitions**

For the source host, the source port keeps a trace of the application where the datagram originated, and informs the destination host of the logical entity where it must send the reply. Generally, in a client-server environment, the source port at the client's station takes on a value between 1024 and 65535. In this series of available ports, several are reserved but not allocated by the IANA.

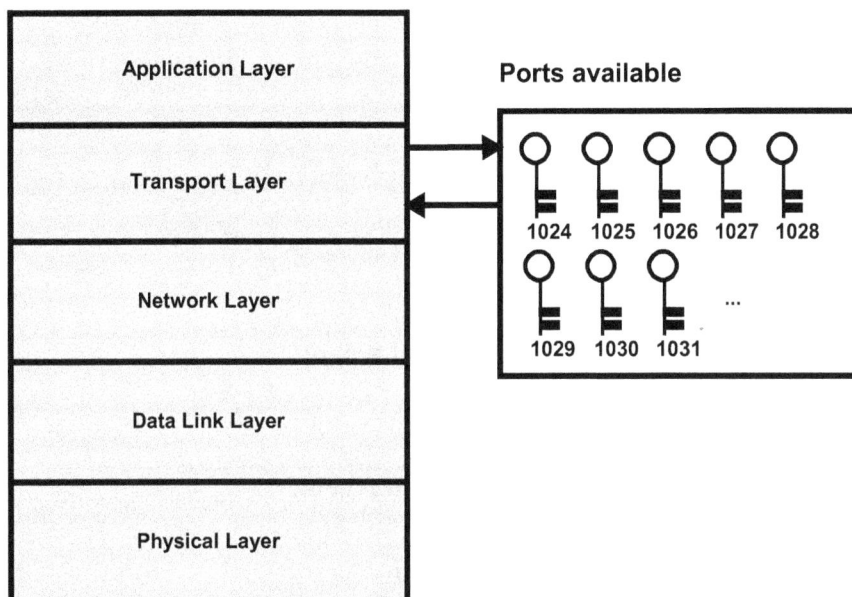

Figure 7-3 **Client Application Port Number Use**

Figure 7-3 shows a client using available socket numbers. The client port can take any number from 1024 to 65535. Computers and embedded systems both use this approach.

The accepted notation used to represent an IP address and port number is to specify the IP address in dotted decimal notation followed by a colon and then the port number. For example: 10.2.43.234:1589.

7-3-1 PORT ADDRESS TRANSLATION (PAT)

Network address translation (NAT) was introduced previously in Chapter 4. It is important to note here that there is a NAT variant called Port Address Translation (PAT) that uses port numbers to reduce the number of public IP addresses required to connect hosts on a private network to hosts on the Internet. Port numbers can be utilized to reuse a single public IP address to allow a private network to access the Internet (see Figure 7-4). This graphic is typical of the mechanism used by our earlier example of gateways in homes that access the Internet.

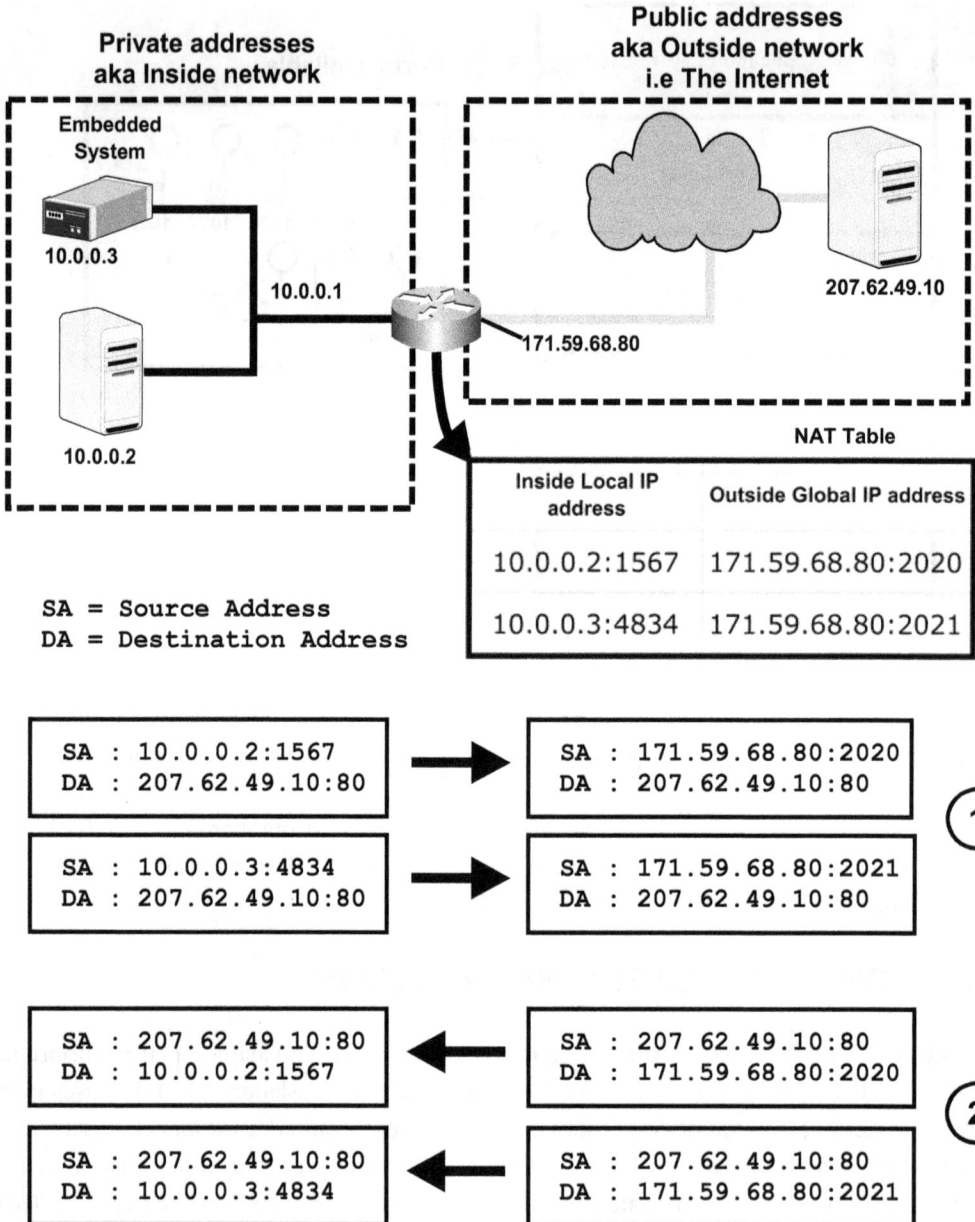

Figure 7-4 **Port Address Translation**

Figure 7-4 shows a 10.0.0.0 private network assigned to the network on the left. The router in the Figure is the default gateway for this network. The gateway has two network interfaces: one facing the network on the left, the private network; and one facing the network on the right, the public network.

F7-4(1)   In this simple case, embedded systems with IP address 10.0.0.2 and 10.0.0.3 on the private network want to connect with a host at 207.62.49.10 on the Internet. The embedded system's private address and source port number (10.0.0.2:1567) is translated into the public address associated with the gateway's public interface of 171.59.68.80 plus a port number (2020). Similarly, the PC's private address and source port number (10.0.0.3:4834) is translated into the public address associated with the gateway's public interface of 171.59.68.80 plus a port number (2021). The Internet Service Provider (ISP) assigns the public address when the private network is registered. When the private network is running, all connection requests from the private network to the Internet will be granted.

The cross-reference between the private addresses and the public addresses is stored in a table in the gateway. The packets sent by the embedded system and PC can now travel on the public network since all addresses are public. In this example, we see that multiple connections are established between the private network and the Internet, reusing a single public address, yet having multiple source port numbers.

F7-4(2)   When the host on the public network answers the query from the host in the private network system with IP translated to 171.59.68.80, it answers the message the same way it would answer another host request on the Internet. When the reply reaches the gateway, it translates the destination address from 171.59.68.80 and associated port number to the correct private address and associated port number using the translation table it created on the initial outgoing packet. This works as long as the communication is established from the private network out.

The same discussion can be made regarding the use of static public addresses to access hosts on the private network from hosts on the public network, as shown in the NAT section in the previous chapter. This process (NAT or PAT) happens in the gateway. When troubleshooting from a private network to a public network or vice-versa, take this process into consideration.

7

7-4 UDP

UDP is a communication protocol at Layer 4, the Transport Layer. It is often believed that UDP is a deprecated protocol because all of the Internet services used on a daily basis including web browsing and e-mail use TCP. This, however, is not the case. As previously stated, there are many services and applications that rely solely on UDP. UDP provides limited services when information is exchanged between two stations on the network; yet it is often all that is required.

When two hosts exchange information using UDP, there is no information regarding the status of the connection between them. Host A knows that it is sending or receiving data from Host B, and vice-versa, but that's all. The UDP layer in both hosts does not know if all of the data was transmitted and received properly. This means that the application layer above UDP in Hosts A and B must implement the necessary mechanisms to guarantee the delivery of data, if necessary. Remember, UDP is a best-effort, connectionless protocol.

UDP encapsulation provides checksum on the payload to detect accidental errors. When the UDP datagram is received, UDP checks for data validity. If validated, UDP will move the data to the application. If the data is invalid, however, the datagram is discarded without additional warning.

0	1	2	3	4	5	6	7	8	9	1 0	1 1	1 2	1 3	1 4	1 5	1 6	1 7	1 8	1 9	2 0	2 1	2 2	2 3	2 4	2 5	2 6	2 7	2 8	2 9	3 0	3 1
Source Port																Destination Port															
Datagram Length																Data Checksum															
Data																															
...																															

Figure 7-5 **UDP Header Fields**

The UDP header format is given in Figure 7-5. This information will be useful when decoding UDP datagrams with a network protocol analyzer as presented in Chapter 6, "Troubleshooting" on page 139.

Because UDP is a simple protocol without control mechanisms, it executes quickly, however datagrams may be lost for many reasons such as network congestion or lack of resources in the receiving host. This can well be the case on an embedded target as typically, embedded targets have scarce resources, especially RAM for buffers.

In a normal application, UDP is used in a system where the exchange of information between the client and server is accomplished with short client requests generating short server replies. Examples of this include DHCP and DNS, which both use UDP.

When a host using DHCP is powered up, it sends a DHCP request as a broadcast message looking for a DHCP server, and asks for an IP address. This is a short request since not many bytes are required to build such a request. Similarly, the reply from the server is fairly short, containing the information required to use the IP address assigned to it by the Server.

Another example is the use of DNS to obtain an IP address associated with a fully qualified domain name or URL. The request is a short question: "What is the IP address of this site?" The answer is also short: "Here's the IP address!"

From here, it is possible to imagine the use of UDP in many industrial-control applications where the amount and therefore duration of data to be transferred is relatively small. Another criteria is that the transfers occur at a reasonable periodic rate easily accommodated by the embedded target hardware. Another requirement is for the system to cope with missing packets discarded somewhere in the network.

If a system meets these requirements, the system TCP/IP stack may not need to implement TCP. The TCP module has a substantially larger code footprint than UDP (see section 3-2-3 "Footprint" on page 78). If UDP alone is used, the total system footprint is substantially smaller, which is an excellent situation for most embedded systems.

Given that UDP is a fairly light protocol, UDP transmission from the target to any other host can maximize throughput performance between the two devices. On many embedded targets, it is quite possible for the target to be a slower consumer, especially if the producer is a PC. UDP transmission from a host PC to an embedded target can flood the network interface. Depending on the processor speed and the number of buffers available, only a certain percentage of the traffic is received by the embedded target. The system designer in this case must consider whether or not the loss of any UDP datagram is critical.

Performance Impact on UDP

When the UDP producer is faster than the UDP consumer, there are potentially limiting factors to performance optimization:

1 The capacity of the Ethernet driver to receive all frames destined to its address.

2 The capacity for the TCP/IP stack and its associated Ethernet driver to move the Ethernet frames into network buffers.

3 In case the CPU cannot process all of the Ethernet frames, the capacity for the stack to have sufficient buffers so that they are kept in a queue for later processing. Of course, this is valid only if this is a transmission burst and not a sustained transmission.

An example of such a design decision is the use of UDP to transport such time-sensitive information as voice or video content. In this case, the timely delivery of the information is more important than the guaranteed delivery of the information.

When control mechanisms are added in a system to guarantee information delivery, it is quite possible that certain data packets will be delayed. Delaying information in a voice conversation or a video stream is not a good idea. This is the cause of clicking sounds, choppiness and delays experienced in early Voice over IP (VoIP) systems. UDP can help. Because UDP is a lighter protocol, it reduces the overhead required to process data. This does not mean that the system will not lose data. The system designer must consider whether or not the application can live with the loss of a few data packets. The new coders/decoders (codecs) in VoIP system do exactly that.

Part II of this book contains a sample project showing how to experiment with this behavior in an evaluation board. It is using the µC/IPerf application previously introduced in Chapter 6, "Troubleshooting" on page 139.

7-5 TCP SPECIFICS

Unlike IP and UDP, which are connectionless protocols, TCP is connection-oriented. This means that this protocol connection requirement involves the following three steps:

- Establishing a connection

- Transferring information

- Closing the connection.

0	1	2	3	4	5	6	7	8	9	1 0	1 1	1 2	1 3	1 4	1 5	1 6	1 7	1 8	1 9	2 0	2 1	2 2	2 3	2 4	2 5	2 6	2 7	2 8	2 9	3 0	3 1
Source Port																Destination Port															
Sequence number																															
Acknowledgment number																															
HLEN				Reserved						Code						Window															
Data checksum																Urgent pointer															
Options																										Pad					
Data																															
...																															

Figure 7-6 **TCP Header Fields**

Figure 7-6 shows s TCP header. It is a useful reference when decoding TCP segments with a network protocol analyzer.

The term "connection oriented" means that both hosts involved in a TCP communication are aware of each other. TCP is not one connection but two connections: one from A to B and one from B to A. The establishment of the full-duplex connection is accomplished using the TCP header "Code" field as shown in Figure 7-6. This field defines the function of the segment or a transmission characteristic.

Each of the six code-field bits corresponds to a command. When the value of a bit is set at 1, the command is active. The six commands in the Code field are:

- URG: Urgent

- ACK: Acknowledge

- PSH: Push

- RST: Reset

- SYN: Synchronize

- FIN: Finalize

The following commands are used in the context of establishing a connection:

URG	Urgent— if the field has a value of 1, it identifies that this segment contains urgent data. The Urgent Pointer field in the TCP header points to the sequence number of the last byte in a sequence of urgent data or, in other words, where the non-urgent data in this segment begins.
ACK	Acknowledge — code used to accept and confirm the TCP connection. This command is used jointly with the Acknowledgement field.
PSH	Push — if the field has a value of 1, the PSH command forces the receiver's TCP protocol to immediately transmit the data to the application without waiting for other segments.
RST	Reset — code used to abruptly interrupt a TCP connection without using the FIN or the ACK commands). This code is used under abnormal transmission conditions. Such browsers as Internet Explorer use it to close a connection without going through the normal closing sequence.
SYN	Synchronize — code used to request the establishment of a connection by defining the first sequence numbers used by the source and by the destination. The first number in the sequence is called the Initial Sequence Number (ISN).
FIN	Finalize — code used to ask the receiver to terminate the TCP connection.

Table 7-4 **TCP Code (6 bits)**

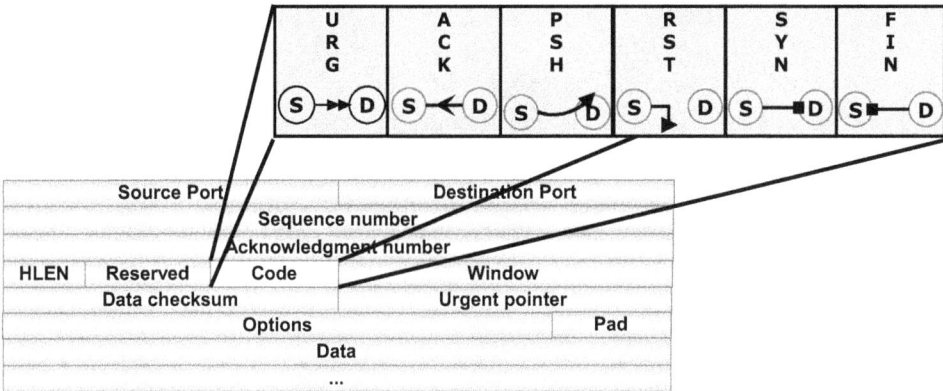

Figure 7-7 **TCP Code (6 bits)**

The six Code bits listed in Table 7-4 and depicted in Figure 7-7 are used in the following connection establishment mechanism.

7-6 TCP CONNECTION PHASES

The basis of the connection mechanism in TCP is called the three-way handshake.

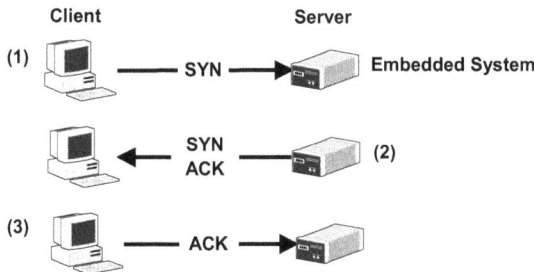

Figure 7-8 **The Three-Way Handshake**

F7-8(1)   The client sends a SYN command to open a connection from the client to the server.

F7-8(2)   The server answers the request for a connection with an ACK command and in the same message also asks to open a connection from the server to the client with a SYN command.

F7-8(3)   The client confirms the connection with an ACK command.

Two connections are established: one from the client to the server and one from the server to the client. Normally, four messages would have been necessary, two per connection. Because the server acknowledges the connection request from the client and in the same message also requests to establish a connection to the client, this saves one message in the process. Three messages are used instead of four resulting in the three-way handshake.

Once the client and the server are aware of the connection, data can be exchanged between the two. For each packet transmitted from the client to the server, the server will acknowledge its reception and vice-versa. The PUSH code used when sending data tells the TCP stack to send this data to the application immediately. Data may also be sent without the PUSH bit. In this case data is accumulated in the receiving stack and, depending on the stack coding, is sent immediately or at a later time.

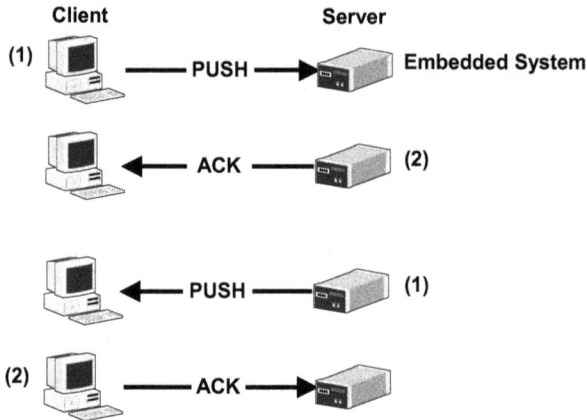

Figure 7-9 **Information Transfer**

F7-9(1)   The PUSH command forces the receiving station to send data to the application.

F7-9(2)   All TCP data received is acknowledged with the ACK command in the following packet transmitted in the opposite direction.

Upon completion of the data transfer, the two connections will be closed by the client and the server. In this case, the FIN command is used.

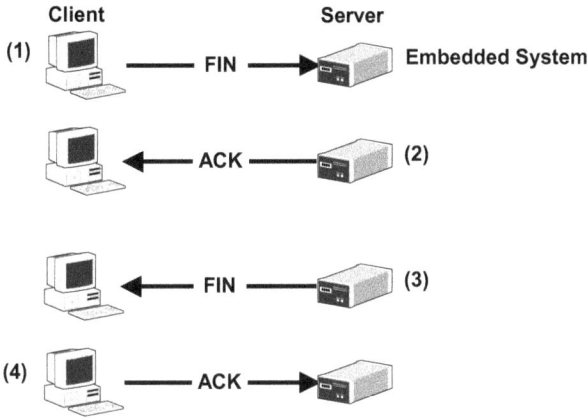

Figure 7-10 **Disconnection**

F7-10(1)   Graceful connection termination is accomplished via the FIN command.

F7-10(2)   The FIN command is also acknowledged with an ACK command.

It is possible to close only one connection of the two. For example, when the client requests a substantial amount of data from the server, the client can close its connection to the server, but the connection from the server to the client will be up until the server completes the data transfer to the client. This mechanism is called a half-close connection. When the server closes the connection steps (3) and (4) of Figure 7-10 above are executed.

7-7 TCP SEQUENCES THE DATA

When we write a letter that is several pages long, we write a sequence number on each page: 1-of-4, 2-of-4, etc. In a similar manner, TCP enters a sequence number into its header that allows for different segments to be put in order at reception.

Figure 7-11 represents the location of the sequence number in the TCP header. The sequence number is a 32-bit field. The initial sequence number in the first TCP segment used to establish connection is a random number selected by TCP. µC/TCP-IP takes care of this for you. The embedded developer does not need to be concerned about the randomness of this field. The sequence number is relative, it is not absolute. From this point, the sequence number is used as a relative pointer to the TCP payload carried by the TCP segment.

185

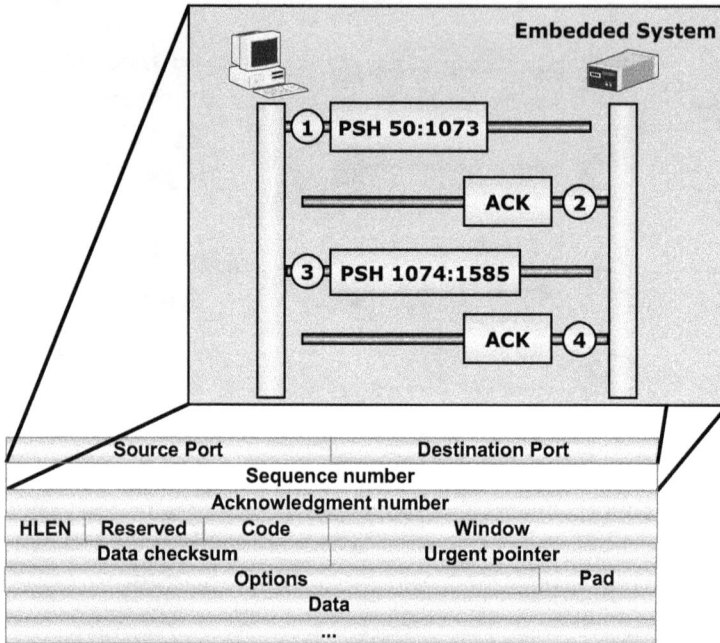

Figure 7-11 **Sequence Number (32 bits)**

F7-11(1)   The sequence number is 50. The segment is carrying 1024 bytes, which means that if the first byte carried by the segment is a byte with index 50, then the last byte has index 1073. The next sequence number is therefore the previous sequence number plus the segment size in bytes (50 + 1024 = 1074).

F7-11(2)   Once the segment is acknowledged, the next segment is ready.

F7-11(3)   512 bytes are transmitted. The sequence number now starts at 1074 which makes the pointer to the last byte carried at 1585.

F7-11(4)   This segment is also acknowledged.

If segments are received out of order, TCP re-orders them. This is a function that is taken for granted today. For example, Simple Mail Transfer Protocol (SMTP) relies on TCP and ensures that the text and attachments in an e-mail are received in order. Similarly, Hyper Text Transfer Protocol (HTTP), which also relies on TCP, ensures that the multimedia content on a web page is placed in the proper location. If that didn't happen, it would not be TCP's error.

7-8 TCP ACKNOWLEDGES THE DATA

The sequence number is also used to check the delivery of data by way of an acknowledgement number based on the sequence number.

When a TCP segment is transmitted by the source host, and received by the destination host, the destination host acknowledges the receipt of the segment. To perform this task, the destination host uses the value of the segment number to create the acknowledgment number that it will use in its next exchange with the corresponding host. As the sequence number is viewed as a pointer to data payload bytes, the acknowledgement number is the value of the pointer to the next byte the destination host expects to receive.

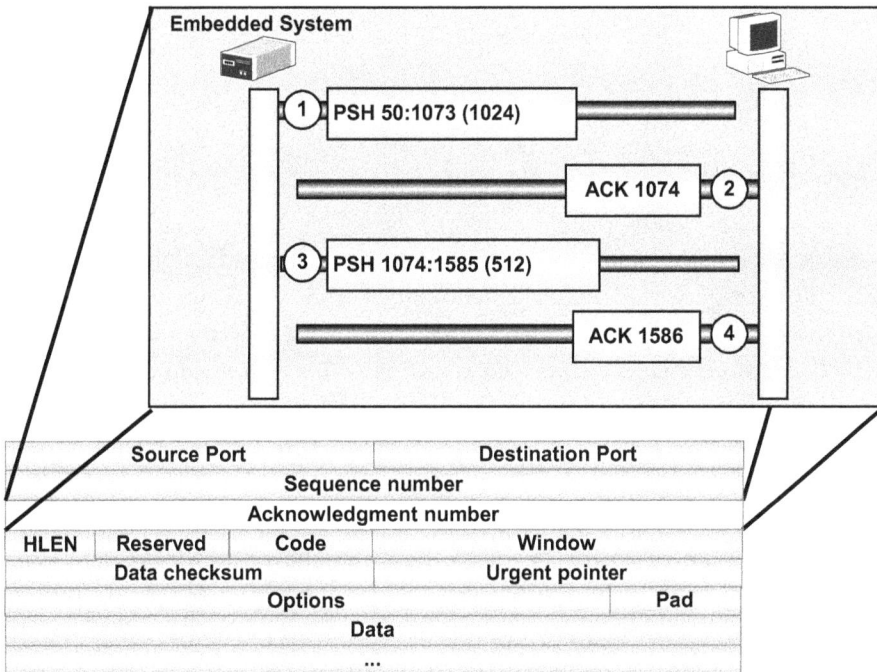

Figure 7-12 **Acknowledgement Number (32 bits)**

The acknowledgement number is related to the sequence number. The same example as in Figure 7-12 is used here, but the ACK number is included in steps (2) and (4).

F7-12(1)   The source host sends 1024 bytes with a sequence number of 50

F7-12(2)   The acknowledgment number is 1074, the pointer to the next byte that follows the byte with index 1073 just received

F7-12(3)   The source host sends 512 bytes with a sequence number of 1074

F7-12(4)   The acknowledgment number is 1586

Acknowledgements use Buffers

When a TCP segment is received, an acknowledgement must be transmitted. If the system is also sending data, an acknowledgement can piggyback on a TCP segment. Otherwise, an empty segment must be generated to acknowledge the TCP segment received.

If the system is low on resources because all of the buffers are used for reception, this presents a problem as buffers are not available to acknowledge data received.

TCP/IP stacks, such as Micrium's µC/TCP-IP, implement delayed acknowledgment as per RFC 1122. Delayed acknowledgement allows for the receiving station to send an acknowledgment for every two segments received instead of for each single segment received. When a system is receiving a stream of data, this technique relieves the receiving task from performing additional processing, making better use of buffers. It is important to know that when you use a network protocol analyzer, you may notice this behavior and believe that the TCP/IP stack is not performing properly. This is in fact the desired behavior.

Another interesting point regarding sequence numbers and acknowledgement numbers is that in the three-way handshake mechanism, the acknowledgement number used in the ACK message to the SYN message is the sequence number of the SYN message plus one (also shown in Figure 7-12). The receiver is telling the sender to send the next byte. The next TCP segment from the sender will use the value of the acknowledgement number as its sequence number.

7-9 TCP GUARANTEES DELIVERY

When segments are not delivered, or are erroneous, TCP uses a mechanism that enables the source host to retransmit. TCP uses the sequence number, acknowledgement number, and timers to guarantee data delivery. After a certain amount of time, when the TCP layer in a transmitting host is not receiving an acknowledgment for one of the segments transmitted, it will retransmit the segment. This is the first attempt at retransmitting a lost or corrupted segment. Special timers are involved in this mechanism.

7-9-1 ROUND-TRIP TIME (RTT)

Round-Trip Time (RTT) is the time that passes between the sending of a TCP segment (SYN or PSH), and the receipt of its acknowledgment (ACK). The RTT is recalculated over the duration of the connection and varies according to network congestion.

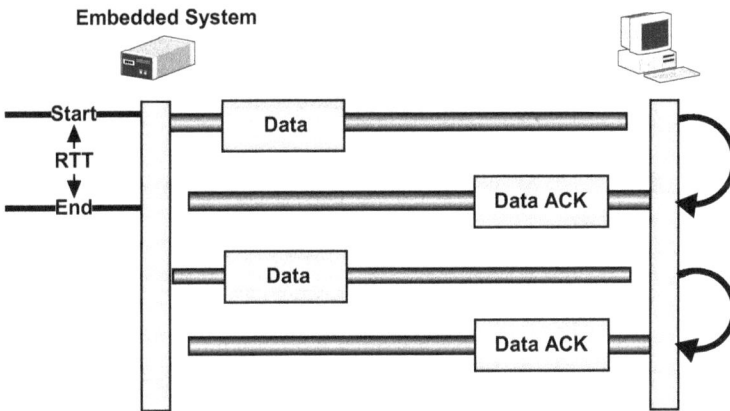

Figure 7-13 **RTT**

Figure 7-13 demonstrates how RTT is measured.

RTT is used to calculate an important timeout used for the retransmission of missing or corrupted segments called the Retransmission Time-Out (RTO). RTO is a function of RTT and has a fixed initial value as implemented in μC/TCP-IP.

When TCP does not receive an acknowledgement message within the RTO limit, the transmitting host retransmits the segment. The RTO is doubled and re-initialized. Each time it expires, the transmitting host retransmits the segment until a maximum of 96 seconds is reached. If an acknowledgement is still not received, the transmitting host closes/resets the connection.

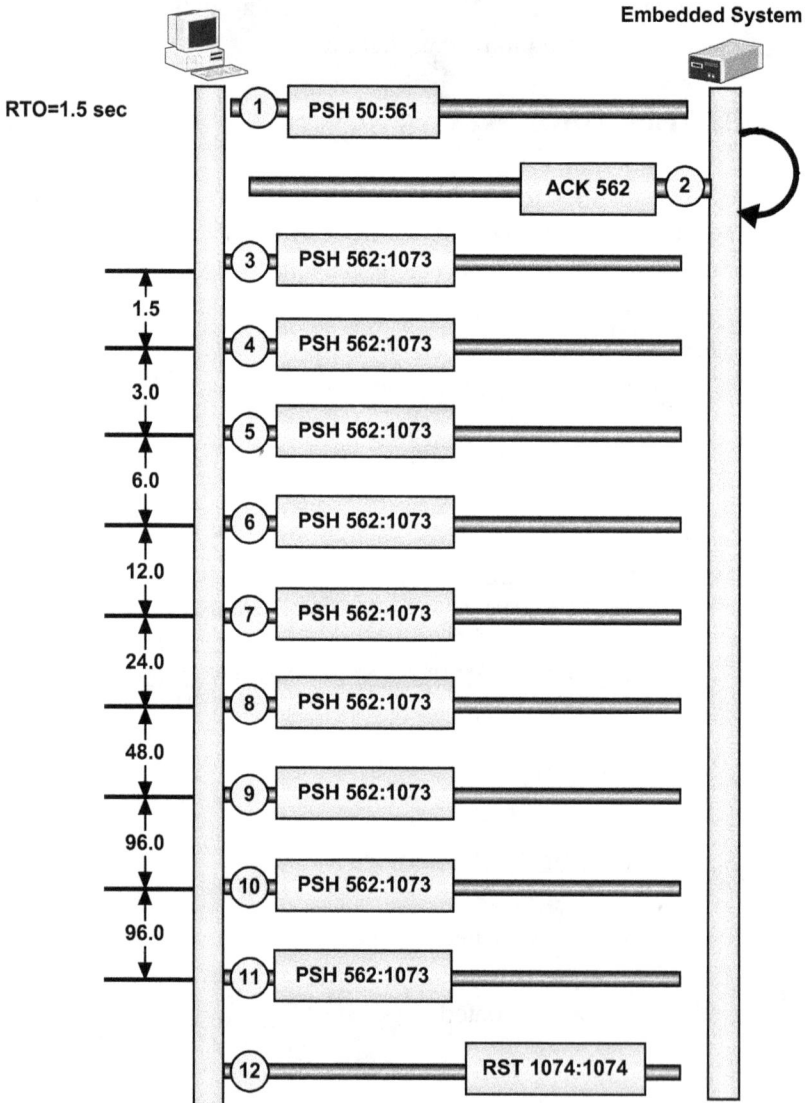

Embedded System

RTO=1.5 sec

①	PSH 50:561
②	ACK 562
③	PSH 562:1073
1.5	
④	PSH 562:1073
3.0	
⑤	PSH 562:1073
6.0	
⑥	PSH 562:1073
12.0	
⑦	PSH 562:1073
24.0	
⑧	PSH 562:1073
48.0	
⑨	PSH 562:1073
96.0	
⑩	PSH 562:1073
96.0	
⑪	PSH 562:1073
⑫	RST 1074:1074

Figure 7-14 **RTO (Retransmission Time Out) Example**

In the RTO example in Figure 7-14, the initial Retransmission Time-out is set to 1.5 seconds.

F7-14(1)   A TCP segment with 512 bytes is transmitted.

F7-14(2)   The segment is acknowledged

F7-14(3)   A second segment with 512 bytes is transmitted.

F7-14(4)   Because the second segment is not acknowledged within the RTO, it is retransmitted and the RTO is doubled to 3 seconds.

F7-14(5)   Because the segment is not acknowledged within the RTO, it is retransmitted and the RTO is doubled to 6 seconds.

F7-14(6)   Because the segment is not acknowledged within the RTO, it is retransmitted and the RTO is doubled to 12 seconds.

F7-14(7)   Because the segment is not acknowledged within the RTO, it is retransmitted and the RTO is doubled to 24 seconds.

F7-14(8)   Because the segment is not acknowledged within the RTO, it is retransmitted and the RTO is doubled to 48 seconds.

F7-14(9)   Because the segment is not acknowledged within the RTO, it is retransmitted and the RTO is doubled to 96 seconds.

F7-14(10)   Because the segment is not acknowledged within the RTO, it is retransmitted and the RTO is kept at 96 seconds.

F7-14(11)   Because the segment is not acknowledged within the RTO, it is retransmitted one last time.

F7-14(12)   The transmitter quits and resets the connection.

The idea is clear after a few steps, but the complete process is required to explain how it ends. When the RTO reaches 96 seconds, TCP resets (RST) the connection.

7

Retransmission Impact on Memory

Retransmission has an important performance impact. To be able to retransmit a segment, the TCP stack must put aside the segment it is transmitting until it receives an acknowledgment. This means that the network buffer(s) remain unavailable until acknowledgment takes place. In an embedded system with limited RAM, this limits system performance.

Sequence number, acknowledge number, and Retransmission Time-Out are TCP header fields and timers used to guarantee delivery. In networks, it is possible for packets to become corrupt or lost. When this happens, and TCP is used, packets will be retransmitted. An application would therefore use TCP when data delivery is more important than its time sensitivity. This is why e-mails, file transfers, and all web services all make use of TCP.

7-10 TCP FLOW CONTROL (CONGESTION CONTROL)

A very important TCP feature is its flow control. With additional features it also becomes a congestion control.

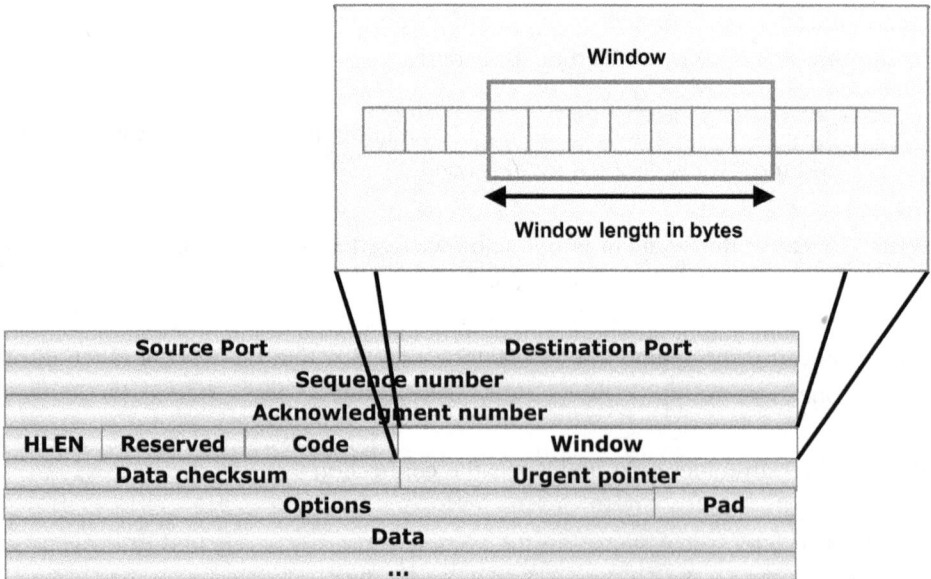

Figure 7-15 **Window (16 bits)**

TCP features a receive window and a transmit window. Figure 7-15 indicates where the window field is located in the TCP header. This field is the TCP receive window size and the field is used to advertise the window size to a corresponding host.

The window field is transmitted to the connected host to advise how many bytes may be transmitted without overflowing the receive buffers. TCP/IP stacks such as µC/TCP-IP allow you to configure the initial value of the receive window. To see how to calculate the size of this parameter (which is important to achieve optimum performance), see section 7-11 "Optimizing TCP Performance" on page 199.

As data is received, the window value is decremented by the number of bytes received. When the receiving target processes the data received, the window value is incremented by the number of bytes processed. In this way, the transmitting TCP host knows if it still can transmit.

If the window size field value is too small, the transmitting host must wait before it can transmit, as it has reached its transmission limit. In the extreme case, the transmitting host will have to wait after each transmitted TCP segment to receive a response before sending the next segment. Having to wait slows throughput considerably. On the other hand, if the window size field is made too large, the transmitting host may transmit many segments and possibly overload the receiving host. The window size field provides flow control. Because it is used by both hosts in the connection, both TCP modules use it to regulate the rate of transmission.

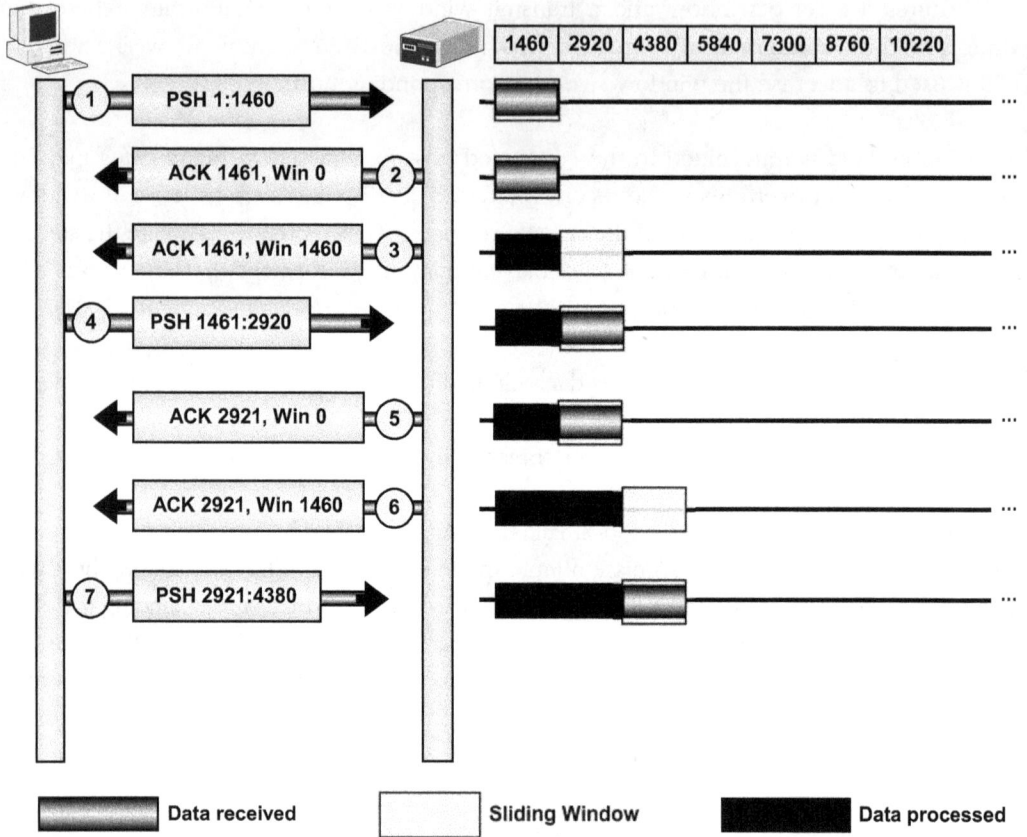

Figure 7-16 **TCP Receive Window Usage**

The TCP Window usage example shown in Figure 7-16 assumes a TCP receive window size of 1460 bytes. This value was selected to immediately show the operation of the windowing mechanism since the first packet received will fill the TCP receive window. For illustration, it was also chosen to use relative sequence and acknowledge numbers. In other words, the first byte sent in the first packet has the sequence number 1.

The example indicates how the TCP receive window size changes as data is received and processed and why it is referred to as the TCP sliding window.

F7-16(1)   A TCP segment with 1460 bytes is transmitted. The receive window is decreased to 0.

F7-16(2)   The first segment is acknowledged. The receive window (currently 0) is sent to the transmitting host. This is a Zero-Window message. The transmitting host now knows that it must stop transmitting.

F7-16(3)   The network buffer used to receive the first segment is now free. The receive window size is increased to 1460 and this is communicated to the transmitting host. This is a Window Update message. The transmitting host now knows that it can resume transmission up to 1460 bytes.

F7-16(4)   A TCP segment with 200 bytes is transmitted. The receive window is decreased to 1260.

F7-16(5)   It is assumed here that the embedded target is busy and cannot process and acknowledge the segment. A Window Update message is sent with the value of the current receive window, which is now 1260.

F7-16(6)   A TCP segment with 1260 bytes is transmitted. The receive window is decreased to 0.

F7-16(7)   The second and third segments are acknowledged. The receive window is decreased to 0.

F7-16(8)   Network buffers that were used to receive the second and third segments are freed. The receive window is increased to 1460 and this is communicated to the transmitting host.

F7-16(9)   A TCP segment with 1460 bytes is transmitted. The receive window is decreased to 0, and so on...

From the example above, it can be extrapolated that this is not an optimal configuration for performance, however on an embedded system with little RAM, it is a configuration that allows TCP to be functional. There are many possible scenarios with this configuration. For example in Step 5 and 6, it is assumed that the receive window size is 1460 and more than one buffer is receiving packets. If using a single receive buffer, the segment transmitted at step 6 would be rejected. Another possibility is for the 200-byte segments to be acknowledged before transmitting the 1260-byte segment. When analyzing the capture of a network protocol analyzer, all of these possible scenarios must be considered.

7

It is recommended to make the TCP receive window a multiple of the Maximum Segment Size (MSS), scaled appropriately as per RFC 1323.

The name "maximum segment size" is in fact a bit misleading. The value actually refers to the maximum amount of data that a segment can hold but it does not include TCP headers. The actual maximum segment size may be larger by 20 for a regular TCP header, or even larger if the segment includes TCP options.

The TCP maximum segment size specifies the maximum number of bytes in the TCP segment's data field, regardless of any other factors that influence segment size. With Ethernet as the preferred Data Link Layer technology, the data carrying capacity is 1500 bytes. The MSS for TCP in this case is 1460, which comes from taking the minimum Ethernet maximum transmission unit (MTU) of 1500 and subtracting 20 bytes each for IP and TCP header. For most computer users, MSS is set automatically by the operating system. This is also the case with μC/TCP-IP. When using μC/TCP-IP, the MTU is defined by the device driver (see Chapter 16, "Device Driver Implementation" on page 365).

SECTION 6-x shows how to calculate an optimal TCP receive window size and how to configure it in μC/TCP-IP.

7-10-1 NAGLE'S ALGORITHM

It is not efficient for an application to repeatedly transmit small packets (for example, 1 byte) because every packet has a 40 byte header (20 bytes for TCP, 20 bytes for IP), which represents substantial overhead. Telnet sessions often produce this situation where most keystrokes generate a single byte that is transmitted immediately. Over slow links, the situation is worse. Many of these small packets may be in transit at the same time, potentially leading to a congestion problem (TCP is not able to ACK packets leading to connections reset). It is referred as the "small packet problem" or "tinygram." This problem is addressed by RFC 896 which describes the Nagle's algorithm.

Nagle's algorithm works by grouping small outgoing TCP segments together, and sending them all at once. Specifically, as long as there is an already transmitted packet not yet acknowledged, the transmitter keeps buffering the output until a full packet is ready and can be transmitted.

In section 7-8 "TCP Acknowledges the Data" on page 187, it is noted that µC/TCP-IP implements delayed acknowledgment. This means that every second packet is acknowledged instead of every packet, to ease the load on the network and protocols.

Nagle's algorithm does not operate well in the presence of delayed acknowledgement. It may prevent an embedded system implementing a real-time application from performing as expected. Any application that needs to send a small quantity of data and expects an immediate answer will not react appropriately because the algorithm's goal is to increase throughput at the expense of network delay (latency). Nagle's algorithm in the transmitting host groups data and will not release a second segment until it has received an acknowledgment for the first.

With delayed acknowledgement, an acknowledgement is not transmitted by the receiving host until two segments are received, or after 200ms of reception of a first segment that is not followed by a second one. When a system uses both Nagle and delayed acknowledgement, an application that performs two successive transmissions and wants to receive data may suffer a delay of up to 500 milliseconds. This delay is the sum of Nagle's waiting for its data to be acknowledged and the 200 ms timer used by the delayed acknowledgment on single segment transmission.

Here is another example where the combination of these two mechanisms may result in poor system performance. If the sum of data to be transmitted fits into an even number of full TCP segments plus a small last segment, all will work fine. The TCP segments will all be acknowledged (automatic ACKs on even segment numbers by the delayed acknowledgment mechanism). The last segment will be released by the Nagle's algorithm since everything was acknowledged and this last segment will be acknowledged by the receiving application, completing the transaction.

However, if the sum of data to transmit ends up being an odd number of full TCP segments, plus a small last segment, the last full segment will suffer a 200 ms delay since it is alone. Nagle's algorithm will wait for this ACK to release the last small segment that completes the transaction. On a high-bandwidth link, all of the data could be transmitted in a few milliseconds. Adding a 200 ms delay greatly degrades performance. In numbers, if 1 Megabyte is transmitted in 500 ms with the system bandwidth, the throughput is 16 Mbps. Applying the additional delay due to the Nagle/Delay acknowledge problem, the throughput falls to 11.43 Mbps.

For real-time data transmission and systems with low bandwidth, disabling the Nagle's algorithm may be desirable. The system design may not allow for delays introduced by the solution to reduce the tinygram problem. The system may be designed to use small packet transmissions only. In practice it is not recommended to disable the Nagle's algorithm. As suggested by Mr. Nagle himself, it is preferable for the application to buffer the data before transmission and avoid sending small segments. If that is not possible, the only solution is to disable the Nagle's algorithm.

BSD sockets (see section "Sockets" on page 209) use the `TCP_NODELAY` option to disable Nagle's algorithm. μC/TCP-IP implements the Nagle algorithm, however the μC/TCP-IP BSD and proprietary socket APIs do not currently implement the `TCP_NODELAY` option.

7-10-2 SILLY WINDOW SYNDROME

There is another issue with the TCP windowing mechanism. It is called the silly window syndrome, and it occurs when the TCP receive window is almost full. The silly window syndrome may create a tinygram problem.

As seen in the windowing mechanism, the TCP receive window will decrease when segments are received and will not be increased until the receiver has processed the data. On an embedded system with few resources, this could easily happen, leading to the silly window syndrome. As the TCP receive window size decreases and is advertised to the sender, the sender will send smaller and smaller segments to meet this requirement. The TCP receive window size is getting small enough to become "silly." Smaller segments transmitted will create Nagle's problem described above.

The solution to the silly window syndrome is described in RFC # 812, Section 4 for transmit and receive. Additionally, RFC #1122, Section 4.2.3.3 adds information about the reception and RFC #1122, Section 4.2.3.4 about transmission. The solution is to wait until the TCP receive window can be increased by the size of at least one full TCP segment (MSS as defined in a previous section). This way the TCP receive window will probably decrease to a small number (or even zero), which the transmitting host will not be able to use until the TCP receive window is restored to at least one full TCP segment. This solution is implemented in μC/TCP-IP.

7-11 OPTIMIZING TCP PERFORMANCE

The performance of data transfer is related to Ethernet controller driver performance and the CPU clock speed as described in Chapter 2. The concept of performance related to the availability of network buffers has also been discussed. Optimizing TCP performance is directly related to the number of buffers available and how they are used. In this section, the most important relation of buffers to performance is the TCP receive window size.

Research on TCP performance resulted in the definition of the Bandwidth-Delay Product (BDP) concept. BDP is an equation that determines the amount of data that can be in transit within the network. It is the product of the available bandwidth of the network interface and network latency.

The available bandwidth of the network interface is fairly simple to calculate, especially with standard Ethernet interfaces at 10, 100 or 1000 Megabits per second. As presented in Chapter 2, we now know that on a typical embedded system, it is quite possible that the system cannot sink or source data at line speeds. A method to evaluate Ethernet controller performance is provided in Part II of this book. μC/IPerf (introduced in Chapter 6, "Troubleshooting" on page 139) can be used to reach this goal.

The latency is the RTT as seen in the previous section. The best way to estimate the round trip time is to use PING from one host to the other and use the response times returned by PING as shown in section 6-1-2 "PING" on page 144.

```
BDP (bytes) = total_available_bandwidth (KBytes/sec) * round_trip_time (ms)
```

The notion here is that Kilobytes multiplied by milliseconds leads to bytes which is the unit of measurement for the BDP. Moreover, the BDP is a very important concept and it is also directly related to the TCP Receive Window Size value which is also expressed in bytes. The TCP Receive Window Size is one of the most important factors in fine tuning TCP. It is the parameter that determines how much data can be transferred before the transmitting host waits for acknowledgement. It is in essence bound by the BDP.

If the BDP (or TCP receive window) is lower than the product of the latency and available bandwidth, the system will not be able to fill the connection at its capacity since the client cannot send acknowledgements back fast enough. A transmission cannot exceed the TCP receive window latency value, therefore the TCP receive window must be large enough to fit the maximum available bandwidth multiplied by the maximum anticipated delay. In other words, there should be enough packets in transit in the network to make sure the TCP module will have enough packets to process due to the longer latency.

The resulting BDP is a measure of an approximation of the TCP receive window value.

Let's assume that the **total_available_bandwidth** is 5 Mbps and that our embedded system is operating on a private network where all of the hosts are located closely, and the RTT to any device is approximately 20 milliseconds.

The BDP in this case is:

```
BDP = 5 Megabits/second * 20 milliseconds
    = 625 kilobytes      * 20 milliseconds
    = 12500 bytes
```

As suggested, the TCP receive window size should be a multiple of the MSS. In our Ethernet-based system, with the MSS at 1460:

```
TCP Receive Window = RoundUp(BDP/1460)     * 1460
                   = RoundUp(12500/1460) * 1460
                   = 9             * 1460
                   = 13140
```

The configuration for the TCP Receive Window from the example above requires nine (9) network buffers. This does not mean that your system needs nine (9) buffers. The system also requires a few network buffers for the data it must transmit. Even if the system does not have data to transmit, it must have network buffers to send ACK messages for TCP segments received. So, more than nine receive buffers need to be configured. As a rule of thumb, adding three to four additional buffers is adequate. In this case, it is close to 50%.

The previous example assumes a private network with all of the nodes in the same local network--not distributed geographically. When a system has to communicate over the public Internet, RTT is substantially larger. Let's take the same system bandwidth of 5 Mbps but with a RTT of 300 ms. In this case, the BDP is:

```
BDP = 5 Mbps        * 300 milliseconds
    = 625 Kbytes    * 300 milliseconds
    = 187500 bytes
```

And, the TCP receive window size:

```
TCP Receive Window = RoundUp(187500/1460) * 1460
                   = 129                   * 1460
                   = 188340
```

It is not far fetched to imagine that an embedded system with limited RAM will not be able to meet the required configuration. This does not mean the system will not work. This only means that system performance will not be optimal. TCP guarantees delivery. However, if there are insufficient buffers, the connection can be extremely slow because of the flow-control effect or because of the large number of retransmissions required.

Part II of this book provides sample code to evaluate system performance based on hardware performance and memory availability.

With µC/TCP-IP the receive window size is configured with a **#define** in the **net_cfg.h** file (see Chapter 12, "Directories and Files" on page 267, and also, Appendix D, "µC/TCP-IP Configuration and Optimization" on page 959).

```
#define NET_TCP_CFG_RX_WIN_SIZE_OCTET       13140
#define NET_TCP_CFG_TX_WIN_SIZE_OCTET       13140
```

Listing 7-1 **TCP Receive and Transmit Window Sizes**

It is a general practice to set the TCP transmit window size and the TCP receive window size to the same value as they are both based on the same BDP calculation and must be configured and negotiated by both ends of the connection. However, as shown in the TCP header, only the receive window size is communicated to the peer.

7

TCP Window Sizes

A poor configuration for the TCP Receive Window size is for it to be larger than the number of receive buffers available. In this case, the transmitter believes it could still send data while the receiver is out of resources for processing. This configuration would result in a substantial number of dropped packets creating unnecessary retransmission and drastically slowing down the connection.

Never configure the TCP receive window size to be larger than the number of configured receive buffers.

Use the bandwidth delay product to estimate the right value for TCP window sizes.

7-11-1 MULTIPLE CONNECTIONS

The discussion in the previous section is valid for the whole system. If the system has a single active TCP connection, all bandwidth and network buffers are used by this TCP connection. If the system has more than one connection, the bandwidth must be shared between all active TCP connections.

Depending on the reasons you are embedding TCP/IP into a product, a system performance assessment is something that must be either calculated if the system parameters are known in advance, or validated with hardware and simulation code. This is covered in Part II of this book.

7-11-2 PERSIST TIMER

With the TCP receive window size, the receiver performs flow control by specifying the amount of data it is willing to accept from the sender.

When the TCP receive window size goes to 0, the sender stops sending data. It is possible for ACKs not to be reliably transmitted, and if ACKs are lost, the receiver will wait to receive data and the sender will wait to receive the TCP window update. This may create a deadlock which can be prevented if the sender uses a persist timer that enables it to query the receiver periodically to find out if the window size has been increased. These segments from the sender are called window probes. They are sent as long as needed – with no timeout.

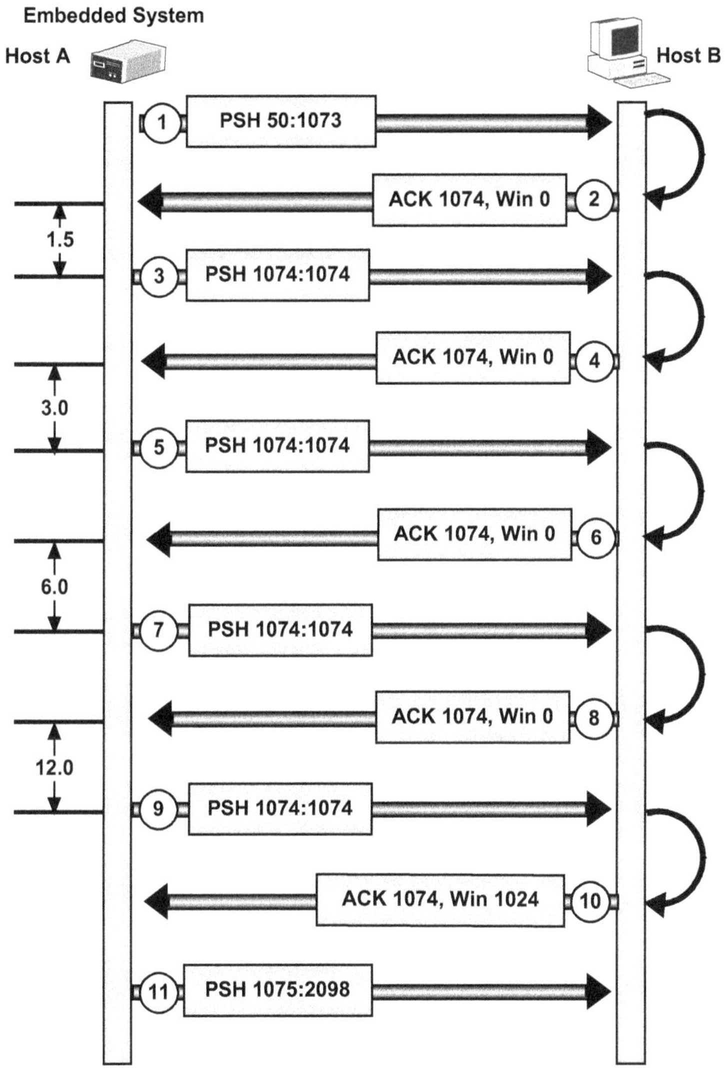

Figure 7-17 **Example of Persist Timer Usage**

F7-17(1)   A TCP segment with 1024 bytes is transmitted.

F7-17(2)   The receiving host acknowledges the segment, but also advertises that its TCP receive window is full (Window = 0).

F7-17(3)   After the first Persist Timer time-out, Host A sends a window probe segment.

F7-17(4)   Host B sends a window update, but it is still 0.

F7-17(5)   After the second Persist Timer time-out, Host A sends a window probe segment.

F7-17(6)   Host B sends a window update, but it is still 0.

F7-17(7)   After the third Persist Timer time-out, Host A sends a window probe segment.

F7-17(8)   Host B sends a window update, but it is still 0.

F7-17(9)   After the fourth Persist Timer time-out, Host A sends a window probe segment.

F7-17(10)   Host B processed packets and has freed space in its TCP receive window.

F7-17(11)   Host A can now transmit more data.

The normal TCP exponential back off is used to calculate the persist timer as shown in Figure 7-17.

■ The first timeout is calculated as 1.5 sec for a typical LAN connection

■ This is multiplied by 2 for a second timeout value of 3 sec

■ A multiplier of 4 gives a value of 6 (4 x 1.5)

■ Then 8 results in 12 (8 x 1.5)

■ And so on… (exponentially)

However, the Persist Timer is always bounded between 5 and 60 seconds.

7-11-3 KEEPALIVE

Keepalive is the maximum period of time between two activities on a TCP connection. Many TCP/IP stacks have the maximum period of inactivity set at two hours. The timer is restarted every time an activity occurs on the connection.

The keepalive concept is very simple. When the keepalive timer reaches zero, the host sends a keepalive probe, which is a packet with no data and the ACK code bit turned on. It acts as a duplicate ACK that is allowed by the TCP/IP specifications. The remote endpoint will not object to the reception of an empty packet, as TCP is a stream-oriented protocol. On the other hand, the transmitting host will receive a reply from the remote host (which doesn't need to support keepalive at all, just TCP/IP), with no data and the ACK set.

If the transmitting host receives a reply to the keepalive probe, we conclude that the connection is still up and running. The user application is totally unaware of this process.

Two main usages for keepalive include:

■ Checking for dead peers

■ Preventing disconnection due to network inactivity

Keepalive is useful since, if other peers lose their connection (for example by rebooting), the TCP/IP stack on the host of interest will notice that the connection is broken, even if there is no active traffic. If keepalive probes are not replied to by the peer host, it can be assumed that the connection is not valid and corrective action can be initiated.

Keepalive is really used to have an idle connection up forever. TCP keepalive is not a mandatory requirement and Micrium did not implement this feature in μC/TCP-IP. But μC/TCP-IP replies to keepalive messages if implemented by the other host.

7

7-12 SUMMARY

For the embedded developer, the transport layer and data link layer are probably the two most important layers. If a system needs to achieve sustained performance, the majority of the parameters to fine tune it are found in the network device driver and transport layer.

This chapter covered transport protocols. Two protocols at the transport layer are very useful and have different goals. Here is a summary of the protocol pros and cons.

With TCP, the analysis and transmission of its parameters generate certain delays, and add data processing overhead, which makes it better suited to non-real-time (data) traffic requiring error-free transmission. When the embedded system needs to guarantee data delivery, TCP is the best solution, yet it comes at a price. TCP code is larger and TCP requires a substantial amount of RAM to properly perform its duties. If the system requires performance and reliable data delivery, it must allocate plenty of RAM for the TCP/IP stack.

TCP handles:

- reliable delivery

- retransmissions of lost packet

- re-ordering

- flow control

UDP can and will be used if:

- TCP congestion avoidance and flow control measures are unsuitable for the embedded application

- The application can cope with some data loss

- More control of the data transported over the network is required

- The application is delay/jitter sensitive (audio, video)

- Delays introduced by TCP ACK are unacceptable

- Maximizing throughput (UDP uses less resources and can achieve better performance. See the Sample Applications in Part II of this book)

- Minimize code and data footprint (see section 3-2-3 "Footprint" on page 78)

Many embedded systems have resource constraints (mainly CPU processing speed and RAM availability) and thus, these systems often use a UDP/IP-only stack instead of a full blown TCP/IP stack.

8

Sockets

The client-server architecture is a familiar concept. Simply, servers contain information and resources, and clients request access to them. The Web and e-mails are examples of client-server architectures. Web servers receive requests from browsers (Internet Explorer, Firefox, Safari, etc.) and e-mail servers receive requests from such mail client as Outlook and Eudora.

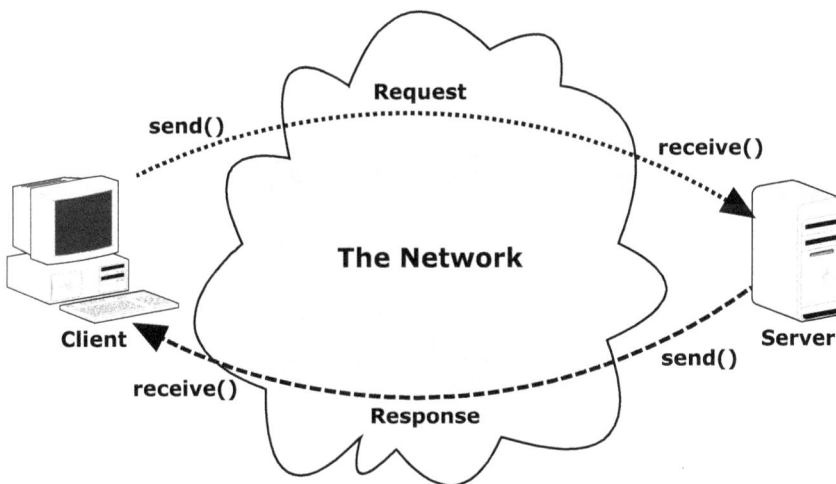

Figure 8-1 **Client and Server**

In contrast with the client-server approach is a peer-to-peer architecture whereby communication between hosts occurs at the same level, with each host offering the same capabilities to each another. Examples of a peer-to-peer approach include applications such as Skype and BitTorrent.

8

In both client-server and peer-to-peer architectures one host must take the initiative and contact a second host. Within IP technology, applications interface with the TCP/IP stack via socket function calls. The use of Transport Layer port numbers makes it possible for one host to establish multiple data exchanges with another host.

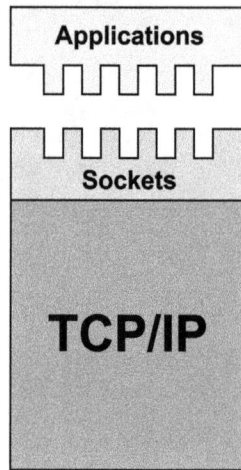

Figure 8-2 **Sockets**

The socket is the data structure used to represent this connection. More than one socket can be active at any point in time, as shown in Figure 8-2. Sockets are used in the same way as household A/C wall plugs in that multiple appliances may be connected simultaneously, throughout the house.

8-1 SOCKET UNIQUENESS

Imagine if several hosts transmit a segment to a given port on a server (P80 for a Web server). The server needs a way to identify each connection so that replies are sent to the correct client. On the client side, source port numbers are dynamically assigned by a TCP/IP stack, from 1024 to 65535. To differentiate between clients, the TCP/IP stack associates port numbers and IP addresses from the source and destination. This data grouping, or association (IP addresses and port numbers) is a "socket."

Therefore, the socket contains the following association:

Socket   =   Source IP address   +   Source port
              +   Destination IP address   +   Destination port

It is common to use nomenclature to identify the IP address and port number as follows:

AAA.BBB.CCC.DDD:1234

where 'AAA.BBB.CCC.DDD' is the IP address in dotted decimal notation and '1234' is the port number. This nomenclature is used in a web browser's address bar to establish a connection to a specific IP address and port number.

A connection using this notation is illustrated in Figure 8-3. Specifically, the host on the left 172.16.10.5:1468 (local host) connects to 172.16.10.8:23 (remote host) on the right.

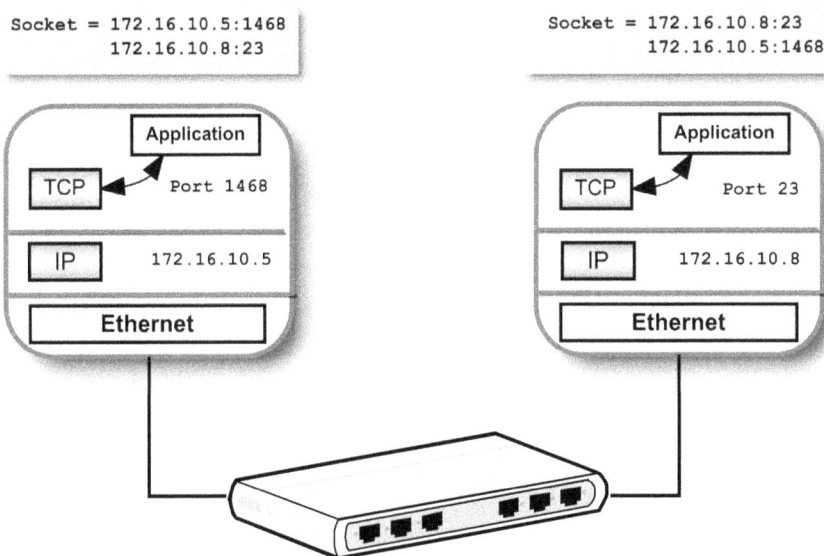

Figure 8-3 **Sockets: Source IP address + Port Number + Destination IP address + Port Number**

The Source IP address, the Source Port number, the Destination IP address and the Destination Port create a unique identifier for the connection. A server, therefore may have multiple connections from the same client yet differentiate them. As long as one of these four fields is different, the connection identifier is different.

In μC/TCP-IP, both the Source and Destination address and port information are stored in a data structure called **NET_CONN** as **AddrLocal** and **AddrRemote** fields. These two fields contain concatenated address/port information for the local address used by the product that embeds the stack and the remote address accessed by the product.

The use of 'Local' vs. 'Remote' addresses as either the source or destination address depends on when they are used to receive or transmit.

For Receive:

■   Local = Destination

■   Remote = Source

For Transmit:

■   Local = Source

■   Remote = Destination

Internally, to identify sockets, μC/TCP-IP uses an index so that each socket is identified by a unique socket ID from 0 to N-1 whereby N is the number of sockets created.

8-2 SOCKET INTERFACE

An application can interface to μC/TCP-IP using one of two network socket interfaces as shown in Figure 8-4. Although both socket interfaces are available, BSD socket interface function calls are converted to their equivalent μC/TCP-IP socket interface function calls. μC/TCP-IP socket interface functions feature greater versatility than their BSD counterparts as they return meaningful error codes to callers instead of just 0 or -1. μC/TCP-IP socket interface functions are also reentrant making them more useful to embedded applications.

A description of all μC/TCP-IP socket error codes is found in section E-7 "IP Error Codes" on page 992 and fatal socket error codes are described in section 18-7-1 "Fatal Socket Error Codes" on page 520.

Micrium layer 7 applications typically use μC/TCP-IP socket interface functions. However, if the system design requires off-the-shelf TCP/IP components that are not provided by Micrium, BSD socket interface functions are typically used. In this case, the BSD socket Application Programming Interface (API) is enabled via the `NET_BSD_CFG_API_EN` configuration constant found in **net_cfg.h** (see section D-17-1 on page 983).

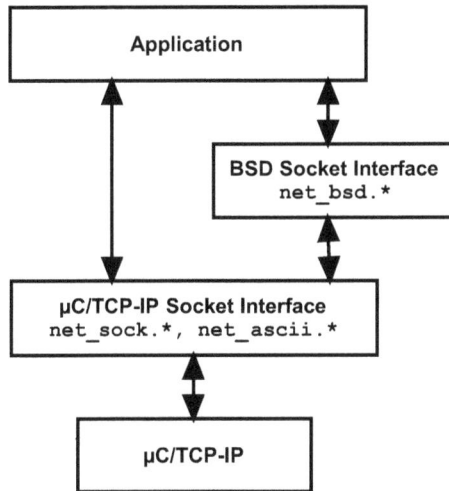

Figure 8-4 **Application relationship to μC/TCP-IP Network Socket Interface**

8-3 SOCKET API

Let's look at socket programming concepts and socket API function calls. A complete list of the μC/TCP-IP socket API functions may be found in Appendix C, "μC/TCP-IP API Reference" on page 649.

BSD socket API	μC/TCP-IP socket API	API description
socket()	NetSock_Open()	Appendix C on page 875
bind()	NetSock_Bind()	Appendix C on page 810
listen()	NetSock_Listen()	Appendix C on page 873
accept()	NetSock_Accept()	Appendix C on page 808
connect()	NetSock_Connect()	Appendix C on page 859
send()	NetSock_TxData()	Appendix C on page 891

BSD socket API	µC/TCP-IP socket API	API description
sendto()	NetSock_TxDataTo()	Appendix C on page 891
recv()	NetSock_RxData()	Appendix C on page 884
recvfrom()	NetSock_RxDataFrom()	Appendix C on page 884
select()	NetSock_Sel()	Appendix C on page 888
close	NetSock_Close()	Appendix C on page 857

Table 8-1 **BSD and µC/TCP-IP proprietary socket API**

Table 8-1 contains examples from the BSD and µC/TCP-IP API lists. The BSD socket interface is used in the following examples as it is the most widely known. Note that Micrium applications use the µC/TCP-IP proprietary socket interface as it provides enhanced error management.

8-3-1 socket()

Before communicating with a remote host, it is necessary to create an empty socket. This is done by calling the **socket()** function which returns a socket descriptor. At this point, the socket is useless until it is assigned a local IP Port. This descriptor is used in subsequent socket API function calls. µC/TCP-IP maintains a "pool" of sockets and the **socket()** call allocates one of the available sockets from this pool to the **socket()** caller.

8-3-2 bind()

The **bind()** function is used to assign a local IP address and port number to a socket. When the port number is assigned, it can not be reused by another socket, allowing for a fixed port to be used as the connection point by the remote host. Standard applications have pre-determined port numbers (FTP, HTTP, SMTP) that must be assigned to socket(s) used for the application so that clients can reach the server.

8-3-3 listen()

Server applications that use TCP, must set a socket to be a listener. As a connection-oriented protocol, TCP requires a connection; however UDP, as a connectionless protocol, does not. Using **listen()** allows an application to receive incoming connection requests. The listen socket contains the IP address and port number of the server, yet it is not aware of a client.A new listen socket will be created when a connection is established and remain open for the lifetime of the server.

8-3-4 accept()

The **accept()** function spawns a new socket. The listen socket used to receive a connection request remains open and a new socket is created that contains the IP address and port number of both client and server. This allows a server to have multiple connections with clients.

8-3-5 connect()

The **connect()** function is the client equivalent of the **listen()** and **accept()** functions used by server applications. **Connect()** allows a client application to open a connection with a server.

8-3-6 send() and sendto()

The **send()** function is used to transmit data through a TCP-based socket, while the **sendto()** function transmits data through a UDP-based socket.

8-3-7 recv() and recvfrom()

The **recv()** function receives data from a TCP-based socket while the **recvfrom()** function receives data through a UDP-based socket.

8-3-8 select()

Select() provides the power to monitor several sockets simultaneously. In fact, **select()** indicates which sockets are ready for reading and writing, or which sockets have raised exceptions.

Select() allows you to specify a timeout period in case there is no activity on the desired sockets. If **select()** times outwit returns with an appropriate error code.

8-3-9 close()

The **close()** function ends a connection and frees the socket to return to the "pool" of available sockets. Note that **close()** will send any remaining buffered data before closing the connection.

8-4 BLOCKING VERSUS NON-BLOCKING SOCKETS

One of the issues a developer faces with sockets is the difference between blocking and non-blocking sockets. When socket operations are performed, the operation may not be able to complete immediately and the function may not be able to return to the application program. For example, a **recv()** on a socket cannot complete until data is sent by the remote host. If there is no data waiting to be received, the socket function call waits until data is received on this socket. The same is true for the **send()**, **connect()** and other socket function calls. The connection blocks until the operation is completed. When the socket waits, it is called a "blocking" socket.

The second case is called a non-blocking socket, and requires that the application recognize an error condition and handle the situation appropriately. Programs that use non-blocking sockets typically use one of two methods when sending and receiving data. In the first method, called polling, a program periodically attempts to read or write data from the socket (typically using a timer). The second, and preferred method, is to use asynchronous notification. This means that the program is notified whenever a socket event takes place, and in turn responds to that event. For example, if the remote program writes data to the socket, a "read event" is generated so that the program knows it can read the data from the socket at that point.

It is also possible for the socket to return immediately with an error condition. The error condition in the previous **recv()** case is -1 (NET_ERR_RX if the µC/TCP-IP proprietary socket interface is used). When using non-blocking sockets in the application, it is important to check the return value from every **recv()** and **send()** operation (assuming a TCP connection). It is possible that the application cannot send or receive all of the data. It is not unusual to develop an application, test it, and find that when used in a different environment, it does not perform in the same way. Always checking the return values of these socket operations ensures that the application will work correctly, regardless of the bandwidth of the connection or configuration of the TCP/IP stack and network.

Be aware that making non-blocking **send()** or **recv()** calls from a high-priority task may cause low-priority tasks to starve. This is especially true if the **send()** or **recv()** functions are called in a tight loop and there is no data to send or none to receive. In fact, if the internal µC/TCP-IP tasks are configured as low-priority tasks, µC/TCP-IP will not have a chance to run and perform its duties. This type of polling is a sign of poor design. In comparison, the use of **select()** creates a more elegant solution.

With µC/TCP-IP, sockets can be configured in "blocking" or "non-blocking" mode using the configuration switches described in section D-15 "Network Socket Configuration" on page 976.

8-5 SOCKET APPLICATIONS

There are two types of sockets: Datagram sockets and Stream sockets. The following sections describing how these sockets work.

8-5-1 DATAGRAM SOCKET (UDP SOCKET)

Datagram sockets use the User Datagram Protocol (UDP). Data received is error-free and may be out of sequence as explained in Chapter 7, "Transport Protocols" on page 169. With datagram sockets, there is no need to maintain an open connection and the protocol is therefore called 'connectionless'. The application simply prepares data to be sent. The TCP/IP stack appends a UDP header containing destination information and sends the packet out. No connection is needed. Datagram sockets are generally used either when TCP is unavailable, or when a few dropped packets here and there is of no consequence. When a short query requires a short reply and if the reply is not received, it is acceptable to re-send the query. Sample applications include: TFTP, BOOTP(DHCP), DNS, multi-player games, and streaming audio and video conferencing.

TFTP and similar programs add their own protocol on top of UDP. For example, for each packet sent with TFTP, the recipient must send back an acknowledgement packet that says, "I got it!" ("ACK"). If the sender of the original packet receives no reply within a timeout period, it retransmits the packet until it finally receives an ACK. This acknowledgment procedure is very important when implementing reliable datagram socket applications. However, it is the responsibility of the application and not the UDP to implement these acknowledgements. For time-sensitive applications such as voice or games that can cope with dropped packets, or perhaps that can cleverly compensate for them, it is the perfect protocol.

8

Figure 8-5 shows a typical UDP client-server application and the BSD socket functions typically used. Figure 8-6 is the same diagram with µC/TCP-IP proprietary socket functions.

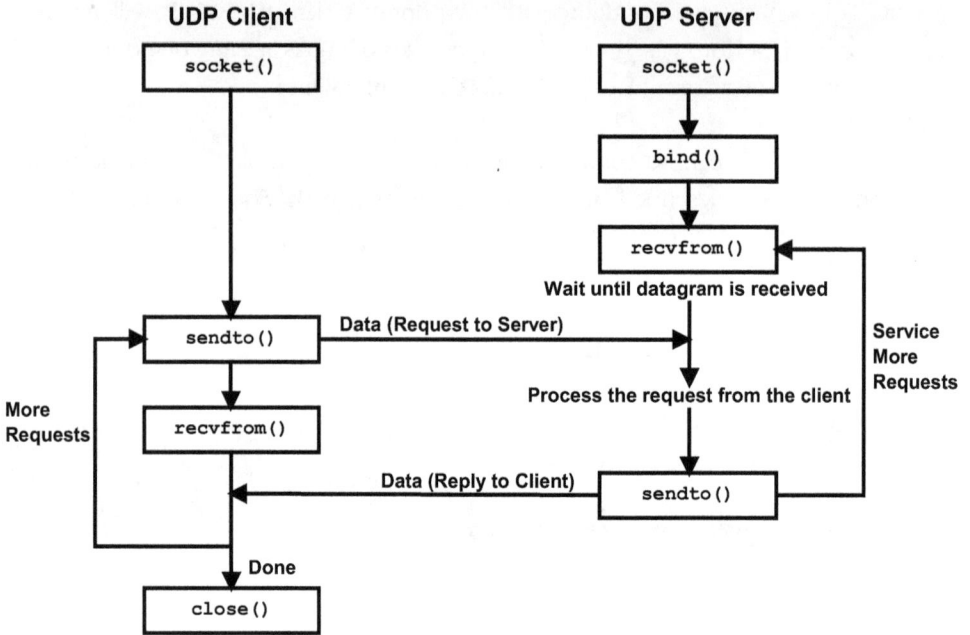

Figure 8-5 **BSD Socket calls used in a typical UDP client-server application**

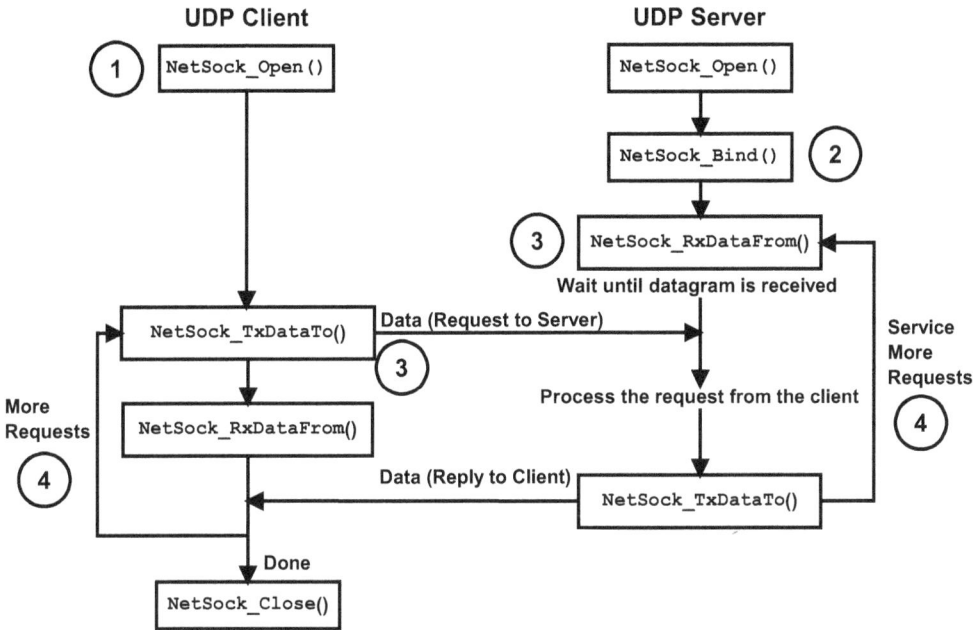

Figure 8-6 **µC/TCP-IP Socket calls used in a typical UDP client-server application**

F8-6(1)   The first step in establishing a UDP communication between two hosts is to open sockets on both hosts.

F8-6(2)   The server binds the IP address and port number to be used to receive data from the client

F8-6(3)   UDP clients do not establish (dedicated) connections with UDP servers. Instead, UDP clients send request datagrams to UDP servers by specifying the socket number of the server. A UDP server waits until data arrives from a client, at which time the server processes the client's request, and responds.

F8-6(4)   The UDP server waits for new client requests. Since UDP clients/servers do not establish dedicated connections, each request from each UDP client to the same UDP server is handled independently as there is no state or connection information preserved between requests.

8

8-5-2 STREAM SOCKET (TCP SOCKET)

Stream sockets are reliable two-way connected communication streams using the Transmission Control Protocol (TCP). Data is received sequentially and error-free. There is a "notion" of a connection. HTTP, FTP, SMTP and Telnet are examples of protocols that use stream sockets.

TCP handles the reliable delivery of data, the retransmissions of lost packets, and the re-ordering of packets and flow control. This additional processing adds overhead to the communication channel. TCP is it best suited for non-real-time (data) traffic requiring error-free transmission, yet extra overhead and the larger size of the TCP code module is the price to pay.

The use of sequence number, acknowledge number and window size in the TCP header guar a tee the delivery of data using a segment acknowledgement mechanism coupled with a retransmission capability.

TCP performance optimization is accomplished by carefully configuring the number of buffers in transmission and reception. In reception, buffers are defined in the Network Device Driver and up into the stack. For transmission, application buffers and network buffers are also required to be of similar number and size for data to flow efficiently from the application down the stack to the network interface. The optimization of the number of buffers can be calculated using the Bandwidth-Delay Product (see Chapter 6).

TCP requires a substantial amount of RAM to properly perform its duties. With the acknowledgment mechanism, TCP will not release a buffer until it has been acknowledged by its peer. While this buffer is in stand-by, it cannot be used for additional transmission or reception. If the system design dictates performance and reliable data delivery, allocate sufficient RAM for the TCP/IP stack.

Figure 8-7 indicates a typical TCP client-server application and the BSD socket functions used. Figure 8-8 is the same diagram with μC/TCP-IP proprietary socket functions.

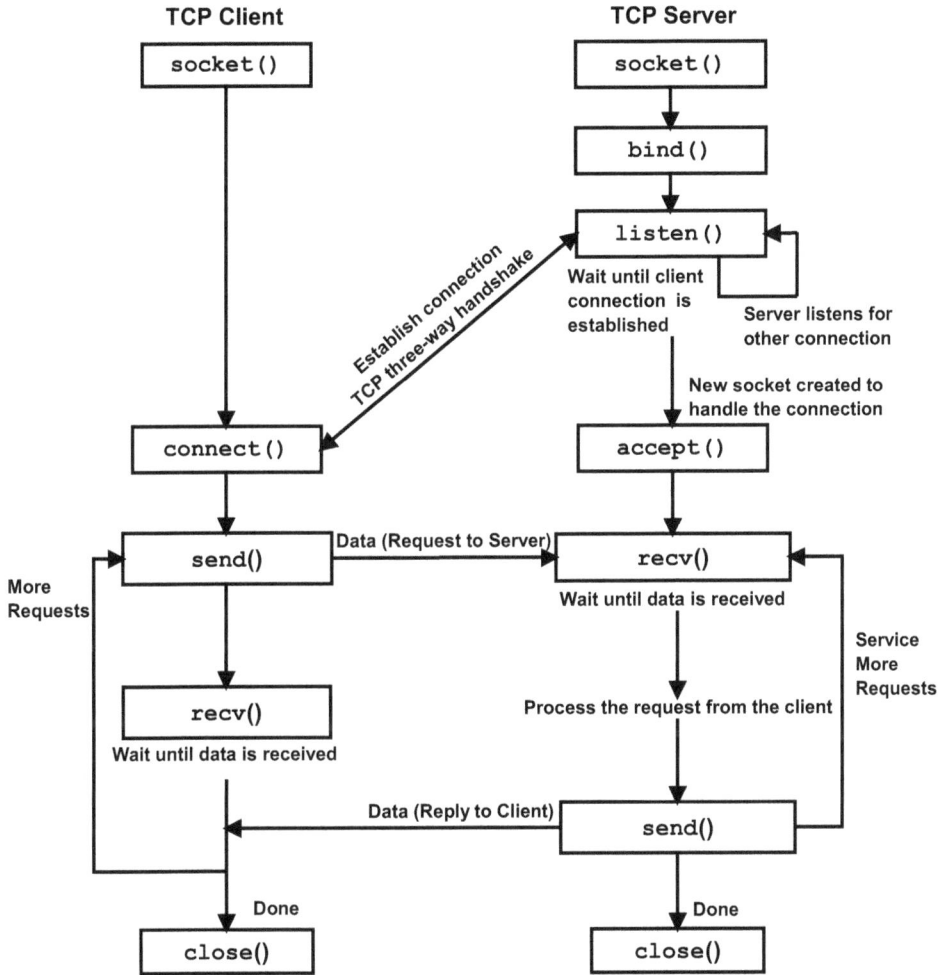

Figure 8-7 **BSD Socket calls used in a typical TCP client-server application**

8

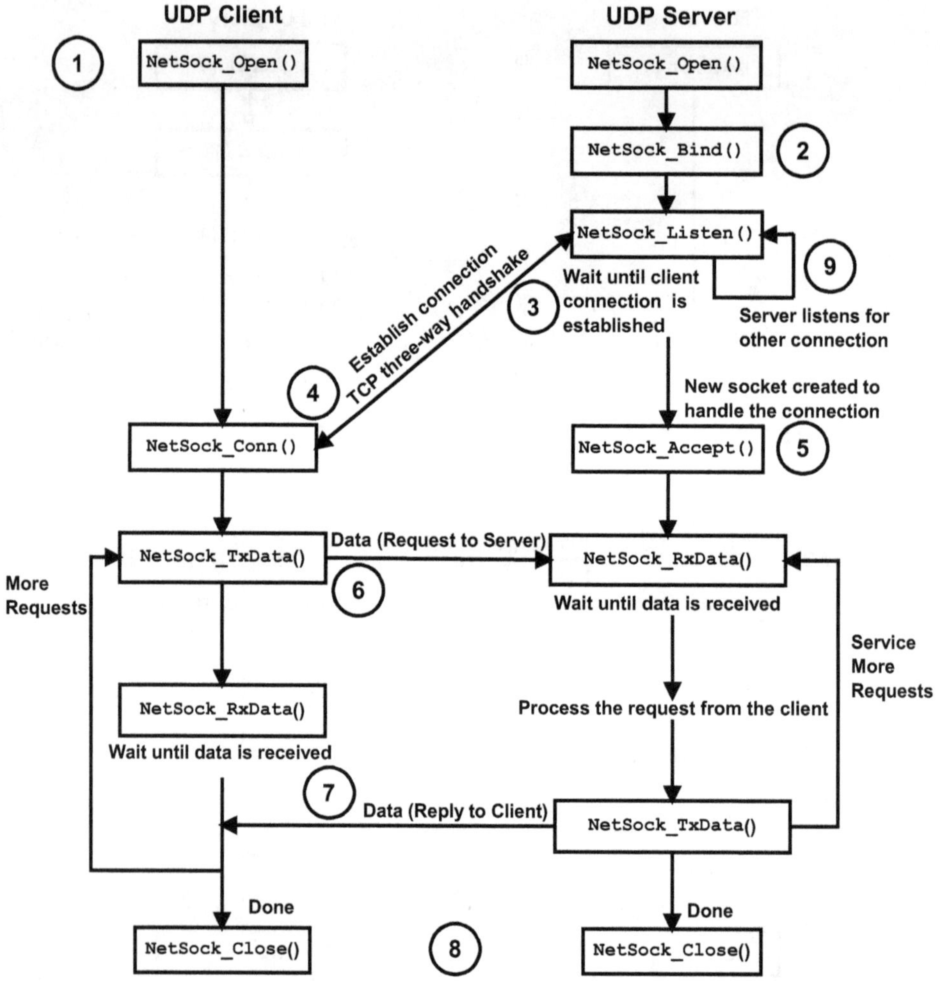

Figure 8-8 µC/TCP-IP Socket calls used in a typical TCP client-server application

F8-8(1)   The first step in establishing TCP communication between two hosts is to open the sockets on both hosts.

F8-8(2)   The server binds the server IP address and port number to be used to receive the connection request from the client.

F8-8(3)   The server waits until a client connection is established using the listen() function call.

F8-8(4)   When the server is ready to receive a connection request it allows clients to connect to the server.

F8-8(5)   The server accepts a connection request from the client. A new socket is created to handle the connection.

F8-8(6)   TCP client sends a request to the server

F8-8(7)   The server replies back to the client (if necessary).

F8-8(8)   This continues until either the client or the server closes the dedicated client-server connection.

F8-8(9)   When handling multiple and simultaneous client-server connections, the TCP server is still available for new client-server connections.

For socket programming information please refer to Chapter 18, "Socket Programming" on page 501. This chapter provides code samples to write UDP and TCP clients and servers. Part II of the book contains sample projects with source code examples.

8

8

Services and Applications

When an IP network is deployed, certain basic services are implemented for the hosts that connect to the network. These services are programs that run at the application layer in servers. There is a basic difference, however, between a service and an application.

A service implements a protocol that is useful to the hosts and engines powering every IP networked device. Two services most often used by embedded systems are the Dynamic Host Configuration Protocol (DHCP) and the Domain Name System (DNS). Additional services also exist such as the Network Information System (NIS), a client-server directory service protocol for distributing system configuration data including user and host names, or the Lightweight Directory Access Protocol (LDAP), an application protocol for querying and modifying directory services. These network services are usually deployed in corporate networks to manage a large number of users. For the scope of this book, we will look specifically at DHCP and DNS.

Any protocol "above" the TCP/IP stack is considered an *application protocol*. The use of these application protocols is valid for network services as described in the previous paragraph and for applications. In the case of the application, you can write your own application protocols, or you can augment the system by purchasing "standard" application-level protocols. There are many available with most TCP/IP stacks including File Transfer Protocol (FTP), web (HTTP), Telnet, Simple Mail Transport Protocol (SMTP), and more.

An application implements a protocol that is useful to the system application and not to the device. Basic TCP/IP protocols provided in a stack such as µC/TCP-IP may not be practical or sufficient for a typical embedded system. For instance, protocols such as FTP and SMTP may be required for the embedded system to transfer files or send e-mails.

9-1 NETWORK SERVICES

9-1-1 DYNAMIC HOST CONFIGURATION PROTOCOL (DHCP)

Since typical embedded systems operate in private networks, it is quite possible that the IP addressing scheme in these networks, is fixed or static. In this case, every device participating in the network receives its IP address and all other network-related parameters from the network administrator and they are hard-coded in the device. This method of parameter assignment is referred to as static addressing, and it provides added security. While no device can be part of a network without the network administrator's knowledge, all servers can be configured to accept requests from specific device IP addresses that correspond to the list of valid devices.

Dynamic addressing, in comparison, was developed as a means to reuse IP addresses in IP networks, especially because of the limited number of IP addresses available. An example is a device often used by home networks. High-speed service delivered by an Internet Service Provider (ISP) is performed by a DSL or cable modem. This modem includes an Ethernet switch and a DHCP server, or another device is connected between the modem and computers on the home network. This additional device often serves such multiple functions as an Ethernet switch, a DHCP server, a router, and a firewall. This is what is shown in Figure 9-1

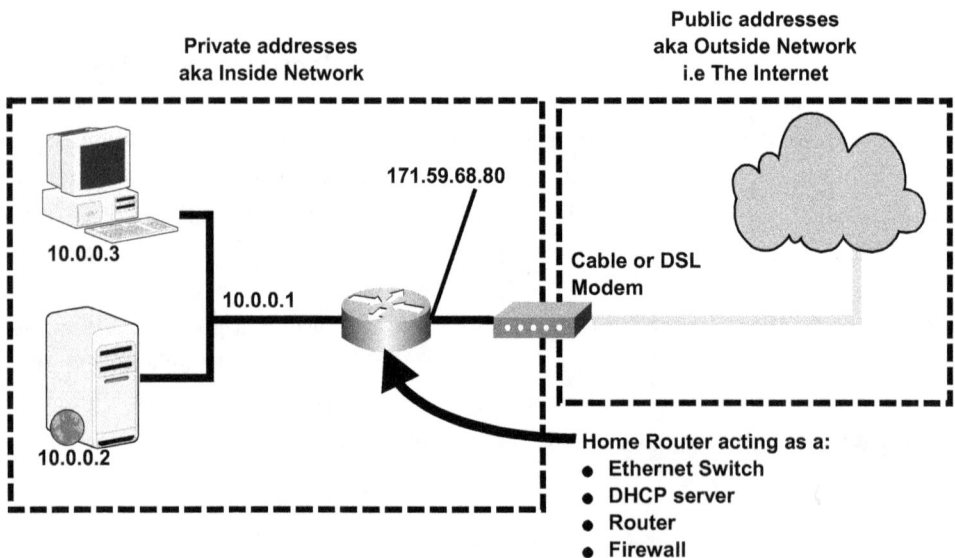

Figure 9-1 **Home Router acting as a DHCP server**

Upon power up, a device running a DHCP client simply sends a request to any DHCP server to obtain an IP address (and other parameters). The DHCP server(s) maintain a "pool" of available IP addresses and assigns a unique IP address to requesting client(s). The DHCP protocol between clients and servers simplifies the work of the network administrator.

DHCP use UDP as the transport protocol. The DHCP server listens for incoming requests on UDP port 67 and sends out offers on UDP port 68 as shown in Figure 9-2 and Figure 9-3.

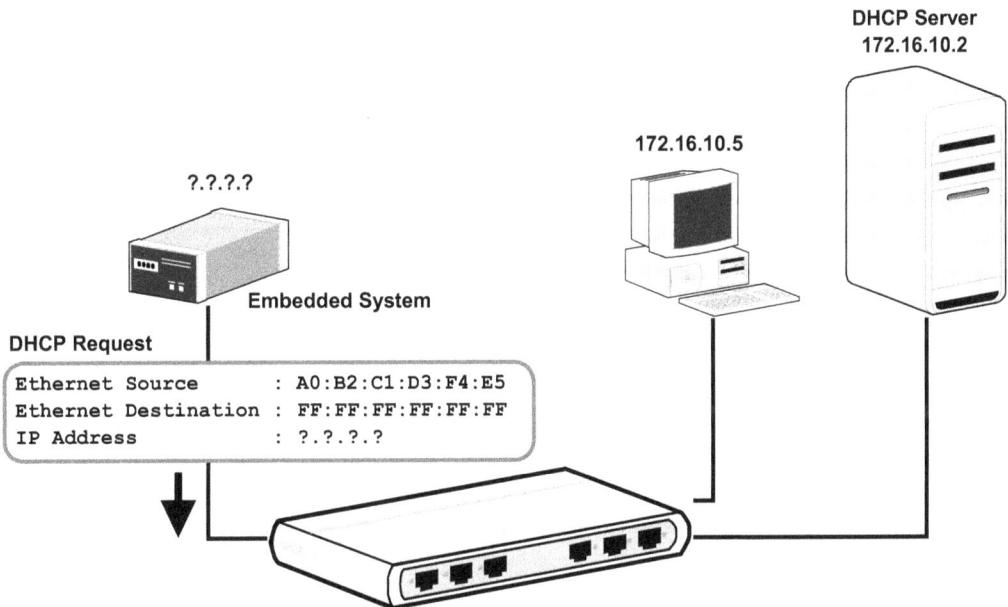

Figure 9-2 **DHCP Request**

DHCP requests are usually transmitted by a device when booting up since that host does not have an IP address and it requires one. The DHCP request message is a broadcast message (Ethernet destination address is FF:FF:FF:FF:FF:FF) since the host does not know anything about the network it is connected to and must obtain that information.

**DHCP Server
172.16.10.2**

172.16.10.5

?.?.?.?

Embedded System

DHCP Offer

```
Ethernet Source       : 80:12:D7:E5:B4:33
Ethernet Destination  : A0:B2:C1:D3:F4:E5
IP Address            : 172.16.10.10
```

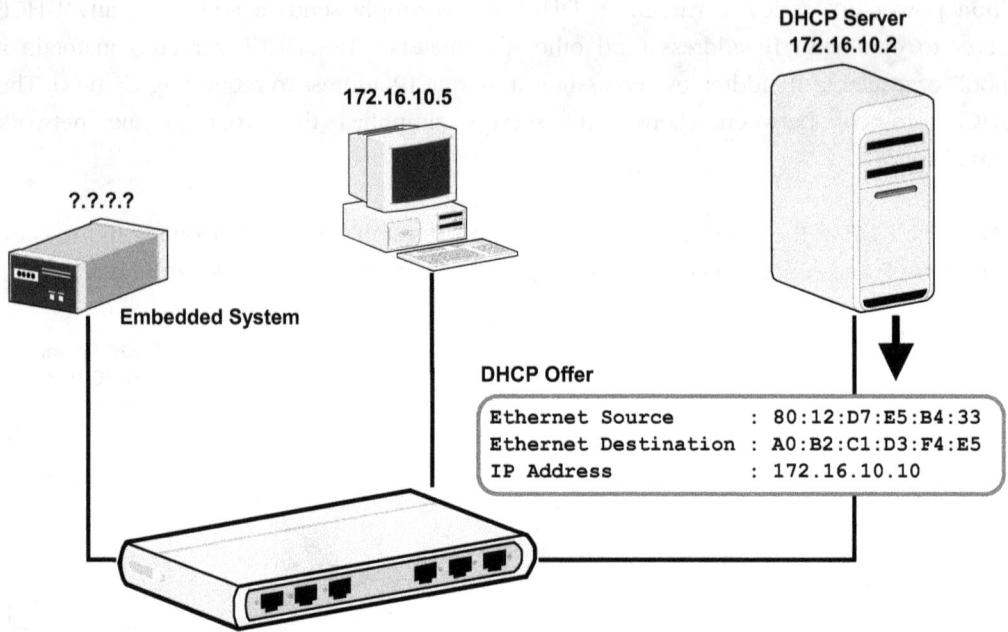

Figure 9-3 **DHCP Offer**

With typical DHCP server implementations, any DHCP server on the network will answer the host DHCP request. Once this offer is received, the host sends an acknowledgement to the DHCP server that the offer is accepted, The DHCP server reserves the address and does not assign it to any other hosts. Again, please note that this is a typical DHCP implementation. Other implementations could work differently.

The IP address and other network parameters required for the host to operate on the network are not assigned permanently. Instead, DHCP uses a leasing principle. After a predefined time-out period, the host must again request for the IP address. The DHCP server refreshes the lease allowing the host to continue using the already assigned address for another time-out period.

There may be more than one DHCP server on a network and the host may receive one offer per DHCP server. Usually, a DHCP client accepts the first offer received and will reject subsequent offers.

If the host disconnects from the network and then reconnects and the IP address previously assigned is still available, the host receives the same address. This is the typical behavior of most DHCP servers. However, it is possible that other DHCP implementations do not reassign previously assigned parameters.

The mandatory parameters the DHCP server provides are:

■ The IP address

■ The subnet mask

The default gateway IP address is not mandatory but is generally included when the host needs to access networks outside of the local network.

The DHCP client is an application invoked by the Application Layer although it impacts the Network Layer. Examples in Part II of this book demonstrate DHCP usage.

There is alternative to obtaining an IP address on single private network referred to as the dynamic configuration of link-local addresses, sometimes called by MIcrosoft and other vendors:

■ Automatic Private IP Addressing (APIPA)

■ AutoNet

■ AutoIP

When a TCP/IP stack in a host requires an IP address using DHCP, and there is no DHCP server present or the DHCP server is not responding, the DHCP client can invoke APIPA.

The Internet Assigned Numbers Authority (IANA) reserves private IP addresses in the range of 169.254.0.0 to 169.254.255.255 for APIPA or written differently, the network reserved is 169.254.0.0/16.

If a DHCP server does not reply, the host selects an IP address within this range and sends a message to this address to see if it is in use. If it receives a reply, the address is in use and another address is selected. This process is repeated until an address is found to be available.

9

After the network adapter is assigned an IP address with APIPA, the host can communicate with any other hosts on the local network also configured by APIPA, or ones that have a static IP address manually set in the 169.254.X.X sub-network with a subnet mask of 255.255.0.0. This is particularly useful for embedded systems where the manual management of IP configuration is not desired or possible.

Whether using DHCP or APIPA, the embedded device must have a way to display the IP address or make it available to other hosts in order for these other hosts to establish communication with the embedded device. If the device is the one to establish the connection, then advertising the IP address is not required.

9-1-2 DOMAIN NAME SYSTEM (DNS)

When communicating with other hosts on the public Internet, it is possible that the only information known regarding these hosts is their 'Fully Qualified Domain Name' (FQDN). For example, it is easier to refer to web servers by their name, i.e., the Web server at Micrium is www.micrium.com.

The DNS is used to establish an association between a system name and its IP address. It is a protocol with two parts:

■ Client: Resolver

■ Server: Name server

DNS uses UDP or TCP as transport protocols to deliver its service on port 53.

The structure of DNS is very similar to the file structures that we find in our existing computers. It is possible, but not recommended, to have up to 127 levels.

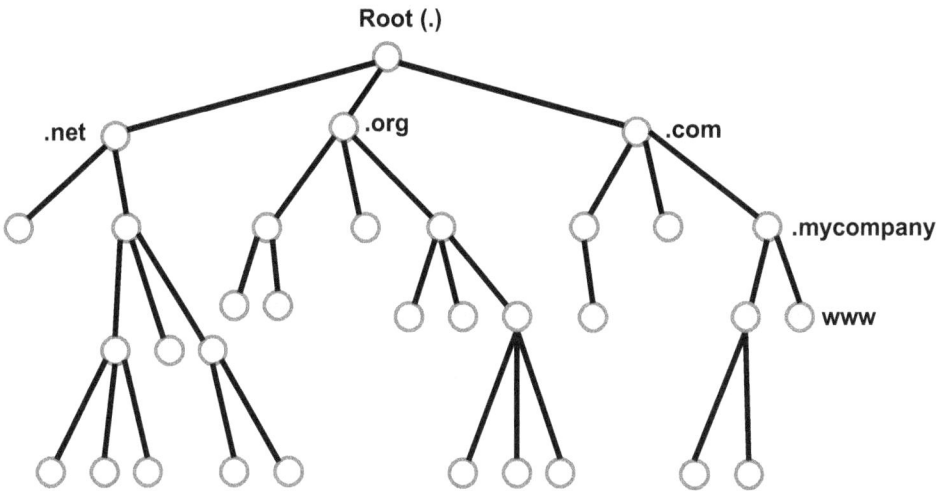

Figure 9-4 **DNS Structure**

Figure 9-4 shows the DNS database, which is depicted as an inverted tree. Each element/node of the tree has a label of up to 63 characters that identifies it relative to its parent. Note that not all nodes at each level are represented. This is only a sample of the DNS structure.

The root, in comparison, uses a reserved label, i.e., « nil character » or « ». The levels are separated from each other by periods « . » The label of each child belonging to a given parent must be unique.

WWW.MYCOMPANY.COM

Service name	Domain name

Figure 9-5 **Syntax of Domain Names**

As shown in Figure 9-5, a FQDN is read from right to left. To the extreme right of the domain defined after the **.com** is the root domain (an empty string). The root domain is also represented by a single dot (.), as shown in Figure 9-4. DNS software does not require that the terminating dot be included when attempting to translate a domain name to an IP address.

Reading from right to left, from the root, the **.com** domain is found, which contains the mycompany domain, and finally contains the web server (www). As you can now see, the service or subdomain is the last field. We are all familiar with the www.mycompany.com

model because web servers are hosts we access often. However, many other services can be available from a domain. For example:

■ An FTP server: `ftp.mycompany.com`

■ A mail server: `mail.mycompanny.com`

When it is required to translate names, an embedded system includes a DNS Client. This software module is also referred to as a DNS resolver or in the case of a DNS server, it is called a network service.

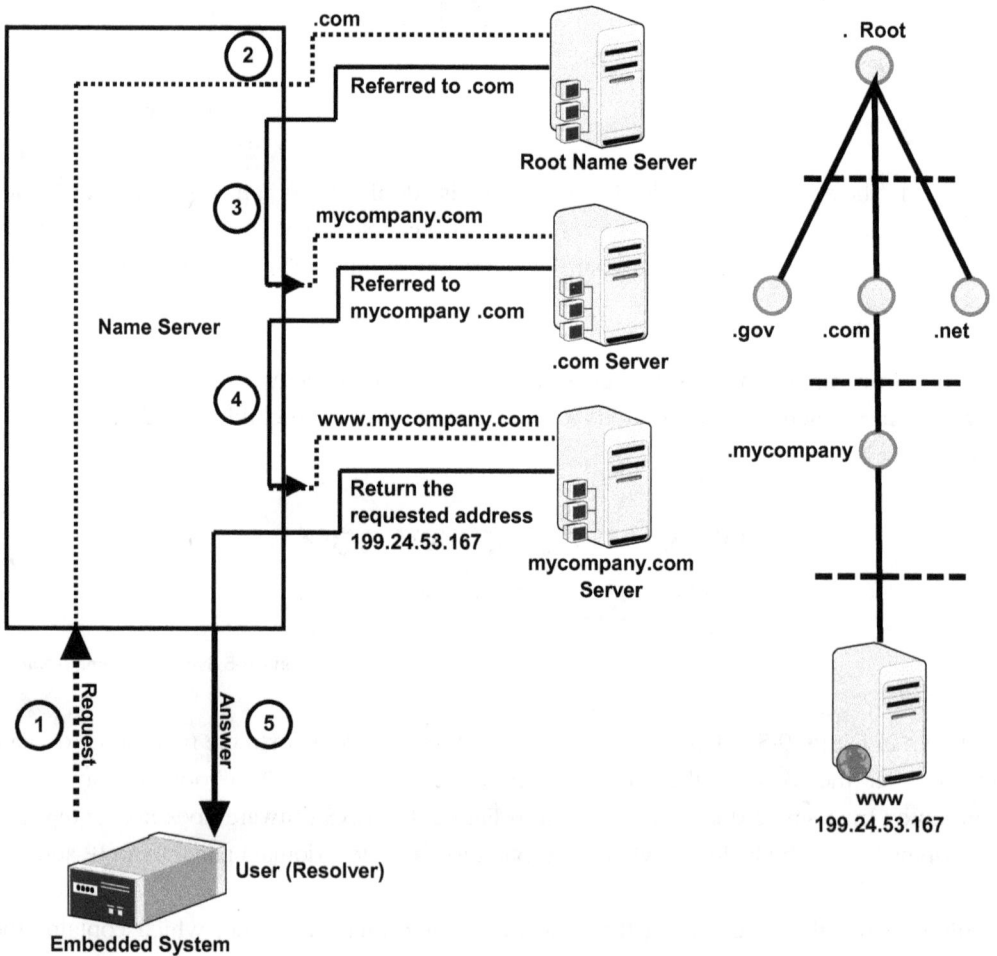

Figure 9-6 **Resolution Mechanism**

F9-6(1)   The first step in converting a FQDN into an IP address is for the host to use its DNS Resolver to send a DNS request to the DNS server on its network, represented by the Name Server box.

F9-6(2)   In this scenario, let's assume the DNS server does not know the answer to the request. The name server must send the request to one of thirteen 'well known' root name servers to find the answer. These thirteen root name servers implement the root name space domain for the Internet's Domain Name System. The root name servers are a critical part of the Internet as they are the first step in resolving human-readable host names into IP addresses. Normally the addresses of these root name servers are configured in the local name server.

            The local DNS server (name server) begins its search by reading the FQDN from right to left and sends a request for each field, one at a time. It sends a request to one of the root name servers to find where the `.com` domain is located.

F9-6(3)   The root name server replies with the address or addresses of the location of the.com domain. This information is stored in the local name server, which now asks the servers for the `.com` domain for the location of the `mycompany.com` domain.

F9-6(4)   The root name server(s) for the `.com` replies with the address or addresses of where the mycompany.com domain is located. This information is stored in the local name server, which can now ask the `mycompany.com` domain name server for the location of the `www.mycompany.com` service.

F9-6(5)   The root name server(s) for the `mycompany.com` replies with the address or addresses of where `www.mycompany.com` service is located. This information is stored in the local name server, which can now answer the request from the resolver with the IP address of the `www.mycompany.com` service.

DNS servers make use of a caching mechanism. Once a request is resolved, the cross-reference between the name and the IP address is kept in the cache so that the next time a DNS request for the same name is received, the server need not reprocess the complete request. This is also one of the reasons that, when a new IP address is assigned to a name, it can take up to 24 hours for the new IP address to propagate through the Internet.

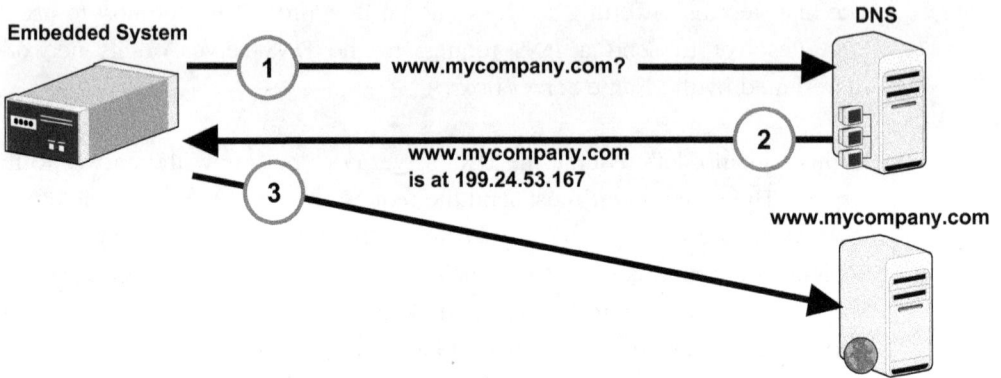

Figure 9-7 **DNS Client (Resolver)**

Figure 9-7 demonstrates the process once the local DNS server knows the IP address for the FQDN submitted to it.

9-2 APPLICATIONS

As previously stated, applications are code running above the TCP/IP stack, and are often referred to as Layer 7 applications. There are standard applications based on standard protocols that are defined by RFCs. These can be used as a software module in embedded systems.

In addition to standard applications, there are any number of user-written applications that are crucial to the embedded product as their code represents a particular field of expertise. Sample code demonstrating how to write a client application, or a server application, is provided in Chapter 19, "Socket programming" and in Part II of this book.

9-3 APPLICATION PERFORMANCE

Performance of the TCP/IP stack has been a constant consideration for this book. Chapter 6, for example, is dedicated to configuring TCP to get the most out of the stack depending on the hardware resources available, particularly RAM.

There is one additional item to consider in order to achieve optimum performance for the complete system. The socket interface between the application and the TCP/IP stack must be configured correctly. When attempting to attain maximum throughput, the most important options involve TCP Window sizes and the number of network device transmit and receive buffers. These are calculated according to the bandwidth-delay product (BDP - see Chapter 7, "Transport Protocols" on page 169). For the connection to achieve an acceptable performance, the flow of packets between the Network Device and TCP and vice-versa is dictated by this configuration.

The same is true between the application layer and the transport layer. Applications usually have their own set of buffers and the number and size of these buffers should match TCP Window sizes based on network buffers, to complete the optimization of a connection (socket). Given the application send and receive buffers and the TCP transmit and receive Windows, the closer their number and size, the more optimal the throughput on the embedded system.

With the BSD socket API, the configuration of the TCP transmit and receive window sizes is accomplished by setting socket send and receive buffer sizes. Most operating systems support separate per connection send and receive buffer limits that can be adjusted by the user application, or other mechanism, as long as they stay within the maximum memory limits of system hardware. These buffer sizes correspond to the **SO_SNDBUF** and **SO_RCVBUF** options of the BSD **setsockopt()** call.

µC/TCP-IP socket API implementation (BSD or proprietary) does not support the **SO_SNDBUF** and **SO_RCVBUF** socket options. With the Micrium application add-ons to µC/TCP-IP such as µC/HTTPs and others, application buffers are specified and configured in the application. This is where the configuration must be performed to optimize the connection throughput. The closer the send and receive buffers configuration for the application is to the TCP Window sizes the better the performance will be. An important performance improvement is to make sure that memory copies between the application buffers and the network buffers are aligned to/from application buffers to network buffers. This means to make sure that application data starts on memory addresses that are optimally-aligned for the memory copy from/to network socket buffers.

Very often, the bandwidth of a TCP connection is restricted by the configuration of transmitter and receiver buffer sizes, resulting in the connection not utilizing the available bandwidth of the links. Making the buffers as large as possible is the preferred approach, in the case of TCP, the size of the MSS (see Chapter 7, "Transport Protocols" on page 169). It is possible to test and validate the buffer and TCP Window sizes configuration. However, very few applications provide you with a way to configure buffer sizes. Network utilities such as **ttcp**, **netperf** and **iperf** allows you to the specify buffer sizes in the command line, and offer the possibility to disable the Nagle's algorithm, assuming you know or can determine what the optimal settings are. With µC/IPerf (see Chapter 6, "Troubleshooting" on page 139), it is possible to configure the buffer size however µC/TCP-IP does not currently have an option to disable the Nagle's algorithm. With µC/IPerf, it is possible to test and validate the buffer and TCP Window sizes configuration. Part II of this book contains UDP and TCP examples using µC/IPerf.

Hardware resources, particularly RAM, may limit the maximum values for certain configurable parameters. The default TCP transmit and receive window sizes can be for ALL connections, as is the case for µC/TCP-IP. While in some applications, that be sub-optimal and wasteful of system memory, in an embedded system, the concurrent number of connections is usually not high so that it is possible to work with default settings for all connections.

Application Performance

When attempting to attain maximum throughput, the most important options involve TCP window sizes and send/receive buffers.

It is crucial to configure the application send/receive buffers. The closer the send and receive buffers configuration for the application is to the TCP Window sizes the better the performance will be.

9-3-1 FILE TRANSFER

FILE TRANSFER PROTOCOL (FTP)

The three most used Internet applications are e-mail, web and FTP. FTP is the standard Internet file transfer protocol and is also one of the oldest application protocols. Its main design goal is to transfer files (computer programs and/or data). When FTP was created, there were many operating systems in use and each OS had its own file system in addition to its own character encoding. FTP was conceived to shield you from variations in file systems between different hosts. Today, FTP's main feature is to reliably and efficiently transfer data between hosts.

FTP is an application-layer protocol using TCP transport service. FTP utilizes separate control and data connections between client and server applications. FTP control uses TCP port 21 while FTP data uses TCP port 20. The use of two separate ports is called "out-of-band control." Dedicated connections are opened on different port numbers for control and data transfers.

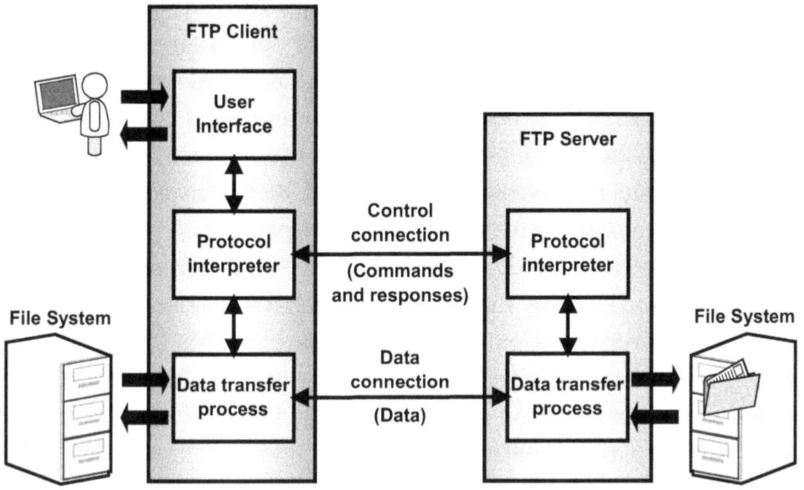

9

Figure 9-8 **File Transfer Protocol (FTP)**

Figure 9-8 shows two TCP connections used by FTP for control and data. A system that utilizes FTP also requires a file system, as shown.

The FTP client and server have different operating modes: active or passive. In each mode, the dynamic port number (another port number picked from the available pool) is used by the client or server to bind the source port of the connection to a different port based on a negotiated connection.

FTP can be used either with user-based password authentication or with anonymous (generic) user access. The latter allows a client to connect to a server without having an account with that given server. Some network administrators can force an anonymous user to enter an e-mail address that contains the domain (see section "Simple Mail Transfer Protocol (SMTP)" on page 242) as the password. With a DNS lookup, the FTP server retrieves the IP address of that e-mail server. By comparing the FTP connection request IP address and the e-mail domain IP address, it is possible to confirm the validity of the connection request as the two addresses should be in the same network.

FTP is an unsecure method of transferring files, as no encryption method is used. User names, passwords, FTP commands, and transferred files are exposed to the "middle man attack" using a network protocol analyzer (see the section "Troubleshooting" on page 139).

9

The Secure Socket Layer (SSL) is an industry standard that represents a solution to this problem. SSL is a layer between the application and socket layers. It is a session layer protocol that encrypts data flowing between the application and the TCP/IP stack, ensuring high-level security over an IP network. SSL is based on standard encryption methods using private and public keys provided by a Certification Authority by the issuance of a SSL Certificate. The certificate resides on the server and the client connecting to the server retrieves the SSL Certificate to receive the public key. Upon connection, the client checks to see if the SSL Certificate is expired, whether or not it is issued by a trusted Certification Authority, and if it is being used by the server for which it was issued. If any checks fail, the client will think the server is not SSL secure. The server matches the SSL Certificate to a private key, allowing data to be encrypted and decrypted. The secure connection is normally represented by a lock icon in the lower right-hand corner of a browser window. Clicking on the icon displays the SSL Certificate.

HTTP, SMTP, and Telnet all use SSL. FTP applies SSL with either SSH (the Unix/Linux Secure Shell) File Transfer Protocol (SFTP), or FTPS (FTP over SSL). μC/TCP-IP does not currently offer an SSL module, but third party modules are readily available.

TRIVIAL FILE TRANSFER PROTOCOL (TFTP)

The Trivial File Transfer Protocol (TFTP) is a similar, yet simplified, non-interoperable, and unauthenticated version of FTP. TFTP is implemented on top of UDP. The TFTP client initially sends a read/write request through port 69. Server and client then determine the port that they will use for the rest of the connections (dynamic port with FTP). The TFTP simple architecture is deliberate for easy implementation For an embedded system, it may very well be the right choice since this simplistic approach has many benefits over traditional FTP. For example, it can be:

■ Used by flash-based devices to download firmware

■ Used by any automated process when it is not possible to assign a user ID or password

■ Used in applications where footprint is limited or resources constrained, allowing it to be implemented inexpensively.

NETWORK FILE SYSTEMS

Network file systems may also provide the necessary functionality to access files on remote hosts. The Network File System (NFS), Andrew File System (AFS), and the Common Internet File System (CIFS - also referred or decoded as Server Message Block (SMB) by a network protocol analyzer), provide this type of functionality.

9-3-2 HYPERTEXT TRANSFER PROTOCOL (HTTP)

Hypertext Transfer Protocol (HTTP) is used to exchange data in all types of formats (text, video, graphics and others) over the World Wide Web. This protocol uses TCP port 80 for sending and receiving data. The protocol works in client/server mode, and HTTP client is the familiar browser used by all.

The server side of HTTP is popular in the embedded industry. Implementing an HTTP server (a web server) in an embedded system allows users or applications to connect to the embedded device with a browser enabling information to be exchanged graphically. Users or applications receive data from the embedded system. Examples are the HTTP interfaces provided by home gateways and printers.

Not so long ago, connecting to configure an embedded system or to retrieve data from it was performed by way of either a console port using RS-232 or Telnet over a network connection. Both provide a terminal I/O interface and are text based. With HTTP, the user interface is more elaborate, using graphical elements, and is accessible from virtually anywhere as long as the embedded device has access to the Internet.

An HTTP server "serves" web pages, files requested by the browser and usually stored on a mass storage medium. A file system is typically required to retrieve these web pages. Some embedded HTTP servers such as Micrium's µC/HTTPs allow for web pages to be stored as part of the code. In this case, a file system is unnecessary, and a custom method is used to read and transfer information. Part II of this book shows an example of using HTTP with web pages stored as code.

HTTP provides the possibility of invoking other protocols. For example, file transfer using FTP can be initiated from a web page. This implies that an FTP client is active on the host that runs the browser. Similarly, an e-mail can be generated from a hyperlink on the page. This implies that a mail client is also running on the host running the browser.

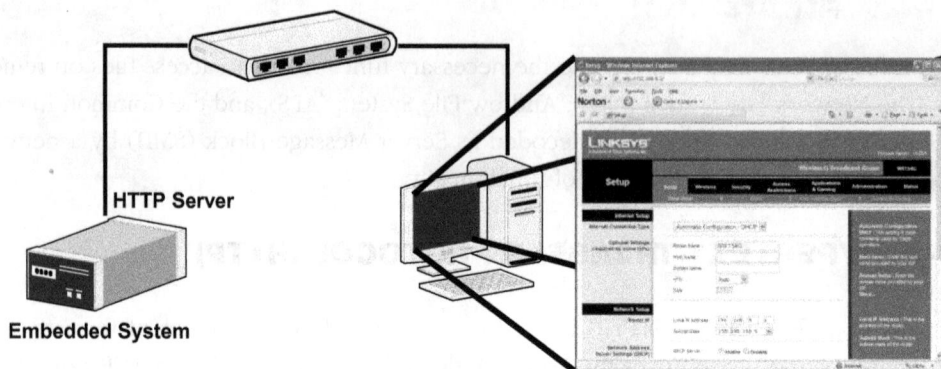

Figure 9-9 **HyperText Transfer Protocol (HTTP)**

Figure 9-9 represents a web page taken from a Linksys Wireless-G Broadband Router (i.e a Home gateway), and is an example of what an embedded system implementing an HTTP server can do.

HTTP is one of the easiest ways to access multimedia content such as music and videos.

A secure HTTP connection can be established using SSL and is referred to as an HTTPS connection which is particularly popular for financial transactions over the Internet, including e-commerce.

On certain embedded systems, the performance of an embedded HTTP server can largely be affected by the memory resources available to dictate the number of buffers and sockets. The current method used by browsers is to retrieve files from the HTTP server and open simultaneous parallel connections to download as many files as possible. This improves the perception of performance. This method is excellent on systems that have sufficient resources and bandwidth. On an embedded system, it may not be possible to operate many sockets in parallel due to the incapacity to allocate sufficient resources.

9-3-3 **TELNET**

Telnet is a standard protocol offered by most TCP/IP implementations. TCP Port 23 is used by the Telnet server to listen for incoming connection requests. Telnet is widely used to establish a connection between a host and a remote system, to manage the system from a distance. Telnet is very popular in the telecom market. Most telecommunications equipment today, such as routers and switches, supports the Telnet protocol.

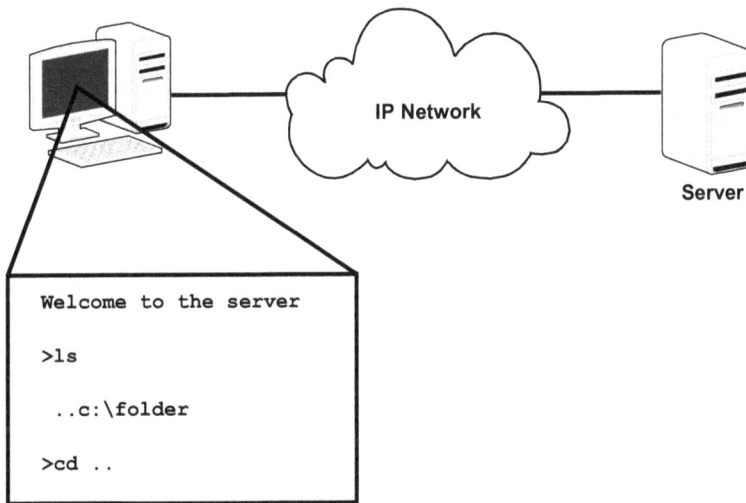

Figure 9-10 **Telnet example**

With Telnet, a virtual session allows the client to run applications via a command-line interface on the remote server in terminal mode (see Figure 9-10). In this case, the remote system may have a shell application allowing the host to issue commands and visualize execution results on the Telnet terminal window. Micrium offers µC/Shell for this purpose.

The two hosts involved in the telnet session begin by exchanging their capabilities (also referred to as options such as binary transmission, echo, reconnection, etc...). After the initial negotiation is complete, the hosts choose a common level to use between them.

Because Telnet uses clear text user name and password, its use has diminished in favor of SSH for secure remote access. Micrium offers µC/Telnet TCP/IP add-on modules.

9

9-3-4 E-MAIL

When designing an embedded system, messages are likely to be exchanged. It is possible that a proprietary messaging system can be developed, and in most cases this is the best solution. At times, sending e-mail instead of a proprietary message may be a clever alternative. For example, when the embedded system detects an alarm condition and needs to report it, sending an e-mail to an iPhone or Blackberry can be the best way to communicate the information.

Or conversely, to send information to an embedded system, sending an e-mail to the embedded system may be a simple way to implement such functionality. The e-mail may be automated and transmit from another device, or it can be sent by a user or administrator telling the embedded system to execute a function.

TCP/IP protocols dealing with e-mail include:

- Simple Mail Transport Protocol (SMTP)

- Sendmail

- Multipurpose Internet Mail Extensions (MIME)

- Post Office Protocol (POP)

- Internet Message Access Protocol (IMAP)

SIMPLE MAIL TRANSFER PROTOCOL (SMTP)

To send an e-mail, a connection is required to an IP network and access to a mail server that forwards the mail. The standard protocol used for sending Internet e-mail is called Simple Mail Transfer Protocol (SMTP). If a system's needs are limited to sending messages, only SMTP is required. However, to receive e-mails, the most popular service is the Post Office Protocol (POP) Version 3 or POP3.

SMTP uses TCP as the transport layer protocol and Port 25 is used by the STMP server to listen to incoming connections. An e-mail client sends an e-mail message to an SMTP server. The server looks at the e-mail address and forwards it to the recipient's mail server, where it's stored until the addressee retrieves it (see Figure 9-11).

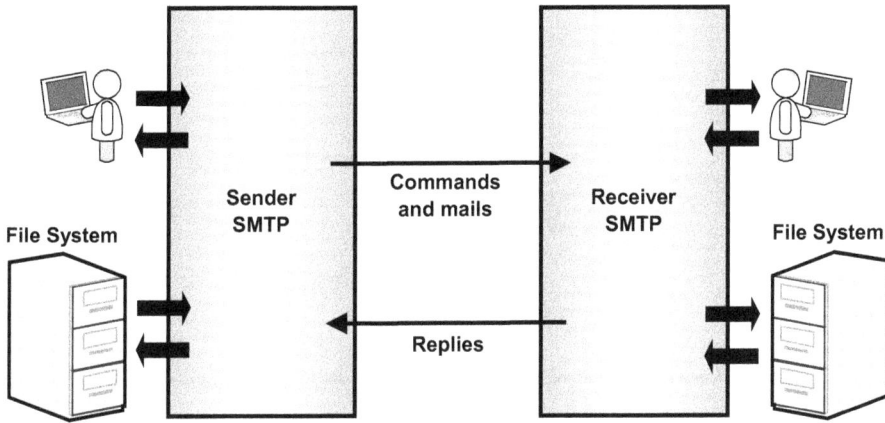

Figure 9-11 **SMTP**

All Internet service providers and major online services offer e-mail accounts (each having an address). The SMTP destination address, also known as the mailbox address, has this general form: User@Domain.

User	A unique user on the Domain
Domain	The domain name of the network to reach.

The e-mail address can also take several other forms, depending of whether the destination is on the same TCP/IP network, a user on a non-SMTP destination remote-host going through the mail gateway-host, or involving a relayed message.

SMTP is an end-to-end delivery system. An SMTP client contacts the destination host's SMTP server directly, on Port 25, to deliver the mail. DNS is invoked, as the domain is part of the e-mail address. The remote Domain Name Server must contain the address of the mail server. The SMTP client ensures that the mail is transmitted until it is successfully copied to the recipient's SMTP server. In this way, SMTP guarantees delivery of the message.

In SMTP, each message has:

▣ A header, or envelope defined by RFC 2822

▣ A mail header terminated by a null line (a line with nothing preceding the <CRLF> sequence).

■ Content: Everything after the null (or blank) line is the message body, which is a sequence of lines containing ASCII characters (characters with a value less than 128 decimal). Content is optional.

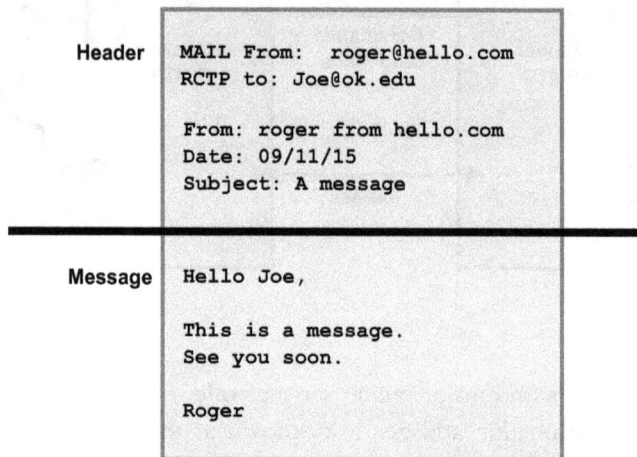

Header	`MAIL From:  roger@hello.com`
	`RCTP to: Joe@ok.edu`
	
	`From: roger from hello.com`
	`Date: 09/11/15`
	`Subject: A message`

Message	`Hello Joe,`
	
	`This is a message.`
	`See you soon.`
	
	`Roger`

Figure 9-12 **SMTP message**

SMTP is simple and light enough to be used on an embedded system when transmission of messages is required. Initially, e-mails were text messages only. Today, given Multipurpose Internet Mail Extension (MIME), and other encoding schemes, such as Base64 and UUencode, formatted documents (Word, PDF, etc.), photos (JPEG and other formats), audio and video files can now be attached to e-mail. An e-mail message containing an attachment has a MIME header in the message body. The encoding schemes used by MIME provide a means for non-text information to be encoded as text. This is how attachments can be carried by SMTP. However, it is important that the recipient has compatible software to open attachments.

MIME is also used by HTTP (www) as it requires data to be transmitted in text-based messages (HTML, DHTML, XML and others).

SENDMAIL

Sendmail is a command-line tool found on most large operating systems. It is a client/server application supporting multiple mail protocols. Sendmail is one of the oldest mail transfer agents on the Internet and is available as open source and with proprietary software packages.

POST OFFICE PROTOCOL (POP)

Post Office Protocol version 3 (POP3) is an e-mail protocol with both client and server functions. POP3 client establishes a TCP connection to the server, using Port 110 and supports basic functions (download and delete) for e-mail retrieval. For more advanced functions IMAP4 is suggested. When retrieving messages on an embedded system, POP3 is simpler and smaller to implement than IMAP4. Micrium currently offers µC/POP3.

INTERNET MESSAGE ACCESS PROTOCOL (IMAP4)

The Internet Message Access Protocol, version 4 (IMAP4) is an e-mail protocol with both client and server functions. As with POP, IMAP4 servers store user account messages to be retrieved upon client request. IMAP4 allows clients to have multiple remote mailboxes from which messages are retrieved. Message download criteria can be specified by IMAP4 clients. For example, a client may be configured to not transfer message bodies or not transfer large messages over slow links. IMAP4 always keeps messages on the server and copies are replicated to clients.

IMAP4 clients can make changes when connected or when disconnected. The changes will be applied when the client is reconnected. POP client must always be connected to make changes to the mailbox. Changes made on the IMAP4 client when disconnected, take effect on the server with automatic periodic re-synchronization of the client to the server. This is why implementing a POP3 client is a lot simpler than implementing an IMAP4 client. For embedded systems with limited resources, these are important considerations.

9

9-4 SUMMARY

On any IP network, there may exist several useful network services in addition to the ones introduced in this chapter. DHCP and DNS, however, remain the two main network services most often used by embedded systems.

On the application level, basic "standard" TCP/IP Application-Layer applications were discussed. Often, these "standard" applications may be complemented by a custom application. This embedded application is used to differentiate devices from the competition. User-written client or server applications leverage the TCP/IP stack.

Application buffer configuration is an important factor in performance considerations. When using a TCP protocol, make sure buffer configurations match TCP Window sizes. If a system uses UDP, allocate sufficient resources (i.e., buffers) to meet system requirements. These assumptions can be tested using the tools and sample applications provided in Part II of this book.

The following chapters explain Micrium's µC/TCP-IP for building efficient TCP/IP-based applications.

Introduction to µC/TCP-IP

µC/TCP-IP is a compact, reliable, high-performance TCP/IP protocol stack. Built from the ground up with Micrium's unique combination of quality, scalability and reliability, µC/TCP-IP, the result of many man-years of development, enables the rapid configuration of required network options to minimize time to market.

The source code for µC/TCP-IP contains over 100,000 lines of the cleanest, most consistent ANSI C source code available in a TCP/IP stack implementation. C was chosen since C is the predominant language in the embedded industry. Over 50% of the code consists of comments and most global variables and all functions are described. References to RFC (Request For Comments) are included in the code where applicable.

10-1 PORTABLE

µC/TCP-IP is ideal for resource-constrained embedded applications. The code was designed for use with nearly any CPU, RTOS, and network device. Although µC/TCP-IP can work on some 8 and 16-bit processors, µC/TCP-IP is optimized for use with 32 or 64-bit CPUs.

10-2 SCALABLE

The memory footprint of µC/TCP-IP can be adjusted at compile time depending on the features required, and the desired level of run-time argument checking appropriate for the design at hand. SinceµC/TCP-IP is rich in its ability to provide statistics computation, unnecessary statistics computation can be disabled to further reduce the footprint.

10

10-3 CODING STANDARDS

Coding standards were established early in the design of µC/TCP-IP. They include:

■ C coding style

■ Naming convention for #define constants, macros, variables and functions

■ Commenting

■ Directory structure

These conventions make µC/TCP-IP the preferred TCP/IP stack implementation in the industry, and result in the ability to attain third party certification more easily as outlined in the next section.

10-4 MISRA C

The source code for µC/TCP-IP follows Motor Industry Software Reliability Association (MISRA) C Coding Standards. These standards were created by MISRA to improve the reliability and predictability of C programs in safety-critical automotive systems. Members of the MISRA consortium include such companies as Delco Electronics, Ford Motor Company, Jaguar Cars Ltd., Lotus Engineering, Lucas Electronics, Rolls-Royce, Rover Group Ltd., and universities dedicated to improving safety and reliability in automotive electronics. Full details of this standard can be obtained directly from the MISRA web site at: www.misra.org.uk.

10-5 SAFETY CRITICAL CERTIFICATION

µC/TCP-IP was designed from the ground up to be certifiable for use in avionics, medical devices, and other safety-critical products. Validated Software's Validation Suite™ for µC/TCP-IP will provide all of the documentation required to deliver µC/TCP-IP as a pre-certifiable software component for avionics RTCA DO-178B and EUROCAE ED-12B, medical FDA 510(k), IEC 61508 industrial control systems, and EN-50128 rail transportation and nuclear systems. The Validation Suite, available through Validated Software, will be immediately certifiable for DO-178B Level A, Class III medical devices, and SIL3/SIL4 IEC-certified systems. For more information, check out the µC/TCP-IP page on the Validated Software web site at: www.ValidatedSoftware.com.

If your product is not safety critical, however, the presence of certification should be viewed as proof that µC/TCP-IP is very robust and highly reliable.

10-6 RTOS

µC/TCP-IP assumes the presence of an RTOS, yet there are no assumptions as to which RTOS to use with µC/TCP-IP. The only requirements are that it must:

■ Be able to support multiple tasks

■ Provide binary and counting semaphore management services

■ Provide message queue services

µC/TCP-IP contains an encapsulation layer that allows for the use of almost any commercial or open source RTOS. Details regarding the RTOS are hidden from µC/TCP-IP. µC/TCP-IP includes the encapsulation layer for µC/OS-II and µC/OS-III real-time kernels.

10-7 NETWORK DEVICES

µC/TCP-IP may be configured with multiple-network devices and network (IP) addresses. Any device may be used as long as a driver with appropriate API and BSP software is provided. The API for a specific device (i.e., chip) is encapsulated in a couple of files and it is quite easy to adapt devices to µC/TCP-IP (see Chapter 21, "Statistics and Error Counters" on page 527).

Although Ethernet devices are supported today, Micrium is currently working on adding Point-to-Point Protocol (PPP) support to µC/TCP-IP.

10-8 µC/TCP-IP PROTOCOLS

µC/TCP-IP consists of the following protocols:

- Device drivers

- Network interfaces (e.g., Ethernet, PPP (TBA), etc.)

- Address Resolution Protocol (ARP)

- Internet Protocol (IP)

- Internet Control Message Protocol (ICMP)

- Internet Group Management Protocol (IGMP)

- User Datagram Protocol (UDP)

- Transport Control Protocol (TCP)

- Sockets (Micrium and BSD v4)

10-9 APPLICATION PROTOCOLS

Micrium offers application layer protocols as add-ons to µC/TCP-IP. A list of these network services and applications includes:

- µC/DCHPc, DHCP Client

- µC/DNSc, DNS Client

- µC/HTTPs, HTTP Server (web server)

- µC/TFTPc, TFTP Client

- µC/TFTPs, TFTP Server

- µC/FTPc, FTP Client

- µC/FTPs, FTP Server

- µC/SMTPc, SMTP Client

- µC/POP3, POP3 Client

- µC/SNTPc, Network Time Protocol Client

Any well known application layer protocols following the BSD socket API standard can be used with µC/TCP-IP.

µC/TCP-IP Architecture

µC/TCP-IP was written to be modular and easy to adapt to a variety of Central Processing Units (CPUs), Real-Time Operating Systems (RTOSs), network devices, and compilers. Figure 11-1 shows a simplified block diagram of µC/TCP-IP modules and their relationships.

Notice that all µC/TCP-IP files start with '**net_**'. This convention allows us to quickly identify which files belong to µC/TCP-IP. Also note that all functions and global variables start with '**Net**', and all macros and **#defines** start with '**net_**'.

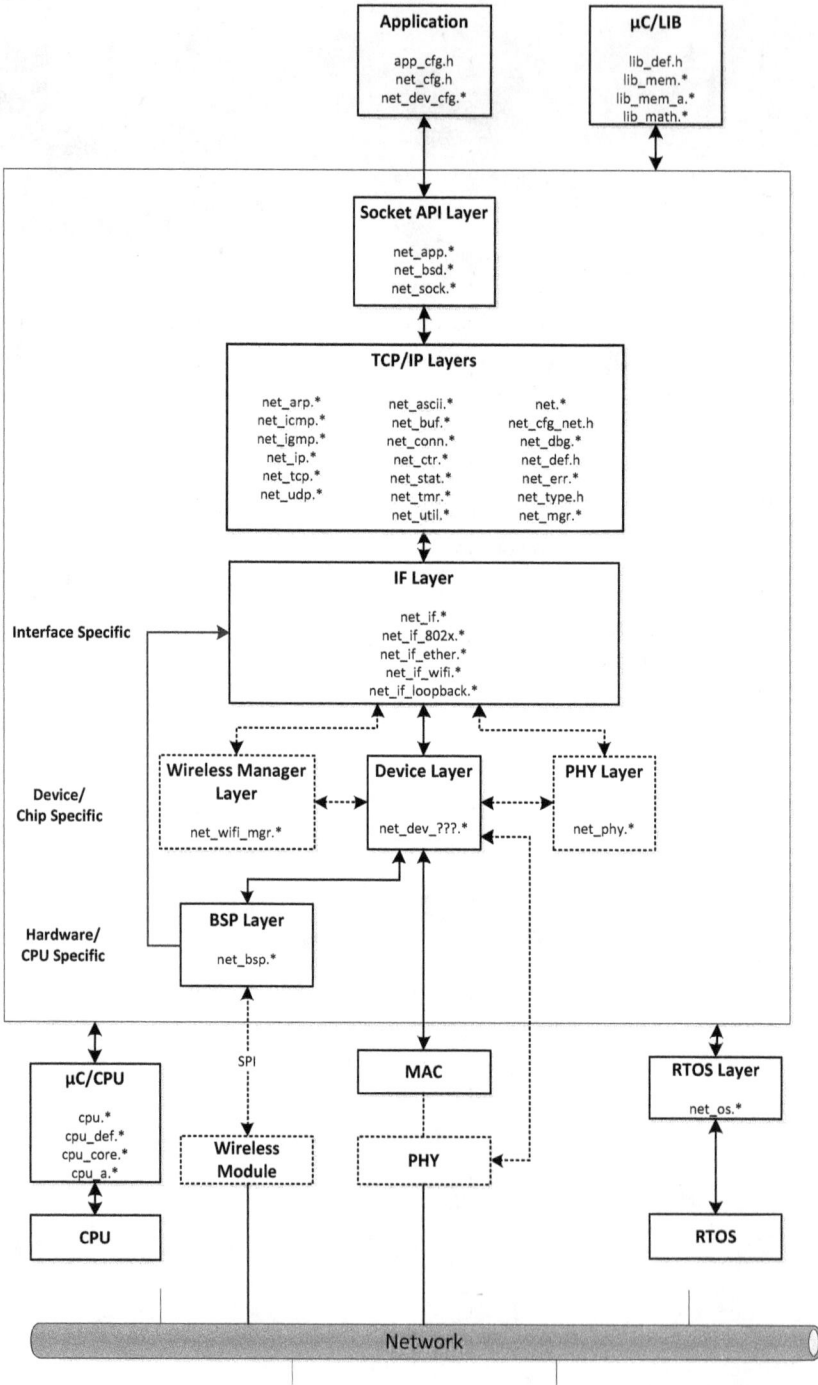

Figure 11-1 **Module Relationships**

11-1 µC/TCP-IP MODULE RELATIONSHIPS

11-1-1 APPLICATION

An application provides configuration information to µC/TCP-IP in the form of four C files: **app_cfg.h**, **net_cfg.h**, **net_dev_cfg.c** and **net_dev_cfg.h**.

app_cfg.h is an application-specific configuration file that *must* be present in the application. **app_cfg.h** contains **#defines** to specify the task priorities of each of the tasks within the application (including those of µC/TCP-IP), and the stack size for those tasks. Task priorities are placed in a file to make it easier to "see" task priorities for the entire application in one place.

Configuration data in **net_cfg.h** consists of specifying the number of timers to allocate to the stack, whether or not statistic counters will be maintained, the number of ARP cache entries, how UDP checksums are computed, and more. One of the most important configurations necessary is the size of the TCP Receive Window. In all, there are approximately 50 **#define** to set. However, most of the **#define** constants can be set to their recommended default value.

Finally, **net_dev_cfg.c** consists of device-specific configuration requirements such as the number of buffers allocated to a device, the MAC address for that device, and necessary physical layer device configuration including physical layer device bus address and link characteristics. Each µC/TCP-IP-compatible device requires that its configuration be specified within **net_dev_cfg.c**.

11-1-2 µC/LIB LIBRARIES

Given that µC/TCP-IP is designed for use in safety critical applications, all "standard" library functions such as **strcpy()**, **memset()**, *etc.* have been rewritten to conform to the same quality as the rest as the protocol stack.

11-1-3 BSD SOCKET API LAYER

The application interfaces to µC/TCP-IP uses the BSD socket Application Programming Interface (API). The software developer can either write their own TCP/IP applications using the BSD socket API or, purchase a number of off-the-shelf TCP/IP components (Telnet, Web server, FTP server, etc.),for use with the BSD socket interface. Note that the BSD socket layer is shown as a separate module but is actually part of µC/TCP-IP.

Alternatively, the software developer can use µC/TCP-IP's own socket interface functions (`net_sock.*`). `net_bsd.*` is a layer of software that converts BSD socket calls to µC/TCP-IP socket calls. Of course, a slight performance gain is achieved by interfacing directly to `net_sock.*` functions. Micrium network products use µC/TCP-IP socket interface functions.

11-1-4 TCP/IP LAYER

The TCP/IP layer contains most of the CPU, RTOS and compiler-independent code for µC/TCP-IP. There are three categories of files in this section:

1 TCP/IP protocol specific files include:

ARP (`net_arp.*`),
ICMP (`net_icmp.*`),
IGMP (`net_igmp.*`),
IP (`net_ip.*`),
TCP (`net_tcp.*`),
UDP (`net_udp.*`)

2 Support files are:

ASCII conversions (`net_ascii.*`),
Buffer management (`net_buf.*`),
TCP/UDP connection management (`net_conn.*`),
Counter management (`net_ctr.*`),
Statistics (`net_stat.*`),
Timer Management (`net_tmr.*`),
Other utilities (`net_util.*`).

3   Miscellaneous header files include:

Master µC/TCP-IP header file (**net.h**)
File containing error codes (**net_err.h**)
Miscellaneous µC/TCP-IP data types (**net_type.h**)
Miscellaneous definitions (**net_def.h**)
Debug (**net_dbg.h**)
Configuration definitions (**net_cfg_net.h**)

11-1-5 NETWORK INTERFACE (IF) LAYER

The IF Layer involves several types of network interfaces (Ethernet, Token Ring, etc.). However, the current version of µC/TCP-IP only supports Ethernet interfaces, wired and wireless. The IF layer is split into two sub-layers.

net_if.* is the interface between higher Network Protocol Suite layers and the link layer protocols. This layer also provides network device management routines to the application.

net_if_*.* contains the link layer protocol specifics independent of the actual device (i.e., hardware). In the case of Ethernet, **net_if_ether.*** understands Ethernet frames, MAC addresses, frame de-multiplexing, and so on, but assumes nothing regarding actual Ethernet hardware.

11-1-6 NETWORK DEVICE DRIVER LAYER

As previously stated, µC/TCP-IP works with just nearly any network device. This layer handles the specifics of the hardware, e.g., how to initialize the device, how to enable and disable interrupts from the device, how to find the size of a received packet, how to read a packet out of the frame buffer, and how to write a packet to the device, etc.

In order for device drivers to have independent configuration for clock gating, interrupt controller, and general purpose I/O, an additional file, **net_bsp.c**, encapsulates such details.

net_bsp.c contains code for the configuration of clock gating to the device, an internal or external interrupt controller, necessary IO pins, as well as time delays, getting a time stamp from the environment, and so on. This file is assumed to reside in the user application.

11-1-7 NETWORK PHYSICAL (PHY) LAYER

Often, devices interface to external physical layer devices, which may need to be initialized and controlled. This layer is shown in Figure 11-1 asa "dotted" area indicating that it is not present with all devices. In fact, some devices have PHY control built-in. Micrium provides a generic PHY driver which controls most external (R)MII compliant Ethernet physical layer devices.

11-1-8 NETWORK WIRELESS MANAGER

Often, wireless device may need to initialize a command and wait to receive the result (i.e. Scan). This layer manages specific wireless management commands. Micrium provides a generic Wireless Manager which should be able to controls most wireless module.

11-1-9 CPU LAYER

µC/TCP-IP can work with either an 8, 16, 32 or even 64-bit CPU, but it must have information about the CPU used. The CPU layer defines such information as the C data type corresponding to 16-bit and 32-bit variables, whether the CPU is little or big endian, and how interrupts are disabled and enabled on the CPU.

CPU-specific files are found in the **...\uC-CPU** directory and are used to adapt µC/TCP-IP to a different CPU, modify either the **cpu*.*** files or, create new ones based on the ones supplied in the uC-CPU directory. In general, it is much easier to modify existing files.

11-1-10 REAL-TIME OPERATING SYSTEM (RTOS) LAYER

µC/TCP-IP assumes the presence of an RTOS, but the RTOS layer allows µC/TCP-IP to be independent of a specific RTOS. µC/TCP-IP consists of three tasks. One task is responsible for handling packet reception, another task for asynchronous transmit buffer de-allocation, and the last task for managing timers. Depending on the configuration, a fourth task may be present to handle loopback operation.

As a minimum, the RTOS:

1   Must be able to create at least three tasks (a Receive task, a Transmit De-allocation task, and a Timer task)

2   Provide semaphore management (or the equivalent) and the μC/TCP-IP needs to be able to create at least two semaphores for each socket and an additional four semaphores for internal use.

3   Provides timer management services

4   Port must also include support for pending on multiple OS objects if BSD socket **select()** is required.

μC/TCP-IP is provided with a μC/OS-II and μC/OS-III interface. If a different RTOS is used, the **net_os.*** for μC/OS-II or μC/OS-III can be used as templates to interface to the RTOS chosen.

11-2 TASK MODEL

The user application interfaces to μC/TCP-IP via a well known API called BSD sockets (or μC/TCP-IP's internal socket interface). The application can send and receive data to/from other hosts on the network via this interface.

The BSD socket API interfaces to internal structures and variables (i.e., data) that are maintained by μC/TCP-IP. A binary semaphore (the global lock in Figure 11-2) is used to guard access to this data to ensure exclusive access. In order to read or write to this data, a task needs to acquire the binary semaphore before it can access the data and release it when finished. Of course, the application tasks do not have to know anything about this semaphore nor the data since its use is encapsulated by functions within μC/TCP-IP.

Figure 11-2 shows a simplified task model of μC/TCP-IP along with application tasks.

11-2-1 μC/TCP-IP TASKS AND PRIORITIES

μC/TCP-IP defines three internal tasks: a Receive task, a Transmit De-allocation task, and a Timer task. The Receive task is responsible for processing received packets from all devices. The Transmit De-allocation task frees transmit buffer resources when they are no longer required. The Timer task is responsible for handling all timeouts related to TCP/IP protocols and network interface management.

When setting up task priorities, we generally recommend that tasks that use µC/TCP-IP's services be configured with higher priorities than µC/TCP-IP's internal tasks. However, application tasks that use µC/TCP-IP should voluntarily relinquish the CPU on a regular basis. For example, they can delay or suspend the tasks or wait on µC/TCP-IP services. This is to reduce starvation issues when an application task sends a substantial amount of data.

We recommend that you configure the network interface Transmit De-allocation task with a higher priority than all application tasks that use µC/TCP-IP network services; but configure the Timer task and network interface Receive task with lower priorities than almost other application tasks.

See also section D-20-1 "Operating System Configuration" on page 985.

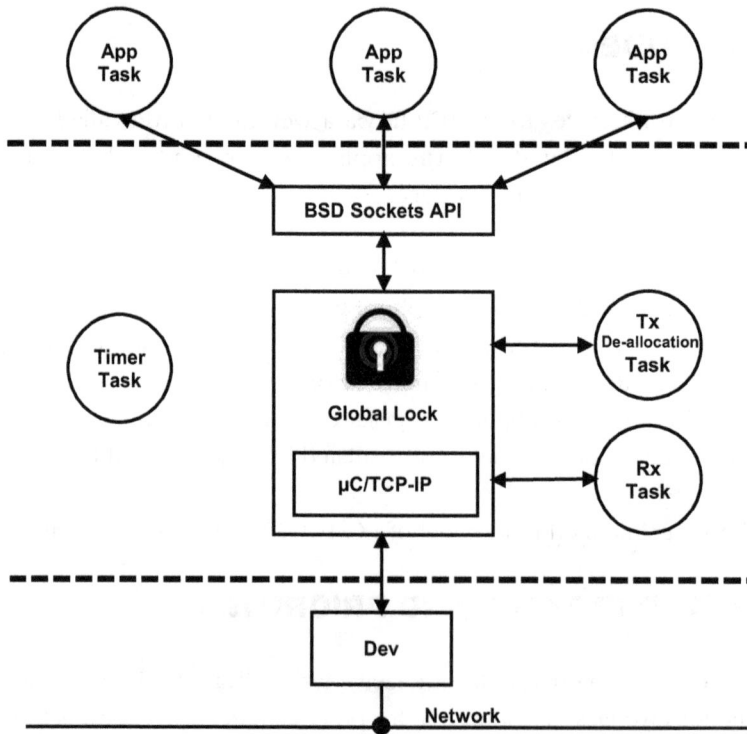

Figure 11-2 **µC/TCP-IP Task model**

11-2-2 RECEIVING A PACKET

Figure 11-3 shows a simplified task model of µC/TCP-IP when packets are received from the device.

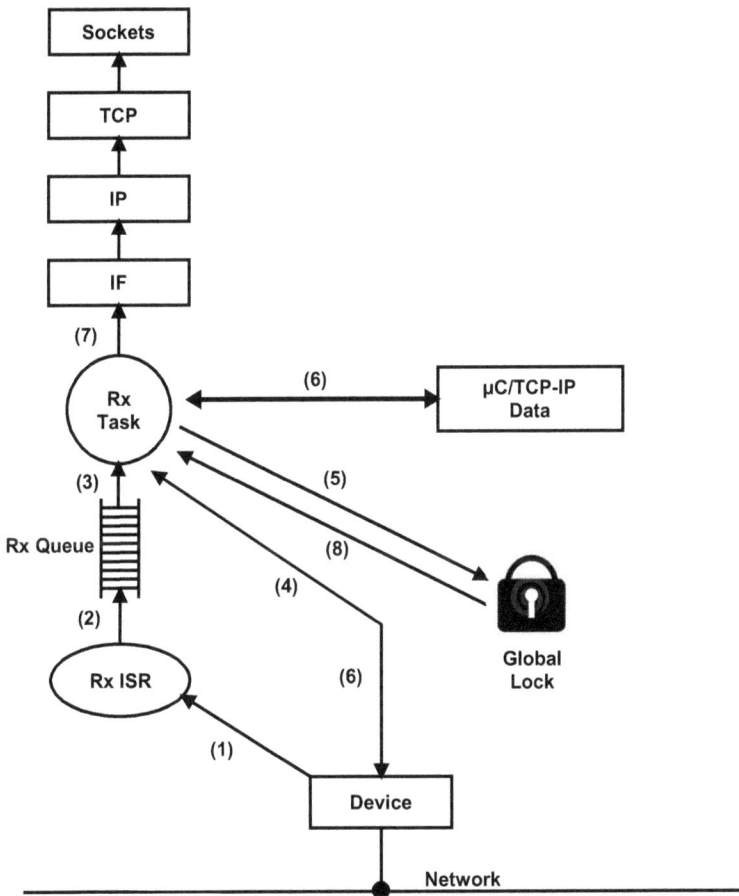

Figure 11-3 **µC/TCP-IP Receiving a Packet**

11

F11-3(1)   A packet is sent on the network and the device recognizes its address as the destination for the packet. The device then generates an interrupt and the BSP global ISR handler is called for non-vectored interrupt controllers. Either the global ISR handler or the vectored interrupt controller calls the Net BSP device specific ISR handler, which in turn indirectly calls the device ISR handler using a predefined Net IF function call. The device ISR handler determines that the interrupt comes from a packet reception (as opposed to the completion of a transmission).

F11-3(2)   Instead of processing the received packet directly from the ISR, it was decided to pass the responsibility to a task. The Rx ISR therefore simply "signals" the Receive task by posting the interface number to the Receive task queue. Note that further Rx interrupts are generally disabled while processing the interrupt within the device ISR handler.

F11-3(3)   The Receive task does nothing until a signal is received from the *Rx ISR*.

F11-3(4)   When a signal is received from an Ethernet device, the Receive task wakes up and extracts the packet from the hardware and places it in a receive buffer. For DMA based devices, the receive descriptor buffer pointer is updated to point to a new data area and the pointer to the receive packet is passed to higher layers for processing.

μC/TCP-IP maintains three types of device buffers: small transmit, large transmit, and large receive. For a common Ethernet configuration, a small transmit buffer typically holds up to 256 bytes of data, a large transmit buffer up to 1500 bytes of data, and a large receive buffer 1500 bytes of data. Note that the large transmit buffer size is generally specified within the device configuration as 1594 or 1614 bytes (see Chapter 9, "Buffer Management" on page 277 for a precise definition). The additional space is used to hold additional protocol header data. These sizes as well as the quantity of these buffers are configurable for each interface during either compile time or run time.

F11-3(5)   Buffers are shared resources and any access to those or any other μC/TCP-IP data structures is guarded by the binary semaphore that guards the data. This means that the Receive task will need to acquire the semaphore before it can receive a buffer from the pool.

F11-3(6)   The Receive task gets a buffer from the buffer pool. The packet is removed from the device and placed in the buffer for further processing. For DMA, the acquired buffer pointer replaces the descriptor buffer pointer that received the current frame. The pointer to the received frame is passed to higher layers for further processing.

F11-3(7)   The Receive task examines received data via the appropriate link layer protocol and determines whether the packet is destined for the ARP or IP layer, and passes the buffer to the appropriate layer for further processing. Note that the Receive task brings the data all the way up to the application layer and therefore the appropriate µC/TCP-IP functions operate within the context of the Receive task.

F11-3(8)   When the packet is processed, the lock is released and the Receive task waits for the next packet to be received.

11-2-3 TRANSMITTING A PACKET

Figure 11-4 shows a simplified task model of μC/TCP-IP when packets are transmitted through the device.

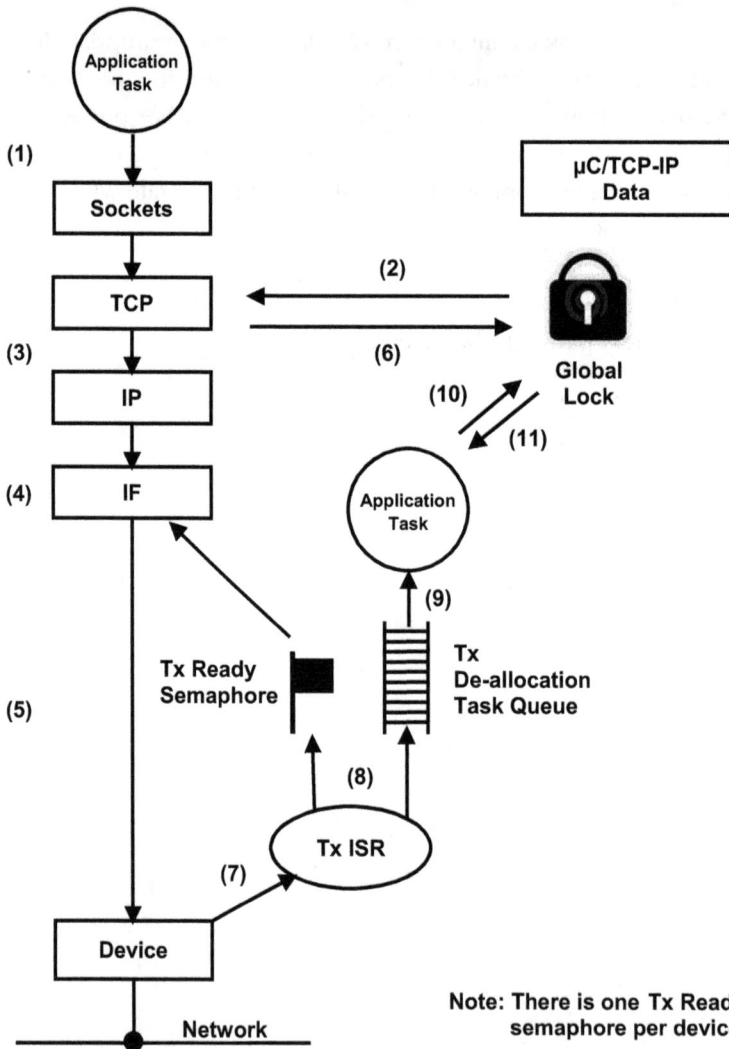

Figure 11-4 μC/TCP-IP Sending a Packet

F11-4(1)   A task (assuming an application task) that wants to send data interfaces to µC/TCP-IP through the BSD socket API.

F11-4(2)   A function within µC/TCP-IP acquires the binary semaphore (i.e., the global lock) in order to place the data to send into µC/TCP-IP's data structures.

F11-4(3)   The appropriate µC/TCP-IP layer processes the data, preparing it for transmission.

F11-4(4)   The task (via the IF layer) then waits on a counting semaphore, which is used to indicate that the transmitter in the device is available to send a packet. If the device is not able to send the packet, the task blocks until the semaphore is signaled by the device. Note that during device initialization, the semaphore is initialized with a value corresponding to the number of packets that can be sent at one time through the device. If the device has sufficient buffer space to be able to queue up four packets, then the counting semaphore is initialized with a count of 4. For DMA-based devices, the value of the semaphore is initialized to the number of available transmit descriptors.

F11-4(5)   When the device is ready, the driver either copies the data to the device internal memory space or configures the DMA transmit descriptor. When the device is fully configured, the device driver issues a transmit command.

F11-4(6)   After placing the packet into the device, the task releases the global data lock and continues execution.

F11-4(7)   When the device finishes sending the data, the device generates an interrupt.

F11-4(8)   The Tx ISR signals the Tx Available semaphore indicating that the device is able to send another packet. Additionally, the Tx ISR handler passes the address of the buffer that completed transmission to the Transmit De-allocation task via a queue which is encapsulated by an OS port function call.

F11-4(9)   The Transmit De-allocation task wakes up when a device driver posts a transmit buffer address to its queue.

11

F11-4(10)   The global data lock is acquired. If the global data lock is held by another task, the Transmit De-allocation task must wait to acquire the global data lock. Since it is recommended that the Transmit De-allocation task be configured as the highest priority µC/TCP-IP task, it will run following the release of the global data lock, assuming the queue has at least one entry present.

F11-4(11)   The lock is released when transmit buffer de-allocation is finished. Further transmission and reception of additional data by application and µC/TCP-IP tasks may resume.

Directories and Files

This chapter will discuss the modules available for µC/TCP-IP, and how they all fit together. A Windows®-based development platform is assumed. The directories and files make references to typical Windows-type directory structures. However, since µC/TCP-IP is available in source form, it can also be used with any ANSI-C compatible compiler/linker and any Operating System.

The names of the files are shown in upper case to make them stand out. However, file names are actually lower case.

12-1 BLOCK DIAGRAM

Figure 12-1 is a block diagram of the modules found in µC/TCP-IP and their relationship. Also included are the names of the files that are related to µC/TCP-IP

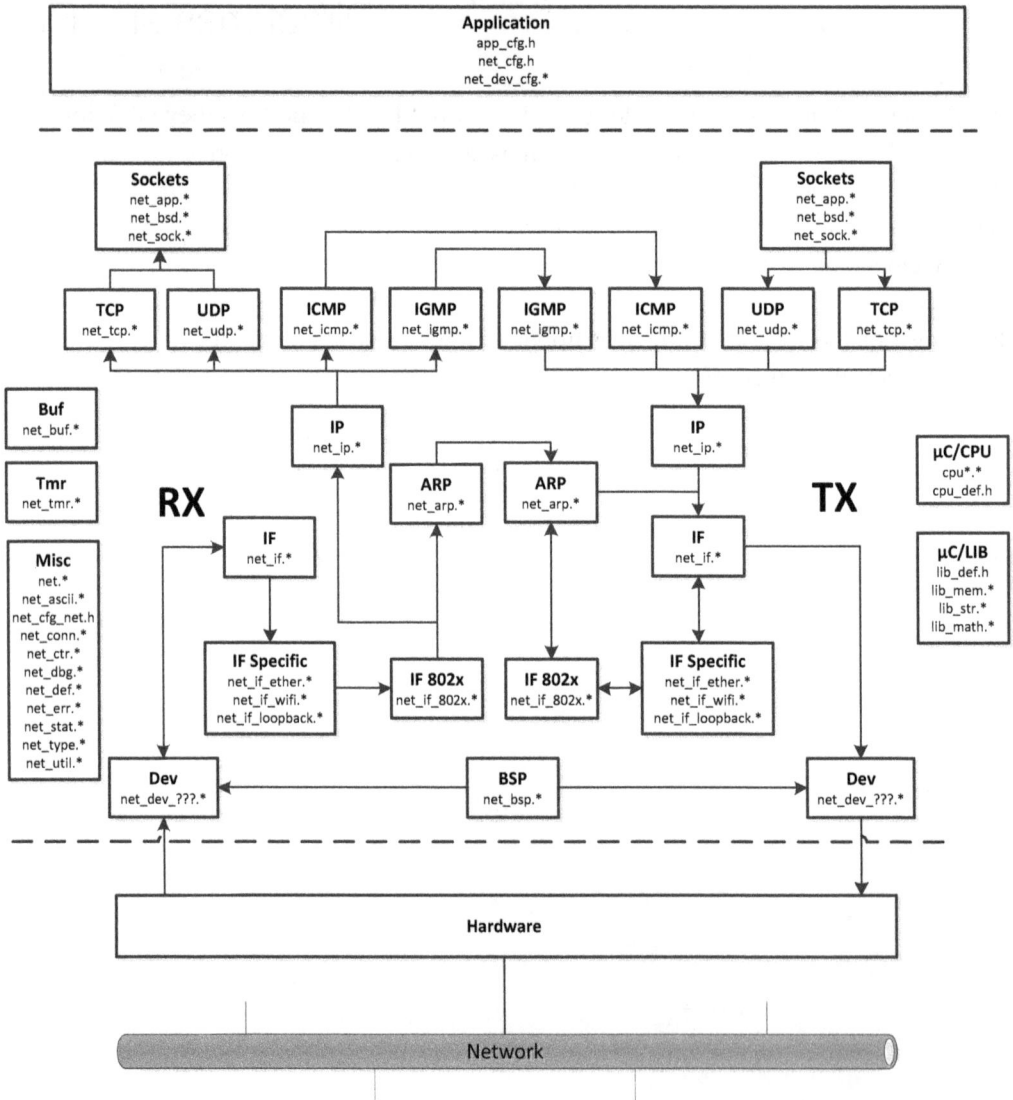

Figure 12-1 µC/TCP-IP Block Diagram

12-2 APPLICATION CODE

When Micrium provides example projects, they are placed in a directory structure shown below. Of course, a directory structure that suits a particular project/product can be used.

```
\Micrium
    \Software
        \EvalBoards
            \<manufacturer>
                \<board_name>
                    \<compiler>
                        \<project name>
                            \*.*
```

\Micrium
This is where we place all software components and projects provided by Micrium. This directory generally starts from the root directory of the computer.

\Software
This sub-directory contains all software components and projects.

\EvalBoards
This sub-directory contains all projects related to evaluation boards supported by Micrium.

\<manufacturer>
This is the name of the manufacturer of the evaluation board. The '<' and '>' are not part of the actual name.

\<board name>
This is the name of the evaluation board. A board from Micrium will typically be called **uC-Eval-xxxx** where **xxxx** represents the CPU or MCU used on the board. The '<' and '>' are not part of the actual name.

\<compiler>
This is the name of the compiler or compiler manufacturer used to build the code for the evaluation board. The '<' and '>' are not part of the actual name.

\<project name>

The name of the project that will be demonstrated. For example a simple µC/TCP-IP project might have a project name of 'OS-Ex1'. The '-Ex1' represents a project containing only µC/OS-III. A project name of **OS-Probe-Ex1** contains µC/TCP-IP and µC/Probe. The '<' and '>' are not part of the actual name.

.

These are the source files for the project. Main files can optionally be called **APP*.***. This directory also contains configuration files **app_cfg.h**, **net_cfg.h**, **net_decv_cfg.h**, **net_dev_cfg.c**, **os_cfg.h**, **os_cfg_app.h** and other project-required source files.

> **includes.h** is the application-specific master include header file. Almost all Micrium products require this file.

> **net_cfg.h** is a configuration file used to configure such µC/TCP-IP parameters as the number of network timers, sockets, and connections created; default timeout values, and more. **net_cfg.h** *must* be included in the application as µC/TCP-IP requires this file. See Chapter 16, "Network Interface Layer" on page 361 for more information.

> **net_dev_cfg.c** and **net_dev_cfg.h** are configuration files used to configure µC/TCP-IP interface parameters such as the number of transmit and receive buffers. See Chapter 14, "Network Interface Configuration" on page 303 for more details.

> **os_cfg.h** is a configuration file used to configure µC/OS-III parameters such as the maximum number of tasks, events, and objects; which µOS-III services are enabled (semaphores, mailboxes, queues); *etc*. **os_cfg.h** is a required file for any µC/OS-III application. See µC/OS-III documentation and books for further information.

> **app.c** contains the application code for the Processor example project. As with most C programs, code execution starts at **main()** which is shown in Listing 13-1 on page 295. The application code starts µC/TCP-IP.

12-3 CPU

The directory shown below contains semiconductor manufacturer peripheral interface source files. Any directory structure that suits the project/product may be used.

```
\Micrium
    \Software
        \CPU
            \<manufacturer>
                \<architecture>
                    \*.*
```

\Micrium
The location of all software components and projects provided by Micrium.

\Software
This sub-directory contains all software components and projects.

\CPU
This sub-directory is always called CPU.

\<manufacturer>
Is the name of the semiconductor manufacturer providing the peripheral library. The < and > are not part of the actual name.

\<architecture>
The name of the specific library, generally associated with a CPU name or an architecture.

.
Indicates library source files. The semiconductor manufacturer names the files.

12-4 BOARD SUPPORT PACKAGE (BSP)

The Board Support Package (BSP) is generally found with the evaluation or target board, and it is specific to that board. In fact, when well written, the BSP should be used for multiple projects.

```
\Micrium
    \Software
        \EvalBoards
            \<manufacturer>
                \<board name>
                    \<compiler>
                        \BSP
                            \*.*
```

\Micrium
Contains all software components and projects provided by Micrium.

\Software
This sub-directory contains all software components and projects.

\EvalBoards
This sub-directory contains all projects related to evaluation boards.

\<manufacturer>
The name of the manufacturer of the evaluation board. The **<** and **>** are not part of the actual name.

\<board name>
The name of the evaluation board. A board from Micrium will typically be called **uC-Eval-xxxx** where **xxxx** is the name of the CPU or MCU used on the evaluation board. The **<** and **>** are not part of the actual name.

\<compiler>
The name of the compiler or compiler manufacturer used to build code for the evaluation board. The **<** and **>** are not part of the actual name.

\BSP
This directory is always called BSP.

.

The source files of the BSP. Typically all of the file names start with BSP. It is therefore normal to find **bsp.c** and **bsp.h** in this directory. BSP code should contain such functions as LED control functions, initialization of timers, interface to Ethernet controllers, and more.

BSP stands for Board Support Package and the 'services' the board provides are placed in such a file. In this case, **bsp.c** contains I/O, timer initialization code, LED control code, and more. The I/Os used on the board are initialized when **BSP_Init()** is called.

The concept of a BSP is to hide the hardware details from the application code. It is important that functions in a BSP reflect the function and do not make references to any CPU specifics. For example, the code to turn on an LED is called **LED_On()** and not **MCU_led()**. If **LED_On()** is used in the code, it can be easily ported to another processor (or board) by simply rewriting **LED_On()** to control the LEDs on a different board. The same is true for other services. Also notice that BSP functions are prefixed with the function's group. LED services start with **LED_**, timer services start with **Tmr_**, etc. In other words, BSP functions do not need to be prefixed by **BSP_**.

12-5 NETWORK BOARD SUPPORT PACKAGE (NET_BSP)

In addition to the general (BSP) there are specific network initialization and configuration requirements. This additional file is generally found with the evaluation or target board as it is specific to that board.

```
\Micrium
    \Software
        \EvalBoards
            \<manufacturer>
                \<board name>
                    \<compiler>
                        \BSP
                            \TCPIP-V2
                                \*.*
```

\Micrium

Contains all software components and projects provided by Micrium.

\Software

This sub-directory contains all software components and projects.

\EvalBoards

This sub-directory contains all projects related to evaluation boards.

\<manufacturer>

The name of the manufacturer of the evaluation board. The '<' and '>' are not part of the actual name.

\<board name>

The name of the evaluation board. A board from Micrium will typically be called **uC-Eval-xxxx** where **xxxx** is the name of the CPU or MCU used on the evaluation board. The '<' and '>' are not part of the actual name.

\<compiler>

The name of the compiler or compiler manufacturer used to build code for the evaluation board. The '<' and '>' are not part of the actual name.

\BSP

This directory is always called BSP.

\TCPIP-V2

This directory is always called TCPIP-V2 as it is the directory for the network related BSP files.

.

The **net_bsp.*** files contain hardware-dependent code specific to the network device(s) and other µC/TCP-IP functions. Specifically, these files may contain code to read data from and write data to network devices, handle hardware-level device interrupts, provide delay functions, and get time stamps, etc.

12-6 µC/OS-III, CPU INDEPENDENT SOURCE CODE

The files in these directories are available to µC/OS-III licensees (see Appendix X, "Licensing Policy").

```
\Micrium
    \Software
        \uCOS-III
            \Cfg\Template
            \Source
```

\Micrium
Contains all software components and projects provided by Micrium.

\Software
This sub-directory contains all software components and projects.

\uCOS-III
This is the main µC/OS-III directory.

\Cfg\Template
This directory contains examples of configuration files to copy to the project directory. These files can be modified to suit the needs of the application.

\Source
The directory contains the CPU-independent source code for µC/OS-III. All files in this directory should be included in the build (assuming the presence of the source code). Features that are not required will be compiled out based on the value of #define constants in **os_cfg.h** and **os_cfg_app.h**.

12-7 µC/OS-III, CPU SPECIFIC SOURCE CODE

The µC/OS-III port developer provides these files. See Chapter 17 in the µC/OS-III book.

```
\Micrium
    \Software
        \uCOS-III
            \Ports
                \<architecture>
                    \<compiler>
```

\Micrium

Contains all software components and projects provided by Micrium.

\Software

This sub-directory contains all software components and projects.

\uCOS-III

The main µC/OS-III directory.

\Ports

The location of port files for the CPU architecture(s) to be used.

\<architecture>

This is the name of the CPU architecture that µC/OS-III was ported to. The '<' and '>' are not part of the actual name.

\<compiler>

The name of the compiler or compiler manufacturer used to build code for the port. The < and > are not part of the actual name.

The files in this directory contain the µC/OS-III port, see Chapter 17 "Porting µC/OS-III" in the µC/OS-III book for details on the contents of these files.

12-8 µC/CPU, CPU SPECIFIC SOURCE CODE

µC/CPU consists of files that encapsulate common CPU-specific functionality and CPU and compiler-specific data types.

```
\Micrium
    \Software
        \uC-CPU
            \cpu_core.c
            \cpu_core.h
            \cpu_def.h
            \Cfg\Template
                \cpu_cfg.h
            \<architecture>
                \<compiler>
                    \cpu.h
                    \cpu_a.asm
                    \cpu_c.c
```

\Micrium
Contains all software components and projects provided by Micrium.

\Software
This sub-directory contains all software components and projects.

\uC-CPU
This is the main µC/CPU directory.

cpu_core.c contains C code that is common to all CPU architectures. Specifically, this file contains functions to measure the interrupt disable time of the CPU_CRITICAL_ENTER() and CPU_CRITICAL_EXIT() macros, a function that emulates a count leading zeros instruction and a few other functions.

cpu_core.h contains function prototypes for the functions provided in cpu_core.c and allocation of the variables used by the module to measure interrupt disable time.

cpu_def.h contains miscellaneous #define constants used by the µC/CPU module.

12

\Cfg\Template

This directory contains a configuration template file (**cpu_cfg.h**) that is required to be copied to the application directory to configure the µC/CPU module based on application requirements.

> **cpu_cfg.h** determines whether to enable measurement of the interrupt disable time, whether the CPU implements a count leading zeros instruction in assembly language, or whether it will be emulated in C, and more.

\<architecture>

The name of the CPU architecture that µC/CPU was ported to. The '<' and '>' are not part of the actual name.

\<compiler>

The name of the compiler or compiler manufacturer used to build code for the µC/CPU port. The '<' and '>' are not part of the actual name.

The files in this directory contain the µC/CPU port, see Chapter 17 of the µC/OS-III book, "Porting µC/OS-III" for details on the contents of these files.

> **cpu.h** contains type definitions to make µC/OS-III and other modules independent of the CPU and compiler word sizes. Specifically, one will find the declaration of the **CPU_INT16U**, **CPU_INT32U**, **CPU_FP32** and many other data types. This file also specifies whether the CPU is a big or little endian machine, defines the **CPU_STK** data type used by µC/OS-III, defines the macros **OS_CRITICAL_ENTER()** and **OS_CRITICAL_EXIT()**, and contains function prototypes for functions specific to the CPU architecture, etc.

> **cpu_a.asm** contains the assembly language functions to implement code to disable and enable CPU interrupts, count leading zeros (if the CPU supports that instruction), and other CPU specific functions that can only be written in assembly language. This file may also contain code to enable caches, and setup MPUs and MMU. The functions provided in this file are accessible from C.

> **cpu_c.c** contains the C code of functions that are based on a specific CPU architecture but written in C for portability. As a general rule, if a function can be written in C then it should be, unless there is significant performance benefits available by writing it in assembly language.

12-9 μC/LIB, PORTABLE LIBRARY FUNCTIONS

μC/LIB consists of library functions meant to be highly portable and not tied to any specific compiler. This facilitates third-party certification of Micrium products. μC/OS-III does not use any μC/LIB functions, however the μC/CPU assumes the presence of **lib_def.h** for such definitions as: DEF_YES, DEF_NO, DEF_TRUE, DEF_FALSE, *etc*.

```
\Micrium
    \Software
        \uC-LIB
            \lib_ascii.c
            \lib_ascii.h
            \lib_def.h
            \lib_math.c
            \lib_math.h
            \lib_mem.c
            \lib_mem.h
            \lib_str.c
            \lib_str.h
            \Cfg\Template
                \lib_cfg.h
            \Ports
                \<architecture>
                    \<compiler>
                        \lib_mem_a.asm
```

\Micrium
Contains all software components and projects provided by Micrium.

\Software
This sub-directory contains all software components and projects.

\uC-LIB
This is the main μC/LIB directory.

\Cfg\Template

This directory contains a configuration template file (**lib_cfg.h**) that is required to be copied to the application directory to configure the µC/LIB module based on application requirements.

> **lib_cfg.h** determines whether to enable assembly language optimization (assuming there is an assembly language file for the processor, i.e., **lib_mem_a.asm**) and a few other **#defines**.

12-10 µC/TCP-IP NETWORK DEVICES

The files in these directories are

```
\Micrium
    \Software
        \uC-TCPIP-V2
            \Dev
                \Ether
                    \PHY
                        \Generic
                    \<Controller>
                \WiFi
                    \Manager
                        \Generic
                    \<Controller>
```

\Micrium

Contains all software components and projects provided by Micrium.

\Software

This sub-directory contains all software components and projects.

\uC-TCPIP-V2

This is the main directory for the µC/TCP-IP code. The name of the directory contains a version number to differentiate it from previous versions of the stack.

\Dev

This directory contains device drivers for different interfaces. Currently, µC/TCP-IP only supports one type of interface, Ethernet. µC/TCP-IP is tested with many types of Ethernet devices.

\Ether

Ethernet controller drivers are placed under the Ether sub-directory. Note that device drivers must also be called **net_dev_<controller>.***.

\WiFi

Wireless controller drivers are placed under the WiFi sub-directory. Note that device drivers must also be called net_dev_<controller>.*.

\PHY

This is the main directory for Ethernet Physical layer drivers.

\Generic

This is the directory for the Micrium provided generic PHY driver. Micrium's generic Ethernet PHY driver provides sufficient support for most (R)MII compliant Ethernet physical layer devices. A specific PHY driver may be developed in order to provide extended functionality such as link state interrupt support.

net_phy.h is the network physical layer header file.

net_phy.c provides the (R)MII interface port that is assumed to be part of the host Ethernet MAC. Therefore, (R)MII reads/writes *must* be performed through the network device API interface via calls to function pointers **Phy_RegRd()** and **Phy_RegWr()**.

\Manager

This is the main directory for Wireless Manager layer.

\Generic

This is the directory for the Micrium provided generic Wireless Manager layer. Micrium's generic Wireless Manager layer provides sufficient support for most wireless devices that embed a wireless supplicant. A specific Wireless Manager may be developed in order to provide extended functionality.

net_wifi_mgr.h is the network Wireless Manager layer header file.

net_wifi_mgr.c provides functionality to access the device for management command that could required asynchronous response such as scan for available network.

\<controller>

The name of the Ethernet or wireless controller or chip manufacturer used in the project. The '<' and '>' are not part of the actual name. This directory contains the network device driver for the Network Controller specified.

net_dev_<controller>.h is the header file for the network device driver.

net_dev_<controller>.c contains C code for the network device driver API.

12-11 µC/TCP-IP NETWORK INTERFACE

This directory contains interface-specific files. Currently, µC/TCP-IP only supports three type of interfaces, Ethernet, wireless and loopback. The Ethernet and wireless interface-specific files are found in the following directories:

```
\Micrium
    \Software
        \uC-TCPIP-V2
            \IF
```

\Micrium

Contains all software components and projects provided by Micrium.

\Software

This sub-directory contains all software components and projects.

\uC-TCPIP-V2

This is the main µC/TCP-IP directory.

\IF

This is the main directory for network interfaces.

net_if.* presents a programming interface between higher µC/TCP-IP layers and the link layer protocols. These files also provide interface management routines to the application.

net_if_802x.* contains common code to receive and transmit 802.3 and Ethernet packets. This file should not need to be modified.

net_if_ether.* contains the Ethernet interface specifics. This file should not need to be modified.

net_if_wifi.* contains the wireless interface specifics. This file should not need to be modified.

net_if_loopback.* contains loopback interface specifics. This file should not need to be modified.

12-12 µC/TCP-IP NETWORK OS ABSTRACTION LAYER

This directory contains the RTOS abstraction layer which allows the use of µC/TCP-IP with nearly any commercial or in-house RTOS. The abstraction layer for the selected RTOS is placed in a sub-directory under OS as follows:

```
\Micrium
    \Software
        \uC-TCPIP-V2
            \OS
                \<rtos_name>
```

\Micrium
Contains all software components and projects provided by Micrium.

\Software
This sub-directory contains all software components and projects.

\uC-TCPIP-V2
This is the main µC/TCP-IP directory.

\OS

This is the main OS directory.

\<rtos_name>

This is the directory that contains the files to perform RTOS abstraction. Note that files for the selected RTOS abstraction layer must always be named **net_os.***.

µC/TCP-IP has been tested with µC/OS-II, µC/OS-III and the RTOS layer files for these RTOS are found in the following directories:

\Micrium\Software\uC-TCPIP-V2\OS\uCOS-II\net_os.*

\Micrium\Software\uC-TCPIP-V2\OS\uCOS-III\net_os.*

12-13 µC/TCP-IP NETWORK CPU SPECIFIC CODE

Some functions can be optimized in assembly to improve the performance of the network protocol stack. An easy candidate is the checksum function. It is used at multiple levels in the stack, and a checksum is generally coded as a long loop.

```
\Micrium
    \Software
        \uC-TCPIP-V2
            \Ports
                \<architecture>
                    \<compiler>
                        \net_util_a.asm
```

\Micrium

Contains all software components and projects provided by Micrium.

\Software

This sub-directory contains all software components and projects.

\uC-TCPIP-V2

This is the main µC/TCP-IP directory.

\Ports
This is the main directory for processor specific code.

\<architecture>
The name of the CPU architecture that was ported to. The '<' and '>' are not part of the actual name.

\<compiler>
The name of the compiler or compiler manufacturer used to build code for the optimized function(s). The '<' and '>' are not part of the actual name.

> **net_util_a.asm** contains assembly code for the specific CPU architecture. All functions that can be optimized for the CPU architecture are located here.

12-14 µC/TCP-IP NETWORK CPU INDEPENDENT SOURCE CODE

This directory contains all the CPU and RTOS independent files for µC/TCP-IP. Nothing should be changed in this directory in order to use µC/TCP-IP.

```
\Micrium
    \Software
        \uC-TCPIP-V2
            \Source
```

\Micrium
Contains all software components and projects provided by Micrium.

\Software
This sub-directory contains all software components and projects.

\uC-TCPIP-V2
This is the main µC/TCP-IP directory.

\Source
This is the directory that contains all the CPU and RTOS independent source code files.

12-15 µC/TCP-IP NETWORK SECURITY MANAGER CPU INDEPENDENT SOURCE CODE

This directory contains all the CPU independent files for µC/TCP-IP Network Security Manager. Nothing should be changed in this directory in order to use µC/TCP-IP.

```
\Micrium
    \Software
        \uC-TCPIP-V2
            \Secure
                \<security_suite_name>
                    \OS
                        \<rtos_name>
```

\Micrium

Contains all software components and projects provided by Micrium.

\Software

This sub-directory contains all software components and projects.

\uC-TCPIP-V2

This is the main µC/TCP-IP directory.

\Secure

This is the directory that contains all the security suite independent source code files. These files must be included in the project even if no security suite is available or if the Network Security Manager is disabled.

\<security_suite_name>

This is the directory that contains the files to perform security suite abstraction. These files should only be included in the project if a security suite (i.e µC/SSL) is available and is to be used by the application.

\<rtos_name>

This is the directory that contains the RTOS dependent files of the security suite layer, if any. These files should only be included in the project if the a security suite (i.e µC/SSL) is available and is to be used by the application. It is possible that a security suite does not require an OS abstraction layer. Please refer to the security suite user's manual for more information.

µC/TCP-IP has been tested with µC/SSL, µC/OS-II and µC/OS-III. The security suite and RTOS files for this security suite are found in the following directories:

\Micrium\Software\uC-TCPIP-V2\Secure\uC-SSL\net_secure.*

\Micrium\Software\uC-TCPIP-V2\Secure\uC-SSL\OS\uCOS-II\net_secure_os.*

\Micrium\Software\uC-TCPIP-V2\Secure\uC-SSL\OS\uCOS-III\net_secure_os.*

12-16 SUMMARY

Below is a summary of all directories and files involved in a µC/TCP-IP-based project. The '**<-Cfg**' on the far right indicates that these files are typically copied into the application (i.e., project) directory and edited based on project requirements.

```
\Micrium
    \Software
        \EvalBoards
            \<manufacturer>
                \<board name>
                    \<compiler>
                        \<project name>
                            \app.c
                            \app.h
                            \other
                        \BSP
                            \bsp.c
                            \bsp.h
                            \others
                            \TCPIP-V2
                                \net_bsp.c
```

```
                          \net_bsp.h
    \CPU
        \<manufacturer>
            \<architecture>
                \*.*
    \uCOS-III
        \Cfg\Template
            \os_app_hooks.c
            \os_cfg.h                          <-Cfg
            \os_cfg_app.h                      <-Cfg
        \Source
            \os_cfg_app.c
            \os_core.c
            \os_dbg.c
            \os_flag.c
            \os_int.c
            \os_mem.c
            \os_msg.c
            \os_mutex.c
            \os_pend_multi.c
            \os_prio.c
            \os_q.c
            \os_sem.c
            \os_stat.c
            \os_task.c
            \os_tick.c
            \os_time.c
            \os_tmr.c
            \os_var.c
            \os.h
            \os_type.h                         <-Cfg
        \Ports
            \<architecture>
                \<compiler>
                    \os_cpu.h
                    \os_cpu_a.asm
                    \os_cpu_c.c
```

```
\uC-CPU
    \cpu_core.c
    \cpu_core.h
    \cpu_def.h
    \Cfg\Template
        \cpu_cfg.h                          <-Cfg
    \<architecture>
        \<compiler>
            \cpu.h
            \cpu_a.asm
            \cpu_c.c
\uC-LIB
    \lib_ascii.c
    \lib_ascii.h
    \lib_def.h
    \lib_math.c
    \lib_math.h
    \lib_mem.c
    \lib_mem.h
    \lib_str.c
    \lib_str.h
    \Cfg\Template
        \lib_cfg.h                          <-Cfg
    \Ports
        \<architecture>
            \<compiler>
                \lib_mem_a.asm
\uC-TCPIP-V2
    \BSP
        Template
            \net_bsp.c                      <-Cfg
            \net_bsp.h                      <-Cfg
            OS
                \<rtos_name>
                    \net_bsp.c              <-Cfg
```

```
\CFG
    \Template
        \net_cfg.h                          <-Cfg
        \net_dev_cfg.c                      <-Cfg
        \net_dev_cfg.h                      <-Cfg
\Dev
    \Ether
        \<controller>
            \net_dev_<controller>.c
            \net_dev_<controller>.h
            \PHY
                \controller>
                    \net_phy_<controller>.c
                    \net_phy_<controller>.h
                \Generic
                    \net_phy.c
                    \net_phy.h
    \WiFi
        \<controller>
            \net_dev_<controller>.c
            \net_dev_<controller>.h
        \Manager
            \Generic
                \net_wifi_mgr.c
                \net_wifi_mgr.h
\IF
    \net_if.c
    \net_if.h
    \net_if_802x.c
    \net_if_802x.h
    \net_if_ether.c
    \net_if_ether.h
    \net_if_wifi.c
    \net_if_wifi.h
    \net_if_loopback.c
    \net_if_loopback.h
\OS
    \<template>
```

```
            \net_os.c                    <-Cfg
            \net_os.h                    <-Cfg
        \<rtos_name>
            \net_os.c
            \net_os.h
    \Ports
        \<architecture>
            \<compiler>
                \net_util_a.asm
    \Secure
        \net_secure_mgr.c
        \net_secure_mgr.h
        \<security_suite_name>
            \net_secure.c
            \NET_secure.h
            \OS
                \<rtos_name>
                    \net_secure_os.c
                    \net_secure_os.h
    \Source
        \net.c
        \net.h
        \net_app.c
        \net_app.h
        \net_arp.c
        \net_arp.h
        \net_ascii.c
        \net_ascii.h
        \net.bsd.c
        \net.bsd.h
        \net.buf.c
        \net.buf.h
        \net.cfg_net.h
        \net.conn.c
        \net.conn.h
        \net.ctr.c
        \net.ctr.h
        \net.dbg.c
```

12

```
\net.dbg.h
\net.def.h
\net.err.c
\net.err.h
\net.icmp.c
\net.icmp.h
\net.igmp.c
\net.igmp.h
\net.ip.c
\net.ip.h
\net.mgr.c
\net.mgr.h
\net.sock.c
\net.sock.h
\net.stat.c
\net.stat.h
\net.tcp.c
\net.tcp.h
\net.tmr.c
\net.tmr.h
\net.type.h
\net.udp.c
\net.udp.h
\net.util.c
\net.util.h
```

13

Getting Started with µC/TCP-IP

As previously stated, the Directories and Files structure used herein assumes you have access to the µC/TCP-IP source code. The samples and examples in Part II of this book, however, use µC/TCP-IP as a library. The project structure is therefore different.

µC/TCP-IP requires an RTOS and, for the purposes of this book, µC/OS-III has been chosen. First, because it is the latest kernel from Micrium, and second, because all the examples in this book were developed with the evaluation board that is available with the µC/OS-III book. This way there is no need for an additional evaluation board.

13-1 INSTALLING µC/TCP-IP

Distribution of µC/TCP-IP is performed through release files. The release archive files contain all of the source code and documentation for µC/TCP-IP. Additional support files such as those located within the CPU directory may or may not be required depending on the target hardware and development tools. Example startup code, if available, may be delivered upon request. Example code is located in the Evalboards directory when applicable.

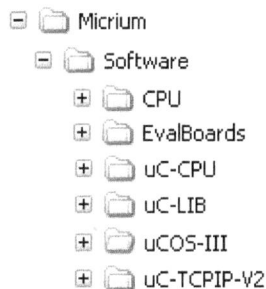

```
☐ 🗁 Micrium
    ☐ 🗁 Software
        ⊞ 🗀 CPU
        ⊞ 🗀 EvalBoards
        ⊞ 🗀 uC-CPU
        ⊞ 🗀 uC-LIB
        ⊞ 🗀 uCOS-III
        ⊞ 🗀 uC-TCPIP-V2
```

Figure 13-1 **Directory tree for µC/TCP-IP**

13-2 µC/TCP-IP EXAMPLE PROJECT

The following example project is used to show the basic architecture of µC/TCP-IP and to build an empty application. The application also uses µC/OS-III as the RTOS. Figure 13-1 shows the project test setup. A Windows-based PC and the target system were connected to a 100 Mbps Ethernet switch or via an Ethernet cross-over cable. The PC's IP address is set to 10.10.10.111 and one of the target's addresses is configured to 10.10.10.64.

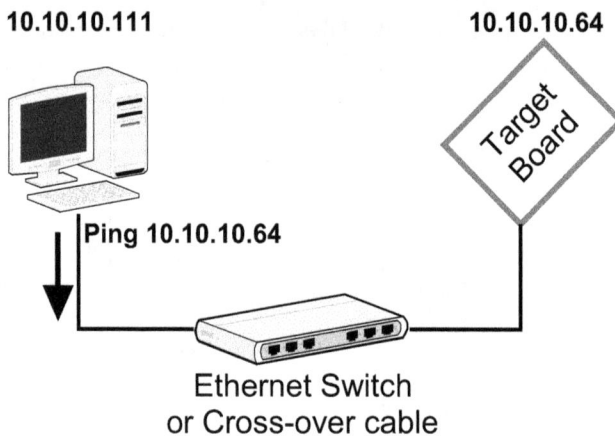

Figure 13-2 **Test setup**

This example contains enough code to be able to ping the board.The IP address of the board is forced to be 10.10.10.64. With a similar setup, the following command from a command-prompt is issued:

```
ping 10.10.10.64
```

Ping (on the PC) should reply back with the ping time to the target. µC/TCP-IP target projects connected to the test PC on the same Ethernet switch or Ethernet cross-over cable achieve ping times of less than 2 milliseconds.

The next sections show the directory tree of different components required to build a µC/TCP-IP example project.

13-3 APPLICATION CODE

File **app.c** contains the application code for the Processor example project. As with most C programs, code execution starts at **main()** which is shown in Listing 13-1. The application code starts µC/TCP-IP.

```
void  main (void)
{
    OS_ERR  err_os;

    BSP_IntDisAll();                                             (1)

    OSInit(&err_os);                                             (2)
    APP_TEST_FAULT(err_os, OS_ERR_NONE);

    OSTaskCreate((OS_TCB     *)&AppTaskStartTCB,                 (3)
                 (CPU_CHAR   *)"App Task Start",                 (4)
                 (OS_TASK_PTR ) AppTaskStart,                    (5)
                 (void       *) 0,                               (6)
                 (OS_PRIO     ) APP_OS_CFG_START_TASK_PRIO,      (7)
                 (CPU_STK    *)&AppTaskStartStk[0],              (8)
                 (CPU_STK_SIZE) APP_OS_CFG_START_TASK_STK_SIZE / 10u,   (9)
                 (CPU_STK_SIZE) APP_OS_CFG_START_TASK_STK_SIZE,        (10)
                 (OS_MSG_QTY  ) 0u,
                 (OS_TICK     ) 0u,
                 (void       *) 0,
                 (OS_OPT      ) (OS_OPT_TASK_STK_CHK | OS_OPT_TASK_STK_CLR),  (11)
                 (OS_ERR     *)&err_os);                         (12)
    APP_TEST_FAULT(err_os, OS_ERR_NONE);

    OSStart(&err_os);                                            (13)
    APP_TEST_FAULT(err_os, OS_ERR_NONE);
}
```

Listing 13-1 **Code execution starts at main()**

L13-1(1) Start **main()** by calling a BSP function that disables all interrupts. On most processors, interrupts are disabled at startup until explicitly enabled by application code. However, it is safer to turn off all peripheral interrupts during startup.

L13-1(2)   Call **OSInit()**, which is responsible for initializing μC/OS-III internal variables and data structures, and also creates two (2) to five (5) internal tasks. At minimum, μC/OS-III creates the idle task (**OS_IdleTask()**), which executes when no other task is ready to run. μC/OS-III also creates the tick task, responsible for keeping track of time.

           Depending on the value of **#define** constants, μC/OS-III will create the statistic task (**OS_StatTask()**), the timer task (**OS_TmrTask()**), and interrupt handler queue management task (**OS_IntQTask()**).

           Most μC/OS-III's functions return an error code via a pointer to an **OS_ERR** variable, err in this case. If **OSInit()** was successful, **err** will be set to **OS_ERR_NONE**. If **OSInit()** encounters a problem during initialization, it will return immediately upon detecting the problem and set err accordingly. If this occurs, look up the error code value in **os.h**. All error codes start with **OS_ERR_**.

           Note that **OSInit()** must be called before any other μC/OS-III function.

L13-1(3)   Create a task by calling **OSTaskCreate()**. **OSTaskCreate()** requires 13 arguments. The first argument is the address of the **OS_TCB** that is declared for this task.

L13-1(4)   **OSTaskCreate()** allows a name to be assigned to each of the tasks. μC/OS-III stores a pointer to the task name inside the **OS_TCB** of the task. There is no limit on the number of ASCII characters used for the name.

L13-1(5)   The third argument is the address of the task code. A typical μC/OS-III task is implemented as an infinite loop as shown:

```
void  MyTask (void *p_arg)
{
    /* Do something with 'p_arg'. */
    while (1) {
        /* Task body */
    }
}
```

The task receives an argument when at inception. The task resembles any C function that can be called by code. However, the code *must not* call **MyTask()**.

L13-1(6)   The fourth argument of **OSTaskCreate()** is the argument that the task receives when it first begins. In other words, the **p_arg** of **MyTask()**. In the example a NULL pointer is passed, and thus **p_arg** for **AppTaskStart()** will be a NULL pointer.

The argument passed to the task can actually be any pointer. For example, you may pass a pointer to a data structure containing parameters for the task.

L13-1(7)   The next argument to **OSTaskCreate()** is the priority of the task. The priority establishes the relative importance of this task with respect to other tasks in the application. A low-priority number indicates a high priority (or more important task). Set the priority of the task to any value between 1 and **OS_CFG_PRIO_MAX-2**, inclusively. Avoid using priority #0, and priority **OS_CFG_PRIO_MAX-1**, because these are reserved for µC/OS-III. **OS_CFG_PRIO_MAX** is a compile time configuration constant, which is declared in **os_cfg.h**.

L13-1(8)   The sixth argument to **OSTaskCreate()** is the base address of the stack assigned to this task. The base address is always the lowest memory location of the stack.

L13-1(9)   The next argument specifies the location of a "watermark" in the task's stack that can be used to determine the allowable stack growth of the task. In the code above, the value represents the amount of stack space (in **CPU_STK** elements) before the stack is empty. In other words, in the example, the limit is reached when 10% of the stack is left.

L13-1(10)   The eighth argument to **OSTaskCreate()** specifies the size of the task's stack in number of **CPU_STK** elements (not bytes). For example, if allocating 1 Kbytes of stack space for a task and the **CPU_STK** is a 32-bit word, pass 256.

L13-1(11)   The next three arguments are skipped as they are not relevant to the current discussion. The next argument to **OSTaskCreate()** specifies options. In this example, it is specified that the stack will be checked at run time (assuming the statistic task was enabled in **os_cfg.h**), and that the contents of the stack will be cleared when the task is created.

L13-1(12)   The last argument of **OSTaskCreate()** is a pointer to a variable that will receive an error code. If **OSTaskCreate()** is successful, the error code will be **OS_ERR_NONE** otherwise, the value of the error code can be looked up in **os.h** (see OS_ERR_xxxx) to determine the problem with the call.

L13-1(13)   The final step in **main()** is to call **OSStart()**, which starts the multitasking process. Specifically, µC/OS-III will select the highest-priority task that was created before calling **OSStart()**. The highest-priority task is always **OS_IntQTask()** if that task is enabled in **os_cfg.h** (through the OS_CFG_ISR_POST_DEFERRED_EN constant). If this is the case, **OS_IntQTask()** will perform some initialization of its own and then µC/OS-III will switch to the next most important task that was created.

A few important points are worth noting. You can create as many tasks as you want before calling **OSStart()**. However, it is recommended to only create one task as shown in the example. Notice that interrupts are not enabled. µC/OS-III and µC/OS-II always start a task with interrupts enabled. As soon as the first task executes, the interrupts are enabled. The first task is **AppTaskStart()** and its contents is examined in can Listing 13-2.

```
static  void  AppTaskStart (void *p_arg)                    (1)
{
    CPU_INT32U  cpu_clk_freq;
    CPU_INT32U  cnts;
    OS_ERR      err_os;

    (void)&p_arg;

    BSP_Init();                                            (2)
    CPU_Init();                                            (3)
    cpu_clk_freq = BSP_CPU_ClkFreq();                      (4)
    cnts = cpu_clk_freq / (CPU_INT32U)OSCfg_TickRate_Hz;
    OS_CPU_SysTickInit(cnts);

    Mem_Init();                                            (5)
    AppInit_TCPIP(&net_err);                               (6)

                                                           (7)
```

```
        BSP_LED_Off(0u);                                    (8)
        while (1) {                                         (9)
            BSP_LED_Toggle(0u);                             (10)
            OSTimeDlyHMSM((CPU_INT16U) 0u,                  (11)
                          (CPU_INT16U) 0u,
                          (CPU_INT16U) 0u,
                          (CPU_INT16U) 100u,
                          (OS_OPT    ) OS_OPT_TIME_HMSM_STRICT,
                          (OS_ERR    *)&err_os);
        }
    }
```

Listing 13-2 **AppTaskStart**

L13-2(1)   As previously mentioned, a task looks like any other C function. The argument **p_arg** is passed to **AppTaskStart()** by **OSTaskCreate()**.

L13-2(2)   **BSP_Init()** is a BSP function responsible for initializing the hardware on an evaluation or target board. The evaluation board might have General Purpose Input Output (GPIO) lines that need to be configured, relays, and sensors, etc. This function is found in a file called **bsp.c**.

L13-2(3)   **Cuprite()** initializes μC/CPU services. μC/CPU provides services to measure interrupt latency, receive time stamps, and provide emulation of the count leading zeros instruction if the processor used does not have that instruction.

L13-2(4)   **BSP_CPU_ClkFreq()** determines the system tick reference frequency of this board. The number of system ticks per OS tick is calculated using **OSCfg_TickRate_Hz**, which is defined in **os_cfg_app.h**. Finally, **OS_CPU_SysTickInit()** sets up the μC/OS-III tick interrupt. For this, the function needs to initialize one of the hardware timers to interrupt the CPU at the **OSCfg_TickRate_Hz** rate calculated previously.

L13-2(5)   **Mem_Init()** initializes the memory management module. μC/TCP-IP object creation uses this module. This function is part of μC/LIB. The memory module *must* be initialized by calling **Mem_Init()** *prior* to calling **Net_Init()**. It is recommended to initialize the memory module before calling **OSStart()**, or near the top of the startup task. The application developer must enable and

299

13

configure the size of the µC/LIB memory heap available to the system. **LIB_MEM_CFG_HEAP_SIZE** should be defined from within **app_cfg.h** and set to match the application requirements.

L13-2(6)   **AppInit_TCPIP()** initializes the TCP/IP stack and the initial parameters to configure it. See section F-1-6 "µC/TCP-IP Initialization" on page 1002 for a description of **AppInit_TCPIP()**.

L13-2(7)   If other IP applications are required this is where they are initialized

L13-2(8)   **BSP_LED_Off()** is a function that will turn off all LEDs because the function is written so that a zero argument refers to all LEDs.

L13-2(9)   Most µC/OS-III tasks will need to be written as an infinite loop.

L13-2(10)   This BSP function toggles the state of the specified LED. Again, a zero indicates that all the LEDs should be toggled on the evaluation board. Simply change the zero to 1 causing LED #1 to toggle. Exactly which LED is LED #1? That depends on the BSP developer. Encapsulate access to LEDs through such functions as **BSP_LED_On()**, **BSP_LED_Off()** and **BSP_LED_Toggle()**. Also, LEDs are assigned logical values (1, 2, 3, etc.) instead of specifying a port and specific bit on each port.

L13-2(11)   Finally, each task in the application must call one of the µC/OS-III functions that will cause the task to "wait for an event." The task can wait for time to expire (by calling **OSTimeDly()**, or **OSTimeDlyHMSM()**), or wait for a signal or a message from an ISR or another task.

AppTaskStart() calls the **AppInit_TCPIP()** to initialize and start the TCP/IP stack. This function is shown in:

```
static  void  AppInit_TCPIP (NET_ERR *perr)
{
    NET_IF_NBR    if_nbr;
    NET_IP_ADDR   ip;
    NET_IP_ADDR   msk;
    NET_IP_ADDR   gateway;
    NET_ERR       err_net;


    err_net = Net_Init();                                         (1)
    APP_TEST_FAULT(err_net, NET_ERR_NONE);

    if_nbr  = NetIF_Add((void    *)&NetIF_API_Ether,              (2)
                        (void    *)&NetDev_API_<controller>,      (3)
                        (void    *)&NetDev_BSP_<controller>,      (4)
                        (void    *)&NetDev_Cfg_<controller>,      (5)
                        (void    *)&NetPhy_API_Generic,           (6)
                        (void    *)&NetPhy_Cfg_<controller>,      (7)
                        (NET_ERR *)&err_net);                     (8)
    APP_TEST_FAULT(err_net, NET_ERR_NONE);


    NetIF_Start(if_nbr, perr);                                    (9)
    APP_TEST_FAULT(err_net, NET_IF_ERR_NONE);


    ip      = NetASCII_Str_to_IP((CPU_CHAR *)"10.10.1.65",        (10)
                                 (NET_ERR *)&err_net);
    msk     = NetASCII_Str_to_IP((CPU_CHAR *)"255.255.255.0",     (11)
                                 (NET_ERR *)&err_net);
    gateway = NetASCII_Str_to_IP((CPU_CHAR *)"10.10.1.1",         (12)
                                 (NET_ERR *)&err_net);


    NetIP_CfgAddrAdd(if_nbr, ip, msk, gateway, &err_net);         (13)
    APP_TEST_FAULT(err_net, NET_IP_ERR_NONE);


}
```

Listing 13-3 **AppInit_TCPIP()**

L13-3(1)   **Net_Init()** is the Network Protocol stack initialization function.

L13-3(2)   **NetIF_Add()** is a network interface function responsible for initializing a Network Device driver. The first parameter is the **address of** the Ethernet API function. **if_nbr** is the interface index number. The first interface is index number 1. If the loopback interface is configured it has interface index number 0.

L13-3(3)   The second parameter is the address of the device API function.

L13-3(4)   The third parameter is the address of the device BSP data structure.

L13-3(5)   The third parameter is the address of the device configuration data structure.

L13-3(6)   The fourth parameter is the address of the PHY API function

L13-3(7)   The fifth and last parameter is the address of the PHY configuration data structure.

L13-3(8)   The error code is used to validate the result of the function execution.

L13-3(9)   **NetIF_Start()** makes the network interface ready to receive and transmit.

L13-3(10)   Definition of the IP address to be used by the network interface. The **NetASCII_Str_to_IP()** converts the human readable address into a format required by the protocol stack. In this example the **10.10.1.65** address out of the 10.10.1.0 network with a subnet mask of **255.255.255.0** is used. To match different network, this address, the subnet mask and the default gateway IP address have to be customized.

L13-3(11)   Definition of the subnet mask to be used by the network interface. The **NetASCII_Str_to_IP()** converts the human readable subnet mask into the format required by the protocol stack.

L13-3(12)   Definition of the default gateway address to be used by the network interface. The **NetASCII_Str_to_IP()** converts the human readable default gateway address into the format required by the protocol stack.

L13-3(13)   **NetIP_CfgAddrAdd()** configures the network parameters (IP address, subnet mask and default gateway IP address) required for the interface. More than one set of network parameters can be configured per interface. Lines from (10) to (13) can be repeated for as many network parameter sets as need to be configured for an interface.

Once the source code is built and loaded into the target, the target will respond to ICMP Echo (ping) requests.

Network Interface Configuration

This chapter describes how to configure a network interface for µC/TCP-IP.

14-1 BUFFER MANAGEMENT

This section describe how µC/TCP-IP uses buffers to receive and transmit application data and network protocol control information. You should understand how network buffers are used by µC/TCP-IP to correctly configure your interface(s).

14-1-1 NETWORK BUFFERS

µC/TCP-IP stores transmitted and received data in data structures known as Network Buffers. Each Network Buffer consists of two parts: the Network Buffer header and the Network Buffer Data Area pointer. Network Buffer headers contain information about the data pointed to via the data area pointer. Data to be received or transmitted is stored in the Network Buffer Data Area.

µC/TCP-IP is designed with the inherent constraints of an embedded system in mind, the most important being the restricted RAM space. µC/TCP-IP defines network buffers for the Maximum Transmission Unit (MTU) of the Data Link technology used, which is most of the time Ethernet.

14-1-2 RECEIVE BUFFERS

Network Buffers used for reception for a Data Link technology are buffers that can hold one maximum frame size. Because it is impossible to predict how much data will be received, only large buffers can be configured. Even if the packet does not contain any payload, a large buffer must be used, as worst case must always be assumed.

14-1-3 TRANSMIT BUFFERS

On transmission, the number of bytes to transmit is always known, so it is possible to use a Network Buffer size smaller than the maximum frame size. µC/TCP-IP allows you to reduce the RAM usage of the system by defining small buffers. When the application does not require a full size frame to transmit, it is possible to use smaller Network Buffers. Depending on the configuration, up to eight pools of Network Buffer related objects may be created per network interface. Only four pools are shown below and the remaining pools are used for maintaining Network Buffer usage statistics for each of the pools shown.

In transmission, the situation is different. The TCP/IP stack knows how much data is being transmitted. In addition to RAM being limited in embedded systems, another feature is the small amount of data that needs to be transmitted. For example, in the case of sensor data to be transmitted periodically, a few hundred bytes every second can be transferred. In this case, a small buffer can be used and save RAM instead of waste a large transmit buffer. Another example is the transmission of TCP acknowledgment packets, especially when they are not carrying any data back to the transmitter. These packets are also small and do not require a large transmit buffer. RAM is also saved.

14-1-4 NETWORK BUFFER ARCHITECTURE

µC/TCP-IP uses both small and large network buffers:

■ Network buffers

■ Small transmit buffers

■ Large transmit buffers

■ Large receive buffers

A single network buffer is allocated for each small transmit, large transmit and large receive buffer. Network buffers contain the control information for the network packet data in the network buffer data area. Currently, network buffers consume approximately 200 bytes each. The network buffers' data areas are used to buffer the actual transmit and receive packet data. Each network buffer is connected to the data area via a pointer to the network buffer data area, and both move through the network protocol stack layers as a single entity. When the data area is no longer required, both the network buffer and the data area are freed. Figure 14-1 depicts the network buffer and data area objects.

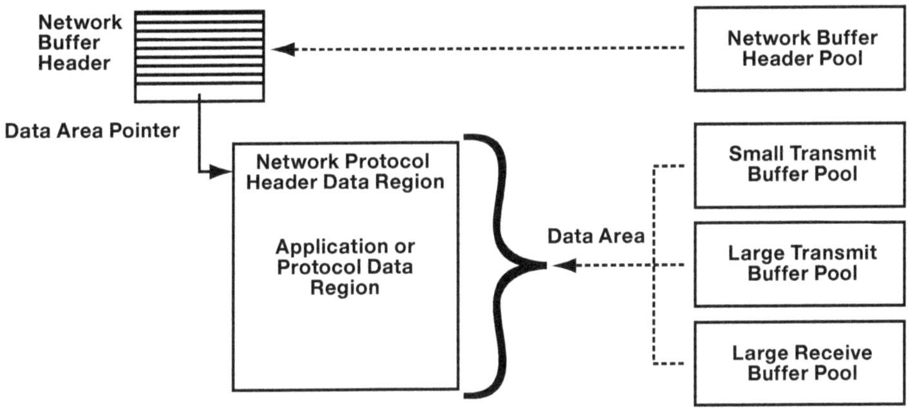

Figure 14-1 **Network Buffer Architecture**

All transmit data areas contain a small region of reserved space located at the top of the data area address space. The reserved space is used for network protocol header data and is currently fixed to 134 bytes in length. In general, not all of this space is required. However, the network protocol header region has been sized according to the maximum network protocol header usage for TCP/IP Ethernet packets.

µC/TCP-IP copies application-specified data from the application buffer into the application data region before writing network protocol header data to the protocol header region. Once the application data has been transferred into the network buffer data area by the highest required µC/TCP-IP layer, the network buffer descends through the remaining layers where additional protocol headers are added to the network protocol header data region.

14-1-5 NETWORK BUFFER SIZES

µC/TCP-IP requires that network buffer sizes configured in **net_dev_cfg.c** satisfy the minimum and maximum packet frame sizes of network interfaces/devices.

Assuming an Ethernet interface (with non-jumbo or VLAN-tagged frames), the minimum frame packet size is 64 bytes (including its 4-byte CRC). If an Ethernet frame is created such that the frame length is less than 60 bytes (before its 4-byte CRC is appended), frame padding must be appended by the network driver or the Ethernet network interface layer to the application data area to meet Ethernet's minimum packet size. For example, the ARP protocol typically creates packets of 42 bytes and therefore 18 bytes of padding must be added. The additional padding must fit within the network buffer's data area.

Ethernet's maximum transmit unit (MTU) size is 1500 bytes. When the TCP is used as the transport protocol, TCP and IP protocol header sizes are subtracted from Ethernet's 1500-byte MTU. A maximum of 1460 bytes of TCP application data may be sent in a full-sized Ethernet frame.

In addition, the variable size of network packet protocol headers must also be considered when configuring buffer sizes. The following computations demonstrate how to configure network buffer sizes to transmit and receive maximum sized network packets.

For transmit buffer size configuration, each layer's maximum header sizes must be assumed/included to achieve the maximum payload for each layer. The maximum header sizes for each layer are:

```
Max Ethernet header :   14 bytes   (this is a fixed size w/o CRC)
Max ARP header      :   28 bytes   (this is a fixed size for Ethernet/IPv4)
Max IP  header      :   60 bytes   (with maximum length IP  options)
Max TCP header      :   60 bytes   (with maximum length TCP options)
Max UDP header      :    8 bytes   (this is a fixed size)
```

Assuming both TCP and UDP are available as transport layer protocols, TCP's maximum header size is the value used as the maximum transport layer header size since it is greater than UDP's header size. Thus, the total maximum header size can then be computed as:

```
Max Hdr Size = Interface Max Header     (Ethernet hdr is 14 bytes)
             + Network    Max Header     (IP   max hdr is 60 bytes)
             + Transport  Max Header     (TCP  max hdr is 60 bytes)
             = 14 + 60 + 60 = 134 bytes
```

µC/TCP-IP configures **NET_BUF_DATA_PROTOCOL_HDR_SIZE_MAX** with this value in **net_cfg_net.h** to use as the starting data area index for transmit buffers' application data.

The next step is to define transmit buffers' total data area size. The issue is that we used the maximum header size for the transport and network layers. However, most of the time, the network and transport layer headers typically do not have any options:

```
Typical IP  header :  20 bytes  (without IP  options)
Typical TCP header :  20 bytes  (without TCP options)
```

These header values are used to determine the maximum payload a Data Link frame can carry. Since a TCP header is larger than UDP headers, the following compares the TCP maximum payload, also known as TCP's Maximum Segment Size (MSS), over an Ethernet data link:

```
TCP payload (max) = Interface Max         (Ethernet 1514 bytes w/o CRC)
                  - Interface Header       (Ethernet   14 bytes w/o CRC)
                  - Min IP  Header         (IP  min hdr is 20 bytes)
                  - Min TCP Header         (TCP min hdr is 20 bytes)
                  = 1514 - 14 - 20 - 20 = 1460 bytes
```

When TCP is used in a system, it is recommended to configure the large buffer size to at least this size in order to transmit maximum size TCP MSS:

```
TCP Max Buf Size = Max TCP payload        (1460 bytes)
                 + Max Hdr sizes          (134 bytes)
                 = 1460 + 134 = 1594 bytes
```

If any IP or TCP options are used, it is possible that the payload must be reduced, but unfortunately, that cannot be known by the application when transmitting. It is possible that, when the packet is at the network layer and because the TCP or IP headers are larger than usual because an option is enabled, a packet is too large and needs to be fragmented to be transmitted. However, µC/TCP-IP does not yet support fragmentation; but since options are seldom used and the standard header sizes for TCP and IP are the ones supported, this is generally not a problem.

For UDP, the UDP header has no options and the size does not change – it is always 8 bytes. Thus, UDP's maximum payload is calculated as follows:

```
UDP payload (max) = Interface Max        (Ethernet 1514 bytes w/o CRC)
                  - Interface Header     (Ethernet   14 bytes w/o CRC)
                  - Min IP  Header       (IP  min hdr is 20 bytes)
                  - Min UDP Header       (UDP     hdr is  8 bytes)
                  = 1514 - 14 - 20 - 8 = 1472 bytes
```

So to transmit maximum-sized UDP packets, configure large buffer sizes to at least:

```
Max UDP Buf Size = Max UDP payload        (1472 bytes)
                 + Max Hdr sizes          (134 bytes)
                 = 1472 + 134 = 1606 bytes
```

ICMP packets which are encapsulated within IP datagrams also have variable-length header sizes from 8 to 20 bytes. However, for certain design reasons, ICMP headers are included in an IP datagram's data area and are not included in the maximum header size calculation. (IGMP packets have a fixed header size of 8 bytes but are also included in an IP datagram's data area.) Thus, ICMP's maximum payload is calculated as follows:

```
ICMP payload (max) = Interface Max        (Ethernet 1514 bytes w/o CRC)
                   - Interface Header     (Ethernet   14 bytes w/o CRC)
                   - Min IP Header        (IP min hdr is 20 bytes)
                   = 1514 - 14 - 20 = 1480 bytes
```

And to transmit maximum-sized ICMP packets, configure large buffer sizes to at least:

```
Max ICMP Buf Size = Max ICMP payload       (1480 bytes)
                  + Max Hdr  sizes         (134 bytes)
                  = 1480 + 134 = 1614 bytes
```

Small transmit buffer sizes must also be appropriately configured to at least the minimum packet frame size for the network interface/device. This means configuring a buffer size that supports sending a minimum sized packet for each layer's minimum header sizes. The minimum header sizes for each layer are:

```
Min Ethernet header :  14 bytes  (this is a fixed size w/o CRC)
Min ARP header      :  28 bytes  (this is a fixed size for Ethernet/IPv4)
Min IP  header      :  20 bytes  (with minimum length IP  options)
Min TCP header      :  20 bytes  (with minimum length TCP options)
Min UDP header      :   8 bytes  (this is a fixed size)
```

For Ethernet frames, the following computation shows that both ARP packets and UDP/IP packets share the smallest minimum header sizes of 42 bytes:

```
ARP packet (min) = Interface Min Header    (Ethernet 14 bytes w/o CRC)
                 + ARP Min Header           (ARP  min hdr is 28 bytes)
                 = 14 + 28 = 42 bytes

UDP packet (min) = Interface Min Header    (Ethernet 14 bytes w/o CRC)
                 + IP  Min Header           (IP   min hdr is 20 bytes)
                 + UDP Min Header           (UDP  min hdr is  8 bytes)
                 = 14 + 20 + 8 = 42 bytes
```

And since Ethernet packets must be at least 60 bytes in length (not including 4-byte CRC), small transmit buffers must be minimally configured to at least 152 bytes to receive the smallest payload for each layer:

```
Min Tx Pkt Size = Interface Min Size      (Ethernet 60 bytes w/o CRC)
                + Max Hdr Sizes            (134 bytes)
                - Min Pkt Size             (42 bytes)
                = 60 + 134 - 42 = 152 bytes
```

Figure 14-2 shows transmit buffers with reserved space of 134 bytes/octets for the maximum protocol header sizes, application data sizes from 0 to 1472 bytes/octets, and the valid range of configured buffer data area sizes for Ethernet of 152 to 1614 bytes/octets.

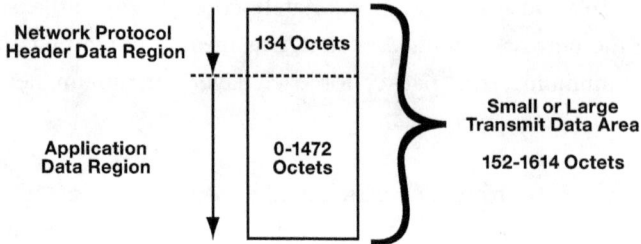

Figure 14-2 **Transmit Buffer Data Areas**

Note that the application data size range plus the maximum header sizes of 134 bytes do not exactly add up to the small or large transmit data area configuration total. This is due to certain protocols (e.g., ICMP) whose protocol headers are not included in the typical network protocol header region but start at index 134. Also note that if no small transmit buffer data areas are available, a data area from the large transmit data area pool is allocated if both small and large transmit data areas are configured.

µC/TCP-IP does *not* require receive buffer data areas to reserve space for maximum header sizes but *does* require that each receive buffer data area be configured to the maximum expected packet frame size for the network interface/device. For Ethernet interfaces, receive buffers must be configured to at least 1514 bytes, assuming the interface's Ethernet device is configured to discard and not buffer the packet's 4-byte CRC, or 1518 bytes, if the device does buffer the CRC. Although network buffers may require additional bytes to properly align each buffer, µC/TCP-IP creates the buffers with the appropriate alignment specified in **net_dev_cfg.c** so no additional bytes need be added to the receive buffer size.

14-2 µC/TCP-IP NETWORK INTERFACE CONFIGURATION

All µC/TCP-IP device drivers require a configuration structure for each device that must be compiled into your driver. You must place all device configuration structures and declarations within a pair of files named **net_dev_cfg.c** and **net_dev_cfg.h**.

Micrium provides sample configuration code free of charge; however, most sample code will likely require modification depending on the combination of compiler, processor, evaluation board, and device hardware used.

14-2-1 MEMORY CONFIGURATION

The first step in creating a device driver configuration for µC/TCP-IP begins with the memory configuration structure. This section describes the memory configuration settings for most device drivers, and should provide you an in-depth understanding of memory configuration. You will also discover which settings to modify in order to enhance the performances of the driver.

Listing 14-1 shows a sample memory configuration structure.

```
const  NET_DEV_CFG  NetDev_Cfg_Dev1 = {
    NET_IF_MEM_TYPE_MAIN, /* Desired receive buffer memory pool type :              */ (1)
                          /* NET_IF_MEM_TYPE_MAIN bufs alloc'd from main memory     */
                          /* NET_IF_MEM_TYPE_DEDICATED bufs alloc'd from dedicated memory */
    1518u,                /* Desired size of device's large receive buffers (in octets)  */ (2)
    9u,                   /* Desired number of device's large receive buffers      */ (3)
    16u,                  /* Desired alignment of device's receive buffers (in octets)  */ (4)
    0u,                   /* Desired offset from base receive index (in octets)    */ (5)
    NET_IF_MEM_TYPE_MAIN, /* Desired transmit buffer memory pool type:             */ (6)
                          /* NET_IF_MEM_TYPE_MAIN buffers allocated from main memory */
                          /* NET_IF_MEM_TYPE_DEDICATED buffers allocated from (device's) */
    1606u,                /* Desired size of device's large transmit buffers (in octets) */ (7)
    4u,                   /* Desired number of device's large transmit buffers     */ (8)
    256u,                 /* Desired size of device's small transmit buffers (in octets) */ (9)
    2u,                   /* Desired number of device's small transmit buffers     */ (10)
    16u,                  /* Desired alignment of device's transmit buffers (in octets)  */ (11)
    0u,                   /* Desired offset from base transmit index (in octets)   */ (12)
    0x00000000u,          /* Base address of dedicated memory                      */ (13)
    0u,                   /* Size of dedicated memory (in octets).                 */ (14)
    NET_DEV_CFG_FLAG_NONE, /* Desired option flags                                 */ (15)
};
```

Listing 14-1 **Sample memory configuration**

L14-1(1)   .RxBufPoolType specifies the memory location for the receive data buffers. Buffers may located either in main memory or in a dedicated memory region. This setting is used by the IF layer to initialize the Rx memory pool. This field must be set to one of two macros: **NET_IF_MEM_TYPE_MAIN** or **NET_IF_MEM_TYPE_DEDICATED**. You may want to set this field when DMA with dedicated memory is used. It is possible that you might have to store descriptors within the dedicated memory if your device requires it.

L14-1(2)   **.RxBufLargeSize** specifies the size of all receive buffers. Specifying a value is required. The buffer length is set to 1518 bytes which corresponds to the Maximum Transmission Unit (MTU) of an Ethernet network. For DMA-based Ethernet controllers, you must set the receive data buffer size to be greater or equal to the size of the largest receivable frame. If the size of the total buffer allocation is greater than the amount of available memory in the chosen memory region, a run-time error will be generated when the device is initialized.

L14-1(3)   **.RxBufLargeNbr** specifies the number of receive buffers that will be allocated to the device. There should be at least one receive buffer allocated, and it is recommended to have at least ten receive buffers. The optimal number of receive buffers depends on your application.

L14-1(4)   **.RxBufAlignOctets** specifies the required alignment of the receive buffers, in bytes. Some devices require that the receive buffers be aligned to a specific byte boundary. Additionally, some processor architectures do not allow multi-byte reads and writes across word boundaries and therefore may require buffer alignment. In general, it is probably a best practice to align buffers to the data bus width of the processor, which may improve performance. For example, a 32-bit processor may benefit from having buffers aligned on a four-byte boundary.

L14-1(5)   **.RxBufIxOffset** specifies the receive buffer offset in bytes. Most devices receive packets starting at base index zero in the network buffer data areas. However, some devices may buffer additional bytes prior to the actual received Ethernet packet. This setting configures an offset to ignore these additional bytes. If a device does not buffer any additional bytes ahead of the received Ethernet packet, then an offset of 0 must be specified. However, if a device does buffer additional bytes ahead of the received Ethernet packet, then you should configure this offset with the number of additional bytes. Also, the receive buffer size must also be adjusted by the number of additional bytes.

L14-1(6)   **.TxBufPoolType** specifies the memory placement of the transmit data buffers. Buffers may be placed either in main memory or in a dedicated memory region. This field is used by the IF layer, and it should be set to one of two macros: **NET_IF_MEM_TYPE_MAIN** or **NET_IF_MEM_TYPE_DEDICATED**. When DMA descriptors are used, they may be stored into the dedicated memory.

L14-1(7)   **.TxBufLargeSize** specifies the size of the large transmit buffers in bytes. This field has no effect if the number of large transmit buffers is configured to zero. Setting the size of the large transmit buffers below 1594 bytes may hinder the µC/TCP-IP module's ability to transmit full sized IP datagrams since IP transmit fragmentation is not yet supported. We recommend setting this field between 1594 and 1614 bytes in order to accommodate the maximum transmit packet sizes all µC/TCP-IP's protocols.

You can optimize the transmit buffer if you know in advance what will be the maximum size of the packets the user will want to transmit through the device.

L14-1(8)   **.TxBufLargeNbr** specifies the number of large transmit buffers allocated to the device. You may set this field to zero to make room for additional small transmit buffers, however, the size of the maximum transmittable packet will then depend on the size of the small transmit buffers.

L14-1(9)   **.TxBufSmallSize** specifies the small transmit buffer size. For devices with a minimal amount of RAM, it is possible to allocate small transmit buffers as well as large transmit buffers. In general, we recommend a 152 byte small transmit buffer size, however, you may adjust this value according to the application requirements. This field has no effect if the number of small transmit buffers is configured to zero.

L14-1(10)   **.TxBufSmallNbr** specifies the numbers of small transmit buffers. This field controls the number of small transmit buffers allocated to the device. You may set this field to zero to make room for additional large transmit buffers if required.

L14-1(11)   **.TxBufAlignOctets** specifies the transmit buffer alignment in bytes. Some devices require that the transmit buffers be aligned to a specific byte boundary. Additionally, some processor architectures do not allow multi-byte reads and writes across word boundaries and therefore may require buffer alignment. In general, it probably a best practice to align buffers to the data bus width of the processor which may improve performance. For example, a 32-bit processor may benefit from having buffers aligned on a four-byte boundary.

L14-1(12)   **.TxBufIxOffset** specifies the transmit buffer offset in bytes. Most devices only need to transmit the actual Ethernet packets as prepared by the higher network layers. However, some devices may need to transmit additional bytes prior to the actual Ethernet packet. This setting configures an offset to prepare space for these additional bytes. If a device does not transmit any additional bytes ahead of the Ethernet packet, the default offset of zero should be configured. However, if a device does transmit additional bytes ahead of the Ethernet packet then configure this offset with the number of additional bytes. Also, the transmit buffer size must be adjusted by the number of additional bytes.

L14-1(13)   **.MemAddr** specifies the starting address of the dedicated memory region for devices with such memory. For devices with non-dedicated memory, you can initialize this field to zero. You may use this setting to put DMA descriptors into the dedicated memory.

L14-1(14)   **.MemSize** specifies the size of the dedicated memory region in bytes for devices with such memory. For devices with non-dedicated memory, you can initialize this field to zero. You may use this setting to put DMA descriptors into the dedicated memory.

L14-1(15)   **.Flags** specify the optional configuration flags. Configure (optional) device features by logically OR'ing bit-field flags:

NET_DEV_CFG_FLAG_NONE	No device configuration flags selected.
NET_DEV_CFG_FLAG_SWAP_OCTETS	Swap data bytes (i.e., swap data words' high-order bytes with data words' low-order bytes, and vice-versa) if required by device-to-CPU data bus wiring and/or CPU endian word order.

14-2-2 µC/TCP-IP MEMORY MANAGEMENT

Memory is allocated to µC/TCP-IP device drivers through the µC/LIB memory module. You must enable and configure the size of the µC/LIB memory heap available to the system. The following configuration constants should be defined from within **app_cfg.h** and set to match the application requirements.

```
#define LIB_MEM_CFG_ALLOC_EN       DEF_ENABLED
#define LIB_MEM_CFG_HEAP_SIZE         58000
```

The heap size is specified in bytes. If the heap size is not configured large enough, an error will be returned during the Network Protocol Stack initialization, or during interface addition.

Since the needed heap size is related to the stack configuration (**net_cfg.h**) and is specific to each device driver, it's not possible to provide an exact formula to calculate it. Thus to optimize the heap size, you should try different heap size until no error is returned for all interfaces added.

Note: The memory module *must* be initialized by the application by calling **Mem_Init()** *prior* to calling **Net_Init()**. We recommend initializing the memory module before calling **OSStart()**, or near the top of the startup task.

14-3 ETHERNET INTERFACE CONFIGURATION

14-3-1 ETHERNET DEVICE CONFIGURATION

Listing 14-2 shows a sample Ethernet configuration structure for Ethernet devices.

```
const  NET_DEV_CFG_ETHER  NetDev_Cfg_Dev1_0 = {
    NET_IF_MEM_TYPE_MAIN, /* Desired receive buffer memory pool type :            */ (1)
                          /* NET_IF_MEM_TYPE_MAIN bufs alloc'd from main memory   */
                          /* NET_IF_MEM_TYPE_DEDICATED bufs alloc'd from dedicated memory */
        1520u,            /* Desired size of device's large receive buffers (in octets) */
           9u,            /* Desired number of device's large receive buffers    */
          16u,            /* Desired alignment of device's receive buffers (in octets) */
           0u,            /* Desired offset from base receive index (in octets)  */
    NET_IF_MEM_TYPE_MAIN, /* Desired transmit buffer memory pool type:           */
                          /* NET_IF_MEM_TYPE_MAIN buffers allocated from main memory */
                          /* NET_IF_MEM_TYPE_DEDICATED buffers allocated from (device's) */
        1606u,            /* Desired size of device's large transmit buffers (in octets) */
           4u,            /* Desired number of device's large transmit buffers   */
         256u,            /* Desired size of device's small transmit buffers (in octets) */
           2u,            /* Desired number of device's small transmit buffers   */
          16u,            /* Desired alignment of device's transmit buffers (in octets) */
           0u,            /* Desired offset from base transmit index (in octets) */
    0x00000000u,          /* Base address of dedicated memory                    */
           0u,            /* Size  of dedicated memory (in octets).              */
    NET_DEV_CFG_FLAG_NONE,/* Desired option flags                                */
           4u,            /* Desired number of device's receive descriptors.     */ (2)
           4u,            /* Desired number of device's transmit descriptors.    */ (3)
    0x40028000u,          /* Base address of device's hardware/registers.        */ (4)
           0u,            /* Size  of device's data bus (in bits)                */ (5)
    "00:50:C2:25:61:00",  /* Desired device hw address; may be NULL address or string ... */ (6)
                          /* ... if device hw address configured or set at run-time.    */
};
```

Listing 14-2 **Memory configuration for Ethernet device**

L14-2(1)   Memory configuration of the Ethernet Device. See "Memory Configuration" on page 311 for further information about how to configure the memory of your Ethernet interface.

L14-2(2)   .RxDescNbr specifies the number of receive descriptors. For DMA-based devices, this value is used by the device driver during initialization in order to allocate a fixed-size pool of receive descriptors to be used by the device. The number of descriptors must be less than the number of configured receive buffers. We recommend setting this value to something within 40% and 70% of the number of receive buffers. Non-DMA based devices may configure this value to zero. You must use this setting with DMA based devices and he must set at least two descriptors. The Device driver could

L14-2(3)   **.TxDescNbr** specifies the number of transmit descriptors. For DMA based devices, this value is used by the device driver during initialization to allocate a fixed size pool of transmit descriptors to be used by the device. For best performance, the number of transmit descriptors it's recommended to set equal to the number of small, plus the number of large transmit buffers configured for the device. Non-DMA based devices may configure this value to zero. You must use this setting with DAM based devices and must set at least two descriptors.

L14-2(4)   **.BaseAddr** specifies the base address of device's hard ware/registers.

L14-2(5)   **.DataBusSizeNbrBits** specifies the size of device's data bus (in bits), if available.

L14-2(6)   **.HW_AddrStr** specifies the desired device hardware address; may be NULL address or string if the device hardware address is configured or set at run-time.

14-3-2 ETHERNET PHY CONFIGURATION

Listing 14-3 shows a typical Ethernet PHY configuration structure.

```
NET_PHY_CFG_ETHER NetPhy_Cfg_FEC_0= {
    NET_PHY_ADDR_AUTO,              (1)
    NET_PHY_BUS_MODE_MII,          (2)
    NET_PHY_TYPE_EXT               (3)
    NET_PHY_SPD_AUTO,              (4)
    NET_PHY_DUPLEX_AUTO,          (5)
};
```

Listing 14-3 **Sample Ethernet PHY Configuration**

L14-3(1)   PHY Address. This field represents the address of the PHY on the (R)MII bus. The value configured depends on the PHY and the state of the PHY pins during power-up. Developers may need to consult the schematics for their board to determine the configured PHY address. Alternatively, the PHY address may be detected automatically by specifying **NET_PHY_ADDR_AUTO**; however, this will increase the initialization latency of μC/TCP-IP and possibly the rest of the application depending on where the application places the call to **NetIF_Start()**.

L14-3(2)   PHY bus mode. This value should be set to one of the following values depending on the hardware capabilities and schematics of the development board. The network device BSP should configure the Phy-level hardware based on this configuration value.

```
NET_PHY_BUS_MODE_MII
NET_PHY_BUS_MODE_RMII
NET_PHY_BUS_MODE_SMII
```

L14-3(3)   PHY bus type. This field represents the type of electrical attachment of the PHY to the Ethernet controller. In some cases, the PHY may be internal to the network controller, while in other cases, it may be attached via an external MII or RMII bus. It is desirable to specify which attachment method is in use so that a device driver can initialize additional hardware resources if an external PHY is attached to a device that also has an internal PHY. Available settings for this field are:

```
NET_PHY_TYPE_INT
NET_PHY_TYPE_EXT
```

L14-3(4)   Initial PHY link speed. This configuration setting will force the PHY to link to the specified link speed. Optionally, auto-negotiation may be enabled. This field must be set to one of the following values:

```
NET_PHY_SPD_AUTO
NET_PHY_SPD_10
NET_PHY_SPD_100
NET_PHY_SPD_1000
```

L14-3(5)   Initial PHY link duplex. This configuration setting will force the PHY to link using the specified duplex. This setting must be set to one of the following values:

```
NET_PHY_DUPLEX_AUTO
NET_PHY_DUPLEX_HALF
NET_PHY_DUPLEX_FULL
```

14-3-3 ADDING AN ETHERNET INTERFACE

Once µC/TCP-IP is initialized, each network interface must be added to the stack via **NetIF_Add()** function. **NetIF_Add()** validates the network interface arguments, initializes the interface, and adds it to the interface list of the TCP/IP stack. µC/TCP-IP uses API functions to access the interface layer, and configuration structures are used to initialize resources needed by the network interface. You must pass the following arguments to the **NetIF_Add()** function:

```
NET_IF_NBR  NetIF_Add (void     *if_api,          (1)
                       void     *dev_api,         (2)
                       void     *dev_bsp,         (3)
                       void     *dev_cfg,         (4)
                       void     *ext_api,         (5)
                       void     *ext_cfg,         (6)
                       NET_ERR  *perr)            (7)
```

Listing 14-4 **NetIF_Add() arguments**

L14-4(1)   The first argument specifies the link layer API that will receive data from the hardware device. For an Ethernet interface, this value will always be defined as **NetIF_API_Ether**. This symbol is defined by µC/TCP-IP and it can be used to add as many Ethernet network interface's as necessary. This API should always be provided with the TCP-IP stack which can be find under the interface folder (**/IF/net_if_ether.***).

L14-4(2)   The second argument represents the hardware device driver API which is defined as a fixed structure of function pointers of the type specified by Micrium for use with µC/TCP-IP. If Micrium supplies the device driver, the symbol name of the device API will be defined within the device driver at the top of the device driver source code file. You can find the device driver under the device folder (/Dev/Ether/<controller>). Otherwise, the driver developer is responsible for creating the device driver and the API structure should start from the device driver template which can be find under the device folder (/Dev/Ether/Template).

L14-4(3)   The third argument specifies the specific device's board-specific (BSP) interface functions which is defined as a fixed structure of function pointers. The application developer must define both the BSP interface structure of function pointers and the actual BSP functions referenced by the BSP interface structure and should start from the BSP template provided with the stack which you can find under the BSP folder (/BSP/Template). Micrium may be able to supply example BSP interface structures and functions for certain evaluation boards. For more information about declaring BSP interface structures and BSP functions device, see Chapter 15, "Network Board Support Package" on page 347 for further information about the BSP API.

L14-4(4)   The fourth argument specifies the device driver configuration structure that will be used to configure the device hardware for the interface being added. The device configuration structure format has been specified by Micrium and must be provided by the application developer since it is specific to the selection of device hardware and design of the evaluation board. Micrium may be able to supply example device configuration structures for certain evaluation boards. For more information about declaring a device configuration structure, See "Ethernet Device Configuration" on page 316.

L14-4(5)   The fifth argument represents the physical layer hardware device API. In most cases, when Ethernet is the link layer API specified in the first argument, the physical layer API may be defined as **NetPHY_API_Generic**. This symbol has been defined by the generic Ethernet physical layer device driver which can be supplied by Micrium. If a custom physical layer device driver is required, then the developer would be responsible for creating the API structure. Often Ethernet devices have built-in physical layer devices which are *not* (R)MII compliant. In this circumstance, the physical layer device driver API field may be left NULL and the Ethernet device driver may implement routines for the built-in PHY.

L14-4(6)   The sixth argument represents the physical layer hardware device configuration structure. This structure is specified by the application developer and contains such information as the physical device connection type, address, and desired link state upon initialization. For devices with built in non (R)MII compliant physical layer devices, this field may be left **NULL**. However, it may be convenient to declare a physical layer device configuration structure and use some of the members for physical layer device initialization from within the Ethernet device driver. For more information about declaring a physical layer hardware configuration structure, see Chapter 14, "Ethernet PHY Configuration" on page 317.

L14-4(7)   The last argument is a pointer to a **NET_ERR** variable that contains the return error code for **NetIF_Add()**. This variable should be checked by the application to ensure that no errors have occurred during network interface addition. Upon success, the return error code will be **NET_IF_ERR_NONE**.

Note: If an error occurs during the call to **NetIF_Add()**, the application *may* attempt to call **NetIF_Add()** a second time for the same interface but unless a temporary hardware fault occured, the application developer should observe the error code, determine and resolve the cause of the error, rebuild the application and try again. If a hardware failure occurred, the application may attempt to add an interface as many times as necessary, but a common problem to watch for is a µC/LIB Memory Manager heap out-of-memory condition. This may occur when adding network interfaces if there is insufficient memory to complete the operation. If this error occurs, the configured size of the µC/LIB heap within **app_cfg.h** must be increased.

Once an interface is added successfully, the next step is to configure the interface with one or more network layer protocol addresses.

For a thorough description of the µC/TCP-IP files and directory structure, see Chapter 12, "Directories and Files" on page 267.

When the network interface is added without error, it must be started via **NetIF_Start()** function to be available and be used by the µC/TCP-IP. The following code example shows how to initialize µC/TCP-IP, add an interface, configure the IP address and start it:

14

```
#include  <net.h>
#include  <net_dev_dev1.h>
#include  <net_bsp.h>
#include  <net_phy.h>


void  App_InitTCPIP (void)
{
    NET_IF_NBR    if_nbr;
    NET_IP_ADDR  ip;
    NET_IP_ADDR  msk;
    NET_IP_ADDR  gateway;
    CPU_BOOLEAN  cfg_success;
    NET_ERR      err;


    err = Net_Init();
    if (err != NET_ERR_NONE) {
        return;
    }

    if_nbr  = NetIF_Add((void    *)&NetIF_API_Ether
                        (void    *)&NetDev_API_Etherxxx,
                        (void    *)&NetDev_BSP_API,
                        (void    *)&NetDev_Cfg_Ether_0,
                        (void    *)&NetPhy_API_Generic,
                        (void    *)&NetPhy_Cfg_0,
                        (NET_ERR *)&err);
    if (err != NET_IF_ERR_NONE) {
        return;
    }

    ip      = NetASCII_Str_to_IP((CPU_CHAR *)"192.168.1.65",  perr);
    msk     = NetASCII_Str_to_IP((CPU_CHAR *)"255.255.255.0", perr);
    gateway = NetASCII_Str_to_IP((CPU_CHAR *)"192.168.1.1",   perr);

    cfg_success = NetIP_CfgAddrAdd(if_nbr, ip, msk, gateway,  perr);
    (void)&cfg_success;

    NetIF_Start(if_nbr, &err);
    if (err != NET_IF_ERR_NONE) {
        return;
    }
}
```

Listing 14-5 **Ethernet interface initialization example**

14-4 WIRELESS INTERFACE CONFIGURATION

14-4-1 WIRELESS DEVICE CONFIGURATION

Listing 14-6 shows a sample wireless configuration structure for wireless devices.

```
const  NET_DEV_CFG_WIFI  NetDev_Cfg_WiFi_0 = {
    NET_IF_MEM_TYPE_MAIN, /* Desired receive buffer memory pool type :                */ (1)
                          /* NET_IF_MEM_TYPE_MAIN bufs alloc'd from main memory       */
                          /* NET_IF_MEM_TYPE_DEDICATED bufs alloc'd from dedicated memory */
    1520u,                /* Desired size of device's large receive buffers (in octets)  */
    3u,                   /* Desired number of device's large receive buffers         */
    16u,                  /* Desired alignment of device's receive buffers (in octets)  */
    0u,                   /* Desired offset from base receive index (in octets)       */
    NET_IF_MEM_TYPE_MAIN, /* Desired transmit buffer memory pool type:                */
                          /* NET_IF_MEM_TYPE_MAIN buffers allocated from main memory  */
                          /* NET_IF_MEM_TYPE_DEDICATED buffers allocated from (device's) */
    1606u,                /* Desired size of device's large transmit buffers (in octets) */
    2u,                   /* Desired number of device's large transmit buffers        */
    256u,                 /* Desired size of device's small transmit buffers (in octets) */
    1u,                   /* Desired number of device's small transmit buffers        */
    16u,                  /* Desired alignment of device's transmit buffers (in octets)  */
    0u,                   /* Desired offset from base transmit index (in octets)      */
    0x00000000u,          /* Base address of dedicated memory                         */
           0u,            /* Size  of dedicated memory (in octets).                   */

    NET_DEV_CFG_FLAG_NONE,  /* Desired option flags                                   */
    NET_DEV_BAND_DUAL,      /* Desired wireless band.                                 */ (2)
                          /*   NET_DEV_BAND_2_4_GHZ     2.4        Ghz.               */
                          /*   NET_DEV_BAND_5_0_GHZ     5.0        Ghz.               */
                          /*   NET_DEV_BAND_DUAL        2.4 and 5.0 Ghz.             */
    25000000L,            /* Desired device's SPI Clock frequency (in Hertz).         */ (3)

    NET_DEV_SPI_CLK_POL_INACTIVE_HIGH,  /* Desired SPI Clock polarity.                */ (4)
                          /*   NET_DEV_SPI_CLK_POL_INACTIVE_LOW  low  when inactive.  */
                          /*   NET_DEV_SPI_CLK_POL_INACTIVE_HIGH high when inactive.  */
                          /* SPI Clock phase:                                         */
    NET_DEV_SPI_CLK_PHASE_FALLING_EDGE, /* Desired SPI Clock Phase.                   */ (5)
                          /*   NET_DEV_SPI_CLK_PHASE_FALLING_EDGE Data on failling edge. */
                          /*   NET_DEV_SPI_CLK_PHASE_RASING_EDGE  Data on rasing  edge. */
```

```
    NET_DEV_SPI_XFER_UNIT_LEN_8_BITS,    /* Desired SPI transfer length:                */ (6)
                            /*    NET_DEV_SPI_XFER_UNIT_LEN_8_BITS     Unit length of  8 bits. */
                            /*    NET_DEV_SPI_XFER_UNIT_LEN_16_BITS    Unit length of 16 bits. */
                            /*    NET_DEV_SPI_XFER_UNIT_LEN_32_BITS    Unit length of 32 bits. */
                            /*    NET_DEV_SPI_XFER_UNIT_LEN_64_BITS    Unit length of 64 bits. */

    NET_DEV_SPI_XFER_SHIFT_DIR_FIRST_MSB, /* Desired SPI shift direction:                */ (7)
                            /*    NET_DEV_SPI_XFER_SHIFT_DIR_FIRST_MSB   Transfer MSB first. */
                            /*    NET_DEV_SPI_XFER_SHIFT_DIR_FIRST_LSB   Transfer LSB first. */
     "00:50:C2:25:60:02",   /* Desired device hw address; may be NULL address or string ... */ (8)
                            /* ... if device hw address configured or set at run-time.       */
};
```

Listing 14-6 **Wireless device memory configuration**

L14-6(1)   Memory configuration of the wireless device. See "Memory Configuration" on page 311 for further information about how to configure the memory of your wireless interface.

L14-6(2)   **.Band** specifies the desired wireless band enabled and used by the wireless device. The network device driver should configure the wireless band based on this configuration value.

NET_DEV_BAND_2_4_GHZ
NET_DEV_BAND_5_0_GHZ
NET_DEV_BAND_DUAL

L14-6(3)   **.SPI_ClkFreq** specifies the SPI controller's clock frequency (in Hertz) configuration for writing and reading on the wireless device.

L14-6(4)   **.SPI_ClkPol** specifies the SPI controller's clock polarity configuration for writing and reading on the wireless device. The network device BSP should configure the SPI controller's clock polarity based on this configuration value.

NET_DEV_SPI_CLK_POL_INACTIVE_LOW
NET_DEV_SPI_CLK_POL_INACTIVE_HIGH

L14-6(5)   **.SPI_ClkPhase** specifies the SPI controller's clock phase configuration for writing and reading on the wireless device. The network device BSP should configure the SPI controller's clock phase based on this configuration value.

```
NET_DEV_SPI_CLK_PHASE_FALLING_EDGE
NET_DEV_SPI_CLK_PHASE_RAISING_EDGE
```

L14-6(6)   **.SPI_XferUnitLen** specifies the SPI controller's transfer unit length configuration for writing and reading on the wireless device. The network device BSP should configure the SPI controller's transfer unit length based on this configuration value.

```
NET_DEV_SPI_XFER_UNIT_LEN_8_BITS
NET_DEV_SPI_XFER_UNIT_LEN_16_BITS
NET_DEV_SPI_XFER_UNIT_LEN_32_BITS
NET_DEV_SPI_XFER_UNIT_LEN_64_BITS
```

L14-6(7)   **.SPI_XferShiftDir** specifies the SPI controller's shift direction configuration for writing and reading on the wireless device. The network device BSP should configure the SPI controller's transfer unit length based on this configuration value.

```
NET_DEV_SPI_XFER_SHIFT_DIR_FIRST_MSB
NET_DEV_SPI_XFER_SHIFT_DIR_FIRST_LSB
```

L14-6(8)   **.HW_AddrStr** specifies the desired device hardware address; may be NULL address or string if the device hardware address is configured or set at run-time.

14-4-2 ADDING A WIRELESS INTERFACE

Once μC/TCP-IP is initialized each network interface must be added to the stack via **NetIF_Add()** function which validates the network interface arguments, initializes the interface and adds it to the interface list. μC/TCP-IP uses API functions to access the interface layer and configuration structures are used to initialize resources needed by the network interface. You must pass the following arguments to the **NetIF_Add()** function:

```
NET_IF_NBR  NetIF_Add (void `   *if_api,              (1)
                       void     *dev_api,             (2)
                       void     *dev_bsp,             (3)
                       void     *dev_cfg,             (4)
                       void     *ext_api,             (5)
                       void     *ext_cfg,             (6)
                       NET_ERR  *perr)                (7)
```

Listing 14-7 **NetIF_Add() arguments**

L14-7(1)   The first argument specifies the link layer API that will receive data from the hardware device. For an wireless interface, this value will always be defined as **NetIF_API_WiFi**. This symbol is defined by μC/TCP-IP and it can be used to add as many wireless network interfaces as necessary. This API should always be provided with the TCP-IP stack which can be find under the interface folder (**/IF/net_if_wifi.***).

L14-7(2)   The second argument represents the hardware device driver API which is defined as a fixed structure of function pointers of the type specified by Micrium for use with μC/TCP-IP. If Micrium supplies the device driver, the symbol name of the device API will be defined within the device driver at the top of the device driver source code file. You can find the device driver under the device folder (**/Dev/WiFi/<device>**). Otherwise, the driver developer is responsible for creating the device driver and the API structure should start from the device driver template which can be find under the device folder (**/Dev/WiFi/Template**).

L14-7(3)   The third argument specifies the specific device's board-specific (BSP) interface functions which is defined as a fixed structure of function pointers. The application developer must define both the BSP interface structure of function pointers and the actual BSP functions referenced by the BSP interface structure and should start from the BSP template provided with the stack which you can find under the BSP folder (**/BSP/Template**). Micrium may be able to supply example BSP interface structures and functions for certain evaluation boards. For more information about declaring BSP interface structures and BSP functions device, see Chapter 15, "Network Board Support Package" on page 347 for further information about the BSP API.

L14-7(4)   The fourth argument specifies the device driver configuration structure that will be used to configure the device hardware for the interface being added. The device configuration structure format has been specified by Micrium and must be provided by the application developer since it is specific to the selection of device hardware and design of the evaluation board. Micrium may be able to supply example device configuration structures for certain evaluation boards. For more information about declaring a device configuration structure, See "Wireless Device Configuration" on page 323

L14-7(5)   The fifth argument represents the extension layer device API. In most cases, when wireless is the Wireless Manager layer API specified in the first argument, the Wireless Manager layer API may be defined as **NetWiFiMgr_API_Generic**. This symbol has been defined by the generic Wireless Manager layer which can be supplied by Micrium. If a custom Wireless Manager layer is required, then the developer would be responsible for creating the API structure.

L14-7(6)   The sixth argument represents the extension layer configuration structure. This structure is specified by the application developer. For devices which uses the generic Wireless Manager this field should be left **NULL**. However, it may be convenient to declare a Wireless Manager layer device configuration structure and use some of the members for Wireless Manager layer initialization from within the wireless device driver or a custom Wireless Manager.

L14-7(7)   The last argument is a pointer to a NET_ERR variable that contains the return error code for NetIF_Add(). This variable *should* be checked by the application to ensure that no errors have occurred during network interface addition. Upon success, the return error code will be NET_IF_ERR_NONE.

Note: If an error occurs during the call to NetIF_Add(), the application *may* attempt to call NetIF_Add() a second time for the same interface but unless a temporary hardware fault occured, the application developer should observe the error code, determine and resolve the cause of the error, rebuild the application and try again. If a hardware failure occurred, the application may attempt to add an interface as many times as necessary, but a common problem to watch for is a μC/LIB Memory Manager heap out-of-memory condition. This may occur when adding network interfaces if there is insufficient memory to complete the operation. If this error occurs, the configured size of the μC/LIB heap within app_cfg.h must be increased.

Once an interface is added successfully, the next step is to configure the interface with one or more network layer protocol addresses.

For a thorough description of the μC/TCP-IP files and directory structure, see Chapter 12, "Directories and Files" on page 267.

Once a network interface is added without error, it must be started via NetIF_Start() function to be see as available and to be use by the μC/TCP-IP. The following code example shows how to initialize μC/TCP-IP, add an interface, add an IP address and start the interface:

```
#include  <net.h>
#include  <net_dev_rs9110n2x.h>
#include  <net_bsp.h>
#include  <net_phy.h>


void  App_InitTCPIP (void)
{
    NET_IF_NBR    if_nbr;
    NET_IP_ADDR   ip;
    NET_IP_ADDR   msk;
    NET_IP_ADDR   gateway;
    CPU_BOOLEAN   cfg_success;
    NET_ERR       err;


    err = Net_Init();
    if (err != NET_ERR_NONE) {
        return;
    }

    if_nbr  = NetIF_Add((void    *)&NetIF_API_WiFi
                        (void    *)&NetDev_API_RS9110N2x,
                        (void    *)&NetDev_BSP_SPI_API,
                        (void    *)&NetDev_Cfg_WiFi_0,
                        (void    *)&NetWiFiMgr_API_Generic,
                        (void    *) 0,
                        (NET_ERR *)&err);
    if (err != NET_IF_ERR_NONE) {
        return;
    }

    ip      = NetASCII_Str_to_IP((CPU_CHAR *)"192.168.1.65",  perr);
    msk     = NetASCII_Str_to_IP((CPU_CHAR *)"255.255.255.0", perr);
    gateway = NetASCII_Str_to_IP((CPU_CHAR *)"192.168.1.1",   perr);

    cfg_success = NetIP_CfgAddrAdd(if_nbr, ip, msk, gateway,  perr);
    (void)&cfg_success;

    NetIF_Start(if_nbr, &err);
    if (err != NET_IF_ERR_NONE) {
        return;
    }
}
```

Listing 14-8 **Wireless interface initialization example**

14-5 LOOPBACK INTERFACE CONFIGURATION

14-5-1 LOOPBACK CONFIGURATION

Configuring the loopback interface requires only a memory configuration, as described in section 14-2-1 on page 311.

Listing 14-9 shows a sample configuration structure for the loopback interface.

```
const  NET_IF_CFG_LOOPBACK  NetIF_Cfg_Loopback = {

        NET_IF_MEM_TYPE_MAIN,                     (1)
        1518,                                     (2)
          10,                                     (3)
           4,                                     (4)
           0,                                     (5)


        NET_IF_MEM_TYPE_MAIN,                     (6)
        1594,                                     (7)
           5,                                     (8)
         134,                                     (9)
           5,                                    (10)
           4,                                    (11)
           0,                                    (12)


        0x00000000,                              (13)
                0,                               (14)


        NET_DEV_CFG_FLAG_NONE                    (15)
};
```

Listing 14-9 **Sample loopback interface configuration**

L14-9(1)   Receive buffer pool type. This configuration setting controls the memory placement of the receive data buffers. Buffers may either be placed in main memory or in a dedicated, possibly higher speed, memory region (see L14-9(13)). This field should be set to one of the two macros:

NET_IF_MEM_TYPE_MAIN
NET_IF_MEM_TYPE_DEDICATED

L14-9(2)   Receive buffer size. This field sets the size of the largest receivable packet, and can be set to match the application's requirements.

Note: If packets are sent from a socket bound to a non local-host address, to the local host address (127.0.0.1), then the receive buffer size must be configured to match the maximum transmit buffer size, or maximum expected data size, that could be generated from a socket bound to any other interface.

L14-9(3)   Number of receive buffers. This setting controls the number of receive buffers that will be allocated to the loopback interface. This value *must* be set greater than or equal to one buffer if loopback is receiving *only* UDP. If TCP data is expected to be transferred across the loopback interface, then there *must* be a minimum of four receive buffers.

L14-9(4)   Receive buffer alignment. This setting controls the alignment of the receive buffers in bytes. Some processor architectures do not allow multi-byte reads and writes across word boundaries and therefore may require buffer alignment. In general, it is probably best practice to align buffers to the data bus width of the processor which may improve performance. For example, a 32-bit processor may benefit from having buffers aligned on a 4-byte boundary.

L14-9(5)   Receive buffer offset. The loopback interface receives packets starting at base index 0 in the network buffer data areas. This setting configures an offset from the base index of 0 to receive loopback packets. The default offset of 0 *should* be configured. However, if loopback receive packets are configured with an offset, the receive buffer size *must* also be adjusted by the additional number of offset bytes.

L14-9(6)   Transmit buffer pool type. This configuration setting controls the memory placement of the transmit data buffers for the loopback interface. Buffers may either be placed in main memory or in a dedicated, possibly higher speed, memory region (see L14-9(13)). This field should be set to one of two macros:

```
NET_IF_MEM_TYPE_MAIN
NET_IF_MEM_TYPE_DEDICATED
```

L14-9(7)   Large transmit buffer size. At the time of this writing, transmit fragmentation is *not* supported; therefore this field sets the size of the largest transmittable buffer for the loopback interface when the application sends from a socket that is bound to the local-host address.

L14-9(8)   Number of large transmit buffers. This field controls the number of large transmit buffers allocated to the loopback interface. The developer may set this field to zero to make room for additional large transmit buffers, however, the number of large plus the number of small transmit buffers *must* be greater than or equal to one for UDP traffic and three for TCP traffic.

L14-9(9)   Small transmit buffer size. For devices with a minimal amount of RAM, it is possible to allocate small transmit buffers as well as large transmit buffers. In general, we recommend 152 byte small transmit buffers, however, the developer may adjust this value according to the application requirements. This field has no effect if the number of small transmit buffers is configured to zero.

L14-9(10)   Number of small transmit buffers. This field controls the number of small transmit buffers allocated to the device. The developer may set this field to zero to make room for additional large transmit buffers, however, the number of large plus the number of small transmit buffers *must* be greater than or equal to one for UDP traffic and three for TCP traffic.

L14-9(11)   Transmit buffer alignment. This setting controls the alignment of the receive buffers in bytes. Some processor architectures do not allow multi-byte reads and writes across word boundaries and therefore may require buffer alignment. In general, it is probably best practice to align buffers to the data bus width of the processor which may improve performance. For example, a 32-bit processor may benefit from having buffers aligned on a 4-byte boundary.

L14-9(12)   Transmit buffer offset. This setting configures an offset from the base transmit index to prepare loopback packets. The default offset of 0 *should* be configured. However, if loopback transmit packets are configured with an offset, the transmit buffer size *must* also be adjusted by the additional number of offset bytes.

L14-9(13)   Memory address. By default, this field is configured to 0x00000000. A value of 0 tells μC/TCP-IP to allocate buffers for the loopback interface from the μC/LIB Memory Manager default heap. If a faster, more specialized memory is available, the loopback interface buffers may be allocated into an alternate region if desired.

L14-9(14)   Memory size. By default, this field is configured to 0. A value of 0 tells μC/TCP-IP to allocate as much memory as required from the μC/LIB Memory Manager default heap. If an alternate memory region is specified in the 'Memory Address' field above, then the maximum size of the specified memory segment must be specified.

L14-9(15)   Optional configuration flags. Configure (optional) loopback features by logically **OR**'ing bit-field flags:

NET_DEV_CFG_FLAG_NONE   No loopback configuration flags selected

14-5-2 ADDING A LOOPBACK INTERFACE

Basically to enable and add the loopback interface you only have to enable the loopback interface within the network configuration (**net_cfg.h**) as follow:

```
#define  NET_IF_CFG_LOOPBACK_EN                DEF_ENABLED
```

14-6 NETWORK INTERFACE API

14-6-1 CONFIGURING AN IP ADDRESS

Each network interface must be configured with at least one IP address. This may be performed using μC/DHCPc or manually during run-time. If run-time configuration is chosen, the following functions may be utilized to set the IP, network mask, and gateway addresses for a specific interface. More than one set of addresses may be configured for a specific network interface by calling the functions below. Note that on the default interface, the first IP address added will be the default address used for all default communication.

```
NetASCII_Str_to_IP()
NetIP_CfgAddrAdd()
```

The first function aids the developer by converting a string format IP address such as "192.168.1.2" to its hexadecimal equivalent. The second function is used to configure an interface with the specified IP, network mask and gateway addresses. An example of each function call is shown below.

```
ip      = NetASCII_Str_to_IP((CPU_CHAR*)"192.168.1.2",   &err);      (1)
msk     = NetASCII_Str_to_IP((CPU_CHAR*)"255.255.255.0", &err);
gateway = NetASCII_Str_to_IP((CPU_CHAR*)"192.168.1.1",   &err);
```

Listing 14-10 Calling NetASCII_Str_to_IP()

L14-10(1)   NetASCII_Str_to_IP() requires two arguments. The first function argument is a string representing a valid IP address, and the second argument is a pointer to a NET_ERR to contain the return error code. Upon successful conversion, the return error will contain the value NET_ASCII_ERR_NONE and the function will return a variable of type NET_IP_ADDR containing the hexadecimal equivalent of the specified address.

```
cfg_success = NetIP_CfgAddrAdd(if_nbr,      (1)
                               ip,          (2)
                               msk,         (3)
                               gateway,     (4)
                               &err);       (5)
```

Listing 14-11 Calling NetIP_CfgAddrAdd()

L14-11(1)   The first argument is the number representing the network interface that is to be configured. This value is obtained as the result of a successful call to NetIF_Add().

L14-11(2)   The second argument is the NET_IP_ADDR value representing the IP address to be configured.

L14-11(3)   The third argument is the NET_IP_ADDR value representing the subnet mask address that is to be configured.

L14-11(4)   The fourth argument is the **NET_IP_ADDR** value representing the default gateway IP address that is to be configured.

L14-11(5)   The fifth argument is a pointer to a **NET_ERR** variable containing the return error code for the function. If the interface address information is configured successfully, then the return error code will contain the value **NET_IP_ERR_NONE**. Additionally, function returns a Boolean value of **DEF_OK** or **DEF_FAIL** depending on the result. Either the return value or the **NET_ERR** variable may be checked for return status; however, the **NET_ERR** contains more detailed information and should therefore be the preferred check.

Note: The application may configure a network interface with more than one set of IP addresses. This may be desirable when a network interface and its paired device are connected to a switch or HUB with more than one network present. Additionally, an application may choose to *not* configure any interface addresses, and thus may *only* receive packets and should not attempt to transmit.

Additionally, addresses may be removed from an interface by calling **NetIP_CfgAddrRemove()** (see section C-12-5 "NetIP_CfgAddrRemove()" on page 781 and section C-12-6 "NetIP_CfgAddrRemoveAll()" on page 783).

Once a network interface has been successfully configured with IP address information, the next step is to start the interface.

14-6-2 STARTING NETWORK INTERFACES

When a network interface is started, it becomes an active interface that is capable of transmitting and receiving data assuming an operational link to the network medium. A network interface may be started any time after the network interface has been successfully "added" to the system. A successful call to **NetIF_Start()** marks the end of the initialization sequence of μC/TCP-IP for a specific network interface. Recall that the first interface added and started will be the default interface.

The application developer may start a network interface by calling the **NetIF_Start()** API function with the necessary parameters. A call to **NetIF_Start()** is shown below.

```
NetIF_Start(if_nbr, &err);    (1)
```

Listing 14-12 **Calling NetIF_Start()**

L14-12(1)   `NetIF_Start()` requires two arguments. The first function argument is the interface number that the application wants to start, and the second argument is a pointer to a **NET_ERR** to contain the return error code. The interface number is acquired upon successful addition of the interface and upon the successful start of the interface; the return error variable will contain the value **NET_IF_ERR_NONE**.

There are very few things that could cause a network interface to not start properly. The application developer should always inspect the return error code and take the appropriate action if an error occurs. Once the error is resolved, the application may again attempt to call `NetIF_Start()`.

14-6-3 STOPPING NETWORK INTERFACES

Under some circumstances, it may be desirable to stop a network interface. A network interface may be stopped any time after it has been successfully "added" to the system. Stopping an interface may be performed by calling `NetIF_Stop()` with the appropriate arguments shown below.

```
NetIF_Stop(if_nbr, &err);    (1)
```

Listing 14-13 **Calling NetIF_Stop()**

L14-13(1)   `NetIF_Stop()` requires two arguments. The first function argument is the interface number that the application wants to stop, and the second argument is a pointer to a **NET_ERR** to contain the return error code. The interface number is acquired upon the successful addition of the interface and upon the successful stop of the interface; the return error variable will contain the value **NET_IF_ERR_NONE**.

There are very few things that may cause a network interface to not stop properly. The application developer should always inspect the return error code and take the appropriate action if an error occurs. Once the error is resolved, the application may attempt to call `NetIF_Stop()` again.

14-6-4 GETTING NETWORK INTERFACE MTU

On occasion, it may be desirable to have the application aware of an interface's Maximum Transmission Unit. The MTU for a particular interface may be acquired by calling `NetIF_MTU_Get()` with the appropriate arguments.

```
mtu = NetIF_MTU_Get(if_nbr, &err);    (1)
```

Listing 14-14 **Calling NetIF_MTU_Get()**

L14-14(1) `NetIF_MTU_Get()` requires two arguments. The first function argument is the interface number to get the current configured MTU, and the second argument is a pointer to a `NET_ERR` to contain the return error code. The interface number is acquired upon the successful addition of the interface, and upon the successful return of the function, the return error variable will contain the value `NET_IF_ERR_NONE`. The result is returned into a local variable of type `NET_MTU`.

14-6-5 SETTING NETWORK INTERFACE MTU

Some networks prefer to operate with a non-standard MTU. If this is the case, the application may specify the MTU for a particular interface by calling `NetIF_MTU_Set()` with the appropriate arguments.

```
NetIF_MTU_Set(if_nbr, mtu, &err);    (1)
```

Listing 14-15 **Calling NetIF_MTU_Set()**

L14-15(1)   `NetIF_MTU_Set()` requires three arguments. The first function argument is the interface number of the interface to set the specified MTU. The second argument is the desired MTU to set, and the third argument is a pointer to a `NET_ERR` variable that will contain the return error code. The interface number is acquired upon the successful addition of the interface, and upon the successful return of the function, the return error variable will contain the value `NET_IF_ERR_NONE` and the specified MTU will be set.

Note: The configured MTU cannot be greater than the largest configured transmit buffer size associated with the specified interfaces' device minus overhead. Transmit buffer sizes are specified in the device configuration structure for the specified interface. For more information about configuring device buffer sizes, refer to section 9-3 "Network Buffer Sizes" on page 279.

14-6-6 GETTING NETWORK INTERFACE HARDWARE ADDRESSES

Many types of network interface hardware require the use of a link layer protocol address. In the case of Ethernet, this address is sometimes known as the hardware address or MAC address. In some applications, it may be desirable to get the current configured hardware address for a specific interface. This may be performed by calling NetIF_AddrHW_Get() with the appropriate arguments.

```
NetIF_AddrHW_Get((NET_IF_NBR  ) if_nbr,                 (1)
                 (CPU_INT08U *)&addr_hw_sender[0],      (2)
                 (CPU_INT08U *)&addr_hw_len,            (3)
                 (NET_ERR    *) perr);                  (4)
```

Listing 14-16 **Calling NetIF_AddrHW_Get()**

L14-16(1) The first argument specifies the interface number from which to get the hardware address. The interface number is acquired upon the successful addition of the interface.

L14-16(2) The second argument is a pointer to a **CPU_INT08U** array used to provide storage for the returned hardware address. This array *must* be sized large enough to hold the returned number of bytes for the given interface's hardware address. The lowest index number in the hardware address array represents the most significant byte of the hardware address.

L14-16(3) The third function is a pointer to a **CPU_INT08U** variable that the function returns the length of the specified interface's hardware address.

L14-16(4) The fourth argument is a pointer to a **NET_ERR** variable containing the return error code for the function. If the hardware address is successfully obtained, then the return error code will contain the value **NET_IF_ERR_NONE**.

14-6-7 SETTING NETWORK INTERFACE HARDWARE ADDRESS

Some applications prefer to configure the hardware device's hardware address via software during run-time as opposed to a run-time auto-loading EEPROM as is common for many Ethernet devices. If the application is to set or change the hardware address during run-time, this may be performed by calling `NetIF_AddrHW_Set()` with the appropriate arguments. Alternatively, the hardware address may be statically configured via the device configuration structure and later changed during run-time.

```
NetIF_AddrHW_Set((NET_IF_NBR  ) if_nbr,            (1)
                 (CPU_INT08U *)&addr_hw[0],        (2)
                 (CPU_INT08U *)&addr_hw_len,       (3)
                 (NET_ERR    *) perr);             (4)
```

Listing 14-17 **Calling NetIF_AddrHW_Set()**

L14-17(1)   The first argument specifies the interface number to set the hardware address. The interface number is acquired upon the successful addition of the interface.

L14-17(2)   The second argument is a pointer to a **CPU_INT08U** array which contains the desired hardware address to set. The lowest index number in the hardware address array represents the most significant byte of the hardware address.

L14-17(3)   The third function is a pointer to a **CPU_INT08U** variable that specifies the length of the hardware address being set. In most cases, this can be specified as **sizeof(addr_hw)** assuming **addr_hw** is declared as an array of **CPU_INT08U**.

L14-17(4)   The fourth argument is a pointer to a **NET_ERR** variable containing the return error code for the function. If the hardware address is successfully obtained, then the return error code will contain the value **NET_IF_ERR_NONE**.

Note: In order to set the hardware address for a particular interface, it *must* first be stopped. The hardware address may then be set, and the interface re-started.

14-6-8 GETTING LINK STATE

Some applications may wish to get the physical link state for a specific interface. Link state information may be obtained by calling `NetIF_IO_Ctrl()` or `NetIF_LinkStateGet()` with the appropriate arguments.

Calling `NetIF_IO_Ctrl()` will poll the hardware for the current link state. Alternatively, `NetIF_LinkStateGet()` gets the approximate link state by reading the interface link state flag. Polling the Ethernet hardware for link state takes significantly longer due to the speed and latency of the MII bus. Consequently, it may not be desirable to poll the hardware in a tight loop. Reading the interface flag is fast, but the flag is only periodically updated by the Net IF every 250mS (default) when using the generic Ethernet PHY driver. PHY drivers that implement link state change interrupts may change the value of the interface flag immediately upon link state change detection. In this scenario, calling `NetIF_LinkStateGet()` is ideal for these interfaces.

```
NetIF_IO_Ctrl((NET_IF_NBR) if_nbr,                          (1)
              (CPU_INT08U) NET_IF_IO_CTRL_LINK_STATE_GET_INFO,   (2)
              (void      *)&link_state,                      (3)
              (NET_ERR   *)&err);                            (4)
```

Listing 14-18 **Calling NetIF_IO_Ctrl()**

L14-18(1)   The first argument specifies the interface number from which to get the physical link state.

L14-18(2)   The second argument specifies the desired function that `NetIF_IO_Ctrl()` will perform. In order to get the current interfaces' link state, the application should specify this argument as either:

NET_IF_IO_CTRL_LINK_STATE_GET

NET_IF_IO_CTRL_LINK_STATE_GET_INFO

L14-18(3)   The third argument is a pointer to a link state variable that must be declared by the application and passed to `NetIF_IO_Ctrl()`.

14

14-6-9 SCANNING FOR A WIRELESS ACCESS POINT

When a wireless network interface is started, it becomes an active interface that is not yet capable of transmitting and receiving data since no operational link to a network medium is configured. The first step to join a network to have an operational link is the scan operation which consists to find the wireless network available in the range of the wireless module.

A wireless network interface should be able to scan any time after the network interface has been successfully started. A successful call to **NetIF_WiFi_Scan()** return the wireless network available to join which can be joined by the wireless network interface. See section C-10-1 "NetIF_WiFi_Scan()" on page 762 for more information.

You can scan for a wireless network by calling the **NetIF_WiFi_Scan()** API function with the necessary parameters. A call to **NetIF_WiFi_Scan()** is shown below.

```
NET_IF_WIFI_AP   ap_buf[NB_AP_MAX]
CPU_INT16U       ap_ctn;
NET_ERR          err;

ap_ctn = NetIF_WiFi_Scan(if_nbr,               (1)
                         ap_buf,               (2)
                         NB_AP_MAX,            (3)
                         0,                    (4)
                         NET_IF_WIFI_CH_ALL,   (5)
                         &err);                (6)
```

Listing 14-19 **Calling NetIF_Start()**

L14-19(1)   **NetIF_WiFi_Scan()** requires six arguments. The first function argument is the interface number that the application wants to scan with. The interface number is acquired upon successful addition of the interface and upon the successful start of the interface.

L14-19(2)   The second argument is a pointer to a wireless access point buffer to contain the wireless network found in the range of the interface.

L14-19(3)   The third argument is the number of wireless access point that can be contained in the wireless access point buffer.

L14-19(4)   The fourth argument is a pointer to a string that can contains the SSID of an hidden wireless access point to find.

L14-19(5)   The fifth argument is the wireless channel to scan.

L14-19(6)   The last argument is a pointer to a **NET_ERR** to contain the return error code. The return error variable will contain the value **NET_IF_WIFI_ERR_NONE** if the scan process has been completed successfully.

There are very few things that could cause a network interface to not scan properly. The application developer should always inspect the return error code and take the appropriate action if an error occurs. Once the error is resolved, the application may again attempt to call **NetIF_WiFi_Scan( )**.

14-6-10 JOINING WIRELESS ACCESS POINT

When a wireless network interface is started, it becomes an active interface that is not yet capable of transmitting and receiving data, since no operational link to a network medium is configured. Once once the interface has found a wireless network, it must be joined to get an operational link. A wireless network interface should be able to join any time after the network interface has been successfully started and before a wireless access point has been joined.

See section C-10-2 "NetIF_WiFi_Join()" on page 764 for more information.

The application developer may join a wireless network by calling the **NetIF_WiFi_Join( )** API function with the necessary parameters. A call to **NetIF_WiFi_Join( )** is shown below.

```
NET_ERR          err;

ap_ctn = NetIF_WiFi_Join(if_nbr,                          (1)
                    NET_IF_WIFI_NET_TYPE_INFRASTRUCTURE, (2)
                    NET_IF_WIFI_DATA_RATE_AUTO,          (3)
                    NET_IF_WIFI_SECURITY_WPA2,           (4)
                    NET_IF_WIFI_PWR_LEVEL_HI,            (5)
                    "network_ssid",                       (6)
                    "network_password",                   (7)
                    &err);                                (8)
```

Listing 14-20 **Calling NetIF_Start()**

L14-20(1)   `NetIF_WiFi_Join()` requires height arguments. The first function argument is the interface number that the application wants to join with. The interface number is acquired upon successful addition of the interface and upon the successful start of the interface.

L14-20(2)   The second argument is wireless network type.

L14-20(3)   The third argument is data rate use to communicate on the wireless network.

L14-20(4)   The fourth argument is the wireless security configured for the wireless network to join.

L14-20(5)   The fifth argument is the wireless radio power level use to communicate on the wireless network.

L14-20(6)   The sixth argument is a pointer to a string that contains the SSID of the wireless access point to join.

L14-20(7)   The seventh argument is a pointer to a string that contains the pre shared key of the wireless access point to join.

L14-20(8)   The last argument is a pointer to a **NET_ERR** to contain the return error code. The return error variable will contain the value **NET_IF_WIFI_ERR_NONE** if the join process has been completed successfully.

There are very few things that could cause a network interface to not join properly. The application developer should always inspect the return error code and take the appropriate action if an error occurs. Once the error is resolved, the application may again attempt to call **NetIF_WiFi_Join()**.

14-6-11 CREATING WIRELESS AD HOC ACCESS POINT

Some applications may need to create an wireless ad hoc access point that can be accessed by other devices. Wireless ad hoc access points can be created by calling the `NetIF_WiFi_CreateAdhoc()` API function with the necessary parameters. See section C-10-3 "NetIF_WiFi_CreateAdhoc()" on page 767 for more information.

A call to `NetIF_WiFi_CreateAdhoc()` is shown below:

```
NET_ERR          err;

ap_ctn = NetIF_WiFi_CreateAdhoc(if_nbr,                    (1)
                         NET_IF_WIFI_DATA_RATE_AUTO,       (2)
                         NET_IF_WIFI_SECURITY_WEP,         (3)
                         NET_IF_WIFI_PWR_LEVEL_HI,         (4)
                         NET_IF_WIFI_CH_1                  (5)
                         "adhoc_ssid",                     (6)
                         "adhoc_password",                 (7)
                         &err);                            (8)
```

Listing 14-21 **Call to NetIF_WiFi_CreateAdhoc()**

L14-21(1)   `NetIF_WiFi_CreateAdhoc()` requires height arguments. The first argument is the interface number, which is acquired upon successful addition and successful start of the interface.

L14-21(2)   The second argument is the data rate used on the wireless network.

L14-21(3)   The third argument is the wireless security type of wireless network.

L14-21(4)   The fourth argument is the radio power level use to communicate on the wireless network.

L14-21(5)   The fifth argument is the wireless channel for the ad hoc network.

L14-21(6)   The sixth argument is a pointer to a string that contains the SSID of the wireless access point.

L14-21(7)   The seventh argument is a pointer to a string that contains the pre-shared key of the wireless access point.

L14-21(8)   The last argument is a pointer to a **NET_ERR** to contain the return error code. The return error variable will contain the value **NET_IF_WIFI_ERR_NONE** if the create process has been completed successfully.

If an error occurs, you should always inspect the return error code and take the appropriate action. There are very few things that could cause a failure to create an ad hoc network properly. Once the error is resolved, the application may again attempt to call `NetIF_WiFi_CreateAdhoc()`.

14-6-12 LEAVING WIRELESS ACCESS POINT

When an application needs to leave a wireless access point, it can do so by calling the `NetIF_WiFi_Leave()` API function with the necessary parameters.

A call to `NetIF_WiFi_Leave()` is shown below.

```
NET_ERR          err;

ap_ctn = NetIF_WiFi_Leave(if_nbr, (1)
                          &err);   (2)
```

Listing 14-22 **Call to NetIF_WiFi_Leave()**

L14-22(1)   **NetIF_WiFi_Leave()** requires two arguments. The first function argument is the interface number. The interface number is acquired upon successful addition of the interface and upon the successful start of the interface.

L14-22(2)   The last argument is a pointer to a **NET_ERR** to contain the return error code. The return error variable will contain the value **NET_IF_WIFI_ERR_NONE** if the leave process has been completed successfully.

There are very few things that could cause a network interface to leave improperly. You should always inspect the return error code and take the appropriate action if an error occurs. Once the error is resolved, the application may again attempt to call `NetIF_WiFi_Leave()`.

Network Board Support Package

This chapter describes all board-specific functions that you may need to implement.

In order for a device driver to be platform independent, it is necessary to provide a layer of code that abstracts details such as configuring clocks, interrupt controllers, general-purpose input/ouput (GPIO) pins, direct-memory access (DMA) modules, and other such hardware modules. The board support package (BSP) code layer enables you to implement certain high-level functionality in µC/TCP-IP that is independent of any specific hardware. It also allows you to reuse device drivers from various architectures and bus configurations without having to customize µC/TCP-IP or the device driver source code for each architecture or hardware platform.

To understand the concepts discussed in this guide, you should be familiar with networking principles, the TCP/IP stack, real-time operating systems, microcontrollers and processors.

Micrium provides sample BSP code free of charge; however, most sample code will likely require modification depending on the combination of compiler, processor, board, and device hardware used.

15-1 ETHERNET BSP LAYER

15-1-1 DESCRIPTION OF THE ETHERNET BSP API

This section describes the BSP API functions that you should implement during the integration of an Ethernet interface for µC/TCP-IP.

For each Ethernet interface/device, an application must implement in **net_bsp.c**, a unique device-specific implementation of each of the following BSP functions:

```
void        NetDev_CfgClk    (NET_IF    *p_if,
                              NET_ERR   *p_err);
void        NetDev_CfgIntCtrl(NET_IF    *p_if,
                              NET_ERR   *p_err);
void        NetDev_CfgGPIO   (NET_IF    *p_if,
                              NET_ERR   *p_err);
CPU_INT32U  NetDev_ClkFreqGet(NET_IF    *p_if,
                              NET_ERR   *p_err);
```

Since each of these functions is called from a unique instantiation of its corresponding device driver, a pointer to the corresponding network interface (**p_if**) is passed in order to access the specific interface's device configuration or data.

Network device driver BSP functions may be arbitrarily named but since development boards with multiple devices require unique BSP functions for each device, it is recommended that each device's BSP functions be named using the following convention:

NetDev_[Device]<Function>[Number]()

[Device]   Network device name or type. For example, MACB. (Optional if the development board does not support multiple devices.)

<Function>   Network device BSP function. For example, **CfgClk.**

[Number]   Network device number for each specific instance of device (optional if the development board does not support multiple instances of the specific device)

For example, the `NetDev_CfgClk()` function for the #2 MACB Ethernet controller on an Atmel AT91SAM9263-EK should be named `NetDev_MACB_CfgClk2()`, or `NetDev_MACB_CfgClk_2()` with additional underscore optional.

Similarly, network devices' BSP-level interrupt service routine (ISR) handlers should be named using the following convention:

`NetDev_[Device]ISR_Handler[Type][Number]()`

[Device]   Network device name or type. For example, MACB. (Optional if the development board does not support multiple devices.)

[Type]   Network device interrupt type. For example, receive interrupt. (Optional if interrupt type is generic or unknown.)

[Number]   Network device number for each specific instance of device (optional if the development board does not support multiple instances of a specific device).

For example, the receive ISR handler for the #2 MACB Ethernet controller on an Atmel AT91SAM9263-EK should be named `NetDev_MACB_ISR_HandlerRx2()`, or `NetDev_MACB_ISR_HandlerRx_2()`, with additional underscore optional.

Next, the BSP functions for each device/interface must be organized into an interface structure. This structure is used by the device driver to call specific devices' BSP functions via function pointer instead of by name. It allows applications to add, initialize, and configure any number of instances of various devices and drivers by creating similar but unique BSP functions and interface structures for each network device/interface. (See Appendix C, "NetIF_Add()" on page 730 for details on how applications add interfaces to µC/TCP-IP.)

The BSP for each device or interface must be declared in the BSP source file (**net_bsp.c**) for each application or development board. The BSP must also be externally declared in the network BSP header file (**net_bsp.h**) with exactly the same name and type as declared in **net_bsp.c**. These BSP interface structures and their corresponding functions must have unique names, and should clearly identify the development board, device name, function name, and possibly the specific device number (assuming the development board supports multiple instances of any given device). BSP interface structures may be given arbitrary names, but it is recommended that they be named using the following convention:

```
NetDev_BSP_<Board><Device>[Number]{}
```

<Board>   Development board name. For example, Atmel AT91SAM9263-EK).

<Device>   Network device name or type. For example, MACB.

[Number]   Network device number for each specific instance of the device (optional if the development board does not support multiple instances of the device).

For example, a BSP interface structure for the #2 MACB Ethernet controller on an Atmel AT91SAM9263-EK board should be named **NetDev_BSP_AT91SAM9263-EK_MACB_2{}** and declared in the AT91SAM9263-EK board's **net_bsp.c**:

```
                        /* AT91SAM9263-EK MACB #2's BSP fnct ptrs :  */
const  NET_DEV_BSP_ETHER  NetDev_BSP_AT91SAM9263-EK_MACB_2 = {
    NetDev_MACB_CfgClk_2,      /*  Cfg MACB #2's clk(s)         */
    NetDev_MACB_CfgIntCtrl_2,  /*  Cfg MACB #2's int ctrl(s)    */
    NetDev_MACB_CfgGPIO_2,     /*  Cfg MACB #2's GPIO           */
    NetDev_MACB_ClkFreqGet_2   /*  Get MACB #2's clk freq       */
};
```

In order for the application to configure an interface with this BSP interface structure, the structure must also be externally declared in the AT91SAM9263-EK board's **net_bsp.h** :

```
extern  const  NET_DEV_BSP_ETHER  NetDev_BSP_AT91SAM9263-EK_MACB_2;
```

Lastly, the AT91SAM9263-EK board's MACB #2 BSP functions must also be declared in **net_bsp.c**:

```
static  void       NetDev_MACB_CfgClk_2     (NET_IF   *pif,
                                             NET_ERR  *perr);
static  void       NetDev_MACB_CfgIntCtrl_2 (NET_IF   *pif,
                                             NET_ERR  *perr);
static  void       NetDev_MACB_CfgGPIO_2    (NET_IF   *pif,
                                             NET_ERR  *perr);
static  CPU_INT32U NetDev_MACB_ClkFreqGet_2 (NET_IF   *pif,
                                             NET_ERR  *perr);
```

Note that since all network device BSP functions are accessed only by function pointer via their corresponding BSP interface structure, they don't need to be globally available and should therefore be declared as **static**.

Also note that although certain device drivers may not need to implement or call all of the above network device BSP function, we recommend that each device's BSP interface structure define all device BSP functions, and not assign any of its function pointers to **NULL**. Instead, for any device's unused BSP functions, create empty functions that return **NET_DEV_ERR_NONE**. This way, if the device driver is ever modified to start using a previously-unused BSP function, there will at least be an empty function for the BSP function pointer to execute.

Details for these functions may be found in their respective sections in Appendix A, "Device Driver BSP Functions" on page 567 and templates for network device BSP functions and BSP interface structures are available in the **\Micrium\Software\uC-TCPIP-V2\BSP\Template** directories.

15-1-2 CONFIGURING CLOCKS FOR AN ETHERNET DEVICE

NetDev_CfgClk() sets a specific network device's clocks to a specific interface.

Each network device's **NetDev_CfgClk()** should configure and enable all required clocks for the specified network device. For example, on some devices it may be necessary to enable clock gating for an embedded Ethernet MAC, as well as various GPIO modules in order to configure Ethernet PHY pins for (R)MII mode and interrupts. See section A-3-1 "NetDev_CfgClk()" on page 567 for more information.

15-1-3 CONFIGURING GENERAL I/O FOR AN ETHERNET DEVICE

NetDev_CfgGPIO() configures a specific network device's general-purpose input/output (GPIO) on a specific interface. This function is called by a device driver's **NetDev_Init()**.

Each network device's **NetDev_CfgGPIO()** should configure all required GPIO pins for the network device. For Ethernet devices, this function is necessary to configure the (R)MII bus pins, depending on whether the user has configured an Ethernet interface to operate in the RMII or MII mode, and optionally the Ethernet PHY interrupt pin.

See section A-3-2 "NetDev_CfgGPIO()" on page 569 for more information.

15-1-4 CONFIGURING THE INTERRUPT CONTROLLER FOR AN ETHERNET DEVICE

NetDev_CfgIntCtrl() is called by a device driver's NetDev_Init() to configure a specific network device's interrupts and/or interrupt controller on a specific interface.

Each network device's NetDev_CfgIntCtrl() function must configure and enable all required interrupt sources for the network device. This means it must configure the interrupt vector address of each corresponding network device BSP interrupt service routine (ISR) handler and enable its corresponding interrupt source.

For NetDev_CfgIntCtrl(), the following actions should be performed:

1   Configure/store each device's network interface number to be available for all necessary NetDev_ISR_Handler() functions (see section 15-3 on page 363 for more information). Even though devices are added dynamically, the device's interface number must be saved in order for each device's ISR handlers to call NetIF_ISR_Handler() with the device's network interface number.

2   Configure each of the device's interrupts on an interrupt controller (either an external or CPU-integrated interrupt comptroller). However, vectored interrupt controllers may not require higher-level interrupt controller sources to be explicitly configured and enabled. In this case, you may need to configure the system's interrupt vector table with the name of the ISR handler functions declared in net_bsp.c.

NetDev_CfgIntCtrl() should enable only each devices' interrupt sources, but not the local device-level interrupts themselves, which are enabled by the device driver only after the device has been fully configured and started.

See section A-3-3 "NetDev_CfgIntCtrl()" on page 571 for more information.

15-1-5 GETTING A DEVICE CLOCK FREQUENCY

NetDev_ClkFreqGet() return a specific network device's clock frequency for a specific interface. This function is called by a device driver's **NetDev_Init()**.

Each network device's **NetDev_ClkFreqGet()** should return the device's clock frequency (in Hz). For Ethernet devices, this is the clock frequency of the device's (R)MII bus. The device driver's **NetDev_Init()** uses the returned clock frequency to configure an appropriate bus divider to ensure that the (R)MII bus logic operates within an allowable range. In general, the device driver should not configure the divider such that the (R)MII bus operates faster than 2.5MHz.

See section A-3-4 "NetDev_ClkGetFreq()" on page 575 for more information.

15-2 WIRELESS BSP LAYER

15-2-1 DESCRIPTION OF THE WIRELESS BSP API

This section describes the BSP API functions that you should implement during the integration of a wireless interface for µC/TCP-IP.

For each wireless interface/device, an application must implement (in **net_bsp.c**) a unique device-specific implementation of each of the following BSP functions:

```
void  NetDev_WiFi_Start       (NET_IF      *p_if,
                               NET_ERR     *p_err);

void  NetDev_WiFi_Stop        (NET_IF      *p_if,
                               NET_ERR     *p_err);

void  NetDev_WiFi_CfgGPIO      (NET_IF      *p_if,
                               NET_ERR     *p_err);

void  NetDev_WiFi_CfgIntCtrl   (NET_IF      *p_if,
                               NET_ERR     *p_err);
void  NetDev_WiFi_IntCtrl      (NET_IF      *p_if,
                               CPU_BOOLEAN  en,
                               NET_ERR     *p_err);
```

353

```
void  NetDev_WiFi_SPI_Init       (NET_IF      *p_if,
                                  NET_ERR     *p_err);


void  NetDev_WiFi_SPI_Lock       (NET_IF      *p_if,
                                  NET_ERR     *p_err);


void  NetDev_WiFi_SPI_Unlock     (NET_IF      *p_if);
void  NetDev_WiFi_SPI_WrRd       (NET_IF      *p_if,
                                  CPU_INT08U  *p_buf_wr,
                                  CPU_INT08U  *p_buf_rd,
                                  CPU_INT16U   len,
                                  NET_ERR     *p_err);


void  NetDev_WiFi_SPI_ChipSelEn (NET_IF      *p_if,
                                  NET_ERR     *p_err);


void  NetDev_WiFi_SPI_ChipSelDis(NET_IF      *p_if);


void  NetDev_WiFi_SPI_Cfg(NET_IF                          *p_if,
                          NET_DEV_CFG_SPI_CLK_FREQ         freq,
                          NET_DEV_CFG_SPI_CLK_POL          pol,
                          NET_DEV_CFG_SPI_CLK_PHASE        phase,
                          NET_DEV_CFG_SPI_XFER_UNIT_LEN    xfer_unit_len,
                          NET_DEV_CFG_SPI_XFER_SHIFT_DIR   xfer_shift_dir,
                          NET_ERR                         *p_err);
```

Since each of these functions is called from a unique instantiation of its corresponding device driver, a pointer to the corresponding network interface (p_if) is passed in order to access the specific interface's device configuration or data.

Network device driver BSP functions may be arbitrarily named but since development boards with multiple devices require unique BSP functions for each device, it is recommended that each device's BSP functions be named using the following convention:

```
NetDev_[Device]<Function>[Number]()
```

[Device]   Network device name or type. For example, MACB (optional if the development board does not support multiple devices).

<Function>   Network device BSP function. For example, **CfgClk**

[Number]   Network device number for each specific instance of device (optional if the development board does not support multiple instances of a specific device)

For example, the **NetDev_CfgGPIO()** function for the #2 RS9110-N-21 wireless module on an Atmel AT91SAM9263-EK should be named **NetDev_RS9110N21_CfgGPIO2()**, or **NetDev_RS9110N21_CfgGPIO_2()** with additional underscore optional.

Similarly, network devices' BSP-level interrupt service routine (ISR) handlers should be named using the following convention:

```
NetDev_[Device]ISR_Handler[Type][Number]()
```

[Device]   Network device name or type. For example, MACB. (Optional if the development board does not support multiple devices.)

[Type]   Network device interrupt type. For example, receive interrupt. (Optional if interrupt type is generic or unknown.)

[Number]   Network device number for each specific instance of device (optional if the development board does not support multiple instances of a specific device).

For example, the receive ISR handler for the #2 RS9110-N-21 wireless module on an Atmel AT91SAM9263-EK should be named **NetDev_RS9110N21_ISR_HandlerRx2()**, or **NetDev_RS9110N21_ISR_HandlerRx_2()** with additional underscore optional.

Next, each device's/interface's BSP functions must be organized into an interface structure used by the device driver to call specific devices' BSP functions via function pointer instead of by name. This allows applications to add, initialize, and configure any number of instances of various devices and drivers by creating similar but unique BSP functions and interface structures for each network device/interface. (See Appendix C, "NetIF_Add()" on page 730 for details on how applications add interfaces to µC/TCP-IP.)

Each device's/interface's BSP interface structure must be declared in the application's/ development board's network BSP source file, **net_bsp.c**, as well as externally declared in network BSP header file, **net_bsp.h**, with the exact same name and type as declared in **net_bsp.c**. These BSP interface structures and their corresponding functions must be uniquely named and should clearly identify the development board, device name, function name, and possibly the specific device number (assuming the development board supports multiple instances of any given device). BSP interface structures may be arbitrarily named but it is recommended that they be named using the following convention:

```
NetDev_BSP_<Board><Device>[Number]{}
```

<Board>   Development board name. For example, Atmel AT91SAM9263-EK.

<Device>   Network device name (or type). For example, RS9110-N-21.

[Number]   Network device number for each specific instance of the device (optional if the development board does not support multiple instances of the device).

For example, a BSP interface structure for the #2 RS9110-N21 wireless module on an Atmel AT91SAM9263-EK board should be named **NetDev_BSP_AT91SAM9263-EK_RS9110N21_2{}** and declared in the AT91SAM9263-EK board's **net_bsp.c**:

```c
                      /* AT91SAM9263-EK RS9110-N21 #2's BSP fnct ptrs :   */
const  NET_DEV_BSP_WIFI_SPI NetDev_BSP_AT91SAM9263-EK_RS9110N21_2 = {
    NetDev_RS9110N21_Start_2
    NetDev_RS9110N21_Stop_2,
    NetDev_RS9110N21_CfgGPIO_2,
    NetDev_RS9110N21_CfgExtIntCtrl_2
    NetDev_RS9110N21_ExtIntCtrl_2,
    NetDev_RS9110N21_SPI_Cfg_2,
    NetDev_RS9110N21_SPI_Lock_2,
    NetDev_RS9110N21_SPI_Unlock_2,
    NetDev_RS9110N21_SPI_WrRd_2,
    NetDev_RS9110N21_SPI_ChipSelEn_2,
    NetDev_RS9110N21_SPI_ChipSelDis_2,
    NetDev_RS9110N21_SetCfg_2
};
```

And in order for the application to configure an interface with this BSP interface structure, the structure must be externally declared in the AT91SAM9263-EK board's **net_bsp.h**:

```
extern  const  NET_DEV_BSP_WIFI_SPI  NetDev_BSP_AT91SAM9263-EK_RS9110N21_2;
```

Lastly, the board's RS9110-N-21 #2 BSP functions must also be declared in **net_bsp.c**:

```
static  void  NetDev_RS9110N21_Start_2        (NET_IF       *p_if,
                                               NET_ERR      *p_err);


static  void  NetDev_RS9110N21_Stop_2         (NET_IF       *p_if,
                                               NET_ERR      *p_err);


static  void  NetDev_RS9110N21_CfgGPIO_2      (NET_IF       *p_if,
                                               NET_ERR      *p_err);


static  void  NetDev_RS9110N21_CfgIntCtrl_2   (NET_IF       *p_if,
                                               NET_ERR      *p_err);


static  void  NetDev_RS9110N21_IntCtrl_2      (NET_IF       *p_if,
                                               CPU_BOOLEAN  en,
                                               NET_ERR      *p_err);


static  void  NetDev_RS9110N21_SPI_Init_2     (NET_IF       *p_if,
                                               NET_ERR      *p_err);


static  void  NetDev_RS9110N21_SPI_Lock_2     (NET_IF       *p_if,
                                               NET_ERR      *p_err);


static  void  NetDev_RS9110N21_SPI_Unlock_2   (NET_IF       *p_if);


static  void  NetDev_RS9110N21_SPI_WrRd_2     (NET_IF       *p_if,
                                               CPU_INT08U   *p_buf_wr,
                                               CPU_INT08U   *p_buf_rd,
                                               CPU_INT16U   len,
                                               NET_ERR      *p_err);
```

```
static  void  NetDev_RS9110N21_SPI_ChipSelEn_2 (NET_IF      *p_if,
                                                NET_ERR     *p_err);


static  void  NetDev_RS9110N21_SPI_ChipSelDis_2(NET_IF      *p_if);


static  void  NetDev_RS9110N21_SPI_Cfg_2(
                      NET_IF                        *p_if,
                      NET_DEV_CFG_SPI_CLK_FREQ       freq,
                      NET_DEV_CFG_SPI_CLK_POL        pol,
                      NET_DEV_CFG_SPI_CLK_PHASE      phase,
                      NET_DEV_CFG_SPI_XFER_UNIT_LEN  xfer_unit_len,
                        NET_DEV_CFG_SPI_XFER_SHIFT_DIR  xfer_shift_dir,
                        NET_ERR                         *p_err);
```

Note that since all network device BSP functions are accessed only by function pointer via their corresponding BSP interface structure, they don't need to be globally available and should therefore be declared as **static**.

Also note that although certain device drivers may not need to implement or call all of the above network device BSP function, we recommend that each device's BSP interface structure define all device BSP functions and not assign any of its function pointers to **NULL**. Instead, for any device's unused BSP functions, create empty functions that return **NET_DEV_ERR_NONE**. This way, if the device driver is ever modified to start using a previously-unused BSP function, there will at least be an empty function for the BSP function pointer to execute.

Details for these functions may be found in their respective sections in section A-3 "Device Driver BSP Functions" on page 567. Templates for network device BSP functions and BSP interface structures can be found in the directory **\Micrium\Software\uC-TCPIP-V2\BSP\Template**.

15-2-2 CONFIGURING GENERAL-PURPOSE I/O FOR A WIRELESS DEVICE

NetDev_WiFi_CfgGPIO() configures a specific network device's general-purpose input/ouput (GPIO) on a specific interface. This function is called by a device driver's NetDev_Init().

Each network device's NetDev_WiFi_CfgGPIO() should configure all required GPIO pins for the network device. For wireless devices, this function is necessary to configure the power, reset and interrupt pins.

See section B-3-3 "NetDev_WiFi_CfgGPIO()" on page 623 for more information.

15-2-3 STARTING A WIRELESS DEVICE

NetDev_WiFi_Start() is used to power up the wireless chip. This function is called by a device driver's NetDev_WiFi_Start() each time the interface is started.

Each network device's NetDev_WiFi_Start() must set GPIO pins to power up and reset the wireless device. For wireless devices, this function is necessary to configure the power pin and other required pins to power up the wireless chip. Note that some wireless device could require a toggle on the Reset pin to be started or restarted correctly.

See section B-3-1 "NetDev_WiFi_Start()" on page 619 for more information.

15-2-4 STOPPING A WIRELESS DEVICE

NetDev_WiFi_Stop() is used to power down a wireless chip. This function is called by a device driver's NetDev_WiFi_Stop() each time the interface is stopped.

Each network device's NetDev_WiFi_Start() must set GPIO pins to power down the wireless chip to reduce the power consumption. For wireless devices, this function is necessary to configure the power pin and other required pins to power down the wireless chip.

See section B-3-2 "NetDev_WiFi_Stop()" on page 621 for more information.

15-2-5 CONFIGURING THE INTERRUPT CONTROLLER FOR A WIRELESS DEVICE

NetDev_WiFi_CfgIntCtrl() is called by a device driver's NetDev_WiFi_Init() to configure a specific wireless device's external interrupts a specific wireless interface.

Each network device's NetDev_WiFi_CfgIntCtrl() function must configure without enabling all required interrupt sources for the network device. This means it must configure the interrupt vector address of each corresponding network device BSP interrupt service routine (ISR) handler and disable its corresponding interrupt source. For NetDev_WiFi_CfgIntCtrl(), the following actions should be performed:

1   Configure/store each device's network interface number to be available for all necessary NetDev_WiFi_ISR_Handler() functions (see section 15-3 on page 363 for more information). Even though devices are added dynamically, the device's interface number must be saved in order for each device's ISR handlers to call NetIF_WiFi_ISR_Handler() with the device's network interface number.

2   Configure each of the device's interrupts on an interrupt controller (either an external or CPU-integrated interrupt comptroller). However, vectored interrupt controllers may not require higher-level interrupt controller sources to be explicitly configured and enabled. In this case, you may need to configure the system's interrupt vector table with the name of the ISR handler functions declared in net_bsp.c.

NetDev_WiFi_CfgIntCtrl() should disable only each devices' interrupt sources. See section B-3-4 "NetDev_WiFi_CfgIntCtrl()" on page 625 for more information.

15-2-6 ENABLING AND DISABLING WIRELESS INTERRUPT

Each network device's NetDev_WiFi_IntCtrl() function must enable or disable all external required interrupt sources for the wireless device. This means enable or disable its corresponding interrupt source following the enable argument received.

See section B-3-5 "NetDev_WiFi_IntCtrl()" on page 629 for more information.

15-2-7 CONFIGURING THE SPI INTERFACE

`NetDev_WiFi_SPI_Init()` initializes a specific network device's SPI controller. This function will be called by a device driver's `NetDev_WiFi_SPI_Init()` when the interface is added.

Each network device's `NetDev_WiFi_SPI_Init()` should configure all required SPI controllers register for the network device. Since more than one device may share the same SPI bus, this function could be empty if the SPI controller is already configured.

If the SPI bus is not shared with other devices, it is recommended that `NetDev_WiFi_SPI_Init()` configures the SPI controller following the SPI device's communication settings and keep `NetDev_WiFi_SPI_Cfg()` empty.

See section B-3-12 "NetDev_WiFi_SPI_Cfg()" on page 643 for more information.

15-2-8 SETTING SPI CONTROLLER FOR A WIRELESS DEVICE

`NetDev_WiFi_SPI_Cfg()` configure a specific network device's SPI communication setting. This function is called by a device driver after the SPI's bus lock has been acquired and before starting to write and read to the SPI bus.

Each network device's `NetDev_WiFi_SPI_Cfg()` should configure all required SPI controllers register for the SPI's communication setting of the network wireless device. Several aspects of SPI communication may need to be configured, including:

■ Clock frequency

■ Clock polarity

■ Clock phase

■ Transfer unit length

■ Shift direction

Since more than one device with different SPI's communication setting may share the same SPI bus, this function must reconfigure the SPI controller following the device's SPI communication setting each time the device driver must access the SPI bus. If the SPI bus is not shared with other devices, it's recommended that **NetDev_SPI_Cfg()** configures SPI controller following the SPI's communication setting of the wireless device and to keep this function empty.

See section B-3-12 "NetDev_WiFi_SPI_Cfg()" on page 643 for more information.

15-2-9 LOCKING AND UNLOCKING SPI BUS

NetDev_WiFi_SPI_Lock() acquires a specific network device's SPI bus access. This function will be called before the device driver begins to access the SPI. The application should not use the same bus to access another device until the matching call to **NetDev_WiFI_SPI_Unlock()** has been made. If no other SPI device shares the same SPI bus, it's recommended to keep this function empty.

See section B-3-7 "NetDev_WiFi_SPI_Lock()" on page 633 for more information.

15-2-10 ENABLING AND DISABLING SPI CHIP SELECT

NetDev_WiFi_SPI_ChipSelEn() enables the chip select pin of the wireless device. This function is called before the device driver begins to access the SPI. The chip select pin should stay enabled until the matching call to **NetDev_WiFi_SPI_ChipSelDis()** has been made. The chip select pin is typically "active low." To enable the device, the chip select pin should be cleared; to disable the device, the chip select pin should be set.

See section B-3-10 "NetDev_WiFi_SPI_ChipSelEn()" on page 639 for more information.

15-2-11 WRITING AND READING TO THE SPI BUS

NetDev_WiFi_SPI_WrRd() writes and reads data to and from the SPI bus. This function is called each time the device driver accesses the SPI bus. **NetDev_WiFi_SPI_WrRd()** must not return until the write/read operation is complete. Writing and reading to the SPI bus by using DMA is possible, but the BSP layer must implement a notification mechanism to return from this function only when the write and read operations are entirely completed. See section B-3-9 "NetDev_WiFi_SPI_WrRd()" on page 637 for more information.

15-3 SPECIFYING THE INTERFACE NUMBER OF THE DEVICE ISR

`NetDev_ISR_Handler()` handles a network device's interrupts on a specific interface.

Each network device's interrupt, or set of device interrupts, must be handled by a unique BSP-level interrupt service routine (ISR) handler, `NetDev_ISR_Handler()`, which maps each specific device interrupt to its corresponding network interface ISR handler, `NetIF_ISR_Handler()`. For some CPUs, this may be a first- or second-level interrupt handler. The application must configure the interrupt controller to call every network device's unique `NetDev_ISR_Handler()` when the device's interrupt occurs (see section A-3-3 "NetDev_CfgIntCtrl()" on page 571). Every unique `NetDev_ISR_Handler()` must then perform the following actions:

1   Call `NetIF_ISR_Handler()` with the device's unique network interface number and appropriate interrupt type. The network interface number should be available in the device's `NetDev_CfgIntCtrl()` function after configuration (see section A-3-3 on page 571). `NetIF_ISR_Handler()` in turn calls the appropriate device driver's interrupt handler.

In most cases, each device requires only a single `NetDev_ISR_Handler()`. This is possible when the device's driver is able determine the device's interrupt type via internal device registers or the interrupt controller. In this case, `NetDev_ISR_Handler()` calls `NetIF_ISR_Handler()` with interrupt type code `NET_DEV_ISR_TYPE_UNKNOWN`.

However, some devices cannot determine the interrupt type when an interrupt occurs and may therefore require multiple, unique `NetDev_ISR_Handler()`'s, each of which calls `NetIF_ISR_Handler()` with the appropriate interrupt type code.

Ethernet physical layer (PHY) interrupts should call `NetIF_ISR_Handler()` with interrupt type code `NET_DEV_ISR_TYPE_PHY`.

2   Clear the device's interrupt source, possibly via an external or CPU-integrated interrupt controller source.

See section B-3-13 "NetDev_WiFi_ISR_Handler()" on page 646 for more information.

15-4 MISCELLANEOUS NETWORK BSP

µC/TCP-IP also implements hardware abstraction code other than the device driver BSP. The following functions *must* be declared and implemented in **net_bsp.c**:

```
NET_TS     NetUtil_TS_Get     (void);
NET_TS_MS  NetUtil_TS_Get_ms  (void);
void       NetTCP_InitTxSeqNbr(void);
```

The first two functions provide internal timestamp µC/TCP-IP functionality (although **NetUtil_TS_Get()** is not absolutely required), while the latter function is only necessary if µC/TCP-IP is configured to include the TCP module. Details for these functions can be found in their respective sections in Appendix C, "µC/TCP-IP API Reference" on page 649, and templates for these BSP functions are available in the **\Micrium\Software\uC-TCPIP-V2\BSP\Template** directories.

Device Driver Implementation

This chapter describes the hardware (device) driver architecture for µC/TCP-IP. In order to understand the concepts discussed in this guide, you should be familiar with networking principles, the TCP/IP stack, real-time operating systems, and microcontrollers and processors.

µC/TCP-IP operates with a variety of network devices. Currently, µC/TCP-IP supports Ethernet type interface controllers wired and wireless, and will support serial, PPP, USB, and other popular interfaces in future releases.

There are many Ethernet controllers available on the market and each requires a driver to work with µC/TCP-IP. The amount of code needed to port a specific device to µC/TCP-IP greatly depends on device complexity.

If a driver for your hardware is not already available, you can develop a driver as described in this book. The best approach is to modify an already device driver with your device's specific code, following the Micrium coding convention for consistency. It is also possible to adapt drivers written for other TCP/IP stacks, especially if the driver code is short and it is a matter of simply copying data to and from the device.

16-1 CONCEPTS

Several aspects of the µC/TCP-IP driver architecture that are discussed in this chapter include:

NETWORK INTERFACE

The network interface is the physical and logical implementation. Currently only network interface which use the IEEE 802.3 and/or Ethernet standards are supported.

DEVICE DRIVER

A device driver is an interface between the common API of the µC/TCP-IP stack and the device specific architecture and available resources (RAM, DMA, IO, Peripheral Registers, etc…).

ETHERNET DEVICE LAYER

The device layer of the Ethernet device driver implements functions to control the Media Access Controller (MAC). µC/TCP-IP supports internal and external wired Ethernet controller and connected to an Ethernet PHY. This layer implements functionality required by other network interface layers which are specific to the device and not to the board such as initializing, receiving and transmitting. This layer may implement functionally by setting and using controller register, DMA, or memory copy.

ETHERNET PHY LAYER

PHY is the physical layer of the TCP/IP stack model between the Media Access Controller (MAC) and physical medium of the network (copper, optical fiber or RF). The PHY accomplishes two tasks: the first is to encode the transmitted data and decode received data; the second is to drive and read the medium with respect to bit timing, signal level and modulation.

WIRELESS DEVICE LAYER

The device layer of the wireless device driver implements functions to control the Media Access Controller (MAC) a wireless module. µC/TCP-IP supports only wireless modules that include an integrated wireless supplicant (which is responsible for making login requests) and which communicate via SPI. Also the packet format used by the module must be 802.3 or Ethernet. This layer implements functionality required by other network interface layers which are specific to the device and not to the board such as initializing, receiving and transmitting. This layer may implement functionally by writing and reading in the wireless device register through SPI.

WIRELESS MANAGER

The Wireless Manager is a set of internal mechanisms to perform management operations on the wireless module such as scan, join, leave, and so on.

DIRECT MEMORY ACCESS (DMA)

Direct Memory Access controller is a common hardware feature of processors and microcontrollers. DMA allows copying memory blocks from peripherals and internal memory while offloading the processor. An interrupt is generated when the transfer is completed to notify the CPU when a data transfer is completed.

MEMORY COPY

In the case where the processor doesn't have DMA controllers, all memory transfers have to be executed by the processor. This method is called Memory Copy. It is less efficient than DMA transfers because the CPU has to move each element of the data, whereas it could do other tasks if a DMA was available to perform the data transfer.

SPI

SPI (Serial Peripheral Interface) is a synchronous serial data link used by peripherals commonly built-in to CPUs. Since the communication can easily be accomplished by software control of GPIO pins ("software SPI" also known as "bit-banging"), SPI devices can be connected to almost any platform. Any SPI device uses four signals, which are used to communicate with the host (CS, DataIn, CLK and DataOut).

The four signals connecting the host and device (also known as master and slave) are named variously in different manuals and documents. The MOSI pin (Master Out Slave In) may be called DI on device pinouts; similarly, MISO pin (Master In Slave Out) may be called DO on device pinouts. The CS and CLK pins (also known as SSEL and SCK) are the chip select and clock pins. The host selects the slave by asserting CS, potentially allowing it to choose a single peripheral among several that are sharing the bus (i.e., by sharing the CLK, MOSI and MISO signals).

16-2 OVERVIEW OF THE µC/TCP-IP INTERFACE LAYERS

This section describe several aspects which are common to all Network interface type, wired or wireless.

16-2-1 CONFIGURATION STRUCTURES AND APIs INTERACTIONS

Once µC/TCP-IP is initialized each type of network interface, wired or wireless, must be added to the stack via **NetIF_Add()** the same function as shown previously in section 14-3-3 "Adding an Ethernet Interface" on page 319 and section 14-4-2 "Adding a Wireless Interface" on page 326.

µC/TCP-IP uses API functions to access the interface layer and configuration structures are used to initialize resources needed by the network interface. When writing a device drive you may have to create device driver and extension APIs and uses configurations structures in your implementation. Thus you must understand what is the interaction between each layer and API.

This is the **NetIF_Add()** prototype with the argument that you must pass:

```
NET_IF_NBR  NetIF_Add (void      *if_api,                    (1)
                       void      *dev_api,                   (2)
                       void      *dev_bsp,                   (3)
                       void      *dev_cfg,                   (4)
                       void      *ext_api,                   (5)
                       void      *ext_cfg,                   (6)
                       NET_ERR   *perr)                      (7)
```

Listing 16-1 **NetIF_Add() arguments**

L16-1(1)   Pointer to specific network interface API. This API should always be provided with the TCP-IP stack, you must only pass the API of your interface type. You can find the API under the interface folder (**/IF**).

L16-1(2)   Pointer to specific network device driver API. If you want to develop your own driver you must implement this API and you should start from the device driver template which can be find under the device folder (**/Dev/Template**). APIs for Ethernet and wireless have some differences; see section 16-5 "Ethernet Device

Driver Implementation" on page 385 and section 16-10 "Wireless Device Driver Implementation" on page 443 for further information about each type of Interface's API.

L16-1(3)   Pointer to specific network device board-specific API. This API is used by the device driver initialization to configure several device aspect which are specific to the board and the application. Thus you must implements the API needed by your network interface. You should start from the BSP template provided with the stack which you can find under the BSP folder (`/BSP/Template`). For further information about the BSP layer to implement, section 15-1 "Ethernet BSP Layer" on page 348 and section 15-2 "Wireless BSP Layer" on page 353.

L16-1(4)   Pointer to specific network device hardware configuration. This configuration structure is used by the interface and the device driver initialize resources needed by the interface. Each interface type has their own configuration structure which always starts with the standard memory configuration. You should start from the interface configuration template which you can find under the configuration template (`CFG/Template/net_dev_cfg.*`). See section 14-3 "Ethernet Interface Configuration" on page 316 and section 14-4 "Wireless Interface Configuration" on page 323 for further information about configurations structures. The device driver should validate the configuration structure before initializing registers and peripherals.

L16-1(5)   Pointer to specific network extension layer API. This API is used by the interface to accomplish some operation specific to the physical type. For an Ethernet interface the extension layer is the PHY API. Micrium provides a generic Ethernet PHY which are compatible with the (R)MII standard, if your PHY is not compatible, you may have to implement an API for it. For further information about the Ethernet PHY API, see section 16-4 "Ethernet PHY API Implementation" on page 382.

For a wireless interface, the extension layer is the Wireless Manager API which can be found under (`Dev/WiFi/Manager`). If you write your own driver you may have to implement the extension API if the provided Wireless Manager doesn't provide the functionality needed by your device driver.

L16-1(6)   Pointer to specific network extension layer configuration. This configuration structure is used by the extension layer to initialize by the interface. For an Ethernet interface you should pass the PHY configuration. This configuration structure might be null for a Wireless Manager.

L16-1(7)   Pointer to variable that will receive the return error code from this function.

For a thorough description of the µC/TCP-IP files and directory structure, see Chapter 12, "Directories and Files" on page 267.

Figure 16-1 shows where these API are used by µC/TCP-IP and also the interaction between each interface layers and API passed to **NetIF_Add()**:

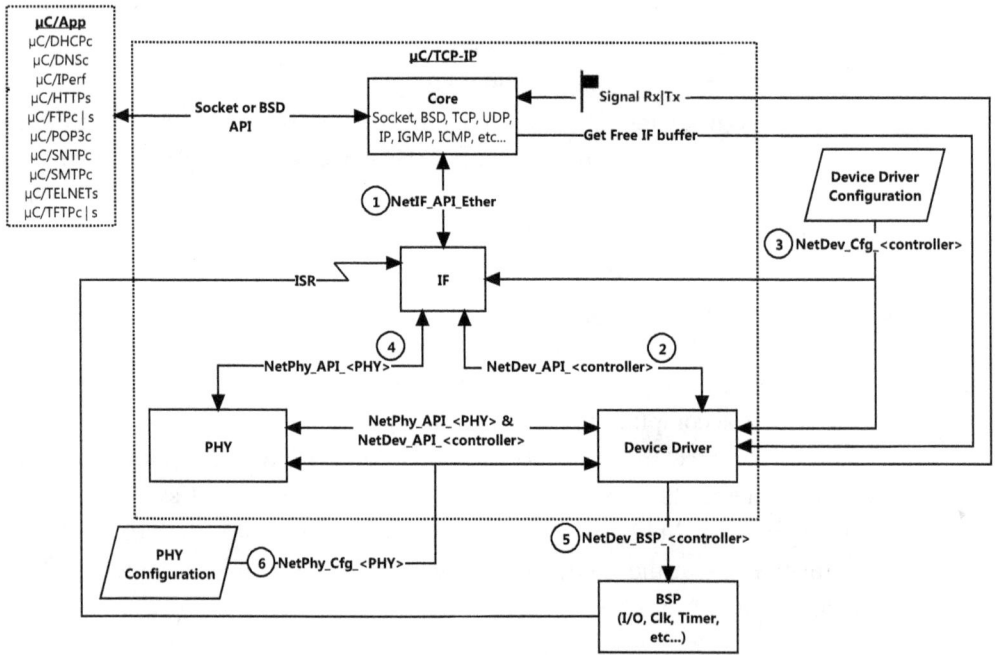

Figure 16-1 **Overview of µC/TCP-IP**

F16-1(1)   **NetIF_API_Ether** and **NetIF_API_WiFi** specify the address of the link layer API structure used by the µC/TCPIP module to transmit and receive data from the hardware device. For an Ethernet interface, this value is always defined as

NetIF_API_Ether. For an wireless interface, this value is always defined as **NetIF_API_WiFi**. So, all you need to do is to add to your project the files contained in the IF folder.

F16-1(2) **NetDev_API_<controller>** is the address of the API structure used by the IF layer to initialize the controller and control transmissions/reception, multicast, controller speed, and so on.

F16-1(3) **NetDev_Cfg_<controller>** is a configuration structure used by the IF and driver layers to configure memory, reserve buffers, reserve descriptor area, and so on. You have to update this structure following your application requirements. Refer to section 14-3 "Ethernet Interface Configuration" on page 316 and section 14-4 "Wireless Interface Configuration" on page 323 for more information about how to configure an interface.

F16-1(4) For an Ethernet interface, a PHY API should be used. **NetPhy_API_<phy>** is the address of the API structure used by the IF and controller layers to control the PHY speed and to get the link state. If a generic (R)MII PHY provides the features you need, you do not have to implement this layer yourself; you can use the generic PHY. However, if the PHY does not support the MII or RMII standard, or necessary features are not provided by the generic (R)MII PHY, you will have to implement a new PHY.

For an wireless interface a Wireless Manager API should be used. **NetWiFiMgr_API_Generic** is the address of the API structure used by the IF and controller layers to control the wireless connection state.

F16-1(5) **NetDev_BSP_<controller>** is the address of the API structure used by the device driver to initialize interfaces specific to the board and the processor.

F16-1(6) For an Ethernet interface, a PHY configuration must be passed. **NetPhy_Cfg_<phy>** is the address of the API structure where the initial PHY configuration settings (such as link speed and link dupex) are defined. More details are provided on that structure in section 14-3 "Ethernet Interface Configuration" on page 316

For an wireless interface no configuration structure is needed.

16-2-2 µC/TCP-IP MEMORY MANAGEMENT

One of the most important aspect when writing a device driver is the memory management since each type of device driver should at least validate the interface memory configuration as shown in section 14-2-1 "Memory Configuration" on page 311. The device driver developer could use the memory configuration of the interface during the initialization to allocate memory uses uniquely within the device driver.

See section 14-2 "µC/TCP-IP Network Interface configuration" on page 310 for further information about the memory management and it's configuration.

For non-DMA based devices, additional memory allocation from within the device driver may not be necessary. However, DMA based devices should allocate memory from the µC/LIB memory module for descriptors. By using the µC/LIB memory module instead of declaring arrays, the driver developer can easily align descriptors to any required boundary and benefit from the run-time flexibility of the device configuration structure.

If you have access to the source code, see the µC/LIB documentation for additional information and usage notes.

Net_dev_cfg_<controller>.c/.h is used to specify how much memory should be reserved by the µC/TCP-IP module for the device buffer and where to map it. As Figure 16-4 shows, the memory regions are managed by the core (**NetBuf** layer) which uses the µC/LIB memory module. The IF layer creates the memory pools for all configured buffers as per the information in **Net_dev_cfg_<controller>.c**.

When the driver requires additional memory, it is the responsibility of the developer to create the additional memory pools. For example, when your device supports DMA access, you have to reserve memory for the Receive/Transmit descriptors. As all memory pools are managed using µC/LIB, when you increase some device configuration value, the heap size of µC/LIB must follow the value modification. If not done properly, the µC/TCP-IP module will run out of memory during the initialization or too much memory will be reserved by µC/LIB.

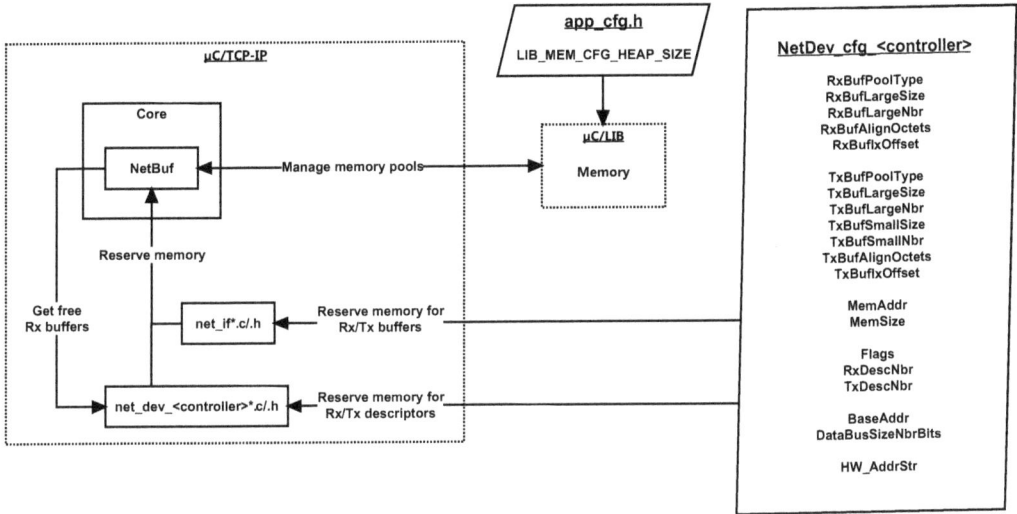

Figure 16-2 **Memory management**

µC/TCP-IP has been designed to operate with several device driver memory configurations. There are four possible memory configuration arrangements which are shown below:

CPU WITH AN INTERNAL MEDIA ACCESS CONTROLLER (MAC)

When a packet is received by the MAC, a DMA transfer from the MAC's internal buffer into main memory is initiated by the MAC. This method generally provides for shortened development time and excellent performance.

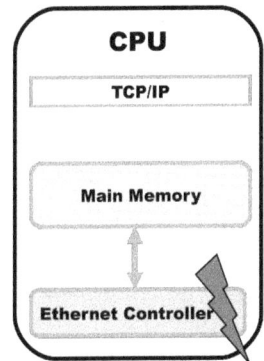

CPU WITH AN INTERNAL MAC BUT WITH DEDICATED MEMORY

When a packet is received, the MAC initiates a DMA transfer into dedicated memory. Generally, most configurations of this type allow for transmission from main memory while reserving dedicated memory for either receive or transmit operations. Both the MAC and the CPU can read and write from dedicated memory and so the stack can process packets directly from dedicated memory.

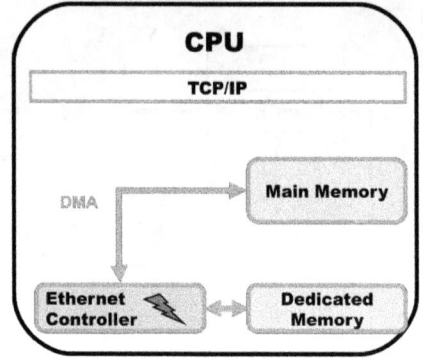

Porting to this architecture is generally not difficult and provides for excellent performance. However, performance may be limited by the size of the dedicated memory; especially in cases where transmit and receive operations share the dedicated memory space.

COOPERATIVE DMA SOLUTION WHERE BOTH THE CPU AND MAC TAKE PART IN THE DMA OPERATION

This configuration is generally found on external devices that are either connected directly to the processor bus or connected via the ISA or PCI standard. This method requires that the CPU contain a DMA peripheral that can be configured to work within the architectural limitations of the external device. This method is more difficult to port to, but generally offers excellent performance.

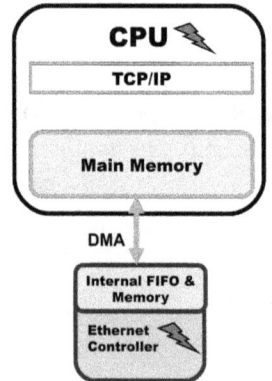

EXTERNAL DEVICE ATTACHED VIA THE CPU'S EXTERNAL BUS

Data is moved between main memory and the external device's internal memory via bus read and write cycles. The amount of data transferred in a given bus operation depends on the width of the data bus. This method requires additional CPU intervention in order to copy all of the data to and from the device when necessary. This method is generally easy to port and offers average performance.

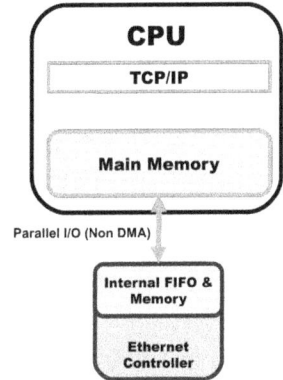

These settings are likely to be influenced by the size of the available memory on the device. You will have to find these specific configuration values for the device driver and provides them to the stack user. An example of a typical device and buffer configuration is available in section F-2-2 "Network and Device Buffer Configuration" on page 1006. The size and number of receive and transmit buffers depends on many factors, including, but not limited to:

■ The desired level of performances

■ The bandwidth required for the application

■ CPU utilization

16-2-3 INTERRUPT HANDLING

This section provides an overview of interrupt handling, which is necessary to understand the reception and transmission of network packets. After reading this section, you should be ready to understand the description and explanations of the follow section of this chapter

Interrupt handling is accomplished using the following multi-level scheme.

1 Processor level interrupt handler

2 µC/TCP-IP BSP interrupt handler (Network BSP)

3 Device driver interrupt handler

During initialization, the device driver registers all necessary interrupt sources with the BSP interrupt management code. This may also be accomplished by plugging an interrupt vector table during compile time. Once the global interrupt vector sources are configured and an interrupt occurs, the system will call the first-level interrupt handler. The first-level handler then calls the network device's BSP handler which in turn calls **NetIF_ISR_Handler()** with the interface number and ISR type. The ISR type may be known if a dedicated interrupt vector is assigned to the source, or it may be de-multiplexed from the device driver by reading a register. If the interrupt type is unknown, then the BSP interrupt handler should call **NetIF_ISR_Handler()** with the appropriate interface number and NET_IF_ISR_TYPE_UNKNOWN.

The following ISR types have been defined from within µC/TCP-IP, however, additional type codes may be defined within each device's **net_dev.h**:

```
NET_DEV_ISR_TYPE_UNKNOWN
NET_DEV_ISR_TYPE_RX
NET_DEV_ISR_TYPE_RX_RUNT
NET_DEV_ISR_TYPE_RX_OVERRUN
NET_DEV_ISR_TYPE_TX_RDY
NET_DEV_ISR_TYPE_TX_COMPLETE
NET_DEV_ISR_TYPE_TX_COLLISION_LATE
NET_DEV_ISR_TYPE_TX_COLLISION_EXCESS
NET_DEV_ISR_TYPE_JABBER
NET_DEV_ISR_TYPE_BABBLE
NET_DEV_ISR_TYPE_TX_DONE
NET_DEV_ISR_TYPE_PHY
```

Depending on the architecture, there may be a network device BSP interrupt handler for each implemented device interrupt type (see also Chapter 15, "Network Board Support Package" on page 347 and section A-3-5 "NetDev_ISR_Handler()" on page 577). PHY interrupts should call **NetIF_ISR_Handler()** with a type code equal to NET_DEV_ISR_TYPE_PHY.

F16-2(1)   The device driver must call the network device BSP during initialization in order to configure any module clocks, GPIO, or external interrupt controllers that require configuration. Note: Network device BSP is processor- and device-specific and must be supplied by the application developer. See Chapter 15, "Network Board Support Package" on page 347 for more details.

16-2-4 NETWORK PACKET RECEPTION OVERVIEW

This section is a quick overview of the mechanism put in place to handle the reception of network packets within the device driver, the µC/TCP-IP module and the OS.

A device's receive interrupt signals the µC/TCP-IP module for each packet received so that each receive is queued and later handled by µC/TCP-IP's network interface Receive task. Processing devices' received packets is deferred to the network interface Receive task to keep device ISRs as short as possible and make the driver easier to write.

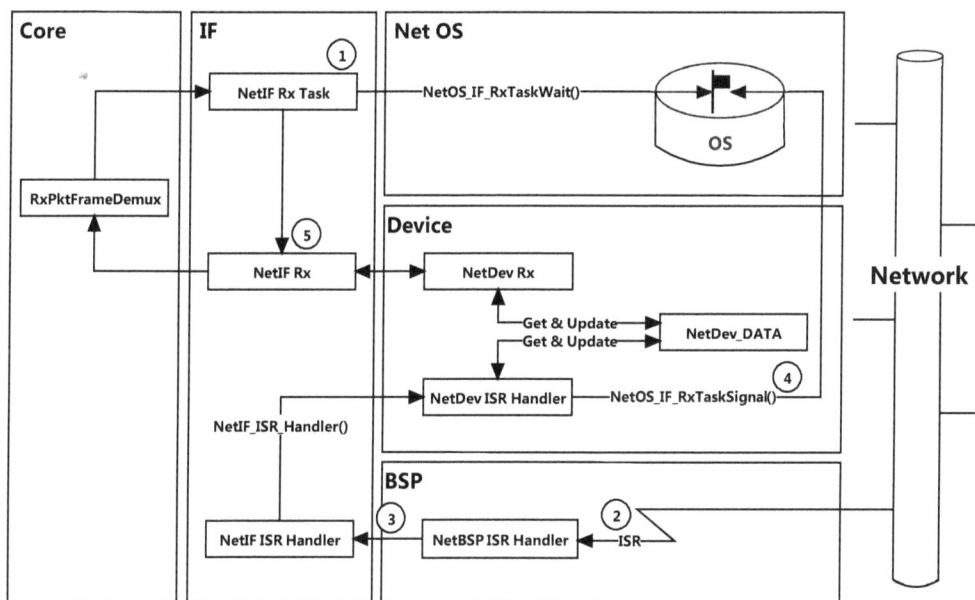

Figure 16-3 **Device Receive interrupt and network receive signaling**

F16-3(1)   The µC/TCP-IP's network interface Receive task calls `NetOS_IF_RxTaskWait()` to wait for device receive packets to arrive by waiting (ideally without timeout) for the Device Rx Signal to be signaled.

F16-3(2)   When a device packet is received, the device generates a receive interrupt which calls the device's BSP-level ISR handler.

F16-3(3)   The device's BSP-level ISR handler determines which network interface number
            the specific device's interrupt is signaling and then calls `NetIF_ISR_Handler()`
            to handle the device's receive interrupt.

F16-3(4)   The network interface and device ISR handlers (i.e., `NetIF_Ether_ISR_Handler()`
            and `NetDev_ISR_Handler()`) call `NetOS_IF_RxTaskSignal()` to signal the
            Device Rx Signal for each received packet.

F16-3(5)   µC/TCP-IP's network interface Receive task's call to `NetOS_IF_RxTaskWait()`
            is made ready for each received packet that signals the Device Rx Signal. The
            network interface Receive task then calls the specific network interface and
            device receive handler functions to retrieve the packet from the device. If the
            packet was not already received directly into a network buffer (e.g., via DMA),
            it is copied into a network buffer data. The network buffer is then
            de-multiplexed to higher-layer protocol(s) for further processing.

16-2-5 NETWORK PACKET TRANSMISSION OVERVIEW

A device's transmit complete interrupt signals µC/TCP-IP that another transmit packet is available to be transmitted or be queued for transmit by the device.

Figure 16-3 shows the relationship between a device's transmit complete interrupt, its transmit complete ISR handling and µC/TCP-IP's network interface transmit.

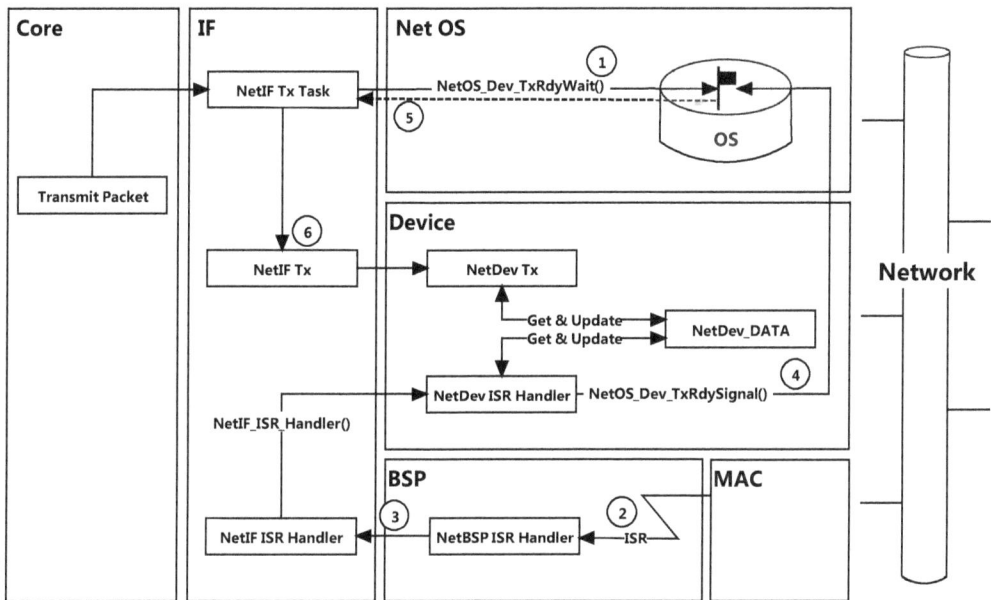

Figure 16-4 **Device transmit complete interrupt and transmit ready signal**

F16-4(1)   The µC/TCP-IP's Network Interface Transmit calls `NetOS_Dev_TxRdyWait()` to wait for a specific network interface device semaphore to become ready and/or available to transmit a packet by waiting (with or without timeout) for the specific network interface's Device Tx Ready Signal to be signaled.

F16-4(2)   When a device is ready and/or available to transmit a packet, the device generates an interrupt which calls the device's BSP-level ISR handler.

F16-4(3)   The device's BSP-level ISR handler determines which network interface number the specific device's interrupt is signaling and then calls `NetIF_ISR_Handler()` to handle the transmit complete interrupt.

F16-4(4)   The specific device ISR handlers **NetDev_ISR_Handler()** calls **NetOS_Dev_TxRdySignal()** to signal the Device Tx Ready Signal for each packet or descriptor that is now available to transmit by the device.

F16-4(5)   µC/TCP-IP's Network Interface Transmit's call to **NetOS_Dev_TxRdyWait()** returns since the semaphore is made ready by each available device transmit complete that signals the Device Tx Ready Signal.

F16-4(6)   The Network Interface Transmit then calls the specific network interface and device transmit handler functions to prepare the packet for transmission by the device.

16-3 ETHERNET LAYERS INTERACTIONS

This sections that follow describe the interactions between the IF layer, the Ethernet device driver API functions, the BSP API functions and the Ethernet PHY API functions. Since the device driver is made of not only logic but also from interactions with the parts on the board, you'll need to understand the calls made to the these layers of the µC/TCP-IP module and to the CPU and board-dependent layers.

Figure 16-5 shows the logical path between the physical layer and the device driver through the function calls and interruptions.

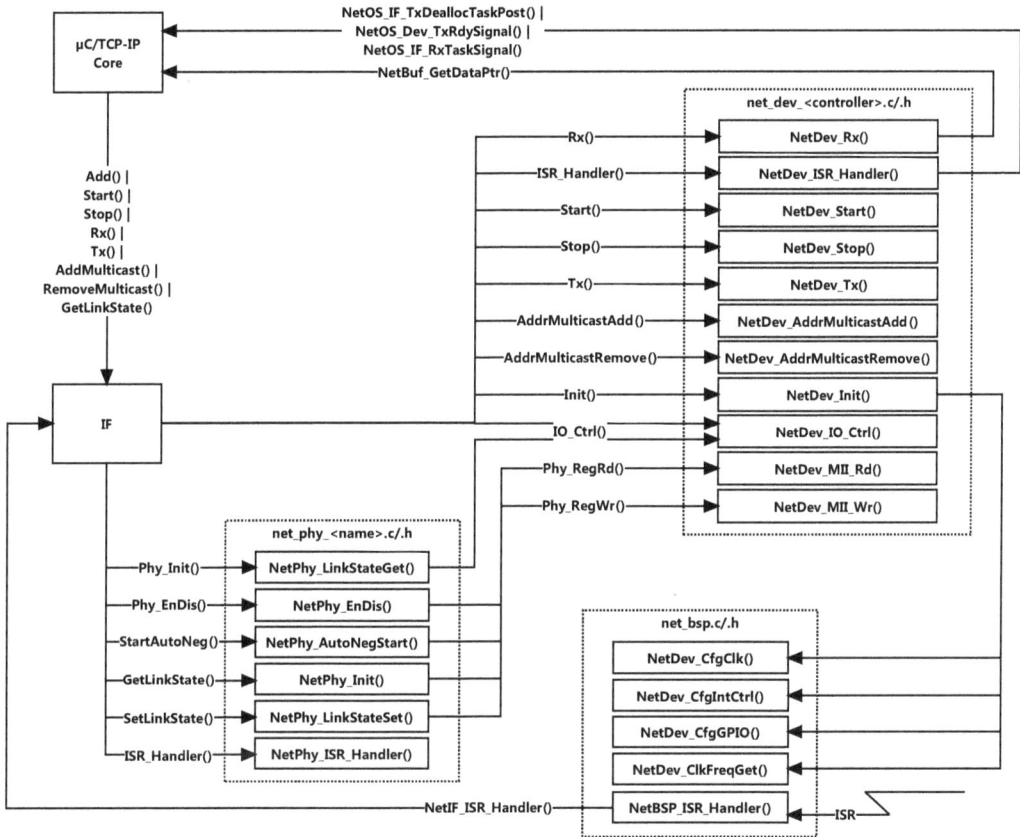

Figure 16-5 **PHY, device driver & BSP interactions**

16-4 ETHERNET PHY API IMPLEMENTATION

16-4-1 DESCRIPTION OF THE ETHERNET PHY API

Many Ethernet devices use external (R)MII compliant physical layers (PHYs) to attach themselves to the Ethernet wire. However, some MACs use embedded PHYs and do not have a MII-compliant communication interface. In this case, it may acceptable to merge the PHY functionality with the MAC device driver, in which case a separate PHY API and configuration structure may not be required. But in the event that an external (R)MII-compliant device is attached to the MAC, the PHY driver must implement the PHY API as follows:

```
const NET_PHY_API_ETHER NetPHY_API_DeviceName = { NetPhy_Init,            (1)
                                                   NetPhy_EnDis,           (2)
                                                   NetPhy_LinkStateGet,    (3)
                                                   NetPhy_LinkStateSet,    (4)
                                                   0                       (5)
};
```

Listing 16-2 **PHY interface API**

L16-2(1)   PHY initialization function pointer

L16-2(2)   PHY enable/disable function pointer

L16-2(3)   PHY link get status function pointer

L16-2(4)   PHY link set status function pointer

L16-2(5)   PHY interrupt service routine (ISR) handler function pointer

µC/TCP-IP provides code that is compatible with most (R)MII compliant PHYs. However, extended functionality, such as link state interrupts, must be implemented on a per-PHY basis. If additional functionality is required, it may be necessary to create an application specific PHY driver.

Note: It is the PHY driver developers' responsibility to ensure that all of the functions listed within the API are properly implemented and that the order of the functions within the API structure is correct. The **NetPhy_ISR_Handler** field is optional and may be populated as **(void *)0** if interrupt functionality is not required.

16-4-2 HOW TO INITIALIZE THE PHY

NetPhy_Init() initializes the PHY driver. It is called by the Ethernet network interface layer after the MAC device driver, if the latter initialized without error.

The PHY initialization function is responsible of the following actions:

1   Reset the PHY and wait with timeout for reset to complete. If a timeout occurs, return **perr** set to **NET_PHY_ERR_RESET_TIMEOUT**.

2   Start the auto-negotiation process. This should configure the PHY registers such that the desired link speed and duplex specified within the PHY configuration are respected. It is not required to wait until the auto-negotiation process has completed, as this can take upwards of many seconds. This action is performed by calling the PHY's **NetPhy_AutoNegStart()** function.

3   If no errors occur, return **perr** set to **NET_PHY_ERR_NONE**.

16-4-3 HOW ENABLE OR DISABLE THE PHY

NetPhy_EnDis() is called by the Ethernet network interface layer when an interface is started or stopped.

Disabling the PHY will causes the PHY to power down which will causes the link state to be disconnected.

16-4-4 HOW TO GET THE NETWORK LINK STATE

The `NetPhy_LinkStateGet()` function returns the current Ethernet link state. Results are passed back to the caller in a `NET_DEV_LINK_ETHER` structure which contains fields for link speed and duplex. This function is called periodically by the µC/TCP-IP module.

The generic PHY driver does not return a link state. Instead, in order to avoid access to extended registers which are PHY specific, the driver attempts to determine link state by analyzing the PHY and PHY partner capabilities. The best combination of auto-negotiated link state is selected as the current link state.

16-4-5 HOW TO SET THE LINK SPEED AND DUPLEX

`NetPhy_LinkStateSet()` function sets the current Ethernet link state. Results are passed back to the caller within a `NET_DEV_LINK_ETHER` structure which contains fields for link speed and duplex. This function is called by `NetIF_Start()`.

16-4-6 HOW TO SPECIFY THE ADDRESS OF THE PHY ISR

`NetPhy_ISR_Handler()` handles PHY's interrupts. See section 16-4-7 on page 384 for more details on how to handle PHY interrupts. µC/TCP-IP does not require PHY drivers to enable or handle PHY interrupts. The generic PHY drivers does not even define a PHY interrupt handler function but instead handles all events by either periodic or event-triggered calls to other PHY API functions.

16-4-7 NetPhy_ISR_Handler()

`NetPhy_ISR_Handler()` is the physical layer interrupt handier. The PHY ISR handler is called though the network device BSP in a similar manner to that of the device ISR handler. The network device BSP is used to initialize the host interrupt controller, clocks, and any necessary I/O pins that are required for configuring and recognizing PHY interrupt sources. When an interrupt occurs, the first level interrupt handler calls the network device BSP interrupt handler which in turn calls `NetIF_ISR_Handler()` with the interface number and interrupt type set to `NET_IF_ISR_TYPE_PHY`. The PHY ISR handler should execute the necessary instructions, clear the PHY interrupt flag and exit.

Note: Link state interrupts must call both the Ethernet device driver and Net IF in order to inform both layers of the current link status. This is performed by calling `pdev_api->IO_Ctrl()` with the option `NET_IF_IO_CTRL_LINK_STATE_UPDATE` as well as a pointer to a `NET_DEV_LINK_ETHER` structure containing the current link state speed and duplex. Additionally, the PHY device driver must call `NetIF_LinkStateSet()` with a pointer to the interface and a Boolean value set to either `NET_IF_LINK_DOWN` or `NET_IF_LINK_UP`.

Note: The Generic PHY driver provided with µC/TCP-IP does not support interrupts. PHY interrupt support requires use of the extended PHY registers which are PHY-specific. However, link state is polled periodically by µC/TCP-IP and you can configure the period during compile time.

16-5 ETHERNET DEVICE DRIVER IMPLEMENTATION

16-5-1 DESCRIPTION OF THE ETHERNET DEVICE DRIVER API

All device drivers must declare an instance of the appropriate device driver API structure as a global variable within the source code. The API structure is an ordered list of function pointers utilized by µC/TCP-IP when device hardware services are required.

A sample Ethernet interface API structure is shown below.

```
const  NET_DEV_API_ETHER  NetDev_API_<controler> = { NetDev_Init,             (1)
                                                      NetDev_Start,            (2)
                                                      NetDev_Stop,             (3)
                                                      NetDev_Rx,               (4)
                                                      NetDev_Tx,               (5)
                                                      NetDev_AddrMulticastAdd, (6)
                                                      NetDev_AddrMulticastRemove, (7)
                                                      NetDev_ISR_Handler,      (8)
                                                      NetDev_IO_Ctrl,          (9)
                                                      NetDev_MII_Rd,           (10)
                                                      NetDev_MII_Wr            (11)
                                                    };
```

Listing 16-3 **Ethernet interface API**

Note: It is the device driver developers' responsibility to ensure that all of the functions listed within the API are properly implemented and that the order of the functions within the API structure is correct.

L16-3(1)   Device initialization/add function pointer

L16-3(2)   Device start function pointer

L16-3(3)   Device stop function pointer

L16-3(4)   Device Receive function pointer

L16-3(5)   Device transmit function pointer

L16-3(6)   Device multicast address add function pointer

L16-3(7)   Device multicast address remove function pointer

L16-3(8)   Device interrupt service routine (ISR) handler function pointer

L16-3(9)   Device I/O control function pointer

L16-3(10)   Physical layer (PHY) register read function pointer

L16-3(11)   Physical layer (PHY) register write function pointer

Note: μC/TCP-IP device driver API function names may not be unique. Name clashes between device drivers are avoided by never globally prototyping device driver functions and ensuring that all references to functions within the driver are obtained by pointers within the API structure. The developer may arbitrarily name the functions within the source file so long as the API structure is properly declared. The user application should never need to call API functions by name. Unless special care is taken, calling device driver functions by name may lead to unpredictable results due to reentrancy.

The following figure describes the call path from the application layer through the Core, Interface and Controller layers.

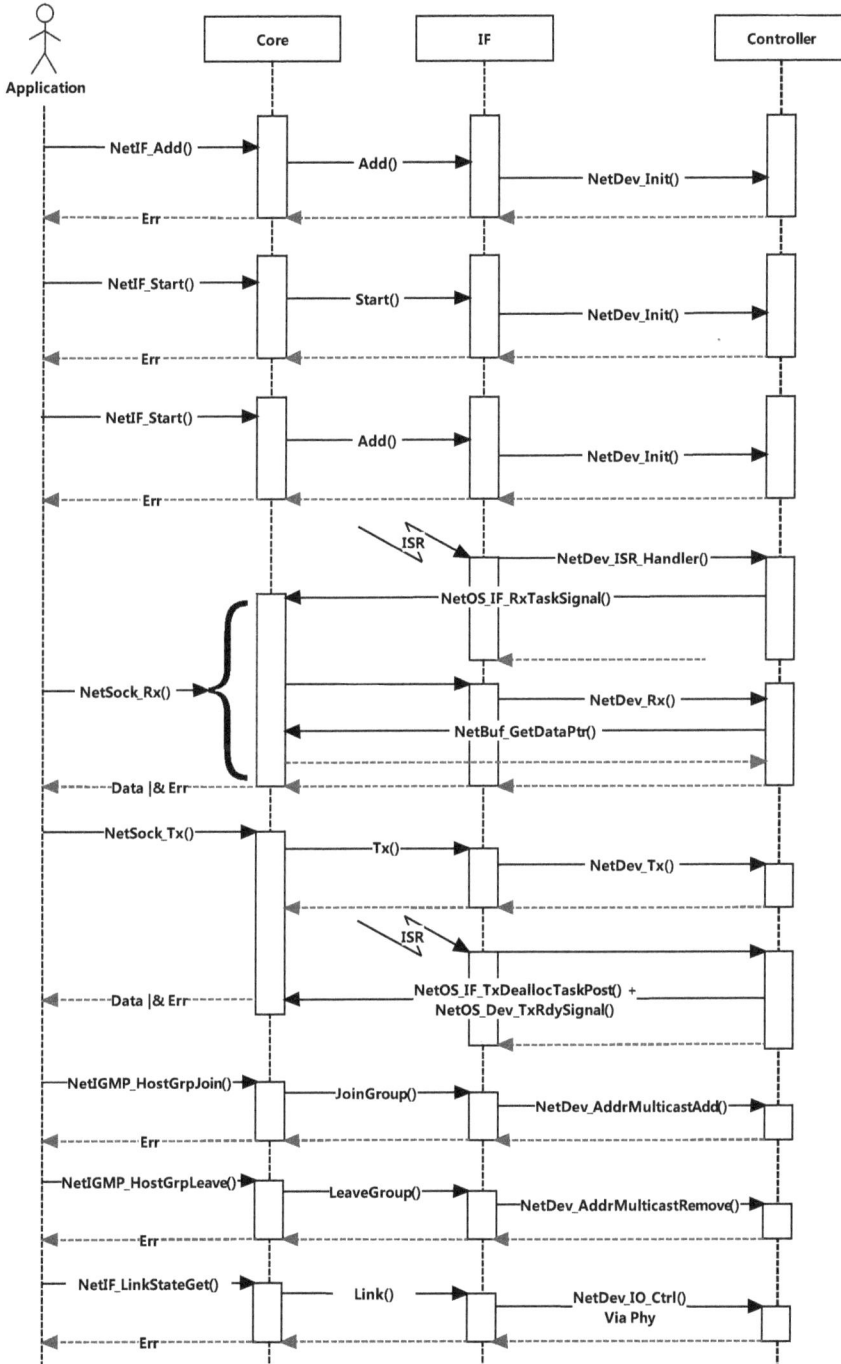

Figure 16-6 **Call path of controller functions**

16-5-2 INITIALIZING A NETWORK DEVICE

NetDev_Init() is called by NetIF_Add() exactly once for each specific network device added by the application. If multiple instances of the same network device are present on the board, then this function is called for each instance of the device. However, applications should not try to add the same specific device more than once. If a network device fails to initialize, we recommend debugging to find and correct the cause of the failure.

NetDev_Init() performs the following operations. However, depending on the device being initialized, functionality may need to be added or removed:

1. Configure clock gating to the MAC device, if applicable. This is performed via the network device's BSP function pointer, NetDev_CfgClk(), implemented in net_bsp.c (see section A-3-1 "NetDev_CfgClk()" on page 567).

2. Configure all necessary I/O pins for both an internal or external MAC and PHY, if present. This is performed via the network device's BSP function pointer, NetDev_CfgGPIO(), implemented in net_bsp.c.

   Configure the host interrupt controller for receive and transmit complete interrupts. Additional interrupt services may be initialized depending on the device and driver requirements. This is performed via the network device's BSP function pointer, NetDev_CfgIntCtrl(), implemented in net_bsp.c.

3. For DMA devices: Allocate memory for all necessary descriptors. This is performed via calls to µC/LIB's memory module.

4. For DMA devices: Initialize all descriptors to their ready states. This may be performed via calls to locally-declared, static functions.

5. Initialize the (R)MII bus interface, if applicable. This entails configuring the (R)MII bus frequency which is dependent on the system clock. Static values for clock frequencies should never be used when determining clock dividers. Instead, the driver should reference the associated clock function(s) for getting the system clock or peripheral bus frequencies, and use these values to compute the correct (R)MII bus clock divider(s). This is performed via the network device's BSP function pointer, NetDev_ClkFreqGet(), implemented in net_bsp.c.

6   Disable the transmitter and receiver (should already be disabled).

7   Disable and clear pending interrupts (should already be cleared).

8   Set **perr** to **NET_DEV_ERR_NONE** if initialization proceeded as expected. Otherwise, set **perr** to an appropriate network device error code.

16-5-3 STARTING A NETWORK DEVICE

NetDev_Start() is called once each time an interface is started. It performs the following actions:

1   Call the **NetOS_Dev_CfgTxRdySignal()** function to configure the transmit ready semaphore count. This function call is optional and is performed if the hardware device supports queuing multiple transmit frames. By default, the semaphore count is initialized to one. However, DMA devices should set the semaphore count equal to the number of configured transmit descriptors for optimal performance. Non-DMA devices that support queuing more than one transmit frame may also benefit from a non-default value.

2   Initialize the device MAC address, if applicable. For Ethernet devices, this step is mandatory. The MAC address data may come from one of three sources and should be set using the following priority scheme:

   ▣   Configure the MAC address using the string found within the device configuration structure. This is a form of static MAC address configuration and may be performed by calling **NetASCII_Str_to_MAC()** and **NetIF_AddrHW_SetHandler()**. If the device configuration string has been left empty, or is specified as all 0's, an error will be returned and the next method should be attempted.

   ▣   Check if the application developer has called **NetIF_AddrHW_Set()** by making a call to **NetIF_AddrHW_GetHandler()** and **NetIF_AddrHW_IsValidHandler()** in order to check if the specified MAC address is valid. This method may be used as a static method for configuring the MAC address during run-time, or a dynamic method should a pre-programmed external memory device exist. If the acquired MAC address does not pass the check function, then:

■ Call **NetIF_AddrHW_SetHandler()** using the data found within the individual MAC address registers. If an auto-loading EEPROM is attached to the MAC, the registers will contain valid data. If not, then a configuration error has occurred. This method is often used with a production process where the MAC supports automatically loading individual address registers from a serial EEPROM. When using this method, you should specify an empty string for the MAC address within the device configuration, and refrain from calling **NetIF_AddrHW_Set()** from within the application.

3 Initialize additional MAC registers required by the MAC for proper operation.

4 Clear all interrupt flags.

5 Locally enable interrupts on the hardware device. The host interrupt controller should have already been configured within the device driver **NetDev_Init()** function.

6 Enable the receiver and transmitter.

7 Set perr equal to **NET_DEV_ERR_NONE** if no errors have occurred. Otherwise, set perr to an appropriate network device error code

16-5-4 STOPPING A NETWORK DEVICE

NetDev_Stop() is called once each time an interface is stopped.

NetDev_Stop() must perform the following operations:

1 Disable the receiver and transmitter.

2 Disable all local MAC interrupt sources.

3 Clear all local MAC interrupt status flags.

4 For DMA devices, re-initialize all receive descriptors.

5 For DMA devices, free all transmit descriptors by calling **NetOS_IF_DeallocTaskPost()** with the address of the transmit descriptor data areas.

6 For DMA devices, re-initialize all transmit descriptors.

7 Set **perr** to **NET_DEV_ERR_NONE** if no error occurs. Otherwise, set **perr** to an appropriate network device error code.

16-5-5 NetDev_ISR_Handler()

NetDev_ISR_Handler() is the device interrupt handler. In general, the device interrupt handler must perform the following functions:

1 Determine which type of interrupt event occurred by switching on the ISR type argument, or reading an interrupt status register if the event type is unknown.

2 If a receive event has occurred, the driver must post the interface number to the μC/TCP-IP Receive task by calling **NetOS_IF_RxTaskSignal()** for each new frame received.

3 If a transmit complete event has occurred, the driver must perform the following items for each transmitted packet.

   a Post the address of the data area that has completed transmission to the transmit buffer de-allocation task by calling **NetOS_IF_TxDeallocTaskPost()** with the pointer to the data area that has completed transmission.

   b Call **NetOS_Dev_TxRdySignal()** with the interface number that has just completed transmission.

4 Clear local interrupt flags.

External or CPU's integrated interrupt controllers should be cleared from within the network device's BSP-level ISR after **NetDev_ISR_Handler()** returns. Additionally, it is highly recommended that device driver ISR handlers be kept as short as possible to reduce the amount of interrupt latency in the system.

Each device's **NetDev_ISR_Handler()** should check all applicable interrupt sources to see if they are active. This additional checking is necessary because multiple interrupt sources may be set within the interrupt response time and will reduce the number and overhead of handling interrupts. **NetDev_ISR_Handler()** should never return early.

16-5-6 RECEIVING PACKETS ON A NETWORK DEVICE

NetDev_Rx() is called by µC/TCP-IP's Receive task after the Interrupt Service Routine handler has signaled to the Receive task that a receive event has occurred. NetDev_Rx() requires that the device driver return a pointer to the data area containing the received data and return the size of the received frame via pointer.

NetDev_Rx() should perform the following actions:

1 Check for receive errors, if applicable. If an error should occur during reception, the driver should set *size to 0 and *p_data to (CPU_INT08U *)0 and return. Additional steps may be necessary depending on the device being serviced.

2 For Ethernet devices, get the size of the received frame and subtract four bytes for the CRC. It's recommended to first check the frame size to ensure that it is larger than four bytes before performing the subtraction, to ensure that an underflow does not occur. Set *size to the adjusted frame size.

3 Get a new data buffer area by calling NetBuf_GetDataPtr(). If memory is not available, an error will be returned and the device driver should set *size to 0 and *p_data to (CPU_INT08U *)0.

4 If an error does not occur while getting a new data area, *p_data must be set to the address of the data area.

5 Set perr to NET_DEV_ERR_NONE and return from the receive function. Otherwise, set perr to an appropriate network device error code.

16-5-7 TRANSMITTING PACKETS ON A NETWORK DEVICE

NetDev_Tx() is used to notify the Ethernet device that a new packet is available to be transmitted. It performs the following actions:

1 For DMA-based hardware, the driver should select the next available transmit descriptor and set the pointer to the data area equal to the address pointer to by **p_data**.

2 For non-DMA hardware, the driver should call **Mem_Copy()** to copy the data stored in the buffer to the device's internal memory. The address of the buffer is specified by **p_data**.

3 Once completed, the driver must configure the device with the number of bytes to transmit. This value contained in the **size** argument. DMA-based devices have a size field within the transmit descriptor. Non-DMA devices have a transmit size register that must be configured.

4 The driver then takes all necessary steps to initiate transmission of the data.

5 NetDev_Tx() sets **perr** to NET_DEV_ERR_NONE and return from the transmit function.

16-5-8 ADDING AN ADDRESS TO THE MULTICAST ADDRESS FILTER OF A NETWORK DEVICE

NetDev_AddrMulticastAdd() is used to configure a device with an (IP-to-Ethernet) multicast hardware address.

Since many network controllers' documentation fails to properly indicate how to add/configure an Ethernet MAC device with a multicast address, the following method is recommended for determining and testing the correct multicast hash bit algorithm.

1 Configure a packet capture program or multicast application to broadcast a multicast packet with Ethernet destination address of 01:00:5E:00:00:01 (which is an IPv4 Ethernet multicast address). This MAC address corresponds to the multicast group IP address of 224.0.0.1 which will be converted to a MAC address by higher layers and passed to this function.

2 Set a break point in the receive ISR handler, and transmit one Send packet to the target. The break point should not be reached as the result of the transmitted packet. Use caution to ensure that other network traffic is not the source of the interrupt when the button is pressed. Sometimes asynchronous network events happen very close in time and the end result can be deceiving. Ideally, these tests should be performed on an isolated network, but if that is not an option, disconnect as many other hosts from the network as possible.

3 Use the debugger to stop the application and program the MAC multicast hash register low bits to 0xFFFFFFFF. Go to step 2. Repeat for the hash bit high register if necessary. The goal is to bracket off which bit in either the high or low hash bit register causes the device to be interrupted when the broadcast frame is received by the target. Once the correct bit is known, the hash algorithm can be easily written and tested.

4 Update the device driver's **NetDev_AddrMulticastAdd()** function to calculate and configure the correct CRC. The sample code in Listing 16-4 can be adjusted as per the network controller's documentation in order to get the hash from the correct subset of CRC bits. Most of the code is similar between various devices and is thus reusable. The hash algorithm is the exclusive OR of every 6th bit of the destination address:

```
hash[5] = da[5] ^ da[11] ^ da[17] ^ da[23] ^ da[29] ^ da[35] ^ da[41] ^ da[47]
hash[4] = da[4] ^ da[10] ^ da[16] ^ da[22] ^ da[28] ^ da[34] ^ da[40] ^ da[46]
hash[3] = da[3] ^ da[09] ^ da[15] ^ da[21] ^ da[27] ^ da[33] ^ da[39] ^ da[45]
hash[2] = da[2] ^ da[08] ^ da[14] ^ da[20] ^ da[26] ^ da[32] ^ da[38] ^ da[44]
hash[1] = da[1] ^ da[07] ^ da[13] ^ da[19] ^ da[25] ^ da[31] ^ da[37] ^ da[43]
hash[0] = da[0] ^ da[06] ^ da[12] ^ da[18] ^ da[24] ^ da[30] ^ da[36] ^ da[42]
```

Where da[0] represents the least significant bit of the first byte of the Ethernet destination address (da) received and where da[47] represents the most significant bit of the last byte of the Ethernet destination address received.

5 Test the device driver's **NetDev_AddrMulticastAdd()** function by ensuring that the group address 224.0.0.1, when joined from the application correctly configures the device to receive multicast packets destined to the 224.0.0.1 address. Then broadcast to 224.0.0.1 to test if the device receives the multicast packet.

16

```
                                        /* ---------- CALCULATE HASH CODE ---------- */
hash = 0;
for (i = 0; i < 6; i++) {               /* For each row in the bit hash table:        */
    bit_val = 0;                        /* Clear initial xor value for each row.       */
    for (j = 0; j < 8; j++) {           /* For each bit in each octet:                 */
        bit_nbr   = (j * 6) + i;        /* Determine which bit in stream, 0-47.        */
        octet_nbr = bit_nbr / 8;        /* Determine which octet bit belongs to.       */
        octet     = paddr_hw[octet_nbr];/* Get octet value.                            */
                                        /* Check if octet's bit is set.                */
        bit       = octet & (1 << (bit_nbr % 8));
        bit_val   ^= (bit > 0) ? 1 : 0; /* Calculate table row's XOR hash value.       */
    }
    hash |= (bit_val << i);             /* Add row's XOR hash value to final hash.     */
}
                                        /* ---- ADD MULTICAST ADDRESS TO DEVICE ---- */
reg_sel = (hash >> 5) & 0x01;           /* Determine hash register      to configure. */
reg_bit = (hash >> 0) & 0x1F;           /* Determine hash register bit to configure.  */
                                        /* (Substitute '0x01'/'0x1F' with device's ..*/
                                        /* .. actual hash register bit masks/shifts.)*/
  paddr_hash_ctrs = &pdev_data->MulticastAddrHashBitCtr[hash];
(*paddr_hash_ctrs)++;                   /* Increment hash bit reference counter.       */
if (reg_sel == 0) {                     /* Set multicast hash register bit.            */
    pdev->MCAST_REG_LO |= (1 << reg_bit);/* (Substitute 'MCAST_REG_LO/HI' with ..      */
} else {                                /* .. device's actual multicast registers.)    */
    pdev->MCAST_REG_HI |= (1 << reg_bit);
}
```

Listing 16-4 **Explicit multicast hash code**

ALTERNATE HASH CODE

Alternatively, Figure 16-7 shows how the CRC hash can be computed with a call to `NetUtil_32BitCRC_CalcCpl()` followed by an optional call to `NetUtil_32BitReflect()`, with four possible combinations:

▨ CRC without complement, without reflection

▨ CRC without complement, with reflection

▨ CRC with complement, without reflection

▨ CRC with complement, with reflection

```
                                           /* ---------- CALCULATE HASH CODE ---------- */
                                           /* Calculate CRC.                            */
crc = NetUtil_32BitCRC_Calc((CPU_INT08U *)paddr_hw,
                            (CPU_INT32U ) addr_hw_len,
                            (NET_ERR    *)perr);
if (*perr != NET_UTIL_ERR_NONE) {
    return;
}
                                           /* ---- ADD MULTICAST ADDRESS TO DEVICE ---- */
crc     = NetUtil_32BitReflect(crc);       /* Optionally, complement CRC.               */
hash    = (crc >> 23u) & 0x3F;             /* Determine hash register    to configure.  */
reg_bit = (hash % 32u);                    /* Determine hash register bit to configure. */
                                           /* (Substitute '23u'/'0x3F' with device's .. */
                                           /* .. actual hash register bit masks/shifts.)*/
   paddr_hash_ctrs = &pdev_data->MulticastAddrHashBitCtr[hash];
(*paddr_hash_ctrs)++;                       /* Increment hash bit reference counter.    */
if (hash <= 31u) {                          /* Set multicast hash register bit.          */
    pdev->MCAST_REG_LO |= (1 << reg_bit);   /* (Substitute 'MCAST_REG_LO/HI' with ..    */
} else {                                    /* .. device's actual multicast registers.) */
    pdev->MCAST_REG_HI |= (1 << reg_bit);
}
```

Listing 16-5 **CRC Multicast Hash Code**

Unfortunately, the network controller's documentation will likely not tell you which combination of complement and reflection is needed to properly compute the hash value. The documentation will likely state 'Standard Ethernet CRC', which when compared to other documents, means any of the four combinations above; different than the actual frame CRC.

Fortunately, if the code is written to perform both the complement and reflection, then you can use the debugger to repeat the code block over and over, skipping either the line that performs the complement or the function call to the reflection, until the output hash bit is computed correctly.

16-5-9 REMOVING AN ADDRESS FROM THE MULTICAST ADDRESS FILTER OF A NETWORK DEVICE

NetDev_AddrMulticastRemove() is used to remove an (IP-to-Ethernet) multicast hardware address from a device.

You can use exactly the same code as in NetDev_AddrMulticastAdd() to calculate the device's CRC hash, but instead remove a multicast address by decrementing the device's hash bit reference counters and clearing the appropriate bits in the device's multicast registers. See Figure 16-8 below.

```c
                                          /* ---------- CALCULATE HASH CODE ---------- */
  /* Use NetDev_AddrMulticastAdd()'s algorithm to calculate CRC hash.                  */
                                          /* - REMOVE MULTICAST ADDRESS FROM DEVICE -- */
  paddr_hash_ctrs = &pdev_data->MulticastAddrHashBitCtr[hash];
  if (*paddr_hash_ctrs > 1u) {            /* If multiple multicast addresses hashed, ..*/
    (*paddr_hash_ctrs)--;                 /* .. decrement hash bit reference counter ..*/
     *perr = NET_DEV_ERR_NONE;            /* .. but do NOT unconfigure hash register.  */
     return;
  }
  *paddr_hash_ctrs = 0u;                  /* Clear hash bit reference counter.         */
  if (hash <= 31u) {                      /* Clear multicast hash register bit.        */
      pdev->MCAST_REG_LO &= ~(1u << reg_bit);  /* (Substitute 'MCAST_REG_LO/HI' with ..  */
  } else {                               /* .. device's actual multicast registers.)  */
      pdev->MCAST_REG_HI &= ~(1u << reg_bit);
  }
```

Listing 16-6 **Removing Multicast Address**

16-5-10 SETTING THE MAC LINK, DUPLEX AND SPEED SETTINGS

NetDev_IO_Ctrl() is used to implement miscellaneous functionality such as setting and getting the PHY link state, as well as updating the MAC link state registers when the PHY link state has changed. An optional void pointer to a data variable is passed into the function and may be used to get device parameters from the caller, or to return device parameters to the caller. µC/TCP-IP defines the following default options: NET_DEV_LINK_STATE_GET_INFO and NET_DEV_LINK_STATE_UPDATE.

The NET_DEV_LINK_STATE_GET_INFO option expects **p_data** to point to a variable of type NET_DEV_LINK_ETHER for the case of an Ethernet driver. This variable has two fields, Speed and Duplex, which are filled in by the PHY device driver via a call through the PHY API. µC/TCP-IP internally uses this option code in order to periodically poll the PHYs for link state. The NET_DEV_LINK_STATE_UPDATE option is used by the PHY driver to communicate with the MAC when either µC/TCP-IP polls the PHY for link status, or when a PHY interrupt occurs. Not all MAC's require PHY link state synchronization. Should this be the case, then the device driver may not need to implement this option.

16-5-11 READING PHY REGISTERS

NetDev_MII_Rd() is implemented within the Ethernet device driver file, since (R)MII bus reads are associated with the MAC device. In the case that the PHY communication mechanism is separate from the MAC, then a handler function may be provided within the **net_bsp.c** file and called from the device driver file instead. Note: This function must be implemented with a timeout and should not block indefinitely should the PHY fail to respond.

16-5-12 WRITING TO PHY REGISTERS

NetDev_MII_Wr() is implemented within the Ethernet device driver file since (R)MII bus writes are associated with the MAC device. In the case that the PHY communication mechanism is separate from the MAC, a handler function may be provided within the **net_bsp.c** file and called from the device driver file instead.

Note: This function must be implemented with a timeout and not block indefinitely should the PHY fail to respond.

16-6 ETHERNET - TRANSMITTING & RECEIVING USING DMA

A DMA controller is a device that moves data through a system independently of the CPU/MCU. It connects internal and peripheral memories via a set of dedicated buses. A DMA controller can also be considered a peripheral itself in the sense that the processor programs it to perform data transfers.

In general, a DMA controller includes an address bus, a data bus, and control registers. An efficient DMA controller possesses the ability to request access to any resource it needs, without involving the CPU. It must have the capability to generate interrupts and to calculate addresses.

A processor might contain multiple DMA controllers, multiple DMA channels, and multiple buses that link the memory banks and peripherals directly. Processors with an integrated Ethernet controller typically have a DMA controller for their Ethernet hardware.

Generally, the processor should need to respond to DMA interrupts only after the data transfers are completed. The DMA controller is programmed by the processor to move data in parallel while the processor is doing its regular processing tasks.

Since the DMA controller has the capability to interface with memory, it can get its own instruction from memory. Picture a DMA controller as a simple processor with a simple instruction set. DMA channels have a finite number of registers that need to be filled with values, each of which gives a description of how to transfer the data.

There are two main classes of DMA transfer: Register Mode and Descriptor Mode. In Register mode, the DMA controller is programmed by the CPU by writing the required parameters in the DMA registers. In Descriptor mode, the DMA can use its read memory circuitry to fetch the register values itself rather than burdening the CPU to write the values. The blocks of memory containing the required register parameters are called *descriptors*. When the DMA runs in Register Mode, the DMA controller simply uses the values contained in the registers.

Descriptor Mode provides the best results, and is mostly found in microprocessor/microcontroller DMA controllers with integrated Ethernet controller. This is the mode described in detail below.

DESCRIPTOR MODE

In Descriptor Mode, the formatting of the descriptor information is provided by the DMA controller. The descriptor contains all of the same parameters that the CPU (operating in Register Mode) would program into the DMA control registers.

Descriptor Mode allows multiple DMA sequences to be chained together so the controller be programmed to automatically set up and start another DMA transfer after the current sequence completes. The descriptor-based model provides the most flexible configuration to manage a system's memory.

The DMA controller provides a main descriptor model method; normally called a *Descriptor List*. Depending on the DMA controller, the descriptor list may reside in consecutive memory locations, but this is not mandatory. μC/TCP-IP reserves consecutive memory blocks for descriptors and both models can be used.

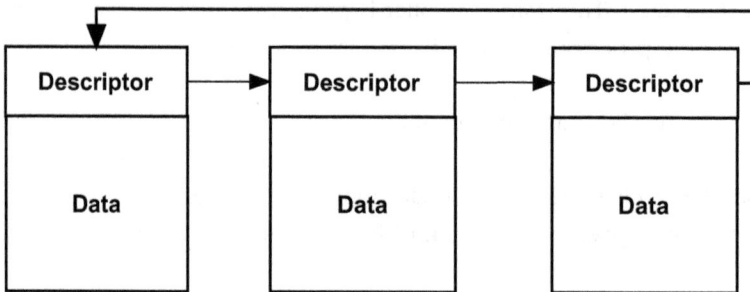

Figure 16-7 **Descriptor link list**

In the μC/TCP-IP device driver, a linked list of descriptors is created, as shown in Figure 16-7. The term *linked* implies that one descriptor points to the next descriptor, which is loaded automatically. To complete the chain, the last descriptor points back to the first descriptor, and the process repeats. This mechanism is used for Ethernet frame reception.

The vast majority of processors that include Ethernet support come with a Direct Memory Access Controller (DMAC). This has the advantage reducing the load on the CPU, as the DMAC handles data transfers from the CPU internal memory to the Ethernet controller memory area or vice versa. If a DMAC is present on your device, we encourage you to take advantage of it.

16-6-1 DRIVER DATA & CONTROL USING DMA

Each driver should have their own data structure **NET_DEV_DATA**, which contains status information about data reception, transmission and statistics. The driver's state structure is stored by the core and can be retrieving within any driver API functions. Figure 16-8 illustrates the structure to track and control Receive & Transmit descriptors.

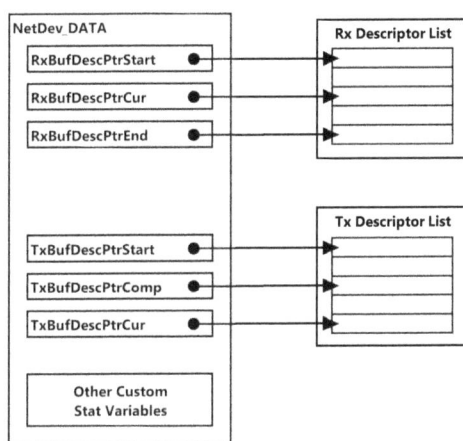

Figure 16-8 **NET_DEV_DATA data structure**

16-6-2 RECEPTION USING DMA

INITIALIZATION

When µC/TCP-IP is initialized, the Network Device Driver allocates a memory block for all Receive descriptors; this is performed via calls to µC/LIB.

Then, the network device driver must allocate a list of descriptors and configure each address field to point to the start address of a Receive buffer. At the same time, the network device driver initializes three pointers: one to track the current descriptor, which is expected to contain the next received frame; a second to remember the descriptor list boundaries; and a third for the descriptor list starting address.

The DMA controller is initialized and the hardware is informed of the address of descriptor list.

**Data
Buffers**

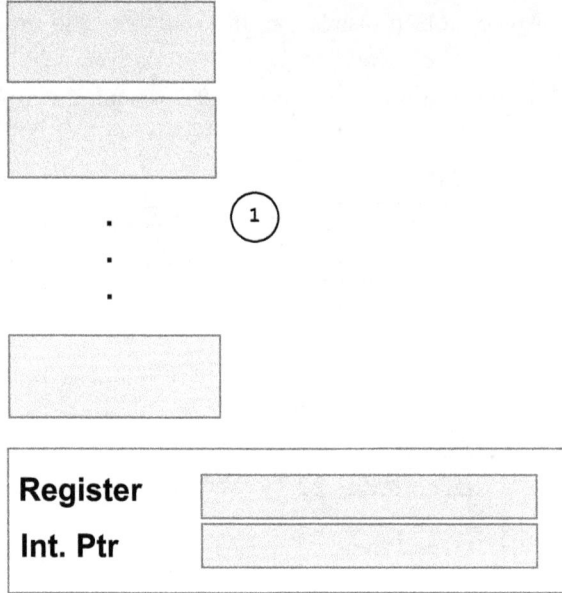

Figure 16-9 **Allocation of buffers**

F16-9(1)   The result of `Mem_Init()` and the first step in the intialization of the Network Device Driver is the allocation of buffers.

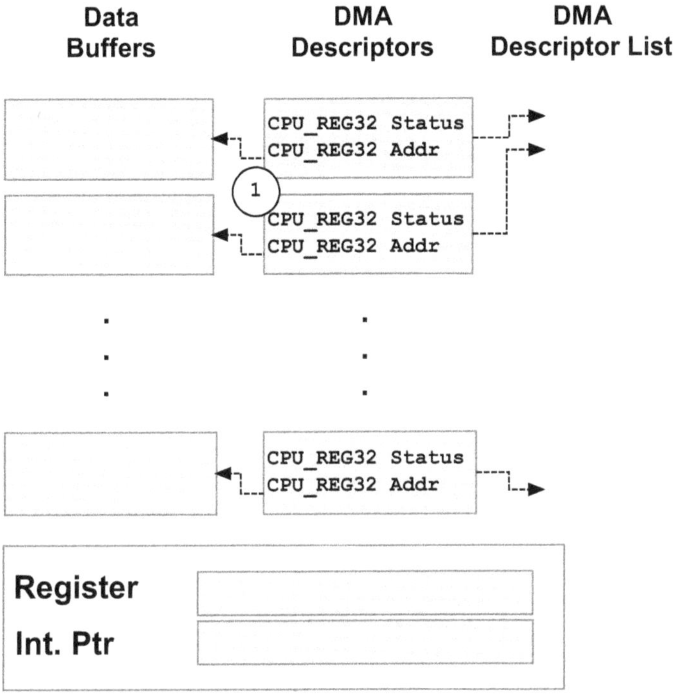

Figure 16-10 **Descriptor allocation**

F16-10(1) μC/TCP-IP allocates a list of descriptors based on the network device driver configuration and sets each address field to point to the start address of a receive buffer.

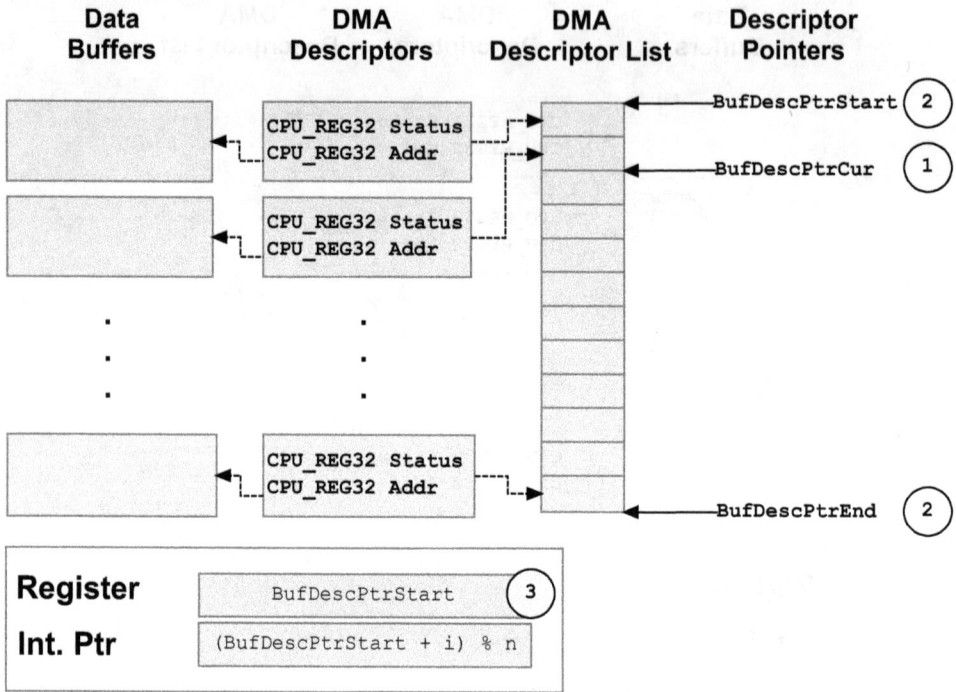

Figure 16-11 **Reception descriptor pointers initialization**

F16-11(1)   The network device driver initializes three pointers. One to track the current descriptor which is expected to contain the next received frame

F16-11(2)   A second pointer to remember the descriptor list boundaries.

F16-11(3)   Finally, the DMA controller is initialized and hardware is informed of the descriptor list starting address.

RECEPTION

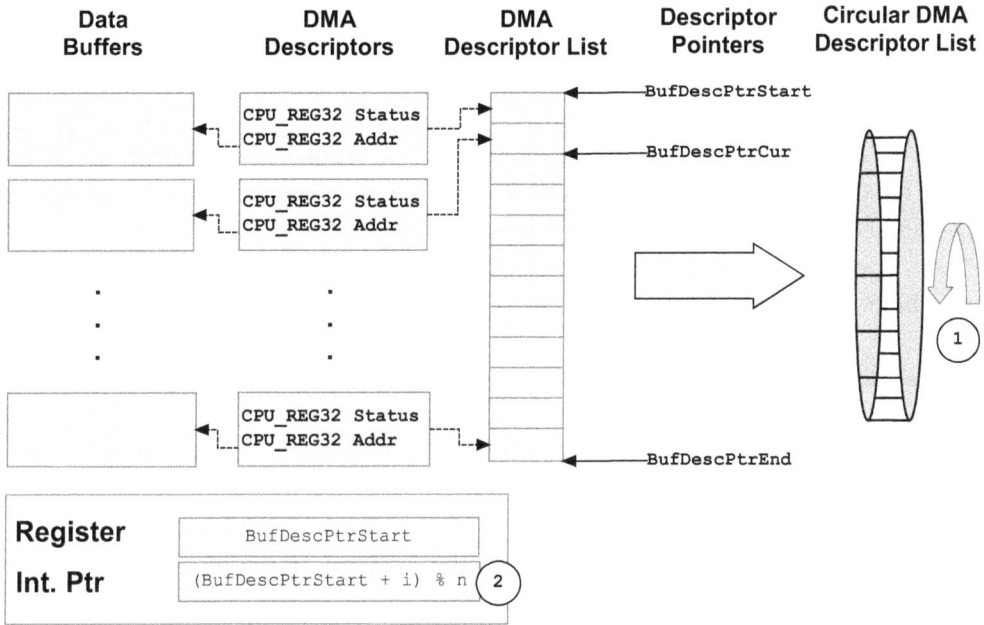

Figure 16-12 **Receiving an Ethernet frame with DMA**

F16-12(1)   With each new received frame, the network device driver increments **BufDescPtrCur** by 1 and wraps around the descriptor list as necessary

F16-12(2)   The hardware applies the same logic to an internal descriptor pointer.

When a received frame is processed, the driver gets a pointer to a new data buffer and updates the current descriptor address field. The previous buffer address is passed to the protocol stack for processing. If a buffer pointer cannot be obtained, the existing pointer remains in place and the frame is dropped.

405

ISR HANDLER

When a frame is received, the DMA controller will generate an interrupt. The ISR handler must signal the network interface. The network interface will automatically call the receive function.

DMA are using a control data structure that indicates the transfer configuration. These data structure are called descriptors and to be able to receive multiple packets at the same time, we need multiple descriptors that we arrange in a list.

We use three pointers to manage and keep track of the Rx descriptors:

`RxBufDescPtrStart`   This pointer doesn't move, it always points to the first descriptor.

`RxBufDescPtrCur`   This pointer must track the current descriptor which data is ready to be processed.

`RxBufDescPtrEnd`   This pointer doesn't move, it always points to the last descriptor.

INITIALIZING DEVICE RECEPTION DESCRIPTORS

`NetDev_Start()` starts the network interface hardware by initializing the receive and transmit descriptors, enabling the transmitter and receiver and starting and enabling the DMA. Initialization the Rx DMA descriptors list can done in a sub-function `NetDev_RxDescInit()`. The memory needed by the descriptors must be reserved by the function `NetDev_Init()`. Initialization of the Rx descriptor list consist of setting the descriptors pointers of the **NET_DEV_DATA** and fill all Receive descriptors with a Receive buffer.

The descriptors should be organized in a ring configuration. This means that each descriptor contains a pointer to the next descriptor and the last descriptor's next pointer refers to the first descriptor of the list.

You also have to initialize each descriptor. You must initialize descriptor field according to the controller documentation. Note that the descriptor must be configured to be owned by the DMA and *not* the software. Here is the pseudo code of the descriptor ring initialization:

```
pdesc                    = (DEV_DESC *)pdev_data->RxBufDescPtrStart;          (1)
pdev_data->RxBufDescPtrCur   = (DEV_DESC *)pdesc;                             (2)
pdev_data->RxBufDescPtrEnd   = (DEV_DESC *)pdesc + (pdev_cfg->RxDescNbr - 1); (3)
for (i = 0; i < pdev_cfg->RxDescNbr; i++) {                                   (4)
    pdesc->Field   = value;                                                   (5)
    pdesc->Status  = ETH_DMA_RX_DESC_OWN;                                     (6)
    pdesc->Buf     = NetBuf_GetDataPtr((NET_IF         *)pif,                 (7)
                                       (NET_TRANSACTION)NET_TRANSACTION_RX,
                                       (NET_BUF_SIZE   )NET_IF_ETHER_FRAME_MAX_SIZE,
                                       (NET_BUF_SIZE   )NET_IF_IX_RX,
                                       (NET_BUF_SIZE  *)0,
                                       (NET_BUF_SIZE  *)0,
                                       (NET_TYPE      *)0,
                                       (NET_ERR       *)perr);
    if (*perr != NET_BUF_ERR_NONE) {                                          (8)
        return;
    }
    pdesc->Next = (DEV_DESC *)(pdesc + 1);                                    (9)
    pdesc++;                                                                  (10)
}
```

Listing 16-7 **Descriptor Ring Initialization**

L16-7(1)   Initialize the descriptor pointer to the first Rx buffer descriptor of **pdev_data**.

L16-7(2)   Initialize current descriptor pointer of **pdev_data** to the first Rx buffer descriptor of **pdev_data**.

L16-7(3)   Initialize last descriptor pointer of **pdev_data** to the last descriptor declared using pointer arithmetic and the Rx descriptor number defined by **RxDescNbr** in **NET_DEV_CFG_ETHER**.

L16-7(4)   Repeat for each descriptor defined in **.RxDescNbr** in **NET_DEV_CFG_ETHER**.

L16-7(5)   Initialize the description fields to their initial value as defined by the DMA Descriptor's documentation in the device data sheet. There might be more than a single field to define depending of the specifications of the DMA used (a field describing the size of associated data buffer might be present and require to be initialized to the length of the requested buffer area below.)

L16-7(6)   Initialize the status bit of the descriptor to specify that it is owned by the DMA engine (not by the software).

L16-7(7) Call **NetBuf_GetDataPtr()** to get a buffer area and initialize the descriptor's buffer start address to the address of the buffer area.

L16-7(8) If an error occurred during the allocation of a buffer area, return as it might mean that there is an issue with the values declared in **NET_DEV_CFG_ETHER** and the available device memory or heap size.

L16-7(9) Initialize the next descriptor location of the current descriptor to the next descriptor using pointer arithmetic.

L16-7(10) Increment the descriptor using pointer arithmetics.

Once the Rx descriptor ring is ready, you have to configure controller register to enable the controller reception. Controller's interrupt generation should be enabled for the following events: reception of a packet with and without errors and completed transmission of a packet with and without errors.

WHAT NEEDS TO BE DONE IN THE ISR FOR RECEPTION

NetDev_ISR_Handler() is the function called by the IF layer when a Ethernet related ISR is generated and handled by the BSP layer. When Rx ISR occur, only **NetOS_IF_RxTaskSignal()** has to be called. Nothing has to be done on **RxBufDescPtrCur**. The complete receive process is delayed in order to have the fastest ISR handler as possible. If an error occurred on RX, you can increment driver statistic into the ISR handler or into **NetDev_Rx()**, it's up to you to determine which of the cases is best. You must always signal the core that a packet is received using **NetOS_IF_RxTaskSignal()**. If you fail to notify the core for each packet, a buffer leak will occur and performance will degrade. **NetDev_Rx()** will discard the packet and it will say to the µC/TCP-IP module that the packet is received with an error.

MOVING BUFFERS FROM THE DEVICE TO THE TCP-IP STACK USING DMA

NetDev_Rx() is called by core once a **NetOS_IF_RxTaskSignal()** call has been made to recover the received packet. If data received is valid, this function must replace the buffer of the current descriptor with a free buffer. Also, the current descriptor must be restarted (owned by the DMA) to be able to receive again. **RxBufDescPtrCur** must be moved to point on the next descriptor. The sub-function **NetDev_RxDescPtrCurInc()** is called to restart the current descriptor and to move the pointer to the next descriptor. If an error has occurred, you have to set data and length pointers to 0 and return an error. If there is no free Rx buffer available, the packet must be discarded by leaving the current data buffer assigned to the DMA, increment the current descriptor and return an error to the µC/TCP-IP module. Here is a pseudo code of **NetDev_Rx()**:

```
static  void  NetDev_Rx (NET_IF      *pif,
                         CPU_INT08U  **p_data,
                         CPU_INT16U  *size,
                         NET_ERR     *perr)
{
    pdesc = (DEV_DESC *)pdev_data->RxBufDescPtrStart;           (1)

    if (pdesc owned by DMA) {                                   (2)
        *perr  = NET_DEV_ERR_RX;
        *size  = 0;
        *p_data = (CPU_INT08U *)0;
        return;
    }

    if (is Rx error) {                                         (3)
        if needed, restart DMA;
        if needed, NetDev_RxDescPtrCurInc();
        *perr  = NET_DEV_ERR_RX;
        *size  = 0;
        *p_data = (CPU_INT08U *)0;
        return;
    }

    if (is Data length valid) {                               (4)
        if needed, NetDev_RxDescPtrCurInc();
        *perr  = NET_DEV_ERR_INVALID_SIZE;
        *size  = 0;
        *p_data = (CPU_INT08U *)0;
        return;
    }

    pbuf_new = NetBuf_GetDataPtr(…, perr);                    (5)
    if (*perr != NET_BUF_ERR_NONE) {
        NetDev_RxDescPtrCurInc();
        *size  = 0;
        *p_data = (CPU_INT08U *)0;
        return;
    }

    *size  = pdesc->Length;                                   (6)
    *p_data = (CPU_INT08U *)pdesc->Buf;                       (7)
    pdesc->Buf = pbuf_new;                                    (8)
    NetDev_RxDescPtrCurInc();                                 (9)
    *perr  = NET_DEV_ERR_NONE;                                (10)
}
```

Listing 16-8 **Packet Reception**

L16-8(1)   Obtain pointer to the next ready descriptor.

L16-8(2)   If this descriptor is owned by the DMA (e.g., the DMA is currently receiving data or hasn't started receiving data yet). The descriptor has to be owned by the software to be processed. If owned by the DMA, set ***perr** to **NET_DEV_ERR_RX** signaling that the interrupt that there was an error within the reception. Set ***size** to 0, ***p_data** to (**CPU_INT08U***)0 and return.

L16-8(3)   If a reception error is reported in the descriptor set ***perr** to **NET_DEV_ERR_RX** notifying that an error occured within the reception. Set ***size** to 0, ***p_data** to (**CPU_INT08U***)0 and return.

L16-8(4)   If the frame length is either runt or overrun set ***perr** to **NET_DEV_ERR_INVALID_SIZE** signaling that the size of the received frame is invalid. Set ***size** to 0, ***p_data** to (**CPU_INT08U***)0 and return.

L16-8(5)   Once every error has been handled, acquire a new data buffer to replace the one we're about to take from the descriptor. If no buffers are available set ***size** to 0, ***p_data** to (**CPU_INT08U***)0, increment **pdev_data** current descriptor and return.

L16-8(6)   Set ***size** to the value of the Length field of the current descriptor. This field should specify how many bytes of data were received by the descriptor.

L16-8(7)   Set ***p_data** to the value of the data buffer of the descriptor.

L16-8(8)   Set the value of the descriptor's data buffer to the newly allocated data area.

L16-8(9)   Increment the current descriptor to the next descriptor.

L16-8(10)   Set ***perr** to **NET_DEV_ERR_NONE** to notify that no errors were found.

The following is the pseudo code for **NetDev_RxDescPtrCurInc()**:

```
pdesc                     = pdev_data->RxBufDescPtrCur;              (1)
pdev_data->RxBufDescPtrCur = pdesc->Next;                            (2)
```

Listing 16-9 **Descriptor Increment**

L16-9(1)   Get current **pdev_data** current descriptor.

L16-9(2)   Set **pdev_data** current descriptor to the next descriptor in the current one.

STOPPING THE RECEPTION OF PACKETS

NetDev_Stop() is called to shutdown a network interface hardware by disabling the receiver and transmitter, disabling receive and transmit interrupts, free all receive descriptors and deallocate all transmit buffers. When the interface is stopped, you must deallocate the DMA descriptor ring. To do that, a sub-function is called **NetDev_RxDescFreeAll()** where each descriptor's buffer is freed and the DMA controller control is disabled:

```
pdesc   = pdev_data->RxBufDescPtrStart;                             (1)
for (i = 0; i < pdev_cfg->RxDescNbr; i++) {                         (2)
    pdesc_data = (CPU_INT08U *)(pdesc->Addr);                       (3)
    NetBuf_FreeBufDataAreaRx(pif->Nbr, pdesc_data);                 (4)
    pdesc->Status = Not owned by the controller                     (5)
    pdesc++;                                                        (6)
}
```

Listing 16-10 **Deallocation of Descriptor Ring**

L16-10(1)   Get **pdev_data**'s first descriptor.

L16-10(2)   For each descriptor defined in **.RxDescNbr** in NET_DEV_CFG_ETHER:

L16-10(3)   Get the address of the descriptor's buffer.

L16-10(4)   Deallocate the buffer area.

L16-10(5)   Set the status of the descriptor to be owned by the software (to disable reception on that descriptor).

L16-10(6)   Increment the current descriptor using pointer arithmetic.

16-6-3 RECEPTION USING DMA WITH LISTS

Micrium provides an alternate method for executing DMA transfers: DMA with Lists. The goal of this implementation is to reduce the number of controller errors (overrun, underrun, etc.), and increase driver performance. The typical implementation of the DMA descriptor initialization still applies here.

In order to keep the interrupt time short as possible, you cannot call the µC/TCP-IP module to get a free buffer from within the ISR. In order manage buffers, you must maintain a list of buffers within the device driver.

To implement the list method, create three lists: the Buffer List, the Ready List and the Free List. The three lists contain nodes which are moved from one list to another. A node is a memory space where you store pointers to the buffer address and the location of the next node.

The device driver data **NET_DEV_DATA** must contain three pointers which point to the first node of each list. The following is a description of the three lists:

Buffers List   This list contains empty nodes. Once a node is filled with the location of a free buffer, you must add this node to the Free List. If a node cannot be filled with the location of a free buffer, or a buffer ready to be processed, you must move the node back into the Buffers List.

Ready List   This list contains buffers which are ready to be processed (i.e., used by the application). When no resources are available to fill a node because they are occupied by the µC/TCP-IP module or by a DMA descriptor, the node must be moved into Buffer List.

Free List   This list contains nodes that point to free buffers. When a buffer is no longer in use by the stack, a node from the Buffer List is moved to the Free List and the pointer in that node set to the free buffer. When a pointer in a node in the Free List is used to replace a pointer to a descriptor buffer, you must move the node from the Free List to the Ready List.

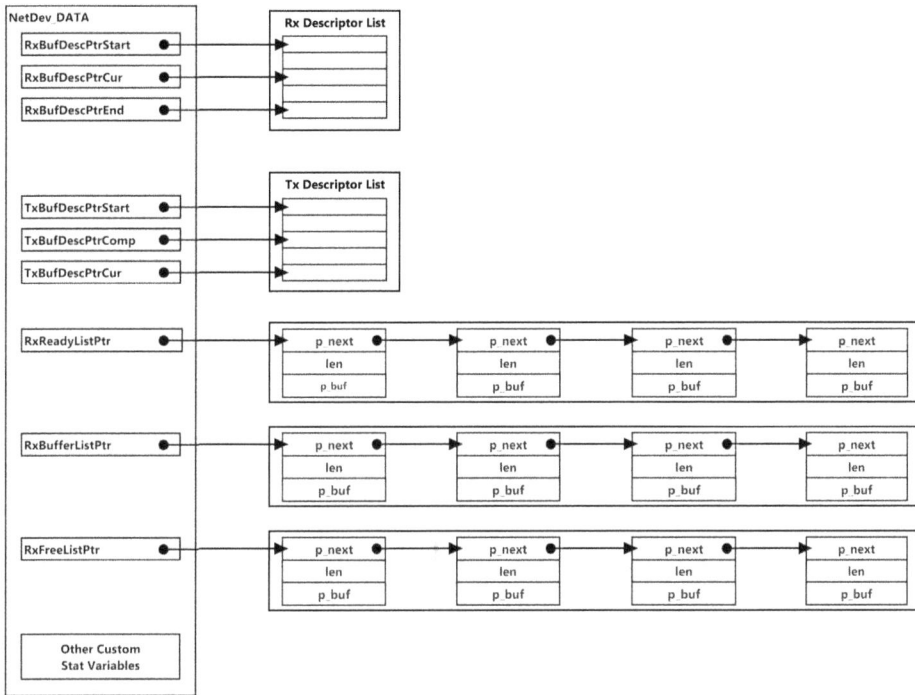

Figure 16-13 **Buffers in lists**

ALLOCATION OF BUFFER LIST NODES

NetDev_Init() is called to allocate memory for the device DMA's descriptors, among other things. You must reserve some memory for each node within the device driver initialization. Since the device is not yet started after the initialization, and no resources are available for the driver, all created nodes must be assigned to the Free List.

Listing Figure 16-13 shows the pseudo code for memory allocation for nodes, and list initialization. These steps should be performed during the device initialization.

```
pdev_data->RxReadyListPtr  = (LIST_ITEM *)0;                              (1)
pdev_data->RxBufferListPtr = (LIST_ITEM *)0;
pdev_data->RxFreeListPtr   = (LIST_ITEM *)0;
cnt = pdev_cfg->RxBufLargeNbr - pdev_cfg->RxDescNbr;                      (2)
for (ix = 0; ix < cnt; ix++) {
    plist = (LIST_ITEM *)Mem_HeapAlloc((CPU_SIZE_T  ) sizeof(LIST_ITEM),  (3)
                                       (CPU_SIZE_T  ) 4,
                                       (CPU_SIZE_T *)&reqd_octets,
                                       (LIB_ERR    *)&lib_err);
    if (plist == (LIST_ITEM *)0) {                                        (4)
       *perr = NET_DEV_ERR_MEM_ALLOC;
        return;
    }
    plist->Buffer = (void *)0;                                           (5)
    plist->Len    = 0;
    plist->Next   = pdev_data->RxFreeListPtr;                            (6)
    pdev_data->RxFreeListPtr = plist;                                    (7)
}
```

Listing 16-11 **Descriptor List Initialization**

L16-11(1)   Initialize **RxReadyListPtr**, **RxBufferListPtr** and **RxFreeListPtr** of **pdev_data** to **(LIST_ITEM *)0**.

L16-11(2)   The initial number of **LIST_ITEM**s in **RxFreeListPtr** is calcuated as the number of **.RxBufLargeNbr** minus **.RxDescNbr**. From the pool of Receive buffers, only that number of buffers needs to be placed in the **RxFreeListPtr** since the rest of the buffers are initially assigned to a descriptor.

L16-11(3)   Allocate a **LIST_ITEM** object from the heap.

L16-11(4)   If an error occurred during the allocation of a **LIST_ITEM** set ***perr** to **NET_DEV_ERR_MEM_ALLOC** to notify that there was an error during memory allocation and then return.

L16-11(5)   Set the **.Buffer** field to **(void *)0** and the **.Len** field to 0 since no buffer is associated with the list nodes yet.

L16-11(6)   Set the **.Next** field of the list node to the current node of **RxFreeListPtr**

L16-11(7)   Insert the newly allocated node to the single ended list of **RxFreeListPtr**.

Thus after the device initialization, all nodes are added into the Free List. The buffers and the ready lists pointers are null.

INITIALIZATION OF BUFFER LIST NODES

NetDev_Start() is used to initialize the reception buffer list. Nodes in the Free List are used to assign a buffer to each of the Receive descriptors, and then removed from the Free List. Any nodes remaining in the Free List should be moved to the Buffer List. Nodes in the Buffer List will be used to replace a descriptor buffer when the ISR handler signals that a new packet has been received. Listing 16-12 shows pseudocode for the Buffer list initialization:

```
cnt = pdev_cfg->RxBufLargeNbr - pdev_cfg->RxDescNbr;              (1)
for (i = 0; i < cnt; i++) {
    plist                 = pdev_data->RxFreeListPtr;            (2)
    pdev_data->RxFreeListPtr = plist->Next;
    plist->Buffer = NetBuf_GetDataPtr(perr);
    if (*perr != NET_BUF_ERR_NONE) {
        plist->Next             = pdev_data->RxFreeListPtr;      (3)
        pdev_data->RxFreeListPtr = plist;
        break;
    }
    plist->Next             = pdev_data->RxBufferListPtr;        (4)
    pdev_data->RxBufferListPtr = plist;
}
```

Listing 16-12 **Buffer List initialization**

L16-12(1)   Get the number of available Receive buffers to put into the **.RxBufferListPtr**. Of the **RxBufLargeNbr** buffers, **RxDescNbr** will be assigned to Receive descriptors; the rest will be put into the **.RxBufferListPtr**.

L16-12(2)   Get the list element pointer from free list.

L16-12(3)   Return the list element pointer to free list in case of error.

L16-12(4)   Store the list element pointer on Buffer list.

Thus after the device start, all nodes should be added into the Buffer List. So the Free and the Ready Lists should be null.

415

DEALLOCATION OF BUFFER LIST NODES

As with typical DMA implementation, you must remove the DMA descriptor ring and free the buffers. Also, you must move all nodes into the Free List. Listing 16-12 shows pseudocode for the node deallocation:

```
plist = pdev_data->RxBufferListPtr;
while (plist != (LIST_ITEM *)0) {                                          (1)
    plist_next = plist->Next;
    pdesc_data = plist->Buffer;
    NetBuf_FreeBufDataAreaRx(pif->Nbr, pdesc_data);                        (2)
    plist->Buffer = (void *)0;
    plist->Len    = 0;
    plist->Next            = pdev_data->RxFreeListPtr;                     (3)
    pdev_data->RxFreeListPtr = plist;
    plist = plist_next;
}
pdev_data->RxBufferListPtr = (LIST_ITEM *)0;                               (4)
plist = pdev_data->RxReadyListPtr;
while (plist != (LIST_ITEM *)0) {                                          (5)
    plist_next = plist->Next;
    pdesc_data = plist->Buffer;
    NetBuf_FreeBufDataAreaRx(pif->Nbr, pdesc_data);                        (6)
    plist->Buffer = (void *)0;
    plist->Len    = 0;
    plist->Next            = pdev_data->RxFreeListPtr;                     (7)
    pdev_data->RxFreeListPtr = plist;
    plist = plist_next;
}
pdev_data->RxReadyListPtr = (LIST_ITEM *)0;                                (8)
```

Listing 16-13 **Descriptor and Buffer List deallocation**

L16-13(1)   Repeat deallocation process for the nodes in **RxBufferListPtr** the until the **.Next** field of the node is null.

L16-13(2)   Return data area to Receive data area pool.

L16-13(3)   Remove the node from **RxBufferListPtr**.

L16-13(4)   Set .**RxBufferListPtr** of **pdev_data** to null.

L16-13(5)   Repeat deallocation process for the nodes in **RxFreeListPtr** until the **.Next** field of the node is null.

L16-13(6)   Return data area to Rx data area pool.

L16-13(7)   Remove the node from **RxFreeListPtr**.

L16-13(8)   Set **.RxFreeListPtr** of **pdev_data** to null.

BUFFER NODE PROCESSING DURING ISR

In order to process received packets, you must call the function **NetDev_ISR_Handler()**.

If there are errors associated with the received packet, the packet must be discarded by returning the control of the descriptor back to the Direct Memory Access Controller. If the Buffer List is empty (meaning that there is no available buffer to exchange with a received DMA buffer) the packet must also be discarded.

On the other hand, if a buffer is available in the Buffer List, you must replace the buffer assigned to the DMAC with the available buffer. You must then move the received buffer from the DMAC to the Ready List in order to be processed by the Receive task. We suggest you to put the ISR Receive task in a separate sub-function. Note that you must call your sub-function for each individual Receive descriptor that is owned by the software, since you might receive only a single interrupt signal for a multiple DMA Receive completions.

Pseudo code of what should be put into the **NetDev_ISR_Handler()** is described below:

```
if ((interrupt source == Receive) ||                              (1)
    (interrupt source == Receive error)) {
    valid = DEF_TRUE;
    while (valid == DEF_TRUE) {
        pdesc = (DEV_DESC *)pdev_data->RxBufDescCurPtr;           (2)

        if (pdesc->status indicates desc' is owned by soft.) {   (3)
            valid = NetDev_ISR_Rx(pif, pdesc);                   (4)

            pdev_data->RxBufDescCurPtr = pdesc->next;            (5)
        } else {
            valid = DEF_FALSE;
        }
    }
}
```

Listing 16-14 **ISR Handling**

L16-14(1)   If the interrupt register indicates a completed reception, or a reception error, proceed with handling of the interrupt.

L16-14(2)   Obtain the pointer to the next ready descriptor.

L16-14(3)   The descriptor is ready to be processed (reception is complete and descriptor is owned by the software).

L16-14(4)   Call **NetDev_ISR_Rx()** to execute the buffer, and list element manipulation required to exchange the buffer of the descriptor with an available buffer.

L16-14(5)   Move to the next descriptor in order to repeat the process with that descriptor, if it is owned by the software.

Your sub-function (**NetDev_ISR_Rx()**) must replace the current descriptor buffer with a buffer from a node into the Buffer List, and then signal the µC/TCP-IP module to process received packets and refill the Buffer list. You must also make sure that the Buffer List is not null (i.e., there is a buffer available). If no buffers are available, you must discard the packet.

The pseudo code for the Receive ISR sub-function is described below:

```
static  CPU_BOOLEAN  NetDev_ISR_Rx (NET_IF    *pif,
                                    DEV_DESC  *pdesc)
{
    NET_DEV_DATA  *pdev_data;
    LIST_ITEM     *plist_buf;
    LIST_ITEM     *plist_ready;
    void          *p_buf;
    CPU_BOOLEAN    valid;
    CPU_BOOLEAN    signal;
    NET_ERR        err;
    pdev_data = (NET_DEV_DATA *)pif->Dev_Data;              (1)
    valid     = DEF_TRUE;
    signal    = DEF_FALSE;

    if (Frame error) {                                     (2)
        valid = DEF_FALSE;
    }
    if (Frame data spans over multiple buffers) {          (3)
        valid = DEF_FALSE;
    }

    if (pdev_data->RxBufferListPtr == (LIST_ITEM *)0) {    (4)
        valid  = DEF_FALSE;
        signal = DEF_TRUE;
    }
```

16

```
Clear Interrupt source;
if (valid == DEF_TRUE) {
    plist_buf                 = pdev_data->RxBufferListPtr;              (5)
    pdev_data->RxBufferListPtr = plist_buf->Next;
    p_buf                     = plist_buf->Buffer;
    plist_buf->Buffer         = pdesc->p_buf;
    plist_buf->Len            = pdesc->size;
    plist_buf->Next           = (LIST_ITEM *)0;
    if (pdev_data->RxReadyListPtr == (LIST_ITEM *)0) {                   (6)
        pdev_data->RxReadyListPtr = plist_buf;
    } else {
        plist_ready = pdev_data->RxReadyListPtr;
        while (plist_ready != (LIST_ITEM *)0) {                          (7)
            if (plist_ready->Next == (LIST_ITEM *)0) {
                break;
            }
            plist_ready = plist_ready->Next;
        }
        plist_ready->Next = plist_buf;
    }
    pdesc->p_buf = p_buf;                                                (8)
    pdesc->size  = 0;
}


if ((valid  == DEF_TRUE) ||
    (signal == DEF_TRUE)) {
    NetOS_IF_RxTaskSignal(pif->Nbr, &err);                              (9)
}
Reset Descriptor;
return (valid);
}
```

Listing 16-15 **Rx ISR Handling**

L16-15(1)   Obtain pointer to **NET_DEV_DATA** object.

L16-15(2)   If there is an error with the received frame, discard it.

L16-15(3)   If the frame doesn't hold in a single buffer, discard it.

L16-15(4)   If there is no node in **RxBufferListPtr** it means that there is no buffer to exchange with the descriptor's buffer and the received frame must be discarded.

L16-15(5)   Remove a node from the **RxBufferListPtr**. Exchange the buffer of that node with the buffer of the descriptor.

L16-15(6)   If the **RxReadyListPtr** is empty, move the node removed from **RxBufferListPtr** to the **RxReadyListPtr**.

L16-15(7)   If the **RxReadyListPtr** is not empty, move the node removed from **RxBufferListPtr** to the end of **RxReadyListPtr**.

L16-15(8)   Assign the buffer removed from **RxBufferListPtr** to the descriptor.

L16-15(9)   Signal the Receive task that there is a new frame available.

MOVING THE NODE'S BUFFER TO THE TCP-IP STACK

NetDev_Rx( ) is called by the Receive task of the µC/TCP-IP module to return a buffer to the application if there is one that is available. This function must return the oldest packet received which should be added into the Ready list by the ISR handler. If the list is empty, you must return an error. If the list is not empty, you must set the **p_data** pointer argument to the current node buffer, set the node buffer to null and move the node to the Free list. Then you have to try to move Free list node to the Buffer list. To do so, you must to get a free buffer from the µC/TCP-IP module, fill a node buffer from the Free List and move the node to the Buffer List.

The following is the pseudo code describing this process:

```
if ((interrupt source == Receive) ||
static  void  NetDev_Rx (NET_IF        *pif,
                         CPU_INT08U  **p_data,
                         CPU_INT16U   *size,
                         NET_ERR      *perr)

{
    NET_DEV_DATA        *pdev_data;
    NET_DEV_CFG_ETHER   *pdev_cfg;
    LIST_ITEM           *plist;
    CPU_INT08U          *pbuf;
    CPU_BOOLEAN          valid;
    NET_ERR              net_err;
    CPU_SR_ALLOC();
    pdev_cfg  = (NET_DEV_CFG_ETHER *)pif->Dev_Cfg;
    pdev_data = (NET_DEV_DATA *)pif->Dev_Data;
```

```
    CPU_CRITICAL_ENTER();                                        (1)
    plist = pdev_data->RxReadyListPtr;                           (2)
    if (plist != (LIST_ITEM *)0) {
        pdev_data->RxReadyListPtr = plist->Next;
       *size    = plist->Len;                                    (3)
       *p_data = (CPU_INT08U *)plist->Buffer;                    (4)
        plist->Len    = 0;
        plist->Buffer = (void *)0;
                                                                 (5)
        plist->Next              = pdev_data->RxFreeListPtr;
        pdev_data->RxFreeListPtr = plist;
        CPU_CRITICAL_EXIT();                                     (6)

       *perr = NET_DEV_ERR_NONE;
    } else {
        CPU_CRITICAL_EXIT();                                     (7)

       *size   = (CPU_INT16U  )0;
       *p_data = (CPU_INT08U *)0;

       *perr = NET_DEV_ERR_RX;
    }
    valid = DEF_TRUE;
    while (valid == DEF_TRUE) {
        pbuf = NetBuf_GetDataPtr((NET_IF          *)pif,
                                 (NET_TRANSACTION)NET_TRANSACTION_RX,
                                 (NET_ERR         *)&net_err);
        if (net_err != NET_BUF_ERR_NONE) {
            valid = DEF_FALSE;
        } else {
            CPU_CRITICAL_ENTER();                                (1)
            plist = pdev_data->RxFreeListPtr;
            if (plist != (LIST_ITEM *)0) {
                pdev_data->RxFreeListPtr   = plist->Next;
                plist->Buffer              = pbuf;
                plist->Next                = pdev_data->RxBufferListPtr;
                pdev_data->RxBufferListPtr = plist;
                CPU_CRITICAL_EXIT();
            } else {
                CPU_CRITICAL_EXIT();
                valid = DEF_FALSE;

                NetBuf_FreeBufDataAreaRx(pif->Nbr, pbuf);        (8)
            }
        }
    }
}
```

Listing 16-16 **Packet Reception**

L16-16(1)   Disable interrupts to alter shared data.

L16-16(2)   Get the next ready buffer.

L16-16(3)   Return the size of the received frame.

L16-16(4)   Return a pointer to the received data area.

L16-16(5)   Move the list header into free list.

L16-16(6)   Restore interrupts.

L16-16(7)   Restore interrupts and mark the received frame as invalid.

L16-16(8)   Return data to received data area pool.

16-6-4 TRANSMISSION USING DMA

When μC/TCP-IP has a packet to transmit, it updates an available descriptor in memory and then writes to a DMA register to start the stalled DMA channel. On transmissions, it is simpler to setup the descriptors. The number and length of the packets to transmit is well defined. This information determines the number of transmit descriptors required and the number of bytes to transmit on each descriptor. The transmit descriptor list is often used in a non-circular fashion. The initial descriptors in the descriptor list are setup for transmission, when the transmission is completed they are cleared, and the process starts over in the next transmission.

INITIALIZATION

Similarly to the receive descriptors, the Network Device Driver should allocate a memory block for all transmit buffers and descriptors shown in Figure 16-9.

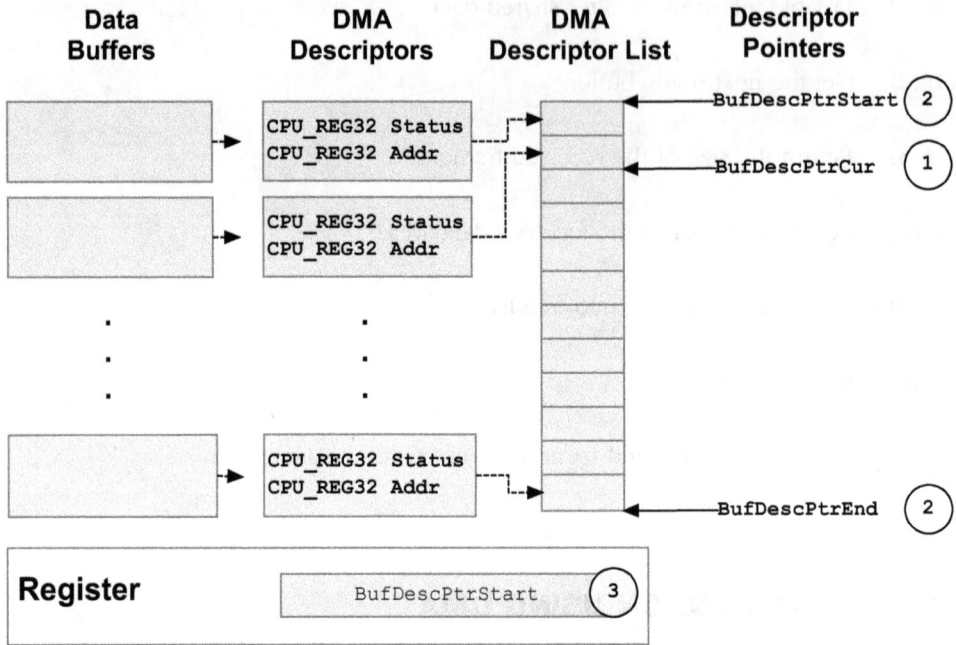

Figure 16-14 **Transmission descriptor pointers initialization**

F16-14(1)   The Network Device Driver must allocate a list of descriptors and configure each address field to point to a null location.

F16-14(2)   The Network Device Driver can initialize three pointers. One to track the current descriptor which is expected to contain the next buffer to transmit. A second points to the beginning of the descriptor list. The last pointer may point to the last descriptor in the list or depending on the implementation, it can also point to the last descriptor to transmit. Another method, depending on the DMA controller used, is to configure a parameter containing the number of descriptors to transmit in one of the DMA controller registers.

Finally, the DMA controller is initialized and hardware is informed of the descriptor list starting address.

TRANSMISSION

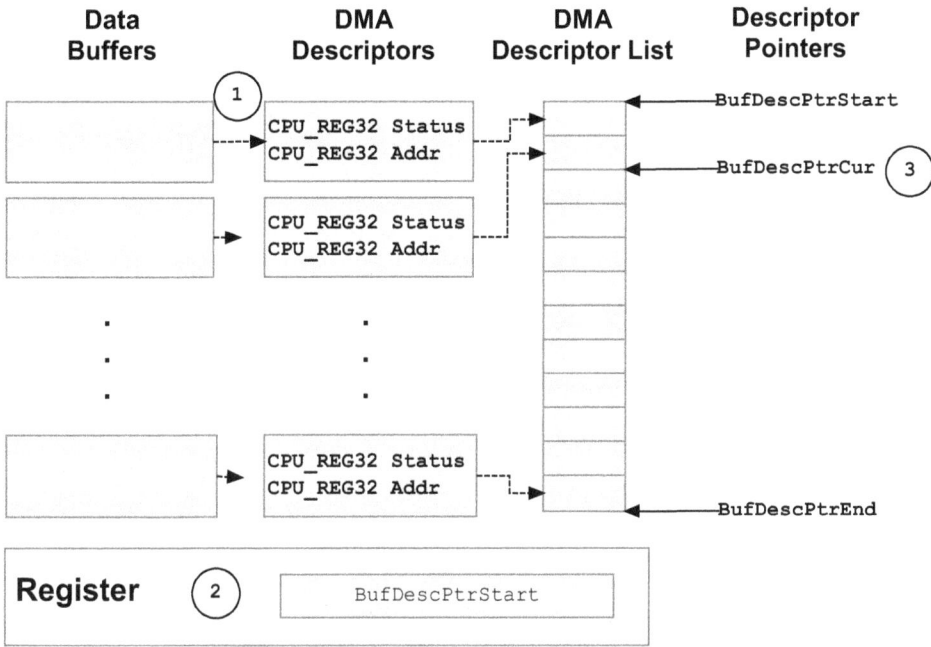

Figure 16-15 **Moving a buffer to the Ethernet controller with DMA**

F16-15(1)   With each new transmit buffer, the current descriptor address is set to the buffer address.

F16-15(2)   DMA transfer is enabled.

F16-15(3)   The current descriptor pointer is set to the next descriptor for the next transmission.

If no descriptor is free an error should be returned to the Network Protocol stack.

ISR HANDLER

When the ISR handler receives a DMA interrupt after the transmission completion, a list of descriptors for the completed transmit buffers is determined. Each completed transmit buffer address is passed to the Network Transmit De-allocation task, where the correspondent buffer gets released if it is not referenced by any other part of the Network stack. The Network interface is also signaled for each one of the completed transmit buffers to allow the Network stack to continue transmission of subsequent packets. To complete the operation, the transmit descriptors are cleared to make room for subsequent transmissions.

Transmission of packets can also benefit from a DMA implementation. Similar to the reception of packets, the DMA can be used to move the packet data from the application memory space to the memory location of the Ethernet controller. By using the DMA, the CPU can work on other tasks and driver performances can be increased.

DESCRIPTION OF THE TRANSMISSION POINTERS

We use three pointers to manage the transmission of buffers:

`TxBufDescPtrStart`	This pointer points to the first descriptor and should not take any other value.
`TxBufDescPtrComp`	This pointer tracks the current descriptor which completed its transmission.
`TxBufDescPtrCur`	This pointer tracks the current descriptor available for transmission.

INITIALIZATION OF THE TRANSMISSION DESCRIPTORS

The function `NetDev_Start()` initializes the Transmit buffer descriptor pointers and the DMA Transmit descriptors. The sub-function `NetDev_TxDescInit()` initializes the Transmit descriptors ring. The descriptors must not filled with buffers and they must be owned by the software. Your code should activate the current Transmit descriptor only when `NetDev_Tx()` is called.

The following is the pseudo code for this initialization:

```
pdesc                        = (DEV_DESC *)pdev_data->TxBufDescPtrStart;      (1)
pdev_data->TxBufDescPtrComp = (DEV_DESC *)pdev_data->TxBufDescPtrStart;
pdev_data->TxBufDescPtrCur  = (DEV_DESC *)pdev_data->TxBufDescPtrStart;
for (i = 0; i < pdev_cfg->TxDescNbr; i++) {                                   (2)
    pdesc->Addr   = 0;
    pdesc->Len    = 0;
    pdesc->Status =  (not started) & (owned by software)
    pdesc->Next   = (DEV_DESC *)(pdesc + 1);
    pdesc++;                                                                  (3)
}
pdesc--;                                                                      (4)
pdesc->Next   = (DEV_DESC *)pdev_data->TxBufDescPtrStart;                     (5)
```

Listing 16-17 **Descriptor Initialization**

L16-17(1)   Initialize descriptor, **.TxBufDescPtrComp** and **.TxBufDescPtrCur** to **.TxBufDescPtrStart** of **pdev_data**

L16-17(2)   For every **.TxDescNbr** in **pdev_cfg**: Set the Transmit Buffer address to null, set the **Len** field to 0, and set the status to "not started" and "owned by the software". Then set the current descriptor's next descriptor to the location of the next descriptor (using pointer arithmetic).

L16-17(3)   Increment descriptor using pointer arithmetic.

L16-17(4)   Decrement descriptor to compensate for over-incrementation in the while loop.

L16-17(5)   Set the **.Next** field of the descriptor to **.TxBufDescPtrStart**.

MOVING PACKETS FROM THE TCP-IP STACK TO THE NETWORK DEVICE

The function **NetDev_Tx()** is called by the µC/TCP-IP module when a packet must be transmitted over the network. This function resets and activates a DMA Transmit descriptor for the packet to transmit. It must first make sure that a Transmit descriptor is available to initialize a transmission. Once the buffer has been assigned to the current Transmit descriptor, an interrupt will be generated to signal that the packet has been transmitted.

The following is the pseudo code for the **NetDev_Tx()** function.

```
static  void  NetDev_Tx (NET_IF        *pif,
                         CPU_INT08U    *p_data,
                         CPU_INT16U     size,
                         NET_ERR       *perr)
{
    NET_DEV_CFG_ETHER  *pdev_cfg;
    NET_DEV_DATA        *pdev_data;
    NET_DEV            *pdev;
    DEV_DESC           *pdesc;
    pdev_cfg  = (NET_DEV_CFG_ETHER *)pif->Dev_Cfg;
    pdev_data = (NET_DEV_DATA       *)pif->Dev_Data;
    pdev      = (NET_DEV            *)pdev_cfg->BaseAddr;
    pdesc     = (DEV_DESC           *)pdev_data->TxBufDescPtrCur;
    if ((pdesc->Status & Hardware) != 0) {                               (1)
        *perr = NET_DEV_ERR_TX_BUSY;
        return;
    }
    pdesc->Addr                 =  p_data;                               (2)
    pdesc->Len                  =  size;                                 (3)

    pdesc->Status               =  Hardware;                             (4)
    pdev->REGISTER              =  Inform harware that a Tx desc has been made avail;
    pdev_data->TxBufDescPtrCur  =  pdesc->Next;                          (5)

    *perr = NET_DEV_ERR_NONE;
}
```

Listing 16-18 **Packet Transmission**

L16-18(1)   If current Transmit Descriptor is still owned by the DMA engine, set ***perr** to **NET_DEV_ERR_TX_BUSY** indicating that the DMA engine is still occupied at transmitting that frame.

L16-18(2)   Configure the descriptor with the transmit data area address.

L16-18(3)   Configure the descriptor frame length.

L16-18(4)   Give the descriptor ownership to hardware.

L16-18(5)   Move the pointer of the current transmit descriptor to the next one.

DEALLOCATING PACKETS AFTER TRANSMISSION

`NetDev_ISR_Handler()` is called when the transmission is completed. Within the ISR handler, you must signal the µC/TCP-IP module for each packet transmitted successfully.

> It is possible that some packets may be transmitted or received during the ISR handler. As a result, sometimes only one ISR is generated for multiple packets transmitted. You must make sure that all descriptors not owned by the hardware and completed have been signaled the µC/TCP-IP module.

```
int_status = pdev->REGISTER;                                        (1)

clear active int;
if ((int_status & TX_INTERRUPT) > 0) {                              (2)

    while(p_desc          != TxBufDescPtrCur ||
        pdev->REGISTER == Owned by software) {                      (3)
        pdesc = pdev_data->TxBufDescPtrComp;
        pdev_data->TxBufDescPtrComp = pdesc->Next;
        NetOS_IF_TxDeallocTaskPost(pdesc->Addr, &err);
        NetOS_Dev_TxRdySignal(pif->Nbr);                            (4)
    }
    pdesc = pdev_data->TxBufDescPtrComp;
    pdev_data->TxBufDescPtrComp = pdesc->Next;                      (5)
}
```

Figure 16-16 **ISR handling**

L16-18(6)   Record the current state of the interrupt register.

L16-18(7)   Verify if there is a transmission interrupt triggered.

L16-18(8)   Cycle through the Transmit descriptor while the working descriptor is not pointing on **.TxBufFescPtrCur** and that the working descriptor pointer is owned by the software (transmission done).

L16-18(9)   Deallocate the transmission buffer used by the descriptor.

L16-18(10)   Signal **NetIF** that the Transmit resources are now available.

L16-18(11)   Move the **.TxBufDescPtrComp** descriptor pointer to the **.Next** one of that descriptor.

DEALLOCATING THE TRANSMIT BUFFERS

NetDev_Stop() is called to free the receive descriptors ring and to deallocate all transmit buffers. To do that, a sub-function is called **NetDev_TxDescFreeAll()** where each descriptor's buffer is freed:

```
pdesc = pdev_data->TxBufDescPtrStart;                              (1)
for (i = 0; i < pdev_cfg->TxDescNbr; i++) {
    NetOS_IF_TxDeallocTaskPost((CPU_INT08U *)pdesc->Addr, &err);   (2)
    (void)&err;                                                    (3)
    pdesc++;
}
```

Listing 16-19 **Transmit descriptor deallocation**

L16-19(1)   Set the current pointer descriptor to **.TxBufDescPtrStart** of **NET_DEV_DATA**.

L16-19(2)   For each descriptor defined in the configuration, deallocate the network buffer associated with the descriptor.

L16-19(3)   Any error returned by **NetOS_IF_TxDeallocTaskPost()** should be ignored since we are doing a best effort to deallocate the buffer and carry on with the rest of the device stopping procedure.

16-7 ETHERNET - TRANSMITTING & RECEIVING USING MEMORY COPY

16-7-1 RECEPTION USING MEMORY COPY

On some devices, the MAC is not part of processor peripherals, and is connected through a serial or a parallel communication scheme. You will have to create specific data transfer functions for writing and reading the data structures of the MAC.

PROCESSING RECEPTION BUFFERS IN THE ISR

The following a list of the actions that must be performed in `NetDev_ISR_Handler()` to receive packets using Memory Copy.

- Read MAC Status Register

- Handle Receive ISR:

    - Signal Net IF Receive task

    - Clear Interrupt

- Handle any other reported interrupts by MAC controller.

Listing 16-20 shows a template for the `NetDev_ISR_Handle()` function:

16

```
static  void  NetDev_ISR_Handler (NET_IF            *pif,
                                  NET_DEV_ISR_TYPE  type)
{
    NET_DEV_CFG_ETHER  *pdev_cfg;
    NET_DEV_DATA       *pdev_data;
    NET_DEV            *pdev;
    CPU_DATA            reg_val;
    CPU_INT08U         *p_data;
    NET_ERR             err;
    (void)&type;                                               (1)
    pdev_cfg  = (NET_DEV_CFG_ETHER *)pif->Dev_Cfg;             (2)
    pdev_data = (NET_DEV_DATA       *)pif->Dev_Data;           (3)
    pdev      = (NET_DEV            *)pdev_cfg->BaseAddr;       (4)
    reg_val = pdev->ISR;                                       (5)
    if ((reg_val & RX_ISR_EVENT_MSK) > 0) {                    (6)
        NetOS_IF_RxTaskSignal(pif->Nbr, &err);                (7)
         switch (err) {
             case NET_IF_ERR_NONE:
                 No error during signalling.
                 break;
             case NET_IF_ERR_RX_Q_FULL:
             case NET_IF_ERR_RX_Q_SIGNAL_FAULT:
             default:
                 An error occurred during signalling.
                 break;
         }
        pdev->ISR |= RX_ISR_EVENT_MSK;                         (8)
    }
                                                               (9)
    if ((reg_val & TX_ISR_EVENT_MSK) > 0) {                    (10)

        p_data = (CPU_INT08U *)pdev_data->TxBufCompPtr;
        NetOS_IF_TxDeallocTaskPost(p_data, &err);
        NetOS_Dev_TxRdySignal(pif->Nbr);                       (11)
        pdev->ISR |= TX_ISR_EVENT_MSK;                         (12)
    }
    pdev->ISR |= UNHANDLED_ISR_EVENT_MASK;                     (13)
}
```

Listing 16-20 **ISR Handler function template**

L16-20(1)   Prevent "variable unused" compiler warning.

L16-20(2)   Obtain pointer to the device configuration structure.

L16-20(3)   Obtain pointer to device data area.

L16-20(4)   Overlay device register structure on top of device base address.

L16-20(5)   Determine interrupt type.

L16-20(6)   Handle reception interrupts.

L16-20(7)   Signal **NetIF** reception queue task for each new ready descriptor.

L16-20(8)   Clear device's reception interrupt event flag.

L16-20(9)   Handle transmission interrupts.

L16-20(10)   Increment transmission packet counter.

L16-20(11)   Signal **NetIF** that transmission resources are now available.

L16-20(12)   Clear device's transmission interrupt event flag.

L16-20(13)   Clear unhandled interrupt event flag.

MOVING BUFFERS FROM THE DEVICE TO THE TCP-IP STACK USING MEMORY COPY

The following a list of the actions that must be performed in **NetDev_Rx()** to receive packets using Memory Copy.

■ Disable interrupts

■ Read the length of the received frame

■ Obtain pointer to new data area

■ Copy frame to new data area

■ Set return values. Pointer to received data area and size

■ Re-Enable interrupts

■ Check for additional ready frames, and signal Net IF receive task

433

Listing 16-21 shows a template for the **NetDev_Rx()** function:

```
static  void  NetDev_Rx (NET_IF       *pif,
                         CPU_INT08U  **p_data,
                         CPU_INT16U   *size,
                         NET_ERR      *perr)
{
    NET_DEV_CFG_ETHER  *pdev_cfg;
    NET_DEV_DATA       *pdev_data;
    NET_DEV            *pdev;
    CPU_INT08U         *pbuf_new;
    CPU_INT16S          length;
    CPU_INT16U          cnt;
    CPU_INT16U          i;
    pdev_cfg  = (NET_DEV_CFG_ETHER *)pif->Dev_Cfg;                            (1)
    pdev_data = (NET_DEV_DATA      *)pif->Dev_Data;                           (2)
    pdev      = (NET_DEV           *)pdev_cfg->BaseAddr;                      (3)

    if ((pdev->RSTAT & RX_STATUS_ERR_MSK) > 0) {                             (4)
        *size   = (CPU_INT16U )0;
        *p_data = (CPU_INT08U *)0;
        *perr   = (NET_ERR    )NET_DEV_ERR_RX;
         return;
    }

    length = (pdev->STATUS & RX_STATUS_SIZE_MSK) - NET_IF_ETHER_FRAME_CRC_SIZE;  (5)
    if (length < NET_IF_ETHER_FRAME_MIN_SIZE) {
        *size   = (CPU_INT16U )0;
        *p_data = (CPU_INT08U *)0;
        *perr   = (NET_ERR    )NET_DEV_ERR_INVALID_SIZE;
         return;
    }

    pbuf_new = NetBuf_GetDataPtr((NET_IF        *)pif,                       (6)
                                 (NET_TRANSACTION)NET_TRANSACTION_RX,
#if (NET_VERSION >= 21000u)
                                 (NET_BUF_SIZE )NET_IF_ETHER_FRAME_MAX_SIZE,
                                 (NET_BUF_SIZE )NET_IF_IX_RX,
                                 (NET_BUF_SIZE *)0,
#else
                                 (NET_BUF_SIZE )pdev_cfg->RxBufLargeSize,
                                 (NET_BUF_SIZE )0u,
#endif
                                 (NET_BUF_SIZE *)0,
                                 (NET_TYPE     *)0,
                                 (NET_ERR      *)perr);
```

```
    if (*perr != NET_BUF_ERR_NONE) {                               (7)
        *size   = (CPU_INT16U )0;
        *p_data = (CPU_INT08U *)0;
        return;
    }

    *size   =  length;                                             (8)
    cnt     =  length / pdev_cfg->DataBusSizeNbrBits;              (9)

    for (i = 0; i < cnt; i++) {
        Read data from device using Memcopy.                       (10)
    }

    *p_data = pbuf_new;                                            (11)
    *perr = NET_DEV_ERR_NONE;
}
```

Listing 16-21 **NetDev_Rx() function template**

F16-16(1)   Obtain pointer to the device configuration structure.

F16-16(2)   Obtain pointer to device data area.

F16-16(3)   Overlay device register structure on top of device base address.

F16-16(4)   If the frame contains reception errors, discard the frame by setting ***size** to 0, ***p_data** to null. Set ***perr** to NET_DEV_ERR_RX to indicate a reception error.

F16-16(5)   If frame is a runt, discard the frame.

F16-16(6)   Request an empty buffer.

F16-16(7)   If unable to get a buffer, discard the frame.

F16-16(8)   Return the size of the received frame.

F16-16(9)   Determine the number of device memory or FIFO reads that are required to complete the memory copy.

F16-16(10)   Read data from device.

F16-16(11)   Return a pointer to the received data.

16-7-2 TRANSMISSION USING MEMORY COPY

The following a list of the actions that must be done in **NetDev_Tx()** in order to implement transmission using Memory Copy:

- Disable interrupts.

- Prepare device to receive the transmit frame in memory.

- Copy frame to transmit to MAC buffer.

- If no frames are queued for transmission, issue a transmission request to the MAC.

- Update the device's list of transmit pointers

- Re-enable interrupts

Listing 16-22 shows a template for the **NetDev_Tx()** function:

```
static  void  NetDev_Tx (NET_IF      *pif,
                         CPU_INT08U  *p_data,
                         CPU_INT16U   size,
                         NET_ERR     *perr)
{
    NET_DEV_CFG_ETHER  *pdev_cfg;
    NET_DEV_DATA       *pdev_data;
    NET_DEV            *pdev;
    CPU_INT16U          cnt;
    CPU_INT16U          i;
    pdev_cfg  = (NET_DEV_CFG_ETHER *)pif->Dev_Cfg;              (1)
    pdev_data = (NET_DEV_DATA      *)pif->Dev_Data;            (2)
    pdev      = (NET_DEV           *)pdev_cfg->BaseAddr;       (3)
    if ((pdev->STATUS & TX_STATUS_BUSY) > 0) {                 (4)
      *perr = NET_DEV_ERR_TX_BUSY;
       return;
    }
    cnt = size / pdev_cfg->DataBusSizeNbrBits;                 (5)
    for (i = 0; i < cnt; i++) {
        Copy data to device using Memcopy                      (6)
    }
    pdev->CTRL = 1;                                            (7)
    pdev_data->TxBufCompPtr = p_data;
}
```

Listing 16-22 **NetDev_Tx() function template**

436

L16-22(1)   Obtain pointer to the device configuration structure.

L16-22(2)   Obtain pointer to device data area.

L16-22(3)   Overlay device register structure on top of the device base address.

L16-22(4)   Check if the device is ready to transmit.

L16-22(5)   Determine the number of device memory or FIFO writes that are required to complete the transfer.

L16-22(6)   Copy data to device using memory copy.

L16-22(7)   Initiate transmission of the packet.

PROCESSING TRANSMISSION BUFFER IN THE ISR

The following is a list of actions that must be performed in **NetDev_ISR_Handler()** to transmit packets using Memory Copy.

■ Setup next frame to transmit if any

■ Signal already transmitted frame for deallocation

■ Signal that Transmit resources have become available

■ Clear interrupt

For the template of **NetDev_ISR_Handler()** refer to the template in Listing 16-20 on page 432.

16-8 WIRELESS LAYERS INTERACTION

This sections that follow describe the interactions between the IF layer, the wireless device driver API functions, the BSP API functions and the Wireless Manager API functions. Since the device driver is made of not only logic but also from interactions with the parts on the board, you'll need to understand the calls made to the these layers of the µC/TCP-IP module and to the CPU and board-dependent layers.

Figure 16-17 shows the logical path between the Wireless Manager layer, BSP APIs functions and the device driver through the function calls and interruptions.

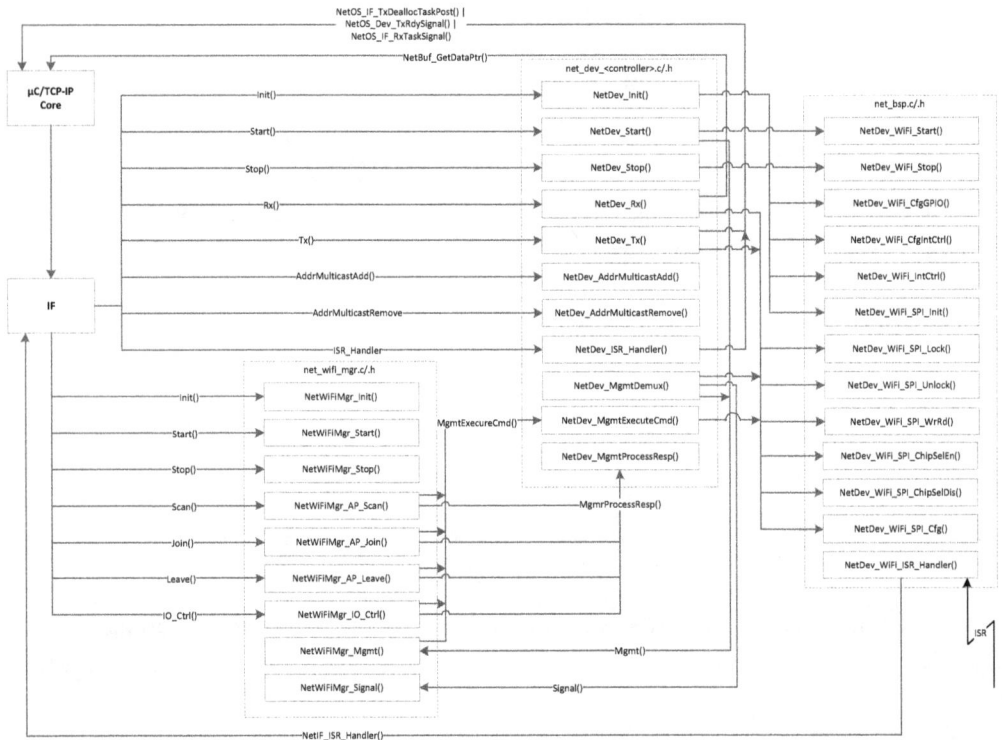

Figure 16-17 **Wireless Manager, device driver & BSP interactions**

16-9 WIRELESS MANAGER API IMPLEMENTATION

µC/TCP-IP supports only wireless devices which include an integrated wireless supplicant (i.e., the client-side software that performs scan and login requests). This kind of hardware requires to send management command to device to accomplish some operation such as scan, join, set MAC address, etc. Some of these management command may take a while to be completed. For those command most of wireless device return the command result via a management frame which must be received like a packet. So, the Wireless Manager must provide mechanisms to send management commands, and then return once the management command is completed.

The Wireless Manager API should be implemented as follows:

```
const  NET_WIFI_MGR_API  NetWiFiMgr_API_Generic = {
                                    &NetWiFiMgr_Init,          (1)
                                    &NetWiFiMgr_Start,         (2)
                                    &NetWiFiMgr_Stop,          (3)
                                    &NetWiFiMgr_AP_Scan,       (4)
                                    &NetWiFiMgr_AP_Join,       (5)
                                    &NetWiFiMgr_AP_Leave,      (6)
                                    &NetWiFiMgr_IO_Ctrl,       (7)
                                    &NetWiFiMgr_Mgmt,          (8)
                                    &NetWiFiMgr_Signal         (9)
                                };
```

Listing 16-23 **Wireless Manager**

L16-23(1)   Wireless Manager initialization function pointer

L16-23(2)   Wireless Manager start function pointer

L16-23(3)   Wireless Manager stop function pointer

L16-23(4)   Wireless Manager access point scan pointer

L16-23(5)   Wireless Manager access point join pointer

L16-23(6)   Wireless Manager access point leave pointer

L16-23(7)   Wireless Manager IO control pointer

L16-23(8)   Wireless Manager device driver management pointer

L16-23(9)   Wireless Manager signal response signal pointer

μC/TCP-IP provides code that is compatible with most wireless device that embed the wireless supplicant. However, extended functionality must be implemented on a per wireless device basis. If additional functionality is required, it may be necessary to create an application specific Wireless Manager.

Note: It is the Wireless Manager developers' responsibility to ensure that all of the functions listed within the API are properly implemented and that the order of the functions within the API structure is correct.

This sections that follow describe the interactions between the device driver and the Wireless Manager layer provided with μC/TCP-IP.

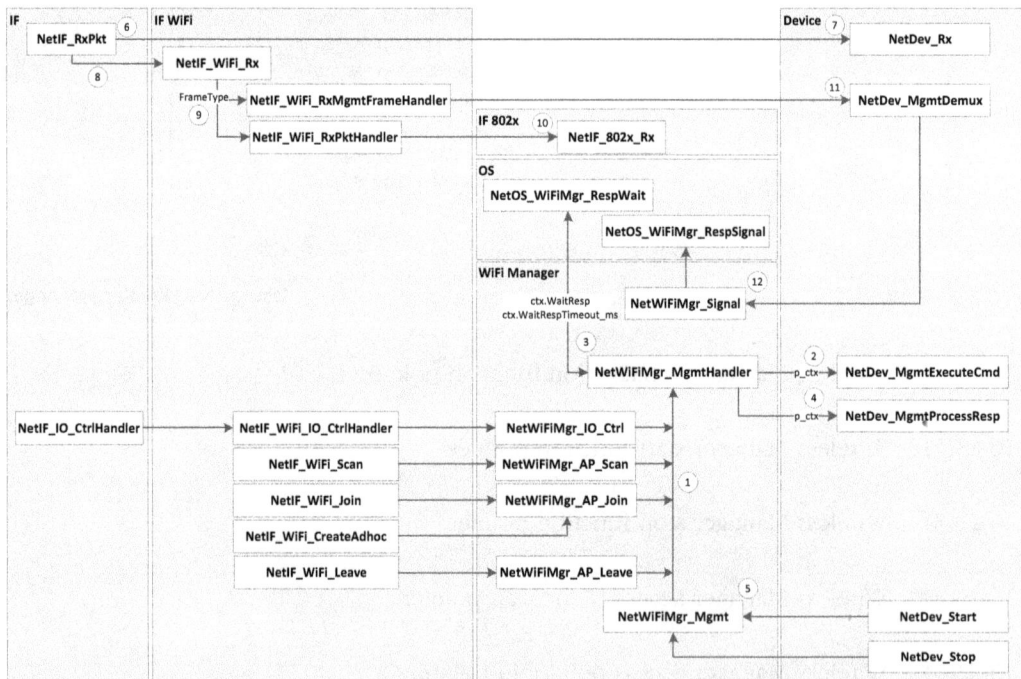

Figure 16-18 **Interactions between the device driver and the Wireless Manager layer**

F16-18(1)   All management functionality present in the Wireless Manager API uses a simple state machine that uses a state machine context set and updated by the device driver. The state machine context contains some fields use by the state machine to know what it should be done after the call. Basically, the state machine is implemented in **NetWiFiMgr_MgmtHadler()** that calls **NetDev_MgmtExecuteCmd()** to start and execute the management command, following the state machine context, the state machine can wait to receive the response and then calls **NetDev_MgmtProcessResp()** to analyze the response data and rearrange the data.

F16-18(2)   **NetDev_MgmtExecuteCmd()** can executes a management command directly if it doesn't require to received a response or just initialize the management command when a response is needed to complete the command. The function let know to the state machine of what should be done after by setting the state machine context that is passed as pointer argument to the function.

F16-18(3)   If no response is needed to complete the command then the **NetWiFiMgr_MgmtHanlder()** returns immediately. If the management command requires a response to complete the command then it returns only if the timeout has expired (i.e. the response not received) or if the Wireless Manager has been signalled and the response is analyzed and translated.

F16-18(4)   When the response of the management command is received **NetDev_MgmtProcessResp()** is called to analyze and to translate the data for upper layers. Also this function must update the state machine context to let know if the management command is completed or if more data must be send to complete the current management command.

F16-18(5)   The device driver can also uses the Wireless Manager to send management command defined within the driver during start and stop of the interface especially when a response is needed to complete the management command such as updating the wireless device firmware. Note that it's not possible to use the Wireless Manager during the initialization since it's not possible to receive packet and management frame before the initialization is completed.

F16-18(6)   When data ready ISR occurs and the interface is signalled, the function **NetIF_RxPkt()** calls the driver to read the data from the wireless device no matter if its management frame or data packet.

F16-18(7)   **NetDev_Rx()** must determine if the data received is a management frame or a packet and must set at least the frame type within the offset of the network buffer. See "Receiving Packets and Management Frames" on page 450. If the data read is a management frame that it's not a response, the processing must be done in **NetDev_DemuxMgmt()** to let the stack increment his statistics.

F16-18(8)   Once the data is read and the frame type set by the device driver then the buffer is passing to the wireless interface layer to be processed.

F16-18(9)   **NetIF_WiFi_Rx()** uses the frame type within the buffer offset and set previously by the device driver to know which layer to call and pass the network buffer.

F16-18(10) If the data received is a packet then the 802x layer is called to process the packet as it's should done for an Ethernet packet.

F16-18(11) If the data received is a management frame then **8** is called to determine what to do with the data. If it's a response for a management command initialized previously then the Wireless Manager must be signalled. If it's information about the wireless device state, then some operation on the stack could be done such as updating the link state of the interface. Note that the buffer offset section could be used by the device driver to help to determine what kind of data is contained in the data section of the buffer.

F16-18(12) When the data is a management response previously initialized then the Wireless Manager must be signalled by using the Wireless Manager API.

16-10 WIRELESS DEVICE DRIVER IMPLEMENTATION

16-10-1 DESCRIPTION OF THE WIRELESS DEVICE DRIVER API

All device drivers must declare an instance of the appropriate device driver API structure as a global variable within the source code. The API structure is an ordered list of function pointers utilized by µC/TCP-IP when device hardware services are required.

A sample Ethernet interface API structure is shown below.

```
const  NET_DEV_API_WIFI  NetDev_API_<controler> = { NetDev_Init,                  (1)
                                                     NetDev_Start,                (2)
                                                     NetDev_Stop,                 (3)
                                                     NetDev_Rx,                   (4)
                                                     NetDev_Tx,                   (5)
                                                     NetDev_AddrMulticastAdd,     (6)
                                                     NetDev_AddrMulticastRemove,  (7)
                                                     NetDev_ISR_Handler,          (8)
                                                     NetDev_MgmtDemux,            (9)
                                                     NetDev_MgmtExcuteCmd,       (10)
                                                     NetDev_mgmtProcessResp      (11)
                                                   };
```

Listing 16-24 **Ethernet interface API**

Note: It is the device driver developers' responsibility to ensure that all of the functions listed within the API are properly implemented and that the order of the functions within the API structure is correct.

L16-24(1)   Device initialization/add function pointer

L16-24(2)   Device start function pointer

L16-24(3)   Device stop function pointer

L16-24(4)   Device Receive function pointer

L16-24(5)   Device transmit function pointer

L16-24(6)   Device multicast address add function pointer

L16-24(7)   Device multicast address remove function pointer

L16-24(8)   Device interrupt service routine (ISR) handler function pointer

L16-24(9)   Device demultiplex management frame function pointer.

L16-24(10)   Device execute management command function pointer.

L16-24(11)   Device process management response function pointer.

Note: µC/TCP-IP device driver API function names may not be unique. Name clashes between device drivers are avoided by never globally prototyping device driver functions and ensuring that all references to functions within the driver are obtained by pointers within the API structure. The developer may arbitrarily name the functions within the source file so long as the API structure is properly declared. The user application should never need to call API functions by name. Unless special care is taken, calling device driver functions by name may lead to unpredictable results due to reentrancy.

16-10-2 HOW TO ACCESS THE SPI BUS

µC/TCP-IP currently supports only wireless devices that communicate with the host via SPI. Also, many other devices/hardware can share the same SPI bus, so each time the device driver need to access the SPI bus it must acquire the access and set the SPI controller following the wireless device's SPI requirement. This procedure must be followed each time the device driver needs to access the SPI:

1   Acquire the SPI lock by calling network device's BSP function pointer, `NetDev_WiFi_SPI_Lock()`.

2   Enable chip select of the wireless device via network device's BSP function pointer, `NetDev_WiFi_SPI_ChipSelEn()`.

3   Configure the SPI controller by calling network device's BSP function pointer, `NetDev_WiFi_SPI_SetCfg()`.

4   Write data and read data from the SPI with appropriate buffer pointer to write buffer and read buffer to the network device's BSP function pointer, `Net_Dev_SPI_WrRd()`.

5   Disable the device's chip select via network device's BSP function pointer, `NetDev_WiFi_SPI_ChipSelDis()`.

6   Release the SPI lock by calling network device's BSP function pointer, `NetDev_WiFi_SPI_Unlock()`.

16-10-3 INITIALIZING A NETWORK DEVICE

`NetDev_Init()` is called by `NetIF_Add()` exactly once for each specific network device added by the application. If multiple instances of the same network device are present on the board, then this function is called for each instance of the device. However, applications should not try to add the same specific device more than once. If a network device fails to initialize, we recommend debugging to find and correct the cause of the failure.

`NetDev_Init()` performs the following operations. However, depending on the device being initialized, functionality may need to be added or removed:

1   Perform device configuration validation. Since some devices require special configuration, the configuration structure received should be examined at the initialization of the device and set `*p_err` if and unacceptable value have been specified to `NET_DEV_ERR_INVALID_CFG` must be returned.

2   Configure all necessary I/O pins for SPI, external interrupt, power pin, reset pin. This is performed via the network device's BSP function pointer, `NetDev_WiFi_CfgGPIO()`, implemented in `net_bsp.c`.

   Configure the host interrupt controller for receive and transmit complete interrupts. Additional interrupt services may be initialized depending on the device and driver requirements. This is performed via the network device's BSP function pointer, `NetDev_WiFi_CfgIntCtrl()`, implemented in `net_bsp.c`. However, receive interrupt should not be enabled before starting the interface.

3   Allocate memory for all necessary local buffers. This is performed via calls to µC/LIB's memory module.

4   Initialize the SPI controller. This is performed via the network device's BSP function pointer, `NetDev_WiFi_SPI_Init()`. The communication between the host and the wireless module should not be initialized, the wireless device should be powered down during and after the initialization.

5   Set `p_err` to `NET_DEV_ERR_NONE` if initialization proceeded as expected. Otherwise, set `p_err` to an appropriate network device error code.

> `NetDev_Init()` can access the SPI bus for command that doesn't requires to receive the command result via a response. Since it's not possible to receive Network packet and management frame before the interface has been started.

16-10-4 STARTING A NETWORK DEVICE

`NetDev_Start()` is called each time an interface is started. It performs the following actions:

1   Call the `NetOS_Dev_CfgTxRdySignal()` function to configure the transmit ready semaphore count. This function call is optional and is performed if the hardware device supports queuing multiple transmit frames. By default, the semaphore count is initialized to one. However, wireless devices should set the semaphore count equal to the number of configured transmit queues size for optimal performance.

2   Power up the wireless module, this is performed via the network device's BSP function pointer, `NetDev_WiFi_Start()`.

3   The wireless device driver must initializes and start the communication between the host and the wireless module.

4   The device driver should validate the current firmware loaded in the wireless device and upgrade the device firmware if required.

Note: After a firmware upgrade, most of the time the wireless device requires to be reset, reinitialized and restarted.

5   Initialize the device MAC address, if applicable. For wireless devices, this step is mandatory. The MAC address data may come from one of three sources and should be set using the following priority scheme:

▨ Configure the MAC address using the string found within the device configuration structure. This is a form of static MAC address configuration and may be performed by calling `NetASCII_Str_to_MAC()` and `NetIF_AddrHW_SetHandler()`. If the device configuration string has been left empty, or is specified as all 0's, an error will be returned and the next method should be attempted.

▨ Check if the application developer has called `NetIF_AddrHW_Set()` by making a call to `NetIF_AddrHW_GetHandler()` and `NetIF_AddrHW_IsValidHandler()` in order to check if the specified MAC address is valid. This method may be used as a static method for configuring the MAC address during run-time, or a dynamic method should a pre-programmed external memory device exist. If the acquired MAC address does not pass the check function, then:

▨ Call `NetIF_AddrHW_SetHandler()` using the data found within the individual MAC address registers. If an auto-loading EEPROM is attached to the MAC, the registers will contain valid data. If not, then a configuration error has occurred. This method is often used with a production process where the MAC supports automatically loading individual address registers from a serial EEPROM. When using this method, you should specify an empty string for the MAC address within the device configuration, and refrain from calling `NetIF_AddrHW_Set()` from within the application.

6   Initialize additional MAC registers required by the MAC for proper operation.

7   Clear all interrupt flags.

8   Locally enable interrupts on the hardware device. This is performed via the network device's BSP function pointer, `NetDev_WiFi_IntCtrl()`. The host interrupt controller should have already been configured within the device driver `NetDev_Init()` function.

9   Enable the receiver and transmitter.

10 Set **perr** equal to **NET_DEV_ERR_NONE** if no errors have occurred. Otherwise, set **perr** to an appropriate network device error code

> Some wireless module return result of commands via a response. The device's Wireless Manager function pointer, `NetWiFiMgr_Mgmt()` should be used to perform these type of command since it will return only when the response is received and processed.

447

16-10-5 STOPPING A NETWORK DEVICE

NetDev_Stop() is called once each time an interface is stopped.

NetDev_Stop() must perform the following operations:

1   Disable the receiver and transmitter.

2   Disable all local MAC interrupt sources.

3   Clear all local MAC interrupt status flags.

4   Power down the wireless device via network device's BSP function pointer, NetDev_WiFi_Stop().

5   For wireless devices which can queued up packet to transmit, free all transmit buffer not yet transmitted by calling NetOS_IF_DeallocTaskPost() with the address of the transmit buffer data areas.

6   Set perr to NET_DEV_ERR_NONE if no error occurs. Otherwise, set **perr** to an appropriate network device error code.

> ⚠ Some wireless module return result of commands via a response. The device's Wireless Manager function pointer, NetWiFiMgr_Mgmt() should be used to perform these type of command since it will return only when the response is received and processed.

16-10-6 HANDLING A WIRELESS DEVICE ISR

NetDev_ISR_Handler() is the device interrupt handler. In general, the device interrupt handler must perform the following functions:

1   Determine which type of interrupt event occurred by switching on the ISR type argument. The ISR handler should not access the SPI bus for reading an interrupt status register.

2   If a receive event has occurred, the driver must post the interface number to the μC/TCP-IP Receive task by calling NetOS_IF_RxTaskSignal() for each new frame received (management or packet).

3   If a transmit complete event has occurred and it is specified in the ISR type argument, the driver must perform the following items for each transmitted packet.

   a   Post the address of the data area that has completed transmission to the transmit buffer de-allocation task by calling NetOS_IF_TxDeallocTaskPost() with the pointer to the data area that has completed transmission.

   b   Call NetOS_Dev_TxRdySignal() with the interface number that has just completed transmission.

4   Interrupt flags on the wireless device should not be cleared. CPU's integrated interrupt controllers should be cleared from within the network device's BSP-level ISR after NetDev_WiFi_ISR_Handler() returns.

Additionally, it is highly recommended that device driver ISR handlers be kept as short as possible to reduce the amount of interrupt latency in the system.

> If the wireless module support transmit complete event, but reading an interrupt status register is required to know it, the receive task must be signaled and in NetDev_Rx() should return a management frame which will be passed to NetDev_MgmtDemux() and then you can perform the transmit complete operations.

16-10-7 RECEIVING PACKETS AND MANAGEMENT FRAMES

NetDev_Rx() is called by µC/TCP-IP's Receive task after the Interrupt Service Routine handler has signaled to the Receive task that a receive event has occurred. NetDev_Rx() requires that the device driver return a pointer to the data area containing the received data and return the size of the received frame via pointer.

RECEIVE BUFFER STRUCTURE

Since NetDev_Rx() can be called to receive management frames and data packets, all wireless receive buffers must contain an offset before the data area to specify the frame type. So to understand data reception, you first need to understand the structure of receive buffers.

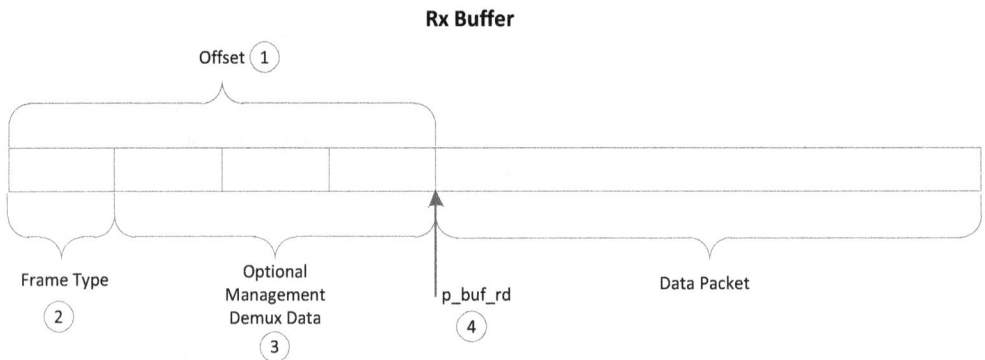

Figure 16-19 **Wireless receive buffer structure**

F16-19(1)   The buffer offset is specified within the device's Memory configuration. The offset must be at least equal to one octet to handle the Frame type. The offset can include option control data for demultiplex and or to respect the buffer alignment.

F16-19(2)   The frame type space is always the first octet of the buffer. If receiving data packet, set the frame type equal to NET_IF_WIFI_DATA_PKT and the packet will be processed by the stack. For a management frame the byte must be set equal to NET_IF_WIFI_MGMT_FRAME, in this case NetDev_MgmtDemux() will be called after return to analyses the management frame and signal the Wireless Manager or update the driver data's state.

F16-19(3)   The receive buffer can include extra space to help to demultiplex a management frame or to respect buffer alignment required by the device's BSP function.

F16-19(4)   The pointer passed to the network device's BSP function pointer, `NetDev_WiFi_SPI_WrRd()`, must point to the frame data area.

RECEIVING FRAMES

`NetDev_Rx()` should perform the following actions:

1   Read the interrupt register which should be done by writing and reading on the SPI bus. This is performed by following the procedure to access the SPI bus. Also, the frame to receive must be know (Management frame or data packet). You should use small local buffer to write and read to complete that step.

2   Check for errors, if applicable. If an error occurs during reception, the driver should set `*size` to 0 and `*p_data` to `(CPU_INT08U *)0` and return. Additional steps may be necessary depending on the device being serviced.

3   Get the size of the received frame and get a new data buffer area by calling `NetBuf_GetDataPtr()`. If memory is not available, an error will be returned and the device driver should set `*size` to 0 and `*p_data` to `(CPU_INT08U *)0`.

4   If an error does not occur while getting a new data area, `*p_data` must be set to the address of the data area.

5   Set the frame type within the receive buffer equal to `NET_IF_WIFI_DATA_PKT` for a packet which must be processed by the stack and equal to `NET_IF_WIFI_MGMT_FRAME` for any management frame which will be passed to `NetDev_MgmtDemux()` to demultiplex the management frame.

6   Read from the device to the receive buffer data area by calling the network device's BSP function pointer, `NetDev_WiFi_SPI_WrRd()`, with an appropriate pointer to the data area of the receive buffer.

7   Set `p_err` to `NET_DEV_ERR_NONE` and return from the receive function. Otherwise, set `p_err` to an appropriate network device error code.

TRANSMIT COMPLETED NOTIFICATION

Since the SPI cannot be accessed within the ISR handler most of time all interrupts type are read in **NetDev_Rx()**. Also, when the ISR type is for a transmit completed notification, it is not recommended to notify the stack by the function and return an error since the reception statistics and errors counter will be affected. Instead it is recommended to return a management frame that contains the address of the data area successfully transmitted. Since all management frame are processed by **NetDev_MgmtDemux()**, the step to notify the stack should be done into it.

16-10-8 TRANSMITTING PACKETS

NetDev_Tx() is used to notify the wireless device that a new packet is available to be transmitted. It performs the following actions:

1 The driver follow the procedure to access the SPI bus, and it takes all necessary steps to initiate transmission of the data by writing to the wireless device's register using appropriate device's BSP functions. The driver must configure the device with the number of bytes to transmit. This value contained in the **size** argument.

2 The driver must write the data stored in the network buffer to the device's memory. The address of the buffer is specified by **p_data** which can be passed directly to 'Write Read' device's BSP function pointer.

3 For wireless devices that do not support transmit completed notifications, the packet is assumed to be transmitted successfully, and the driver must perform the following actions.

    a Post the address of the just-used network buffer to the transmit buffer de-allocation task by calling **NetOS_IF_TxDeallocTaskPost()** with the pointer **p_data**.

    b Call **NetOS_Dev_TxRdySignal()** with the number of the interface that had just completed transmission.

4 For wireless devices that do support transmit completed notifications, the previous transmit complete steps should be performed by **NetDev_MgmtDemux()**.

5 **NetDev_Tx()** sets **p_err** to **NET_DEV_ERR_NONE** and return from the transmit function.

16-10-9 ADDING AN ADDRESS TO THE MULTICAST ADDRESS FILTER OF A NETWORK DEVICE

NetDev_AddrMulticastAdd() is used to configure a device with an (IP-to-Ethernet) multicast hardware address.

You should follow the same steps described in section 16-5-8 "Adding an Address to the Multicast Address Filter of a Network Device" on page 393, except that the device's registers must be accessed through SPI.

> If the wireless device return the result through a response, NetDev_AddrMulticastAdd() should calls the device's Wireless Manager function pointer, NetWiFiMgr_Mgmt(), to complete the operation.

16-10-10 REMOVING AN ADDRESS FROM THE MULTICAST ADDRESS FILTER OF A NETWORK DEVICE

NetDev_AddrMulticastRemove() is used to remove an (IP-to-Ethernet) multicast hardware address from a device.

You should follow the same steps described in section 16-5-9 "Removing an Address from the Multicast Address Filter of a Network Device" on page 397 should be followed, except that the device's registers must be accessed through SPI.

> If the wireless device return the result through a response, NetDev_AddrMulticastAdd() should calls the device's Wireless Manager function pointer, NetWiFiMgr_Mgmt(), to complete the operation.

16-10-11 HOW TO DEMULTIPLEX MANAGEMENT FRAMES

NetDev_MgmtDemux() is called by µC/TCP-IP's Receive task after the device's receive function has returned a management frame. NetDev_MgmtDemux() requires that the device driver analyses management frames received and it must performs all necessary operations. It performs the following actions:

1   Determine if the management frame is a response of a previous management command sent or if it is a management frame which require the driver to update driver's state.

2   If the management frame is a response, the device's Wireless Manager must be signaled using the function pointer **NetWiFiMgr_Signal()**. No other steps are required in that case.

3   If the management frame is a state update, the driver should update device's data or interface's link state or perform transmit complete operations.

4   **NetDev_MgmtDemux()** sets **p_err** to **NET_DEV_ERR_NONE** and return from the demultiplex function.

> If the management frame is only used within **NetDev_MgmtDemux()** (i.e., device's Wireless Manager not signaled), the network buffer must be freed by calling **NetBuf_Free()**.

16-10-12 HOW TO EXECUTE MANAGEMENT COMMAND

NetDev_MgmtExcuteCmd() is used to notify the wireless device that a new management command must be executed. It performs the following actions:

1   The driver follow the procedure to access the SPI bus and it takes all necessary steps to initiate the management command by writing to the wireless device's register using appropriate device's BSP functions. The driver must use the command data argument to send the data needed by the wireless device to perform the management command.

2   Update the pointer to the device's Wireless Manager context state argument following how the command result must be handled by the Wireless Manager.

    a   If the management command requires multiple calls to **NetDev_MgmtExecuteCmd()** before completion, **MgmtCompleted** should be set to false. By doing this, **NetDev_MgmtExecuteCmd** is called in loop until **MgmtCompleted** comes equal to true or an error is returned.

    b   If the management command requires to wait a response before completing the management command process, **WaitResp** must be set equal to true. In this case, once the response is received **NetDev_MgmtProcessResp** will be called. Also, **WaitRespTimeout_ms** should be set to let the Wireless Manager return an error when the response is not received.

3   If the result is not sent via a response, `NetDev_MgmtProcessCmd()` must fill the return buffer with appropriate data following the stack format.

4   `NetDev_MgmtExecuteCmd()` sets `p_err` to `NET_DEV_ERR_NONE` and returns from the execute management command function.

16-10-13 HOW TO PROCESS MANAGEMENT RESPONSE

`NetDev_MgmtProcessResp()` is called when the response of the current management command is received which means that `NetDev_Demux()` has signaled the device's Wireless Manager and the response must be analyzed and translated. `NetDev_MgmtProcessResp()` performs the following actions:

1   The function must translate the response and it must fills the return buffer with appropriate data following the stack format.

2   Update the device's Wireless Manager context state argument pointer following how the command result must be handled by the Wireless Manager.

   a   If the management command is completed, `MgmtCompleted` must be set to true.

   b   If the management command is not completed and more calls to `NetDev_MgmtExecuteCmd()` are required before completing the current management command, `MgmtCompleted` should be set to false. `NetDev_MgmtExecuteCmd` will be called and the management command will not return until `MgmtCompleted` comes equal to true.

3   `NetDev_MgmtProcessResp()` sets `p_err` to `NET_DEV_ERR_NONE` and return from the Process management response function.

16

Device Driver Validation

To help in the development of the Ethernet driver, Micrium provides a Windows-based tool called the Network Driver Integrated Tester (NDIT). The NDIT encapsulates many of the performance tests that you perform on your driver during development. It handles synchronisation between the test station and the target device, and parses and displays test results, all in one interface.

Tools that may help you during the design or tuning phase are presented in this chapter. These tools test and exercise different parts of the Ethernet device driver and can help uncovering flaws in the implementation of the driver. A set of test procedures is also provided in order to validate the proper behavior of the driver.

17-1 CHECKLIST

It is strongly suggested that you use the following checklist when writing a new device driver or when an existing driver is modified. You can fill it out as you develop your device driver and perform the tests described in the document.

Element of Validation	Directly connected	Networked
Hardware Address configuration	❏	❏
Answer to all received ping	❏	❏
Answer to all received ping via fping	❏	❏
Transmit UDP Test 1 (transmit UDP packet of 1472 bytes)	❏	❏
Receive UDP Test 1 (Receive UDP packet of 1472 bytes)	❏	❏
Receive UDP Test 2 (Receive UDP packet with different length)	❏	❏
Transmit TCP Test 1	❏	❏
Receive TCP Test 1 (Receive with default RX windows size)	❏	❏
Receive TCP Test 2 (Receive with optimized RX windows size)	❏	❏
No buffers leak	❏	❏
Configuration & Performance results are logged	❏	❏
Multicast	❏	❏
IF Start/Stop	❏	❏

17-2 TEST MANAGEMENT INTERFACE

NDIT requires a connection with the target to configure the tests. There are two connection protocols available: RS-232 or TCP/IP (Ethernet). The use of TCP/IP requires a functional Ethernet driver and TCP/IP stack. It is common to start with RS-232, when a UART is available.

Upon starting NDIT, the following dialog box appears:

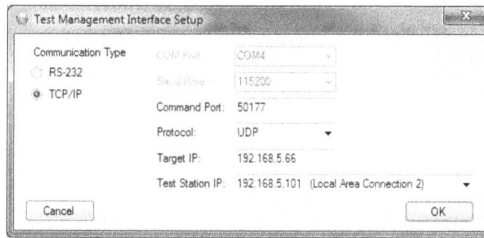

Figure 17-1 **Test management interface setup dialog**

The connection setup options are as followed:

Connection type	RS-232	COM port (ex: COM1).
		Baud rate (8 bits, no parity, 1 stop bit and no flow control)
	TCP/IP	Command port (UDP or TCP port)
		The test station and target exchange commands and return results on this port. It must match the port number defined in **app_cfg.h** (#define **NDIT_PORT**).
Transport protocol		TCP or UDP. Either one of the protocol can be chosen as long as the target's TCP/IP implementation supports it.
Target IP		The target IP address must be the one used by **App_TCPIP_Init()** in **app.c** in order for the test station to reach the target board. This parameter is also used when the NDIT is setup for RS-232 communication.

459

Network   The network interface used to communicate with the target. By default, the first IPv4 network interface found is used. In order for the tests to work, the target has to be reachable via the selected network interface.

Once you click 'OK' the NDIT main window (see next section) appears, and your chosen connection settings are stored and will be reloaded at the next startup of NDIT.

17-2-1 NDIT MAIN WINDOW

The features of the main window are described in the following section. Below is a screen shot of the main window:

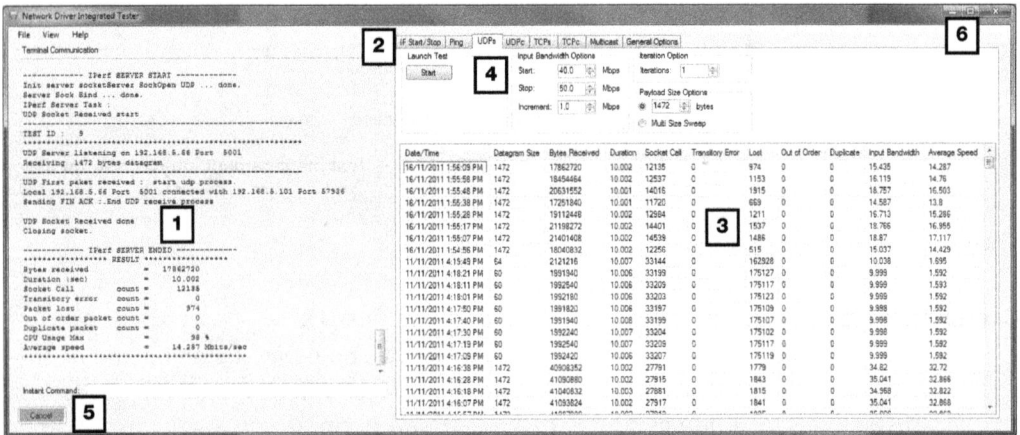

Figure 17-2 **NDIT Main Window**

F17-2(1)   The target's communication log: The target received data is displayed in this scrollable text box.

F17-2(2)   Test tabs: Each tab contains tests and test options:

    1   IF Start/Stop: The network interface of the device is turned off and on again after a specified delay.

    2   Ping: The target receives an ICMP echo request.

    3   UDPs (UDP server): The target receives UDP frames from the test station at a specified bandwidth.

4   UDPc (UDP client): The target transmits UDP frames to the test station computer at the highest possible bandwidth achievable by the target.

5   TCPs (TCP server): The target receives TCP frames from the test station computer.

6   TCPc (TCP client): The target transmits TCP frames to the test station computer.

7   Multicast: The test station computer sends multicast packets to the target.

8   General Options: Common parameters for all the tests.

F17-2(3)   Test results table: Each tab has its own test results table that displays the input information and the output results for each test ,along with the date and time at which that test was executed. When the NDIT is launched, it loads the test results logs from previous tests and displays them in the test results table.

F17-2(4)   Tests and test options: This section contains the different tests and test options that can be performed from the selected tab.

In addition to the options specified in the current test tab, there is another set of options located in the General Option tab. These options, like test duration and target IP address, are common to more than one test.

F17-2(5)   Cancel button: When an iterative or a parameter sweep test is launched, it can be cancelled by clicking the Cancel button. The current test will finish and the results will be displayed in the test result table.

F17-2(6)   Exit button: Upon clicking the Exit button, the test results will be saved, and connections, if any, will be closed with the target.

17-2-2 GENERAL OPTIONS TAB

The General Options tab contains common test properties that are used throughout the test cases.

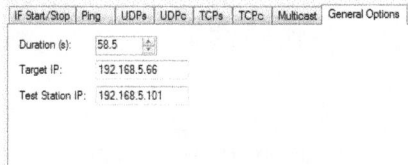

Figure 17-3 **General Options tab**

This tab contains three options:

■ Duration (s): Used for IPerf testing. Specifies the duration of the data transfer between the test station and the target.

■ Target IP: The target IP address as specified in **app.c**.

■ Test Station IP: The test station IP address to which the target will reply when using IPerf.

17-3 VALIDATING A DEVICE DRIVER

This section describes how a driver should be validated. These tests must be performed for each new driver and any modifications to an existing driver. The tests provided have been chosen to highlight potential flaws that may be present in the device driver.

17-3-1 FILES NEEDED

The required source files needed to validate a device driver are as follows:

```
$/Micrium/Software/uC-IPerf/Source/iperf.c
$/Micrium/Software/uC-IPerf/Source/iperf.h
$/Micrium/Software/uC-IPerf/Source/iperf-c.c
$/Micrium/Software/uC-IPerf/Source/iperf-s.c
$/Micrium/Software/uC-IPerf/Reporter/Terminal/iperf_rep.c
$/Micrium/Software/uC-IPerf/Reporter/Terminal/iperf_rep.h
$/Micrium/Software/uC-TCPIP-V2/App/NDIT/Source/ndit.c
$/Micrium/Software/uC-TCPIP-V2/App/NDIT/Source/ndit.h
$/Micrium/Software/uC-TCPIP-V2/App/NDIT/Source/ndit_ifss.c
$/Micrium/Software/uC-TCPIP-V2/App/NDIT/Source/ndit_ifss.h
$/Micrium/Software/uC-TCPIP-V2/App/NDIT/Source/ndit_mcast.c
$/Micrium/Software/uC-TCPIP-V2/App/NDIT/Source/ndit_mcast.h
```

When using µC/OS-II:

```
$/Micrium/Software/uC-IPerf/Source/uCOS-II.c
$/Micrium/Software/uC-TCPIP-V2/App/NDIT/OS/uCOS-II/ndit_os.c
$/Micrium/Software/uC-TCPIP-V2/App/NDIT/OS/uCOS-II/ndit_mcast_os.c
```

Or when using µC/OS-III:

```
$/Micrium/Software/uC-IPerf/Source/uCOS-III.c
$/Micrium/Software/uC-TCPIP-V2/App/NDIT/OS/uCOS-III/ndit_os.c
$/Micrium/Software/uC-TCPIP-V2/App/NDIT/OS/uCOS-III/ndit_mcast_os.c
```

Copy the contents of

```
$/Micrium/Software/uC-IPerf/Cfg/Template/iperf_cfg.h
```

and

```
$/Micrium/Software/uC-TCPIP-V2/App/NDIT/Cfg/Template/ndit_cfg.h
```

into your **app_cfg.h**.

17-3-2 PROJECT EXAMPLE

Figure 17-4 shows the workspace with groups expanded for a development board with NDIT and IPerf modules included.

The **APP group** is where the actual code for the example is located.

The **BSP group** contains the 'Board Support Package' code to use for several of the Input/Output (I/O) devices on the development board.

The **NDIT group** contains the necessary files to interact with the NDIT software on the test station host. In hold the executive code for the test procedures describes in Section 10 of this document.

The **µC/CPU group** contains source and header files for the µC/CPU module. Header files contain definitions and declaration that are required by some of the application code.

The **µC/IPerf group** contains the source and header for the µC/IPerf module. It also contains the IPerf Reporter module which formats and displays IPerf's test results.

The **µC/LIB group** contains the source and header for the µC/LIB module. Again, the header files are needed as some of the application code requires definitions and declarations found in these files.

The **µC/OS-III group** contains the source and header files for the µC/OS-III module.

The **µC/TCP-IP group** contains the source and header files for the µC/TCP-IP module.

```
OSIII-TCPIP                              cpu_core.c          os_task.c               net_icmp.c
  APP                                    cpu_core.h          os_tick.c               net_icmp.h
    app.c                                cpu_def.h           os_time.c               net_igmp.c
    app_cfg.h                          uC/IPerf              os_tmr.c                net_igmp.h
    app_vect.c                           APP                 os_var.c                net_ip.c
    cpu_cfg.h                              app_iperf.c     uC/TCP-IP                 net_ip.h
    dhcp-c_cfg.h                           app_iperf.h       Dev                     net_mgr.c
    includes.h                           OS                    Ether                 net_mgr.h
    net_cfg.h                              iperf_os.c            DEVICEXXX           net_sock.c
    net_dev_cfg.c                        Reporter                net_dev_etherxxx.c  net_sock.h
    net_dev_cfg.h                          iperf_rep.c           net_dev_etherxxx.h  net_stat.c
    os_app_hooks.c                         iperf_rep.h         PHY                   net_stat.h
    os_app_hooks.h                       Source                  net_phy.c           net_tcp.c
    os_cfg.h                               iperf-c.c             net_phy.h           net_tcp.h
    os_cfg_app.h                           iperf-s.c         IF                      net_tmr.c
    os_type.h                              iperf.c             net_if.c              net_tmr.h
    dev1_conf.h                            iperf.h             net_if.h              net_type.h
  BSP                                  uC/LIB                  net_if_ether.c        net_udp.c
    FWlib                                Ports                 net_if_ether.h        net_udp.h
    uCOS-III                              lib_mem_a.asm       net_if_loopback.c      net_util.c
      bsp_os.c                           lib_ascii.c          net_if_loopback.h      net_util.h
      bsp_os.h                           lib_ascii.h        OS                    Output
    bsp.c                                lib_def.h            net_os.c                OSIII-TCPIP-IPerf.out
    bsp.h                                lib_math.c           net_os.h
    bsp_int.c                            lib_math.h         Port
    bsp_periph.c                         lib_mem.c            net_util_a.asm
    bsp_ser.c                            lib_mem.h          Source
    bsp_ser.h                            lib_str.c            net.c
    bsp_stlm75.c                         lib_str.h            net.h
    bsp_stlm75.h                       uC/OS-III              net_app.c
    net_bsp.c                            Port                 net_app.h
    net_bsp.h                              os_cpu.h           net_arp.c
  NDIT                                     os_cpu_a.asm       net_arp.h
    OS                                     os_cpu_c.c         net_ascii.c
      ndit_mcast_os.c                    Source               net_ascii.h
      ndit_os.c                            os.h               net_bsd.c
    Source                                 os_cfg_app.c       net_bsd.h
      ndit.c                               os_core.c          net_buf.c
      ndit.h                               os_dbg.c           net_buf.h
      ndit_ifss.c                          os_flag.c          net_cfg_net.h
      ndit_ifss.h                          os_int.c           net_conn.c
      ndit_mcast.c                         os_mem.c           net_conn.h
      ndit_mcast.h                         os_msg.c           net_ctr.c
  uC/CPU                                   os_mutex.c         net_ctr.h
    cpu.h                                  os_pend_multi.c    net_dbg.c
    cpu_a.asm                              os_prio.c          net_dbg.h
    cpu_c.c                                os_q.c             net_def.h
    cpu_core.c                             os_sem.c           net_err.c
                                           os_stat.c          net_err.h
```

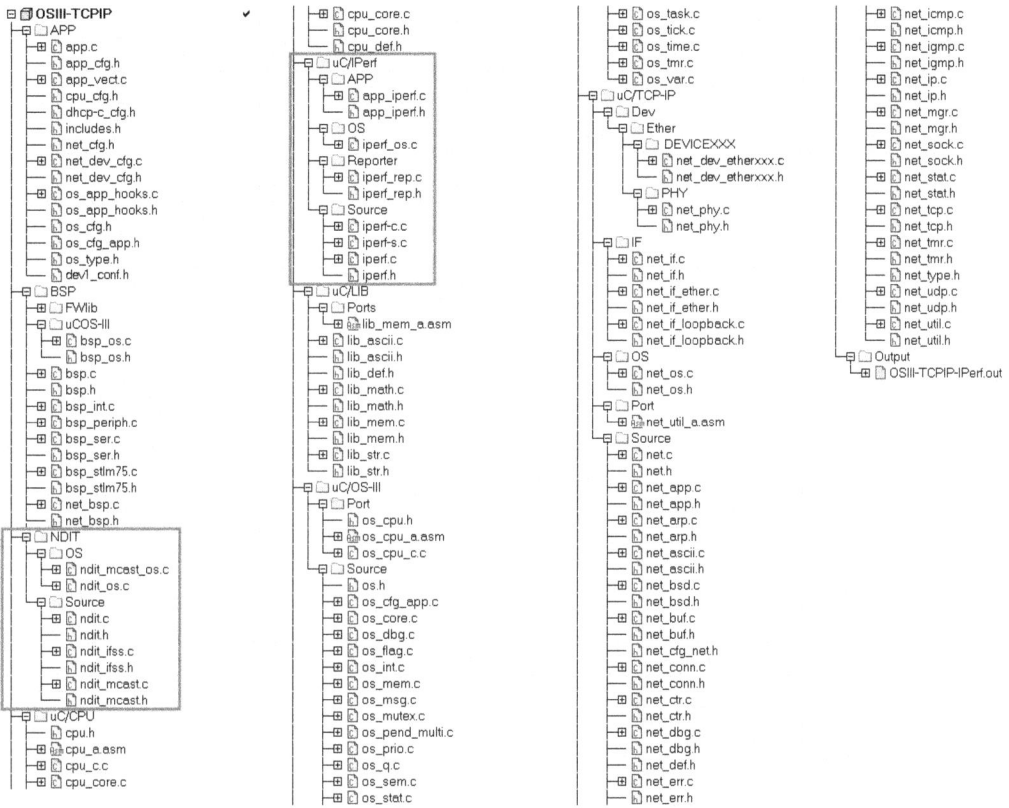

Figure 17-4 **Project Workspace with NDIT and IPerf modules highlighted**

17-3-3 HARDWARE ADDRESS CONFIGURATION

It is important to validate the configuration of the Ethernet interface's hardware address. The physical hardware address should be configured from within **NetDev_Start()** to allow for the proper use of **NetIF_Ether_HW_AddrSet()**, hard coded hardware addresses from the device configuration structure, or auto-loading EEPROM's. Changes to the physical address only take effect when the device transitions from the **NET_IF_LINK_DOWN** to **NET_IF_LINK_UP** state. These states are defined in **net_if.h**, and the current state of the controller can be found by calling **NetIF_LinkStateGet()** from your application.

The device hardware address is set from one of the data sources below, listed in the order of precedence.

1 From the device configuration structure (`NET_DEV_CFG_ETHER`) defined in `net_dev_cfg.c`. Configure a valid hardware address (i.e., not null) for `.HW_AddrStr[]` in `NetDev_Cfg_<device>_<Nbr>` in `net_dev_cfg.c` at compilation time.

2 From a call to `NetIF_Ether_HW_AddrSet()`:

The value of `.HW_AddrStr[]` must be set to "00:00:00:00:00:00", or an empty string. `NetIF_Ether_HW_AddrSet()` must be called with the desired hardware address before calling `NetIF_Start()`.

3 From Auto-Loading via EEPROM

If `.HW_AddrStr[]` is set to "00:00:00:00:00:00", and `NetIF_Ether_HW_AddrSet()` is not called, then `NetDev_Start()` will attempt to configure the hardware address with the network hardware address registers. These registers are the low and high hardware address register from the MAC device registers.

Note that this test is not available in NDIT since automatic source code compilation and binary download to the target are not supported by NDIT.

TESTING

In order to verify that the three hardware address configuration methods work, there are a few steps that you will have to perform:

1 Set the value of `.HW_AddrStr[]` in `NetDev_Cfg_<device>_<Nbr>` in `net_dev_cfg.c` to a valid unicast MAC address. Then set up Wireshark to capture the ARP and ICMP traffic on the network interface used by your target. Send an ICMP echo request to the IP address of the target and verify that the device responds with the hardware address specified by `.HW_AddrStr[]` in the Wireshark trace.

2 Set the value of `.HW_AddrStr[]` in `NetDev_Cfg_<device>_<Nbr>` in `net_dev_cfg.c` to "00:00:00:00:00:00", before calling `NetIF_Start()` in your application code call `NetIF_AddrHW_Set()` with a valid unicast MAC address (i.e., not null) Then set up Wireshark to capture the ARP and ICMP traffic on the network interfece on which your target is connected. Send an ICMP echo request to the IP address of the target and verify that the device responds with the hardware address specified with `NetIF_AddrHW_Set()` in the Wireshark trace.

3 The third method can be tested if the MAC on your device stores the MAC address registers in an EEPROM. If the EEPROM is accessible from the program loader, you can configure the high and low address registers with a valid HW address. Then setup Wireshark to capture the ARP and ICMP traffic on the network interface on which your target is connected. Send an ICMP echo request to the IP address of the target and verify, in the Wireshark trace, that the device responds with the hardware address specified.

17-3-4 IF START / STOP

The purpose of the Interface Start / Stop test is to validate that the driver can successfully stop a network interface and restart it again. Testing the driver's ability to stop the network interface is often skipped, but it is an essential function. Stopping and starting the network interface of your device is one of the ways to detect buffer leaks since stopping the device will deallocate all the network buffers and descriptors. If restarting the network interface fails, it might indicate that you have a buffer leak situation.

IF START / STOP TEST USING NDIT

To validate the start/stop function, the NDIT verifies tthat the network device should:

▣ Respond to an echo request (ping) before stopping the network interface.

▣ Ignore an echo request after the network interface has been stopped.

▣ Respond again to an echo request after restarting the network interface.

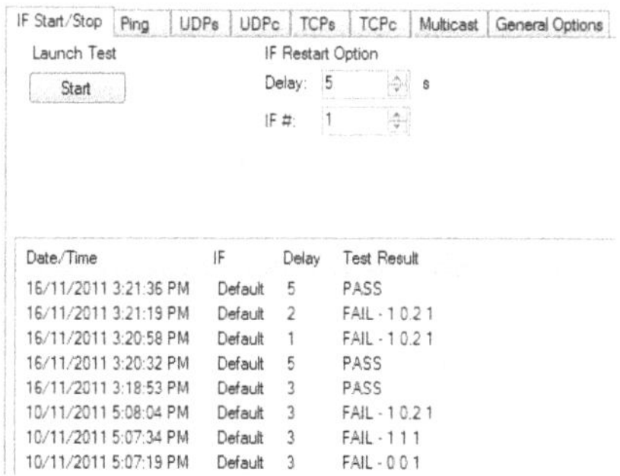

Figure 17-5 **Interface Start / Stop test tab**

There is a single option for the Interface Start / Stop test:

Delay   The time between the Interface Stops and the Interface Starts (in seconds).

IF #   The Interface number to Start / Stop.

ANALYZING THE RESULTS

If the Test Result column does not indicate a PASS, it will show a FAIL followed by three echo request results. The first result should be 1 and represents a 100% echo reply success rate before the interface is stopped. The second result should be 0 and represents a 0% echo reply success rate while the interface is stopped. The final result should be 1 and represents a 100% echo reply success rate after the interface is restarted.

In the example shown in Figure 17-5, the test result that shows "FAIL – 1 1 1" indicates that the Interface continued replying to the test station host after it has sent the `ifss` stop command. Since all commands sent by the NDIT are acknowledged by the target, it is unlikely that the command wasn't received and processed by the target. Furthermore, the 100% success rate for the ICMP echo shows that the target is responsive. Therefore the error should be in the implementation of the `NetDev_Stop()` function.

17-3-5 ICMP ECHO REQUEST (PING) TESTS

The ping can be used as a starting point to validate the driver. But keep in mind that if your target answers to a ping request, it doesn't mean that your work is done. Since a ping request sends only a small payload to the target, and the device sends back an equally small payload to the test station, it is not a test for reliability or performance. The goal of this test is only to quickly determine whether or not the basic mechanism for receiving and transmitting a packet are implemented in your device driver.

```
ping <target.ip.address>
```

The μC/TCP-IP module need to be given a heavier load to see if the device driver is robust and stable. Your device driver must be able to answer (for a of minimum 15 seconds) this command:

```
ping <target.ip.address> -n 15 -l 1472
```

Once your driver is able to handle the previous ping command, you can increase the load by using fping.

A Windows version of fping can be downloaded from this site: `http://www.kwakkelflap.com/fping.html`. Additional download sites are available for Linux and other operating systems. Note that NDIT is a Windows-only tool.

Your driver must be able to handle these fping commands:

`fping <target.ip.address> -t 1 -c -i`

−t 1   Sets the interval between two subsequent ICMP echo request to 1 ms

−c   Send the request indefinitely

−i   Disables an annoying fping warning

A good result would be if your device can sustain that rate of request without ever stalling. Otherwise, you might have a buffer leak issue or a device configuration issue you should fix first before continuing with the subsequent tests.

`fping <target.ip.address> -t 1 -S 1/1464`

17-3-6 TARGET BOARD CONFIGURATION

The following sections require interactions between the NDIT on the test station and the code in your target. To be able to communicate with the test station, both the target and the test station must share the same configuration.

The first thing to configure is the communication protocol. The NDIT supports either serial port RS-232 communication or network TCP-IP communication. The communication protocol is configured in **app_cfg.h**.

FOR RS-232 COMMUNICATION

```
#define  NDIT_COM                          NDIT_SERIAL_COM
```

The data rate of the serial communication has to be defined to one of the available bit rates supported by the NDIT: 1200, 2400, 4800, 9600, 14400, 19200, 38400, 57600 or 115200 bits/sec. If your device has a serial port, the bit rate parameter should be defined in the BSP layer of the software architecture of the device. Your device must also implement a framing of 8 data bits, no parity and 1 stop bit. Also, flow control should not be used with NDIT.

FOR TCP/IP CONNECTION

```
#define  NDIT_COM                          NDIT_NETWORK_COM
```

The command port can be changed in **app_cfg.h** to any available port number:

```
#define  NDIT_PORT                         50177u
```

17-4 USING IPERF

Perf is a tool designed to perform performance tests and to measure various variables of a network. IPerf is a benchmaring tool for measuring performance between two systems. It can be used as a server or a client for both the TCP and UDP protocols. Many IPerf applications are available for different operating systems. IPerf applications for the PC are easily found on the web. However, we suggest to use the IPerf function integrated in the Network Driver Integrated Tester for version compatibility purposes with the target software.

It is strongly recommended that you use IPerf to validate your driver and find the best target configuration. Perform four tests (Receive and Transmit are from the target point of view):

■ TCP Server (Receive)

■ TCP Client (Transmit)

■ UDP Server (Receive)

■ UDP Client (Transmit)

You have to test your driver with different TCP/IP stack configuration (**net_cfg.h**). Tests must be performed with the target directly connected to the test station and on a network and you it is recommended to log all performances results and configurations into a device drivers test result document.

You can find more information on IPerf at **http://sourceforge.net/projects/iperf/**.

17-4-1 GETTING STARTED WITH IPERF

Mircium's implementation of IPerf is called µC/IPerf. It can be used in many ways, the most practical being to launch a test on the target using the NDIT test management interface via a string command. µC/IPerf doesn't generate output by itself. Rather, statistics are compiled by IPerf for your test. To get the results, you must query IPerf using your own application or an existing tool. µC/IPerf comes with two built-in applications to query test status and output test results.

IPerf is available within the NDIT. It allows you to test the performance of your driver quickly, since the NDIT tests are using predefined IPerf commands. The results are logged and displayed in a table which makes it easier to track the driver's performances.

17-4-2 IPERF TOOLS

TERMINAL REPORTER ON THE TARGET

If your target board has a serial interface, you should use the Terminal Reporter. You must create a function which will transmit a string buffer via the serial interface. The NDIT module must be able to use this function to send back the menu or any command errors. Listing 17-1 shows an example.

```
/*
************************************************************************************************
*                                    NDIT_OutputFnct()
*
* Description : Output a string on the display.
*
* Argument(s) : p_buf        Pointer to buffer to output.
*
*               p_param      Pointer to IPerf output parameters. (unused)
*
* Return(s)   : none.
*
* Caller(s)   : various.
*
* Note(s)     : (1) The string pointed to by p_buf has to be NUL ('\0') terminated.
************************************************************************************************
*/
#if (NDIT_COM == NDIT_SERIAL_COM)
void  NDIT_OutputFnct (CPU_CHAR          *p_buf,
                       IPERF_OUT_PARAM   *p_param)
{
   (void)&p_param;                                                            (1)

   if (p_buf == (CPU_CHAR *)0) {                                              (2)
       return;
   }
   APP_TRACE_INFO((p_buf));                                                   (3)
}
#endif
```

Listing 17-1 **Terminal reporter output function**

L17-1(1)   Prevent "variable unused" compiler warning.

L17-1(2)   Validate that the pointer to the string is not null.

L17-1(3)   Display the string on the serial port of the board. **BSP_Ser_WrStr()** is a
            BSP-specific function that outputs each character of the string passed in the
            parameter until it reaches the NULL character ("\0"). It terminates the string
            with the Carriage Return symbol ("\r") followed by the Line Feed symbol
            ("\n"). The null is not transmitted.

You will also need to implement the task **NDIT_TaskTerminal()** which performs Terminal I/O. It must be able to:

1   Receive a string from the serial interface.

2   Launch IPerf or other NDIT commands with the string received on the serial interface.

Listing 17-2 shows a Terminal I/O task example.

```
/*
**********************************************************************************************
*                                  NDIT_TaskTerminal()
*
* Description : Task that reads the serial port input, processes the commands and verifies
*               that the cmd has been correctly executed.
*
* Argument(s) : p_arg              Pointer to task input parameter (unused).
*
* Return(s)   : none.
*
* Caller(s)   : AppTaskCreateTerminal().
*
* Note(s)     : none.
**********************************************************************************************
*/
#if (NDIT_COM == NDIT_SERIAL_COM)
void  NDIT_TaskTerminal (void  *p_arg)
{
    CPU_CHAR       cmd_str[TASK_TERMINAL_CMD_STR_MAX_LEN];
    CPU_SIZE_T     cmd_len;
    NDIT_ERR       err;

#if (IPERF_REPORTER == DEF_ENABLED)
    APP_TRACE_INFO(("\r\nTerminal I/O\r\n\r\n"));
    while (DEF_ON) {
        APP_TRACE(("\r\n>  "));
        BSP_Ser_RdStr((CPU_CHAR *)&cmd_str[0],                                    (1)
                      (CPU_INT16U) TASK_TERMINAL_CMD_STR_MAX_LEN);

        cmd_len = Str_Len(&cmd_str[0]);

        NDIT_ProcessCommand((CPU_CHAR      *)&cmd_str[0],                         (2)
                            (CPU_INT16U     ) cmd_len,
                            (NDIT_OUT_FNCT )&NDIT_Output,
                            (IPERF_OUT_FNCT)&NDIT_OutputFnct,
                            (NDIT_ERR      *)&err);
```

```
        switch(err) {                                              (3)
            case NDIT_NO_ERR:
            case NDIT_ERR_NO_CMD:
                break;
            case NDIT_ERR_IPERF:                                   (4)
                NDIT_Output(("Error in IPerf Test\r\n\r\n"));
                break;
            case NDIT_ERR_MCAST:                                   (5)
                NDIT_Output(("Error in Mcast Test\r\n\r\n"));
                break;
            case NDIT_ERR_IFSS:                                    (6)
                NDIT_Output(("Error in IFSS Test\r\n\r\n"));
                break;
            case NDIT_ERR_NO_MATCH:                                (7)
                NDIT_Output(("Command not recognized\r\n\r\n"));
                break;
        }
    }
#endif
}
#endif
```

Listing 17-2 **Terminal I/O task**

L17-2(1)   Read string command from serial port.

L17-2(2)   The command read from the serial port is processed and executed by the **NDIT_ProcessCommand( )** function.

L17-2(3)   Verify test executed correctly based on the return error from the **NDIT_ProcessCommand( )** function.

L17-2(4)   An error occurred during an IPerf test.

L17-2(5)   An error occurred during a Multicast test.

L17-2(6)   An error occurred during an Interface Start/Stop test.

L17-2(7)   The provided command was neither recognized by the IPerf, Multicast or Interface Start/Stop test modules.

Note that you must initialize µC/IPerf before using the "Terminal Reporter."

SERVER REPORTER ON THE TARGET

You can also use the network interface of your device to send commands to the NDIT. This way, if you don't have a Serial Port on your device, you can still send commands and receive results through the **NDIT_TaskServer()** task and **NDIT_NetOutputFnct()** display function.

The source of **NDIT_NetOutputFnct()** is displayed in Listing 17-3:

```
/*
*********************************************************************************
*                                   NDIT_NetOutputFnct()
*
* Description : Outputs a string to the test host application.
*
* Argument(s) : p_buf        Pointer to buffer to output.
*
*               p_param      Pointer to IPERF_OUT_PARAM object.
*
* Return(s)   : none.
*
* Caller(s)   : various.
*
* Note(s)     : (1) The string pointed to by p_buf has to be NUL ('\0') terminated.
*********************************************************************************
*/
#if (NDIT_COM == NDIT_NETWORK_COM)
void  NDIT_NetOutputFnct (CPU_CHAR         *p_buf,
                          IPERF_OUT_PARAM  *p_param)
{
    CPU_INT16U  tx_len;
    NET_ERR     net_err;

    (void)&p_param;                                                   (1)

    if (p_buf == (CPU_CHAR *)0) {                                     (2)
        return;
    }
```

```
    if (NDIT_TS_SockInfo.NetSockID != NET_SOCK_BSD_ERR_OPEN) {

        tx_len = (CPU_INT16U)Str_Len(p_buf);                                          (3)

        (void)NetApp_SockTx ((NET_SOCK_ID        ) NDIT_TS_SockInfo.NetSockID,        (4)
                             (void             *) p_buf,
                             (CPU_INT16U        ) tx_len,
                             (CPU_INT16S        ) NET_SOCK_FLAG_NONE,
                             (NET_SOCK_ADDR     *)&NDIT_TS_SockInfo.NetSockAddr,
                             (NET_SOCK_ADDR_LEN) NDIT_TS_SockInfo.NetSockAddrLen,
                             (CPU_INT16U        ) NDIT_SERVER_RETRY_MAX,
                             (CPU_INT32U        ) NDIT_SERVER_DELAY_MS,
                             (CPU_INT32U        ) NDIT_SERVER_DELAY_MS,
                             (NET_ERR           *)&net_err);      }
    }
}
#endif
```

Listing 17-3 **NDIT_NetOutputFnct display function**

L17-3(1)   Prevent "variable unused" compiler warning.

L17-3(2)   Verify that the pointer is not null.

L17-3(3)   Calculate buffer length.

L17-3(4)   Send the buffer to the test station host using the test station host information found in the DIS_TS_SockInfo global variable.

Listing 17-4 shows the **NDIT_TaskServer()** function, which reads the commands from the test station host, processes them, and gives back the results to the test station host.

476

```
typedef   struct  host_sock_info {                                              (1)
    NET_SOCK_ID        NetSockID;
    NET_SOCK_ADDR      NetSockAddr;
    NET_SOCK_ADDR_LEN  NetSockAddrLen;
} HOST_SOCK_INFO;
static  HOST_SOCK_INFO    NDIT_TS_SockInfo;                                      (2)
/*
*************************************************************************************
*                               NDIT_TaskServer()
*
* Description:  This function creates a input/output ethernet communication link to use iPerf.
*
* Argument(s) : p_arg      Pointer to arg. (unused)
*
* Return(s)   : none.
*
* Caller(s)   : NDIT_TaskCreateServer().
*
* Note(s)     : (1) NDIT_COM must be defined to NDIT_NETWORK_COM in app_cfg.h for this function
* to be used.
*
*************************************************************************************
*/
#if (NDIT_COM == NDIT_NETWORK_COM)
void  NDIT_TaskServer (void  *p_arg)
{
    NET_SOCK_ID        net_sock_id;
    NET_SOCK_ADDR_IP   server_addr_port;
    NET_SOCK_ADDR      client_addr_port;
    NET_SOCK_ADDR_LEN  client_addr_port_len;
    CPU_CHAR           buf[TASK_TERMINAL_CMD_STR_MAX_LEN];
    CPU_INT16S         rx_len;
    CPU_BOOLEAN        socket_connected;
    NET_ERR            net_err;
    NDIT_ERR           test_err;

    (void)&p_arg;                                                               (3)

    Mem_Clr((void     *)&server_addr_port,                                      (4)
            (CPU_SIZE_T) sizeof(server_addr_port));

    server_addr_port.AddrFamily = NET_SOCK_ADDR_FAMILY_IP_V4;
    server_addr_port.Port       = NET_UTIL_HOST_TO_NET_16(NDIT_PORT);
    server_addr_port.Addr       = NET_SOCK_ADDR_IP_WILDCARD;
```

```
while (DEF_TRUE){
    socket_connected = DEF_YES;

    net_sock_id = NetApp_SockOpen((NET_SOCK_PROTOCOL_FAMILY) NET_SOCK_FAMILY_IP_V4,          (5)
                                  (NET_SOCK_TYPE          ) NET_SOCK_TYPE_DATAGRAM,
                                  (NET_SOCK_PROTOCOL      ) NET_SOCK_PROTOCOL_UDP,
                                  (CPU_INT16U             ) NDIT_SERVER_RETRY_MAX,
                                  (CPU_INT32U             ) NDIT_SERVER_DELAY_MS,
                                  (NET_ERR                *)&net_err);

    if (net_err != NET_APP_ERR_NONE) {
        APP_TRACE_INFO(("\r\nFail to open socket.\r\n\r\n"));                                 (6)
        socket_connected = DEF_NO;
    } else {

        (void)NetApp_SockBind((NET_SOCK_ID      ) net_sock_id,                                (7)
                              (NET_SOCK_ADDR    *)&server_addr_port,
                              (NET_SOCK_ADDR_LEN) NET_SOCK_ADDR_SIZE,
                              (CPU_INT16U       ) NDIT_SERVER_RETRY_MAX,
                              (CPU_INT32U       ) NDIT_SERVER_DELAY_MS,
                              (NET_ERR          *)&net_err);

        if (net_err != NET_APP_ERR_NONE) {

            (void)NetApp_SockClose((NET_SOCK_ID) net_sock_id,                                 (8)
                                   (CPU_INT32U ) 0u,
                                   (NET_ERR    *)&net_err);

            socket_connected = DEF_NO;
        }
    }

    while(socket_connected == DEF_YES) {                                                      (9)

        rx_len = NetApp_SockRx ((NET_SOCK_ID        ) net_sock_id,                            (10)
                                (void               *)&buf[0],
                                (CPU_INT16U         ) TASK_TERMINAL_CMD_STR_MAX_LEN,
                                (CPU_INT16U         ) 0,
                                (CPU_INT16S         ) NET_SOCK_FLAG_NONE,
                                (NET_SOCK_ADDR      *)&client_addr_port,
                                (NET_SOCK_ADDR_LEN  *)&client_addr_port_len,
                                (CPU_INT16U         ) 1,
                                (CPU_INT32U         ) 0,
                                (CPU_INT32U         ) 0,
                                (NET_ERR            *)&net_err);
```

```
            switch (net_err) {
                case NET_APP_ERR_CONN_CLOSED:                             (11)
                    socket_connected = DEF_NO;
                    break;
                case NET_APP_ERR_NONE:
                default:
                    break;
            }


            NDIT_TS_SockInfo.NetSockID      = net_sock_id;               (12)
            NDIT_TS_SockInfo.NetSockAddr    = client_addr_port;
            NDIT_TS_SockInfo.NetSockAddrLen = client_addr_port_len;


            buf[rx_len] = '\0';
            NDIT_NetOutput(&buf[0]);                                     (13)
            NDIT_NetOutput(NEW_LINE);


            NDIT_ProcessCommand((CPU_CHAR      *)&buf[0],                (14)
                                (CPU_INT16U    ) rx_len,
                                (NDIT_OUT_FNCT )&NDIT_NetOutput,
                                (IPERF_OUT_FNCT)&NDIT_NetOutputFnct,
                                (NDIT_ERR      *)&test_err);
            switch(test_err) {                                          (15)
                case NDIT_NO_ERR:
                case NDIT_ERR_NO_CMD:
                    break;
                case NDIT_ERR_IPERF:
                    NDIT_NetOutput("\r\nError in IPerf Test\r\n\r\n");   (16)
                    break;
                case NDIT_ERR_MCAST:
                    NDIT_NetOutput("\r\nError in Mcast Test\r\n\r\n");   (17)
                    break;
                case NDIT_ERR_IFSS:
                    NDIT_NetOutput("\r\nError in IFSS Test\r\n\r\n");    (18)
                    break;
                case NDIT_ERR_NO_MATCH:
                default:
                    NDIT_NetOutput("\r\nCommand not recognized\r\n\r\n"); (19)
                    break;
            }


            NDIT_Delay (0, 0, 0, 100);
        }
    }
}
#endif
```

Listing 17-4 **NDIT_TaskServer() task**

479

L17-4(1)   Structure that contains the test station host socket id, socket address and socket address length.

L17-4(2)   The global variable that hold the necessary information for the NDIT display function to return the test results and information messages to the test station host.

L17-4(3)   Prevent the "variable unused" warning from the compiler.

L17-4(4)   Initialize NDIT Server Address and Port.

L17-4(5)   Open socket for receiving host commands and publish results.

L17-4(6)   An error has occurred during the opening of the socket.

L17-4(7)   Bind the socket to a local port.

L17-4(8)   If binding fails, close the socket.

L17-4(9)   Server reading and command processing loop.

L17-4(10)   Read the incoming command from the test station host.

L17-4(11)   If socket is closed, then exit the while loop and restart connection process.

L17-4(12)   Update remote host socket information for displaying test results and messages to the test station host.

L17-4(13)   Reply to test station for acknowledgement.

L17-4(14)   The command read from the serial port is processed and executed by the **NDIT_ProcessCommand( )** function.

L17-4(15)   Verify test executed correctly based on the return error from the **NDIT_ProcessCommand( )** function.

L17-4(16)   An error occurred during an IPerf test.

L17-4(17)   An error occurred during a Multicast test.

L17-4(18)   An error occurred during an Interface Start/Stop test.

L17-4(19)   The provided command was neither recognized by the IPerf, Multicast or Interface Start/Stop test modules.

17-5 IPERF TEST CASE

Once the target answers to ping requests on a switched network, you should perform additional IPerf tests with the target connected directly to the test station, and on a network. It is best to perform standard tests, and log the results into a device driver test result document.

BUFFER LEAKS

For each IPerf test, make sure that your driver does not have any buffer leaks. If the driver performance decrease over time, or if the driver suddenly stops, you might have a buffer leak.

Buffer leaks can happen in many cases. The root cause of a buffer leak is when the program loses track of memory allocation pointers. Assigning a newly allocated buffer to a pointer without deallocating the previous memory block that the pointer associated with will also cause a buffer leak. If no other pointer refers to that memory location, then there is no way it can be deallocated in the future, and that memory block will remain unusable unless the system is reset.

Transmit buffer leaks can be detected by having the target transmit a large buffer to the test station using TCP. A good example would be an FTP test. If a given buffer is not transmitted because it has leaked, the test station will request its retransmission by the target. This operation should fail since the leaked buffer is lost.

In Figure 17-6, the test station (192.168.5.110) requests the retransmission of a lost segment and the target (192.168.5.217) fails to retransmit it:

No.	Time	Delta	Source	Destination	Protocol	Size	Scr Port	Dest Port	Info
1595	12.970545	0.000083	192.168.5.110	192.168.5.217	TCP	54	57885	2000	57885 > 2000 [ACK] Seq=1 Ack=49641 Win=65535 Len=0
1596	12.971298	0.000753	192.168.5.217	192.168.5.110	FTP-DAT	1514	2000	57885	FTP Data: 1460 bytes
1597	12.971889	0.000591	192.168.5.217	192.168.5.110	FTP-DAT	1514	2000	57885	FTP Data: 1460 bytes
1598	12.971979	0.000090	192.168.5.110	192.168.5.217	TCP	54	57885	2000	57885 > 2000 [ACK] Seq=1 Ack=52561 Win=65535 Len=0
1599	12.972781	0.000802	192.168.5.217	192.168.5.110	FTP-DAT	1514	2000	57885	FTP Data: 1460 bytes
1600	12.973357	0.000576	192.168.5.217	192.168.5.110	FTP-DAT	1514	2000	57885	FTP Data: 1460 bytes
1601	12.973435	0.000078	192.168.5.110	192.168.5.217	TCP	54	57885	2000	57885 > 2000 [ACK] Seq=1 Ack=55481 Win=65535 Len=0
1602	12.974747	0.001312	192.168.5.217	192.168.5.110	FTP-DAT	1514	2000	57885	[TCP Previous segment lost] FTP Data: 1460 bytes
1603	12.974777	0.000030	192.168.5.110	192.168.5.217	TCP	54	57885	2000	[TCP Dup ACK 1601#1] 57885 > 2000 [ACK] Seq=1 Ack=55481 Win=65535 Len=0
1604	12.975633	0.000856	192.168.5.217	192.168.5.110	FTP-DAT	1514	2000	57885	FTP Data: 1460 bytes
1605	12.975662	0.000029	192.168.5.110	192.168.5.217	TCP	54	57885	2000	[TCP Dup ACK 1601#2] 57885 > 2000 [ACK] Seq=1 Ack=55481 Win=65535 Len=0
1606	12.976184	0.000522	192.168.5.217	192.168.5.110	FTP-DAT	1514	2000	57885	FTP Data: 1460 bytes
1607	12.976208	0.000024	192.168.5.110	192.168.5.217	TCP	54	57885	2000	[TCP Dup ACK 1601#3] 57885 > 2000 [ACK] Seq=1 Ack=55481 Win=65535 Len=0
1608	12.977069	0.000861	192.168.5.217	192.168.5.110	FTP-DAT	1514	2000	57885	FTP Data: 1460 bytes
1609	12.977094	0.000025	192.168.5.110	192.168.5.217	TCP	54	57885	2000	[TCP Dup ACK 1601#4] 57885 > 2000 [ACK] Seq=1 Ack=55481 Win=65535 Len=0
1610	12.977700	0.000606	192.168.5.217	192.168.5.110	FTP-DAT	1514	2000	57885	FTP Data: 1460 bytes
1611	12.977752	0.000052	192.168.5.110	192.168.5.217	TCP	54	57885	2000	[TCP Dup ACK 1601#5] 57885 > 2000 [ACK] Seq=1 Ack=55481 Win=65535 Len=0
1612	12.978609	0.000857	192.168.5.217	192.168.5.110	FTP-DAT	1514	2000	57885	FTP Data: 1460 bytes
1613	12.978631	0.000022	192.168.5.110	192.168.5.217	TCP	54	57885	2000	[TCP Dup ACK 1601#6] 57885 > 2000 [ACK] Seq=1 Ack=55481 Win=65535 Len=0
1614	12.979151	0.000520	192.168.5.217	192.168.5.110	FTP-DAT	1514	2000	57885	FTP Data: 1460 bytes
1615	12.979203	0.000052	192.168.5.110	192.168.5.217	TCP	54	57885	2000	[TCP Dup ACK 1601#7] 57885 > 2000 [ACK] Seq=1 Ack=55481 Win=65535 Len=0
1616	13.053527	0.074324	192.168.5.110	192.168.5.217	TCP	54	57881	21	57881 > 21 [ACK] Seq=122 Ack=623 Win=63585 Len=0

Figure 17-6 **Transmission Buffer Leak Example**

NO RETRANSMISSION

Retransmissions should never happen unless they are requested by the communication protocol. Erroneous retransmissions can happen if a transmitted buffer remains assigned to a descriptor, and the buffer is not deallocated.

While performing performance tests on the target, you should use Wireshark or another packet capture tool to monitoring the trafic. Unrequested packets retransmission can be detected by searching for frames marked with "[This frame is a (suspected) retransmission]" in Wireshark.

ADVERTISED WINDOW SIZE

The total memory available for the reception buffer should always be equal to or greater than the window size advertised by the target. If it is not the case, the test station might send too many packets before waiting for an acknowledge message, and the target might lose packets. Loosing those packets will trigger a retransmission of the lost packets, and thus slow down the data transfer.

PERFORMANCE RESULTS

You should log your driver performance in the driver document. This document is used as a reference for support requests, so it's very important to log performance when you write or update a driver. The performance data that you should log is described in the following sections.

Certain TCP/IP features reduce performance, so you should disable these features before logging the results. The µC/TCP-IP configuration switches for these features are shown in Listing 17-5, and can be found in **net_cfg.h**.

```
Net Configuration:
#define   NET_DBG_CFG_INFO_EN                 DEF_DISABLED
#define   NET_DBG_CFG_STATUS_EN               DEF_DISABLED
#define   NET_DBG_CFG_MEM_CLR_EN              DEF_DISABLED
#define   NET_DBG_CFG_TEST_EN                 DEF_DISABLED
#define   NET_ERR_CFG_ARG_CHK_EXT_EN          DEF_DISABLED
#define   NET_ERR_CFG_ARG_CHK_DBG_EN          DEF_DISABLED
#define   NET_CTR_CFG_STAT_EN                 DEF_DISABLED
#define   NET_CTR_CFG_ERR_EN                  DEF_DISABLED
#define   NET_IF_CFG_LOOPBACK_EN              DEF_DISABLED
#define   NET_ICMP_CFG_TX_SRC_QUENCH_EN       DEF_DISABLED
```

Listing 17-5 **Net Configuration for optimal performances**

TASK PRIORITIES

In order to obtain the best possible performance for your tests, you should use appropriate task priorities.

When setting up task priorities, we recommend that tasks that use µC/TCP-IP's services be given higher priorities than µC/TCP-IP's internal tasks. However, application tasks that use µC/TCP-IP should voluntarily relinquish the CPU on a regular basis. For example, they can delay or suspend the tasks, or wait on µC/TCP-IP services. The purpose is to reduce starvation issues when an application task sends a substantial amount of data.

We recommend that you configure the network interface Transmit De-allocation task with a higher priority than all application tasks that use µC/TCP-IP network services; but configure the Timer task and network interface Receive task with lower priorities than almost other application tasks.

Listing 17-6 shows an example of task priorities and stack sizes for a typical device performance measurement application.

```
 *
 ********************************************************************************
 *                              TASK PRIORITIES
 ********************************************************************************
 */
#define  IPERF_OS_CFG_TASK_PRIO                        11u
#define  APP_TASK_START_PRIO                           13u
#define  NDIT_TASK_TERMINAL_PRIO                       15u
#define  NDIT_TASK_MULTICAST_PRIO                      12u
#define  NDIT_TASK_SERVER_PRIO                         16u
#define  NET_OS_CFG_IF_TX_DEALLOC_TASK_PRIO             2u
#define  NET_OS_CFG_TMR_TASK_PRIO                      15u
#define  NET_OS_CFG_IF_RX_TASK_PRIO                    18u
#define  NDIT_MCAST_TASK_PRIO                          20u
 /*
 ********************************************************************************
 *                              TASK STACK SIZES
 *                 Size of the task stacks (# of OS_STK entries)
 ********************************************************************************
 */
#define  APP_TASK_START_STK_SIZE                      128u
#define  NDIT_TASK_TERMINAL_STK_SIZE                  512u
#define  IPERF_OS_CFG_TASK_STK_SIZE                   512u
#define  NDIT_TASK_SERVER_STK_SIZE                    512u
#define  NDIT_MCAST_TASK_STK_SIZE                     512u
#define  NET_OS_CFG_TMR_TASK_STK_SIZE                 512u
#define  NET_OS_CFG_IF_TX_DEALLOC_TASK_STK_SIZE       128u
#define  NET_OS_CFG_IF_RX_TASK_STK_SIZE               512u
```

Listing 17-6 **Example of task priorities and stack sizes**

17-5-1 TESTING UDP TRANSMISSION

The first IPerf test you should perform is UDP transmission. Your target must be able to transmit UDP packets reliably and with acceptable throughput. Also, your target must be able to transmit packets that have the maximum UDP packet length, which is 1472 bytes (make sure to have the correct Transmit buffer size).

TEST: TRANSMIT UDP PACKET (1472 BYTES) USING NDIT

Selecting the UDPc test tab in the main NDIT window. The UDPc test tab appears:

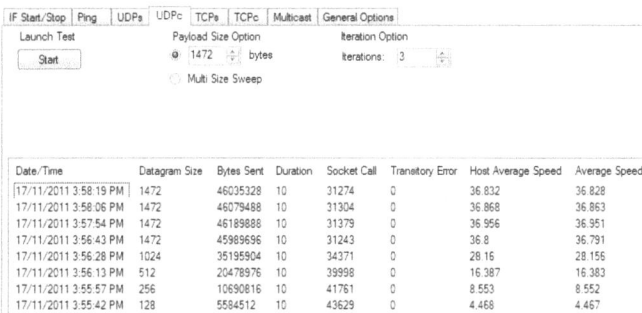

IF Start/Stop	Ping	UDPs	UDPc	TCPs	TCPc	Multicast	General Options

Launch Test   Payload Size Option   Iteration Option

Start   ◉ 1472 ⇕ bytes   Iterations: 3 ⇕

   ○ Multi Size Sweep

Date/Time	Datagram Size	Bytes Sent	Duration	Socket Call	Transitory Error	Host Average Speed	Average Speed
17/11/2011 3:58:19 PM	1472	46035328	10	31274	0	36.832	36.828
17/11/2011 3:58:06 PM	1472	46079488	10	31304	0	36.868	36.863
17/11/2011 3:57:54 PM	1472	46189888	10	31379	0	36.956	36.951
17/11/2011 3:56:43 PM	1472	45989696	10	31243	0	36.8	36.791
17/11/2011 3:56:28 PM	1024	35195904	10	34371	0	28.16	28.156
17/11/2011 3:56:13 PM	512	20478976	10	39998	0	16.387	16.383
17/11/2011 3:55:57 PM	256	10690816	10	41761	0	8.553	8.552
17/11/2011 3:55:42 PM	128	5584512	10	43629	0	4.468	4.467

Figure 17-7 **UDPc test tab**

There are three options for this test. The first is the size of the datagram (either a single 1472 or a sweep of multiple packets that are 64, 128, 256, 512, 1024 and 1472 bytes in size). The second option is the number of times the test is repeated. The third is the test duration (in seconds), which is located in the General Options tab.

EXPECTED RESULTS

▪ Highest throughput possible.

Although it is difficult to estimate the achievable throughput with a particular device, it is possible to compare with other drivers sharing roughly the same quantity of network buffers or processor speed.

Table 17-1 shows an example of performance results for different devices and configurations:

Development Board	Device 1	Device 2
CPU Speed	72 MHz	70 MHz
CPU Architecture	ARM® Cortex-M3™	ARM® Cortex-M4™
Tx Buffers	4	3
Tx Descr.	4	3
64 byte Datagram		
Socket Call	44253	29994
Throughput (Mbps)	2.265	1.535
1472 byte Datagram		
Socket Call	31245	29991
Throughput (Mbps)	36.794	35.317

Table 17-1 **UDPc Performance Example**

Tweaking the task priorities might help increasing the throughput out the network driver.

■ Few transitory errors.

Transitory errors are errors that temporarily prevent the transmission of packets. Transitory errors are often recoverable. These errors include:

■ Trying to receive on a socket where the host has disconnected prematurely.

■ Trying to receive on a socket before the network initialization is completed.

■ Trying to receive on a socket that is in use by another process.

To solve these issues, make sure that you use valid parameters for your tests. Make sure that the resources you use are still valid, and not already used by another task.

- Ability to send packets with a size equal to the MTU.

  To find out the MTU size for your network type, enter the following command in the command shell in Windows:

  `netsh interface ipv4 show subinterfaces`

  The results you should get is something like this:

```
Microsoft Windows [Version 6.1.7601]
Copyright (c) 2009 Microsoft Corporation.  All rights reserved.
C:\Users\user01>netsh interface ipv4 show subinterfaces
      MTU  MediaSenseState   Bytes In  Bytes Out  Interface
----------  ---------------  ---------  ---------  --------------
      1500                5          0          0  Wireless Network Connection
      1500                5          0          0  Local Area Connection
      1500                1  693970658   90284509  Local Area Connection 2
```

  In the above example, the MTU size is set to 1500 for all the network interfaces. For this reason, we use 1472 bytes as the length for the payload in our UDP test. Since the MAC-IP-UDP headers account for 28 bytes that leaves 1472 bytes left for the payload.

  In subsequent TCP tests, we use a value of 1460 or multiple of that value to set buffer sizes, window sizes, and so on. Since the size of the TCP header is slightly larger than the UDP header, this yields a smaller payload.

- Comparable results for the target directly connected, or on a network.

- No buffer leaks.

  See section "Buffer leaks" on page 481 for more details.

- Logging performance results (with the target directly connected, and networked).

17-5-2 TESTING UDP RECEPTION

Your target must be able to receive UDP packets reliably and with acceptable throughput. It must also be able to receive UDP packets with a size equal to the MTU.

TEST 1: MAXIMUM BANDWIDTH RECEIVE UDP TEST USING NDIT

Select the UDPs test tab in the NDIT main window. The UDP test tab appears

The first test we suggest you to run is a 100 Mbps, 1472-byte payload test. It is the most demanding test in terms of data reception, as UDP is a light transport protocol and the CPU will be strained with a flood of UDP datagrams.

Figure 17-8 shows the UDPs test tab.

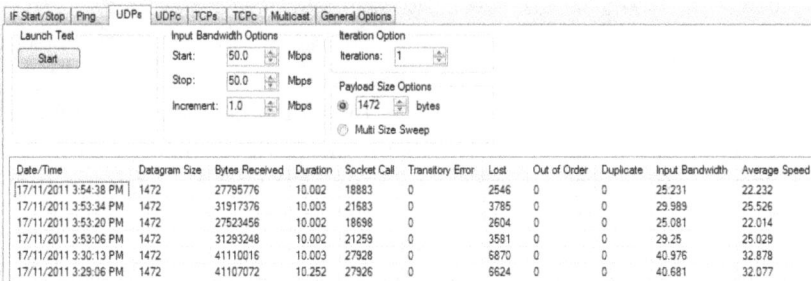

Figure 17-8 **UDPs test tab**

There are four options for the UDP receive test:

Input Bandwidth   To test at a single bandwidth, set the Start and Stop values to the same bandwidth value. Values are in megabits per seconds.

If the Start and Stop values are different, a UDP receive test will be launch with the Start bandwidth. The bandwidth of the subsequent tests will increase by the value of Increment until the Stop bandwidth is reached.

Iterations   NDIT will repeat the UDP receive test and its conditions for the specified number of times.

Payload Size   1472 bytes is maximum value for the payload size, and will maximize throughput.

Multi Size Sweep will repeat the test with payloads of 64, 128, 256, 512, 1024 and 1472 bytes.

Test Duration   This option can be found in the General Options tab.

EXPECTED RESULTS

■ Highest throughput possible

Although it is difficult to estimate the achievable throughput with a particular device, it is possible to compare with other drivers sharing roughly the same quantity of network buffers or processor speed.

Development Board	Device 1	Device 2
CPU Speed	72 MHz	70 MHz
CPU Architecture	ARM® Cortex-M3™	ARM® Cortex-M4™
Rx Buffers	4	3
Rx Descr.	4	3
64 byte Datagram		
Socket Call	33144	58652
Throughput (Mbps)	1.695	3.002
1472 byte Datagram		
Socket Call	27915	31788.91
Throughput (Mbps)	32.866	37.433

Listing 17-7 **UDPs Performance Example**

There is also a practical limit at which the network driver can operate. At one point, as you increase the input data rate, the network driver will be overwhelmed and will start dropping the excess of packets it cannot handle.

As shown in Figure 17-9, there is a point where the rate of increase in throughput will slow down, and the error rate will increase until the throughput reaches its limit. Depending on the driver's architecture, increasing the input data rate will decrease the performances of the driver. This is due to an increase in the number of receive interrupts that have to be handled.

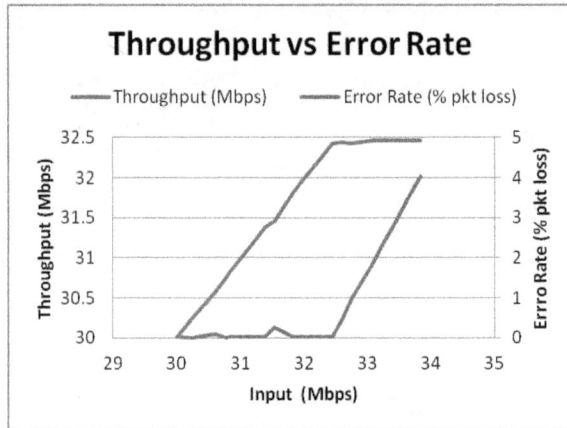

Throughput vs Error Rate

Figure 17-9 **Throughput and Error Rate**

▩ Few transitory errors.

See the section on transitory errors on page 486 for more information.

▩ Low packet loss.

Packet loss should begin to happen only near or after the driver reached maximum throughput (close to 32 Mbps as in the example in Figure 17-9). If there is a constant packet loss throughout the input data rate range, than something is wrong.

▩ Ability to receive packets with a size equal to the MTU.

See the section on sending packets on page 487 for more information.

▩ Similar results with target directly connected and on a network.

Unless there is a heavy broadcasting of packets on the real network, the results should be fairly similar.

▧   No buffer leaks.

See section "Buffer leaks" on page 481 for more details.

▧   Logging performance results (with the target directly connected, and networked).

TEST 2: PAYLOAD SIZE SWEEP RECEIVE UDP TEST USING NDIT

This test is similar to the previous one, except that we are modifying the size of the payload received by the target. We will set the payload size to 64, 128, 256, 512 and 1024 bytes. By reducing the size of the packet, we can increase the number of packets processed by the target in the same amount of time. By using a payload size of 64 bytes (the smallest payload for a Ethernet frame) you can get the maximum packet rate that you driver can handle.

EXPECTED RESULTS

▧   Highest throughput possible

Once again predicting the achievable throughput might be difficult. As the length of the payload decreases, the packet rate increases to sustain the required data rate. This decrease is likely due to the fact that it is more time consuming to execute the µC/TCP-IP module operation than the transfer the packet from the network device to the processor memory.

▧   Few transitory errors

See the section on transitory errors on page 486 for more information.

▧   Ability to send packets with a size equal to the MTU.

See the section on sending packets on page 487 for more information.

▧   Similar results with the target directly connected and on a network.

▧   No buffer leaks

See section "Buffer leaks" on page 481 for more details.

▧   Logging performance results (with the target directly connected, and networked).

17-5-3 TESTING TCP TRANSMISSION

Your target must be able to transmit TCP packets reliably, and with acceptable throughput. You should also validate the driver with various TCP window sizes.

TRANSMIT TCP TEST USING NDIT

This test measures the capacity of the target to send packets to a server located on the test station. To optimize performance, the value of NET_TCP_CFG_TX_WIN_SIZE_OCTET in net_cfg.h should be set to the number of transmit descriptors multiplied by 1460 bytes. The TCP Transmit Window Size should be set to the target's number of transmit buffers multiplied by 1460 bytes.

Select the TCPc test tab in the NDIT main window. The TCP transmit test panel appears.

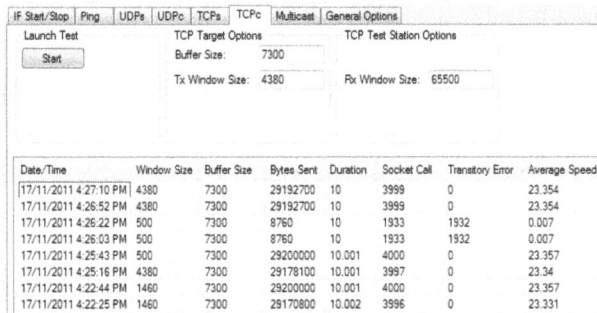

Figure 17-10 **TCPc test tab**

There are four options for the TCP transmit test:

Buffer Size   The length of the buffer to transmit.

Tx Window Size   The size of the transmit socket window on the target host.

Rx Window Size   The size of the receive socket window on the test station.

Test Duration   Located in the General Options tab.

EXPECTED RESULTS

- Highest throughput possible

  Although it is difficult to estimate the achievable throughput with a particular device, it is possible to compare with other drivers sharing roughly the same quantity of network buffers or processor speed. Tweaking the task priorities might help increasing the throughput out the network driver.

- Few transitory errors

  See the section on transitory errors on page 486 for more information.

- No retransmission

  See the section on retransmission on page 482 for more details.

- No buffer leaks

  See section "Buffer leaks" on page 481 for more details.

- Logging performance results (with the target directly connected, and networked).

17-5-4 TESTING TCP RECEPTION

Along with the reception of UDP traffic, you should test your device driver for TCP traffic. The following are two tests that measure the driver performance under different conditions.

TEST 1: RECEIVE TCP TEST WITH USING NDIT

To achieve the best possible throughput, you might have to increase the number of receive descriptors and receive buffers. On the other hand, it is also possible to reserve too many buffers for reception. To find out the ideal number of descriptors and buffers, there are two things you need to measure.

First, you must determine the rate at which the target can receive data. This value, in bits per second, will be referred to as the bandwidth. You can obtain this value by running the receive UDP test.

Second, you must determine the round trip time (RTT) of a message between the test station and the target. This is achieved by sending an ICMP echo request to the target and measuring the RTT of the reply. You can use ping (or preferably fping) to acquire this value.

Then take these two value and multiply them to determine the *Bandwidth-Delay Product.*

```
BDP (bytes) = total_available_bandwidth (KBytes/sec) • round_trip_time (ms)
```

The BDP is approximately equal to the Receive TCP Window Size. It is recommended to round up the calculated value to a multiple of the Maximum Segment Size (MSS), typically 1460 bytes.

For example, the bandwidth of a test station-target link is 32.461 Mbps as found by the Receive UDP test. The measured RTT is 0.9 millisecond. It gives us a BDP of 28315 bits (32.461 Mbps x 0.9 ms) or 3539 bytes. Rounding up this result to a multiple of the MSS value gives us 4380 bytes. If the combined size of the receive buffers cannot hold the BDP, the receive buffers must be increased in order to have optimal performances. It is important to increase the number of receive descriptors (**RxDescNbr**) accordingly.

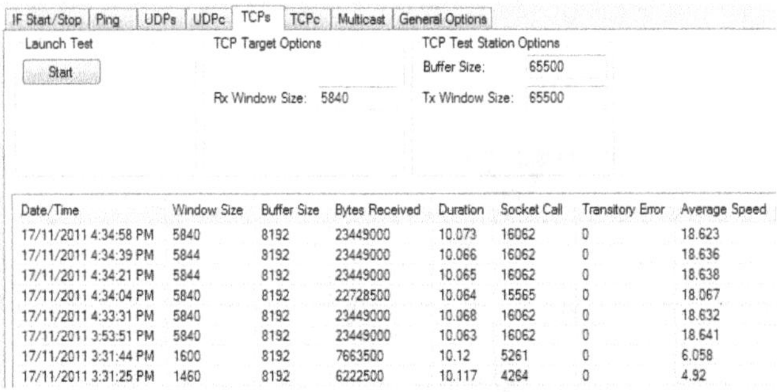

IF Start/Stop	Ping	UDPs	UDPc	TCPs	TCPc	Multicast	General Options

Launch Test	TCP Target Options	TCP Test Station Options	
Start		Buffer Size:	65500
	Rx Window Size: 5840	Tx Window Size:	65500

Date/Time	Window Size	Buffer Size	Bytes Received	Duration	Socket Call	Transitory Error	Average Speed
17/11/2011 4:34:58 PM	5840	8192	23449000	10.073	16062	0	18.623
17/11/2011 4:34:39 PM	5844	8192	23449000	10.066	16062	0	18.636
17/11/2011 4:34:21 PM	5844	8192	23449000	10.065	16062	0	18.638
17/11/2011 4:34:04 PM	5840	8192	22728500	10.064	15565	0	18.067
17/11/2011 4:33:31 PM	5840	8192	23449000	10.068	16062	0	18.632
17/11/2011 3:53:51 PM	5840	8192	23449000	10.063	16062	0	18.641
17/11/2011 3:31:44 PM	1600	8192	7663500	10.12	5261	0	6.058
17/11/2011 3:31:25 PM	1460	8192	6222500	10.117	4264	0	4.92

Figure 17-11 **TCPs test tab**

There are four options for the TCP receive test:

Rx Window Size   The size of the receive socket window on the target host.

Buffer Size   The length of the buffer to transmit to the target.

Tx Window Size   The size of the transmit socket window on the test station.

Test Duration   Located in the General Options tab.

The TCPs test parameters must be adjusted to the following: both Buffer Size and Tx Window Size should be set to 65500. These settings will minimize the overhead of socket creation on the test station, and make full use of the available processing power of the target. The Receive Window Size must be set to the value of the BDP, rounded up to a multiple of the MSS.

You should set the TCP Receive Window size in **net_cfg.h** as follows:

```
#define  NET_TCP_CFG_RX_WIN_SIZE_OCTET        (RxDescNbr * 1460)u
```

EXPECTED RESULTS

- Driver throughput should be optimized.

- Few transitory errors.

  See the section on transitory errors on page 486 for more information.

- No retransmission.

  See the section on retransmission on page 482 for more details.

- The messages "Window update", "Zero window" and "Window probe" are acceptable.

  These messages are part of a flow control mechanism that prevents the receiver from getting more packets that it can actually handle, or for the transmitter to wait indefinitely for acknowledgement to resume the transmission.

- No buffer leaks.

  See section "Buffer leaks" on page 481 for more details.

- Logging performance results (with the target directly connected, and networked).

17-6 MULTICAST

Multicast is a routing scheme that enables data delivery to a group of hosts. Multicast allows the source to transmit the data once, while routers in the network take care of duplicating the data and transmitting it to the registered hosts. Multicast requires UDP support. TCP is not designed to work with Multicast, but there are some reliable Multicast protocols that can replace TCP such as Pragmatic General Multicast (PGM).

17-6-1 MULTICAST TEST SETUP

In order for multicast to work, the source and the destination must be linked by multicast-enabled routers. Multicast cannot operate when the target is directly connected to the test station. Moreover, the router(s) between the target and the test station must support the IGMP protocol.

The goal of this test is to validate that the driver properly configures the MAC filter to allow the multicast packets to be passed by the µC/TCP-IP module when the target is registered to a multicast group. Also, the test ensures that, when the target is unregistered from the multicast group, multicast packets are dropped by the MAC filter.

The following steps are performed by NDIT to validate the behavior of the driver:

■ Register the target to an IP multicast group.

■ Have the test station send a packet to the IP multicast group.

■ Upon reception of the multicast packet, the target replies to the test station to acknowledge the reception of the multicast packet.

■ Unregister the target from the IP multicast group.

■ Have the test station to send a packet to the IP multicast group.

■ Verify that, after a certain timeout, no reply was received by the test station.

17-6-2 MULTICAST TEST USING NDIT

This section describes how to run a multicast test using NDIT. Select the Multicast test tab in the NDIT main window. The Multicast test panel appears.

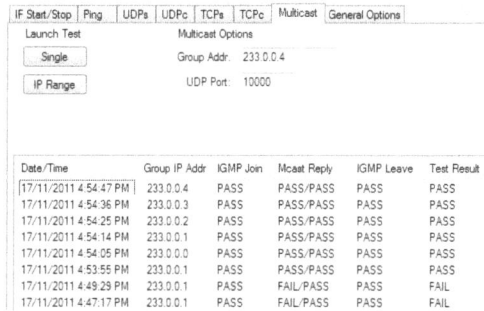

Launch Test		Multicast Options	
Single		Group Addr.	233.0.0.4
IP Range		UDP Port:	10000

Date/Time	Group IP Addr	IGMP Join	Mcast Reply	IGMP Leave	Test Result
17/11/2011 4:54:47 PM	233.0.0.4	PASS	PASS/PASS	PASS	PASS
17/11/2011 4:54:36 PM	233.0.0.3	PASS	PASS/PASS	PASS	PASS
17/11/2011 4:54:25 PM	233.0.0.2	PASS	PASS/PASS	PASS	PASS
17/11/2011 4:54:14 PM	233.0.0.1	PASS	PASS/PASS	PASS	PASS
17/11/2011 4:54:05 PM	233.0.0.0	PASS	PASS/PASS	PASS	PASS
17/11/2011 4:53:55 PM	233.0.0.1	PASS	PASS/PASS	PASS	PASS
17/11/2011 4:49:29 PM	233.0.0.1	PASS	FAIL/PASS	PASS	FAIL
17/11/2011 4:47:17 PM	233.0.0.1	PASS	FAIL/PASS	PASS	FAIL

Figure 17-12 **Multicast test tab**

There are two options for the multicast test:

Group Address   The Group IP multicast address at which the test station will send the packets.

UDP Port   The UDP port at which the packets will be delivered.

To run a multicast test, click either the Single or IP Range button in the Launch Text box.

Clicking the Single button will send a command to the target to create an IGMP Join request for the specified Group Address, and create a UDP socket that listens for incoming traffic on the specified UDP port. Upon receiving a packet on the specified UDP port, the target will reply to the packet source with the received payload. In return, NDIT will listen to the target reply, and determine if the multicast test was successful.

Clicking the IP Range button will do the exact same test as the Single button, but will do the test for the IP address range from xxx.xxx.xxx.0 to xxx.xxx.xxx.255

17-6-3 ANALYZING THE RESULTS

The Mcast Reply column contains two results. The first one refers to the success of the reception of a multicast message while it is registered to the specified IP multicast group. The second one refers to the success of the multicast message being not received while the target is unregistered from the specified IP multicast group.

ROUND-TRIP TIME

Payload size	Average Round-Trip Time (ms)
32	
64	
128	
256	
512	
1024	
1464	

PING RESULTS

ICMP Payload Size	Round Trip Time (ms)

UDP SERVER

Payload size	Socket Calls	Packets Lost	Throughput (Mbps)
64			
128			
256			
512			
1024			
1472			

UDP CLIENT

Payload size	Socket Calls	Throughput (Mbps)
64		
128		
256		
512		
1024		
1472		

TCP SERVER

Buffer size	Socket Calls	Throughput (Mbps)
1460		
2920		
4380		
5840		
7300		
8192		

TCP CLIENT

Buffer size	Socket Calls	Throughput (Mbps)
1460		
2920		
4380		
5840		
7300		
8192		

Chapter

18

Socket Programming

The two network socket interfaces supported by µC/TCP-IP were previously introduced. Now, in this chapter, we will discuss socket programming, data structures, and API functions calls.

18-1 NETWORK SOCKET DATA STRUCTURES

Communication using sockets requires configuring or reading network addresses from network socket address structures. The BSD socket API defines a generic socket address structure as a blank template with no address-specific configuration...

```
struct  sockaddr {                        /* Generic BSD   socket address structure   */
    CPU_INT16U  sa_family;                /* Socket address family                    */
    CPU_CHAR    sa_data[14];              /* Protocol-specific address informatio     */
};


typedef  struct  net_sock_addr {          /* Generic µC/TCP-IP socket address structure */
    NET_SOCK_ADDR_FAMILY   AddrFamily;
    CPU_INT08U             Addr[NET_SOCK_BSD_ADDR_LEN_MAX = 14];
} NET_SOCK_ADDR;
```

Listing 18-1 **Generic (non-address-specific) address structures**

...as well as specific socket address structures to configure each specific protocol address family's network address configuration (e.g., IPv4 socket addresses):

```
struct  in_addr {
    NET_IP_ADDR  s_addr;                        /* IPv4 address (32 bits)                    */
};


struct  sockaddr_in {                           /* BSD    IPv4 socket address structure   */
    CPU_INT16U      sin_family;                 /*  Internet address family (e.g. AF_INET) */
    CPU_INT16U      sin_port;                   /*  Socket  address port number (16 bits)  */
    struct in_addr  sin_addr;                   /*  IPv4    address       (32 bits)        */
    CPU_CHAR        sin_zero[8];                /*  Not used (all zeroes)                  */
};


typedef  struct  net_sock_addr_ip {             /* µC/TCP-IP socket address structure     */
    NET_SOCK_ADDR_FAMILY    AddrFamily;
    NET_PORT_NBR            Port;
    NET_IP_ADDR            Addr;
    CPU_INT08U              Unused[NET_SOCK_ADDR_IP_NBR_OCTETS_UNUSED = 8];
} NET_SOCK_ADDR_IP;
```

Listing 18-2 **Internet (IPv4) address structures**

A socket address structure's **AddrFamily/sa_family/sin_family** value *must* be read/written in host CPU byte order, while all **Addr/sa_data** values *must* be read/written in network byte order (big endian).

Even though socket functions – both µC/TCP-IP and BSD – pass pointers to the generic socket address structure, applications *must* declare and pass an instance of the specific protocol's socket address structure (e.g., an IPv4 address structure). For microprocessors that require data access to be aligned to appropriate word boundaries, this forces compilers to declare an appropriately-aligned socket address structure so that all socket address members are correctly aligned to their appropriate word boundaries.

Caution: Applications should avoid, or be cautious when, declaring and configuring a generic byte array as a socket address structure, since the compiler may not correctly align the array to or the socket address structure's members to appropriate word boundaries.

Figure 18-1 shows an example IPv4 instance of the µC/TCP-IP **NET_SOCK_ADDR_IP** (**sockaddr_in**) structure overlaid on top of **NET_SOCK_ADDR** (**sockaddr**) the structure

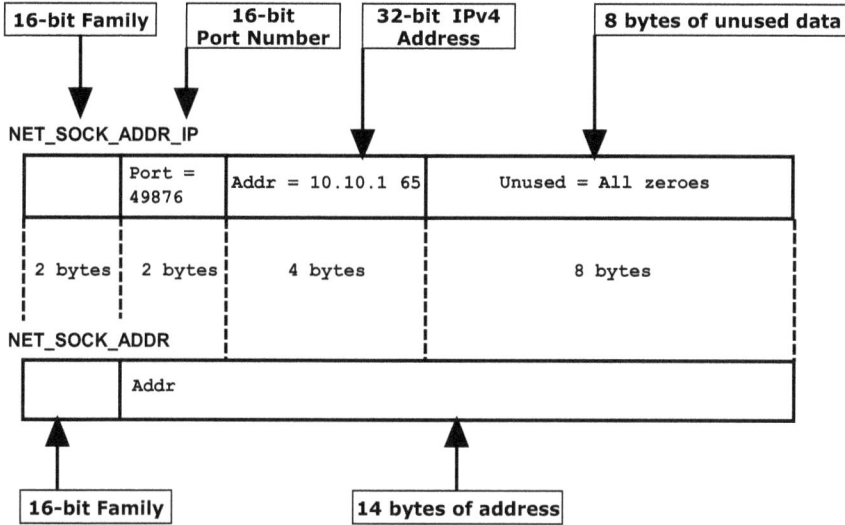

Figure 18-1 **NET_SOCK_ADDR_IP is the IPv4 specific instance of the generic NET_SOCK_ADDR data structure**

A socket could configure the example socket address structure in Figure 18-1 to bind on IP address 10.10.1.65 and port number 49876 with the following code:

```
NET_SOCK_ADDR_IP    addr_local;
NET_IP_ADDR         addr_ip;
NET_PORT_NBR        addr_port;
NET_SOCK_RTN_CODE   rtn_code;
NET_ERR             err;


addr_ip   = NetASCII_Str_to_IP("10.10.1.65", &err);
addr_port = 49876;
Mem_Clr((void   *)&addr_local,
        (CPU_SIZE_T) sizeof(addr_local));
addr_local.AddrFamily = NET_SOCK_ADDR_FAMILY_IP_V4;               /* = AF_INET†† Figure 18-1
*/
addr_local.Addr    = NET_UTIL_HOST_TO_NET_32(addr_ip);
addr_local.Port    = NET_UTIL_HOST_TO_NET_16(addr_port);
rtn_code           = NetSock_Bind((NET_SOCK_ID      ) sock_id,
                                  (NET_SOCK_ADDR    *)&addr_local, /* Cast to generic addr† */
                                  (NET_SOCK_ADDR_LEN) sizeof(addr_local),
                                  (NET_ERR          *)&err);
```

Listing 18-3 **Bind on 10.10.1.65**

† The address of the specific IPv4 socket address structure is cast to a pointer to the generic socket address structure.

18-2 COMPLETE SEND() OPERATION

send( ) returns the number of bytes actually sent out. This might be less than the number that are available to send. The function will send as much of the data as it can. The developer must make sure that the rest of the packet is sent later.

```
{
    int  total    = 0;        /* how many bytes we've sent       */
    int  bytesleft = *len;    /* how many we have left to send   */
    int  n;


    while (total < *len) {
        n = send(s, buf + total, bytesleft, 0);                       (1)
        if (n == -1) {
            break;
        }
        total += n;                                                   (2)
        bytesleft -= n;                                               (3)
    }
}
```

Listing 18-4 **Completing a send()**

L18-4(1)   Send as many bytes as there are transmit network buffers available.

L18-4(2)   Increase the number of bytes sent.

L18-4(3)   Calculate how many bytes are left to send.

This is another example that, for a TCP/IP stack to operate smoothly, sufficient memory to define enough buffers for transmission and reception is a design decision that requires attention if optimum performance for the given hardware is desired.

18-3 SOCKET APPLICATIONS

Two socket types are identified: Datagram sockets and Stream sockets. The following sections provide sample code describing how these sockets work.

In addition to the BSD 4.x sockets application interface (API), the µC/TCP-IP stack gives the developer the opportunity to use Micrium's own socket functions with which to interact.

Although there is a great deal of similarity between the two APIs, the parameters of the two sets of functions differ slightly. The purpose of the following sections is o give developers a first look at Micrium's functions by providing concrete examples of how to use the API.

For those interested in BSD socket programming, there are plenty of books, online references, and articles dedicated to this subject.

The examples have been designed to be as simple as possible. Hence, only basic error checking is performed. When it comes to building real applications, those checks should be extended to deliver a product that is as robust as possible.

18-3-1 DATAGRAM SOCKET (UDP SOCKET)

Figure 18-2 reproduces a diagram that introduces sample code using the typical socket functions for a UDP client-server application. The example uses the Micrium proprietary socket API function calls. A similar example could be written using the BSD socket API.

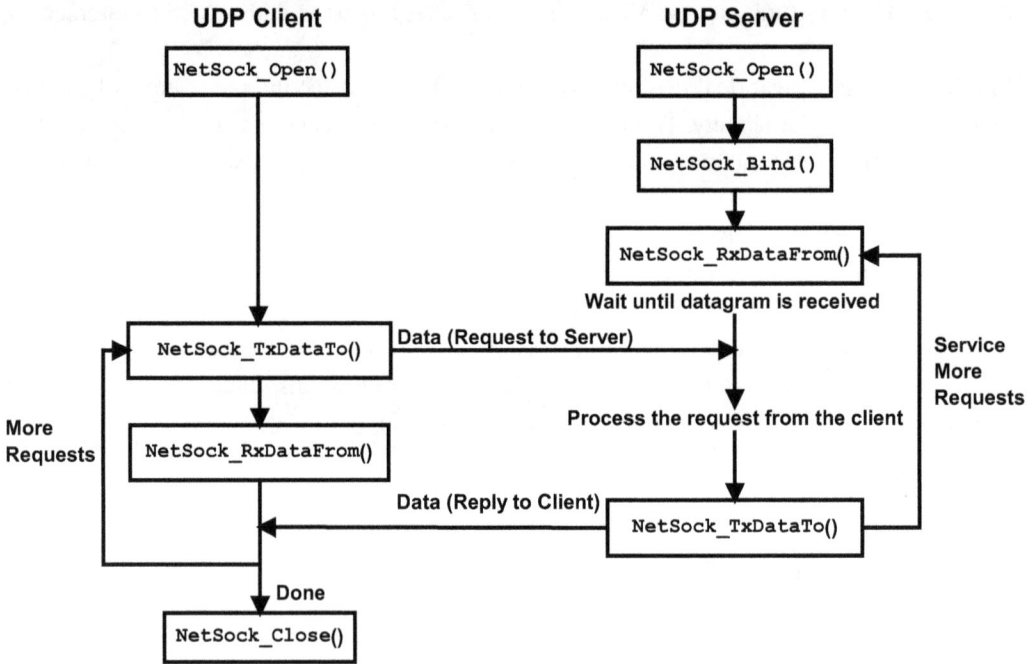

Figure 18-2 μC/TCP-IP Socket calls used in a typical UDP client-server application

The code in Listing 18-5 implements a UDP server. It opens a socket and binds an IP address, listens and waits for a packet to arrive at the specified port. See Appendix C, "μC/TCP-IP API Reference" on page 649 for a list of all μC/TCP-IP socket API functions.

DATAGRAM SERVER (UDP SERVER)

```
#define  UDP_SERVER_PORT  10001
#define  RX_BUF_SIZE         15
CPU_BOOLEAN  TestUDPServer (void)
{
    NET_SOCK_ID        sock;
    NET_SOCK_ADDR_IP   server_sock_addr_ip;
    NET_SOCK_ADDR_LEN  server_sock_addr_ip_size;
    NET_SOCK_ADDR_IP   client_sock_addr_ip;
    NET_SOCK_ADDR_LEN  client_sock_addr_ip_size;
    NET_SOCK_RTN_CODE  rx_size;
    CPU_CHAR           rx_buf[RX_BUF_SIZE];
    CPU_BOOLEAN        attempt_rx;
    NET_ERR            err;


    sock = NetSock_Open( NET_SOCK_ADDR_FAMILY_IP_V4,                         (1)
                         NET_SOCK_TYPE_DATAGRAM,
                         NET_SOCK_PROTOCOL_UDP,
                       &err);
    if (err != NET_SOCK_ERR_NONE) {
        return (DEF_FALSE);
    }


    server_sock_addr_ip_size = sizeof(server_sock_addr_ip);                  (2)
    Mem_Clr((void      *)&server_sock_addr_ip,
            (CPU_SIZE_T) server_sock_addr_ip_size);
    server_sock_addr_ip.AddrFamily = NET_SOCK_ADDR_FAMILY_IP_V4;
    server_sock_addr_ip.Addr       = NET_UTIL_HOST_TO_NET_32(NET_SOCK_ADDR_IP_WILD_CARD);
    server_sock_addr_ip.Port       = NET_UTIL_HOST_TO_NET_16(UDP_SERVER_PORT);


    NetSock_Bind((NET_SOCK_ID      ) sock,                                   (3)
                 (NET_SOCK_ADDR    *)&server_sock_addr_ip,
                 (NET_SOCK_ADDR_LEN) NET_SOCK_ADDR_SIZE,
                 (NET_ERR          *)&err);
    if (err != NET_SOCK_ERR_NONE) {
        NetSock_Close(sock, &err);
        return (DEF_FALSE);
    }
```

```
    do {
        client_sock_addr_ip_size = sizeof(client_sock_addr_ip);

        rx_size = NetSock_RxDataFrom((NET_SOCK_ID ) sock,                    (4)
                                     (void *) rx_buf,
                                     (CPU_INT16S ) RX_BUF_SIZE,
                                     (CPU_INT16S ) NET_SOCK_FLAG_NONE,
                                     (NET_SOCK_ADDR *)&client_sock_addr_ip,
                                     (NET_SOCK_ADDR_LEN *)&client_sock_addr_ip_size,
                                     (void *) 0,
                                     (CPU_INT08U ) 0,
                                     (CPU_INT08U *) 0,
                                     (NET_ERR *)&err);
        switch (err) {
            case NET_SOCK_ERR_NONE:
                attempt_rx = DEF_NO;
                break;
            case NET_SOCK_ERR_RX_Q_EMPTY:
            case NET_OS_ERR_LOCK:
                attempt_rx = DEF_YES;
                break;
            default:
                attempt_rx = DEF_NO;
                break;
        }
    } while (attempt_rx == DEF_YES);

    NetSock_Close(sock, &err);                                              (5)

    if (err != NET_SOCK_ERR_NONE) {
        return (DEF_FALSE);
    }

    return (DEF_TRUE);
}
```

Listing 18-5 **Datagram Server**

L18-5(1)   Open a datagram socket (UDP protocol).

L18-5(2)   Populate the **NET_SOCK_ADDR_IP** structure for the server address and port, and convert it to network order.

L18-5(3)   Bind the newly created socket to the address and port specified by **server_sock_addr_ip**.

L18-5(4)   Receive data from any host on port **DATAGRAM_SERVER_PORT**.

L18-5(5)   Close the socket.

DATAGRAM CLIENT (UDP CLIENT)

The code in Listing 18-6 implements a UDP client. It sends a **'Hello World!'** message to a server that listens on the **UDP_SERVER_PORT**.

```
#define   UDP_SERVER_IP_ADDR   "192.168.1.100"
#define   UDP_SERVER_PORT              10001
#define   UDP_SERVER_TX_STR    "Hello World!"


CPU_BOOLEAN  TestUDPClient (void)
{
    NET_SOCK_ID        sock;
    NET_IP_ADDR        server_ip_addr;
    NET_SOCK_ADDR_IP   server_sock_addr_ip;
    NET_SOCK_ADDR_LEN  server_sock_addr_ip_size;
    CPU_CHAR          *pbuf;
    CPU_INT16S         buf_len;
    NET_SOCK_RTN_CODE  tx_size;
    NET_ERR            err;
    pbuf    = UDP_SERVER_TX_STR;
    buf_len = Str_Len(UDP_SERVER_TX_STR);

    sock = NetSock_Open( NET_SOCK_ADDR_FAMILY_IP_V4,                    (1)
                         NET_SOCK_TYPE_DATAGRAM,
                         NET_SOCK_PROTOCOL_UDP,
                         &err);
    if (err != NET_SOCK_ERR_NONE) {
        return (DEF_FALSE);
    }

    server_ip_addr = NetASCII_Str_to_IP(UDP_SERVER_IP_ADDR, &err);      (2)
    if (err != NET_ASCII_ERR_NONE) {
        NetSock_Close(sock, &err);
        return (DEF_FALSE);
    }
```

```
    server_sock_addr_ip_size = sizeof(server_sock_addr_ip);                    (3)
    Mem_Clr((void      *)&server_sock_addr_ip,
            (CPU_SIZE_T) server_sock_addr_ip_size);
    server_sock_addr_ip.AddrFamily = NET_SOCK_ADDR_FAMILY_IP_V4;
    server_sock_addr_ip.Addr       = NET_UTIL_HOST_TO_NET_32(server_ip_addr);
    server_sock_addr_ip.Port       = NET_UTIL_HOST_TO_NET_16(UDP_SERVER_PORT);


    tx_size = NetSock_TxDataTo((NET_SOCK_ID ) sock,                            (4)
                              (void *) pbuf,
                              (CPU_INT16S ) buf_len,
                              (CPU_INT16S ) NET_SOCK_FLAG_NONE,
                              (NET_SOCK_ADDR *)&server_sock_addr_ip,
                              (NET_SOCK_ADDR_LEN) sizeof(server_sock_addr_ip),
                              (NET_ERR *)&err);


    NetSock_Close(sock, &err);                                                 (5)
    if (err != NET_SOCK_ERR_NONE) {
        return (DEF_FALSE);
    }
    return (DEF_TRUE);
}
```

Listing 18-6 **Datagram Client**

L18-6(1)   Open a datagram socket (UDP protocol).

L18-6(2)   Convert an IPv4 address from ASCII dotted-decimal notation to a network
            protocol IPv4 address in host-order.

L18-6(3)   Populate the NET_SOCK_ADDR_IP structure for the server address and port,
            and convert it to network order.

L18-6(4)   Transmit data to host DATAGRAM_SERVER_IP_ADDR on port
            DATAGRAM_SERVER_PORT.

L18-6(5)   Close the socket.

18-3-2 STREAM SOCKET (TCP SOCKET)

Figure 18-3 reproduces Figure 8-8, which introduced sample code using typical socket functions for a TCP client-server application. The example uses the Micrium proprietary socket API function calls. A similar example could be written using the BSD socket API.

Typically, after a TCP server starts, TCP clients can connect and send requests to the server. A TCP server waits until client connections arrive and then creates a dedicated TCP socket connection to process the client's requests and reply back to the client (if necessary). This continues until either the client or the server closes the dedicated client-server connection. Also while handling multiple, simultaneous client-server connections, the TCP server can wait for new client-server connections

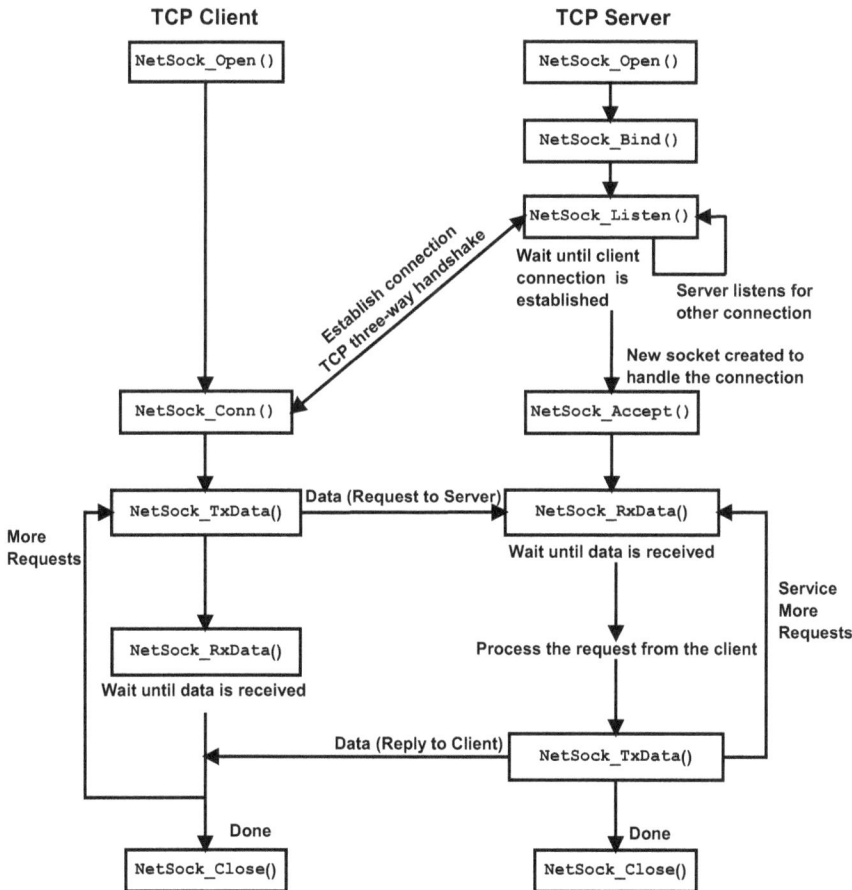

Figure 18-3 **µC/TCP-IP Socket calls used in a typical TCP client-server application**

STREAM SERVER (TCP SERVER)

This example presents a very basic client-server application over a TCP connection. The server presented is simply waits for a connection and send the string **'Hello World!'**. See section "µC/TCP-IP API Reference" on page 649 for a list of all µC/TCP-IP socket API functions.

```
#define  TCP_SERVER_PORT                10000
#define  TCP_SERVER_CONN_Q_SIZE             1
#define  TCP_SERVER_TX_STR       "Hello World!"

CPU_BOOLEAN  TestTCPServer (void)
{
    NET_SOCK_ID        sock_listen;
    NET_SOCK_ID        sock_req;
    NET_SOCK_ADDR_IP   server_sock_addr_ip;
    NET_SOCK_ADDR_LEN  server_sock_addr_ip_size;
    NET_SOCK_ADDR_IP   client_sock_addr_ip;
    NET_SOCK_ADDR_LEN  client_sock_addr_ip_size;
    CPU_BOOLEAN        attempt_conn;
    CPU_CHAR           *pbuf;
    CPU_INT16S         buf_len;
    NET_SOCK_RTN_CODE  tx_size;
    NET_ERR            err;
    pbuf    = TCP_SERVER_TX_STR;
    buf_len = Str_Len(TCP_SERVER_TX_STR);


    sock_listen = NetSock_Open( NET_SOCK_ADDR_FAMILY_IP_V4,               (1)
                                NET_SOCK_TYPE_STREAM,
                                NET_SOCK_PROTOCOL_TCP,
                               &err);
    if (err != NET_SOCK_ERR_NONE) {
        return (DEF_FALSE);
    }


    server_sock_addr_ip_size = sizeof(server_sock_addr_ip);              (2)
    Mem_Clr((void      *)&server_sock_addr_ip,
            (CPU_SIZE_T) server_sock_addr_ip_size);
    server_sock_addr_ip.AddrFamily = NET_SOCK_ADDR_FAMILY_IP_V4;
    server_sock_addr_ip.Addr       = NET_UTIL_HOST_TO_NET_32(NET_SOCK_ADDR_IP_WILD_CARD);
    server_sock_addr_ip.Port       = NET_UTIL_HOST_TO_NET_16(TCP_SERVER_PORT);
```

```
    NetSock_Bind((NET_SOCK_ID ) sock_listen,                                    (3)
               (NET_SOCK_ADDR *)&server_sock_addr_ip,
               (NET_SOCK_ADDR_LEN) NET_SOCK_ADDR_SIZE,
               (NET_ERR *)&err);
    if (err != NET_SOCK_ERR_NONE) {
        NetSock_Close(sock_listen, &err);
        return (DEF_FALSE);
    }
}


    NetSock_Listen( sock_listen,                                                (4)
                   TCP_SERVER_CONN_Q_SIZE,
                   &err);
    if (err != NET_SOCK_ERR_NONE) {
        NetSock_Close(sock_listen, &err);
        return (DEF_FALSE);
    }

    do {
        client_sock_addr_ip_size = sizeof(client_sock_addr_ip);

        sock_req = NetSock_Accept((NET_SOCK_ID ) sock_listen,                   (5)
                               (NET_SOCK_ADDR *)&client_sock_addr_ip,
                               (NET_SOCK_ADDR_LEN *)&client_sock_addr_ip_size,
                               (NET_ERR *)&err);
        switch (err) {
            case NET_SOCK_ERR_NONE:
                attempt_conn = DEF_NO;
                break;
            case NET_ERR_INIT_INCOMPLETE:
            case NET_SOCK_ERR_NULL_PTR:
            case NET_SOCK_ERR_NONE_AVAIL:
            case NET_SOCK_ERR_CONN_ACCEPT_Q_NONE_AVAIL:
            case NET_SOCK_ERR_CONN_SIGNAL_TIMEOUT:
            case NET_OS_ERR_LOCK:
                attempt_conn = DEF_YES;
                break;

            default:
                attempt_conn = DEF_NO;
                break;
        }
    } while (attempt_conn == DEF_YES);

    if (err != NET_SOCK_ERR_NONE) {
        NetSock_Close(sock_req, &err);
        return (DEF_FALSE);
    }
```

```
    tx_size = NetSock_TxData( sock_req,                                    (6)
                              pbuf,
                              buf_len,
                              NET_SOCK_FLAG_NONE,
                              &err);

    NetSock_Close(sock_req, &err);                                        (7)
    NetSock_Close(sock_listen, &err);

    return (DEF_TRUE);
}
```

Listing 18-7 **Stream Server**

L18-7(1)   Open a stream socket (TCP protocol).

L18-7(2)   Populate the **NET_SOCK_ADDR_IP** structure for the server address and port, and convert it to network order.

L18-7(3)   Bind the newly created socket to the address and port specified by **server_sock_addr_ip**.

L18-7(4)   Set the socket to listen for a connection request coming on the specified port.

L18-7(5)   Accept the incoming connection request, and return a new socket for this particular connection. Note that this function call is being called from inside a loop because it might timeout (no client attempts to connect to the server).

L18-7(6)   One the connection has been established between the server and a client, transmit the message. Note that the return value of this function is not used here, but a real application should make sure all the message has been sent by comparing that value with the length of the message.

L18-7(7)   Close both listen and request sockets. When the server need to stay active, the listen socket stays open so that I can accept additional connection requests. Usually, the server will wait for a connection, **accept()** it, and **OSTaskCreate()** a task to handle it.

STREAM CLIENT (TCP CLIENT)

The client of Listing 18-8 connects to the specified server and receives the string the
server sends.

```
#define  TCP_SERVER_IP_ADDR  "192.168.1.101"
#define  TCP_SERVER_PORT           10000
#define  RX_BUF_SIZE                  15

CPU_BOOLEAN  TestTCPClient (void)
{
    NET_SOCK_ID        sock;
    NET_IP_ADDR        server_ip_addr;
    NET_SOCK_ADDR_IP   server_sock_addr_ip;
    NET_SOCK_ADDR_LEN  server_sock_addr_ip_size;
    NET_SOCK_RTN_CODE  conn_rtn_code;
    NET_SOCK_RTN_CODE  rx_size;
    CPU_CHAR           rx_buf[RX_BUF_SIZE];
    NET_ERR            err;


    sock = NetSock_Open( NET_SOCK_ADDR_FAMILY_IP_V4,              (1)
                         NET_SOCK_TYPE_STREAM,
                         NET_SOCK_PROTOCOL_TCP,
                        &err);
    if (err != NET_SOCK_ERR_NONE) {
        return (DEF_FALSE);
    }

    server_ip_addr = NetASCII_Str_to_IP(TCP_SERVER_IP_ADDR, &err);    (2)
    if (err != NET_ASCII_ERR_NONE) {
        NetSock_Close(sock, &err);
        return (DEF_FALSE);
    }

    server_sock_addr_ip_size = sizeof(server_sock_addr_ip);          (3)
    Mem_Clr((void     *)&server_sock_addr_ip,
            (CPU_SIZE_T) server_sock_addr_ip_size);
    server_sock_addr_ip.AddrFamily = NET_SOCK_ADDR_FAMILY_IP_V4;
    server_sock_addr_ip.Addr       = NET_UTIL_HOST_TO_NET_32(server_ip_addr);
    server_sock_addr_ip.Port       = NET_UTIL_HOST_TO_NET_16(TCP_SERVER_PORT);
```

18

515

```
    conn_rtn_code = NetSock_Conn((NET_SOCK_ID ) sock,                          (4)
                                 (NET_SOCK_ADDR *)&server_sock_addr_ip,
                                 (NET_SOCK_ADDR_LEN) sizeof(server_sock_addr_ip),
                                 (NET_ERR *)&err);
    if (err != NET_SOCK_ERR_NONE) {
        NetSock_Close(sock, &err);
        return (DEF_FALSE);
    }

    rx_size = NetSock_RxData( sock,                                             (5)
                             rx_buf,
                             RX_BUF_SIZE,
                             NET_SOCK_FLAG_NONE,
                             &err);
    if (err != NET_SOCK_ERR_NONE) {
        NetSock_Close(sock, &err);
        return (DEF_FALSE);
    }

    NetSock_Close(sock, &err);                                                 (6)
    return (DEF_TRUE);
}
```

Listing 18-8 **Stream Client**

L18-8(1)   Open a stream socket (TCP protocol).

L18-8(2)   Convert an IPv4 address from ASCII dotted-decimal notation to a network
            protocol IPv4 address in host-order.

L18-8(3)   Populate the **NET_SOCK_ADDR_IP** structure for the server address and port, and
            convert it to network order.

L18-8(4)   Connect the socket to a remote host.

L18-8(5)   Receive data from the connected socket. Note that the return value for this
            function is not used here.However, a real application should make sure
            everything has been received.

L18-8(6)   Close the socket.

TCP CONNECTION CONFIGURATION

µC/TCP-IP provides a set of APIs to configure TCP connections on an individual basis. These APIs are listed below and detailed in section C-15 "TCP Functions" on page 896:

- ▣ NetTCP_ConnCfgIdleTimeout()

- ▣ NetTCP_ConnCfgMaxSegSizeLocal()

- ▣ NetTCP_ConnCfgReTxMaxTh()

- ▣ NetTCP_ConnCfgReTxMaxTimeout()

- ▣ NetTCP_ConnCfgRxWinSize()

- ▣ NetTCP_ConnCfgTxWinSize()

- ▣ NetTCP_ConnCfgTxAckImmedRxdPushEn()

- ▣ NetTCP_ConnCfgTxNagleEn()

- ▣ NetTCP_ConnCfgTxKeepAliveEn()

- ▣ NetTCP_ConnCfgTxKeepAliveTh()

- ▣ NetTCP_ConnCfgTxAckDlyTimeout()

18-4 SOCKET CONFIGURATION

µC/TCP-IP provides a set of APIs to configure sockets on an individual basis. These APIs are listed below and detailed in section C-14 "Network Socket Functions" on page 808:

- ▣ NetSock_CfgBlock() (TCP/UDP)

- ▣ NetSock_CfgSecure() (TCP)

- ▣ NetSock_CfgRxQ_Size() (TCP/UDP)

■ NetSock_CfgTxQ_Size() (TCP/UDP)

■ NetSock_CfgTxIP_TOS() (TCP/UDP)

■ NetSock_CfgTxIP_TTL() (TCP/UDP)

■ NetSock_CfgTxIP_TTL_Multicast() (TCP/UDP)

■ NetSock_CfgTimeoutConnAcceptDflt() (TCP)

■ NetSock_CfgTimeoutConnAcceptGet_ms() (TCP)

■ NetSock_CfgTimeoutConnAcceptSet() (TCP)

■ NetSock_CfgTimeoutConnCloseDflt() (TCP)

■ NetSock_CfgTimeoutConnCloseGet_ms() (TCP)

■ NetSock_CfgTimeoutConnCloseSet() (TCP)

■ NetSock_CfgTimeoutConnReqDflt() (TCP)

■ NetSock_CfgTimeoutConnReqGet_ms() (TCP)

■ NetSock_CfgTimeoutConnReqSet() (TCP)

■ NetSock_CfgTimeoutRxQ_Dflt() (TCP/UDP)

■ NetSock_CfgTimeoutRxQ_Get_ms() (TCP/UDP)

■ NetSock_CfgTimeoutRxQ_Set() (TCP/UDP)

■ NetSock_CfgTimeoutTxQ_Dflt() (TCP)

■ NetSock_CfgTimeoutTxQ_Get_ms() (TCP)

■ NetSock_CfgTimeoutTxQ_Set() (TCP)

18-4-1 SOCKET OPTIONS

µC/TCP-IP provides two APIs to read and configure socket option values. These APIs are listed below and detailed in section C-14 "Network Socket Functions" on page 808:

- NetSock_OptGet()

- NetSock_OptSet()

Their BSD equivalent are listed below. See also section C-19 "BSD Functions" on page 938.

- getsockopt() (TCP/UDP)

- setsockopt() (TCP/UDP)

18-5 SECURE SOCKETS

If a network security module (such as µC/SSL) is available, µC/TCP-IP network security manager can be used to secure sockets. Basically, it provides APIs to install the required keying material and to set the secure flag on a specific socket. For details about the network security manager configuration, please refer to Appendix D, "Network Socket Configuration" on page 976. An example that shows how to use the network security manager can be found in section F-6 "Using Network Security Manager" on page 1023.

18-6 2MSL

Maximum Segment Lifetime (MSL) is the time a TCP segment can exist in the network, and is defined as two minutes. 2MSL is twice this lifetime. It is the maximum lifetime of a TCP segment on the network because it supposes segment transmission and acknowledgment.

Currently, Micrium does not support multiple sockets with identical connection information. This prevents new sockets from binding to the same local addresses as other sockets. Thus, for TCP sockets, each **close()** incurs the TCP 2MSL timeout and prevents the next **bind()** from the same client from occurring until after the timeout expires. This is why the 2MSL value is used. This can lead to a long delay before the socket resource is released and reused. µC/TCP-IP configures the TCP connection's default maximum segment lifetime (MSL) timeout value, specified in integer seconds. A starting value of 3 seconds is recommended.

If TCP connections are established and closed rapidly, it is possible that this timeout may further delay new TCP connections from becoming available. Thus, an even lower timeout value may be desirable to free TCP connections and make them available for new connections as rapidly as possible. However, a 0 second timeout prevents µC/TCP-IP from performing the complete TCP connection close sequence and will instead send TCP reset (RST) segments.

For UDP sockets, the sockets **close()** without delay. Thus, the next **bind()** is not blocked.

18-7 µC/TCP-IP SOCKET ERROR CODES

When socket functions return error codes, the error codes should be inspected to determine if the error is a temporary, non-fault condition (such as no data to receive) or fatal (such as the socket has been closed).

18-7-1 FATAL SOCKET ERROR CODES

Whenever any of the following fatal error codes are returned by any µC/TCP-IP socket function, that socket *must* be immediately **closed()**'d without further access by any other socket functions:

```
NET_SOCK_ERR_INVALID_FAMILY
NET_SOCK_ERR_INVALID_PROTOCOL
NET_SOCK_ERR_INVALID_TYPE
NET_SOCK_ERR_INVALID_STATE
NET_SOCK_ERR_FAULT
```

Whenever any of the following fatal error codes are returned by any µC/TCP-IP socket function, that socket *must not* be accessed by any other socket functions but must also *not* be **closed()**'d:

```
NET_SOCK_ERR_NOT_USED
```

18-7-2 SOCKET ERROR CODE LIST

See section E-7 "IP Error Codes" on page 992 for a brief explanation of all µC/TCP-IP socket error codes.

Timer Management

µC/TCP-IP manages software timers used to keep track of various network-related timeouts. Timer management functions are found in **net_tmr.***. Timers are required for:

- Network interface/device driver link-layer monitor   1 total

- Network interface performance statistics   1 total

- ARP cache management   1 per ARP cache entry

- IP fragment reassembly   1 per fragment chain

- Various TCP connection timeouts   up to 7 per TCP connection

- Debug monitor task   1 total

- Performance monitor task   1 total

Of the three mandatory µC/TCP-IP tasks, one of them, the timer task, is used to manage and update timers. The timer task updates timers periodically. **NET_TMR_CFG_TASK_FREQ** determines how often (in Hz) network timers are to be updated. This value *must not* be configured as a floating-point number. This value is typically set to **10 Hz**.

See section D-5-1 on page 966 for more information on timer usage and configuration.

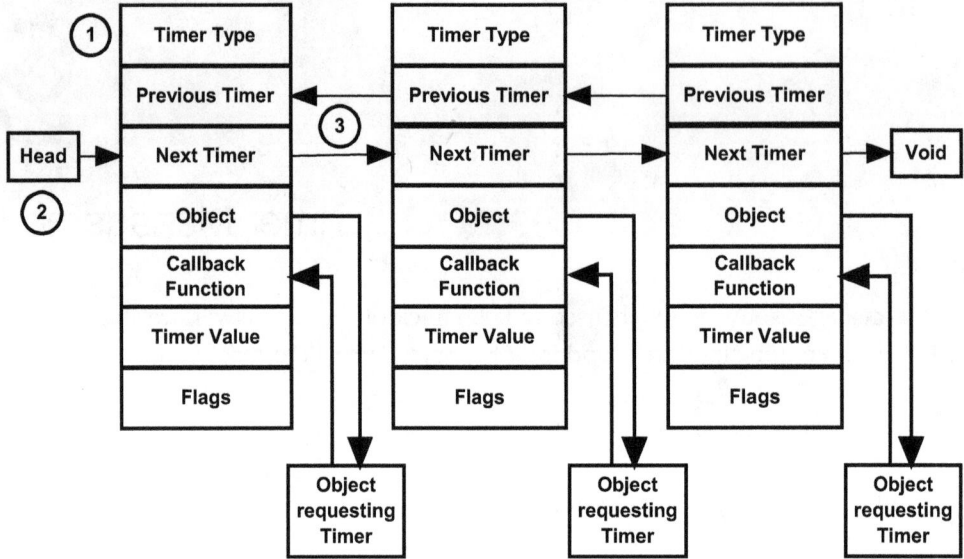

Figure 19-1 **Timer List**

L19-0(1)   Timer types are either **NONE** or **TMR**, meaning unused or used. This field is defined as ASCII representations of network timer types. Memory displays of network timers will display the timer TYPEs with their chosen ASCII name.

L19-0(2)   To manage the timers, the head of the timer list is identified by **NetTmr_TaskListHead**, a pointer to the head of the Timer List.

L19-0(3)   **PrevPtr** and **NextPtr** doubly link each timer to form the Timer List.

The flags field is currently unused.

Network timers are managed by the Timer task in a doubly-linked Timer List. The function that executes these operation is the **NetTmr_TaskHandler()** function. This function is an operating system (OS) function and *should* be called only by appropriate network-operating system port function(s). **NetTmr_TaskHandler()** is blocked until network initialization completes.

NetTmr_TaskHandler() handles the network timers in the Timer List by acquiring the global network lock first. This function blocks all other network protocol tasks by pending on and acquiring the global network lock. Then it handles every network timer in Timer List by decrementing the network timer(s) and for any timer that expires, execute the timer's callback function and free the timer from Timer List. When a network timer expires, the timer is be freed *prior* to executing the timer callback function. This ensures that at least one timer is available if the timer callback function requires a timer. Finally, `NetTmr_TaskHandler()` releases the global network lock.

New timers are added at the head of the Timer List. As timers are added into the list, older timers migrate to the tail of the Timer List. Once a timer expires or is discarded, it is removed.

`NetTmr_TaskHandler()` handles of all the valid timers in the Timer List, up to the first corrupted timer. If a corrupted timer is detected, the timer is discarded/unlinked from the List. Consequently, any remaining valid timers are unlinked from Timer List and are not handled. Finally, the Timer task is aborted.

Since `NetTmr_TaskHandler()` is asynchronous to ANY timer Get/Set, one additional tick is added to each timer's count-down so that the requested timeout is *always* satisfied. This additional tick is added by NOT checking for zero ticks after decrementing; any timer that expires is recognized at the next tick.

A timer value of 0 ticks/seconds is allowed. The next tick will expire the timer.

The `NetTmr_***()` functions are internal functions and should not be called by application functions. This is the reason they are not described here or in Appendix C, "µC/TCP-IP API Reference" on page 649. For more details on these functions, please refer to the `net_tmr.*` files.

19

Debug Management

µC/TCP-IP contains debug constants and functions that may be used by applications to determine network RAM usage, check run-time network resource usage, and check network error or fault conditions. These constants and functions are found in **net_dbg.***. Most of these debug features must be enabled by appropriate configuration constants (see Appendix D, "µC/TCP-IP Configuration and Optimization" on page 959).

20-1 NETWORK DEBUG INFORMATION CONSTANTS

Network debug information constants provide the developer with run-time statistics on µC/TCP-IP configuration, data type and structure sizes, and data RAM usage. The list of debug information constants can be found in **net_dbg.c**, sections GLOBAL NETWORK MODULE DEBUG INFORMATION CONSTANTS & GLOBAL NETWORK MODULE DATA SIZE CONSTANTS. These debug constants are enabled by configuring NET_DBG_CFG_DBG_INFO_EN to DEF_ENABLED.

For example, these constants can be used as follows:

```
CPU_INT16U    net_version;
CPU_INT32U    net_data_size;
CPU_INT32U    net_data_nbr_if;


net_version     = Net_Version;
net_data_size   = Net_DataSize;
net_data_nbr_if = NetIF_CfgMaxNbrIF;
printf("µC/TCP-IP Version        : %05d\n", net_version);
printf("Total Network RAM Used   : %05d\n", net_data_size);
printf("Number Network Interfaces : %05d\n", net_data_nbr_if);
```

20-2 NETWORK DEBUG MONITOR TASK

The Network Debug Monitor task periodically checks the current run-time status of certain µC/TCP-IP conditions and saves that status to global variables which may be queried by other network modules.

Currently, the Network Debug Monitor task is only enabled when ICMP Transmit Source Quenches are enabled (see section D-10-1 on page 971) because this is the only network functionality that requires a periodic update of certain network status conditions. Applications do not need Debug Monitor task functionality since applications have access to the same debug status functions that the Monitor task calls and may call them asynchronously.

Statistics and Error Counters

μC/TCP-IP maintains counters and statistics for a variety of expected or unexpected error conditions. Some of these statistics are optional since they require additional code and memory and are enabled only if **NET_CTR_CFG_STAT_EN** or **NET_CTR_CFG_ERR_EN** is enabled (see section D-4 "Network Counter Configuration" on page 965).

21-1 STATISTICS

μC/TCP-IP maintains run-time statistics on interfaces and most μC/TCP-IP object pools. If desired, an application can thus query μC/TCP-IP to find out how many frames have been processed on a particular interface, transmit and receive performance metrics, buffer utilization and more. An application can also reset the statistic pools back to their initialization values (see **net_stat.h**).

Applications may choose to monitor statistics for various reasons. For example, examining buffer statistics allows you to better manage the memory usage. Typically, more buffers can be allocated than necessary and, by examining buffer usage statistics, adjustments can be made to reduce their number.

Network protocol and interface statistics are kept in an instance of a data structure named **Net_StatCtrs**. This variable may be viewed within a debugger or referenced externally by the application for run-time analysis.

Unlike network protocol statistics, object pool statistics have functions to get a copy of the specified statistic pool and functions for resetting the pools to their default values. These statistics are kept in a data structure called **NET_STAT_POOL** which can be declared by the application and used as a return variable from the statistics API functions.

The data structure is shown below

```
typedef struct net_stat_pool {
    NET_TYPE            Type;
    NET_STAT_POOL_QTY   EntriesInit;
    NET_STAT_POOL_QTY   EntriesTotal;
    NET_STAT_POOL_QTY   EntriesAvail;
    NET_STAT_POOL_QTY   EntriesUsed;
    NET_STAT_POOL_QTY   EntriesUsedMax;
    NET_STAT_POOL_QTY   EntriesLostCur;
    NET_STAT_POOL_QTY   EntriesLostTotal;
    CPU_INT32U          EntriesAllocatedCtr;
    CPU_INT32U          EntriesDeallocatedCtr;
} NET_STAT_POOL;
```

NET_STAT_POOL_QTY is a data type currently set to CPU_INT16U and thus contains a maximum count of 65535.

Access to buffer statistics is obtained via interface functions that the application can call (described in the next sections). Most likely, only the following variables in NET_STAT_POOL need to be examined, because the **.Type** member is configured at initialization time as NET_STAT_TYPE_POOL :

.EntriesAvail

This variable indicates how many buffers are available in the pool.

.EntriesUsed

This variable indicates how many buffers are currently used by the TCP/IP stack.

.EntriesUsedMax

This variable indicates the maximum number of buffers used since it was last reset.

.EntriesAllocatedCtr

This variable indicates the total number of times buffers were allocated (i.e., used by the TCP/IP stack).

.EntriesDeallocatedCtr

This variable indicates the total number of times buffers were returned back to the buffer pool.

In order to enable run-time statistics, the macro NET_CTR_CFG_STAT_EN located within net_cfg.h must be defined to DEF_ENABLED.

21-2 ERROR COUNTERS

µC/TCP-IP maintains run-time counters for tracking error conditions within the Network Protocol Stack. If desired, the application may view the error counters in order to debug run-time problems such as low memory conditions, slow performance, packet loss, *etc*.

Network protocol error counters are kept in an instance of a data structure named **Net_ErrCtrs**. This variable may be viewed within a debugger or referenced externally by the application for run-time analysis (see **net_stat.h**).

In order to enable run-time error counters, the macro **NET_CTR_CFG_ERR_EN** located within **net_cfg.h** must be defined to **DEF_ENABLED**.

21

µC/TCP-IP Ethernet Device Driver APIs

This appendix provides a reference to the µC/TCP-IP Device Driver API. Each user-accessible service is presented in alphabetical order. The following information is provided for each of the services:

- A brief description

- The function prototype

- The filename of the source code

- A description of the arguments passed to the function

- A description of the returned value(s)

- Specific notes and warnings on the use of the service

A-1 DEVICE DRIVER FUNCTIONS FOR MAC

A-1-1 NetDev_Init()

The first function within the Ethernet API is the device driver initialization/**Init()** function. This function is called by **NetIF_Add()** exactly once for each specific network device added by the application. If multiple instances of the same network device are present on the development board, then this function is called for each instance of the device. However, applications should not try to add the same specific device more than once. If a network device fails to initialize, we recommend debugging to find and correct the cause of failure.

Note: This function relies heavily on the implementation of several network device board support package (BSP) functions. See Chapter 15, "Network Board Support Package" on page 347 and Appendix A, "Device Driver BSP Functions" on page 567 for more information on network device BSP functions.

FILES

Every device driver's **net_dev.c**

PROTOTYPE

```
static void NetDev_Init (NET_IF   *pif,
                         NET_ERR *perr);
```

Note that since every device driver's **Init()** function is accessed only by function pointer via the device driver's API structure, it doesn't need to be globally available and should therefore be declared as '**static**'.

ARGUMENTS

pif   Pointer to the interface to initialize a network device.

perr   Pointer to variable that will receive the return error code from this function.

None.

None.

The **Init( )** function generally performs the following operations, however, depending on the device being initialized, functionality may need to be added or removed:

1 Configure clock gating to the MAC device, if applicable. This is generally performed via the network device's BSP function pointer, **CfgClk( )**, implemented in **net_bsp.c** (see section A-3-1 on page 567).

2 Configure all necessary I/O pins for both an internal or external MAC and PHY, if present. This is generally performed via the network device's BSP function pointer, **CfgGPIO( )**, implemented in **net_bsp.c** (see section A-3-2 on page 569).

   ■ Configure the host interrupt controller for receive and transmit complete interrupts. Additional interrupt services may be initialized depending on the device and driver requirements. This is generally performed via the network device's BSP function pointer, **CfgIntCtrl( )**, implemented in **net_bsp.c** (see section A-3-3 on page 571).

3 For DMA devices: Allocate memory for all necessary descriptors. This is performed via calls to μC/LIB's memory module.

4 For DMA devices: Initialize all descriptors to their ready states. This may be performed via calls to locally-declared, '**static**' functions.

5 Initialize the (R)MII bus interface, if applicable. This generally entails configuring the (R)MII bus frequency which is dependent on the system clock. Static values for clock frequencies should never be used when determining clock dividers. Instead, the driver should reference the associated clock function(s) for getting the system clock or peripheral bus frequencies, and use these values to compute the correct (R)MII bus clock divider(s). This is generally performed via the network device's BSP function pointer, **ClkFreqGet( )**, implemented in **net_bsp.c** (see section A-3-4 on page 575).

6   Disable the transmitted and receiver (should already be disabled).

7   Disable and clear pending interrupts (should already be cleared).

8   Set **perr** to **NET_DEV_ERR_NONE** if initialization proceeded as expected. Otherwise, set **perr** to an appropriate network device error code.

A-1-2 NetDev_Start()

The second function is the device driver **Start()** function. This function is called once each time an interface is started.

FILES

Every device driver's **net_dev.c**

PROTOTYPE

```
static void NetDev_Start (NET_IF  *pif,
                          NET_ERR *perr);
```

Note that since every device driver's **Start()** function is accessed only by function pointer via the device driver's API structure, it doesn't need to be globally available and should therefore be declared as '**static**'.

ARGUMENTS

pif   Pointer to the interface to start a network device.

perr   Pointer to variable that will receive the return error code from this function.

RETURNED VALUE

None.

REQUIRED CONFIGURATION

None.

NOTES / WARNINGS

The **Start()** function performs the following items:

1   Configure the transmit ready semaphore count via a call to **NetOS_Dev_CfgTxRdySignal()**. This function call is optional and is generally performed when the hardware device supports the queuing of multiple transmit frames. By default, the count is initialized to one. However, DMA devices should set the semaphore count equal to the number of configured transmit descriptors for optimal

performance. Non-DMA devices that support the queuing of more than one transmit frame may also benefit from a non-default value.

2   Initialize the device MAC address if applicable. For Ethernet devices, this step is mandatory. The MAC address data may come from one of three sources and should be set using the following priority scheme:

a. Configure the MAC address using the string found within the device configuration structure. This is a form of static MAC address configuration and may be performed by calling `NetASCII_Str_to_MAC()` and `NetIF_AddrHW_SetHandler()`. If the device configuration string has been left empty, or is specified as all 0's, an error will be returned and the next method should be attempted.

b. Check if the application developer has called `NetIF_AddrHW_Set()` by making a call to `NetIF_AddrHW_GetHandler()` and `NetIF_AddrHW_IsValidHandler()` in order to check if the specified MAC address is valid. This method may be used as a static method for configuring the MAC address during run-time, or a dynamic method should a pre-programmed external memory device exist. If the acquired MAC address does not pass the check function, then:

c. Call `NetIF_AddrHW_SetHandler()` using the data found within the MAC individual address registers. If an auto-loading EEPROM is attached to the MAC, the registers will contain valid data. If not, then a configuration error has occurred. This method is often used with a production process where the MAC supports the automatic loading of individual address registers from a serial EEPROM. When using this method, the developer should specify an empty string for the MAC address within the device configuration and refrain from calling `NetIF_AddrHW_Set()` from within the application.

3   Initialize additional MAC registers required by the MAC for proper operation.

4   Clear all interrupt flags.

5   Locally enable interrupts on the hardware device. The host interrupt controller should have already been configured within the device driver `Init()` function.

6   Enable the receiver and transmitter.

7   Set **perr** equal to **NET_DEV_ERR_NONE** if no errors have occurred. Otherwise, set **perr** to an appropriate network device error code.

A-1-3 NetDev_Stop()

The next function within the device API structure is the device **Stop()** function. This function is called once each time an interface is stopped.

FILES

Every device driver's **net_dev.c**

PROTOTYPE

```
static void NetDev_Stop (NET_IF  *pif,
                         NET_ERR *perr);
```

Note that since every device driver's **Stop()** function is accessed only by function pointer via the device driver's API structure, it doesn't need to be globally available and should therefore be declared as '**static**'.

ARGUMENTS

pif   Pointer to the interface to start a network device.

perr   Pointer to variable that will receive the return error code from this function.

RETURNED VALUE

None.

REQUIRED CONFIGURATION

None.

NOTES / WARNINGS

The **Stop( )** function must perform the following operations:

1   Disable the receiver and transmitter.

2   Disable all local MAC interrupt sources.

3   Clear all local MAC interrupt status flags.

4   For DMA devices, re-initialize all receive descriptors.

5   For DMA devices, free all transmit descriptors by calling **NetOS_IF_DeallocTaskPost( )** with the address of the transmit descriptor data areas.

6   For DMA devices, re-initialize all transmit descriptors.

7   Set **perr** to **NET_DEV_ERR_NONE** if no error occurs. Otherwise, set **perr** to an appropriate network device error code.

A-1-4 NetDev_Rx()

The receive/**Rx()** function is called by µC/TCP-IP's Receive task after the Interrupt Service Routine handler has signaled to the Receive task that a receive event has occurred. The Receive function requires that the device driver return a pointer to the data area containing the received data and return the size of the received frame via pointer.

FILES

Every device driver's **net_dev.c**

PROTOTYPE

```
static void NetDev_Rx (NET_IF      *pif,
                       CPU_INT08U **p_data,
                       CPU_INT16U  *size,
                       NET_ERR     *perr);
```

Note that since every device driver's **Rx()** function is accessed only by function pointer via the device driver's API structure, it doesn't need to be globally available and should therefore be declared as '**static**'.

ARGUMENTS

pif Pointer to the interface to receive data from a network device.

p_data Pointer to return the address of the received data.

size Pointer to return the size of the received data.

perr Pointer to variable that will receive the return error code from this function.

RETURNED VALUE

None.

REQUIRED CONFIGURATION

None.

NOTES / WARNINGS

The receive function should perform the following actions:

1   Check for receive errors if applicable. If an error should occur during reception, the driver should set ***size** to 0 and ***p_data** to **(CPU_INT08U *)**0 and return. Additional steps may be necessary depending on the device being serviced.

2   For Ethernet devices, get the size of the received frame and subtract 4 bytes for the CRC. It it always recommended that the frame size is checked to ensure that it is greater than 4 bytes before performing the subtraction to ensure that an underflow does not occur. Set ***size** equal to the adjusted frame size.

3   Get a new data buffer area by calling **NetBuf_GetDataPtr()**. If memory is not available, an error will be returned and the device driver should set ***size** to 0 and ***p_data** to **(CPU_INT08U *)**0. For DMA devices, the current receive descriptor should be marked as available or owned by hardware. The device driver should then return from the receive function.

4   If an error does not occur while getting a new data area, DMA devices should perform the following operations:

   a. Set ***p_data** equal to the address of the data area within the descriptor being serviced.

   b. Set the data area pointer within the receive descriptor to the address of the data area obtained by calling **NetBuf_GetDataPtr()**.

   c. Update any descriptor ring pointers if applicable.

5   Non DMA devices should **Mem_Copy()** the data stored within the device to the address of the buffer obtained by calling **NetBuf_GetDataPtr()** and set ***p_data** equal to the address of the obtained data area.

6   Set **perr** to **NET_DEV_ERR_NONE** and return from the receive function. Otherwise, set **perr** to an appropriate network device error code.

A-1-5 NetDev_Tx()

The next function in the device API structure is the transmit/**Tx( )** function.

FILES

Every device driver's **net_dev.c**

PROTOTYPE

```
static void NetDev_Tx (NET_IF      *pif,
                       CPU_INT08U *p_data,
                       CPU_INT16U  size,
                       NET_ERR     *perr);
```

Note that since every device driver's **Tx( )** function is accessed only by function pointer via the device driver's API structure, it doesn't need to be globally available and should therefore be declared as '**static**'.

ARGUMENTS

pif   Pointer to the interface to start a network device.

p_data   Pointer to address of the data to transmit.

size   Size of the data to transmit.

perr   Pointer to variable that will receive the return error code from this function.

RETURNED VALUE

None.

REQUIRED CONFIGURATION

None.

NOTES / WARNINGS

The transmit function should perform the following actions:

1   For DMA-based hardware, the driver should select the next available transmit descriptor and set the pointer to the data area equal to the address pointer to by **p_data**.

2   Non-DMA hardware should **Mem_Copy()** the data stored within the buffer pointed to by **p_data** to the device's internal memory.

3   Once completed, the driver must configure the device with the number of bytes to transmit. This is passed directly by value within the size argument. DMA-based devices generally have a size field within the transmit descriptor. Non-DMA devices generally have a transmit size register that needs to be configured.

4   The driver should then take all necessary steps to initiate transmission of the data.

5   Set **perr** to **NET_DEV_ERR_NONE** and return from the transmit function.

A-1-6 NetDev_AddrMulticastAdd()

The next API function is the **AddrMulticastAdd( )** function used to configure a device with an (IP-to-Ethernet) multicast hardware address.

Every device driver's **net_dev.c**

```
static void NetDev_AddrMulticastAdd (NET_IF      *pif,
                                     CPU_INT08U *paddr_hw,
                                     CPU_INT08U  addr_hw_len,
                                     NET_ERR     *perr);
```

Note that since every device driver's **AddrMulticastAdd( )** function is accessed only by function pointer via the device driver's API structure, it doesn't need to be globally available and should therefore be declared as '**static**'.

pif   Pointer to the interface to add/configure a multicast address.

paddr_hw   Pointer to multicast hardware address to add.

addr_hw_len Length of multicast hardware address.

perr   Pointer to variable that will receive the return error code from this function.

None.

Necessary only if **NET_IP_CFG_MULTICAST_SEL** is configured for transmit and receive multicasting (see section D-9-2 on page 971).

NOTES / WARNINGS

Since many network controllers' documentation fail to properly indicate how to add/configure an Ethernet MAC device with a multicast address, the following methodology is recommended for determining and testing the correct multicast hash bit algorithm.

1   Configure a packet capture program or multicast application to broadcast a multicast packet with Ethernet destination address of 01:00:5E:00:00:01. This MAC address corresponds to the multicast group IP address of 224.0.0.1 which will be converted to a MAC address by higher layers and passed to this function.

2   Set a break point in the receive ISR handler and transmit one send packet to the target. The break point should *not* be reached as the result of the transmitted packet. Use caution to ensure that other network traffic is not the source of the interrupt when the button is pressed. Sometimes asynchronous network events happen very close in time and the end result can be deceiving. Ideally, these tests should be performed on an isolated network but disconnect as many other hosts from the network as possible.

3   Use the debugger to stop the application and program the MAC multicast hash register low bits to 0xFFFFFFFF. Go to step 2. Repeat for the hash bit high register if necessary. The goal is to bracket off which bit in either the high or low hash bit register causes the device to be interrupted when the broadcast frame is received by the target. Once the correct bit is known, the hash algorithm can be easily written and tested.

4   The following hash bit algorithm code below could be adjusted per the network controller's documentation in order to get the hash from the correct subset of CRC bits. Most of the code is similar between various devices and is thus reusable. The hash algorithm is the exlusive **OR** of every 6th bit of the destination address:

```
hash[5] = da[5] ^ da[11] ^ da[17] ^ da[23] ^ da[29] ^ da[35] ^ da[41] ^ da[47]
hash[4] = da[4] ^ da[10] ^ da[16] ^ da[22] ^ da[28] ^ da[34] ^ da[40] ^ da[46]
hash[3] = da[3] ^ da[09] ^ da[15] ^ da[21] ^ da[27] ^ da[33] ^ da[39] ^ da[45]
hash[2] = da[2] ^ da[08] ^ da[14] ^ da[20] ^ da[26] ^ da[32] ^ da[38] ^ da[44]
hash[1] = da[1] ^ da[07] ^ da[13] ^ da[19] ^ da[25] ^ da[31] ^ da[37] ^ da[43]
hash[0] = da[0] ^ da[06] ^ da[12] ^ da[18] ^ da[24] ^ da[30] ^ da[36] ^ da[42]
```

Where **da0** represents the least significant bit of the first byte of the destination address received and where **da47** represents the most significant bit of the last byte of the destination address received.

```
                                      /* ---------- CALCULATE HASH CODE ---------- */
hash = 0;
for (i = 0; i < 6; i++) {             /* For each row in the bit hash table:      */
    bit_val = 0;                      /* Clear initial xor value for each row.     */
    for (j = 0; j < 8; j++) {         /* For each bit in each octet:               */
        bit_nbr   = (j * 6) + i;      /* Determine which bit in stream, 0-47.      */
        octet_nbr = bit_nbr / 8;      /* Determine which octet bit belongs to.     */
        octet     = paddr_hw[octet_nbr];   /* Get octet value.                     */
        bit       = octet & (1 << (bit_nbr % 8));  /* Check if octet's bit is set.  */
        bit_val  ^= (bit > 0) ? 1 : 0;     /* Calculate table row's XOR hash value. */
    }
    hash |= (bit_val << i);           /* Add row's XOR hash value to final hash.   */
}
                                      /* ---- ADD MULTICAST ADDRESS TO DEVICE ---- */
reg_sel = (hash >> 5) & 0x01;         /* Determine hash register    to configure. */
reg_bit = (hash >> 0) & 0x1F;         /* Determine hash register bit to configure. */
                                      /* (Substitute '0x01'/'0x1F' with device's ..*/
                                      /* .. actual hash register bit masks/shifts.)*/

  paddr_hash_ctrs = &pdev_data->MulticastAddrHashBitCtr[hash];
(*paddr_hash_ctrs)++;                 /* Increment hash bit reference counter.     */

if (reg_sel == 0) {                   /* Set multicast hash register bit.          */
    pdev->MCAST_REG_LO |= (1 << reg_bit);  /* (Substitute 'MCAST_REG_LO/HI' with ..  */
} else {                              /* .. device's actual multicast registers.)  */
    pdev->MCAST_REG_HI |= (1 << reg_bit);
}
                                      /* ---------- CALCULATE HASH CODE ---------- */
                                      /* Calculate CRC.                            */
crc = NetUtil_32BitCRC_Calc((CPU_INT08U *)paddr_hw,
                            (CPU_INT32U  ) addr_hw_len,
                            (NET_ERR    *)perr);
```

Listing A-1 **Example device multicast address configuration using CRC hash code algorithm**

Alternatively, you may be able to compute the CRC hash with a call to `NetUtil_32BitCRC_CalcCpl()` followed by an optional call to `NetUtil_32BitReflect()`, with four possible combinations:

a. CRC without complement and without reflection

b. CRC without complement and with reflection

c. CRC with complement and without reflection

d. CRC with complement and with reflection

```
if (*perr != NET_UTIL_ERR_NONE) {
    return;
}
                                        /* ---- ADD MULTICAST ADDRESS TO DEVICE ---- */
crc      = NetUtil_32BitReflect(crc);   /* Optionally, complement CRC.               */
hash     = (crc >> 23u) & 0x3F;          /* Determine hash register    to configure. */
reg_bit = (hash % 32u);                 /* Determine hash register bit to configure. */
                                        /* (Substitute '23u'/'0x3F' with device's .. */
                                        /* .. actual hash register bit masks/shifts.)*/


  paddr_hash_ctrs = &pdev_data->MulticastAddrHashBitCtr[hash];
(*paddr_hash_ctrs)++;                    /* Increment hash bit reference counter.     */

if (hash <= 31u) {                       /* Set multicast hash register bit.          */
    pdev->MCAST_REG_LO |= (1 << reg_bit); /* (Substitute 'MCAST_REG_LO/HI' with ..     */
} else {                                 /* .. device's actual multicast registers.)  */
    pdev->MCAST_REG_HI |= (1 << reg_bit);
}
```

Listing A-2 **Example device multicast address configuration using CRC and reflection functions**

Unfortunately, the product documentation will *not* likely tell you which combination of complement and reflection is necessary in order to properly compute the hash value. Most likely, the documentation will simply state 'Standard Ethernet CRC' which when compared to other documents, means any of the four combinations above; different than the actual frame CRC.

Fortunately, if the code is written to perform both the complement and reflection, then the debugger may be used to repeat the code block over and over skipping either the line that performs the complement or the function call to the reflection until the output hash bit is computed correctly.

5   Update the device driver's **AddrMulticastAdd()** function to calculate and configure the correct CRC.

6   Test the device driver's **AddrMulticastAdd()** function by ensuring that the group address 224.0.0.1, when joined from the application (see section C-11-1 on page 771), correctly configures the device to receive multicast packets destined to the 224.0.0.1 address. Then broadcast the 224.0.0.1 (see step 1) to test if the device receives the multicast packet.

A-1-7 NetDev_AddrMulticastRemove()

The next API function is the **AddrMulticastRemove()** function used to remove an (IP-to-Ethernet) multicast hardware address from a device.

FILES

Every device driver's **net_dev.c**

PROTOTYPE

```
static void NetDev_AddrMulticastRemove (NET_IF     *pif,
                                        CPU_INT08U *paddr_hw,
                                        CPU_INT08U  addr_hw_len,
                                        NET_ERR    *perr);
```

Note that since every device driver's **AddrMulticastRemove()** function is accessed only by function pointer via the device driver's API structure, it doesn't need to be globally available and should therefore be declared as '**static**'.

ARGUMENTS

pif   Pointer to the interface to remove a multicast address.

paddr_hw   Pointer to multicast hardware address to remove.

addr_hw_len   Length of multicast hardware address.

perr   Pointer to variable that will receive the return error code from this function.

RETURNED VALUE

None.

REQUIRED CONFIGURATION

Necessary only if **NET_IP_CFG_MULTICAST_SEL** is configured for transmit and receive multicasting (see section D-9-2 on page 971).

NOTES / WARNINGS

Use same exact code as in **NetDev_AddrMulticastAdd()** to calculate the device's CRC hash (see section A-1-6 on page 543), but remove a multicast address by decrementing the device's hash bit reference counters and clearing the appropriate bits in the device's multicast registers.

```
                                       /* ---------- CALCULATE HASH CODE ---------- */
/* Use NetDev_AddrMulticastAdd()'s algorithm to calculate CRC hash.              */
                                       /* - REMOVE MULTICAST ADDRESS FROM DEVICE -- */
paddr_hash_ctrs = &pdev_data->MulticastAddrHashBitCtr[hash];
if (*paddr_hash_ctrs > 1u) {           /* If multiple multicast addresses hashed, ..*/
    (*paddr_hash_ctrs)--;              /* .. decrement hash bit reference counter ..*/
     *perr = NET_DEV_ERR_NONE;         /* .. but do NOT unconfigure hash register.  */
      return;
}
*paddr_hash_ctrs = 0u;                 /* Clear hash bit reference counter.        */

if (hash <= 31u) {                     /* Clear multicast hash register bit.       */
    pdev->MCAST_REG_LO &= ~(1u << reg_bit);  /* (Substitute 'MCAST_REG_LO/HI' with ..  */
} else {                               /* .. device's actual multicast registers.) */
    pdev->MCAST_REG_HI &= ~(1u << reg_bit);
}
```

Listing A-3 **Example device multicast address removal**

A-1-8 NetDev_ISR_Handler()

A device's `ISR_Handler()` function is used to handle each device's interrupts. See section 16-5-5 on page 391 for more details on how to handle each device's interrupts.

FILES

Every device driver's `net_dev.c`

PROTOTYPE

```
static void NetDev_ISR_Handler (NET_IF            *pif,
                                NET_DEV_ISR_TYPE  type);
```

Note that since every device driver's `ISR_Handler()` function is accessed only by function pointer via the device driver's API structure, it doesn't need to be globally available and should therefore be declared as '**static**'.

ARGUMENTS

pif   Pointer to the interface to handle network device interrupts.

type   Device's interrupt type:

        NET_DEV_ISR_TYPE_UNKNOWN

        NET_DEV_ISR_TYPE_RX

        NET_DEV_ISR_TYPE_RX_RUNT

        NET_DEV_ISR_TYPE_RX_OVERRUN

        NET_DEV_ISR_TYPE_TX_RDY

        NET_DEV_ISR_TYPE_TX_COMPLETE

        NET_DEV_ISR_TYPE_TX_COLLISION_LATE

        NET_DEV_ISR_TYPE_TX_COLLISION_EXCESS

NET_DEV_ISR_TYPE_JABBER

NET_DEV_ISR_TYPE_BABBLE

NET_DEV_ISR_TYPE_PHY

RETURNED VALUE

None.

REQUIRED CONFIGURATION

None.

NOTES / WARNINGS

Each device's **NetDev_ISR_Handler()** should never return early but check all applicable interrupt sources to see if they are active. This additional checking is necessary because multiple interrupt sources may be set within the interrupt response time and will reduce the number and overhead of handling interrupts.

A-1-9 NetDev_IO_Ctrl()

A device's input/output control/**IO_Ctrl()** function is used to implement miscellaneous functionality such as setting and getting the PHY link state, as well as updating the MAC link state registers when the PHY link state has changed. An optional void pointer to a data variable is passed into the function and may be used to get device parameters from the caller, or to return device parameters to the caller.

FILES

Every device driver's **net_dev.c**

PROTOTYPE

```
static void NetDev_IO_Ctrl (NET_IF      *pif,
                            CPU_INT08U  opt,
                            void        *p_data,
                            NET_ERR     *perr);
```

Note that since every device driver's **IO_Ctrl()** function is accessed only by function pointer via the device driver's API structure, it doesn't need to be globally available and should therefore be declared as '**static**'.

ARGUMENTS

pif   Pointer to the interface to handle network device I/O operations.

opt   I/O operation to perform.

p_data   A pointer to a variable containing the data necessary to perform the operation or a pointer to a variable to store data associated with the result of the operation.

perr   Pointer to variable that will receive the return error code from this function.

RETURNED VALUE

None.

REQUIRED CONFIGURATION

None.

NOTES / WARNINGS

µC/TCP-IP defines the following default options:

```
NET_DEV_LINK_STATE_GET_INFO
NET_DEV_LINK_STATE_UPDATE
```

The `NET_DEV_LINK_STATE_GET_INFO` option expects **p_data** to point to a variable of type `NET_DEV_LINK_ETHER` for the case of an Ethernet driver. This variable has two fields, **Spd** and **Duplex**, which are filled in by the PHY device driver via a call through the PHY API. µC/TCP-IP internally uses this option code in order to periodically poll the PHYs for link state.

The `NET_DEV_LINK_STATE_UPDATE` option is used by the PHY driver to communicate with the MAC when either µC/TCP-IP polls the PHY for link status, or when a PHY interrupt occurs. Not all MAC's require PHY link state synchronization. Should this be the case, then the device driver may not need to implement this option.

A-1-10 NetDev_MII_Rd()

The next function to implement is the (R)MII read/**Phy_RegRd( )** function. This function is generally implemented within the Ethernet device driver file, since (R)MII bus reads are generally associated with the MAC device. In the case that the PHY communication mechanism is separate from the MAC, then a handler function may be provided within the **net_bsp.c** file and called from the device driver file instead.

Note: This function must be implemented with a timeout and should *not* block indefinitely should the PHY fail to respond.

FILES

Every device driver's **net_dev.c**

PROTOTYPE

```
static void NetDev_MII_Rd (NET_IF      *pif,
                           CPU_INT08U  phy_addr,
                           CPU_INT08U  reg_addr,
                           CPU_INT16U *p_data,
                           NET_ERR     *perr);
```

Note that since every device driver's **Phy_RegRd( )/MII_Rd( )** function is accessed only by function pointer via the device driver's API structure, it doesn't need to be globally available and should therefore be declared as '**static**'.

ARGUMENTS

pif   Pointer to the interface to read a (R)MII PHY register.

phy_addr   The bus address of the PHY.

reg_addr   The MII register number to read.

p_data   Pointer to a address to store the content of the PHY register being read.

perr   Pointer to variable that will receive the return error code from this function.

RETURNED VALUE

None.

REQUIRED CONFIGURATION

None.

NOTES/WARNINGS

None.

A-1-11 NetDev_MII_Wr()

Next is the (R)MII write/**Phy_RegWr( )** function. This function is generally implemented within the Ethernet device driver file since (R)MII bus writes are generally associated with the MAC device. In the case that the PHY communication mechanism is separate from the MAC, a handler function may be provided within the **net_bsp.c** file and called from the device driver file instead.

Note: This function must be implemented with a timeout and not block indefinitely should the PHY fail to respond.

FILES

Every device driver's **net_dev.c**

PROTOTYPE

```
static void NetDev_MII_Wr (NET_IF      *pif,
                           CPU_INT08U  phy_addr,
                           CPU_INT08U  reg_addr,
                           CPU_INT16U  data,
                           NET_ERR     *perr);
```

Note that since every device driver's **Phy_RegWr( )/MII_Wr( )** function is accessed only by function pointer via the device driver's API structure, it doesn't need to be globally available and should therefore be declared as '**static**'.

ARGUMENTS

pif   Pointer to the interface to read a (R)MII PHY register.

phy_addr   The bus address of the PHY.

reg_addr   The MII register number to write to.

p_data   Pointer to the data to write to the specified PHY register.

perr   Pointer to variable that will receive the return error code from this function.

RETURNED VALUE

None.

REQUIRED CONFIGURATION

None.

NOTES/WARNINGS

None.

A-2 DEVICE DRIVER FUNCTIONS FOR PHY

A-2-1 NetPhy_Init()

The first function within the Ethernet PHY API is the PHY driver initialization/Init()
function which is called by the Ethernet network interface layer after the MAC device driver
is initialized without error.

FILES

Every physical layer driver's **net_phy.c**

PROTOTYPE

```
static void NetPhy_Init (NET_IF  *pif,
                         NET_ERR *perr)
```

Note that since every PHY driver's **Init()** function is accessed only by function pointer via
the PHY driver's API structure, it doesn't need to be globally available and should therefore
be declared as '**static**'.

ARGUMENTS

pif   Pointer to the interface to initialize a PHY.

perr   Pointer to variable that will receive the return error code from this function.

RETURNED VALUE

None.

REQUIRED CONFIGURATION

None.

NOTES/WARNINGS

The PHY initialization function is responsible for the following actions:

1   Reset the PHY and wait with timeout for reset to complete. If a timeout occurs, return **perr** set to `NET_PHY_ERR_RESET_TIMEOUT`.

2   Start the auto-negotiation process. This should configure the PHY registers such that the desired link speed and duplex specified within the PHY configuration are respected. It is not necessary to wait until the auto-negotiation process has completed, as this can take upwards of many seconds. Generally, this action is performed by calling the PHY's `NetPhy_AutoNegStart()` function.

3   If no errors occur, return **perr** set to `NET_PHY_ERR_NONE`.

A-2-2 NetPhy_EnDis()

The next Ethernet PHY function is the enable-disable/**EnDis()** function. This function is called by the Ethernet network interface layer when an interface is started or stopped.

FILES

Every physical layer driver's **net_phy.c**

PROTOTYPE

```
static void NetPhy_EnDis (NET_IF      *pif,
                          CPU_BOOLEAN  en,
                          NET_ERR     *perr);
```

Note that since every PHY driver's **EnDis()** function is accessed only by function pointer via the PHY driver's API structure, it doesn't need to be globally available and should therefore be declared as '**static**'.

ARGUMENTS

pif   Pointer to the interface to enable/disable a PHY.

en   A flag representing the next desired state of the PHY:

            DEF_ENABLED

            DEF_DISABLED

perr   Pointer to variable that will receive the return error code from this function.

RETURNED VALUE

None.

None.

NOTES/WARNINGS

Disabling the PHY will generally cause the PHY to power down which will cause link state to be disconnected.

A-2-3 NetPhy_LinkStateGet()

The Ethernet PHY's **LinkStateGet()** function determines the current Ethernet link state. Results are passed back to the caller in a **NET_DEV_LINK_ETHER** structure which contains fields for link speed and duplex. This function is called periodically by µC/TCP-IP.

FILES

Every physical layer driver's **net_phy.c**

PROTOTYPE

```
static void NetPhy_LinkStateGet (NET_IF             *pif,
                                 NET_DEV_LINK_ETHER *plink_state,
                                 NET_ERR            *perr);
```

Note that since every PHY driver's **LinkStateGet()** function is accessed only by function pointer via the PHY driver's API structure, it doesn't need to be globally available and should therefore be declared as '**static**'.

ARGUMENTS

pif   Pointer to the interface to get a PHY's current link state.

plink_state Pointer to a link state structure to return link state information. The **NET_DEV_LINK_ETHER** structure contains two fields for link speed and duplex. Link speed is returned via **plink_state->Spd** :

NET_PHY_SPD_0

NET_PHY_SPD_10

NET_PHY_SPD_100

And link duplex is returned via **plink_state->Duplex** :

NET_PHY_DUPLEX_UNKNOWN

NET_PHY_DUPLEX_HALF

NET_PHY_DUPLEX_FULL

NET_PHY_SPD_0 and NET_PHY_DUPLEX_UNKNOWN represent an unlinked or unknown link state if an error occurs.

perr   Pointer to variable that will receive the return error code from this function.

RETURNED VALUES

None.

REQUIRED CONFIGURATION

None.

NOTES/WARNINGS

The generic PHY driver does not return a link state. Instead, in order to avoid access to extended registers which are PHY specific, the driver attempts to determine link state by analyzing the PHY and PHY partner capabilities. The best combination of auto-negotiated link state is selected as the current link state.

A-2-4 NetPhy_LinkStateSet()

The Ethernet PHY's `LinkStateSet()` function determines the current Ethernet link state. Results are passed back to the caller within a `NET_DEV_LINK_ETHER` structure which contains fields for link speed and duplex. This function is called periodically by µC/TCP-IP.

FILES

Every physical layer driver's `net_phy.c`

PROTOTYPE

```
static void NetPhy_LinkStateSet (NET_IF               *pif,
                                 NET_DEV_LINK_ETHER *plink_state,
                                 NET_ERR              *perr);
```

Note that since every PHY driver's `LinkStateSet()` function is accessed only by function pointer via the PHY driver's API structure, it doesn't need to be globally available and should therefore be declared as '**static**'.

ARGUMENTS

pif   Pointer to the interface to set a PHY's current link state.

plink_state Pointer to a link state structure with link state information to configure. The `NET_DEV_LINK_ETHER` structure contains two fields for link speed and duplex. Link speed is set via `plink_state->Spd` :

NET_PHY_SPD_10

NET_PHY_SPD_100

And link duplex is set via `plink_state->Duplex` :

NET_PHY_DUPLEX_HALF

NET_PHY_DUPLEX_FULL

perr   Pointer to variable that will receive the return error code from this function.

RETURNED VALUE

None.

REQUIRED CONFIGURATION

None.

NOTES/WARNINGS

None.

A-2-5 NetPhy_ISR_Handler()

An Ethernet PHY's **ISR_Handler( )** function is used to handle a PHY's interrupts. See section 16-4-7 "NetPhy_ISR_Handler()" on page 384 for more details on how to handle PHY interrupts. µC/TCP-IP does not require PHY drivers to enable or handle PHY interrupts. The generic PHY drivers does not even define a PHY interrupt handler function but instead handles all events by either periodic or event-triggered calls to other PHY API functions.

FILES

Every physical layer driver's **net_phy.c**

PROTOTYPE

```
static void NetPhy_ISR_Handler (NET_IF *pif);
```

Note that since every PHY driver's **ISR_Handler( )** function is accessed only by function pointer via the PHY driver's API structure, it doesn't need to be globally available and should therefore be declared as '**static**'.

ARGUMENTS

pif   Pointer to the interface to handle PHY interrupts.

RETURNED VALUE

None.

REQUIRED CONFIGURATION

None.

NOTES/WARNINGS

None.

A-3 DEVICE DRIVER BSP FUNCTIONS

A-3-1 NetDev_CfgClk()

This function is called by a device driver's `NetDev_Init()` to configure a specific network device's clocks on a specific interface.

FILES

net_bsp.c

PROTOTYPE

```
static void NetDev_CfgClk (NET_IF  *pif,
                           NET_ERR *perr);
```

Note: since `NetDev_CfgClk()` is accessed only by function pointer via a BSP interface structure, it doesn't need to be globally available and should therefore be declared as '**static**'.

ARGUMENTS

pif   Pointer to specific interface to configure device's clocks.

perr   Pointer to variable that will receive the return error code from this function:

        NET_DEV_ERR_NONE

        NET_DEV_ERR_FAULT

This is *not* an exclusive list of return errors and specific network device's or device BSP functions may return any other specific errors as required.

RETURNED VALUE

None.

REQUIRED CONFIGURATION

None.

NOTES / WARNINGS

Each network device's `NetDev_CfgClk()` should configure and enable all required clocks for the network device. For example, on some devices it may be necessary to enable clock gating for an embedded Ethernet MAC as well as various GPIO modules in order to configure Ethernet Phy pins for (R)MII mode and interrupts.

Since each network device requires a unique `NetDev_CfgClk()`, it is recommended that each device's `NetDev_CfgClk()` function be named using the following convention:

`NetDev_[Device]CfgClk[Number]()`

`[Device]`   Network device name or type, e.g. MACB (optional if the development board does not support multiple devices)

`[Number]`   Network device number for each specific instance of device (optional if the development board does not support multiple instances of the specific device)

For example, the `NetDev_CfgClk()` function for the #2 MACB Ethernet controller on an Atmel AT91SAM9263-EK should be named `NetDev_MACB_CfgClk2()`, or `NetDev_MACB_CfgClk_2()` with additional underscore optional.

See also Chapter 15, "Network Board Support Package" on page 347.

A-3-2 NetDev_CfgGPIO()

This function is called by a device driver's **NetDev_Init()** to configure a specific network device's general-purpose input/ouput (GPIO) on a specific interface.

FILES

net_bsp.c

PROTOTYPE

```
static void NetDev_CfgGPIO (NET_IF  *pif,
                            NET_ERR *perr);
```

Note that since **NetDev_CfgGPIO()** is accessed only by function pointer via a BSP interface structure, it doesn't need to be globally available and should therefore be declared as 'static'.

ARGUMENTS

pif   Pointer to specific interface to configure device's GPIO.

perr   Pointer to variable that will receive the return error code from this function:

        NET_DEV_ERR_NONE

        NET_DEV_ERR_FAULT

This is *not* an exclusive list of return errors and specific network device's or device BSP functions may return any other specific errors as required.

RETURNED VALUE

None.

REQUIRED CONFIGURATION

None.

569

NOTES / WARNINGS

Each network device's **NetDev_CfgGPIO()** should configure all required GPIO pins for the network device. For Ethernet devices, this function is usually necessary to configure the (R)MII bus pins, depending on whether you have configured an Ethernet interface to operate in the RMII or MII mode, and optionally the Ethernet Phy interrupt pin.

Since each network device requires a unique **NetDev_CfgGPIO()**, it is recommended that each device's **NetDev_CfgGPIO()** function be named using the following convention:

NetDev_[Device]CfgGPIO[Number]()

[Device]   Network device name or type, e.g. MACB (optional if the development board does not support multiple devices)

[Number]   Network device number for each specific instance of device (optional if the development board does not support multiple instances of the specific device)

For example, the **NetDev_CfgGPIO()** function for the #2 MACB Ethernet controller on an Atmel AT91SAM9263-EK should be named **NetDev_MACB_CfgGPIO2()**, or NetDev_MACB_CfgGPIO_2() with additional underscore optional.

See also Chapter 15, "Network Board Support Package" on page 347.

A-3-3 NetDev_CfgIntCtrl()

This function is called by a device driver's **NetDev_Init()** to configure a specific network device's interrupts and/or interrupt controller on a specific interface.

FILES

net_bsp.c

PROTOTYPE

```
static void NetDev_CfgIntCtrl (NET_IF   *pif,
                               NET_ERR  *perr);
```

Note that since **NetDev_CfgIntCtrl()** is accessed only by function pointer via a BSP interface structure, it doesn't need to be globally available and should therefore be declared as '**static**'.

ARGUMENTS

pif   Pointer to specific interface to configure device's interrupts.

perr   Pointer to variable that will receive the return error code from this function:

        NET_DEV_ERR_NONE

        NET_DEV_ERR_FAULT

This is *not* an exclusive list of return errors and specific network device's or device BSP functions may return any other specific errors as required.

RETURNED VALUE

None.

REQUIRED CONFIGURATION

None.

NOTES / WARNINGS

Each network device's **NetDev_CfgIntCtrl()** should configure and enable all required interrupt sources for the network device. This usually means configuring the interrupt vector address of each corresponding network device BSP interrupt service routine (ISR) handler and enabling its corresponding interrupt source. Thus, for most **NetDev_CfgIntCtrl()**, the following actions *should* be performed:

1   Configure/store each device's network interface number to be available for all necessary **NetDev_ISR_Handler()** functions (see section A-3-5 on page 577). Even though devices are added dynamically, the device's interface number must be saved in order for each device's ISR handlers to call **NetIF_ISR_Handler()** with the device's network interface number.

Since each network device maps to a unique network interface number, it is recommended that each instance of network devices' interface numbers be named using the following convention:

<Board><Device>[Number]_IF_Nbr

<Board>   Development board name

<Device>   Network device name (or type)

[Number]   Network device number for each specific instance of device (optional if the development board does not support multiple instances of the specific device)

For example, the network device interface number variable for the #2 MACB Ethernet controller on an Atmel AT91SAM9263-EK should be named **AT91SAM9263-EK_MACB_2_IF_Nbr**.

Network device interface number variables *should* be initialized to **NET_IF_NBR_NONE** at system initialization prior to being configured by their respective devices.

2 Configure each of the device's interrupts on either an external or CPU's integrated interrupt controller. However, vectored interrupt controllers may not require the explicit configuration and enabling of higher-level interrupt controller sources. In this case, the application developer may need to configure the system's interrupt vector table with the name of the ISR handler functions declared in **net_bsp.c**.

NetDev_CfgIntCtrl() should only enable each devices' interrupt sources but *not* the local device-level interrupts themselves, which are enabled by the device driver only after the device has been fully configured and started.

Since each network device requires a unique **NetDev_CfgIntCtrl()**, it is recommended that each device's **NetDev_CfgIntCtrl()** function be named using the following convention:

NetDev_[Device]CfgIntCtrl[Number]()

[Device] Network device name or type, e.g. MACB (optional if the development board does not support multiple devices)

[Number] Network device number for each specific instance of device (optional if the development board does not support multiple instances of the specific device)

For example, the **NetDev_CfgIntCtrl()** function for the #2 MACB Ethernet controller on an Atmel AT91SAM9263-EK should be named **NetDev_MACB_CfgIntCtrl2()**, or **NetDev_MACB_CfgIntCtrl_2()** with additional underscore optional.

See also Chapter 15, "Network Board Support Package" on page 347.

EXAMPLES

```
static  void  NetDev_MACB_CfgIntCtrl (NET_IF   *pif,
                                      NET_ERR  *perr)
{
                            /* Configure AT91SAM9263-EK MACB #2's specific IF number.    */
   AT91SAM9263-EK_MACB_2_IF_Nbr = pif->Nbr;
                            /* Configure AT91SAM9263-EK MACB #2's interrupts:            */
   BSP_IntVectSet(BSP_INT, &NetDev_MACB_ISR_Handler_2);/* Configure interrupt vector.    */
   BSP_IntEn(BSP_INT);                                  /* Enable    interrupts.         */


   *perr = NET_DEV_ERR_NONE;
}


static  void  NetDev_MACB_CfgIntCtrlRx_2 (NET_IF   *pif,
                                          NET_ERR  *perr)
{
                            /* Configure AT91SAM9263-EK MACB #2's specific IF number.    */
   AT91SAM9263-EK_MACB_2_IF_Nbr = pif->Nbr;
                            /* Configure AT91SAM9263-EK MACB #2's receive interrupt:     */
   BSP_IntVectSet(BSP_INT_RX, &NetDev_MACB_ISR_HandlerRx_2);  /* Configure interrupt vector. */
   BSP_IntEn(BSP_INT_RX);                               /* Enable    interrupt.          */


   *perr = NET_DEV_ERR_NONE;
}
```

A-3-4 NetDev_ClkGetFreq()

This function is called by a device driver's **NetDev_Init( )** to return a specific network device's clock frequency for a specific interface.

FILES

net_bsp.c

PROTOTYPE

```
static CPU_INT32U NetDev_ClkGetFreq (NET_IF  *pif,
                                     NET_ERR *perr);
```

Note that since **NetDev_ClkFreqGet( )** is accessed only by function pointer via a BSP interface structure, it doesn't need to be globally available and should therefore be declared as '**static**'.

ARGUMENTS

pif   Pointer to specific interface to return device's clock frequency.

perr   Pointer to variable that will receive the return error code from this function:

       NET_DEV_ERR_NONE

       NET_DEV_ERR_FAULT

This is *not* an exclusive list of return errors and specific network device's or device BSP functions may return any other specific errors as required.

RETURNED VALUE

Network device's clock frequency (in Hz).

REQUIRED CONFIGURATION

None.

NOTES / WARNINGS

Each network device's **NetDev_ClkFreqGet()** should return the device's clock frequency (in Hz). For Ethernet devices, this is usually the clock frequency of the device's (R)MII bus. The device driver's **NetDev_Init()** uses the returned clock frequency to configure an appropriate bus divider to ensure that the (R)MII bus logic operates within an allowable range. In general, the device driver should not configure the divider such that the (R)MII bus operates faster than 2.5MHz.

Since each network device requires a unique **NetDev_ClkFreqGet()**, it is recommended that each device's **NetDev_ClkFreqGet()** function be named using the following convention:

NetDev_[Device]ClkGetFreq[Number]()

[Device]   Network device name or type, e.g. MACB (optional if the development board does not support multiple devices)

[Number]   Network device number for each specific instance of device (optional if the development board does not support multiple instances of the specific device)

For example, the **NetDev_ClkFreqGet()** function for the #2 MACB Ethernet controller on an Atmel AT91SAM9263-EK should be named **NetDev_MACB_ClkGetFreq2()**, or **NetDev_MACB_ClkGetFreq_2()** with additional underscore optional.

See also Chapter 15, "Network Board Support Package" on page 347.

A-3-5 NetDev_ISR_Handler()

Handle a network device's interrupts on a specific interface.

FILES

net_bsp.c

PROTOTYPE

```
static void NetDev_ISR_Handler (void);
```

Note that since **NetDev_ISR_Handler()** is accessed only by function pointer usually via an interrupt vector table, it doesn't need to be globally available and should therefore be declared as '**static**'.

ARGUMENTS

None.

RETURNED VALUE

None.

REQUIRED CONFIGURATION

None.

NOTES / WARNINGS

Each network device's interrupt, or set of device interrupts, must be handled by a unique BSP-level interrupt service routine (ISR) handler, **NetDev_ISR_Handler()**, which maps each specific device interrupt to its corresponding network interface ISR handler, **NetIF_ISR_Handler()**. For some CPUs this may be a first- or second-level interrupt handler. Generally, the application must configure the interrupt controller to call every network device's unique **NetDev_ISR_Handler()** when the device's interrupt occurs (see section A-3-3 on page 571). Every unique **NetDev_ISR_Handler()** *must* then perform the following actions:

1   Call **NetIF_ISR_Handler()** with the device's unique network interface number and appropriate interrupt type. The device's network interface number should be available after configuration in the device's **NetDev_CfgIntCtrl()** function (see section A-3-3 "NetDev_CfgIntCtrl()" on page 571). **NetIF_ISR_Handler()** in turn calls the appropriate device driver's interrupt handler.

In most cases, each device requires only a single **NetDev_ISR_Handler()** which calls **NetIF_ISR_Handler()** with interrupt type code **NET_DEV_ISR_TYPE_UNKNOWN**. This is possible when the device's driver can determine the device's interrupt type to via internal device registers or the interrupt controller. However, some devices cannot generically determine the interrupt type when an interrupt occurs and may therefore require multiple, unique **NetDev_ISR_Handler()**'s each of which calls **NetIF_ISR_Handler()** with the appropriate interrupt type code.

Ethernet Physical layer (Phy) interrupts should call **NetIF_ISR_Handler()** with interrupt type code **NET_DEV_ISR_TYPE_PHY**.

See also section C-9-12 "NetIF_ISR_Handler()" on page 751.

2   Clear the device's interrupt source, possibly via an external or CPU-integrated interrupt controller source.

Since each network device requires a unique **NetDev_ISR_Handler()** for each device interrupt, it is recommended that each device's **NetDev_ISR_Handler()** function be named using the following convention:

NetDev_[Device]ISR_Handler[Type][Number]()

[Device]   Network device name or type, e.g., MACB (optional if the development board does not support multiple devices)

[Type]   Network device interrupt type, e.g., receive interrupt (optional if interrupt type is generic or unknown)

[Number]   Network device number for each specific instance of device (optional if the development board does not support multiple instances of the specific device)

For example, the receive ISR handler for the #2 MACB Ethernet controller on an Atmel AT91SAM9263-EK should be named **NetDev_MACB_ISR_HandlerRx2()**.

See also Chapter 15, "Network Board Support Package" on page 347.

```
static void NetDev_MACB_ISR_Handler_2 (void)
{
    NET_ERR  err;

    NetIF_ISR_Handler(AT91SAM9263-EK_MACB_2_IF_Nbr, NET_DEV_ISR_TYPE_UNKNOWN, &err);
    /* Clear external or CPU's integrated interrupt controller. */
}


static void NetDev_MACB_ISR_HandlerRx_2 (void)
{
    NET_ERR  err;

    NetIF_ISR_Handler(AT91SAM9263-EK_MACB_2_IF_Nbr, NET_DEV_ISR_TYPE_RX, &err);
    /* Clear external or CPU's integrated interrupt controller. */
}
```

μC/TCP-IP Wireless Device Driver APIs

This appendix provides a reference to the μC/TCP-IP Device Driver API. Each user-accessible service is presented in alphabetical order. The following information is provided for each of the services:

- A brief description

- The function prototype

- The filename of the source code

- A description of the arguments passed to the function

- A description of the returned value(s)

- Specific notes and warnings on the use of the service

B-1 DEVICE DRIVER FUNCTIONS FOR WIRELESS MODULE

B-1-1 NetDev_Init()

The first function within the wireless API is the device driver initialization/**Init()** function. This function is called by **NetIF_Add()** exactly once for each specific network device added by the application. If multiple instances of the same network device are present on the development board, then this function is called for each instance of the device. However, applications should not try to add the same specific device more than once. If a network device fails to initialize, we recommend debugging to find and correct the cause of failure.

Note: This function relies heavily on the implementation of several network device board support package (BSP) functions. See Chapter 15, "Network Board Support Package" on page 347 and Appendix B, "Device Driver BSP Functions" on page 619 for more information on network device BSP functions.

FILES

Every device driver's **net_dev.c**

PROTOTYPE

```
static void NetDev_Init (NET_IF  *p_if,
                         NET_ERR *p_err);
```

Note that since every device driver's **Init()** function is accessed only by function pointer via the device driver's API structure, it doesn't need to be globally available and should therefore be declared as '**static**'.

ARGUMENTS

p_if   Pointer to the interface to initialize a network device.

p_err   Pointer to variable that will receive the return error code from this function.

RETURNED VALUE

None.

REQUIRED CONFIGURATION

None.

NOTES / WARNINGS

The `Init()` function generally performs the following operations, however, depending on the device being initialized, functionality may need to be added or removed:

1   Validate all wireless configuration values.

2   Configure all necessary I/O pins for the wireless device such as power enable or reset pin. This is generally performed via the network device's BSP function pointer, `CfgGPIO()`, implemented in **net_bsp.c** (see section A-3-2 on page 569).

3   Initialize SPI controller for writing and reading from the wireless module.

4   Configure the host interrupt controller for receive and transmit complete interrupts. Additional interrupt services may be initialized depending on the device and driver requirements. This is generally performed via the network device's BSP function pointer, `CfgIntCtrl()`, implemented in **net_bsp.c** (see section B-3-4 on page 625).

5   Allocate memory for all necessary driver buffers that will be reuse only by the driver such as a read buffer to validate the command sent. This is performed via calls to µC/LIB's memory module.

6   Disable the transmitted and receiver (should already be disabled).

7   Set **p_err** to **NET_DEV_ERR_NONE** if initialization proceeded as expected. Otherwise, set **p_err** to an appropriate network device error code.

B-1-2 NetDev_Start()

The second function is the device driver **Start()** function. This function is called once each time an interface is started.

FILES

Every device driver's **net_dev.c**

PROTOTYPE

```
static void NetDev_Start (NET_IF  *p_if,
                          NET_ERR *p_err);
```

Note that since every device driver's **Start()** function is accessed only by function pointer via the device driver's API structure, it doesn't need to be globally available and should therefore be declared as '**static**'.

ARGUMENTS

p_if   Pointer to the interface to start a network device.

p_err   Pointer to variable that will receive the return error code from this function.

RETURNED VALUE

None.

REQUIRED CONFIGURATION

None.

NOTES / WARNINGS

The **Start()** function performs the following items:

1 Configure the transmit ready semaphore count via a call to **NetOS_Dev_CfgTxRdySignal()**. This function call is optional and is generally performed when the hardware device supports the queuing of multiple transmit frames. By default, the count is initialized to one.

2   Send command to start and initialize wireless device. If a specific firmware must be loaded on the device, the firmware should be validated and updated if necessary.

3   Initialize the device MAC address if applicable. For Ethernet devices, this step is mandatory. The MAC address data may come from one of three sources and should be set using the following priority scheme:

a. Configure the MAC address using the string found within the device configuration structure. This is a form of static MAC address configuration and may be performed by calling `NetASCII_Str_to_MAC()` and `NetIF_AddrHW_SetHandler()`. If the device configuration string has been left empty, or is specified as all 0's, an error will be returned and the next method should be attempted.

b. Check if the application developer has called `NetIF_AddrHW_Set()` by making a call to `NetIF_AddrHW_GetHandler()` and `NetIF_AddrHW_IsValidHandler()` in order to check if the specified MAC address is valid. This method may be used as a static method for configuring the MAC address during run-time, or a dynamic method should a pre-programmed external memory device exist. If the acquired MAC address does not pass the check function, then:

c. Call `NetIF_AddrHW_SetHandler()` using the data found within the MAC individual address registers. If an auto-loading EEPROM is attached to the MAC, the registers will contain valid data. If not, then a configuration error has occurred. This method is often used with a production process where the MAC supports the automatic loading of individual address registers from a serial EEPROM. When using this method, the developer should specify an empty string for the MAC address within the device configuration and refrain from calling `NetIF_AddrHW_Set()` from within the application.

4   Initialize additional MAC registers required by the MAC for proper operation.

5   Clear all interrupt flags.

6   Locally enable interrupts on the hardware device. The host interrupt controller should have already been configured within the device driver `Init()` function.

7   Enable the receiver and transmitter.

8   Set `p_err` equal to `NET_DEV_ERR_NONE` if no errors have occurred. Otherwise, set `p_err` to an appropriate network device error code.

B-1-3 NetDev_Stop()

The next function within the device API structure is the device **Stop()** function. This function is called once each time an interface is stopped.

FILES

Every device driver's **net_dev.c**

PROTOTYPE

```
static void NetDev_Stop (NET_IF  *p_if,
                         NET_ERR *p_err);
```

Note that since every device driver's **Stop()** function is accessed only by function pointer via the device driver's API structure, it doesn't need to be globally available and should therefore be declared as '**static**'.

ARGUMENTS

p_if   Pointer to the interface to start a network device.

p_err   Pointer to variable that will receive the return error code from this function.

RETURNED VALUE

None.

REQUIRED CONFIGURATION

None.

NOTES / WARNINGS

The **Stop( )** function must perform the following operations:

1   Disable the receiver and transmitter.

2   Disable all local MAC interrupt sources.

3   Clear all local MAC interrupt status flags.

4   Power down the wireless device.

5   Set **p_err** to **NET_DEV_ERR_NONE** if no error occurs. Otherwise, set **p_err** to an appropriate network device error code.

B-1-4 NetDev_Rx()

The receive/**Rx()** function is called by µC/TCP-IP's Receive task after the Interrupt Service Routine handler has signaled to the Receive task that a receive event has occurred. The Receive function requires that the device driver return a pointer to the data area containing the received data and return the size of the received frame via pointer.

FILES

Every device driver's **net_dev.c**

PROTOTYPE

```
static void NetDev_Rx (NET_IF      *p_if,
                       CPU_INT08U **p_data,
                       CPU_INT16U  *p_size,
                       NET_ERR     *p_err);
```

Note that since every device driver's **Rx()** function is accessed only by function pointer via the device driver's API structure, it doesn't need to be globally available and should therefore be declared as '**static**'.

ARGUMENTS

   p_if Pointer to the interface to receive data from a network device.

   p_data Pointer to return the address of the received data.

   p_size Pointer to return the size of the received data.

   p_err Pointer to variable that will receive the return error code from this function.

RETURNED VALUE

None.

REQUIRED CONFIGURATION

None.

NOTES / WARNINGS

The receive function should perform the following actions:

1 For SPI wireless device, get the access to the SPI bus by performing the following operation:

   a. Acquire the SPI lock by calling **p_dev_bsp->SPI_Lock()**.

   b. Enable the chip select by calling **p_dev_bsp->SPI_ChipSelEn()**.

   c. Configure the SPI controller for the wireless device by calling **p_dev_bsp->SPI_SetCfg()**.

2 Check for receive errors if applicable. If an error should occur during reception, the driver should set ***size** to 0 and ***p_data** to **(CPU_INT08U *)0** and return. Additional steps may be necessary depending on the device being serviced.

3 For wireless devices, get the size of the received frame and subtract 4 bytes for the CRC. It is always recommended that the frame size is checked to ensure that it is greater than 4 bytes before performing the subtraction to ensure that an underflow does not occur. Set ***size** equal to the adjusted frame size.

4 Get a new data buffer area by calling **NetBuf_GetDataPtr()**. If memory is not available, an error will be returned and the device driver should set ***size** to 0 and ***p_data** to **(CPU_INT08U *)0**.

5 If an error does not occur while getting a new data area, the function should perform the following operations:

   a. Set the frame type of the data received (**NET_IF_WIFI_MGMT_FRAME** or **NET_IF_WIFI_DATA_PKT**) at the beginning of the network buffer.

   b. The data stored within the device should be transferred to the address of the data section (after the frame type) of the network buffer by calling **p_dev_bsp->SPI_WrRd()** and by using a global buffer to write data and set ***p_data** equal to the address of the obtained data area.

6   Sidable the device chip select by calling **p_dev_bsp->SPI_ChipSelDis()** and unlock the SPI bus access by calling **p_dev_bsp->SPI_Unlock()**.

7   Set **p_err** to **NET_DEV_ERR_NONE** and return from the receive function. Otherwise, set **p_err** to an appropriate network device error code.

B-1-5 NetDev_Tx()

The next function in the device API structure is the transmit/**Tx( )** function.

FILES

Every device driver's **net_dev.c**

PROTOTYPE

```
static void NetDev_Tx (NET_IF     *p_if,
                       CPU_INT08U *p_data,
                       CPU_INT16U  size,
                       NET_ERR    *p_err);
```

Note that since every device driver's **Tx( )** function is accessed only by function pointer via the device driver's API structure, it doesn't need to be globally available and should therefore be declared as '**static**'.

ARGUMENTS

p_if   Pointer to the interface to start a network device.

p_data   Pointer to address of the data to transmit.

size   Size of the data to transmit.

p_err   Pointer to variable that will receive the return error code from this function.

RETURNED VALUE

None.

REQUIRED CONFIGURATION

None.

NOTES / WARNINGS

The transmit function should perform the following actions:

1   For SPI wireless device, get the access to the SPI bus by performing the following operation:

   a. Acquire the SPI lock by calling **p_dev_bsp->SPI_Lock()**.

   b. Enable the chip select by calling **p_dev_bsp->SPI_ChipSelEn()**.

   c. Configure the SPI controller for the wireless device by calling **p_dev_bsp->SPI_SetCfg()**.

2   Write data to the device by calling **p_dev_bsp->SPI_WrRd()** and by using the network buffer passed as argument and by using a global buffer to read data.

3   The driver should then take all necessary steps to initiate transmission of the data.

4   Set **perr** to **NET_DEV_ERR_NONE** and return from the transmit function.

B-1-6 NetDev_AddrMulticastAdd()

The next API function is the **AddrMulticastAdd()** function used to configure a device with an (IP-to-Ethernet) multicast hardware address.

FILES

Every device driver's **net_dev.c**

PROTOTYPE

```
static void NetDev_AddrMulticastAdd (NET_IF     *p_if,
                                     CPU_INT08U *p_addr_hw,
                                     CPU_INT08U  addr_hw_len,
                                     NET_ERR    *p_err);
```

Note that since every device driver's **AddrMulticastAdd()** function is accessed only by function pointer via the device driver's API structure, it doesn't need to be globally available and should therefore be declared as '**static**'.

ARGUMENTS

p_if   Pointer to the interface to add/configure a multicast address.

p_addr_hw   Pointer to multicast hardware address to add.

addr_hw_len Length of multicast hardware address.

p_err   Pointer to variable that will receive the return error code from this function.

RETURNED VALUE

None.

REQUIRED CONFIGURATION

Necessary only if **NET_IP_CFG_MULTICAST_SEL** is configured for transmit and receive multicasting (see section D-9-2 on page 971).

NOTES / WARNINGS

Since many network controllers' documentation fail to properly indicate how to add/configure an MAC device with a multicast address, the following methodology is recommended for determining and testing the correct multicast hash bit algorithm.

1   Configure a packet capture program or multicast application to broadcast a multicast packet with destination address of 01:00:5E:00:00:01. This MAC address corresponds to the multicast group IP address of 224.0.0.1 which will be converted to a MAC address by higher layers and passed to this function.

2   Set a break point in the receive ISR handler and transmit one send packet to the target. The break point should *not* be reached as the result of the transmitted packet. Use caution to ensure that other network traffic is not the source of the interrupt when the button is pressed. Sometimes asynchronous network events happen very close in time and the end result can be deceiving. Ideally, these tests should be performed on an isolated network but disconnect as many other hosts from the network as possible.

3   Use the debugger to stop the application and program the MAC multicast hash register low bits to 0xFFFFFFFF. Go to step 2. Repeat for the hash bit high register if necessary. The goal is to bracket off which bit in either the high or low hash bit register causes the device to be interrupted when the broadcast frame is received by the target. Once the correct bit is known, the hash algorithm can be easily written and tested.

4   The following hash bit algorithm code below could be adjusted per the network controller's documentation in order to get the hash from the correct subset of CRC bits. Most of the code is similar between various devices and is thus reusable. The hash algorithm is the exlusive **OR** of every 6th bit of the destination address:

```
hash[5] = da[5] ^ da[11] ^ da[17] ^ da[23] ^ da[29] ^ da[35] ^ da[41] ^ da[47]
hash[4] = da[4] ^ da[10] ^ da[16] ^ da[22] ^ da[28] ^ da[34] ^ da[40] ^ da[46]
hash[3] = da[3] ^ da[09] ^ da[15] ^ da[21] ^ da[27] ^ da[33] ^ da[39] ^ da[45]
hash[2] = da[2] ^ da[08] ^ da[14] ^ da[20] ^ da[26] ^ da[32] ^ da[38] ^ da[44]
hash[1] = da[1] ^ da[07] ^ da[13] ^ da[19] ^ da[25] ^ da[31] ^ da[37] ^ da[43]
hash[0] = da[0] ^ da[06] ^ da[12] ^ da[18] ^ da[24] ^ da[30] ^ da[36] ^ da[42]
```

Where **da0** represents the least significant bit of the first byte of the destination address received and where **da47** represents the most significant bit of the last byte of the destination address received.

```
                                        /* ---------- CALCULATE HASH CODE ---------- */
hash = 0;
for (i = 0; i < 6; i++) {               /* For each row in the bit hash table:       */
    bit_val = 0;                        /* Clear initial xor value for each row.      */
    for (j = 0; j < 8; j++) {           /* For each bit in each octet:                */
        bit_nbr   = (j * 6) + i;        /* Determine which bit in stream, 0-47.       */
        octet_nbr = bit_nbr / 8;        /* Determine which octet bit belongs to.      */
        octet     = paddr_hw[octet_nbr];  /* Get octet value.                         */
        bit       = octet & (1 << (bit_nbr % 8));  /* Check if octet's bit is set.    */
        bit_val   ^= (bit > 0) ? 1 : 0;   /* Calculate table row's XOR hash value.    */
    }
    hash |= (bit_val << i);             /* Add row's XOR hash value to final hash.    */
}

                                        /* ---- ADD MULTICAST ADDRESS TO DEVICE ---- */
reg_sel = (hash >> 5) & 0x01;           /* Determine hash register    to configure. */
reg_bit = (hash >> 0) & 0x1F;           /* Determine hash register bit to configure. */
                                        /* (Substitute '0x01'/'0x1F' with device's ..*/
                                        /* .. actual hash register bit masks/shifts.)*/

  paddr_hash_ctrs = &pdev_data->MulticastAddrHashBitCtr[hash];
(*paddr_hash_ctrs)++;                   /* Increment hash bit reference counter.     */

if (reg_sel == 0) {                     /* Set multicast hash register bit.          */
    pdev->MCAST_REG_LO |= (1 << reg_bit);  /* (Substitute 'MCAST_REG_LO/HI' with ..  */
} else {                                /* .. device's actual multicast registers.)  */
    pdev->MCAST_REG_HI |= (1 << reg_bit);
}
                                        /* ---------- CALCULATE HASH CODE ---------- */
                                        /* Calculate CRC.                            */
crc = NetUtil_32BitCRC_Calc((CPU_INT08U *)paddr_hw,
                            (CPU_INT32U  ) addr_hw_len,
                            (NET_ERR    *)perr);
```

Listing B-1 **Example device multicast address configuration using CRC hash code algorithm**

Alternatively, you may be able to compute the CRC hash with a call to **NetUtil_32BitCRC_CalcCpl()** followed by an optional call to **NetUtil_32BitReflect()**, with four possible combinations:

a. CRC without complement and without reflection

b. CRC without complement and with reflection

c. CRC with complement and without reflection

d. CRC with complement and with reflection

```
if (*perr != NET_UTIL_ERR_NONE) {
    return;
}
                                        /* ---- ADD MULTICAST ADDRESS TO DEVICE ---- */
crc     = NetUtil_32BitReflect(crc);    /* Optionally, complement CRC.               */
hash    = (crc >> 23u) & 0x3F;          /* Determine hash register     to configure. */
reg_bit = (hash % 32u);                 /* Determine hash register bit to configure. */
                                        /* (Substitute '23u'/'0x3F' with device's .. */
                                        /* .. actual hash register bit masks/shifts.)*/


  paddr_hash_ctrs = &pdev_data->MulticastAddrHashBitCtr[hash];
(*paddr_hash_ctrs)++;                   /* Increment hash bit reference counter.    */

if (hash <= 31u) {                      /* Set multicast hash register bit.         */
    pdev->MCAST_REG_LO |= (1 << reg_bit);   /* (Substitute 'MCAST_REG_LO/HI' with ..   */
} else {                                /* .. device's actual multicast registers.) */
    pdev->MCAST_REG_HI |= (1 << reg_bit);
}
```

Listing B-2 **Example device multicast address configuration using CRC and reflection functions**

Unfortunately, the product documentation will *not* likely tell you which combination of complement and reflection is necessary in order to properly compute the hash value. Most likely, the documentation will simply state 'Standard Ethernet CRC' which when compared to other documents, means any of the four combinations above; different than the actual frame CRC.

Fortunately, if the code is written to perform both the complement and reflection, then the debugger may be used to repeat the code block over and over skipping either the line that performs the complement or the function call to the reflection until the output hash bit is computed correctly.

5   Update the device driver's **AddrMulticastAdd()** function to calculate and configure the correct CRC.

6   Test the device driver's **AddrMulticastAdd()** function by ensuring that the group address 224.0.0.1, when joined from the application (see section C-11-1 on page 771), correctly configures the device to receive multicast packets destined to the 224.0.0.1 address. Then broadcast the 224.0.0.1 (see step 1) to test if the device receives the multicast packet.

B-1-7 NetDev_AddrMulticastRemove()

The next API function is the **AddrMulticastRemove()** function used to remove an (IP-to-Ethernet) multicast hardware address from a device.

FILES

Every device driver's **net_dev.c**

PROTOTYPE

```
static void NetDev_AddrMulticastRemove (NET_IF      *p_if,
                                        CPU_INT08U *p_addr_hw,
                                        CPU_INT08U  addr_hw_len,
                                        NET_ERR     *p_err);
```

Note that since every device driver's **AddrMulticastRemove()** function is accessed only by function pointer via the device driver's API structure, it doesn't need to be globally available and should therefore be declared as '**static**'.

ARGUMENTS

p_if   Pointer to the interface to remove a multicast address.

p_addr_hw   Pointer to multicast hardware address to remove.

addr_hw_len   Length of multicast hardware address.

p_err   Pointer to variable that will receive the return error code from this function.

RETURNED VALUE

None.

REQUIRED CONFIGURATION

Necessary only if **NET_IP_CFG_MULTICAST_SEL** is configured for transmit and receive multicasting (see section D-9-2 on page 971).

NOTES / WARNINGS

Use same exact code as in **NetDev_AddrMulticastAdd()** to calculate the device's CRC hash (see section B-1-6 on page 593), but remove a multicast address by decrementing the device's hash bit reference counters and clearing the appropriate bits in the device's multicast registers.

```
                                         /* ---------- CALCULATE HASH CODE ---------- */
    /* Use NetDev_AddrMulticastAdd()'s algorithm to calculate CRC hash.              */
                                         /* - REMOVE MULTICAST ADDRESS FROM DEVICE -- */
    paddr_hash_ctrs = &pdev_data->MulticastAddrHashBitCtr[hash];
    if (*paddr_hash_ctrs > 1u) {         /* If multiple multicast addresses hashed, ..*/
       (*paddr_hash_ctrs)--;             /* .. decrement hash bit reference counter ..*/
        *perr = NET_DEV_ERR_NONE;        /* .. but do NOT unconfigure hash register.  */
         return;
    }
    *paddr_hash_ctrs = 0u;               /* Clear hash bit reference counter.         */

    if (hash <= 31u) {                   /* Clear multicast hash register bit.        */
       pdev->MCAST_REG_LO &= ~(1u << reg_bit);  /* (Substitute 'MCAST_REG_LO/HI' with ..   */
    } else {                             /* .. device's actual multicast registers.)  */
       pdev->MCAST_REG_HI &= ~(1u << reg_bit);
    }
```

Listing B-3 **Example device multicast address removal**

B-1-8 NetDev_ISR_Handler()

A device's `ISR_Handler()` function is used to handle each device's interrupts. See section 16-5-5 "NetDev_ISR_Handler()" on page 391 for more details on how to handle each device's interrupts.

FILES

Every device driver's **net_dev.c**

PROTOTYPE

```
static void NetDev_ISR_Handler (NET_IF          *pif,
                                NET_DEV_ISR_TYPE  type);
```

Note that since every device driver's `ISR_Handler()` function is accessed only by function pointer via the device driver's API structure, it doesn't need to be globally available and should therefore be declared as '**static**'.

ARGUMENTS

pif   Pointer to the interface to handle network device interrupts.

type   Device's interrupt type:

           NET_DEV_ISR_TYPE_UNKNOWN

           NET_DEV_ISR_TYPE_RX

           NET_DEV_ISR_TYPE_RX_RUNT

           NET_DEV_ISR_TYPE_RX_OVERRUN

           NET_DEV_ISR_TYPE_TX_RDY

           NET_DEV_ISR_TYPE_TX_COMPLETE

           NET_DEV_ISR_TYPE_TX_COLLISION_LATE

NET_DEV_ISR_TYPE_TX_COLLISION_EXCESS

NET_DEV_ISR_TYPE_JABBER

NET_DEV_ISR_TYPE_BABBLE

NET_DEV_ISR_TYPE_PHY

RETURNED VALUE

None.

REQUIRED CONFIGURATION

None.

NOTES / WARNINGS

Each device's **NetDev_ISR_Handler()** should never return early but check all applicable interrupt sources to see if they are active. This additional checking is necessary because multiple interrupt sources may be set within the interrupt response time and will reduce the number and overhead of handling interrupts.

B-1-9 NetDev_MgmtDemux()

A device's management demultiplex() function is used to demultiplex a management frame to signal the Wireless Manager the response or to implement miscellaneous functionality such as updating the link state when the wireless network is out of the range and the connection is lost.

FILES

Every wireless device driver's **net_dev.c**

PROTOTYPE

```
static void NetDev_MgmtDemux (NET_IF    *p_if,
    void        *p_buf,
    NET_ERR     *p_err);
```

Note that since every device driver's **MgmtDemux()** function is accessed only by function pointer via the device driver's API structure, it doesn't need to be globally available and should therefore be declared as '**static**'.

ARGUMENTS

p_if   Pointer to the interface to handle network device I/O operations.

p_buf   Pointer to the network buffer that contains the management frame.

p_err   Pointer to variable that will receive the return error code from this function.

RETURNED VALUE

None.

REQUIRED CONFIGURATION

None.

NOTES / WARNINGS

1   When a management command has been sent and the Wireless Manager is waiting for the response, the Wireless Manager MUST be signaled by calling `p_mgr_api->Signal()`.

   a. The network buffer MUST be freed by the function if the Wireless Manager is not signaled and no error are returned by calling `NetBuf_Free()`.

B-1-10 NetDev_MgmtExecuteCmd()

A device's execute management command() function is used to implement miscellaneous wireless management functionality such as scanning for available wireless network.

FILES

Every wireless device driver's **net_dev.c**

PROTOTYPE

```
static void NetDev_IO_Ctrl (NET_IF     *p_if,
NET_IF_WIFI_CMD cmf,
NET_WIFI_MGR_CTX *p_ctx,
void *p_cmd_data,
CPU_INT16U cmd_data_len,
CPU_INT08U *p_buf_rtn,
CPU_INT08U buf_rtn_len_max,
NET_ERR    *p_err);
```

Note that since every device driver's **MgmtDemux()** function is accessed only by function pointer via the device driver's API structure, it doesn't need to be globally available and should therefore be declared as '**static**'.

ARGUMENTS

p_if   Pointer to the interface to handle network device I/O operations.

cmd   Management command to execute:

        NET_IF_WIFI_CMD_SCAN

        NET_IF_WIFI_CMD_JOIN

        NET_IF_WIFI_CMD_LEAVE

        NET_IF_IO_CTRL_LINK_STATE_GET

        NET_IF_IO_CTRL_LINK_STATE_GET_INFO

NET_IF_IO_CTRL_LINK_STATE_UPDATE

Others management commands defined by the driver.

p_ctx   Pointer to the Wireless Manager context.

p_cmd_data   Pointer to a buffer that contains data to be used by the driver to execute the command.

cmd_data_len   Command data length.

p_buf_rtn   Pointer to buffer that will receive return data.

buf_rtn_len_max   Return maximum data length.

p_err   Pointer to variable that will receive the return error code from this function.

RETURNED VALUE

None.

REQUIRED CONFIGURATION

None.

NOTES / WARNINGS

(1) The state machine context is used by the Wireless Manager to know what it MUST do after the call such as waiting for a management response.

B-1-11 NetDev_MgmtProcessResp()

A device's process management response() function is used to analyse the response, set the state machine context of the Wireless Manager and fill the return buffer.

FILES

Every wireless device driver's **net_dev.c**

PROTOTYPE

```
static void NetDev_IO_Ctrl (NET_IF      *p_if,
NET_IF_WIFI_CMD cmf,
NET_WIFI_MGR_CTX *p_ctx,
void *p_cmd_data,
CPU_INT16U cmd_data_len,
CPU_INT08U *p_buf_rtn,
CPU_INT08U buf_rtn_len_max,
NET_ERR     *p_err);
```

Note that since every device driver's **MgmtDemux()** function is accessed only by function pointer via the device driver's API structure, it doesn't need to be globally available and should therefore be declared as '**static**'.

ARGUMENTS

p_if   Pointer to the interface to handle network device I/O operations.

cmd   Management command to execute:

        NET_IF_WIFI_CMD_SCAN

        NET_IF_WIFI_CMD_JOIN

        NET_IF_WIFI_CMD_LEAVE

        NET_IF_IO_CTRL_LINK_STATE_GET

        NET_IF_IO_CTRL_LINK_STATE_GET_INFO

NET_IF_IO_CTRL_LINK_STATE_UPDATE

Others management commands defined by the driver.

p_ctx	Pointer to the Wireless Manager context.
p_buf_rxd	Pointer to a network buffer that contains the command response
cmd_data_len	Length of the data response.
p_buf_rtn	Pointer to buffer that will receive return data.
buf_rtn_len_max	Return maximum data length.
p_err	Pointer to variable that will receive the return error code from this function.

RETURNED VALUE

None.

REQUIRED CONFIGURATION

None.

NOTES / WARNINGS

None.

B-2 WIRELESS MANAGER API

B-2-1 NetWiFiMgr_Init()

The first function within the Wireless Manager API is the manager initialization/**Init()** function which is called by the wireless network interface layer.

FILES

Every Wireless Manager layer **net_wifi_mgr.c**

PROTOTYPE

```
static void NetWiFiMgr_Init (NET_IF  *p_if,
NET_ERR *p_err)
```

Note that since every Wireless Manager's **Init()** function is accessed only by function pointer via the Wireless Manager's API structure, it doesn't need to be globally available and should therefore be declared as '**static**'.

ARGUMENTS

pif   Pointer to the interface to initialize a Wireless Manager.

perr   Pointer to variable that will receive the return error code from this function.

RETURNED VALUE

None.

REQUIRED CONFIGURATION

None.

NOTES/WARNINGS

None.

B-2-2 NetWiFiMgr_Start()

The next Wireless Manager function is the **Start()** function. This function is called by the wireless network interface layer when an interface is started.

FILES

Every Wireless Manager layer **net_wifi_mgr.c**

PROTOTYPE

```
static void NetWiFiMgr_Start (NET_IF     *p_if,
                         NET_ERR     *p_err);
```

Note that since every Wireless Manager's **Start()** function is accessed only by function pointer via the Wireless Manager's API structure, it doesn't need to be globally available and should therefore be declared as '**static**'.

ARGUMENTS

p_if   Pointer to the interface to start the Wireless Manager.

perr   Pointer to variable that will receive the return error code from this function.

RETURNED VALUE

None.

REQUIRED CONFIGURATION

None.

NOTES/WARNINGS

None.

B-2-3 NetWiFiMgr_Stop()

The Wireless Manager function **Stop()** function is called by the wireless network interface layer when an interface is stopped.

FILES

Every Wireless Manager layer **net_wifi_mgr.c**

PROTOTYPE

```
static void NetWiFiMgr_Stop (NET_IF      *p_if,
                             NET_ERR     *p_err);
```

Note that since every Wireless Manager's **Stop()** function is accessed only by function pointer via the Wireless Manager's API structure, it doesn't need to be globally available and should therefore be declared as '**static**'.

ARGUMENTS

p_if   Pointer to the interface to stop the Wireless Manager.

perr   Pointer to variable that will receive the return error code from this function.

RETURNED VALUE

None.

REQUIRED CONFIGURATION

None.

NOTES/WARNINGS

None.

B-2-4 NetWiFiMgr_AP_Scan()

The Wireless Manager's **AP_Scan()** function start the scan process. Results are passed back to the caller in a table of **NET_IF_WIFI_AP** structure which contains fields for link network SSID, channel, network type, Security type and signal strength.

FILES

Every Wireless Manager layer **net_wifi_mgr.c**

PROTOTYPE

```
static void NetWiFiMgr_AP_Scan (NET_IF              *p_if,
                                NET_IF_WIFI_AP *p_buf_scan,
CPU_INT16U scna_len_max,
const NET_IF_WIFI_SSID *p_ssid,
NET_IF_WIFI_CH ch,
NET_ERR            *perr);
```

Note that since every Wireless Manager's **AP_Scan()** function is accessed only by function pointer via the Wireless Manager's API structure, it doesn't need to be globally available and should therefore be declared as '**static**'.

ARGUMENTS

p_if   Pointer to the interface to scan with.

p_buf_scan   Pointer to table that will receive the return network found.

scan_len_max Length of the scan buffer (i.e. Number of network that can be found).

p_ssid   Pointer to variable that contains the SSID to find.

ch   The wireless channel to scan:

                  NET_IF_WIFI_CH_ALL

                  NET_IF_WIFI_CH_1

NET_IF_WIFI_CH_2

NET_IF_WIFI_CH_3

NET_IF_WIFI_CH_4

NET_IF_WIFI_CH_5

NET_IF_WIFI_CH_6

NET_IF_WIFI_CH_7

NET_IF_WIFI_CH_8

NET_IF_WIFI_CH_9

NET_IF_WIFI_CH_10

NET_IF_WIFI_CH_11

NET_IF_WIFI_CH_12

NET_IF_WIFI_CH_13

NET_IF_WIFI_CH_14

perr   Pointer to variable that will receive the return error code from this function.

RETURNED VALUES

None.

REQUIRED CONFIGURATION

None.

NOTES/WARNINGS

None.

B-2-5 NetWiFiMgr_AP_Join()

The Wireless Manager's **AP_Join( )** function completes the join process.

FILES

Every Wireless Manager layer **net_wifi_mgr.c**

PROTOTYPE

```
static void NetWiFiMgr_AP_Join (NET_IF              *p_if,
                                NET_IF_WIFI_AP_JOIN *p_join,
         NET_ERR            *p_err);
```

Note that since every Wireless Manager's **AP_Join( )** function is accessed only by function pointer via the Wireless Manager's API structure, it doesn't need to be globally available and should therefore be declared as '**static**'.

ARGUMENTS

p_if   Pointer to the interface to join with.

p_join   Pointer to variable that contains the wireless network to join.

p_err   Pointer to variable that will receive the return error code from this function.

RETURNED VALUES

None.

REQUIRED CONFIGURATION

None.

NOTES/WARNINGS

None.

B-2-6 NetWiFiMgr_AP_Leave()

The Wireless Manager's **AP_Leave( )** function completes the disconnect.

FILES

Every Wireless Manager layer **net_wifi_mgr.c**

PROTOTYPE

```
static void NetWiFiMgr_AP_Leave (NET_IF          *p_if,
NET_ERR           *p_err);
```

Note that since every Wireless Manager's **AP_Leace( )** function is accessed only by function pointer via the Wireless Manager's API structure, it doesn't need to be globally available and should therefore be declared as '**static**'.

ARGUMENTS

p_if   Pointer to the interface to join with.

p_join   Pointer to variable that contains the wireless network to join.

p_err   Pointer to variable that will receive the return error code from this function.

RETURNED VALUES

None.

REQUIRED CONFIGURATION

None.

NOTES/WARNINGS

None.

B-2-7 NetWiFiMgr_IO_Ctrl()

A device's input/output control/IO_Ctrl() function is used to implement miscellaneous functionality such as setting and getting the link state. An optional void pointer to a data variable is passed into the function and may be used to get device parameters from the caller, or to return device parameters to the caller.

FILES

Every Wireless Manager layer **net_wifi_mgr.c**

PROTOTYPE

```
static void NetWiFiMgr_IO_Ctrl (NET_IF          *p_if,
CPU_INT08U opt,
void *p_data,
NET_ERR         *p_err);
```

Note that since every Wireless Manager's **IO_Ctrl()** function is accessed only by function pointer via the Wireless Manager's API structure, it doesn't need to be globally available and should therefore be declared as '**static**'.

ARGUMENTS

p_if   Pointer to the interface to handle network device I/O operations.

opt   I/O operation to perform.

p_data   A pointer to a variable containing the data necessary to perform the operation or a pointer to a variable to store data associated with the result of the operation.

p_err   Pointer to variable that will receive the return error code from this function.

RETURNED VALUES

None.

REQUIRED CONFIGURATION

None.

NOTES/WARNINGS

µC/TCP-IP defines the following default options:

`NET_DEV_LINK_STATE_GET_INFO`

`NET_DEV_LINK_STATE_UPDATE`

The `NET_DEV_LINK_STATE_GET_INFO` option expects **p_data** to point to a variable of type `NET_DEV_LINK_WIFI` for the case of an Ethernet driver. This variable has one field, link state, which are filled in by the device driver API. µC/TCP-IP internally uses this option code in order to periodically poll the driver for linkstate.

B-2-8 NetWiFiMgr_Mgmt()

A wireless management/Mgmt() function is used to implement miscellaneous functionality needed by the driver such as command that need response.

FILES

Every Wireless Manager layer **net_wifi_mgr.c**

PROTOTYPE

```
static void NetWiFiMgr_Mgmt (NET_IF            *p_if,
NET_IF_WIFI_CMD cmd,
CPU_INT08U *p_buf_cmd,
CPU_INT16U buf_cmd_len,
CPU_INT08U *p_buf_rtn,
CPU_INT16U buf_rtn_len_max,
NET_ERR           *p_err);
```

Note that since every Wireless Manager's **Mgmt()** function is accessed only by function pointer via the Wireless Manager's API structure, it doesn't need to be globally available and should therefore be declared as '**static**'.

ARGUMENTS

p_if   Pointer to the interface to wireless device to manage.

cmd   Management command to send.

             The driver can define and implement its own management commands which
             need a response by calling the Wireless Manager api (p_mgr_api->Mgmt()) to
             send the management command and to receive the response.

             Driver management command code '100' series reserved for driver.

p_buf_cmd   Pointer to variable that contains the data to send.

buf_cmd_len Length of the command buffer.

p_buf_rtn   Pointer to variable that will receive the return data.

buf_rtn_len_max   Length of the return buffer.

p_err   Pointer to variable that will receive the return error code from this function.

RETURNED VALUES

None.

REQUIRED CONFIGURATION

None.

NOTES/WARNINGS

Prior calling this function, the network lock must be acquired.

B-3 DEVICE DRIVER BSP FUNCTIONS

B-3-1 NetDev_WiFi_Start()

This function is called by a device driver's NetDev_Start() to start and power up the wireless hardware.

FILES

net_bsp.c

PROTOTYPE

```
static void NetDev_WiFi_Start (NET_IF  *p_if,
                               NET_ERR *p_err);
```

Note: since NetDev_WiFi_Start() is accessed only by function pointer via a BSP interface structure, it doesn't need to be globally available and should therefore be declared as '**static**'.

ARGUMENTS

p_if   Pointer to specific interface to start device's hardware.

p_err   Pointer to variable that will receive the return error code from this function:

            NET_DEV_ERR_NONE

            NET_DEV_ERR_FAULT

This is *not* an exclusive list of return errors and specific network device's or device BSP functions may return any other specific errors as required.

RETURNED VALUE

None.

REQUIRED CONFIGURATION

None.

NOTES / WARNINGS

Since each network device requires a unique NetDev_WiFi_Start(), it is recommended that each device's NetDev_WiFi_Start() function be named using the following convention:

NetDev_WiFi_[Device]_Start[Number]()

[Device]   Network device name or type, e.g. RS9110 (optional if the development board does not support multiple devices)

[Number]   Network device number for each specific instance of device (optional if the development board does not support multiple instances of the specific device)

For example, the NetDev_WiFi_Start() function for the #2 RS9110 wireless devie should be named NetDev_WiFi_RS9110_Start2(), or NetDev_WiFI_RS9110_Start_2() with additional underscore optional.

B-3-2 NetDev_WiFi_Stop()

This function is called by a device driver's `NetDev_Stop()` to stop &/or power down the wireless hardware.

FILES

`net_bsp.c`

PROTOTYPE

```
static void NetDev_WiFi_Stop (NET_IF  *p_if,
                              NET_ERR *p_err);
```

Note: since `NetDev_WiFi_Stop()` is accessed only by function pointer via a BSP interface structure, it doesn't need to be globally available and should therefore be declared as '**static**'.

ARGUMENTS

`p_if`   Pointer to specific interface to stop device's hardware.

`p_err`   Pointer to variable that will receive the return error code from this function:

         `NET_DEV_ERR_NONE`

         `NET_DEV_ERR_FAULT`

This is *not* an exclusive list of return errors and specific network device's or device BSP functions may return any other specific errors as required.

RETURNED VALUE

None.

REQUIRED CONFIGURATION

None.

NOTES / WARNINGS

Since each network device requires a unique `NetDev_WiFi_Stop()`, it is recommended that each device's `NetDev_WiFi_Stop()` function be named using the following convention:

`NetDev_WiFi_[Device]_Stop[Number]()`

`[Device]`   Network device name or type, e.g. RS9110 (optional if the development board does not support multiple devices)

`[Number]`   Network device number for each specific instance of device (optional if the development board does not support multiple instances of the specific device)

For example, the `NetDev_WiFi_Stop()` function for the #2 RS9110 wireless devie should be named `NetDev_WiFi_RS9110_Stop2()`, or `NetDev_WiFI_RS9110_Stop_2()` with additional underscore optional.

B-3-3 NetDev_WiFi_CfgGPIO()

This function is called by a device driver's **NetDev_Init()** to configure a specific network device's general-purpose input/ouput (GPIO) on a specific interface such as SPI, external interrupt, power & reset pins.

FILES

net_bsp.c

PROTOTYPE

```
static void NetDev_WiFi_CfgGPIO (NET_IF  *p_if,
NET_ERR *p_err);
```

Note that since **NetDev_WiFi_CfgGPIO()** is accessed only by function pointer via a BSP interface structure, it doesn't need to be globally available and should therefore be declared as '**static**'.

ARGUMENTS

p_if   Pointer to specific interface to configure device's GPIO.

p_err   Pointer to variable that will receive the return error code from this function:

NET_DEV_ERR_NONE

NET_DEV_ERR_FAULT

This is *not* an exclusive list of return errors and specific network device's or device BSP functions may return any other specific errors as required.

RETURNED VALUE

None.

REQUIRED CONFIGURATION

None.

NOTES / WARNINGS

Since each network device requires a unique NetDev_WiFi_CfgGPIO(), it is recommended that each device's NetDev_WiFi_CfgGPIO() function be named using the following convention:

NetDev_WiFi_[Device]_CfgGPIO[Number]()

[Device]   Network device name or type, e.g. RS9110 (optional if the development board does not support multiple devices)

[Number]   Network device number for each specific instance of device (optional if the development board does not support multiple instances of the specific device)

For example, the NetDev_WiFi_CfgGPIO() function for the #2 RS9110 wireless device should be named NetDev_WiFi_RS9110_CfgGPIO2(), or NetDev_WiFI_RS9110_CfgGPIO_2() with additional underscore optional.

See also Chapter 15, "Network Board Support Package" on page 347.

B-3-4 NetDev_WiFi_CfgIntCtrl()

This function is called by a device driver's **NetDev_Init()** to configure a specific network device's interrupts and/or interrupt controller on a specific interface.

FILES

net_bsp.c

PROTOTYPE

```
static void NetDev_CfgIntCtrl (NET_IF  *pif,
                               NET_ERR *perr);
```

Note that since **NetDev_WiFi_CfgIntCtrl()** is accessed only by function pointer via a BSP interface structure, it doesn't need to be globally available and should therefore be declared as '**static**'.

ARGUMENTS

p_if   Pointer to specific interface to configure device's interrupts.

p_err   Pointer to variable that will receive the return error code from this function:

        NET_DEV_ERR_NONE

        NET_DEV_ERR_FAULT

This is *not* an exclusive list of return errors and specific network device's or device BSP functions may return any other specific errors as required.

RETURNED VALUE

None.

REQUIRED CONFIGURATION

None.

625

NOTES / WARNINGS

Each network device's **NetDev_WiFi_CfgIntCtrl()** should configure and enable all required interrupt sources for the network device. This usually means configuring the interrupt vector address of each corresponding network device BSP interrupt service routine (ISR) handler and enabling its corresponding interrupt source. Thus, for most **NetDev_WiFi_CfgIntCtrl()**, the following actions *should* be performed:

1   Configure/store each device's network interface number to be available for all necessary **NetDev_WiFi_ISR_Handler()** functions (see section B-3-13 "NetDev_WiFi_ISR_Handler()" on page 646). Even though devices are added dynamically, the device's interface number must be saved in order for each device's ISR handlers to call **NetIF_ISR_Handler()** with the device's network interface number.

Since each network device maps to a unique network interface number, it is recommended that each instance of network devices' interface numbers be named using the following convention:

<Board><Device>[Number]_IF_Nbr

<Board>   Development board name

<Device>   Network device name (or type)

[Number]   Network device number for each specific instance of device (optional if the development board does not support multiple instances of the specific device)

For example, the network device interface number variable for the #2 RS9110 wireless device on an Atmel AT91SAM9263-EK should be named **AT91SAM9263-EK_RS9110_2_IF_Nbr**.

Network device interface number variables *should* be initialized to **NET_IF_NBR_NONE** at system initialization prior to being configured by their respective devices.

2   Configure each of the device's interrupts on either an external or CPU's integrated interrupt controller. However, vectored interrupt controllers may not require the explicit configuration and enabling of higher-level interrupt controller sources. In this case, the application developer may need to configure the system's interrupt vector table with the name of the ISR handler functions declared in **net_bsp.c**.

NetDev_WiFi_CfgIntCtrl() should only enable each devices' interrupt sources but *not* the local device-level interrupts themselves, which are enabled by the device driver only after the device has been fully configured and started.

Since each network device requires a unique **NetDev_WiFi_CfgIntCtrl()**, it is recommended that each device's **NetDev_WiFi_CfgIntCtrl()** function be named using the following convention:

NetDev_WiFi_[Device]CfgIntCtrl[Number]()

[Device]   Network device name or type, e.g. RS9110 (optional if the development board does not support multiple devices)

[Number]   Network device number for each specific instance of device (optional if the development board does not support multiple instances of the specific device)

For example, the **NetDev_CfgIntCtrl()** function for the #2 RS9110 wireless device on an Atmel AT91SAM9263-EK should be named **NetDev_WiFi_RS9110_CfgIntCtrl2()**, or **NetDev_WiFi_RS9110_CfgIntCtrl_2()** with additional underscore optional.

See also Chapter 15, "Network Board Support Package" on page 347.

EXAMPLES

```
static void NetDev_WiFi_RS9110_CfgIntCtrl (NET_IF  *p_if,
NET_ERR *p_err)
{
                        /* Configure AT91SAM9263-EK RS9110 #2's specific IF number.   */
   AT91SAM9263-EK__WiFi_RS9110_2_IF_Nbr = pif->Nbr;
                        /* Configure AT91SAM9263-EK RS9110 #2's interrupts:           */
  BSP_IntVectSet(BSP_INT, &NetDev_WiFi_RS9110_ISR_Handler_2);/* Configure interrupt vector.
*/
   BSP_IntEn(BSP_INT);                              /* Enable    interrupts.          */

   *perr = NET_DEV_ERR_NONE;
}


static void NetDev_WiFi_RS9110_CfgIntCtrlRx_2 (NET_IF  *p_if,
                                    NET_ERR *p_err)
{
                        /* Configure AT91SAM9263-EK RS9110 #2's specific IF number.   */
   AT91SAM9263-EK_WiFi_RS9110_2_IF_Nbr = pif->Nbr;
                        /* Configure AT91SAM9263-EK RS9110 #2's receive interrupt:    */
   BSP_IntVectSet(BSP_INT_RX, &NetDev_WiFi_RS9100_ISR_HandlerRx_2);  /* Configure interrupt
vector. */
   BSP_IntEn(BSP_INT_RX);                              /* Enable    interrupt.        */

   *perr = NET_DEV_ERR_NONE;
}
```

B-3-5 NetDev_WiFi_IntCtrl()

This function is called by a device driver **to** enable or disable interface's/device's interrupt.

FILES

net_bsp.c

PROTOTYPE

```
static CPU_INT32U NetDev_WiFi_IntCtrl (NET_IF  *p_if,
CPU_BOOLEAN en,
                                    NET_ERR *p_err);
```

Note that since **NetDev_WiFi_IntCtrl()** is accessed only by function pointer via a BSP interface structure, it doesn't need to be globally available and should therefore be declared as '**static**'.

ARGUMENTS

p_if   Pointer to specific interface to enable or disable the interrupt.

en   Enable or disable the interrupt.

p_err   Pointer to variable that will receive the return error code from this function:

             NET_DEV_ERR_NONE

             NET_DEV_ERR_FAULT

This is *not* an exclusive list of return errors and specific network device's or device BSP functions may return any other specific errors as required.

RETURNED VALUE

None.

REQUIRED CONFIGURATION

None.

NOTES / WARNINGS

Since each network device requires a unique `NetDev_WiFi_IntCtrl()`, it is recommended that each device's `NetDev_WiFi_IntCtrl()` function be named using the following convention:

`NetDev_WiFi_[Device]IntCtrl[Number]()`

`[Device]`   Network device name or type, e.g. RS9110 (optional if the development board does not support multiple devices)

`[Number]`   Network device number for each specific instance of device (optional if the development board does not support multiple instances of the specific device)

For example, the `NetDev_WiFi_IntCtrl()` function for the #2 RS9110 wireless device on an Atmel AT91SAM9263-EK should be named `NetDev_WiFi_RS9110_IntCtrl2()`, or `NetDev_WiFi_RS9110_IntCtrl_2()` with additional underscore optional.

See also Chapter 15, "Network Board Support Package" on page 347.

B-3-6 NetDev_WiFi_SPI_Init()

This function is called by a device driver **to** initialize interface's/device's SPI bus.

FILES

net_bsp.c

PROTOTYPE

```
static CPU_INT32U NetDev_WiFi_SPI_Init (NET_IF  *p_if,
                                        NET_ERR *p_err);
```

Note that since **NetDev_WiFi_SPI_Init()** is accessed only by function pointer via a BSP interface structure, it doesn't need to be globally available and should therefore be declared as '**static**'.

ARGUMENTS

p_if   Pointer to specific interface to initialize the SPI.

p_err   Pointer to variable that will receive the return error code from this function:

        NET_DEV_ERR_NONE

        NET_DEV_ERR_FAULT

This is *not* an exclusive list of return errors and specific network device's or device BSP functions may return any other specific errors as required.

RETURNED VALUE

None.

REQUIRED CONFIGURATION

None.

NOTES / WARNINGS

1   This function can configure the SPI mode by accessing the device configuration if no other device's hardware sahre the same SPI bus.

2   Since each network device requires a unique `NetDev_WiFi_SPI_Init()`, it is recommended that each device's `NetDev_WiFi_SPI_Init()` function be named using the following convention:

`NetDev_WiFi_[Device]SPI_Init[Number]()`

`[Device]`   Network device name or type. For example, RS9110 (optional if the development board does not support multiple devices)

`[Number]`   Network device number for each specific instance of device (optional if the development board does not support multiple instances of the specific device)

For example, the `NetDev_WiFi_SPI_Init()` function for the #2 RS9110 wireless device on an Atmel AT91SAM9263-EK should be named `NetDev_WiFi_RS9110_SPI_Init2()`, or `NetDev_WiFi_RS9110_SPI_Init_2()` with additional underscore optional.

See also Chapter 15, "Network Board Support Package" on page 347.

B-3-7 NetDev_WiFi_SPI_Lock()

This function is called by a device driver to acquire the SPI lock and restrict the access to the SPI bus only to the wireless driver.

net_bsp.c

```
static CPU_INT32U NetDev_WiFi_SPI_Lock (NET_IF  *p_if,
                                        NET_ERR *p_err);
```

Note that since **NetDev_WiFi_SPI_Lock()** is accessed only by function pointer via a BSP interface structure, it doesn't need to be globally available and should therefore be declared as '**static**'.

p_if   Pointer to specific interface to lock.

p_err   Pointer to variable that will receive the return error code from this function:

            NET_DEV_ERR_NONE

            NET_DEV_ERR_FAULT

This is *not* an exclusive list of return errors and specific network device's or device BSP functions may return any other specific errors as required.

None.

None.

NOTES / WARNINGS

1   `NetDev_WiFi_SPI_Lock` must be implemented if more than one device's hardware share the same SPI bus.

2   Since each network device requires a unique `NetDev_WiFi_SPI_Lock()`, it is recommended that each device's `NetDev_WiFi_SPI_Lock()` function be named using the following convention:

`NetDev_WiFi_[Device]SPI_Lock[Number]()`

`[Device]`	Network device name or type, e.g. RS9110 (optional if the development board does not support multiple devices)
`[Number]`	Network device number for each specific instance of device (optional if the development board does not support multiple instances of the specific device)

For example, the `NetDev_WiFi_SPI_Lock()` function for the #2 RS9110 wireless device on an Atmel AT91SAM9263-EK should be named `NetDev_WiFi_RS9110_SPI_Lock2()`, or `NetDev_WiFi_RS9110_SPI_Lock_2()` with additional underscore optional.

See also Chapter 15, "Network Board Support Package" on page 347.

B-3-8 NetDev_WiFi_SPI_Unlock()

This function is called by a device driver **to** release the SPI lock and give the access to the SPI bus to other device's hardware.

FILES

net_bsp.c

PROTOTYPE

```
static CPU_INT32U NetDev_WiFi_SPI_Unlock (NET_IF  *p_if);
```

Note that since **NetDev_WiFi_SPI_Unlock()** is accessed only by function pointer via a BSP interface structure, it doesn't need to be globally available and should therefore be declared as '**static**'.

ARGUMENTS

p_if   Pointer to specific interface to unlock.

RETURNED VALUE

None.

REQUIRED CONFIGURATION

None.

NOTES / WARNINGS

1   **NetDev_WiFi_SPI_Unlock must be** implemented if more than one hardware device share the same SPI bus.

2   Since each network device requires a unique **NetDev_WiFi_SPI_Unlock()**, it is recommended that each device's **NetDev_WiFi_SPI_Unlock()** function be named using the following convention:

`NetDev_WiFi_[Device]SPI_Unlock[Number]()`

[Device]   Network device name or type, e.g. RS9110 (optional if the development board does not support multiple devices)

[Number]   Network device number for each specific instance of device (optional if the development board does not support multiple instances of the specific device)

For example, the `NetDev_WiFi_SPI_Unlock()` function for the #2 RS9110 wireless device on an Atmel AT91SAM9263-EK should be named `NetDev_WiFi_RS9110_SPI_Unlock2()`, or `NetDev_WiFi_RS9110_SPI_Unlock_2()` with additional underscore optional.

See also Chapter 15, "Network Board Support Package" on page 347.

B-3-9 NetDev_WiFi_SPI_WrRd()

This function is called by a device driver **each time some data must be written &/or read from the wireless device/interface**.

FILES

net_bsp.c

PROTOTYPE

```
static CPU_INT32U NetDev_WiFi_SPI_WrRd (NET_IF  *p_if,
CPU_INT08U *p_buf_wr,
CPU_INT08U *p_buf_rd,
CPU_INT16U wr_rd_len,
NET_ERR *p_err);
```

Note that since **NetDev_WiFi_SPI_Unlock( )** is accessed only by function pointer via a BSP interface structure, it doesn't need to be globally available and should therefore be declared as '**static**'.

ARGUMENTS

p_if   Pointer to specific interface to write and read data to SPI bus.

p_buf_wr   Pointer to a buffer that contains the data to write.

p_buf_rd   Pointer to a buffer that will receive the data read.

wr_rd_len   Number of octet to write and read.

p_err   Pointer to variable that will receive the return error code from this function:

            NET_DEV_ERR_NONE

            NET_DEV_ERR_FAULT

This is *not* an exclusive list of return errors and specific network device's or device BSP functions may return any other specific errors as required.

RETURNED VALUE

None.

REQUIRED CONFIGURATION

None.

NOTES / WARNINGS

1 NetDev_WiFi_SPI_ChipSelEn() should be called only after the SPI lock has been acquired by calling NetDev_WiFi_SPI_Lock().

2 Since each network device requires a unique NetDev_WiFi_SPI_WrRd(), it is recommended that each device's NetDev_WiFi_SPI_WrRd() function be named using the following convention:

NetDev_WiFi_[Device]SPI_WrRd[Number]()

[Device]	Network device name or type, e.g. RS9110 (optional if the development board does not support multiple devices)
[Number]	Network device number for each specific instance of device (optional if the development board does not support multiple instances of the specific device)

For example, the NetDev_WiFi_SPI_WrRd() function for the #2 RS9110 wireless device on an Atmel AT91SAM9263-EK should be named NetDev_WiFi_RS9110_SPI_WrRd2(), or NetDev_WiFi_RS9110_SPI_WrRd_2() with additional underscore optional.

See also Chapter 15, "Network Board Support Package" on page 347.

B-3-10 NetDev_WiFi_SPI_ChipSelEn()

This function is called by a device driver to enable the SPI chip select of the wireless device.

FILES

net_bsp.c

PROTOTYPE

```
static CPU_INT32U NetDev_WiFi_SPI_ChipSelEn (NET_IF  *p_if,
                                             NET_ERR *p_err);
```

Note that since **NetDev_WiFi_SPI_ChipSelEn()** is accessed only by function pointer via a BSP interface structure, it doesn't need to be globally available and should therefore be declared as '**static**'.

ARGUMENTS

p_if   Pointer to specific interface to enable the chip select.

p_err   Pointer to variable that will receive the return error code from this function:

        NET_DEV_ERR_NONE

        NET_DEV_ERR_FAULT

This is *not* an exclusive list of return errors and specific network device's or device BSP functions may return any other specific errors as required.

RETURNED VALUE

None.

REQUIRED CONFIGURATION

None.

NOTES / WARNINGS

1   NetDev_WiFi_SPI_ChipSelEn() should be called only after the SPI lock has been acquired by calling NetDev_WiFi_SPI_Lock().

2   Since each network device requires a unique NetDev_WiFi_SPI_ChipSelEn(), it is recommended that each device's NetDev_WiFi_SPI_ChipSelEn() function be named using the following convention:

NetDev_WiFi_[Device]SPI_ChipSelEn[Number]()

[Device]	Network device name or type, e.g. RS9110 (optional if the development board does not support multiple devices)
[Number]	Network device number for each specific instance of device (optional if the development board does not support multiple instances of the specific device)

For example, the NetDev_WiFi_SPI_ChipSelEn() function for the #2 RS9110 wireless device on an Atmel AT91SAM9263-EK should be named NetDev_WiFi_RS9110_SPI_ChipSelEn2(), or NetDev_WiFi_RS9110_SPI_ChipSelEn_2() with additional underscore optional.

See also Chapter 15, "Network Board Support Package" on page 347.

B-3-11 NetDev_WiFi_SPI_ChipSelDis()

This function is called by a device driver **to** disable the SPI chip select of the wireless device.

FILES

net_bsp.c

PROTOTYPE

```
static CPU_INT32U NetDev_WiFi_SPI_ChipSelDis (NET_IF  *p_if);
```

Note that since **NetDev_WiFi_SPI_ChipSelDis()** is accessed only by function pointer via a BSP interface structure, it doesn't need to be globally available and should therefore be declared as '**static**'.

ARGUMENTS

p_if   Pointer to specific interface to enable the chip select.

RETURNED VALUE

None.

REQUIRED CONFIGURATION

None.

NOTES / WARNINGS

1   NetDev_WiFi_SPI_ChipSelDis() should be called only after the SPI lock has been acquired by calling NetDev_WiFi_SPI_Lock().

2   Since each network device requires a unique NetDev_WiFi_SPI_ChipSelDis(), it is recommended that each device's NetDev_WiFi_SPI_ChipSelDis() function be named using the following convention:

`NetDev_WiFi_[Device]SPI_ChipSelDis[Number]()`

`[Device]`	Network device name or type, e.g. RS9110 (optional if the development board does not support multiple devices)
`[Number]`	Network device number for each specific instance of device (optional if the development board does not support multiple instances of the specific device)

For example, the `NetDev_WiFi_SPI_ChipSelDis()` function for the #2 RS9110 wireless device on an Atmel AT91SAM9263-EK should be named `NetDev_WiFi_RS9110_SPI_ChipSelDis2()`, or `NetDev_WiFi_RS9110_SPI_ChipSelDis_2()` with additional underscore optional.

See also Chapter 15, "Network Board Support Package" on page 347.

B-3-12 NetDev_WiFi_SPI_Cfg()

This function is called by a device driver **to** configure the SPI controller accordingly with device's SPI setting.

net_bsp.c

```
static CPU_INT32U NetDev_WiFi_SPI_Cfg (NET_IF   *p_if,
NET_DEV_CFG_SPI_CLK_FREQ freq,
NET_DEV_CFG_SPI_CLK_POL pol,
NET_DEV_CFG_SPI_CLK_PHASE phase,
NET_DEV_CFG_SPI_XFER_UNIT_LEN xfer_unit_len,
NET_DEV_CFG_SPI_XFER_SHIFT_DIR xfer_shift_dir,
NET_ERR *p_err);
```

Note that since **NetDev_WiFi_SPI_Cfg()** is accessed only by function pointer via a BSP interface structure, it doesn't need to be globally available and should therefore be declared as '**static**'.

p_if   Pointer to specific interface to configure the SPI controller.

freq   SPI system clock frequency in hertz.

pol   SPI clock polarity:

            NET_DEV_SPI_CLK_POL_INACTIVE_LOW

            NET_DEV_SPI_CLK_POL_INACTIVE_HIGH

phase   SPI clock phase:

            NET_DEV_SPI_CLK_PHASE_FALLING_EDGE

            NET_DEV_SPI_CLK_PHASE_RASING_EDGE

xfer_unit_len   SPI Transfer unit length:

                       NET_DEV_SPI_XFER_UNIT_LEN_8_BITS

                       NET_DEV_SPI_XFER_UNIT_LEN_16_BITS

                       NET_DEV_SPI_XFER_UNIT_LEN_32_BITS

                       NET_DEV_SPI_XFER_UNIT_LEN_64_BITS

xfer_shift_dir   SPI transfer shift direction:

                       NET_DEV_SPI_XFER_SHIFT_DIR_FIRST_MSB

                       NET_DEV_SPI_XFER_SHIFT_DIR_FIRST_LSB

p_err   Pointer to variable that will receive the return error code from this function:

               NET_DEV_ERR_NONE

               NET_DEV_ERR_FAULT

This is *not* an exclusive list of return errors and specific network device's or device BSP functions may return any other specific errors as required.

RETURNED VALUE

None.

REQUIRED CONFIGURATION

None.

NOTES / WARNINGS

1 NetDev_WiFi_SPI_Cfg() should be called only after the SPI lock has been acquired by calling NetDev_WiFi_SPI_Lock().

2 If no other device's hardware share the same SPI controller, the configuration can be applied only at the initialization when NetDev_WiFi_SPI_Init() is called.

3   Since each network device requires a unique `NetDev_WiFi_SPI_ChipSelEn()`, it is recommended that each device's `NetDev_WiFi_SPI_ChipSelEn()` function be named using the following convention:

`NetDev_WiFi_[Device]SPI_ChipSelEn[Number]()`

`[Device]`   Network device name or type, e.g. RS9110 (optional if the development board does not support multiple devices)

`[Number]`   Network device number for each specific instance of device (optional if the development board does not support multiple instances of the specific device)

For example, the `NetDev_WiFi_SPI_ChipSelEn()` function for the #2 RS9110 wireless device on an Atmel AT91SAM9263-EK should be named `NetDev_WiFi_RS9110_SPI_ChipSelEn2()`, or `NetDev_WiFi_RS9110_SPI_ChipSelEn_2()` with additional underscore optional.

See also Chapter 15, "Network Board Support Package" on page 347.

B-3-13 NetDev_WiFi_ISR_Handler()

Handle a network device's interrupts on a specific interface.

FILES

net_bsp.c

PROTOTYPE

```
static void NetDev_ISR_Handler (void);
```

Note that since **NetDev_ISR_Handler()** is accessed only by function pointer usually via an interrupt vector table, it doesn't need to be globally available and should therefore be declared as '**static**'.

ARGUMENTS

None.

RETURNED VALUE

None.

REQUIRED CONFIGURATION

None.

NOTES / WARNINGS

Each network device's interrupt, or set of device interrupts, must be handled by a unique BSP-level interrupt service routine (ISR) handler, **NetDev_WiFi_ISR_Handler()**, which maps each specific device interrupt to its corresponding network interface ISR handler, **NetIF_ISR_Handler()**. For some CPUs this may be a first- or second-level interrupt handler. Generally, the application must configure the interrupt controller to call every network device's unique **NetDev_WiFi_ISR_Handler()** when the device's interrupt occurs (see section B-3-4 on page 625). Every unique **NetDev_WiFi_ISR_Handler()** *must* then perform the following actions:

1   Call `NetIF_ISR_Handler()` with the device's unique network interface number and appropriate interrupt type. The device's network interface number should be available after configuration in the device's `NetDev_WiFi_CfgIntCtrl()` function (see section B-3-4 "NetDev_WiFi_CfgIntCtrl()" on page 625). `NetIF_ISR_Handler()` in turn calls the appropriate device driver's interrupt handler.

In most cases, each device requires only a single `NetDev_WiFi_ISR_Handler()` which calls `NetIF_ISR_Handler()` with interrupt type code `NET_DEV_ISR_TYPE_UNKNOWN`. This is possible when the device's driver can determine the device's interrupt type to via the interrupt controller. However, some devices cannot generically determine the interrupt type when an interrupt occurs and may therefore require multiple, unique `NetDev_WiFi_ISR_Handler()`'s each of which calls `NetIF_ISR_Handler()` with the appropriate interrupt type code.

See also section C-9-12 "NetIF_ISR_Handler()" on page 751.

2   Clear the device's interrupt source, possibly via an external or CPU-integrated interrupt controller source.

Since each network device requires a unique `NetDev_WiFi_ISR_Handler()` for each device interrupt, it is recommended that each device's `NetDev_WiFi_ISR_Handler()` function be named using the following convention:

`NetDev_WiFi_[Device]ISR_Handler[Type][Number]()`

`[Device]`   Network device name or type, e.g., RS9110 (optional if the development board does not support multiple devices)

`[Type]`   Network device interrupt type, e.g., receive interrupt (optional if interrupt type is generic or unknown)

`[Number]`   Network device number for each specific instance of device (optional if the development board does not support multiple instances of a specific device)

For example, the receive ISR handler for the #2 RS9110 wireless device on an Atmel AT91SAM9263-EK should be named `NetDev_WiFi_RS9110_ISR_HandlerRx2()`.

See also Chapter 15, "Network Board Support Package" on page 347.

EXAMPLES

```
static void NetDev_WiFi_RS9110_ISR_Handler_2 (void)
{
    NET_ERR  err;

    NetIF_ISR_Handler(AT91SAM9263-EK_RS9110_2_IF_Nbr, NET_DEV_ISR_TYPE_UNKNOWN, &err);
    /* Clear external or CPU's integrated interrupt controller. */
}


static void NetDev_WiFi_RS9110_ISR_HandlerRx_2 (void)
{
    NET_ERR  err;

    NetIF_ISR_Handler(AT91SAM9263-EK_RS9110_2_IF_Nbr, NET_DEV_ISR_TYPE_RX, &err);
    /* Clear external or CPU's integrated interrupt controller. */
}
```

µC/TCP-IP API Reference

The application programming interfaces (APIs) to µC/TCP-IP using any of the functions or macros are described in this appendix. The functions/macros in this appendix are organized alphabetically with the exception of alphabetizing all BSD functions/macros in their own section, section C-19 on page 938.

C-1 GENERAL NETWORK FUNCTIONS

C-1-1 Net_Init()

Initializes µC/TCP-IP and *must* be called prior to calling any other µC/TCP-IP API functions.

FILES

net.h/net.c

PROTOTYPE

```
NET_ERR Net_Init(void);
```

ARGUMENTS

None.

RETURNED VALUE

NET_ERR_NONE,   if successful;

Specific initialization error code,   otherwise.

Return value *should* be inspected to determine whether or not µC/TCP-IP successfully initialized. If µC/TCP-IP did *not* successfully initialize, search for the returned error code in **net_err.h** and source files to locate where the µC/TCP-IP initialization failed.

REQUIRED CONFIGURATION

None.

NOTES / WARNINGS

µC/LIB memory management function **Mem_Init()** *must* be called prior to calling **Net_Init()**.

C-1-2 Net_InitDflt()

Initialize default values for all µC/TCP-IP configurable parameters.

FILES

net.h/net.c

PROTOTYPE

```
void Net_InitDflt(void);
```

ARGUMENTS

None.

RETURNED VALUE

None.

REQUIRED CONFIGURATION

None.

NOTES / WARNINGS

Some default parameters are specified in **net_cfg.h** (see Appendix D, "µC/TCP-IP Configuration and Optimization" on page 959).

C-1-3 Net_VersionGet()

Get the µC/TCP-IP software version.

FILES

net.h/net.c

PROTOTYPE

```
CPU_INT16U Net_VersionGet(void);
```

ARGUMENTS

None.

RETURNED VALUE

µC/TCP-IP software version.

REQUIRED CONFIGURATION

None.

NOTES / WARNINGS

µC/TCP-IP's software version is denoted as follows:

   Vx.yy.zz

      where
      V denotes Version label
      x denotes major software version revision number
      yy denotes minor software version revision number
      zz denotes sub-minor software version revision number

The software version is returned as follows:

ver = x.yyzz * 100 * 100

> where
> ver denotes software version number scaled as an integer value
> x.yyzz denotes software version number, where the unscaled integer portion denotes the major version number and the unscaled fractional portion denotes the (concatenated) minor version numbers

For example, (version) V2.11.01 would be returned as **21101**.

C-2 NETWORK APPLICATION INTERFACE FUNCTIONS

C-2-1 NetApp_SockAccept() (TCP)

Return a new application socket accepted from a listen application socket, with error handling. See section C-14-1 on page 808 for more information.

FILES

net_app.h/net_app.c

PROTOTYPE

```
NET_SOCK_ID  NetApp_SockAccept (NET_SOCK_ID        sock_id,
                                NET_SOCK_ADDR      *paddr_remote,
                                NET_SOCK_ADDR_LEN  *paddr_len,
                                CPU_INT16U         retry_max,
                                CPU_INT32U         timeout_ms,
                                CPU_INT32U         time_dly_ms,
                                NET_ERR            *perr);
```

ARGUMENTS

sock_id   This is the socket ID returned by **NetApp_SockOpen()/
                   NetSock_Open()/socket()** when the socket was created. This
                   socket is assumed to be bound to an address and listening for
                   new connections (see section C-14-34 on page 873).

paddr_remote   Pointer to a socket address structure (see section 18-1 "Network
                   Socket Data Structures" on page 501) to return the remote host
                   address of the new accepted connection.

paddr_len   Pointer to the size of the socket address structure which *must* be
                   passed the size of the socket address structure [e.g.,
                   sizeof(NET_SOCK_ADDR_IP)]. Returns size of the accepted
                   connection's socket address structure, if no errors; returns 0,
                   otherwise.

retry_max   Maximum number of consecutive socket accept retries.

`timeout_ms`   Socket accept timeout value per attempt/retry.

`time_dly_ms` Socket accept delay value, in milliseconds.

`perr`   Pointer to variable that will receive the error code from this function:

                NET_APP_ERR_NONE

                NET_APP_ERR_NONE_AVAIL

                NET_APP_ERR_INVALID_ARG

                NET_APP_ERR_INVALID_OP

                NET_APP_ERR_FAULT

                NET_APP_ERR_FAULT_TRANSITORY

RETURNED VALUE

Socket descriptor/handle identifier of new accepted socket, if no errors.

NET_SOCK_BSD_ERR_ACCEPT, otherwise.

REQUIRED CONFIGURATION

Available only if NET_APP_CFG_API_EN is enabled (see section D-18-1 on page 984) *and* NET_CFG_TRANSPORT_LAYER_SEL is configured for TCP (see section D-12-1 on page 972).

NOTES / WARNINGS

Some socket arguments and/or operations are validated only if validation code is enabled (see section D-3-1 on page 965).

If a non-zero number of retries is requested (**retry_max**) *and* socket blocking is configured for non-blocking operation (see section D-15-3 on page 977); then a non-zero timeout (**timeout_ms**) and/or a non-zero time delay (**time_dly_ms**) should also be requested. Otherwise, all retries will most likely fail immediately since no time will elapse to wait for and allow socket operations to successfully complete.

C-2-2 NetApp_SockBind() (TCP/UDP)

Bind an application socket to a local address, with error handling. See section C-14-2 on page 810 for more information.

FILES

net_app.h/net_app.c

PROTOTYPE

```
CPU_BOOLEAN  NetApp_SockBind (NET_SOCK_ID        sock_id,
                              NET_SOCK_ADDR     *paddr_local,
                              NET_SOCK_ADDR_LEN  addr_len,
                              CPU_INT16U         retry_max,
                              CPU_INT32U         time_dly_ms,
                              NET_ERR           *perr);
```

ARGUMENTS

sock_id   This is the socket ID returned by **NetApp_SockOpen()/**
              NetSock_Open()/socket() when the socket was created.

paddr_local   Pointer to a socket address structure (see section 8-2 "Socket Interface" on
              page 212) which contains the local host address to bind the socket to.

addr_len   Size of the socket address structure which *must* be passed the size of the
              socket address structure [for example, **sizeof(NET_SOCK_ADDR_IP)**].

retry_max   Maximum number of consecutive socket bind retries.

time_dly_ms   Socket bind delay value, in milliseconds.

perr   Pointer to variable that will receive the error code from this function:

        NET_APP_ERR_NONE
        NET_APP_ERR_NONE_AVAIL
        NET_APP_ERR_INVALID_ARG
        NET_APP_ERR_INVALID_OP
        NET_APP_ERR_FAULT

RETURNED VALUE

DEF_OK,   Application socket successfully bound to a local address.

DEF_FAIL,   otherwise.

REQUIRED CONFIGURATION

Available only if **NET_APP_CFG_API_EN** is enabled (see section D-18-1 on page 984) **AND** either **NET_CFG_TRANSPORT_LAYER_SEL** is configured for TCP (see section D-12-1 on page 972) and/or **NET_UDP_CFG_APP_API_SEL** is configured for sockets (see section D-13-1 on page 973).

NOTES / WARNINGS

Some socket arguments and/or operations are validated only if validation code is enabled (see section D-3-1 on page 965).

If a non-zero number of retries is requested (**retry_max**) then a non-zero time delay (**time_dly_ms**) should also be requested. Otherwise, all retries will most likely fail immediately since no time will elapse to wait for and allow socket operations to successfully complete.

C-2-3 NetApp_SockClose() (TCP/UDP)

Close an application socket, with error handling. See section C-14-25 on page 857 for more information.

FILES

net_app.h/net_app.c

PROTOTYPE

```
CPU_BOOLEAN  NetApp_SockClose (NET_SOCK_ID   sock_id,
                               CPU_INT32U    timeout_ms,
                               NET_ERR       *perr);
```

ARGUMENTS

sock_id   This is the socket ID returned by **NetApp_SockOpen()/**
            NetSock_Open()/socket() when the socket was created *or* by
            NetApp_SockAccept()/NetSock_Accept()/accept() when a connection
            was accepted.

timeout_ms Socket close timeout value per attempt/retry.

perr   Pointer to variable that will receive the error code from this function:

            NET_APP_ERR_NONE
            NET_APP_ERR_INVALID_ARG
            NET_APP_ERR_FAULT
            NET_APP_ERR_FAULT_TRANSITORY

RETURNED VALUE

DEF_OK,   Application socket successfully closed.

DEF_FAIL,   otherwise.

REQUIRED CONFIGURATION

Available only if `NET_APP_CFG_API_EN` is enabled (see section D-18-1 on page 984) **AND** either `NET_CFG_TRANSPORT_LAYER_SEL` is configured for TCP (see section D-12-1 on page 972) and/or `NET_UDP_CFG_APP_API_SEL` is configured for sockets (see section D-13-1 on page 973).

NOTES / WARNINGS

Some socket arguments and/or operations are validated only if validation code is enabled (see section D-3-1 on page 965).

C-2-4 NetApp_SockConn() (TCP/UDP)

Connect an application socket to a remote address, with error handling. See section C-14-26 on page 859 for more information.

FILES

net_app.h/net_app.c

PROTOTYPE

```
CPU_BOOLEAN  NetApp_SockConn (NET_SOCK_ID          sock_id,
                             NET_SOCK_ADDR        *paddr_remote,
                             NET_SOCK_ADDR_LEN    addr_len,
                             CPU_INT16U           retry_max,
                             CPU_INT32U           timeout_ms,
                             CPU_INT32U           time_dly_ms,
                             NET_ERR              *perr);
```

ARGUMENTS

sock_id   This is the socket ID returned by **NetApp_SockOpen()/**
                   NetSock_Open()/socket() when the socket was created.

paddr_remote   Pointer to a socket address structure (see section 8-2 "Socket
                   Interface" on page 212) which contains the remote socket
                   address to connect the socket to.

addr_len   Size of the socket address structure which *must* be passed the
                   size   of   the   socket   address   structure   [e.g.,
                   sizeof(NET_SOCK_ADDR_IP)].

retry_max   Maximum number of consecutive socket connect retries.

timeout_ms   Socket connect timeout value per attempt/retry.

time_dly_ms   Socket connect delay value, in milliseconds.

perr   Pointer to variable that will receive the error code from this function:

            NET_APP_ERR_NONE

            NET_APP_ERR_NONE_AVAIL

            NET_APP_ERR_INVALID_ARG

            NET_APP_ERR_INVALID_OP

            NET_APP_ERR_FAULT

            NET_APP_ERR_FAULT_TRANSITORY

RETURNED VALUE

DEF_OK,   Application socket successfully connected to a remote address.

DEF_FAIL,   otherwise.

REQUIRED CONFIGURATION

Available only if **NET_APP_CFG_API_EN** is enabled (see section D-18-1 on page 984) *and* either **NET_CFG_TRANSPORT_LAYER_SEL** is configured for TCP (see section D-12-1 on page 972) and/or **NET_UDP_CFG_APP_API_SEL** is configured for sockets (see section D-13-1 on page 973).

NOTES / WARNINGS

Some socket arguments and/or operations are validated only if validation code is enabled (see section D-3-1 on page 965).

If a non-zero number of retries is requested (**retry_max**) *and* socket blocking is configured for non-blocking operation (see section D-15-3 on page 977); then a non-zero timeout (**timeout_ms**) and/or a non-zero time delay (**time_dly_ms**) should also be requested. Otherwise, all retries will most likely fail immediately since no time will elapse to wait for and allow socket operations to successfully complete.

C-2-5 NetApp_SockListen() (TCP)

Set an application socket to listen for connection requests, with error handling. See section C-14-34 on page 873 for more information.

FILES

net_app.h/net_app.c

PROTOTYPE

```
CPU_BOOLEAN  NetApp_SockListen (NET_SOCK_ID      sock_id,
                                NET_SOCK_Q_SIZE  sock_q_size,
                                NET_ERR          *perr);
```

ARGUMENTS

sock_id   This is the socket ID returned by **NetApp_SockOpen()**/ **NetSock_Open()/socket()** when the socket was created.

sock_q_size Maximum number of new connections allowed to be waiting. In other words, this argument specifies the maximum queue length of pending connections while the listening socket is busy servicing the current request.

perr   Pointer to variable that will receive the error code from this function:

             NET_APP_ERR_NONE
             NET_APP_ERR_INVALID_ARG
             NET_APP_ERR_INVALID_OP
             NET_APP_ERR_FAULT
             NET_APP_ERR_FAULT_TRANSITORY

RETURNED VALUE

DEF_OK,   Application socket successfully set to listen.

DEF_FAIL,   otherwise.

REQUIRED CONFIGURATION

Available only if `NET_APP_CFG_API_EN` is enabled (see section D-18-1 on page 984) **AND** `NET_CFG_TRANSPORT_LAYER_SEL` is configured for TCP (see section D-12-1 on page 972).

NOTES / WARNINGS

Some socket arguments and/or operations are validated only if validation code is enabled (see section D-3-1 on page 965).

C-2-6 NetApp_SockOpen() (TCP/UDP)

Open an application socket, with error handling. See section C-14-35 on page 875 for more information.

FILES

net_app.h/net_app.c

PROTOTYPE

```
NET_SOCK_ID  NetApp_SockOpen (NET_SOCK_PROTOCOL_FAMILY    protocol_family,
                              NET_SOCK_TYPE               sock_type,
                              NET_SOCK_PROTOCOL           protocol,
                              CPU_INT16U                  retry_max,
                              CPU_INT32U                  time_dly_ms,
                              NET_ERR                     *perr);
```

ARGUMENTS

protocol_family   This field establishes the socket protocol family domain. Always use **NET_SOCK_FAMILY_IP_V4/PF_INET** for TCP/IP sockets.

sock_type   Socket type:

NET_SOCK_TYPE_DATAGRAM/PF_DGRAM for datagram sockets (i.e., UDP)

NET_SOCK_TYPE_STREAM/PF_STREAM for stream sockets (i.e., TCP)

NET_SOCK_TYPE_DATAGRAM sockets preserve message boundaries. Applications that exchange single request and response messages are examples of datagram communication.

NET_SOCK_TYPE_STREAM sockets provides a reliable byte-stream connection, where bytes are received from the remote application in the same order as they were sent. File transfer and terminal emulation are examples of applications that require this type of protocol.

protocol   Socket protocol:
             NET_SOCK_PROTOCOL_UDP/IPPROTO_UDP for UDP
             NET_SOCK_PROTOCOL_TCP/IPPROTO_TCP for TCP

             0 for default-protocol:
             UDP for NET_SOCK_TYPE_DATAGRAM/PF_DGRAM
             TCP for NET_SOCK_TYPE_STREAM/PF_STREAM

retry_max   Maximum number of consecutive socket open retries.

time_dly_ms Socket open delay value, in milliseconds.

perr   Pointer to variable that will receive the error code from this function:

             NET_APP_ERR_NONE
             NET_APP_ERR_NONE_AVAIL
             NET_APP_ERR_INVALID_ARG
             NET_APP_ERR_FAULT

RETURNED VALUE

Socket descriptor/handle identifier of new socket, if no errors.

NET_SOCK_BSD_ERR_OPEN, otherwise.

REQUIRED CONFIGURATION

Available only if NET_APP_CFG_API_EN is enabled (see section D-18-1 on page 984) *and* either NET_CFG_TRANSPORT_LAYER_SEL is configured for TCP (see section D-12-1 on page 972) and/or NET_UDP_CFG_APP_API_SEL is configured for sockets (see section D-13-1 on page 973).

NOTES / WARNINGS

Some socket arguments and/or operations are validated only if validation code is enabled (see section D-3-1 on page 965).

If a non-zero number of retries is requested (retry_max) then a non-zero time delay (time_dly_ms) should also be requested. Otherwise, all retries will likely fail immediately since no time will elapse to wait for and allow socket operations to successfully complete.

C-2-7 NetApp_SockRx() (TCP/UDP)

Receive application data via socket, with error handling. See section C-14-40 on page 884 for more information.

FILES

net_app.h/net_app.c

PROTOTYPE

```
CPU_INT16U  NetApp_SockRx (NET_SOCK_ID        sock_id,
                           void               *pdata_buf,
                           CPU_INT16U         data_buf_len,
                           CPU_INT16U         data_rx_th,
                           CPU_INT16S         flags,
                           NET_SOCK_ADDR      *paddr_remote,
                           NET_SOCK_ADDR_LEN  *paddr_len,
                           CPU_INT16U         retry_max,
                           CPU_INT32U         timeout_ms,
                           CPU_INT32U         time_dly_ms,
                           NET_ERR            *perr);
```

ARGUMENTS

sock_id   This is the socket ID returned by **NetApp_SockOpen()/** **NetSock_Open()/socket()** when the socket was created *or* by **NetApp_SockAccept()/NetSock_Accept()/accept()** when a connection was accepted.

pdata_buf   Pointer to the application memory buffer to receive data.

data_buf_len   Size of the destination application memory buffer (in bytes).

data_rx_th   Application data receive threshold:

               0, no minimum receive threshold; i.e. receive any amount of data. Recommended for datagram sockets;

               Minimum amount of application data to receive (in bytes) within maximum number of retries, otherwise.

flags   Flag to select receive options; bit-field flags logically **OR**'d:

               NET_SOCK_FLAG_NONE/0   No socket flags selected
               NET_SOCK_FLAG_RX_DATA_PEEK/
               MSG_PEEK   Receive socket data without consuming it
               NET_SOCK_FLAG_RX_NO_BLOCK/
               MSG_DONTWAIT   Receive socket data without blocking

               In most cases, this flag would be set to NET_SOCK_FLAG_NONE/0.

paddr_remote   Pointer to a socket address structure (see section 8-2 "Socket Interface" on page 212) to return the remote host address that sent the received data.

paddr_len   Pointer to the size of the socket address structure which *must* be passed the size of the socket address structure [e.g., sizeof(NET_SOCK_ADDR_IP)]. Returns size of the accepted connection's socket address structure, if no errors; returns 0, otherwise.

retry_max   Maximum number of consecutive socket receive retries.

timeout_ms   Socket receive timeout value per attempt/retry.

time_dly_ms   Socket receive delay value, in milliseconds.

perr   Pointer to variable that will receive the error code from this function:

               NET_APP_ERR_NONE
               NET_APP_ERR_INVALID_ARG
               NET_APP_ERR_INVALID_OP
               NET_APP_ERR_FAULT
               NET_APP_ERR_FAULT_TRANSITORY
               NET_APP_ERR_CONN_CLOSED
               NET_APP_ERR_DATA_BUF_OVF
               NET_ERR_RX

RETURNED VALUE

Number of data bytes received, if no errors.

0, otherwise.

REQUIRED CONFIGURATION

Available only if `NET_APP_CFG_API_EN` is enabled (see section D-18-1 on page 984) *and* either `NET_CFG_TRANSPORT_LAYER_SEL` is configured for TCP (see section D-12-1 on page 972) and/or `NET_UDP_CFG_APP_API_SEL` is configured for sockets (see section D-13-1 on page 973).

NOTES / WARNINGS

Some socket arguments and/or operations are validated only if validation code is enabled (see section D-3-1 on page 965).

If a non-zero number of retries is requested (`retry_max`) *and* socket blocking is configured for non-blocking operation (see section D-15-3 on page 977); then a non-zero timeout (`timeout_ms`) and/or a non-zero time delay (`time_dly_ms`) should also be requested. Otherwise, all retries will most likely fail immediately since no time will elapse to wait for and allow socket operations to successfully complete.

C-2-8 NetApp_SockTx() (TCP/UDP)

Transmit application data via socket, with error handling. See section C-14-42 on page 891 for more information.

FILES

net_app.h/net_app.c

PROTOTYPE

```
CPU_INT16U  NetApp_SockTx (NET_SOCK_ID        sock_id,
                           void               *p_data,
                           CPU_INT16U         data_len,
                           CPU_INT16S         flags,
                           NET_SOCK_ADDR      *paddr_remote,
                           NET_SOCK_ADDR_LEN  addr_len,
                           CPU_INT16U         retry_max,
                           CPU_INT32U         timeout_ms,
                           CPU_INT32U         time_dly_ms,
                           NET_ERR            *perr);
```

ARGUMENTS

sock_id   The socket ID returned by **NetApp_SockOpen()/NetSock_Open()/socket()** when the socket was created *or* by **NetApp_SockAccept()/ NetSock_Accept()/accept()** when a connection was accepted.

p_data   Pointer to the application data memory buffer to send.

data_len   Size of the application data memory buffer (in bytes).

flags   Flag to select transmit options; bit-field flags logically **OR**'d:

NET_SOCK_FLAG_NONE/0
NET_SOCK_FLAG_TX_NO_BLOCK/   No socket flags selected
MSG_DONTWAIT   Send socket data without blocking

In most cases, this flag would be set to **NET_SOCK_FLAG_NONE/0**.

paddr_remote Pointer to a socket address structure (see section 8-2 "Socket Interface" on page 212) which contains the remote socket address to send data to.

addr_len Size of the socket address structure which *must* be passed the size of the socket address structure [e.g., **sizeof(NET_SOCK_ADDR_IP)**].

retry_max Maximum number of consecutive socket transmit retries.

timeout_ms Socket transmit timeout value per attempt/retry.

time_dly_ms Socket transmit delay value, in milliseconds.

perr Pointer to variable that will receive the error code from this function:

NET_APP_ERR_NONE
NET_APP_ERR_INVALID_ARG
NET_APP_ERR_INVALID_OP
NET_APP_ERR_FAULT
NET_APP_ERR_FAULT_TRANSITORY
NET_APP_ERR_CONN_CLOSED
NET_ERR_TX

RETURNED VALUE

Number of data bytes transmitted, if no errors.

0, otherwise.

REQUIRED CONFIGURATION

Available only if **NET_APP_CFG_API_EN** is enabled (see section D-18-1 on page 984) *and* either **NET_CFG_TRANSPORT_LAYER_SEL** is configured for TCP (see section D-12-1 on page 972) and/or **NET_UDP_CFG_APP_API_SEL** is configured for sockets (see section D-13-1 on page 973).

NOTES / WARNINGS

Some socket arguments and/or operations are validated only if validation code is enabled (see section D-3-1 on page 965).

If a non-zero number of retries is requested (**retry_max**) *and* socket blocking is configured for non-blocking operation (see section D-15-3 on page 977); then a non-zero timeout (**timeout_ms**) and/or a non-zero time delay (**time_dly_ms**) should also be requested. Otherwise, all retries will most likely fail immediately since no time will elapse to wait for and allow socket operations to successfully complete.

C-2-9 NetApp_TimeDly_ms()

Delay for specified time, in milliseconds.

FILES

net_app.h/net_app.c

PROTOTYPE

```
void  NetApp_TimeDly_ms (CPU_INT32U   time_dly_ms,
                         NET_ERR     *perr);
```

ARGUMENTS

time_dly_ms Time delay value, in milliseconds.

perr Pointer to variable that will receive the error code from this function:

　　　　　NET_APP_ERR_NONE
　　　　　NET_APP_ERR_INVALID_ARG
　　　　　NET_APP_ERR_FAULT

RETURNED VALUE

None.

REQUIRED CONFIGURATION

Available only if **NET_APP_CFG_API_EN** is enabled (see section D-18-1 on page 984).

NOTES / WARNINGS

Time delay of **0** milliseconds allowed. Time delay limited to the maximum possible time delay supported by the system/OS.

C-3 ARP FUNCTIONS

C-3-1 NetARP_CacheCalcStat()

Calculate ARP cache found percentage statistics.

FILES

net_arp.h/net_arp.c

PROTOTYPE

```
CPU_INT08U NetARP_CacheCalcStat(void);
```

ARGUMENTS

None.

RETURNED VALUE

ARP cache found percentage, if no errors.

NULL cache found percentage, otherwise.

REQUIRED CONFIGURATION

Available only if an appropriate network interface layer is present (e.g., Ethernet; see section D-7-3 on page 968).

NOTES / WARNINGS

None.

C-3-2 NetARP_CacheGetAddrHW()

Get the hardware address corresponding to a specific ARP cache's protocol address.

FILES

net_arp.h/net_arp.c

PROTOTYPE

```
NET_ARP_ADDR_LEN NetARP_CacheGetAddrHW (CPU_INT08U        *paddr_hw
                                        NET_ARP_ADDR_LEN   addr_hw_len_buf,
                                        CPU_INT08U        *paddr_protocol,
                                        NET_ARP_ADDR_LEN   addr_protocol_len,
                                        NET_ERR           *perr);
```

ARGUMENTS

paddr_hw   Pointer to a memory buffer that will receive the hardware
                    address:

                    Hardware address that corresponds to the desired protocol
                    address, if no errors; hardware address cleared to all zeros,
                    otherwise.

addr_hw_len_buf   Size of hardware address memory buffer (in bytes).

paddr_protocol   Pointer to the specific protocol address.

addr_protocol_len   Length of protocol address (in bytes).

perr   Pointer to variable that will receive the error code from this function:

            NET_ARP_ERR_NONE
            NET_ARP_ERR_NULL_PTR
            NET_ARP_ERR_INVALID_HW_ADDR_LEN
            NET_ARP_ERR_INVALID_PROTOCOL_ADDR_LEN
            NET_ARP_ERR_CACHE_NOT_FOUND
            NET_ARP_ERR_CACHE_PEND

RETURNED VALUE

Length of returned hardware address, if available;

0, otherwise.

REQUIRED CONFIGURATION

Available only if an appropriate network interface layer is present (e.g., Ethernet; see section D-7-3 on page 968).

NOTES / WARNINGS

`NetARP_CacheGetAddrHW()` may be used in conjunction with `NetARP_ProbeAddrOnNet()` to determine if a specific protocol address is available on the local network.

C-3-3 NetARP_CachePoolStatGet()

Get ARP caches' statistics pool.

FILES

net_arp.h/net_arp.c

PROTOTYPE

```
NET_STAT_POOL NetARP_CachePoolStatGet(void);
```

ARGUMENTS

None.

RETURNED VALUE

ARP caches' statistics pool, if no errors.

NULL statistics pool, otherwise.

REQUIRED CONFIGURATION

Available only if an appropriate network interface layer is present (e.g., Ethernet; see section D-7-3 on page 968).

NOTES / WARNINGS

None.

C-3-4 NetARP_CachePoolStatResetMaxUsed()

Reset ARP caches' statistics pool's maximum number of entries used.

FILES

net_arp.h/net_arp.c

PROTOTYPE

```
void NetARP_CachePoolStatResetMaxUsed(void);
```

ARGUMENTS

None.

RETURNED VALUE

None.

REQUIRED CONFIGURATION

Available only if an appropriate network interface layer is present (e.g., Ethernet; see section D-7-3 on page 968).

NOTES / WARNINGS

None.

C-3-5 NetARP_CfgCacheAccessedTh()

Configure ARP cache access promotion threshold.

FILES

net_arp.h/net_arp.c

PROTOTYPE

```
CPU_BOOLEAN NetARP_CfgCacheAccessedTh(CPU_INT16U nbr_access);
```

ARGUMENTS

nbr_access   Desired number of ARP cache accesses before ARP cache entry
                    is promoted.

RETURNED VALUE

DEF_OK,   ARP cache access promotion threshold successfully configured;

DEF_FAIL,   otherwise.

REQUIRED CONFIGURATION

Available only if an appropriate network interface layer is present (e.g., Ethernet; see section D-7-3 on page 968).

NOTES / WARNINGS

None.

C-3-6 NetARP_CfgCacheTimeout()

Configure ARP cache timeout for ARP Cache List. ARP cache entries will be retired if they are not used within the specified timeout.

FILES

net_arp.h/net_arp.c

PROTOTYPE

```
CPU_BOOLEAN NetARP_CfgCacheTimeout(CPU_INT16U timeout_sec);
```

ARGUMENTS

timeout_sec   Desired value for ARP cache timeout (in seconds)

RETURNED VALUE

DEF_OK,   ARP cache timeout successfully configured;

DEF_FAIL,   otherwise.

REQUIRED CONFIGURATION

Available only if an appropriate network interface layer is present (e.g., Ethernet; see section D-7-3 on page 968).

NOTES / WARNINGS

None.

C-3-7 NetARP_CfgReqMaxRetries()

Configure maximum number of ARP request retries.

FILES

net_arp.h/net_arp.c

PROTOTYPE

```
CPU_BOOLEAN NetARP_CfgReqMaxRetries(CPU_INT08U max_nbr_retries);
```

ARGUMENTS

max_nbr_retries   Desired maximum number of ARP request retries.

RETURNED VALUE

DEF_OK,   maximum number of ARP request retries configured.

DEF_FAIL,   otherwise.

REQUIRED CONFIGURATION

Available only if an appropriate network interface layer is present (e.g., Ethernet; see section D-7-3 on page 968).

NOTES / WARNINGS

None.

C-3-8 NetARP_CfgReqTimeout()

Configure timeout between ARP request timeouts.

FILES

net_arp.h/net_arp.c

PROTOTYPE

```
CPU_BOOLEAN NetARP_CfgReqTimeout(CPU_INT08U timeout_sec);
```

ARGUMENTS

timeout_sec   Desired value for ARP request pending ARP reply timeout (in seconds).

RETURNED VALUE

DEF_OK,   ARP request timeout successfully configured,

DEF_FAIL,   otherwise.

REQUIRED CONFIGURATION

Available only if an appropriate network interface layer is present (e.g., Ethernet; see section D-7-3 on page 968).

NOTES / WARNINGS

None.

C-3-9 NetARP_IsAddrProtocolConflict()

Check interface's protocol address conflict status between this interface's ARP host protocol address(es) and any other host(s) on the local network.

FILES

net_arp.h/net_arp.c

PROTOTYPE

```
CPU_BOOLEAN NetARP_IsAddrProtocolConflict (NET_IF_NBR  if_nbr,
                                           NET_ERR    *perr);
```

ARGUMENTS

if_nbr   Interface number to get protocol address conflict status.

perr   Pointer to variable that will receive the return error code from this function:

        NET_ARP_ERR_NONE
        NET_IF_ERR_INVALID_IF
        NET_OS_ERR_LOCK

RETURNED VALUE

DEF_YES   if address conflict detected;
DEF_NO   otherwise.

REQUIRED CONFIGURATION

Available only if an appropriate network interface layer is present (e.g., Ethernet; see section D-7-3 on page 968).

NOTES / WARNINGS

None.

C-3-10 NetARP_ProbeAddrOnNet()

Transmit an ARP request to probe the local network for a specific protocol address.

FILES

net_arp.h/net_arp.c

PROTOTYPE

```
void NetARP_ProbeAddrOnNet(NET_PROTOCOL_TYPE  protocol_type,
                          CPU_INT08U        *paddr_protocol_sender,
                          CPU_INT08U        *paddr_protocol_target
                          NET_ARP_ADDR_LEN   addr_protocol_len,
                          NET_ERR           *perr);
```

ARGUMENTS

protocol_type   Address protocol type.

paddr_protocol_sender Pointer to protocol address to send probe from.

paddr_protocol_target Pointer to protocol address to probe local network.

addr_protocol_len   Length of protocol address (in bytes).

perr   Pointer to variable that will receive the return error code from this function:

        NET_ARP_ERR_NONE
        NET_ARP_ERR_NULL_PTR
        NET_ARP_ERR_INVALID_PROTOCOL_ADDR_LEN
        NET_ARP_ERR_CACHE_INVALID_TYPE
        NET_ARP_ERR_CACHE_NONE_AVAIL
        NET_MGR_ERR_INVALID_PROTOCOL
        NET_MGR_ERR_INVALID_PROTOCOL_ADDR
        NET_MGR_ERR_INVALID_PROTOCOL_ADDR_LEN
        NET_TMR_ERR_NULL_OBJ
        NET_TMR_ERR_NULL_FNCT
        NET_TMR_ERR_NONE_AVAIL
        NET_TMR_ERR_INVALID_TYPE
        NET_OS_ERR_LOCK

RETURNED VALUE

None.

REQUIRED CONFIGURATION

Available only if an appropriate network interface layer is present (e.g., Ethernet; see section D-7-3 on page 968).

NOTES / WARNINGS

`NetARP_ProbeAddrOnNet()` may be used in conjunction with `NetARP_CacheGetAddrHW()` to determine if a specific protocol address is available on the local network.

C-4 NETWORK ASCII FUNCTIONS

C-4-1 NetASCII_IP_to_Str()

Convert an IPv4 address in host-order into an IPv4 dotted-decimal notation ASCII string.

FILES

net_ascii.h/net_ascii.c

PROTOTYPE

```
void  NetASCII_IP_to_Str(NET_IP_ADDR    addr_ip,
                         CPU_CHAR      *paddr_ip_ascii,
                         CPU_BOOLEAN    lead_zeros,
                         NET_ERR       *perr);
```

ARGUMENTS

addr_ip   IPv4 address (in host-order).

paddr_ip_ascii   Pointer to a memory buffer of size greater than or equal to
                        NET_ASCII_LEN_MAX_ADDR_IP bytes to receive the IPv4 address
                        string. Note that the first ASCII character in the string is the most
                        significant nibble of the IP address's most significant byte and
                        that the last character in the string is the least significant nibble
                        of the IP address's least significant byte. Example: "10.10.1.65" =
                        0x0A0A0141

lead_zeros   Select formatting the IPv4 address string with leading zeros ('0') prior to the
              first non-zero digit in each IP address byte. The number of leading zeros
              added is such that each byte's total number of decimal digits is equal to the
              maximum number of digits for each byte (i.e., 3).

              DEF_NO   Do *not* prepend leading zeros to each IP
                                                  address byte
              DEF_YES   Prepend leading zeros to each IP address
                                                  byte

perr   Pointer to variable that will receive the return error code from this function:

    NET_ASCII_ERR_NONE
    NET_ASCII_ERR_NULL_PTR
    NET_ASCII_ERR_INVALID_CHAR_LEN

RETURNED VALUE

None.

REQUIRED CONFIGURATION

None.

NOTES / WARNINGS

RFC 1983 states that "dotted-decimal notation... refers [to] IP addresses of the form A.B.C.D; where each letter represents, in decimal, one byte of a four-byte IP address." In other words, the dotted-decimal notation separates four decimal byte values by the dot, or period, character ('.'). Each decimal value represents one byte of the IP address starting with the most significant byte in network order.

IPv4 Address Examples:

DOTTED DECIMAL NOTATION	HEXADECIMAL EQUIVALENT
127.0.0.1	0x7F000001
192.168.1.64	0xC0A80140
255.255.255.0	0xFFFFFF00
MSB .... LSB	MSB .... LSB

MSB   Most Significant Byte in Dotted-Decimal IP Address

LSB   Least Significant Byte in Dotted-Decimal IP Address

C-4-2 NetASCII_MAC_to_Str()

Convert a Media Access Control (MAC) address into a hexadecimal address string.

net_ascii.h/net_ascii.c

```
void NetASCII_MAC_to_Str(CPU_INT08U   *paddr_mac,
                         CPU_CHAR     *paddr_mac_ascii,
                         CPU_BOOLEAN   hex_lower_case,
                         CPU_BOOLEAN   hex_colon_sep,
                         NET_ERR      *perr);
```

paddr_mac   Pointer to a memory buffer of **NET_ASCII_NBR_OCTET_ADDR_MAC** bytes in size that contains the MAC address.

paddr_mac_ascii   Pointer to a memory buffer of size greater than or equal to **NET_ASCII_LEN_MAX_ADDR_MAC** bytes to receive the MAC address string. Note that the first ASCII character in the string is the most significant nibble of the MAC address's most significant byte and that the last character in the string is the least significant nibble of the MAC address's least significant address byte.

                               Example: **"00:1A:07:AC:22:09"** = 0x001A07AC2209

hex_lower_case   Select formatting the MAC address string with upper- or lower-case ASCII characters:

DEF_NO	Format MAC address string with upper-case characters
DEF_YES	Format MAC address string with lower-case characters

hex_colon_sep Select formatting the MAC address string with colon (':') or dash ('-') characters to separate the MAC address hexadecimal bytes:

> **DEF_NO** Separate MAC address bytes with hyphen characters
>
> **DEF_YES** Separate MAC address bytes with colon characters

perr Pointer to variable that will receive the return error code from this function:

> NET_ASCII_ERR_NONE
> NET_ASCII_ERR_NULL_PTR

RETURNED VALUE

None.

REQUIRED CONFIGURATION

None.

NOTES / WARNINGS

None.

C-4-3 NetASCII_Str_to_IP()

Convert a string of an IPv4 address in dotted-decimal notation to an IPv4 address in host-order.

FILES

net_ascii.h/net_ascii.c

PROTOTYPE

```
NET_IP_ADDR NetASCII_Str_to_IP(CPU_CHAR  *paddr_ip_ascii,
                                NET_ERR   *perr);
```

ARGUMENTS

paddr_ip_ascii   Pointer to an ASCII string that contains a dotted-decimal IPv4 address. Each decimal byte of the IPv4 address string must be separated by a dot, or period, character ('.'). Note that the first ASCII character in the string is the most significant nibble of the IP address's most significant byte and that the last character in the string is the least significant nibble of the IP address's least significant byte.

Example: "10.10.1.65" = 0x0A0A0141

perr   Pointer to variable that will receive the return error code from this function:

NET_ASCII_ERR_NONE
NET_ASCII_ERR_NULL_PTR
NET_ASCII_ERR_INVALID_STR_LEN
NET_ASCII_ERR_INVALID_CHAR
NET_ASCII_ERR_INVALID_CHAR_LEN
NET_ASCII_ERR_INVALID_CHAR_VAL
NET_ASCII_ERR_INVALID_CHAR_SEQ

RETURNED VALUE

Returns the IPv4 address, represented by the IPv3 address string, in host-order, if no errors.

`NET_IP_ADDR_NONE`, otherwise.

REQUIRED CONFIGURATION

None.

NOTES / WARNINGS

RFC 1983 states that "dotted decimal notation… refers [to] IP addresses of the form A.B.C.D; where each letter represents, in decimal, one byte of a four-byte IP address". In other words, the dotted-decimal notation separates four decimal byte values by the dot, or period, character ('.'). Each decimal value represents one byte of the IP address starting with the most significant byte in network order.

IPv4 Address Examples:

DOTTED DECIMAL NOTATION	HEXADECIMAL EQUIVALENT
127.0.0.1	0x7F000001
192.168.1.64	0xC0A80140
255.255.255.0	0xFFFFFF00
MSB .... LSB	MSB .... LSB

MSB   Most Significant Byte in Dotted-Decimal IP Address

LSB   Least Significant Byte in Dotted-Decimal IP Address

The IPv4 dotted-decimal ASCII string *must* include *only* decimal values and the dot, or period, character ('.'); all other characters are trapped as invalid, including any leading or trailing characters. The ASCII string *must* include exactly four decimal values separated by exactly three dot characters. Each decimal value *must not* exceed the maximum byte value (i.e., 255), or exceed the maximum number of digits for each byte (i.e., 3) including any leading zeros.

C-4-4 NetASCII_Str_to_MAC()

Convert a hexadecimal address string to a Media Access Control (MAC) address.

FILES

net_ascii.h/net_ascii.c

PROTOTYPE

```
void NetASCII_Str_to_MAC(CPU_CHAR    *paddr_mac_ascii,
                         CPU_INT08U  *paddr_mac,
                         NET_ERR     *perr);
```

ARGUMENTS

paddr_mac_ascii   Pointer to an ASCII string that contains hexadecimal bytes
                     separated by colons or dashes that represents the MAC address.
                     Each hexadecimal byte of the MAC address string must be
                     separated by either the colon (':') or dash ('-') characters. Note
                     that the first ASCII character in the string is the most significant
                     nibble of the MAC address's most significant byte and that the
                     last character in the string is the least significant nibble of the
                     MAC address's least significant address byte.

                     Example: "00:1A:07:AC:22:09" = 0x001A07AC2209

paddr_mac   Pointer to a memory buffer of size greater than or equal to
            NET_ASCII_NBR_OCTET_ADDR_MAC bytes to receive the MAC address.

perr   Pointer to variable that will receive the return error code from this function:

            NET_ASCII_ERR_NONE
            NET_ASCII_ERR_NULL_PTR
            NET_ASCII_ERR_INVALID_STR_LEN
            NET_ASCII_ERR_INVALID_CHAR
            NET_ASCII_ERR_INVALID_CHAR_LEN
            NET_ASCII_ERR_INVALID_CHAR_SEQ

RETURNED VALUE

None.

REQUIRED CONFIGURATION

None.

NOTES / WARNINGS

None.

C-5 NETWORK BUFFER FUNCTIONS

C-5-1 NetBuf_PoolStatGet()

Get an interface's Network Buffers' statistics pool.

FILES

net_buf.h/net_buf.c

PROTOTYPE

```
NET_STAT_POOL NetBuf_PoolStatGet(NET_IF_NBR if_nbr);
```

ARGUMENTS

if_nbr   Interface number to get Network Buffer statistics.

RETURNED VALUE

Network Buffers' statistics pool, if no errors.

NULL statistics pool, otherwise.

REQUIRED CONFIGURATION

None.

NOTES / WARNINGS

None.

C-5-2 NetBuf_PoolStatResetMaxUsed()

Reset an interface's Network Buffers' statistics pool's maximum number of entries used.

FILES

net_buf.h/net_buf.c

PROTOTYPE

```
void NetBuf_PoolStatResetMaxUsed(NET_IF_NBR if_nbr);
```

ARGUMENTS

if_nbr   Interface number to reset Network Buffer statistics.

RETURNED VALUE

None.

REQUIRED CONFIGURATION

None.

NOTES / WARNINGS

None.

C-5-3 NetBuf_RxLargePoolStatGet()

Get an interface's large receive buffers' statistics pool.

FILES

net_buf.h/net_buf.c

PROTOTYPE

```
NET_STAT_POOL NetBuf_RxLargePoolStatGet(NET_IF_NBR if_nbr);
```

ARGUMENTS

if_nbr   Interface number to get Network Buffer statistics.

RETURNED VALUE

Large receive buffers' statistics pool, if no errors.

NULL statistics pool, otherwise.

REQUIRED CONFIGURATION

None.

NOTES / WARNINGS

None.

C-5-4 NetBuf_RxLargePoolStatResetMaxUsed()

Reset an interface's large receive buffers' statistics pool's maximum number of entries used.

FILES

net_buf.h/net_buf.c

PROTOTYPE

```
void NetBuf_RxLargePoolStatResetMaxUsed(NET_IF_NBR if_nbr);
```

ARGUMENTS

if_nbr   Interface number to reset Network Buffer statistics.

RETURNED VALUE

None.

REQUIRED CONFIGURATION

None.

NOTES / WARNINGS

None.

C-5-5 NetBuf_TxLargePoolStatGet()

Get an interface's large transmit buffers' statistics pool.

FILES

net_buf.h/net_buf.c

PROTOTYPE

```
NET_STAT_POOL NetBuf_TxLargePoolStatGet(NET_IF_NBR if_nbr);
```

ARGUMENTS

if_nbr   Interface number to get Network Buffer statistics.

RETURNED VALUE

Large transmit buffers' statistics pool, if no errors.

NULL statistics pool, otherwise.

REQUIRED CONFIGURATION

None.

NOTES / WARNINGS

None.

C-5-6 NetBuf_TxLargePoolStatResetMaxUsed()

Reset an interface's large transmit buffers' statistics pool's maximum number of entries used.

FILES

net_buf.h/net_buf.c

PROTOTYPE

```
void NetBuf_TxLargePoolStatResetMaxUsed(NET_IF_NBR if_nbr);
```

ARGUMENTS

if_nbr   Interface number to reset Network Buffer statistics.

RETURNED VALUE

None.

REQUIRED CONFIGURATION

None.

NOTES / WARNINGS

None.

C-5-7 NetBuf_TxSmallPoolStatGet()

Get an interface's small transmit buffers' statistics pool.

FILES

net_buf.h/net_buf.c

PROTOTYPE

```
NET_STAT_POOL NetBuf_TxSmallPoolStatGet(NET_IF_NBR if_nbr);
```

ARGUMENTS

if_nbr   Interface number to get Network Buffer statistics.

RETURNED VALUE

Small transmit buffers' statistics pool, if no errors.

NULL statistics pool, otherwise.

REQUIRED CONFIGURATION

None.

NOTES / WARNINGS

None.

C-5-8 NetBuf_TxSmallPoolStatResetMaxUsed()

Reset an interface's small transmit buffers' statistics pool's maximum number of entries used.

FILES

net_buf.h/net_buf.c

PROTOTYPE

```
void NetBuf_TxSmallPoolStatResetMaxUsed(NET_IF_NBR if_nbr);
```

ARGUMENTS

if_nbr   Interface number to reset Network Buffer statistics.

RETURNED VALUE

None.

REQUIRED CONFIGURATION

None.

NOTES / WARNINGS

None.

C-6 NETWORK CONNECTION FUNCTIONS

C-6-1 NetConn_CfgAccessedTh()

Configure network connection access promotion threshold.

FILES

net_conn.h/net_conn.c

PROTOTYPE

```
CPU_BOOLEAN NetConn_CfgAccessedTh(CPU_INT16U nbr_access);
```

ARGUMENTS

nbr_access   Desired number of accesses before network connection is promoted.

RETURNED VALUE

DEF_OK,   network connection access promotion threshold configured.

DEF_FAIL,   otherwise.

REQUIRED CONFIGURATION

Available only if either NET_CFG_TRANSPORT_LAYER_SEL is configured for TCP (see section D-12-1 on page 972) and/or NET_UDP_CFG_APP_API_SEL is configured for sockets (see section D-13-1 on page 973).

NOTES / WARNINGS

None.

C-6-2 NetConn_PoolStatGet()

Get Network Connections' statistics pool.

FILES

net_conn.h/net_conn.c

PROTOTYPE

```
NET_STAT_POOL NetConn_PoolStatGet(void);
```

ARGUMENTS

None.

RETURNED VALUE

Network Connections' statistics pool, if no errors.

NULL statistics pool, otherwise.

REQUIRED CONFIGURATION

Available only if either **NET_CFG_TRANSPORT_LAYER_SEL** is configured for TCP (see section D-12-1 on page 972) and/or **NET_UDP_CFG_APP_API_SEL** is configured for sockets (see section D-13-1 on page 973).

NOTES / WARNINGS

None.

C-6-3 NetConn_PoolStatResetMaxUsed()

Reset Network Connections' statistics pool's maximum number of entries used.

FILES

net_conn.h/net_conn.c

PROTOTYPE

```
void NetConn_PoolStatResetMaxUsed(void);
```

ARGUMENTS

None.

RETURNED VALUE

None.

REQUIRED CONFIGURATION

Available only if either **NET_CFG_TRANSPORT_LAYER_SEL** is configured for TCP (see section D-12-1 on page 972) and/or **NET_UDP_CFG_APP_API_SEL** is configured for sockets (see section D-13-1 on page 973).

NOTES / WARNINGS

None.

C-7 NETWORK DEBUG FUNCTIONS

C-7-1 NetDbg_CfgMonTaskTime()

Configure Network Debug Monitor time.

FILES

net_dbg.h/net_dbg.c

PROTOTYPE

```
CPU_BOOLEAN NetDbg_CfgMonTaskTime(CPU_INT16U time_sec);
```

ARGUMENTS

time_sec   Desired value for Network Debug Monitor task time (in seconds).

RETURNED VALUE

DEF_OK,   Network Debug Monitor task time successfully configured.

DEF_FAIL,   otherwise.

REQUIRED CONFIGURATION

Available only if the Network Debug Monitor task is enabled (see section 20-2 "Network Debug Monitor Task" on page 526).

NOTES / WARNINGS

None.

C-7-2 NetDbg_CfgRsrcARP_CacheThLo()

Configure ARP caches' low resource threshold.

net_dbg.h/net_dbg.c

```
CPU_BOOLEAN NetDbg_CfgRsrcARP_CacheThLo(CPU_INT08U th_pct,
                                        CPU_INT08U hyst_pct);
```

th_pct   Desired percentage of ARP caches available to trip low resources.

hyst_pct   Desired percentage of ARP caches freed to clear low resources.

DEF_OK,   ARP caches' low resource threshold successfully configured.

DEF_FAIL,   otherwise.

Available only if **NET_DBG_CFG_DBG_STATUS_EN** is enabled (see section D-2-2 on page 964) and/or if the Network Debug Monitor task is enabled (Se section 20-2 on page 526) **AND** if an appropriate network interface layer is present (e.g., Ethernet; see section D-7-3 on page 968).

None.

C-7-3 NetDbg_CfgRsrcBufThLo()

Configure an interface's network buffers' low resource threshold.

FILES

net_dbg.h/net_dbg.c

PROTOTYPE

```
CPU_BOOLEAN NetDbg_CfgRsrcBufThLo(NET_IF_NBR if_nbr,
                                  CPU_INT08U  th_pct,
                                  CPU_INT08U  hyst_pct);
```

ARGUMENTS

if_nbr   Interface number to configure low threshold and hysteresis.

th_pct   Desired percentage of network buffers available to trip low resources.

hyst_pct   Desired percentage of network buffers freed to clear low resources.

RETURNED VALUE

DEF_OK,   Network buffers' low resource threshold successfully configured.

DEF_FAIL,   otherwise.

REQUIRED CONFIGURATION

Available only if NET_DBG_CFG_DBG_STATUS_EN is enabled (see section D-2-2 on page 964) and/or if the Network Debug Monitor task is enabled (see section 20-2 on page 526).

NOTES / WARNINGS

None.

C-7-4 NetDbg_CfgRsrcBufRxLargeThLo()

Configure an interface's large receive buffers' low resource threshold.

FILES

net_dbg.h/net_dbg.c

PROTOTYPE

```
CPU_BOOLEAN NetDbg_CfgRsrcBufRxLargeThLo(NET_IF_NBR if_nbr,
                                         CPU_INT08U th_pct,
                                         CPU_INT08U hyst_pct);
```

ARGUMENTS

if_nbr   Interface number to configure low threshold & hysteresis.

th_pct   Desired percentage of large receive buffers available to trip low resources.

hyst_pct   Desired percentage of large receive buffers freed to clear low resources.

RETURNED VALUE

DEF_OK,   Large receive buffers' low resource threshold successfully configured.

DEF_FAIL,   otherwise.

REQUIRED CONFIGURATION

Available only if NET_DBG_CFG_DBG_STATUS_EN is enabled (see section D-2-2 on page 964) and/or if the Network Debug Monitor task is enabled (see section 20-2 on page 526).

NOTES / WARNINGS

None.

C-7-5 NetDbg_CfgRsrcBufTxLargeThLo()

Configure an interface's large transmit buffers' low resource threshold.

FILES

net_dbg.h/net_dbg.c

PROTOTYPE

```
CPU_BOOLEAN NetDbg_CfgRsrcBufTxLargeThLo(NET_IF_NBR if_nbr,
                                         CPU_INT08U th_pct,
                                         CPU_INT08U hyst_pct);
```

ARGUMENTS

if_nbr   Interface number to configure low threshold and hysteresis.

th_pct   Desired percentage of large transmit buffers available to trip low resources.

hyst_pct   Desired percentage of large transmit buffers freed to clear low resources.

RETURNED VALUE

DEF_OK,   Large transmit buffers' low resource threshold successfully configured.

DEF_FAIL,   otherwise.

REQUIRED CONFIGURATION

Available only if NET_DBG_CFG_DBG_STATUS_EN is enabled (see section D-2-2 on page 964) and/or if the Network Debug Monitor task is enabled (see section 20-2 on page 526).

NOTES / WARNINGS

None.

C-7-6 NetDbg_CfgRsrcBufTxSmallThLo()

Configure an interface's small transmit buffers' low resource threshold.

FILES

net_dbg.h/net_dbg.c

PROTOTYPE

```
CPU_BOOLEAN NetDbg_CfgRsrcBufTxSmallThLo(NET_IF_NBR if_nbr,
                                         CPU_INT08U th_pct,
                                         CPU_INT08U hyst_pct);
```

ARGUMENTS

if_nbr   Interface number to configure low threshold & hysteresis.

th_pct   Desired percentage of small transmit buffers available to trip low resources.

hyst_pct   Desired percentage of small transmit buffers freed to clear low resources.

RETURNED VALUE

DEF_OK,   Small transmit buffers' low resource threshold successfully configured.

DEF_FAIL,   otherwise.

REQUIRED CONFIGURATION

Available only if NET_DBG_CFG_DBG_STATUS_EN is enabled (see section D-2-2 on page 964) and/or if the Network Debug Monitor task is enabled (see section 20-2 on page 526).

NOTES / WARNINGS

None.

C-7-7 NetDbg_CfgRsrcConnThLo()

Configure network connections' low resource threshold.

FILES

net_dbg.h/net_dbg.c

PROTOTYPE

```
CPU_BOOLEAN NetDbg_CfgRsrcConnThLo(CPU_INT08U th_pct,
                                   CPU_INT08U hyst_pct);
```

ARGUMENTS

th_pct   Desired percentage of network connections available to trip low resources.

hyst_pct   Desired percentage of network connections freed to clear low resources.

RETURNED VALUE

DEF_OK,   Network connections' low resource threshold successfully configured.

DEF_FAIL,   otherwise.

REQUIRED CONFIGURATION

Available only if NET_DBG_CFG_DBG_STATUS_EN is enabled (see section D-2-2 on page 964) and/or if the Network Debug Monitor task is enabled (see section 20-2 on page 526) *and* if either NET_CFG_TRANSPORT_LAYER_SEL is configured for TCP (see section D-12-1 on page 972) and/or NET_UDP_CFG_APP_API_SEL is configured for sockets (see section D-13-1 on page 973).

NOTES / WARNINGS

None.

C-7-8 NetDbg_CfgRsrcSockThLo()

Configure network sockets' low resource threshold.

FILES

net_dbg.h/net_dbg.c

PROTOTYPE

```
CPU_BOOLEAN NetDbg_CfgRsrcSockThLo(CPU_INT08U th_pct,
                                   CPU_INT08U hyst_pct);
```

ARGUMENTS

th_pct   Desired percentage of network sockets available to trip low resources.

hyst_pct   Desired percentage of network sockets freed to clear low resources.

RETURNED VALUE

DEF_OK,   Network sockets' low resource threshold successfully configured.

DEF_FAIL,   otherwise.

REQUIRED CONFIGURATION

Available only if NET_DBG_CFG_DBG_STATUS_EN is enabled (see section D-2-2 on page 964) and/or if the Network Debug Monitor task is enabled (see section 20-2 on page 526) **AND** if either NET_CFG_TRANSPORT_LAYER_SEL is configured for TCP (see section D-12-1 on page 972) and/or NET_UDP_CFG_APP_API_SEL is configured for sockets (see section D-13-1 on page 973).

NOTES / WARNINGS

None.

C-7-9 NetDbg_CfgRsrcTCP_ConnThLo()

Configure TCP connections' low resource threshold.

FILES

net_dbg.h/net_dbg.c

PROTOTYPE

```
CPU_BOOLEAN NetDbg_CfgRsrcTCP_ConnThLo(CPU_INT08U th_pct,
                                       CPU_INT08U hyst_pct);
```

ARGUMENTS

th_pct   Desired percentage of TCP connections available to trip low resources.

hyst_pct   Desired percentage of TCP connections freed to clear low resources.

RETURNED VALUE

DEF_OK,   TCP connections' low resource threshold successfully configured.

DEF_FAIL,   otherwise.

REQUIRED CONFIGURATION

Available only if NET_DBG_CFG_DBG_STATUS_EN is enabled (see section D-2-2 on page 964) and/or if the Network Debug Monitor task is enabled (see section 20-2 on page 526) **AND** if NET_CFG_TRANSPORT_LAYER_SEL is configured for TCP (see section D-12-1 on page 972).

NOTES / WARNINGS

None.

C-7-10 NetDbg_CfgRsrcTmrThLo()

Configure network timers' low resource threshold.

FILES

net_dbg.h/net_dbg.c

PROTOTYPE

```
CPU_BOOLEAN NetDbg_CfgRsrcTmrThLo(CPU_INT08U th_pct,
                                  CPU_INT08U hyst_pct);
```

ARGUMENTS

th_pct   Desired percentage of network timers available to trip low resources.

hyst_pct   Desired percentage of network timers freed to clear low resources.

RETURNED VALUE

DEF_OK,   Network timers' low resource threshold successfully configured.

DEF_FAIL,   otherwise.

REQUIRED CONFIGURATION

Available only if NET_DBG_CFG_DBG_STATUS_EN is enabled (see section D-2-2 on page 964) and/or if the Network Debug Monitor task is enabled (see section 20-2 on page 526).

NOTES / WARNINGS

None.

C-7-11 NetDbg_ChkStatus()

Return the current run-time status of certain µC/TCP-IP conditions.

FILES

net_dbg.h/net_dbg.c

PROTOTYPE

```
NET_DBG_STATUS NetDbg_ChkStatus(void);
```

ARGUMENTS

None.

RETURNED VALUE

NET_DBG_STATUS_OK, if all network conditions are OK (i.e., no warnings, faults, or errors currently exist);

Otherwise, returns the following status condition codes logically **OR**'d:

NET_DBG_STATUS_FAULT   Some network status fault(s)

NET_DBG_STATUS_RSRC_LOST   Some network resources lost.

NET_DBG_STATUS_RSRC_LO   Some network resources low.

NET_DBG_STATUS_FAULT_BUF   Some network buffer management fault(s).

NET_DBG_STATUS_FAULT_TMR   Some network timer management fault(s).

NET_DBG_STATUS_FAULT_CONN   Some network connection management fault(s).

NET_DBG_STATUS_FAULT_TCP   Some TCP layer fault(s).

REQUIRED CONFIGURATION

Available only if `NET_DBG_CFG_DBG_STATUS_EN` is enabled (see section D-2-2 on page 964).

NOTES / WARNINGS

None.

C-7-12 NetDbg_ChkStatusBufs()

Return the current run-time status of µC/TCP-IP network buffers.

FILES

net_dbg.h/net_dbg.c

PROTOTYPE

```
NET_DBG_STATUS NetDbg_ChkStatusBufs(void);
```

ARGUMENTS

None.

RETURNED VALUE

NET_DBG_STATUS_OK, if all network buffer conditions are OK (i.e., no warnings, faults, or errors currently exist);

Otherwise, returns the following status condition codes logically **OR**'d:

NET_DBG_SF_BUF   Some Network Buffer management fault(s).

REQUIRED CONFIGURATION

Available only if NET_DBG_CFG_DBG_STATUS_EN is enabled (see section D-2-2 on page 964).

NOTES / WARNINGS

Debug status information for network buffers has been deprecated in µC/TCP-IP.

C-7-13 NetDbg_ChkStatusConns()

Return the current run-time status of µC/TCP-IP network connections.

FILES

net_dbg.h/net_dbg.c

PROTOTYPE

```
NET_DBG_STATUS NetDbg_ChkStatusConns(void);
```

ARGUMENTS

None.

RETURNED VALUE

NET_DBG_STATUS_OK, if all network connection conditions are OK (i.e., no warnings, faults, or errors currently exist);

Otherwise, returns the following status condition codes logically **OR**'d:

NET_DBG_SF_CONN	Some network connection management fault(s).
NET_DBG_SF_CONN_TYPE	Network connection invalid type.
NET_DBG_SF_CONN_FAMILY	Network connection invalid family.
NET_DBG_SF_CONN_PROTOCOL_IX_NBR_MAX	Network connection invalid protocol list index number.
NET_DBG_SF_CONN_ID	Network connection invalid ID.
NET_DBG_SF_CONN_ID_NONE	Network connection with no connection IDs.

NET_DBG_SF_CONN_ID_UNUSED	Network connection linked to unused connection.
NET_DBG_SF_CONN_LINK_TYPE	Network connection invalid link type.
NET_DBG_SF_CONN_LINK_UNUSED	Network connection link unused.
NET_DBG_SF_CONN_LINK_BACK_TO_CONN	Network connection invalid link back to same connection.
NET_DBG_SF_CONN_LINK_NOT_TO_CONN	Network connection invalid link not back to same connection.
NET_DBG_SF_CONN_LINK_NOT_IN_LIST	Network connection not in appropriate connection list.
NET_DBG_SF_CONN_POOL_TYPE	Network connection invalid pool type.
NET_DBG_SF_CONN_POOL_ID	Network connection invalid pool id.
NET_DBG_SF_CONN_POOL_DUP	Network connection pool contains duplicate connection(s).
NET_DBG_SF_CONN_POOL_NBR_MAX	Network connection pool number of connections greater than maximum number of connections.
NET_DBG_SF_CONN_LIST_NBR_NOT_SOLITARY	Network connection lists number of connections not equal to solitary connection.
NET_DBG_SF_CONN_USED_IN_POOL	Network connection used but in pool.
NET_DBG_SF_CONN_USED_NOT_IN_LIST	Network connection used but not in list.
NET_DBG_SF_CONN_UNUSED_IN_LIST	Network connection unused but in list.

`NET_DBG_SF_CONN_UNUSED_NOT_IN_POOL`	Network connection unused but not in pool.
`NET_DBG_SF_CONN_IN_LIST_IN_POOL`	Network connection in list and in pool.
`NET_DBG_SF_CONN_NOT_IN_LIST_NOT_IN_POOL`	Network connection not in list nor in pool.

REQUIRED CONFIGURATION

Available only if `NET_DBG_CFG_DBG_STATUS_EN` is enabled (see section D-2-2 on page 964) *and* if either `NET_CFG_TRANSPORT_LAYER_SEL` is configured for TCP (see section D-12-1 on page 972) and/or `NET_UDP_CFG_APP_API_SEL` is configured for sockets (see section D-13-1 on page 973).

NOTES / WARNINGS

None.

C-7-14 NetDbg_ChkStatusRsrcLost() / NetDbg_MonTaskStatusGetRsrcLost()

Return whether any µC/TCP-IP resources are currently lost.

FILES

net_dbg.h/net_dbg.c

PROTOTYPES

```
NET_DBG_STATUS NetDbg_ChkStatusRsrcLost(void);
NET_DBG_STATUS NetDbg_MonTaskStatusGetRsrcLost(void);
```

ARGUMENTS

None.

RETURNED VALUE

NET_DBG_STATUS_OK, if no network resources are lost; otherwise, returns the following status condition codes logically **OR**'d:

NET_DBG_SF_RSRC_LOST   Some network resources lost.

NET_DBG_SF_RSRC_LOST_BUF_SMALL Some network SMALL buffer resources lost.

NET_DBG_SF_RSRC_LOST_BUF_LARGE Some network LARGE buffer resources lost.

NET_DBG_SF_RSRC_LOST_TMR   Some network timer resources lost.

NET_DBG_SF_RSRC_LOST_CONN   Some network connection resources lost.

NET_DBG_SF_RSRC_LOST_ARP_CACHE Some network ARP cache resources lost.

NET_DBG_SF_RSRC_LOST_TCP_CONN   Some network TCP connection resources lost.

NET_DBG_SF_RSRC_LOST_SOCK   Some network socket resources lost.

REQUIRED CONFIGURATION

NetDbg_ChkStatusRsrcLost() available only if NET_DBG_CFG_DBG_STATUS_EN is enabled (see section D-2-2 on page 964). NetDbg_MonTaskStatusGetRsrcLost() available only if the Network Debug Monitor task is enabled (see section 20-2 on page 526).

NOTES / WARNINGS

NetDbg_ChkStatusRsrcLost() checks network conditions lost status inline, whereas NetDbg_MonTaskStatusGetRsrcLost() checks the Network Debug Monitor task's last known lost status.

C-7-15 NetDbg_ChkStatusRsrcLo() / NetDbg_MonTaskStatusGetRsrcLo()

Return whether any µC/TCP-IP resources are currently low.

FILES

net_dbg.h/net_dbg.c

PROTOTYPES

```
NET_DBG_STATUS NetDbg_ChkStatusRsrcLo(void);
NET_DBG_STATUS NetDbg_MonTaskStatusGetRsrcLo(void);
```

ARGUMENTS

None.

RETURNED VALUE

NET_DBG_STATUS_OK, if no network resources are low; otherwise, returns the following status condition codes logically **OR**'d:

NET_DBG_SF_RSRC_LO	Some network resources low.
NET_DBG_SF_RSRC_LO_BUF_SMALL	Network SMALL buffer resources low
NET_DBG_SF_RSRC_LO_BUF_LARGE	Network LARGE buffer resources low.
NET_DBG_SF_RSRC_LO_TMR	Network timer resources low.
NET_DBG_SF_RSRC_LO_CONN	Network connection resources low.
NET_DBG_SF_RSRC_LO_ARP_CACHE	Network ARP cache resources low.
NET_DBG_SF_RSRC_LO_TCP_CONN	Network TCP connection resources low.
NET_DBG_SF_RSRC_LO_SOCK	Network socket resources low.

REQUIRED CONFIGURATION

NetDbg_ChkStatusRsrcLo() available only if NET_DBG_CFG_DBG_STATUS_EN is enabled (see section D-2-2 on page 964). NetDbg_MonTaskStatusGetRsrcLo() available only if the Network Debug Monitor task is enabled (see section 20-2 on page 526).

NOTES / WARNINGS

NetDbg_ChkStatusRsrcLo() checks network conditions low status inline, whereas NetDbg_MonTaskStatusGetRsrcLo() checks the Network Debug Monitor task's last known low status.

C-7-16 NetDbg_ChkStatusTCP()

Return the current run-time status of µC/TCP-IP TCP connections.

FILES

net_dbg.h/net_dbg.c

PROTOTYPE

```
NET_DBG_STATUS NetDbg_ChkStatusTCP(void);
```

ARGUMENTS

None.

RETURNED VALUE

NET_DBG_STATUS_OK, if all TCP layer conditions are OK (i.e., no warnings, faults, or errors currently exist); otherwise, returns the following status condition codes logically **OR**'d:

NET_DBG_SF_TCP	Some TCP layer fault(s).
NET_DBG_SF_TCP_CONN_TYPE	TCP connection invalid type.
NET_DBG_SF_TCP_CONN_ID	TCP connection invalid id.
NET_DBG_SF_TCP_CONN_LINK_TYPE	TCP connection invalid link type.
NET_DBG_SF_TCP_CONN_LINK_UNUSED	TCP connection link unused.
NET_DBG_SF_TCP_CONN_POOL_TYPE	TCP connection invalid pool type.
NET_DBG_SF_TCP_CONN_POOL_ID	TCP connection invalid pool id.
NET_DBG_SF_TCP_CONN_POOL_DUP	TCP connection pool contains duplicate connection(s).

NET_DBG_SF_TCP_CONN_POOL_NBR_MAX	TCP connection pool number of connections greater than maximum number of connections.
NET_DBG_SF_TCP_CONN_USED_IN_POOL	TCP connection used in pool.
NET_DBG_SF_TCP_CONN_UNUSED_NOT_IN_POOL	TCP connection unused *not* in pool.
NET_DBG_SF_TCP_CONN_Q	Some TCP connection queue fault(s).
NET_DBG_SF_TCP_CONN_Q_BUF_TYPE	TCP connection queue buffer invalid type.
NET_DBG_SF_TCP_CONN_Q_BUF_UNUSED	TCP connection queue buffer unused.
NET_DBG_SF_TCP_CONN_Q_LINK_TYPE	TCP connection queue buffer invalid link type.
NET_DBG_SF_TCP_CONN_Q_LINK_UNUSED	TCP connection queue buffer link unused.
NET_DBG_SF_TCP_CONN_Q_BUF_DUP	TCP connection queue contains duplicate buffer(s).

REQUIRED CONFIGURATION

Available only if NET_DBG_CFG_DBG_STATUS_EN is enabled (see section D-2-2 on page 964) **AND** if NET_CFG_TRANSPORT_LAYER_SEL is configured for TCP (see section D-12-1 on page 972).

NOTES / WARNINGS

None.

C-7-17 NetDbg_ChkStatusTmrs()

Return the current run-time status of µC/TCP-IP network timers.

FILES

net_dbg.h/net_dbg.c

PROTOTYPE

```
NET_DBG_STATUS NetDbg_ChkStatusTmrs(void);
```

ARGUMENTS

None.

RETURNED VALUE

NET_DBG_STATUS_OK, if all network timer conditions are OK (i.e., no warnings, faults, or errors currently exist);

Otherwise, returns the following status condition codes logically **OR**'d:

NET_DBG_SF_TMR	Some network timer management fault(s).
NET_DBG_SF_TMR_TYPE	Network timer invalid type.
NET_DBG_SF_TMR_ID	Network timer invalid id.
NET_DBG_SF_TMR_LINK_TYPE	Network timer invalid link type.
NET_DBG_SF_TMR_LINK_UNUSED	Network timer link unused.
NET_DBG_SF_TMR_LINK_BACK_TO_TMR	Network timer invalid link back to same timer.
NET_DBG_SF_TMR_LINK_TO_TMR	Network timer invalid link back to timer.

`NET_DBG_SF_TMR_POOL_TYPE`	Network timer invalid pool type.
`NET_DBG_SF_TMR_POOL_ID`	Network timer invalid pool id.
`NET_DBG_SF_TMR_POOL_DUP`	Network timer pool contains duplicate timer(s).
`NET_DBG_SF_TMR_POOL_NBR_MAX`	Network timer pool number of timers greater than maximum number of timers.
`NET_DBG_SF_TMR_LIST_TYPE`	Network Timer task list invalid type.
`NET_DBG_SF_TMR_LIST_ID`	Network Timer task list invalid id.
`NET_DBG_SF_TMR_LIST_DUP`	Network Timer task list contains duplicate timer(s).
`NET_DBG_SF_TMR_LIST_NBR_MAX`	Network Timer task list number of timers greater than maximum number of timers.
`NET_DBG_SF_TMR_LIST_NBR_USED`	Network Timer task list number of timers *not* equal to number of used timers.
`NET_DBG_SF_TMR_USED_IN_POOL`	Network timer used but in pool.
`NET_DBG_SF_TMR_UNUSED_NOT_IN_POOL`	Network timer unused but *not* in pool.
`NET_DBG_SF_TMR_UNUSED_IN_LIST`	Network timer unused but in Timer task list.

REQUIRED CONFIGURATION

Available only if `NET_DBG_CFG_DBG_STATUS_EN` is enabled (see section D-2-2 on page 964).

NOTES / WARNINGS

None.

C-7-18 NetDbg_MonTaskStatusGetRsrcLost()

Return whether any µC/TCP-IP resources are currently lost.

See section C-7-14 on page 720 for more information.

FILES

net_dbg.h/net_dbg.c

PROTOTYPE

```
NET_DBG_STATUS NetDbg_MonTaskStatusGetRsrcLost(void);
```

C-7-19 NetDbg_MonTaskStatusGetRsrcLo()

Return whether any µC/TCP-IP resources are currently low.

See section C-7-15 on page 722 for more information.

FILES

net_dbg.h/net_dbg.c

PROTOTYPE

```
NET_DBG_STATUS NetDbg_MonTaskStatusGetRsrcLo(void);
```

C-8 ICMP FUNCTIONS

C-8-1 NetICMP_CfgTxSrcQuenchTh()

Configure ICMP transmit source quench entry's access transmit threshold.

FILES

net_icmp.h/net_icmp.c

PROTOTYPE

```
CPU_BOOLEAN NetICMP_CfgTxSrcQuenchTh(CPU_INT16U th);
```

ARGUMENTS

th   Desired number of received IP packets from a specific IP source host that trips the transmission of an additional ICMP Source Quench Error Message.

RETURNED VALUE

DEF_OK,   ICMP transmit source quench threshold configured.

DEF_FAIL,   otherwise.

REQUIRED CONFIGURATION

None.

NOTES / WARNINGS

None.

C-9 NETWORK INTERFACE FUNCTIONS

C-9-1 NetIF_Add()

Add a network device and hardware as a network interface.

FILES

net_if.h/net_if.c

PROTOTYPE

```
NET_IF_NBR NetIF_Add(void    *if_api,
                     void    *dev_api,
                     void    *dev_bsp,
                     void    *dev_cfg,
                     void    *phy_api,
                     void    *phy_cfg,
                     NET_ERR *perr);
```

ARGUMENTS

if_api   Pointer to the desired link-layer API for this network interface and device
            hardware. In most cases, the desired link-layer interface will point to the
            Ethernet API, **NetIF_API_Ether** (see also section L16-1(1) on page 362).

dev_api   Pointer to the desired device driver API for this network interface (see also
            section 14-3-3 "Adding an Ethernet Interface" on page 319 and section 14-4-2
            "Adding a Wireless Interface" on page 326).

dev_bsp   Pointer to the specific device's BSP interface for this network interface (see
            also Chapter 15, "Network Board Support Package" on page 347).

dev_cfg   Pointer to a configuration structure used to configure the device hardware for
            the specific network interface (see also Chapter 14, "Network Interface
            Configuration" on page 303).

phy_api   Pointer to an optional physical layer device driver API for this network interface. In most cases, the generic physical layer device API will be used, **NetPhy_API_Generic**, but for Ethernet devices that have non-MII or non-RMII compliant physical layer components, another device-specific physical layer device driver API may be necessary. See also section 16-4 "Ethernet PHY API Implementation" on page 382.

phy_cfg   Pointer to a configuration structure used to configure the physical layer hardware for the specific network interface (see also section 14-3-2 "Ethernet PHY Configuration" on page 317).

perr   Pointer to variable that will receive the return error code from this function:

            NET_IF_ERR_NONE
            NET_IF_ERR_NULL_PTR
            NET_IF_ERR_INVALID_IF
            NET_IF_ERR_INVALID_CFG
            NET_IF_ERR_NONE_AVAIL
            NET_BUF_ERR_POOL_INIT
            NET_BUF_ERR_INVALID_POOL_TYPE
            NET_BUF_ERR_INVALID_POOL_ADDR
            NET_BUF_ERR_INVALID_POOL_SIZE
            NET_BUF_ERR_INVALID_POOL_QTY
            NET_BUF_ERR_INVALID_SIZE
            NET_OS_ERR_INIT_DEV_TX_RDY
            NET_OS_ERR_INIT_DEV_TX_RDY_NAME
            NET_OS_ERR_LOCK

RETURNED VALUE

Network interface number, if device and hardware successfully added;

NET_IF_NBR_NONE, otherwise.

REQUIRED CONFIGURATION

None.

NOTES / WARNINGS

The first network interface added and started is the default interface used for all default communication. See also section C-12-1 on page 774 and section C-12-2 on page 776.

Both physical layer API and configuration parameters *must* ,either be specified or passed **NULL** pointers.

Additional error codes may be returned by the specific interface or device driver.

See section 16-1-1 "Adding Network Interfaces" on page 361 for a detailed example of how to add an interface.

C-9-2 NetIF_AddrHW_Get()

Get network interface's hardware address.

FILES

net_if.h/net_if.c

PROTOTYPE

```
void NetIF_AddrHW_Get(NET_IF_NBR  if_nbr,
                      CPU_INT08U *paddr_hw,
                      CPU_INT08U *paddr_len,
                      NET_ERR    *perr);
```

ARGUMENTS

if_nbr   Network interface number to get the hardware address.

paddr_hw   Pointer to variable that will receive the hardware address.

paddr_len   Pointer to a variable to pass the length of the address buffer pointed to by
             paddr_hw and return the size of the returned hardware address, if no errors.

perr   Pointer to variable that will receive the return error code from this function:

             NET_IF_ERR_NONE
             NET_IF_ERR_NULL_PTR
             NET_IF_ERR_NULL_FNCT
             NET_IF_ERR_INVALID_IF
             NET_IF_ERR_INVALID_CFG
             NET_IF_ERR_INVALID_ADDR_LEN
             NET_OS_ERR_LOCK

RETURNED VALUE

None.

REQUIRED CONFIGURATION

None.

NOTES / WARNINGS

The hardware address is returned in network-order; i.e., the pointer to the hardware address points to the highest-order byte. Additional error codes may be returned by the specific interface or device driver.

C-9-3 NetIF_AddrHW_IsValid()

Validate a network interface hardware address.

FILES

net_if.h/net_if.c

PROTOTYPE

```
CPU_BOOLEAN NetIF_AddrHW_IsValid(NET_IF_NBR  if_nbr,
                                 CPU_INT08U  *paddr_hw,
                                 NET_ERR     *perr);
```

ARGUMENTS

if_nbr   Network interface number to validate the hardware address.

paddr_hw   Pointer to a network interface hardware address.

perr   Pointer to variable that will receive the return error code from this function:

        NET_IF_ERR_NONE
        NET_IF_ERR_NULL_PTR
        NET_IF_ERR_NULL_FNCT
        NET_IF_ERR_INVALID_IF
        NET_IF_ERR_INVALID_CFG
        NET_OS_ERR_LOCK

RETURNED VALUE

DEF_YES   if hardware address valid;

DEF_NO   otherwise.

REQUIRED CONFIGURATION

None.

NOTES / WARNINGS

None.

C-9-4 NetIF_AddrHW_Set()

Set network interface's hardware address.

FILES

net_if.h/net_if.c

PROTOTYPE

```
void NetIF_AddrHW_Set(NET_IF_NBR  if_nbr,
                      CPU_INT08U *paddr_hw,
                      CPU_INT08U  addr_len,
                      NET_ERR    *perr);
```

ARGUMENTS

if_nbr   Network interface number to set hardware address.

paddr_hw   Pointer to a hardware address.

addr_len   Length of hardware address.

perr   Pointer to variable that will receive the return error code from this function:

              NET_IF_ERR_NONE
              NET_IF_ERR_NULL_PTR
              NET_IF_ERR_NULL_FNCT
              NET_IF_ERR_INVALID_IF
              NET_IF_ERR_INVALID_CFG
              NET_IF_ERR_INVALID_STATE
              NET_IF_ERR_INVALID_ADDR
              NET_IF_ERR_INVALID_ADDR_LEN
              NET_OS_ERR_LOCK

RETURNED VALUE

None.

REQUIRED CONFIGURATION

None.

NOTES / WARNINGS

The hardware address *must* be in network-order (i.e., the pointer to the hardware address *must* point to the highest-order byte).

The network interface *must* be stopped *before* setting a new hardware address, which does *not* take effect until the interface is re-started.

Additional error codes may be returned by the specific interface or device driver.

C-9-5 NetIF_CfgPerfMonPeriod()

Configure the network interface Performance Monitor Handler timeout.

FILES

net_if.h/net_if.c

PROTOTYPE

```
CPU_BOOLEAN NetIF_CfgPerfMonPeriod(CPU_INT16U timeout_ms);
```

ARGUMENTS

timeout_ms   Desired value for network interface Performance Monitor Handler timeout (in milliseconds).

RETURNED VALUE

DEF_OK,   Network interface Performance Monitor Handler timeout configured;

DEF_FAIL,   otherwise.

REQUIRED CONFIGURATION

Available only if NET_CTR_CFG_STAT_EN is enabled (see section D-4-1 on page 966).

NOTES / WARNINGS

None.

C-9-6 NetIF_CfgPhyLinkPeriod()

Configure network interface Physical Link State Handler timeout.

FILES

net_if.h/net_if.c

PROTOTYPE

```
CPU_BOOLEAN NetIF_CfgPhyLinkPeriod(CPU_INT16U timeout_ms);
```

ARGUMENTS

timeout_ms   Desired value for network interface Link State Handler timeout   (in milliseconds).

RETURNED VALUE

DEF_OK,   Network interface Physical Link State Handler timeout configured;

DEF_FAIL,   otherwise.

REQUIRED CONFIGURATION

None.

NOTES / WARNINGS

None.

C-9-7 NetIF_GetRxDataAlignPtr()

Get an aligned pointer into a receive application data buffer.

FILES

net_if.h/net_if.c

PROTOTYPE

```
void  *NetIF_GetRxDataAlignPtr(NET_IF_NBR   if_nbr,
                               void        *p_data,
                               NET_ERR     *perr);
```

ARGUMENTS

if_nbr   Network interface number to get a receive application buffer's aligned data
             pointer.

p_data   Pointer to receive application data buffer to get an aligned pointer into (see
             also Note #2).

perr   Pointer to variable that will receive the return error code from this function :

             NET_IF_ERR_NONE
             NET_IF_ERR_NULL_PTR
             NET_IF_ERR_INVALID_IF
             NET_IF_ERR_ALIGN_NOT_AVAIL
             NET_ERR_INIT_INCOMPLETE
             NET_ERR_INVALID_TRANSACTION
             NET_OS_ERR_LOCK

RETURNED VALUE

Pointer to aligned receive application data buffer address, if no errors.

Pointer to NULL, otherwise.

NOTES/WARNINGS #1

1 Optimal alignment between application data buffers and the network interface's network buffer data areas is *not* guaranteed, and is possible if, and only if, all of the following conditions are true:

- Network interface's network buffer data areas *must* be aligned to a multiple of the CPU's data word size.

Otherwise, a single, fixed alignment between application data buffers and network interface's buffer data areas is *not* possible.

2 Even when application data buffers and network buffer data areas are aligned in the best case, optimal alignment is *not* guaranteed for every read/write of data to/from application data buffers and network buffer data areas.

For any single read/write of data to/from application data buffers and network buffer data areas, optimal alignment occurs if, and only if, all of the following conditions are true:

- Data read/written to/from application data buffers to network buffer data areas *must* start on addresses with the same relative offset from CPU word-aligned addresses.

In other words, the modulus of the specific read/write address in the application data buffer with the CPU's data word size *must* be equal to the modulus of the specific read/write address in the network buffer data area with the CPU's data word size.

This condition *might not* be satisfied whenever:

- Data is read/written to/from fragmented packets

- Data is *not* maximally read/written to/from stream-type packets (e.g., TCP data segments)

- Packets include variable number of header options (e.g., IP options)

However, even though optimal alignment between application data buffers and network buffer data areas is *not* guaranteed for every read/write; optimal alignment SHOULD occur more frequently, leading to improved network data throughput.

NOTES/WARNINGS #2

Since the first aligned address in the application data buffer may be 0 to `(CPU_CFG_DATA_SIZE-1)` bytes after the application data buffer's starting address, the application data buffer *should* allocate and reserve an additional `(CPU_CFG_DATA_SIZE-1)` number of bytes.

However, the application data buffer's effective, useable size is still limited to its original declared size (before reserving additional bytes), and *should not* be increased by the additional, reserved bytes.

C-9-8 NetIF_GetTxDataAlignPtr()

Get an aligned pointer into a transmit application data buffer.

FILES

net_if.h/net_if.c

PROTOTYPE

```
void  *NetIF_GetTxDataAlignPtr(NET_IF_NBR   if_nbr,
                               void        *p_data,
                               NET_ERR     *perr);
```

ARGUMENTS

if_nbr   Network interface number to get a transmit application buffer's aligned data
             pointer.

p_data   Pointer to transmit application data buffer to get an aligned pointer into (see
             also Note #2b).

perr   Pointer to variable that will receive the return error code from this function :

             NET_IF_ERR_NONE
             NET_IF_ERR_NULL_PTR
             NET_IF_ERR_INVALID_IF
             NET_IF_ERR_ALIGN_NOT_AVAIL
             NET_ERR_INIT_INCOMPLETE
             NET_ERR_INVALID_TRANSACTION
             NET_OS_ERR_LOCK

RETURNED VALUE

Pointer to aligned transmit application data buffer address, if no errors.

Pointer to NULL, otherwise.

REQUIRED CONFIGURATION

None.

NOTES/WARNINGS #1

1   Optimal alignment between application data buffers and the network interface's network buffer data areas is *not* guaranteed, and is possible if, and only if, all of the following conditions are true:

- Network interface's network buffer data areas *must* be aligned to a multiple of the CPU's data word size.

   Otherwise, a single, fixed alignment between application data buffers and network interface's buffer data areas is *not* possible.

2   Even when application data buffers and network buffer data areas are aligned in the best case, optimal alignment is *not* guaranteed for every read/write of data to/from application data buffers and network buffer data areas.

   For any single read/write of data to/from application data buffers and network buffer data areas, optimal alignment occurs if, and only if, all of the following conditions are true:

- Data read/written to/from application data buffers to network buffer data areas *must* start on addresses with the same relative offset from CPU word-aligned addresses.

   In other words, the modulus of the specific read/write address in the application data buffer with the CPU's data word size *must* be equal to the modulus of the specific read/write address in the network buffer data area with the CPU's data word size.

   This condition *might not* be satisfied whenever:

- Data is read/written to/from fragmented packets

- Data is *not* maximally read/written to/from stream-type packets (e.g., TCP data segments)

- Packets include variable number of header options (e.g., IP options)

However, even though optimal alignment between application data buffers and network buffer data areas is *not* guaranteed for every read/write; optimal alignment SHOULD NOT occur more frequently, leading to improved network data throughput.

NOTES/WARNINGS #2

Since the first aligned address in the application data buffer may be 0 to **(CPU_CFG_DATA_SIZE-1)** bytes after the application data buffer's starting address, the application data buffer *should* allocate and reserve an additional **(CPU_CFG_DATA_SIZE-1)** number of bytes.

However, the application data buffer's effective, useable size is still limited to its original declared size (before reserving additional bytes), and *should not* be increased by the additional, reserved bytes.

C-9-9 NetIF_IO_Ctrl()

Handle network interface &/or device specific (I/O) control(s).

FILES

net_if.h/net_if.c

PROTOTYPE

```
void NetIF_IO_Ctrl(NET_IF_NBR  if_nbr,
                   CPU_INT08U  opt,
                   void        *p_data,
                   NET_ERR     *perr);
```

ARGUMENTS

if_nbr   Network interface number to handle (I/O) controls.

opt   Desired I/O control option code to perform; additional control options may
            be defined by the device driver:

            NET_IF_IO_CTRL_LINK_STATE_GET
            NET_IF_IO_CTRL_LINK_STATE_UPDATE

p_data   Pointer to variable that will receive the I/O control information.

perr   Pointer to variable that will receive the return error code from this function:

            NET_IF_ERR_NONE
            NET_IF_ERR_NULL_PTR
            NET_IF_ERR_NULL_FNCT
            NET_IF_ERR_INVALID_IF
            NET_IF_ERR_INVALID_CFG
            NET_IF_ERR_INVALID_IO_CTRL_OPTNET_OS_ERR_LOCK

RETURNED VALUE

None.

REQUIRED CONFIGURATION

None.

NOTES / WARNINGS

Additional error codes may be returned by the specific interface or device driver.

C-9-10 NetIF_IsEn()

Validate network interface as enabled.

FILES

net_if.h/net_if.c

PROTOTYPE

```
CPU_BOOLEAN NetIF_IsEn(NET_IF_NBR  if_nbr,
                       NET_ERR     *perr);
```

ARGUMENTS

if_nbr   Network interface number to validate.

perr   Pointer to variable that will receive the return error code from this function:

        NET_IF_ERR_NONE
        NET_IF_ERR_INVALID_IF
        NET_OS_ERR_LOCK

RETURNED VALUE

DEF_YES   network interface valid and enabled;

DEF_NO   network interface invalid or disabled.

REQUIRED CONFIGURATION

None.

NOTES / WARNINGS

None.

C-9-11 NetIF_IsEnCfgd()

Validate configured network interface as enabled.

FILES

net_if.h/net_if.c

PROTOTYPE

```
CPU_BOOLEAN NetIF_IsEnCfgd(NET_IF_NBR  if_nbr,
                           NET_ERR    *perr);
```

ARGUMENTS

if_nbr   Network interface number to validate.

perr   Pointer to variable that will receive the return error code from this function:

        NET_IF_ERR_NONE
        NET_IF_ERR_INVALID_IF
        NET_OS_ERR_LOCK

RETURNED VALUE

DEF_YES   network interface valid and enabled;

DEF_NO   network interface invalid or disabled.

REQUIRED CONFIGURATION

None.

NOTES / WARNINGS

None.

C-9-12 NetIF_ISR_Handler()

Handle a network interface's device interrupts.

FILES

net_if.h/net_if.c

PROTOTYPE

```
void NetIF_ISR_Handler (NET_IF_NBR       if_nbr,
                        NET_DEV_ISR_TYPE type,
                        NET_ERR          *perr);
```

ARGUMENTS

if_nbr   Network interface number to handler device interrupts.

type   Device interrupt type(s) to handle:

NET_DEV_ISR_TYPE_UNKNOWN	Handle unknown device interrupts.
NET_DEV_ISR_TYPE_RX	Handle device receive interrupts.
NET_DEV_ISR_TYPE_RX_OVERRUN	Handle device receive overrun interrupts.
NET_DEV_ISR_TYPE_TX_RDY	Handle device transmit ready interrupts.
NET_DEV_ISR_TYPE_TX_COMPLETE	Handle device transmit complete interrupts.

This is *not* an exclusive list of interrupt types and specific network device's may handle other types of interrupts.

perr   Pointer to variable that will receive the return error code from this function:

NET_IF_ERR_NONE

NET_IF_ERR_INVALID_CFG

NET_IF_ERR_NULL_FNCT

NET_IF_ERR_INVALID_STATE

NET_ERR_INIT_INCOMPLETE

NET_IF_ERR_INVALID_IF

This is *not* an exclusive list of return errors and specific network interface's or device's may return any other specific errors as required.

RETURNED VALUE

None.

REQUIRED CONFIGURATION

None.

NOTES / WARNINGS

None.

C-9-13 NetIF_IsValid()

Validate network interface number.

FILES

net_if.h/net_if.c

PROTOTYPE

```
CPU_BOOLEAN NetIF_IsValid(NET_IF_NBR  if_nbr,
                          NET_ERR     *perr);
```

ARGUMENTS

if_nbr   Network interface number to validate.

perr   Pointer to variable that will receive the return error code from this function:

            NET_IF_ERR_NONE
            NET_IF_ERR_INVALID_IF
            NET_OS_ERR_LOCK

RETURNED VALUE

DEF_YES   network interface number valid;

DEF_NO   network interface number invalid/*not* yet configured.

REQUIRED CONFIGURATION

None.

NOTES / WARNINGS

None.

C-9-14 NetIF_IsValidCfgd()

Validate configured network interface number.

net_if.h/net_if.c

```
CPU_BOOLEAN NetIF_IsValidCfgd(NET_IF_NBR  if_nbr,
                             NET_ERR    *perr);
```

if_nbr   Network interface number to validate.

perr   Pointer to variable that will receive the return error code from this function:

　　　　　　NET_IF_ERR_NONE
　　　　　　NET_IF_ERR_INVALID_IF
　　　　　　NET_OS_ERR_LOCK

DEF_YES   network interface number valid;

DEF_NO   network interface number invalid/*not* yet configured or reserved.

None.

None.

C-9-15 NetIF_LinkStateGet()

Get network interface's last known physical link state.

FILES

net_if.h/net_if.c

PROTOTYPE

```
CPU_BOOLEAN NetIF_LinkStateGet(NET_IF_NBR  if_nbr,
                               NET_ERR    *perr);
```

ARGUMENTS

if_nbr   Network interface number to get last known physical link state.

perr   Pointer to variable that will receive the return error code from this function:

            NET_IF_ERR_NONE
            NET_IF_ERR_INVALID_IF
            NET_OS_ERR_LOCK

RETURNED VALUE

NET_IF_LINK_UP   if no errors and network interface's last known physical link state was 'UP';

NET_IF_LINK_DOWN   otherwise.

REQUIRED CONFIGURATION

None.

NOTES / WARNINGS

Use NetIF_IO_Ctrl() with option NET_IF_IO_CTRL_LINK_STATE_GET to get a network interface's current physical link state.

C-9-16 NetIF_LinkStateWaitUntilUp()

Wait for a network interface's physical link state to be UP.

FILES

net_if.h/net_if.c

PROTOTYPE

```
CPU_BOOLEAN NetIF_LinkStateWaitUntilUp(NET_IF_NBR   if_nbr,
                                       CPU_INT16U   retry_max,
                                       CPU_INT32U   time_dly_ms,
                                       NET_ERR      *perr);
```

ARGUMENTS

if_nbr   Network interface number to wait for link state to be UP.

retry_max   Maximum number of consecutive socket open retries.

time_dly_ms Transitory socket open delay value, in milliseconds.

perr   Pointer to variable that will receive the return error code from this function:

   NET_IF_ERR_NONE
   NET_IF_ERR_INVALID_IF
   NET_IF_ERR_LINK_DOWN
   NET_ERR_INIT_INCOMPLETE
   NET_OS_ERR_LOCK

RETURNED VALUE

NET_IF_LINK_UP   if no errors and network interface's physical link state is UP;

NET_IF_LINK_DOWN   otherwise.

REQUIRED CONFIGURATION

None.

NOTES / WARNINGS

If a non-zero number of retries is requested (**retry_max**) then a non-zero time delay (**time_dly_ms**) should also be requested. Otherwise, all retries will most likely fail immediately since no time will elapse to wait for and allow the network interface's link state to successfully be UP.

C-9-17 NetIF_MTU_Get()

Get network interface's MTU.

FILES

net_if.h/net_if.c

PROTOTYPE

```
NET_MTU NetIF_MTU_Get(NET_IF_NBR  if_nbr,
                      NET_ERR    *perr);
```

ARGUMENTS

if_nbr   Network interface number to get MTU.

perr   Pointer to variable that will receive the return error code from this function:

            NET_IF_ERR_NONE
            NET_IF_ERR_INVALID_IF
            NET_OS_ERR_LOCK

RETURNED VALUE

Network interface's MTU, if no errors.

0, otherwise.

REQUIRED CONFIGURATION

None.

NOTES / WARNINGS

None.

C-9-18 NetIF_MTU_Set()

Set network interface's MTU.

FILES

net_if.h/net_if.c

PROTOTYPE

```
void NetIF_MTU_Set(NET_IF_NBR  if_nbr,
                   NET_MTU     mtu,
                   NET_ERR     *perr);
```

ARGUMENTS

if_nbr   Network interface number to set MTU.

mtu   Desired maximum transmission unit size to configure.

perr   Pointer to variable that will receive the return error code from this function:

NET_IF_ERR_NONE
NET_IF_ERR_NULL_FNCT
NET_IF_ERR_INVALID_IF
NET_IF_ERR_INVALID_CFG
NET_IF_ERR_INVALID_MTU
NET_OS_ERR_LOCK

RETURNED VALUE

None.

REQUIRED CONFIGURATION

None.

NOTES / WARNINGS

Additional error codes may be returned by the specific interface or device driver.

C-9-19 NetIF_Start()

Start a network interface.

FILES

net_if.h/net_if.c

PROTOTYPE

```
void NetIF_Start(NET_IF_NBR  if_nbr,
                 NET_ERR     *perr);
```

ARGUMENTS

if_nbr   Network interface number to start.

perr   Pointer to variable that will receive the return error code from this function:

            NET_IF_ERR_NONE
            NET_IF_ERR_NULL_FNCT
            NET_IF_ERR_INVALID_IF
            NET_IF_ERR_INVALID_CFG
            NET_IF_ERR_INVALID_STATE
            NET_OS_ERR_LOCK

RETURNED VALUE

None.

REQUIRED CONFIGURATION

None.

NOTES / WARNINGS

Additional error codes may be returned by the specific interface or device driver.

C-9-20 NetIF_Stop()

Stop a network interface.

FILES

net_if.h/net_if.c

PROTOTYPE

```
void NetIF_Stop(NET_IF_NBR  if_nbr,
                NET_ERR    *perr);
```

ARGUMENTS

if_nbr   Network interface number to stop.

perr   Pointer to variable that will receive the return error code from this function:

            NET_IF_ERR_NONE
            NET_IF_ERR_NULL_FNCT
            NET_IF_ERR_INVALID_IF
            NET_IF_ERR_INVALID_CFG
            NET_IF_ERR_INVALID_STATE
            NET_OS_ERR_LOCK

RETURNED VALUE

None.

REQUIRED CONFIGURATION

None.

NOTES / WARNINGS

Additional error codes may be returned by the specific interface or device driver.

C-10 WIRELESS NETWORK INTERFACE FUNCTION

C-10-1 NetIF_WiFi_Scan()

Scan available wireless access point.

FILES

net_if_wifi.h/net_if_wifi.c

PROTOTYPE

```
void NetIF_WiFi_Scan (NET_IF_NBR          if_nbr,
                      NET_IF_WIFI_AP      *p_buf_scan,
                      CPU_INT16U          buf_scan_len_max,
                const NET_IF_WIFI_SSID    *p_ssid,
                      NET_IF_WIFI_CH      ch,
                      NET_ERR             *p_err);
```

ARGUMENTS

if_nbr   Interface number to scan wireless access point.

p_buf_scan   Pointer to a buffer that will receive wireless access point found.

buf_scan_len_max   Maximum number of access point that can be stored in the scan
                       buffer.

p_ssid   Pointer to a:

                       a. string that contains the hidden SSID to scan for

                       b. null pointer, if the scan is for all SSID broadcasted.

ch   Wireless channel number to scan:

             NET_IF_WIFI_CH_ALL
             NET_IF_WIFI_CH_1
             NET_IF_WIFI_CH_2

```
NET_IF_WIFI_CH_3
NET_IF_WIFI_CH_4
NET_IF_WIFI_CH_5
NET_IF_WIFI_CH_6
NET_IF_WIFI_CH_7
NET_IF_WIFI_CH_8
NET_IF_WIFI_CH_9
NET_IF_WIFI_CH_10
NET_IF_WIFI_CH_11
NET_IF_WIFI_CH_12
NET_IF_WIFI_CH_13
NET_IF_WIFI_CH_14
```

perr   Pointer to variable that will receive the return error code from this function:

```
NET_IF_WIFI_ERR_NONE
NET_IF_WIFI_ERR_CH_INVALID
NET_IF_WIFI_ERR_SCAN
NET_IF_ERR_NULL_PTR
```

RETURNED VALUE

Number of wireless access point found and set in the scan buffer.

REQUIRED CONFIGURATION

None.

NOTES / WARNINGS

None.

C-10-2 NetIF_WiFi_Join()

Join an wireless access point.

FILES

net_if_wifi.h/net_if_wifi.c

PROTOTYPE

```
void NetIF_WiFi_Join (NET_IF_NBR              if_nbr,
                      NET_IF_WIFI_NET_TYPE     net_type,
                      NET_IF_WIFI_DATA_RATE    data_rate,
                      NET_IF_WIFI_SECURITY_TYPE security_type,
                      NET_IF_WIFI_PWR_LEVEL    pwr_level,
                      NET_IF_WIFI_SSID         ssid,
                      NET_IF_WIFI_PSK          psk,
                      NET_ERR                 *p_err);
```

ARGUMENTS

if_nbr   Interface number to join wireless access point.

net_type   Wireless network type of the access point:

        NET_IF_WIFI_NET_TYPE_INFRASTRUCTURE
        NET_IF_WIFI_NET_TYPE_ADHOC

data_rate   Wireless data rate to configure:

        NET_IF_WIFI_DATA_RATE_AUTO
        NET_IF_WIFI_DATA_RATE_1_MBPS
        NET_IF_WIFI_DATA_RATE_2_MBPS
        NET_IF_WIFI_DATA_RATE_5_5_MBPS
        NET_IF_WIFI_DATA_RATE_6_MBPS
        NET_IF_WIFI_DATA_RATE_9_MBPS
        NET_IF_WIFI_DATA_RATE_11_MBPS
        NET_IF_WIFI_DATA_RATE_12_MBPS
        NET_IF_WIFI_DATA_RATE_18_MBPS
        NET_IF_WIFI_DATA_RATE_24_MBPS

```
                NET_IF_WIFI_DATA_RATE_36_MBPS
                NET_IF_WIFI_DATA_RATE_48_MBPS
                NET_IF_WIFI_DATA_RATE_54_MBPS
                NET_IF_WIFI_DATA_RATE_MCS0
                NET_IF_WIFI_DATA_RATE_MCS1
                NET_IF_WIFI_DATA_RATE_MCS2
                NET_IF_WIFI_DATA_RATE_MCS3
                NET_IF_WIFI_DATA_RATE_MCS4
                NET_IF_WIFI_DATA_RATE_MCS5
                NET_IF_WIFI_DATA_RATE_MCS6
                NET_IF_WIFI_DATA_RATE_MCS7
                NET_IF_WIFI_DATA_RATE_MCS8
                NET_IF_WIFI_DATA_RATE_MCS9
                NET_IF_WIFI_DATA_RATE_MCS10
                NET_IF_WIFI_DATA_RATE_MCS11
                NET_IF_WIFI_DATA_RATE_MCS12
                NET_IF_WIFI_DATA_RATE_MCS13
                NET_IF_WIFI_DATA_RATE_MCS14
                NET_IF_WIFI_DATA_RATE_MCS15
```

security_type   Wireless security type:

```
                NET_IF_WIFI_SECURITY_OPEN
                NET_IF_WIFI_SECURITY_WEP
                NET_IF_WIFI_SECURITY_WPA
                NET_IF_WIFI_SECURITY_WPA2
```

pwr_level   Wireless radio power to configure:

```
                NET_IF_WIFI_PWR_LEVEL_LO
                NET_IF_WIFI_PWR_LEVEL_MED
                NET_IF_WIFI_PWR_LEVEL_HI
```

ssid   SSID of the access point to join.

psk   Pre shared key of the access point to join.

p_err   Pointer to variable that will receive the return error code from this function:

          `NET_IF_WIFI_ERR_NONE`
          `NET_IF_WIFI_ERR_JOIN`
          `NET_IF_WIFI_ERR_INVALID_NET_TYPE`
          `NET_IF_WIFI_ERR_INVALID_DATA_RATE`
          `NET_IF_WIFI_ERR_INVALID_SECURITY`
          `NET_IF_WIFI_ERR_INVALID_PWR_LEVEL`

RETURNED VALUE

None.

REQUIRED CONFIGURATION

None.

NOTES / WARNINGS

Prior joining an access point a scan should be performed to find the access point.

C-10-3 NetIF_WiFi_CreateAdhoc()

Create an wireless adhoc access point.

FILES

net_if_wifi.h/net_if_wifi.c

PROTOTYPE

```
void NetIF_WiFi_CreateAdhoc (NET_IF_NBR              if_nbr,
                             NET_IF_WIFI_DATA_RATE   data_rate,
                             NET_IF_WIFI_SECURITY_TYPE security_type,
                             NET_IF_WIFI_PWR_LEVEL   pwr_level,
                             NET_IF_WIFI_CGH,        ch,
                             NET_IF_WIFI_SSID        ssid,
                             NET_IF_WIFI_PSK         psk,
                             NET_ERR                 *p_err);
```

ARGUMENTS

if_nbr   Interface number to join wireless access point.

data_rate   Wireless data rate to configure:

            NET_IF_WIFI_DATA_RATE_AUTO
            NET_IF_WIFI_DATA_RATE_1_MBPS
            NET_IF_WIFI_DATA_RATE_2_MBPS
            NET_IF_WIFI_DATA_RATE_5_5_MBPS
            NET_IF_WIFI_DATA_RATE_6_MBPS
            NET_IF_WIFI_DATA_RATE_9_MBPS
            NET_IF_WIFI_DATA_RATE_11_MBPS
            NET_IF_WIFI_DATA_RATE_12_MBPS
            NET_IF_WIFI_DATA_RATE_18_MBPS
            NET_IF_WIFI_DATA_RATE_24_MBPS
            NET_IF_WIFI_DATA_RATE_36_MBPS
            NET_IF_WIFI_DATA_RATE_48_MBPS
            NET_IF_WIFI_DATA_RATE_54_MBPS
            NET_IF_WIFI_DATA_RATE_MCS0
            NET_IF_WIFI_DATA_RATE_MCS1

```
            NET_IF_WIFI_DATA_RATE_MCS2
            NET_IF_WIFI_DATA_RATE_MCS3
            NET_IF_WIFI_DATA_RATE_MCS4
            NET_IF_WIFI_DATA_RATE_MCS5
            NET_IF_WIFI_DATA_RATE_MCS6
            NET_IF_WIFI_DATA_RATE_MCS7
            NET_IF_WIFI_DATA_RATE_MCS8
            NET_IF_WIFI_DATA_RATE_MCS9
            NET_IF_WIFI_DATA_RATE_MCS10
            NET_IF_WIFI_DATA_RATE_MCS11
            NET_IF_WIFI_DATA_RATE_MCS12
            NET_IF_WIFI_DATA_RATE_MCS13
            NET_IF_WIFI_DATA_RATE_MCS14
            NET_IF_WIFI_DATA_RATE_MCS15
```

security_type   Wireless security type:

```
            NET_IF_WIFI_SECURITY_OPEN
            NET_IF_WIFI_SECURITY_WEP
            NET_IF_WIFI_SECURITY_WPA
            NET_IF_WIFI_SECURITY_WPA2
```

pwr_level   Wireless radio power to configure:

```
            NET_IF_WIFI_PWR_LEVEL_LO
            NET_IF_WIFI_PWR_LEVEL_MED
            NET_IF_WIFI_PWR_LEVEL_HI
```

ch   Wireless channel number of the access point:

```
            NET_IF_WIFI_CH_1
            NET_IF_WIFI_CH_2
            NET_IF_WIFI_CH_3
            NET_IF_WIFI_CH_4
            NET_IF_WIFI_CH_5
            NET_IF_WIFI_CH_6
            NET_IF_WIFI_CH_7
            NET_IF_WIFI_CH_8
```

```
NET_IF_WIFI_CH_9
NET_IF_WIFI_CH_10
NET_IF_WIFI_CH_11
NET_IF_WIFI_CH_12
NET_IF_WIFI_CH_13
NET_IF_WIFI_CH_14
```

ssid   SSID of the access point.

psk   Pre shared key of the access point.

p_err   Pointer to variable that will receive the return error code from this function:

```
NET_IF_WIFI_ERR_NONE
NET_IF_WIFI_ERR_CREATE_ADHOC
NET_IF_WIFI_ERR_INVALID_CH
NET_IF_WIFI_ERR_INVALID_NET_TYPE
NET_IF_WIFI_ERR_INVALID_DATA_RATE
NET_IF_WIFI_ERR_INVALID_SECURITY
NET_IF_WIFI_ERR_INVALID_PWR_LEVEL
```

RETURNED VALUE

None.

REQUIRED CONFIGURATION

None.

NOTES / WARNINGS

None.

C-10-4 NetIF_WiFi_Leave()

Leave the access point previously joined.

FILES

net_if_wifi.h/net_if_wifi.c

PROTOTYPE

```
void NetIF_WiFi_Leave (NET_IF_NBR   if_nbr,
                       NET_ERR     *p_err);
```

ARGUMENTS

if_nbr   Interface number to join wireless access point.

p_err   Pointer to variable that will receive the return error code from this function:

            NET_IF_WIFI_ERR_NONE
            NET_IF_WIFI_ERR_LEAVE

RETURNED VALUE

None.

REQUIRED CONFIGURATION

None.

NOTES / WARNINGS

None.

C-11 IGMP FUNCTIONS

C-11-1 NetIGMP_HostGrpJoin()

Join a host group.

FILES

net_igmp.h/net_igmp.c

PROTOTYPE

```
void NetIGMP_HostGrpJoin (NET_IF_NBR   if_nbr,
                          NET_IP_ADDR  addr_grp,
                          NET_ERR      *perr);
```

ARGUMENTS

if_nbr   Interface number to join host group.

addr_grp   IP address of host group to join.

perr   Pointer to variable that will receive the return error code from this function:

        NET_IGMP_ERR_NONE
        NET_IGMP_ERR_INVALID_ADDR_GRP
        NET_IGMP_ERR_HOST_GRP_NONE_AVAIL
        NET_IGMP_ERR_HOST_GRP_INVALID_TYPE
        NET_IF_ERR_INVALID_IF
        NET_ERR_INIT_INCOMPLETE
        NET_OS_ERR_LOCK

RETURNED VALUE

DEF_OK,   if host group successfully joined.

DEF_FAIL,   otherwise.

REQUIRED CONFIGURATION

Available only if **NET_IP_CFG_MULTICAST_SEL** is configured for transmit and receive multicasting (see section D-9-2 on page 971).

NOTES / WARNINGS

addr_grp *must* be in host-order.

C-11-2 NetIGMP_HostGrpLeave()

Leave a host group.

FILES

net_igmp.h/net_igmp.c

PROTOTYPE

```
void NetIGMP_HostGrpLeave (NET_IF_NBR   if_nbr,
                           NET_IP_ADDR  addr_grp,
                           NET_ERR      *perr);
```

ARGUMENTS

if_nbr   Interface number to leave host group.

addr_grp   IP address of host group to leave.

err   Pointer to variable that will receive the return error code from this function:

        NET_IGMP_ERR_NONE
        NET_IGMP_ERR_HOST_GRP_NOT_FOUND
        NET_ERR_INIT_INCOMPLETE
        NET_OS_ERR_LOCK

RETURNED VALUE

DEF_OK,   if host group successfully left.

DEF_FAIL,   otherwise.

REQUIRED CONFIGURATION

Available only if **NET_IP_CFG_MULTICAST_SEL** is configured for transmit and receive multicasting (see section D-9-2 on page 971).

NOTES / WARNINGS

addr_grp *must* be in host-order.

C-12 IP FUNCTIONS

C-12-1 NetIP_CfgAddrAdd()

Add a static IP host address, subnet mask, and default gateway to an interface.

FILES

net_ip.h/net_ip.c

PROTOTYPE

```
CPU_BOOLEAN NetIP_CfgAddrAdd(NET_IF_NBR   if_nbr,
                            NET_IP_ADDR  addr_host,
                            NET_IP_ADDR  addr_subnet_mask,
                            NET_IP_ADDR  addr_dflt_gateway,
                            NET_ERR      *perr);
```

ARGUMENTS

if_nbr   Interface number to configure.

addr_host   Desired IP address to add to this interface.

addr_subnet_mask   Desired IP address subnet mask.

addr_dflt_gateway   Desired IP default gateway address.

perr   Pointer to variable that will receive the error code from this function:

NET_IP_ERR_NONE
NET_IP_ERR_INVALID_ADDR_HOST
NET_IP_ERR_INVALID_ADDR_GATEWAY
NET_IP_ERR_ADDR_CFG_STATE
NET_IP_ERR_ADDR_TBL_FULL
NET_IP_ERR_ADDR_CFG_IN_USE
NET_IF_ERR_INVALID_IF
NET_OS_ERR_LOCK

RETURNED VALUE

DEF_OK,   if valid IP address, subnet mask, and default gateway statically-configured;

DEF_FAIL,   otherwise.

REQUIRED CONFIGURATION

None.

NOTES / WARNINGS

IP addresses *must* be configured in host-order.

An interface may be configured with either:

- One or more statically- configured IP addresses (default configuration) **OR**

- Exactly one dynamically-configured IP address (see section C-12-2 on page 776).

If an interface's address(es) are dynamically-configured, no statically-configured address(es) may be added until all dynamically-configured address(es) are removed.

The maximum number of IP address(es) configured on any interface is limited to NET_IP_CFG_IF_MAX_NBR_ADDR (see section D-9-1 on page 970).

Note that on the default interface, the first IP address added will be the default address used for all default communication. See also section C-9-1 on page 730.

A host *may* be configured without a gateway address to allow communication only with other hosts on its local network. However, any configured gateway address *must* be on the same network as the configured host IP address (i.e., the network portion of the configured IP address and the configured gateway addresses *must* be identical).

C-12-2 NetIP_CfgAddrAddDynamic()

Add a dynamically-configured IP host address, subnet mask, and default gateway to an interface.

FILES

net_ip.h/net_ip.c

PROTOTYPE

```
CPU_BOOLEAN NetIP_CfgAddrAddDynamic(NET_IF_NBR   if_nbr,
                                    NET_IP_ADDR  addr_host,
                                    NET_IP_ADDR  addr_subnet_mask,
                                    NET_IP_ADDR  addr_dflt_gateway,
                                    NET_ERR      *perr);
```

ARGUMENTS

if_nbr   Interface number to configure.

addr_host   Desired IP address to add to this interface.

addr_subnet_mask   Desired IP address subnet mask.

addr_dflt_gateway   Desired IP default gateway address.

perr   Pointer to variable that will receive the return error code from this function:

NET_IP_ERR_NONE
NET_IP_ERR_INVALID_ADDR_HOST
NET_IP_ERR_INVALID_ADDR_GATEWAY
NET_IP_ERR_ADDR_CFG_STATE
NET_IP_ERR_ADDR_CFG_IN_USE
NET_IF_ERR_INVALID_IF
NET_ERR_INIT_INCOMPLETE
NET_OS_ERR_LOCK

RETURNED VALUE

DEF_OK, if valid IP address, subnet mask, and default gateway dynamically configured;

DEF_FAIL, otherwise.

REQUIRED CONFIGURATION

None.

NOTES / WARNINGS

IP addresses *must* be configured in host-order.

An interface may be configured with either:

■ One or more statically- configured IP addresses (see section C-12-1 on page 774) **OR**

■ Exactly one dynamically-configured IP address.

This function should *only* be called by appropriate network application function(s) [e.g., DHCP initialization functions]. However, if the application attempts to dynamically configure IP address(es), it *must* call **NetIP_CfgAddrAddDynamicStart()** before calling **NetIP_CfgAddrAddDynamic()**. Note that on the default interface, the first IP address added will be the default address used for all default communication. See also section C-9-1 on page 730.

A host *may* be configured without a gateway address to allow communication only with other hosts on its local network. However, any configured gateway address *must* be on the same network as the configured host IP address (i.e., the network portion of the configured IP address and the configured gateway addresses *must* be identical).

C-12-3 NetIP_CfgAddrAddDynamicStart()

Start dynamic IP address configuration for an interface.

FILES

net_ip.h/net_ip.c

PROTOTYPE

```
CPU_BOOLEAN NetIP_CfgAddrAddDynamicStart(NET_IF_NBR  if_nbr,
                                         NET_ERR    *perr);
```

ARGUMENTS

if_nbr   Interface number to start dynamic address configuration.

perr   Pointer to variable that will receive the return error code from this function:

            NET_IP_ERR_NONE
            NET_IP_ERR_ADDR_CFG_STATE
            NET_IP_ERR_ADDR_CFG_IN_PROGRESS
            NET_IF_ERR_INVALID_IF
            NET_OS_ERR_LOCK

RETURNED VALUE

DEF_OK,   if dynamic IP address configuration successfully started;

DEF_FAIL,   otherwise.

REQUIRED CONFIGURATION

None.

NOTES / WARNINGS

This function should *only* be called by appropriate network application function(s) [e.g., DHCP initialization functions]. However, if the application attempts to dynamically configure IP address(es), it *must* call `NetIP_CfgAddrAddDynamicStart()` before calling `NetIP_CfgAddrAddDynamic()`.

C-12-4 NetIP_CfgAddrAddDynamicStop()

Stop dynamic IP address configuration for an interface.

FILES

net_ip.h/net_ip.c

PROTOTYPE

```
CPU_BOOLEAN NetIP_CfgAddrAddDynamicStop(NET_IF_NBR  if_nbr,
                                        NET_ERR    *perr);
```

ARGUMENTS

if_nbr   Interface number to stop dynamic address configuration.

perr   Pointer to variable that will receive the return error code from this function:

            NET_IP_ERR_NONE
            NET_IP_ERR_ADDR_CFG_STATE
            NET_IF_ERR_INVALID_IF
            NET_OS_ERR_LOCK

RETURNED VALUE

DEF_OK,   if dynamic IP address configuration successfully stopped;

DEF_FAIL,   otherwise.

REQUIRED CONFIGURATION

None.

NOTES / WARNINGS

This function should *only* be called by appropriate network application function(s) [e.g., DHCP initialization functions]. However, if the application attempts to dynamically configure IP address(es), it must call **NetIP_CfgAddrAddDynamicStop()** *only* after calling **NetIP_CfgAddrAddDynamicStart()** and dynamic IP address configuration has failed.

C-12-5 NetIP_CfgAddrRemove()

Remove a configured IP host address from an interface.

FILES

net_ip.h/net_ip.c

PROTOTYPE

```
CPU_BOOLEAN NetIP_CfgAddrRemove(NET_IF_NBR   if_nbr,
                                NET_IP_ADDR  addr_host,
                                NET_ERR      *perr);
```

ARGUMENTS

if_nbr   Interface number to remove configured IP host address.

addr_host   IP address to remove.

perr   Pointer to variable that will receive the return error code from this function:

            NET_IP_ERR_NONE
            NET_IP_ERR_INVALID_ADDR_HOST
            NET_IP_ERR_ADDR_CFG_STATE
            NET_IP_ERR_ADDR_TBL_EMPTY
            NET_IP_ERR_ADDR_NOT_FOUND
            NET_IF_ERR_INVALID_IF
            NET_OS_ERR_LOCK

RETURNED VALUE

DEF_OK,   if interface's configured IP host address successfully removed;

DEF_FAIL,   otherwise.

REQUIRED CONFIGURATION

None.

NOTES / WARNINGS

None.

C-12-6 NetIP_CfgAddrRemoveAll()

Remove all configured IP host address(es) from an interface.

FILES

net_ip.h/net_ip.c

PROTOTYPE

```
CPU_BOOLEAN NetIP_CfgAddrRemoveAll(NET_IF_NBR  if_nbr,
                                   NET_ERR     *perr);
```

ARGUMENTS

if_nbr   Interface number to remove all configured IP host address(es).

perr   Pointer to variable that will receive the return error code from this function:

            NET_IP_ERR_NONE
            NET_IP_ERR_ADDR_CFG_STATE
            NET_IF_ERR_INVALID_IF
            NET_OS_ERR_LOCK

RETURNED VALUE

DEF_OK,   if all interface's configured IP host address(es) successfully removed;

DEF_FAIL,   otherwise.

REQUIRED CONFIGURATION

None.

NOTES / WARNINGS

None.

C-12-7 NetIP_CfgFragReasmTimeout()

Configure IP fragment reassembly timeout.

FILES

net_ip.h/net_ip.c

PROTOTYPE

```
CPU_BOOLEAN NetIP_CfgFragReasmTimeout(CPU_INT08U timeout_sec);
```

ARGUMENTS

timeout_sec Desired value for IP fragment reassembly timeout (in seconds).

RETURNED VALUE

DEF_OK,   IP fragment reassembly timeout successfully configured.

DEF_FAIL,   otherwise.

REQUIRED CONFIGURATION

None.

NOTES / WARNINGS

Fragment reassembly timeout is the maximum time allowed between received fragments of the same IP datagram.

C-12-8 NetIP_GetAddrDfltGateway()

Get the default gateway IP address for a host's configured IP address.

net_ip.h/net_ip.c

```
NET_IP_ADDR NetIP_GetAddrDfltGateway(NET_IP_ADDR  addr,
                                     NET_ERR      *perr);
```

addr   Configured IP host address.

perr   Pointer to variable that will receive the return error code from this function:

        NET_IP_ERR_NONE
        NET_IP_ERR_INVALID_ADDR_HOST
        NET_OS_ERR_LOCK

Configured IP host address's default gateway (in host-order), if no errors.

NET_IP_ADDR_NONE, otherwise.

None.

All IP addresses in host-order.

C-12-9 NetIP_GetAddrHost()

Get an interface's configured IP host address(es).

FILES

net_ip.h/net_ip.c

PROTOTYPE

```
CPU_BOOLEAN NetIP_GetAddrHost(NET_IF_NBR       if_nbr,
                             NET_IP_ADDR      *paddr_tbl,
                             NET_IP_ADDRS_QTY *paddr_tbl_qty,
                             NET_ERR          *perr);
```

ARGUMENTS

if_nbr   Interface number to get configured IP host address(es).

paddr_tbl   Pointer to IP address table that will receive the IP host address(es) in host-order for this interface.

paddr_tbl_qty   Pointer to a variable to:

Pass the size of the address table, in number of IP addresses, pointed to by **paddr_tbl**.

Returns the actual number of IP addresses, if no errors.

Returns **0**, otherwise.

perr   Pointer to variable that will receive the error code from this function:

NET_IP_ERR_NONE
NET_IP_ERR_NULL_PTR
NET_IP_ERR_ADDR_NONE_AVAIL
NET_IP_ERR_ADDR_CFG_IN_PROGRESS
NET_IP_ERR_ADDR_TBL_SIZE
NET_IF_ERR_INVALID_IF
NET_OS_ERR_LOCK

RETURNED VALUE

DEF_OK,   if interface's configured IP host address(es) successfully returned;

DEF_FAIL,   otherwise.

REQUIRED CONFIGURATION

None.

NOTES / WARNINGS

IP addresses returned in host-order.

C-12-10 NetIP_GetAddrHostCfgd()

Get corresponding configured IP host address for a remote IP address.

FILES

net_ip.h/net_ip.c

PROTOTYPE

```
NET_IP_ADDR NetIP_GetAddrHostCfgd(NET_IP_ADDR addr_remote);
```

ARGUMENTS

addr_remote   Remote address to get configured IP host address

RETURNED VALUE

Configured IP host address,   if available;

NET_IP_ADDR_NONE,   otherwise.

REQUIRED CONFIGURATION

None.

NOTES / WARNINGS

IP addresses returned in host-order.

C-12-11 NetIP_GetAddrSubnetMask()

Get the IP address subnet mask for a host's configured IP address.

net_ip.h/net_ip.c

```
NET_IP_ADDR NetIP_GetAddrSubnetMask(NET_IP_ADDR  addr,
                                    NET_ERR      *perr);
```

addr   Configured IP host address.

perr   Pointer to variable that will receive the return error code from this function:

            NET_IP_ERR_NONE
            NET_IP_ERR_INVALID_ADDR_HOST
            NET_OS_ERR_LOCK

Configured IP host address's subnet mask (in host-order), if no errors.

NET_IP_ADDR_NONE, otherwise.

None.

IP addresses in host-order.

C-12-12 NetIP_IsAddrBroadcast()

Validate an IP address as the limited broadcast IP address.

FILES

net_ip.h/net_ip.c

PROTOTYPE

```
CPU_BOOLEAN NetIP_IsAddrBroadcast(NET_IP_ADDR addr);
```

ARGUMENTS

addr   IP address to validate.

RETURNED VALUE

DEF_YES   if IP address is a limited broadcast IP address;

DEF_NO   otherwise.

REQUIRED CONFIGURATION

None.

NOTES / WARNINGS

IP address *must* be in host-order.

The broadcast IP address is 255.255.255.255.

C-12-13 NetIP_IsAddrClassA()

Validate an IP address as a Class-A IP address.

FILES

net_ip.h/net_ip.c

PROTOTYPE

```
CPU_BOOLEAN NetIP_IsAddrClassA(NET_IP_ADDR addr);
```

ARGUMENTS

addr   IP address to validate.

RETURNED VALUE

DEF_YES   if IP address is a Class-A IP address;

DEF_NO   otherwise.

REQUIRED CONFIGURATION

None.

NOTES / WARNINGS

IP address *must* be in host-order.

Class-A IP addresses have their most significant bit be '0'.

C-12-14 NetIP_IsAddrClassB()

Validate an IP address as a Class-B IP address.

FILES

net_ip.h/net_ip.c

PROTOTYPE

```
CPU_BOOLEAN NetIP_IsAddrClassB(NET_IP_ADDR addr);
```

ARGUMENTS

addr   IP address to validate.

RETURNED VALUE

DEF_YES   if IP address is a Class-B IP address;

DEF_NO   otherwise.

REQUIRED CONFIGURATION

None.

NOTES / WARNINGS

IP address *must* be in host-order.

Class-B IP addresses have their most significant bits be '10'.

C-12-15 NetIP_IsAddrClassC()

Validate an IP address as a Class-C IP address.

net_ip.h/net_ip.c

```
CPU_BOOLEAN NetIP_IsAddrClassC(NET_IP_ADDR addr);
```

addr   IP address to validate.

DEF_YES   if IP address is a Class-C IP address;

DEF_NO   otherwise.

None.

IP address *must* be in host-order.

Class-C IP addresses have their most significant bits be '110'.

C-12-16 NetIP_IsAddrHost()

Validate an IP address as one the host's IP address(es).

FILES

net_ip.h/net_ip.c

PROTOTYPE

```
CPU_BOOLEAN NetIP_IsAddrHost(NET_IP_ADDR addr);
```

ARGUMENTS

addr   IP address to validate.

RETURNED VALUE

DEF_YES   if IP address is any one of the host's IP address(es);

DEF_NO   otherwise.

REQUIRED CONFIGURATION

None.

NOTES / WARNINGS

IP address *must* be in host-order.

C-12-17 NetIP_IsAddrHostCfgd()

Validate an IP address as one the host's configured IP address(es).

FILES

net_ip.h/net_ip.c

PROTOTYPE

```
CPU_BOOLEAN NetIP_IsAddrHostCfgd(NET_IP_ADDR addr);
```

ARGUMENTS

addr   IP address to validate.

RETURNED VALUE

DEF_YES   if IP address is any one of the host's configured IP address(es);

DEF_NO   otherwise.

REQUIRED CONFIGURATION

None.

NOTES / WARNINGS

IP address *must* be in host-order.

C-12-18 NetIP_IsAddrLocalHost()

Validate an IP address as a Localhost IP address.

FILES

net_ip.h/net_ip.c

PROTOTYPE

```
CPU_BOOLEAN NetIP_IsAddrLocalHost(NET_IP_ADDR addr);
```

ARGUMENTS

addr   IP address to validate.

RETURNED VALUE

DEF_YES   if IP address is a Localhost IP address;

DEF_NO   otherwise.

REQUIRED CONFIGURATION

None.

NOTES / WARNINGS

IP address *must* be in host-order.

Localhost IP addresses are any host address in the '127.<host>' subnet.

C-12-19 NetIP_IsAddrLocalLink()

Validate an IP address as a link-local IP address.

FILES

net_ip.h/net_ip.c

PROTOTYPE

```
CPU_BOOLEAN NetIP_IsAddrLocalLink(NET_IP_ADDR addr);
```

ARGUMENTS

addr   IP address to validate.

RETURNED VALUE

DEF_YES   if IP address is a link-local IP address;

DEF_NO   otherwise.

REQUIRED CONFIGURATION

None.

NOTES / WARNINGS

IP address *must* be in host-order.

Link-local IP addresses are any host address in the '169.254.<host>' subnet.

C-12-20 NetIP_IsAddrsCfgdOnIF()

Check if any IP address(es) are configured on an interface.

FILES

net_ip.h/net_ip.c

PROTOTYPE

```
CPU_BOOLEAN NetIP_IsAddrsHostCfgdOnIF(NET_IF_NBR  if_nbr,
NET_ERR    *perr);
```

ARGUMENTS

if_nbr   Interface number to check for configured IP host address(es).

perr   Pointer to variable that will receive the return error code from this function:

NET_IP_ERR_NONE
NET_IF_ERR_INVALID_IF
NET_OS_ERR_LOCK

RETURNED VALUE

DEF_YES   if ANY IP host address(es) are configured on the interface;

DEF_NO   otherwise.

REQUIRED CONFIGURATION

None.

NOTES / WARNINGS

None.

C-12-21 NetIP_IsAddrThisHost()

Validate an IP address as the 'This Host' initialization IP address.

FILES

net_ip.h/net_ip.c

PROTOTYPE

```
CPU_BOOLEAN NetIP_IsAddrThisHost(NET_IP_ADDR addr);
```

ARGUMENTS

addr   IP address to validate.

RETURNED VALUE

DEF_YES   if IP address is a 'This Host' initialization IP address;

DEF_NO   otherwise.

REQUIRED CONFIGURATION

None.

NOTES / WARNINGS

IP address *must* be in host-order.

The 'This Host' initialization IP address is 0.0.0.0.

C-12-22 NetIP_IsValidAddrHost()

Validate an IP address as a valid IP host address.

FILES

net_ip.h/net_ip.c

PROTOTYPE

```
CPU_BOOLEAN NetIP_IsValidAddrHost(NET_IP_ADDR addr_host);
```

ARGUMENTS

addr_host   IP host address to validate.

RETURNED VALUE

DEF_YES   if valid IP host address;

DEF_NO   otherwise.

REQUIRED CONFIGURATION

None.

NOTES / WARNINGS

IP address *must* be in host-order. A valid IP host address must *not* be one of the following:

- This Host (see section C-12-21 on page 799)

- Specified Host

- Localhost (see section C-12-18 on page 796)

- Limited Broadcast (see section C-12-12 on page 790)

- Directed Broadcast

C-12-23 NetIP_IsValidAddrHostCfgd()

Validate an IP address as a valid, configurable IP host address.

FILES

net_ip.h/net_ip.c

PROTOTYPE

```
CPU_BOOLEAN NetIP_IsValidAddrHostCfgd(NET_IP_ADDR addr_host,
                                      NET_IP_ADDR addr_subnet_mask);
```

ARGUMENTS

addr_host   IP host address to validate.

addr_subnet_mask   IP host address subnet mask.

RETURNED VALUE

DEF_YES   if configurable IP host address;

DEF_NO   otherwise.

REQUIRED CONFIGURATION

None.

NOTES / WARNINGS

IP addresses *must* be in host-order.

A configurable IP host address must *not* be one of the following:

- This Host (see section C-12-21 on page 799)

- Specified Host

- Localhost (see section C-12-18 on page 796)

- Limited Broadcast (see section C-12-12 on page 790)

- Directed Broadcast

- Subnet Broadcast

C-12-24 NetIP_IsValidAddrSubnetMask()

Validate an IP address subnet mask.

FILES

net_ip.h/net_ip.c

PROTOTYPE

```
CPU_BOOLEAN NetIP_IsValidAddrSubnetMask(NET_IP_ADDR addr_subnet_mask);
```

ARGUMENTS

addr_subnet_mask   IP host address subnet mask.

RETURNED VALUE

DEF_YES   if valid IP address subnet mask;

DEF_NO   otherwise.

REQUIRED CONFIGURATION

None.

NOTES / WARNINGS

IP address *must* be in host-order.

C-13 NETWORK SECURITY FUNCTIONS

C-13-1 NetSecureMgr_InstallBuf()

Install a certificate authority (CA), a certificate (CERT), or a private key (KEY) from a buffer.

FILE

net_secure_mgr.h/net_secure_mgr.c

CALLED FROM

Application

PROTOTYPE

```
CPU_BOOLEAN NetSecureMgr_InstallBuf(void       *p_buf,
                                    CPU_INT08U  type,
                                    CPU_INT08U  fmt,
                                    CPU_SIZE_T  size,
                                    NET_ERR     *p_err);
```

ARGUMENTS

p_buf   Pointer to the CA, CERT or KEY buffer to install.

type   Type of the CA, CERT or KEY to install:

        NET_SECURE_MGR_INSTALL_TYPE_CA   Certificate authority (CA)
        NET_SECURE_INSTALL_TYPE_CERT   Public key certificate
        NET_SECURE_INSTALL_TYPE_KEY   Private key

fmt   Format of the CA, CERT or KEY to install:

        NET_SECURE_MGR_INSTALL_FMT_PEM
        NET_SECURE_MGR_INSTALL_FMT_DER

size   Size of the CA, CERT or KEY buffer to install.

p_err   Pointer to variable that will receive the return error code from this function:

                NET_SECURE_MGR_ERR_NONE
                NET_SECURE_MGR_ERR_NULL_PTR
                NET_SECURE_MGR_ERR_TYPE
                NET_SECURE_MGR_ERR_FMT
                NET_SECURE_ERR_INSTALL_NOT_TRUSTED
                NET_SECURE_ERR_INSTALL_DATE_EXPIRATION
                NET_SECURE_ERR_INSTALL_DATE_CREATION
                NET_SECURE_ERR_INSTALL_CA_SLOT
                NET_SECURE_ERR_INSTALL

RETURNED VALUE

DEF_OK,   CA, CERT or KEY successfully installed;

DEF_FAIL,   otherwise.

REQUIRED CONFIGURATION

Available only if **NET_SECURE_CFG_EN** is enabled (see section D-16-1 on page 980) *and* **NET_CFG_TRANSPORT_LAYER_SEL** is configured for TCP (see section D-12-1 on page 972).

NOTES / WARNINGS

None.

C-13-2 NetSecureMgr_InstallFile()

Install a certificate authority (CA), a certificate (CERT), or a private key (KEY) from a file.

FILE

net_secure_mgr.h/net_secure_mgr.c

CALLED FROM

Application

PROTOTYPE

```
CPU_BOOLEAN NetSecureMgr_InstallFile(CPU_CHAR   *p_filename,
                                     CPU_INT08U  type,
                                     CPU_INT08U  fmt,
                                     NET_ERR    *p_err);
```

ARGUMENTS

p_filename Pointer to the CA, CERT or KEY filename to install.

type   Type of the CA, CERT or KEY to install:

NET_SECURE_MGR_INSTALL_TYPE_CA	Certificate authority (CA)
NET_SECURE_INSTALL_TYPE_CERT	Public key certificate
NET_SECURE_INSTALL_TYPE_KEY	Private key

fmt   Format of the CA, CERT or KEY to install:

NET_SECURE_MGR_INSTALL_FMT_PEM
NET_SECURE_MGR_INSTALL_FMT_DER

p_err   Pointer to variable that will receive the return error code from this function:

NET_SECURE_MGR_ERR_NONE
NET_SECURE_MGR_ERR_NULL_PTR
NET_SECURE_MGR_ERR_TYPE
NET_SECURE_MGR_ERR_FMT
NET_SECURE_ERR_INSTALL_NOT_TRUSTED
NET_SECURE_ERR_INSTALL_DATE_EXPIRATION
NET_SECURE_ERR_INSTALL_DATE_CREATION
NET_SECURE_INSTALL_CA_SLOT
NET_SECURE_ERR_INSTALL

RETURNED VALUE

DEF_OK,   CA, CERT or KEY successfully installed;

DEF_FAIL,   otherwise.

REQUIRED CONFIGURATION

Available only if **NET_SECURE_CFG_EN** is enabled (see section D-16-1 on page 980) *and* **NET_CFG_TRANSPORT_LAYER_SEL** is configured for TCP (see section D-12-1 on page 972).

NOTES / WARNINGS

p_filename must point to the full path filename of the CA, CERT or KEY file to install. The following are some example files:

\server-cert.der
\<Your Target Path>\server-key.pem

...and corresponding filename strings:

"\\server-cert.der"
"\\<Your Target Path>\\server-key.pem"

where:

<Your Target Path>   directory path on your target file system (FS)

C-14 NETWORK SOCKET FUNCTIONS

C-14-1 NetSock_Accept() / accept() (TCP)

Wait for new socket connections on a listening server socket (see section C-14-34 on page 873). When a new connection arrives and the TCP handshake has successfully completed, a new socket ID is returned for the new connection with the remote host's address and port number returned in the socket address structure.

FILES

net_sock.h/net_sock.c
net_bsd.h/net_bsd.c

PROTOTYPES

```
NET_SOCK_ID NetSock_Accept(NET_SOCK_ID        sock_id,
                           NET_SOCK_ADDR     *paddr_remote,
                           NET_SOCK_ADDR_LEN *paddr_len,
                           NET_ERR           *perr);

int accept(int               sock_id,
           struct sockaddr  *paddr_remote,
           socklen_t        *paddr_len);
```

ARGUMENTS

sock_id   This is the socket ID returned by **NetSock_Open()/socket()** when the socket was created. This socket is assumed to be bound to an address and listening for new connections (see section C-14-34 on page 873).

paddr_remote Pointer to a socket address structure (see section 18-1 "Network Socket Data Structures" on page 501) to return the remote host address of the new accepted connection.

paddr_len   Pointer to the size of the socket address structure which *must* be passed the size of the socket address structure [e.g., **sizeof(NET_SOCK_ADDR_IP)**]. Returns size of the accepted connection's socket address structure, if no errors; returns **0**, otherwise.

perr   Pointer to variable that will receive the return error code from this function:

NET_SOCK_ERR_NONE
NET_SOCK_ERR_NULL_PTR
NET_SOCK_ERR_NONE_AVAIL
NET_SOCK_ERR_NOT_USED
NET_SOCK_ERR_CLOSED
NET_SOCK_ERR_INVALID_SOCK
NET_SOCK_ERR_INVALID_FAMILY
NET_SOCK_ERR_INVALID_TYPE
NET_SOCK_ERR_INVALID_STATE
NET_SOCK_ERR_INVALID_OP
NET_SOCK_ERR_CONN_ACCEPT_Q_NONE_AVAIL
NET_SOCK_ERR_CONN_SIGNAL_TIMEOUT
NET_SOCK_ERR_CONN_FAIL
NET_SOCK_ERR_FAULT
NET_ERR_INIT_INCOMPLETE
NET_OS_ERR_LOCK

RETURNED VALUE

Returns a non-negative socket descriptor ID for the new accepted connection, if successful;
NET_SOCK_BSD_ERR_ACCEPT/-1, otherwise.

If the socket is configured for non-blocking, a return value of
NET_SOCK_BSD_ERR_ACCEPT/-1 may indicate that the no requests for connection were
queued when NetSock_Accept()/accept() was called. In this case, the server can "poll"
for a new connection at a later time.

REQUIRED CONFIGURATION

NetSock_Accept() is available only if NET_CFG_TRANSPORT_LAYER_SEL is configured for
TCP (see section D-12-1 on page 972).

In addition, accept() is available only if NET_BSD_CFG_API_EN is enabled (see section
D-17-1 on page 983).

NOTES / WARNINGS

See section 8-2 "Socket Interface" on page 212 for socket address structure formats.

C-14-2 NetSock_Bind() / bind() (TCP/UDP)

Assign network addresses to sockets. Typically, server sockets bind to addresses but client sockets do not. Servers may bind to one of the local host's addresses but usually bind to the wildcard address (**NET_SOCK_ADDR_IP_WILDCARD/INADDR_ANY**) on a specific, well-known port number. Whereas client sockets usually bind to one of the local host's addresses but with a random port number (by configuring the socket address structure's port number field with a value of 0).

FILES

net_sock.h/net_sock.c
net_bsd.h/net_bsd.c

PROTOTYPES

```
NET_SOCK_RTN_CODE NetSock_Bind(NET_SOCK_ID        sock_id,
                               NET_SOCK_ADDR      *paddr_local,
                               NET_SOCK_ADDR_LEN  addr_len,
                               NET_ERR            *perr);

int bind(int               sock_id,
         struct sockaddr   *paddr_local,
         socklen_t         addr_len);
```

ARGUMENTS

sock_id   This is the socket ID returned by **NetSock_Open()/socket()** when the socket was created.

paddr_local Pointer to a socket address structure (see section 8-2 "Socket Interface" on page 212) which contains the local host address to bind the socket to.

addr_len   Size of the socket address structure which *must* be passed the size of the socket address structure [for example, **sizeof(NET_SOCK_ADDR_IP)**].

perr	Pointer to variable that will receive the return error code from this function:

```
NET_SOCK_ERR_NONE
NET_SOCK_ERR_NOT_USED
NET_SOCK_ERR_CLOSED
NET_SOCK_ERR_INVALID_SOCK
NET_SOCK_ERR_INVALID_FAMILY
NET_SOCK_ERR_INVALID_PROTOCOL
NET_SOCK_ERR_INVALID_TYPE
NET_SOCK_ERR_INVALID_STATE
NET_SOCK_ERR_INVALID_OP
NET_SOCK_ERR_INVALID_ADDR
NET_SOCK_ERR_ADDR_IN_USE
NET_SOCK_ERR_PORT_NBR_NONE_AVAIL
NET_SOCK_ERR_CONN_FAIL
NET_IF_ERR_INVALID_IF
NET_IP_ERR_ADDR_NONE_AVAIL
NET_IP_ERR_ADDR_CFG_IN_PROGRESS
NET_CONN_ERR_NULL_PTR
NET_CONN_ERR_NOT_USED
NET_CONN_ERR_NONE_AVAIL
NET_CONN_ERR_INVALID_CONN
NET_CONN_ERR_INVALID_FAMILY
NET_CONN_ERR_INVALID_TYPE
NET_CONN_ERR_INVALID_PROTOCOL_IX
NET_CONN_ERR_INVALID_ADDR_LEN
NET_CONN_ERR_ADDR_NOT_USED
NET_CONN_ERR_ADDR_IN_USE
NET_ERR_INIT_INCOMPLETE
NET_OS_ERR_LOCK
```

RETURNED VALUE

NET_SOCK_BSD_ERR_NONE/0, if successful;

NET_SOCK_BSD_ERR_BIND/-1, otherwise.

REQUIRED CONFIGURATION

NetSock_Bind() is available only if either NET_CFG_TRANSPORT_LAYER_SEL is configured for TCP (see section D-12-1 on page 972) and/or NET_UDP_CFG_APP_API_SEL is configured for sockets (see section D-13-1 on page 973).

In addition, **bind()** is available only if NET_BSD_CFG_API_EN is enabled (see section D-17-1 on page 983).

NOTES / WARNINGS

See section 8-2 "Socket Interface" on page 212 for socket address structure formats.

Sockets may bind to any of the host's configured addresses, any localhost address (127.x.y.z network; e.g., 127.0.0.1), any link-local address (169.254.y.z network; e.g., 169.254.65.111), as well as the wildcard address (NET_SOCK_ADDR_IP_WILDCARD/INADDR_ANY, i.e., 0.0.0.0).

Sockets may bind to specific port numbers or request a random, ephemeral port number by configuring the socket address structure's port number field with a value of 0. Sockets may *not* bind to a port number that is within the configured range of random port numbers (see section D-15-2 on page 976 and section D-15-7 on page 978):

```
NET_SOCK_CFG_PORT_NBR_RANDOM_BASE <= RandomPortNbrs <=
(NET_SOCK_CFG_PORT_NBR_RANDOM_BASE + NET_SOCK_CFG_NBR_SOCK + 10)
```

C-14-3 NetSock_CfgBlock() (TCP/UDP)

Configure a socket's blocking mode.

net_sock.h/net_sock.c

```
CPU_BOOLEAN NetSock_CfgBlock(NET_SOCK_ID  sock_id,
                            CPU_INT08U   block,
                            NET_ERR      *perr);
```

sock_id   This is the socket ID returned by **NetSock_Open()/socket()** when the
            socket was created *or* by **NetSock_Accept()/accept()** when a connection
            was accepted.

block   Desired value for socket blocking mode:

NET_SOCK_BLOCK_SEL_DFLT	Socket operations will block
NET_SOCK_BLOCK_SEL_BLOCK	Socket operations will block
NET_SOCK_BLOCK_SEL_NO_BLOCK	Socket operations will not block

perr   Pointer to variable that will receive the return error code from this function:

NET_SOCK_ERR_NONE
NET_SOCK_ERR_NOT_USED
NET_SOCK_ERR_INVALID_SOCK
NET_SOCK_ERR_INVALID_ARG
NET_ERR_INIT_INCOMPLETE
NET_OS_ERR_LOCK

RETURNED VALUE

DEF_OK,   Socket blocking mode successfully configured;

DEF_FAIL,   otherwise.

REQUIRED CONFIGURATION

Available only if **NET_CFG_TRANSPORT_LAYER_SEL** is configured for TCP (see section D-12-1 on page 972) and/or **NET_UDP_CFG_APP_API_SEL** is configured for sockets (see section D-13-1 on page 973).

NOTES / WARNINGS

None.

C-14-4 NetSock_CfgSecure() (TCP)

Configure a socket's secure mode.

net_sock.h/net_sock.c

```
CPU_BOOLEAN NetSock_CfgBlock(NET_SOCK_ID  sock_id,
                            CPU_INT08U   secure,
                            NET_ERR      *perr);
```

sock_id   This is the socket ID returned by **NetSock_Open()/socket()** when the
            socket was created.

block   Desired value for socket secure mode:

            DEF_ENABLED   Socket operations will be secured.
            DEF_DISABLED   Socket operations will not be secured.

perr   Pointer to variable that will receive the return error code from this function:

            NET_SOCK_ERR_NONE
            NET_SOCK_ERR_NOT_USED
            NET_SOCK_ERR_INVALID_ARG
            NET_SOCK_ERR_INVALID_TYPE
            NET_SOCK_ERR_INVALID_STATE
            NET_SOCK_ERR_INVALID_SOCK
            NET_ERR_INIT_INCOMPLETE
            NET_SECURE_ERR_NOT_AVAIL
            NET_OS_ERR_LOCK

RETURNED VALUE

DEF_OK,   Socket secure mode successfully configured;

DEF_FAIL,   otherwise.

REQUIRED CONFIGURATION

Available only if **NET_CFG_TRANSPORT_LAYER_SEL** is configured for TCP (see section D-12-1 on page 972) *and* if **NET_SECURE_CFG_EN** is enabled (see section D-15 on page 976).

NOTES / WARNINGS

Available only for stream-type sockets (e.g., TCP sockets).

C-14-5 NetSock_CfgRxQ_Size() (TCP/UDP)

Configure socket's receive queue size.

FILES

net_sock.h/net_sock.c

PROTOTYPE

```
CPU_BOOLEAN NetSock_CfgRxQ_Size(NET_SOCK_ID        sock_id,
                                NET_SOCK_DATA_SIZE  size
                                NET_ERR            *perr);
```

ARGUMENTS

sock_id   This is the socket ID of socket to configure receive queue size.

size   Desired receive queue size.

perr   Pointer to variable that will receive the return error code from this function:

           NET_SOCK_ERR_NONE
           NET_SOCK_ERR_INVALID_TYPE
           NET_SOCK_ERR_INVALID_PROTOCOL
           NET_SOCK_ERR_INVALID_DATA_SIZE
           NET_ERR_INIT_INCOMPLETE
           NET_SOCK_ERR_INVALID_SOCK
           NET_SOCK_ERR_NOT_USED
           NET_TCP_ERR_INVALID_CONN
           NET_TCP_ERR_INVALID_ARG
           NET_TCP_ERR_CONN_NOT_USED
           NET_CONN_ERR_INVALID_CONN
           NET_CONN_ERR_NOT_USED
           NET_OS_ERR_LOCK

RETURNED VALUE

DEF_OK,   Socket receive queue size successfully configured;

DEF_FAIL,   otherwise.

REQUIRED CONFIGURATION

None.

NOTES / WARNINGS

For datagram sockets, configured size does NOT:

- Limit or remove any received data currently queued but becomes effective for later received data.

- Partially truncate any received data but instead allows data from exactly one received packet buffer to overflow the configured size since each datagram MUST be received atomically (see section C-14-40 "NetSock_RxData() / recv() (TCP) NetSock_RxDataFrom() / recvfrom() (UDP)" on page 884).

For steam sockets, size MAY be required to be configured prior to connecting (see section C-15-5 "NetTCP_ConnCfgRxWinSize()" on page 904).

C-14-6 NetSock_CfgTxQ_Size() (TCP/UDP)

Configure socket's transmit queue size.

net_sock.h/net_sock.c

```
CPU_BOOLEAN NetSock_CfgTxQ_Size(NET_SOCK_ID         sock_id,
                                NET_SOCK_DATA_SIZE  size
                                NET_ERR            *perr);
```

sock_id   This is the socket ID of socket to configure transmit queue size.

size   Desired transmit queue size.

perr   Pointer to variable that will receive the return error code from this function:

            NET_SOCK_ERR_NONE
            NET_SOCK_ERR_INVALID_TYPE
            NET_SOCK_ERR_INVALID_PROTOCOL
            NET_SOCK_ERR_INVALID_DATA_SIZE
            NET_ERR_INIT_INCOMPLETE
            NET_SOCK_ERR_INVALID_SOCK
            NET_SOCK_ERR_NOT_USED
            NET_TCP_ERR_INVALID_CONN
            NET_TCP_ERR_INVALID_ARG
            NET_TCP_ERR_CONN_NOT_USED
            NET_CONN_ERR_INVALID_CONN
            NET_CONN_ERR_NOT_USED
            NET_OS_ERR_LOCK

RETURNED VALUE

DEF_OK,   Socket transmit queue size successfully configured;

DEF_FAIL,   otherwise.

REQUIRED CONFIGURATION

None.

NOTES / WARNINGS

For datagram sockets, configured size does *not*:

▓ Partially truncate any transmitted data but instead allows data from exactly one transmitted packet buffer to overflow the configured size since each datagram MUST be transmitted atomically (see section C-14-42 "NetSock_TxData() / send() (TCP) NetSock_TxDataTo() / sendto() (UDP)" on page 891).

For steam sockets, size *may* be required to be configured prior to connecting (see section C-15-6 "NetTCP_ConnCfgTxWinSize()" on page 906).

C-14-7 NetSock_CfgTxIP_TOS() (TCP/UDP)

Configure socket's transmit IP TOS.

FILES

net_sock.h/net_sock.c

PROTOTYPE

```
CPU_BOOLEAN NetSock_CfgTxIP_TOS(NET_SOCK_ID  sock_id,
                                NET_IP_TOS   ip_tos
                                NET_ERR      *perr);
```

ARGUMENTS

sock_id   This is the socket ID of socket to configure transmit IP TOS.

size   Desired transmit IP TOS.

perr   Pointer to variable that will receive the return error code from this function:

           NET_SOCK_ERR_NONE
           NET_SOCK_ERR_NOT_USED
           NET_SOCK_ERR_INVALID_STATE
           NET_SOCK_ERR_INVALID_OP
           NET_ERR_INIT_INCOMPLETE
           NET_SOCK_ERR_INVALID_SOCK
           NET_CONN_ERR_INVALID_ARG
           NET_CONN_ERR_INVALID_CONN
           NET_CONN_ERR_NOT_USED
           NET_OS_ERR_LOCK

RETURNED VALUE

DEF_OK,   Socket transmit IP TOS successfully configured;

DEF_FAIL,   otherwise.

REQUIRED CONFIGURATION

None.

NOTES / WARNINGS

None.

C-14-8 NetSock_CfgTxIP_TTL() (TCP/UDP)

Configure socket's transmit IP TTL.

FILES

net_sock.h/net_sock.c

PROTOTYPE

```
CPU_BOOLEAN NetSock_CfgTxIP_TTL(NET_SOCK_ID  sock_id,
                                NET_IP_TTL   ip_ttl
                                NET_ERR      *perr);
```

ARGUMENTS

sock_id   This is the socket ID of socket to configure transmit IP TTL.

size   Desired transmit IP TTL:

NET_IP_TTL_MIN	Minimum TTL transmit value (1)
NET_IP_TTL_MAX	Maximum TTL transmit value (255)
NET_IP_TTL_DFLT	Default TTL transmit value (128)
NET_IP_TTL_NONE	Replace with default TTL

perr   Pointer to variable that will receive the return error code from this function:

             NET_SOCK_ERR_NONE
             NET_SOCK_ERR_NOT_USED
             NET_SOCK_ERR_INVALID_STATE
             NET_SOCK_ERR_INVALID_OP
             NET_ERR_INIT_INCOMPLETE
             NET_SOCK_ERR_INVALID_SOCK
             NET_CONN_ERR_INVALID_ARG
             NET_CONN_ERR_INVALID_CONN
             NET_CONN_ERR_NOT_USED
             NET_OS_ERR_LOCK

RETURNED VALUE

DEF_OK,   Socket transmit IP TTL successfully configured;

DEF_FAIL,   otherwise.

REQUIRED CONFIGURATION

None.

NOTES / WARNINGS

None.

C-14-9 NetSock_CfgTxIP_TTL_Multicast() (TCP/UDP)

Configure socket's transmit IP multicast TTL.

net_sock.h/net_sock.c

```
CPU_BOOLEAN NetSock_CfgTxIP_TTL_Multicast(NET_SOCK_ID  sock_id,
                                          NET_IP_TTL   ip_ttl
                                          NET_ERR      *perr);
```

sock_id   This is the socket ID of socket to configure transmit IP TTL.

size   Desired transmit IP multicast TTL:

NET_IP_TTL_MIN	Minimum TTL transmit value (1)
NET_IP_TTL_MAX	Maximum TTL transmit value (255)
NET_IP_TTL_DFLT	Default TTL transmit value (1)
NET_IP_TTL_NONE	Replace with default TTL

perr   Pointer to variable that will receive the return error code from this function:

NET_SOCK_ERR_NONE
NET_SOCK_ERR_NOT_USED
NET_SOCK_ERR_INVALID_STATE
NET_SOCK_ERR_INVALID_OP
NET_SOCK_ERR_API_DIS
NET_ERR_INIT_INCOMPLETE
NET_SOCK_ERR_INVALID_SOCK
NET_CONN_ERR_INVALID_ARG
NET_CONN_ERR_INVALID_CONN
NET_CONN_ERR_NOT_USED
NET_OS_ERR_LOCK

RETURNED VALUE

DEF_OK,   Socket transmit IP multicast TTL successfully configured;

DEF_FAIL,   otherwise.

REQUIRED CONFIGURATION

Available only if NET_SOCK_CFG_FAMILY is configured for IPv4 sockets (see section D-15-1 "NET_SOCK_CFG_FAMILY" on page 976).

NOTES / WARNINGS

None.

C-14-10 NetSock_CfgTimeoutConnAcceptDflt() (TCP)

Set socket's connection accept timeout to configured-default value.

FILES

net_sock.h/net_sock.c

PROTOTYPE

```
CPU_BOOLEAN NetSock_CfgTimeoutConnAcceptDflt(NET_SOCK_ID  sock_id,
                                             NET_ERR      *perr);
```

ARGUMENTS

sock_id   This is the socket ID returned by **NetSock_Open()/socket()** when the socket was created *or* by **NetSock_Accept()/accept()** when a connection was accepted.

perr   Pointer to variable that will receive the return error code from this function:

                    NET_SOCK_ERR_NONE
                    NET_SOCK_ERR_NOT_USED
                    NET_SOCK_ERR_INVALID_SOCK
                    NET_ERR_INIT_INCOMPLETE
                    NET_OS_ERR_INVALID_TIME
                    NET_OS_ERR_LOCK

RETURNED VALUE

DEF_OK,   Socket connection accept configured-default timeout successfully set;

DEF_FAIL,   otherwise.

REQUIRED CONFIGURATION

Available only if `NET_CFG_TRANSPORT_LAYER_SEL` is configured for TCP (see section D-12-1 on page 972).

NOTES / WARNINGS

None.

C-14-11 NetSock_CfgTimeoutConnAcceptGet_ms() (TCP)

Get socket's connection accept timeout value.

FILES

net_sock.h/net_sock.c

PROTOTYPE

```
CPU_INT32U NetSock_CfgTimeoutConnAcceptGet_ms(NET_SOCK_ID  sock_id,
                                              NET_ERR     *perr);
```

ARGUMENTS

sock_id   This is the socket ID returned by **NetSock_Open()/socket()** when the
             socket was created *or* by **NetSock_Accept()/accept()** when a connection
             was accepted.

perr   Pointer to variable that will receive the return error code from this function:

             NET_SOCK_ERR_NONE
             NET_SOCK_ERR_NOT_USED
             NET_SOCK_ERR_INVALID_SOCK
             NET_ERR_INIT_INCOMPLETE
             NET_OS_ERR_LOCK

RETURNED VALUE

0, on any errors;

NET_TMR_TIME_INFINITE, if infinite (i.e., no timeout) value configured.

Timeout in number of milliseconds, otherwise.

REQUIRED CONFIGURATION

Available only if **NET_CFG_TRANSPORT_LAYER_SEL** is configured for TCP (see section D-12-1 on page 972).

NOTES / WARNINGS

None.

C-14-12 NetSock_CfgTimeoutConnAcceptSet() (TCP)

Set socket's connection accept timeout value.

FILES

net_sock.h/net_sock.c

PROTOTYPE

```
CPU_BOOLEAN NetSock_CfgTimeoutConnAcceptSet(NET_SOCK_ID  sock_id,
                                            CPU_INT32U   timeout_ms,
                                            NET_ERR      *perr);
```

ARGUMENTS

sock_id   This is the socket ID returned by **NetSock_Open()/socket()** when the
             socket was created *or* by **NetSock_Accept()/accept()** when a connection
             was accepted.

timeout_ms   Desired timeout value:

             NET_TMR_TIME_INFINITE, if infinite (i.e., no timeout) value desired.

             In number of milliseconds, otherwise.

perr   Pointer to variable that will receive the return error code from this function:

             NET_SOCK_ERR_NONE
             NET_SOCK_ERR_NOT_USED
             NET_SOCK_ERR_INVALID_SOCK
             NET_ERR_INIT_INCOMPLETE
             NET_OS_ERR_INVALID_TIME
             NET_OS_ERR_LOCK

RETURNED VALUE

DEF_OK,   Socket connection accept timeout successfully set;

DEF_FAIL,   otherwise.

REQUIRED CONFIGURATION

Available only if **NET_CFG_TRANSPORT_LAYER_SEL** is configured for TCP (see section D-12-1 on page 972).

NOTES / WARNINGS

None.

C-14-13 NetSock_CfgTimeoutConnCloseDflt() (TCP)

Set socket's connection close timeout to configured-default value.

FILES

net_sock.h/net_sock.c

PROTOTYPE

```
CPU_BOOLEAN NetSock_CfgTimeoutConnCloseDflt(NET_SOCK_ID  sock_id,
                                            NET_ERR      *perr);
```

ARGUMENTS

sock_id   This is the socket ID returned by **NetSock_Open()/socket()** when the
            socket was created *or* by **NetSock_Accept()/accept()** when a connection
            was accepted.

perr   Pointer to variable that will receive the return error code from this function:

            NET_SOCK_ERR_NONE
            NET_SOCK_ERR_NOT_USED
            NET_SOCK_ERR_INVALID_SOCK
            NET_ERR_INIT_INCOMPLETE
            NET_OS_ERR_INVALID_TIME
            NET_OS_ERR_LOCK

RETURNED VALUE

DEF_OK,   Socket connection close configured-default timeout successfully set;

DEF_FAIL,   otherwise.

C

REQUIRED CONFIGURATION

Available only if **NET_CFG_TRANSPORT_LAYER_SEL** is configured for TCP (see section D-12-1 on page 972).

NOTES / WARNINGS

None.

C-14-14 NetSock_CfgTimeoutConnCloseGet_ms() (TCP)

Get socket's connection close timeout value.

FILES

net_sock.h/net_sock.c

PROTOTYPE

```
CPU_INT32U NetSock_CfgTimeoutConnCloseGet_ms(NET_SOCK_ID  sock_id,
                                             NET_ERR      *perr);
```

ARGUMENTS

sock_id   This is the socket ID returned by **NetSock_Open()/socket()** when the
            socket was created *or* by **NetSock_Accept()/accept()** when a connection
            was accepted.

perr   Pointer to variable that will receive the return error code from this function:

            NET_SOCK_ERR_NONE
            NET_SOCK_ERR_NOT_USED
            NET_SOCK_ERR_INVALID_SOCK
            NET_ERR_INIT_INCOMPLETE
            NET_OS_ERR_LOCK

RETURNED VALUE

0, on any errors;

NET_TMR_TIME_INFINITE, if infinite (i.e., no timeout) value configured;

Timeout in number of milliseconds, otherwise.

REQUIRED CONFIGURATION

Available only if **NET_CFG_TRANSPORT_LAYER_SEL** is configured for TCP (see section D-12-1 on page 972).

NOTES / WARNINGS

None.

C-14-15 NetSock_CfgTimeoutConnCloseSet() (TCP)

Set socket's connection close timeout value.

FILES

net_sock.h/net_sock.c

PROTOTYPE

```
CPU_BOOLEAN NetSock_CfgTimeoutConnCloseSet(NET_SOCK_ID  sock_id,
                                           CPU_INT32U   timeout_ms,
                                           NET_ERR      *perr);
```

ARGUMENTS

sock_id   This is the socket ID returned by **NetSock_Open()/socket()** when the socket was created *or* by **NetSock_Accept()/accept()** when a connection was accepted.

timeout_ms Desired timeout value:

NET_TMR_TIME_INFINITE, if infinite (i.e., no timeout) value desired.

In number of milliseconds, otherwise.

perr   Pointer to variable that will receive the return error code from this function:

NET_SOCK_ERR_NONE
NET_SOCK_ERR_NOT_USED
NET_SOCK_ERR_INVALID_SOCK
NET_ERR_INIT_INCOMPLETE
NET_OS_ERR_INVALID_TIME
NET_OS_ERR_LOCK

RETURNED VALUE

DEF_OK,   Socket connection close timeout successfully set;

DEF_FAIL,   otherwise.

REQUIRED CONFIGURATION

Available only if **NET_CFG_TRANSPORT_LAYER_SEL** is configured for TCP (see section D-12-1 on page 972).

NOTES / WARNINGS

None.

C-14-16 NetSock_CfgTimeoutConnReqDflt() (TCP)

Set socket's connection request timeout to configured-default value.

FILES

net_sock.h/net_sock.c

PROTOTYPE

```
CPU_BOOLEAN NetSock_CfgTimeoutConnReqDflt(NET_SOCK_ID  sock_id,
                                          NET_ERR   *perr);
```

ARGUMENTS

sock_id   This is the socket ID returned by **NetSock_Open()/socket()** when the
            socket was created *or* by **NetSock_Accept()/accept()** when a connection
            was accepted.

perr   Pointer to variable that will receive the return error code from this function:

            NET_SOCK_ERR_NONE
            NET_SOCK_ERR_NOT_USED
            NET_SOCK_ERR_INVALID_SOCK
            NET_ERR_INIT_INCOMPLETE
            NET_OS_ERR_INVALID_TIME
            NET_OS_ERR_LOCK

RETURNED VALUE

DEF_OK,   Socket connection request configured-default timeout successfully set;

DEF_FAIL,   otherwise.

REQUIRED CONFIGURATION

Available only if **NET_CFG_TRANSPORT_LAYER_SEL** is configured for TCP (see section D-12-1 on page 972).

NOTES / WARNINGS

None.

C-14-17 NetSock_CfgTimeoutConnReqGet_ms() (TCP)

Get socket's connection request timeout value.

FILES

net_sock.h/net_sock.c

PROTOTYPE

```
CPU_INT32U NetSock_CfgTimeoutConnReqGet_ms(NET_SOCK_ID  sock_id,
                                           NET_ERR      *perr);
```

ARGUMENTS

sock_id   This is the socket ID returned by **NetSock_Open()/socket()** when the socket was created *or* by **NetSock_Accept()/accept()** when a connection was accepted.

perr   Pointer to variable that will receive the return error code from this function:

        NET_SOCK_ERR_NONE
        NET_SOCK_ERR_NOT_USED
        NET_SOCK_ERR_INVALID_SOCK
        NET_ERR_INIT_INCOMPLETE
        NET_OS_ERR_LOCK

RETURNED VALUE

0, on any errors;

NET_TMR_TIME_INFINITE, if infinite (i.e., no timeout) value configured;

Timeout in number of milliseconds, otherwise.

REQUIRED CONFIGURATION

Available only if **NET_CFG_TRANSPORT_LAYER_SEL** is configured for TCP (see section D-12-1 on page 972).

NOTES / WARNINGS

None.

C-14-18 NetSock_CfgTimeoutConnReqSet() (TCP)

Set socket's connection request timeout value.

FILES

net_sock.h/net_sock.c

PROTOTYPE

```
CPU_BOOLEAN NetSock_CfgTimeoutConnReqSet(NET_SOCK_ID  sock_id,
                                         CPU_INT32U   timeout_ms,
                                         NET_ERR      *perr);
```

ARGUMENTS

sock_id   This is the socket ID returned by **NetSock_Open()/socket()** when the
          socket was created *or* by **NetSock_Accept()/accept()** when a connection
          was accepted.

timeout_ms Desired timeout value:

            NET_TMR_TIME_INFINITE, if infinite (i.e., no timeout) value desired.

            In number of milliseconds, otherwise.

perr   Pointer to variable that will receive the return error code from this function:

            NET_SOCK_ERR_NONE
            NET_SOCK_ERR_NOT_USED
            NET_SOCK_ERR_INVALID_SOCK
            NET_ERR_INIT_INCOMPLETE
            NET_OS_ERR_INVALID_TIME
            NET_OS_ERR_LOCK

RETURNED VALUE

DEF_OK, Socket connection request timeout successfully set;

DEF_FAIL, otherwise.

REQUIRED CONFIGURATION

Available only if **NET_CFG_TRANSPORT_LAYER_SEL** is configured for TCP (see section D-12-1 on page 972).

NOTES / WARNINGS

None.

C-14-19 NetSock_CfgTimeoutRxQ_Dflt() (TCP/UDP)

Set socket's connection receive queue timeout to configured-default value.

FILES

net_sock.h/net_sock.c

PROTOTYPE

```
CPU_BOOLEAN NetSock_CfgTimeoutRxQ_Dflt(NET_SOCK_ID  sock_id,
                                       NET_ERR      *perr);
```

ARGUMENTS

sock_id   This is the socket ID returned by **NetSock_Open()/socket()** when the
           socket was created *or* by **NetSock_Accept()/accept()** when a connection
           was accepted.

perr   Pointer to variable that will receive the return error code from this function:

           NET_SOCK_ERR_NONE
           NET_SOCK_ERR_NOT_USED
           NET_SOCK_ERR_INVALID_SOCK
           NET_SOCK_ERR_INVALID_TYPE
           NET_SOCK_ERR_INVALID_PROTOCOL
           NET_TCP_ERR_CONN_NOT_USED
           NET_TCP_ERR_INVALID_CONN
           NET_CONN_ERR_NOT_USED
           NET_CONN_ERR_INVALID_CONN
           NET_ERR_INIT_INCOMPLETE
           NET_OS_ERR_INVALID_TIME
           NET_OS_ERR_LOCK

RETURNED VALUE

DEF_OK,   Socket receive queue configured-default timeout successfully set;

DEF_FAIL,   otherwise.

REQUIRED CONFIGURATION

Available only if either **NET_CFG_TRANSPORT_LAYER_SEL** is configured for TCP (see section D-12-1 on page 972) and/or **NET_UDP_CFG_APP_API_SEL** is configured for sockets (see section D-13-1 on page 973).

NOTES / WARNINGS

None.

C-14-20 NetSock_CfgTimeoutRxQ_Get_ms() (TCP/UDP)

Get socket's receive queue timeout value.

FILES

net_sock.h/net_sock.c

PROTOTYPE

```
CPU_INT32U NetSock_CfgTimeoutRxQ_Get_ms(NET_SOCK_ID  sock_id,
                                        NET_ERR      *perr);
```

ARGUMENTS

sock_id   This is the socket ID returned by **NetSock_Open()/socket()** when the socket was created *or* by **NetSock_Accept()/accept()** when a connection was accepted.

perr   Pointer to variable that will receive the return error code from this function:

            NET_SOCK_ERR_NONE
            NET_SOCK_ERR_NOT_USED
            NET_SOCK_ERR_INVALID_SOCK
            NET_SOCK_ERR_INVALID_TYPE
            NET_SOCK_ERR_INVALID_PROTOCOL
            NET_TCP_ERR_CONN_NOT_USED
            NET_TCP_ERR_INVALID_CONN
            NET_CONN_ERR_NOT_USED
            NET_CONN_ERR_INVALID_CONN
            NET_ERR_INIT_INCOMPLETE
            NET_OS_ERR_LOCK

RETURNED VALUE

0, on any errors;

NET_TMR_TIME_INFINITE, if infinite (i.e., no timeout) value configured;

Timeout in number of milliseconds, otherwise.

REQUIRED CONFIGURATION

Available only if either **NET_CFG_TRANSPORT_LAYER_SEL** is configured for TCP (see section D-12-1 on page 972) and/or **NET_UDP_CFG_APP_API_SEL** is configured for sockets (see section D-13-1 on page 973).

NOTES / WARNINGS

None.

C-14-21 NetSock_CfgTimeoutRxQ_Set() (TCP/UDP)

Set socket's connection receive queue timeout value.

FILES

net_sock.h/net_sock.c

PROTOTYPE

```
CPU_BOOLEAN NetSock_CfgTimeoutRxQ_Set(NET_SOCK_ID  sock_id,
                                      CPU_INT32U   timeout_ms,
                                      NET_ERR      *perr);
```

ARGUMENTS

sock_id   This is the socket ID returned by **NetSock_Open()/socket()** when the
              socket was created *or* by **NetSock_Accept()/accept()** when a connection
              was accepted.

timeout_ms   Desired timeout value:

              NET_TMR_TIME_INFINITE, if infinite (i.e., no timeout) value desired. In
              number of milliseconds, otherwise.

perr   Pointer to variable that will receive the return error code from this function:

              NET_SOCK_ERR_NONE
              NET_SOCK_ERR_NOT_USED
              NET_SOCK_ERR_INVALID_SOCK
              NET_SOCK_ERR_INVALID_TYPE
              NET_SOCK_ERR_INVALID_PROTOCOL
              NET_TCP_ERR_CONN_NOT_USED
              NET_TCP_ERR_INVALID_CONN
              NET_CONN_ERR_NOT_USED
              NET_CONN_ERR_INVALID_CONN
              NET_ERR_INIT_INCOMPLETE
              NET_OS_ERR_INVALID_TIME
              NET_OS_ERR_LOCK

RETURNED VALUE

DEF_OK,   Socket receive queue timeout successfully set;

DEF_FAIL,   otherwise.

REQUIRED CONFIGURATION

Available only if either **NET_CFG_TRANSPORT_LAYER_SEL** is configured for TCP (see section D-12-1 on page 972) and/or **NET_UDP_CFG_APP_API_SEL** is configured for sockets (see section D-13-1 on page 973).

NOTES / WARNINGS

None.

C-14-22 NetSock_CfgTimeoutTxQ_Dflt() (TCP)

Set socket's connection transmit queue timeout to configured-default value.

FILES

net_sock.h/net_sock.c

PROTOTYPE

```
CPU_BOOLEAN NetSock_CfgTimeoutTxQ_Dflt(NET_SOCK_ID  sock_id,
                                       NET_ERR      *perr);
```

ARGUMENTS

sock_id   This is the socket ID returned by **NetSock_Open()/socket()** when the
            socket was created *or* by **NetSock_Accept()/accept()** when a connection
            was accepted.

perr   Pointer to variable that will receive the return error code from this function:

            NET_SOCK_ERR_NONE
            NET_SOCK_ERR_NOT_USED
            NET_SOCK_ERR_INVALID_SOCK
            NET_SOCK_ERR_INVALID_TYPE
            NET_SOCK_ERR_INVALID_PROTOCOL
            NET_TCP_ERR_CONN_NOT_USED
            NET_TCP_ERR_INVALID_CONN
            NET_CONN_ERR_NOT_USED
            NET_CONN_ERR_INVALID_CONN
            NET_ERR_INIT_INCOMPLETE
            NET_OS_ERR_INVALID_TIME
            NET_OS_ERR_LOCK

RETURNED VALUE

DEF_OK,   Socket transmit queue configured-default timeout successfully set;

DEF_FAIL,   otherwise.

REQUIRED CONFIGURATION

Available only if **NET_CFG_TRANSPORT_LAYER_SEL** is configured for TCP (see section D-12-1 on page 972).

NOTES / WARNINGS

None.

C-14-23 NetSock_CfgTimeoutTxQ_Get_ms() (TCP)

Get socket's transmit queue timeout value.

FILES

net_sock.h/net_sock.c

PROTOTYPE

```
CPU_INT32U NetSock_CfgTimeoutTxQ_Get_ms(NET_SOCK_ID  sock_id,
                                        NET_ERR      *perr);
```

ARGUMENTS

sock_id   This is the socket ID returned by **NetSock_Open()/socket()** when the socket was created *or* by **NetSock_Accept()/accept()** when a connection was accepted.

perr   Pointer to variable that will receive the return error code from this function:

           NET_SOCK_ERR_NONE
           NET_SOCK_ERR_NOT_USED
           NET_SOCK_ERR_INVALID_SOCK
           NET_SOCK_ERR_INVALID_TYPE
           NET_SOCK_ERR_INVALID_PROTOCOL
           NET_TCP_ERR_CONN_NOT_USED
           NET_TCP_ERR_INVALID_CONN
           NET_CONN_ERR_NOT_USED
           NET_CONN_ERR_INVALID_CONN
           NET_ERR_INIT_INCOMPLETE
           NET_OS_ERR_LOCK

RETURNED VALUE

0, on any errors;

NET_TMR_TIME_INFINITE, if infinite (i.e., no timeout) value configured;

Timeout in number of milliseconds, otherwise.

REQUIRED CONFIGURATION

Available only if **NET_CFG_TRANSPORT_LAYER_SEL** is configured for TCP (see section D-12-1 on page 972).

NOTES / WARNINGS

None.

C-14-24 NetSock_CfgTimeoutTxQ_Set() (TCP)

Set socket's connection transmit queue timeout value.

FILES

net_sock.h/net_sock.c

PROTOTYPE

```
CPU_BOOLEAN NetSock_CfgTimeoutTxQ_Set(NET_SOCK_ID  sock_id,
                                      CPU_INT32U   timeout_ms,
                                      NET_ERR      *perr);
```

ARGUMENTS

sock_id   This is the socket ID returned by **NetSock_Open()/socket()** when the
            socket was created *or* by **NetSock_Accept()/accept()** when a connection
            was accepted.

timeout_ms Desired timeout value:

            NET_TMR_TIME_INFINITE, if infinite (i.e., no timeout) value desired. In
            number of milliseconds, otherwise.

perr   Pointer to variable that will receive the return error code from this function:

            NET_SOCK_ERR_NONE
            NET_SOCK_ERR_NOT_USED
            NET_SOCK_ERR_INVALID_SOCK
            NET_SOCK_ERR_INVALID_TYPE
            NET_SOCK_ERR_INVALID_PROTOCOL
            NET_TCP_ERR_CONN_NOT_USED
            NET_TCP_ERR_INVALID_CONN
            NET_CONN_ERR_NOT_USED
            NET_CONN_ERR_INVALID_CONN
            NET_ERR_INIT_INCOMPLETE
            NET_OS_ERR_INVALID_TIME
            NET_OS_ERR_LOCK

RETURNED VALUE

DEF_OK,   Socket transmit queue timeout successfully set;

DEF_FAIL,   otherwise.

REQUIRED CONFIGURATION

Available only if **NET_CFG_TRANSPORT_LAYER_SEL** is configured for TCP (see section D-12-1 on page 972).

NOTES / WARNINGS

None.

C-14-25 NetSock_Close() / close() (TCP/UDP)

Terminate communication and free a socket.

FILES

net_sock.h/net_sock.c
net_bsd.h/net_bsd.c

PROTOTYPES

```
NET_SOCK_RTN_CODE NetSock_Close(NET_SOCK_ID  sock_id,
                                NET_ERR    *perr);

int close(int sock_id);
```

ARGUMENTS

sock_id   The socket ID returned by **NetSock_Open()/socket()** when the socket is
           created *or* by **NetSock_Accept()/accept()** when a connection is accepted.

perr   Pointer to variable that will receive the return error code from this function:

        NET_SOCK_ERR_NONE

        NET_SOCK_ERR_NOT_USED

        NET_SOCK_ERR_CLOSED

        NET_SOCK_ERR_INVALID_SOCK

        NET_SOCK_ERR_INVALID_FAMILY

        NET_SOCK_ERR_INVALID_STATE

        NET_SOCK_ERR_CLOSE_IN_PROGRESS

        NET_SOCK_ERR_CONN_SIGNAL_TIMEOUT

        NET_SOCK_ERR_CONN_FAIL

        NET_SOCK_ERR_FAULT

        NET_CONN_ERR_NULL_PTR

        NET_CONN_ERR_NOT_USED

        NET_CONN_ERR_INVALID_CONN

        NET_CONN_ERR_INVALID_ADDR_LEN

        NET_CONN_ERR_ADDR_IN_USE

        NET_ERR_INIT_INCOMPLETE

        NET_OS_ERR_LOCK

RETURNED VALUE

NET_SOCK_BSD_ERR_NONE/0, if successful;

NET_SOCK_BSD_ERR_CLOSE/-1, otherwise.

REQUIRED CONFIGURATION

NetSock_Close() is available only if either NET_CFG_TRANSPORT_LAYER_SEL is configured for TCP (see section D-12-1 on page 972) and/or NET_UDP_CFG_APP_API_SEL is configured for sockets (see section D-13-1 on page 973).

In addition, close() is available only if NET_BSD_CFG_API_EN is enabled (see section D-17-1 on page 983).

NOTES / WARNINGS

After closing a socket, no further operations should be performed with the socket.

C-14-26 NetSock_Conn() / connect() (TCP/UDP)

Connect a local socket to a remote socket address. If the local socket was not previously bound to a local address and port, the socket is bound to the default interface's default address and a random port number. When successful, a connected socket has access to both local and remote socket addresses.

Although both UDP and TCP sockets may both connect to remote servers or hosts, UDP and TCP connections are inherently different:

For TCP sockets, **NetSock_Conn( )/connect( )** returns successfully only after completing the three-way TCP handshake with the remote TCP host. Success implies the existence of a dedicated connection to the remote socket similar to a telephone connection. This dedicated connection is maintained for the life of the connection until one or both sides close the connection.

For UDP sockets, **NetSock_Conn( )/connect( )** merely saves the remote socket's address for the local socket for convenience. All UDP datagrams from the socket will be transmitted to the remote socket. This pseudo-connection is not permanent and may be re-configured at any time.

FILES

net_sock.h/net_sock.c
net_bsd.h/net_bsd.c

PROTOTYPES

```
NET_SOCK_RTN_CODE NetSock_Conn(NET_SOCK_ID        sock_id,
                               NET_SOCK_ADDR      *paddr_remote,
                               NET_SOCK_ADDR_LEN  addr_len,
                               NET_ERR            *perr);

int connect(int               sock_id,
            struct sockaddr   *paddr_remote,
            socklen_t         addr_len);
```

ARGUMENTS

sock_id   This is the socket ID returned by `NetSock_Open()/socket()` when the socket was created.

paddr_remote Pointer to a socket address structure (see section 8-2 "Socket Interface" on page 212) which contains the remote socket address to connect the socket to.

addr_len   Size of the socket address structure which *must* be passed the size of the socket address structure [e.g., `sizeof(NET_SOCK_ADDR_IP)`].

perr   Pointer to variable that will receive the return error code from this function:

        NET_SOCK_ERR_NONE
        NET_SOCK_ERR_NOT_USED
        NET_SOCK_ERR_CLOSED
        NET_SOCK_ERR_INVALID_SOCK
        NET_SOCK_ERR_INVALID_FAMILY
        NET_SOCK_ERR_INVALID_PROTOCOL
        NET_SOCK_ERR_INVALID_TYPE
        NET_SOCK_ERR_INVALID_STATE
        NET_SOCK_ERR_INVALID_OP
        NET_SOCK_ERR_INVALID_ADDR
        NET_SOCK_ERR_INVALID_ADDR_LEN
        NET_SOCK_ERR_ADDR_IN_USE
        NET_SOCK_ERR_PORT_NBR_NONE_AVAIL
        NET_SOCK_ERR_CONN_SIGNAL_TIMEOUT
        NET_SOCK_ERR_CONN_IN_USE
        NET_SOCK_ERR_CONN_FAIL
        NET_SOCK_ERR_FAULT
        NET_IF_ERR_INVALID_IF
        NET_IP_ERR_ADDR_NONE_AVAIL
        NET_IP_ERR_ADDR_CFG_IN_PROGRESS
        NET_CONN_ERR_NULL_PTR
        NET_CONN_ERR_NOT_USED
        NET_CONN_ERR_NONE_AVAIL
        NET_CONN_ERR_INVALID_CONN
        NET_CONN_ERR_INVALID_FAMILY
        NET_CONN_ERR_INVALID_TYPE

NET_CONN_ERR_INVALID_PROTOCOL_IX

NET_CONN_ERR_INVALID_ADDR_LEN

NET_CONN_ERR_ADDR_NOT_USED

NET_CONN_ERR_ADDR_IN_USE

NET_ERR_INIT_INCOMPLETE

NET_OS_ERR_LOCK

RETURNED VALUE

NET_SOCK_BSD_ERR_NONE/0, if successful;

NET_SOCK_BSD_ERR_CONN/-1, otherwise.

REQUIRED CONFIGURATION

NetSock_Conn() is available only if either NET_CFG_TRANSPORT_LAYER_SEL is configured for TCP (see section D-12-1 on page 972) and/or NET_UDP_CFG_APP_API_SEL is configured for sockets (see section D-13-1 on page 973).

In addition, connect() is available only if NET_BSD_CFG_API_EN is enabled (see section D-17-1 on page 983).

NOTES / WARNINGS

See section 8-2 "Socket Interface" on page 212 for socket address structure formats.

C-14-27 NET_SOCK_DESC_CLR() / FD_CLR() (TCP/UDP)

Remove a socket file descriptor ID as a member of a file descriptor set. See also section C-14-41 "NetSock_Sel() / select() (TCP/UDP)" on page 888.

FILES

net_sock.h

PROTOTYPE

```
NET_SOCK_DESC_CLR(desc_nbr, pdesc_set);
```

ARGUMENTS

desc_nbr This is the socket file descriptor ID returned by **NetSock_Open()/socket()** when the socket was created *or* by **NetSock_Accept()/accept()** when a connection was accepted.

pdesc_set Pointer to a socket file descriptor set.

RETURNED VALUE

None.

REQUIRED CONFIGURATION

Available only if either **NET_CFG_TRANSPORT_LAYER_SEL** is configured for TCP (see section D-12-1 on page 972) and/or **NET_UDP_CFG_APP_API_SEL** is configured for sockets (see section D-13-1 on page 973) *and* if **NET_SOCK_CFG_SEL_EN** is enabled (see section D-15-4 on page 977).

In addition, **FD_CLR()** is available only if **NET_BSD_CFG_API_EN** is enabled (see section D-17-1 on page 983).

NOTES / WARNINGS

NetSock_Sel()/select() checks or waits for available operations or error conditions on any of the socket file descriptor members of a socket file descriptor set.

No errors are returned even if the socket file descriptor ID or the file descriptor set is invalid, or the socket file descriptor ID is *not* set in the file descriptor set.

C-14-28 NET_SOCK_DESC_COPY() (TCP/UDP)

Copy a file descriptor set to another file descriptor set. See also section C-14-41
"NetSock_Sel() / select() (TCP/UDP)" on page 888.

FILES

net_sock.h

PROTOTYPE

```
NET_SOCK_DESC_COPY(pdesc_set_dest, pdesc_set_src);
```

ARGUMENTS

pdesc_set_dest   Pointer to the destination socket file descriptor set.

pdesc_set_src   Pointer to the source socket file descriptor set to copy.

RETURNED VALUE

None.

REQUIRED CONFIGURATION

Available only if either **NET_CFG_TRANSPORT_LAYER_SEL** is configured for TCP (see section
D-12-1 on page 972) and/or **NET_UDP_CFG_APP_API_SEL** is configured for sockets (see
section D-13-1 on page 973) *and if* **NET_SOCK_CFG_SEL_EN** is enabled (see section D-15-4
on page 977).

NOTES / WARNINGS

NetSock_Sel()/select() checks or waits for available operations or error conditions on
any of the socket file descriptor members of a socket file descriptor set.

No errors are returned even if either file descriptor set is invalid.

C-14-29 NET_SOCK_DESC_INIT() / FD_ZERO() (TCP/UDP)

Initialize/zero-clear a file descriptor set. See also section C-14-41 "NetSock_Sel() / select() (TCP/UDP)" on page 888.

net_sock.h

```
NET_SOCK_DESC_INIT(pdesc_set);
```

pdesc_set   Pointer to a socket file descriptor set.

None.

Available only if either NET_CFG_TRANSPORT_LAYER_SEL is configured for TCP (see section D-12-1 on page 972) and/or NET_UDP_CFG_APP_API_SEL is configured for sockets (see section D-13-1 on page 973) *and* if NET_SOCK_CFG_SEL_EN is enabled (see section D-15-4 on page 977).

In addition, FD_ZERO() is available only if NET_BSD_CFG_API_EN is enabled (see section D-17-1 on page 983).

NetSock_Sel()/select() checks or waits for available operations or error conditions on any of the socket file descriptor members of a socket file descriptor set.

No errors are returned even if the file descriptor set is invalid.

C-14-30 NET_SOCK_DESC_IS_SET() / FD_IS_SET() (TCP/UDP)

Check if a socket file descriptor ID is a member of a file descriptor set. See also section C-14-41 "NetSock_Sel() / select() (TCP/UDP)" on page 888.

FILES

net_sock.h

PROTOTYPE

```
NET_SOCK_DESC_IS_SET(desc_nbr, pdesc_set);
```

ARGUMENTS

desc_nbr   This is the socket file descriptor ID returned by **NetSock_Open()/socket()** when the socket was created *or* by **NetSock_Accept()/accept()** when a connection was accepted.

pdesc_set   Pointer to a socket file descriptor set.

RETURNED VALUE

1, if the socket file descriptor ID is a member of the file descriptor set;

0, otherwise.

REQUIRED CONFIGURATION

Available only if either **NET_CFG_TRANSPORT_LAYER_SEL** is configured for TCP (see section D-12-1 on page 972) and/or **NET_UDP_CFG_APP_API_SEL** is configured for sockets (see section D-13-1 on page 973) *and* if **NET_SOCK_CFG_SEL_EN** is enabled (see section D-15-4 on page 977).

In addition, **FD_IS_SET()** is available only if **NET_BSD_CFG_API_EN** is enabled (see section D-17-1 on page 983).

NOTES / WARNINGS

`NetSock_Sel()`/`select()` checks or waits for available operations or error conditions on any of the socket file descriptor members of a socket file descriptor set.

0 is returned if the socket file descriptor ID or the file descriptor set is invalid.

C-14-31 NET_SOCK_DESC_SET() / FD_SET() (TCP/UDP)

Add a socket file descriptor ID as a member of a file descriptor set. See also section C-14-41 "NetSock_Sel() / select() (TCP/UDP)" on page 888.

FILES

net_sock.h

PROTOTYPE

```
NET_SOCK_DESC_SET(desc_nbr, pdesc_set);
```

ARGUMENTS

desc_nbr   This is the socket file descriptor ID returned by NetSock_Open()/socket() when the socket was created *or* by NetSock_Accept()/accept() when a connection was accepted.

pdesc_set   Pointer to a socket file descriptor set.

RETURNED VALUE

None.

REQUIRED CONFIGURATION

Available only if either NET_CFG_TRANSPORT_LAYER_SEL is configured for TCP (see section D-12-1 on page 972) and/or NET_UDP_CFG_APP_API_SEL is configured for sockets (see section D-13-1 on page 973) *and* if NET_SOCK_CFG_SEL_EN is enabled (see section D-15-4 on page 977). In addition, FD_SET() is available only if NET_BSD_CFG_API_EN is enabled (see section D-17-1 on page 983).

NOTES / WARNINGS

NetSock_Sel()/select() checks or waits for available operations or error conditions on any of the socket file descriptor members of a socket file descriptor set.

No errors are returned even if the socket file descriptor ID or the file descriptor set is invalid, or the socket file descriptor ID is *not* cleared in the file descriptor set.

C-14-32 NetSock_GetConnTransportID()

Gets a socket's transport layer connection handle ID (e.g., TCP connection ID) if available.

FILES

net_sock.h/net_sock.c

PROTOTYPE

```
NET_CONN_ID NetSock_GetConnTransportID(NET_SOCK_ID  sock_id,
                                       NET_ERR      *perr);
```

ARGUMENTS

sock_id   This is the socket ID returned by **NetSock_Open()/socket()** when the socket was created *or* by **NetSock_Accept()/accept()** when a connection was accepted.

perr   Pointer to variable that will receive the return error code from this function:

NET_SOCK_ERR_NONE
NET_SOCK_ERR_NOT_USED
NET_SOCK_ERR_INVALID_SOCK
NET_SOCK_ERR_INVALID_TYPE
NET_CONN_ERR_NOT_USED
NET_CONN_ERR_INVALID_CONN
NET_ERR_INIT_INCOMPLETE
NET_OS_ERR_LOCK

RETURNED VALUE

Socket's transport connection handle ID (e.g., TCP connection ID), if no errors.

NET_CONN_ID_NONE, otherwise.

REQUIRED CONFIGURATION

Available only if either **NET_CFG_TRANSPORT_LAYER_SEL** is configured for TCP (see section D-12-1 on page 972) and/or **NET_UDP_CFG_APP_API_SEL** is configured for sockets (see section D-13-1 on page 973).

NOTES / WARNINGS

None.

C-14-33 NetSock_IsConn() (TCP/UDP)

Check if a socket is connected to a remote socket.

FILES

net_sock.h/net_sock.c

PROTOTYPE

```
CPU_BOOLEAN NetSock_IsConn(NET_SOCK_ID  sock_id,
                           NET_ERR      *perr);
```

ARGUMENTS

sock_id   This is the socket ID returned by **NetSock_Open()/socket()** when the socket was created *or* by **NetSock_Accept()/accept()** when a connection was accepted.

perr   Pointer to variable that will receive the return error code from this function:

            NET_SOCK_ERR_NONE
            NET_SOCK_ERR_NOT_USED
            NET_SOCK_ERR_INVALID_SOCK
            NET_ERR_INIT_INCOMPLETE
            NET_OS_ERR_LOCK

RETURNED VALUE

DEF_YES   if the socket is valid and connected;

DEF_NO   otherwise.

REQUIRED CONFIGURATION

Available only if either NET_CFG_TRANSPORT_LAYER_SEL is configured for TCP (see section D-12-1 on page 972) and/or NET_UDP_CFG_APP_API_SEL is configured for sockets (see section D-13-1 on page 973).

NOTES / WARNINGS

None.

C-14-34 NetSock_Listen() / listen() (TCP)

Set a socket to accept incoming connections. The socket must already be bound to a local address. If successful, incoming TCP connection requests addressed to the socket's local address will be queued until accepted by the socket (see section C-14-1 "NetSock_Accept() / accept() (TCP)" on page 808).

FILES

net_sock.h/net_sock.c
net_bsd.h/net_bsd.c

PROTOTYPES

```
NET_SOCK_RTN_CODE NetSock_Listen(NET_SOCK_ID      sock_id,
                                 NET_SOCK_Q_SIZE  sock_q_size,
                                 NET_ERR          *perr);

int listen(int sock_id,
           int sock_q_size);
```

ARGUMENTS

sock_id   This is the socket ID returned by **NetSock_Open()/socket()** when the socket was created.

sock_q_size Maximum number of new connections allowed to be waiting. In other words, this argument specifies the maximum queue length of pending connections while the listening socket is busy servicing the current request.

perr   Pointer to variable that will receive the return error code from this function:

             NET_SOCK_ERR_NONE
             NET_SOCK_ERR_NOT_USED
             NET_SOCK_ERR_CLOSED
             NET_SOCK_ERR_INVALID_SOCK
             NET_SOCK_ERR_INVALID_FAMILY
             NET_SOCK_ERR_INVALID_PROTOCOL
             NET_SOCK_ERR_INVALID_TYPE
             NET_SOCK_ERR_INVALID_STATE

```
NET_SOCK_ERR_INVALID_OP
NET_SOCK_ERR_CONN_FAIL
NET_CONN_ERR_NOT_USED
NET_CONN_ERR_INVALID_CONN
NET_ERR_INIT_INCOMPLETE
NET_OS_ERR_LOCK
```

RETURNED VALUE

`NET_SOCK_BSD_ERR_NONE/0`, if successful;

`NET_SOCK_BSD_ERR_LISTEN/-1`, otherwise.

REQUIRED CONFIGURATION

`NetSock_Listen()` is available only if either `NET_CFG_TRANSPORT_LAYER_SEL` is configured for TCP (see section D-12-1 on page 972) and/or `NET_UDP_CFG_APP_API_SEL` is configured for sockets (see section D-13-1 on page 973).

In addition, `listen()` is available only if `NET_BSD_CFG_API_EN` is enabled (see section D-17-1 on page 983).

NOTES / WARNINGS

None.

C-14-35 NetSock_Open() / socket() (TCP/UDP)

Create a datagram (i.e., UDP) or stream (i.e., TCP) type socket.

FILES

net_sock.h/net_sock.c
net_bsd.h/net_bsd.c

PROTOTYPES

```
NET_SOCK_ID NetSock_Open(NET_SOCK_PROTOCOL_FAMILY  protocol_family,
                         NET_SOCK_TYPE             sock_type,
                         NET_SOCK_PROTOCOL         protocol,
                         NET_ERR                   *perr);

int socket(int protocol_family,
           int sock_type,
           int protocol);
```

ARGUMENTS

protocol_family   This field establishes the socket protocol family domain. Always
                    use **NET_SOCK_FAMILY_IP_V4/PF_INET** for TCP/IP sockets.

sock_type   Socket type:

              NET_SOCK_TYPE_DATAGRAM/PF_DGRAM for datagram sockets (i.e., UDP)

              NET_SOCK_TYPE_STREAM/PF_STREAM for stream sockets (i.e., TCP)

              NET_SOCK_TYPE_DATAGRAM sockets preserve message boundaries.
              Applications that exchange single request and response messages are
              examples of datagram communication.

              NET_SOCK_TYPE_STREAM sockets provides a reliable byte-stream connection,
              where bytes are received from the remote application in the same order as
              they were sent. File transfer and terminal emulation are examples of
              applications that require this type of protocol.

protocol   Socket protocol:

`NET_SOCK_PROTOCOL_UDP`/`IPPROTO_UDP` for UDP

`NET_SOCK_PROTOCOL_TCP`/`IPPROTO_TCP` for TCP

0 for default-protocol:

UDP for `NET_SOCK_TYPE_DATAGRAM`/`PF_DGRAM`

TCP for `NET_SOCK_TYPE_STREAM`/`PF_STREAM`

perr   Pointer to variable that will receive the return error code from this function:

```
NET_SOCK_ERR_NONE
NET_SOCK_ERR_NONE_AVAIL
NET_SOCK_ERR_INVALID_FAMILY
NET_SOCK_ERR_INVALID_PROTOCOL
NET_SOCK_ERR_INVALID_TYPE
NET_ERR_INIT_INCOMPLETE
NET_OS_ERR_LOCK
```

The table below shows you the different ways you can specify the three arguments.

TCP/IP Protocol	Arguments		
	protocol_family	sock_type	protocol
UDP	NET_SOCK_FAMILY_IP_V4	NET_SOCK_TYPE_DATAGRAM	NET_SOCK_PROTOCOL_UDP
UDP	NET_SOCK_FAMILY_IP_V4	NET_SOCK_TYPE_DATAGRAM	0
TCP	NET_SOCK_FAMILY_IP_V4	NET_SOCK_TYPE_STREAM	ET_SOCK_PROTOCOL_TCP
TCP	NET_SOCK_FAMILY_IP_V4	NET_SOCK_TYPE_STREAM	0

RETURNED VALUE

Returns a non-negative socket descriptor ID for the new socket connection, if successful;

NET_SOCK_BSD_ERR_OPEN/-1 otherwise.

REQUIRED CONFIGURATION

NetSock_Open() is available only if either NET_CFG_TRANSPORT_LAYER_SEL is configured for TCP (see section D-12-1 on page 972) and/or NET_UDP_CFG_APP_API_SEL is configured for sockets (see section D-13-1 on page 973).

In addition, socket() is available only if NET_BSD_CFG_API_EN is enabled (see section D-17-1 on page 983).

NOTES / WARNINGS

The family, type, and protocol of a socket is fixed once a socket is created. In other words, you cannot change a TCP stream socket to a UDP datagram socket (or vice versa) at run-time.

To connect two sockets, both sockets must share the same socket family, type, and protocol.

C-14-36 NetSock_OptGet()

Get the specified socket option from the **sock_id** socket.

FILES

net_sock.h/net_sock.c

PROTOTYPE

```
NET_SOCK_RTN_CODE_ID NetSock_OptGet(NET_SOCK_ID        sock_id,
                                    NET_SOCK_PROTOCOL  level,
                                    NET_SOCK_OPT_NAME  opt_name,
                                    void               *popt_val,
                                    NET_SOCK_OPT_LEN   *popt_len,
                                    NET_ERR            *perr);
```

ARGUMENTS

sock_id   This is the socket ID returned by **NetSock_Open()/socket()** when the socket was created *or* by **NetSock_Accept()/accept()** when a connection was accepted.

level   Protocol level from which to retrieve the socket option.

opt_name   Socket option to get the value.

popt_val   Pointer to a socket option value buffer.

popt_len   Pointer to variable a socket option value buffer length.

perr   Pointer to variable that will receive the return error code from this function:

            NET_SOCK_ERR_NONE
            NET_SOCK_ERR_INVALID_OPT
            NET_SOCK_ERR_INVALID_ARG
            NET_SOCK_ERR_INVALID_OPT_LEN
            NET_CONN_ERR_INVALID_OPT_GET
            NET_CONN_ERR_INVALID_OPT_LEVEL

RETURNED VALUE

NET_SOCK_BSD_ERR_NONE/0, if successful; NET_SOCK_BSD_ERR_OPT_GET/-1, otherwise.

REQUIRED CONFIGURATION

NetSock_OptGet() is available only if either NET_CFG_TRANSPORT_LAYER_SEL is configured for TCP (see section D-12-1 on page 972) and/or NET_UDP_CFG_APP_API_SEL is configured for sockets (see section D-13-1 on page 973).

In addition, getsockopt() is available only if NET_BSD_CFG_API_EN is enabled (see section D-17-1 on page 983).

NOTES / WARNINGS

The supported options are:

- Protocol level NET_SOCK_PROTOCOL_SO:

  - NET_SOCK_OPT_SOCK_TYPE

  - NET_SOCK_OPT_SOCK_KEEP_ALIVE

  - NET_SOCK_OPT_SOCK_ACCEPT_CONN

  - NET_SOCK_OPT_SOCK_TX_BUF_SIZE / NET_SOCK_OPT_SOCK_RX_BUF_SIZE

  - NET_SOCK_OPT_SOCK_TX_TIMEOUT / NET_SOCK_OPT_SOCK_RX_TIMEOUT

- Protocol level NET_SOCK_PROTOCOL_IP:

  - NET_SOCK_OPT_IP_TOS

  - NET_SOCK_OPT_IP_TTL

  - NET_SOCK_OPT_IP_RX_IF

- Protocol level NET_SOCK_PROTOCOL_TCP:

  - NET_SOCK_OPT_TCP_NO_DELAY

  - NET_SOCK_OPT_TCP_KEEP_CNT

  - NET_SOCK_OPT_TCP_KEEP_IDLE

  - NET_SOCK_OPT_TCP_KEEP_INTVL

C-14-37 NetSock_OptSet()

Set the specified socket option to the **sock_id** socket.

FILES

net_sock.h/net_sock.c

PROTOTYPE

```
NET_SOCK_RTN_CODE_ID NetSock_OptSet(NET_SOCK_ID        sock_id,
                                    NET_SOCK_PROTOCOL  level,
                                    NET_SOCK_OPT_NAME  opt_name,
                                    void               *popt_val,
                                    NET_SOCK_OPT_LEN   opt_len,
                                    NET_ERR            *perr);
```

ARGUMENTS

sock_id   This is the socket ID returned by **NetSock_Open()/socket()** when the
                socket was created *or* by **NetSock_Accept()/accept()** when a connection
                was accepted.

level   Protocol level from which to set the socket option.

opt_name   Name of the option to set.

popt_val   Pointer to the value to set the socket option.

opt_len   Option length.

perr   Pointer to variable that will receive the return error code from this function:

                NET_SOCK_ERR_NONE
                NET_SOCK_ERR_INVALID_DATA_SIZE
                NET_SOCK_ERR_NULL_PTR
                NET_SOCK_ERR_INVALID_OPT

RETURNED VALUE

NET_SOCK_BSD_ERR_NONE/0, if successful;

NET_SOCK_BSD_ERR_OPT_SET/-1, otherwise.

REQUIRED CONFIGURATION

NetSock_OptSet() is available only if either NET_CFG_TRANSPORT_LAYER_SEL is configured for TCP (see section D-12-1 on page 972) and/or NET_UDP_CFG_APP_API_SEL is configured for sockets (see section D-13-1 on page 973).

In addition, setsockopt() is available only if NET_BSD_CFG_API_EN is enabled (see section D-17-1 on page 983).

NOTES / WARNINGS

The supported options are:

- Protocol level NET_SOCK_PROTOCOL_SO:

    - NET_SOCK_OPT_SOCK_KEEP_ALIVE

    - NET_SOCK_OPT_SOCK_TX_BUF_SIZE / NET_SOCK_OPT_SOCK_RX_BUF_SIZE

    - NET_SOCK_OPT_SOCK_TX_TIMEOUT / NET_SOCK_OPT_SOCK_RX_TIMEOUT

- Protocol level NET_SOCK_PROTOCOL_IP:

    - NET_SOCK_OPT_IP_TOS

    - NET_SOCK_OPT_IP_TTL

- Protocol level NET_SOCK_PROTOCOL_TCP:

    - NET_SOCK_OPT_TCP_NO_DELAY

    - NET_SOCK_OPT_TCP_KEEP_CNT

    - NET_SOCK_OPT_TCP_KEEP_IDLE

    - NET_SOCK_OPT_TCP_KEEP_INTVL

C-14-38 NetSock_PoolStatGet()

Get Network Sockets' statistics pool.

FILES

net_sock.h/net_sock.c

PROTOTYPE

```
NET_STAT_POOL NetSock_PoolStatGet(void);
```

ARGUMENTS

None.

RETURNED VALUE

Network Sockets' statistics pool, if no errors.

NULL statistics pool, otherwise.

REQUIRED CONFIGURATION

Available only if either NET_CFG_TRANSPORT_LAYER_SEL is configured for TCP (see section D-12-1 on page 972) and/or NET_UDP_CFG_APP_API_SEL is configured for sockets (see section D-13-1 on page 973).

NOTES / WARNINGS

None.

C-14-39 NetSock_PoolStatResetMaxUsed()

Reset Network Sockets' statistics pool's maximum number of entries used.

net_sock.h/net_sock.c

```
void NetSock_PoolStatResetMaxUsed(void);
```

None.

None.

Available only if either NET_CFG_TRANSPORT_LAYER_SEL is configured for TCP (see section D-12-1 on page 972) and/or NET_UDP_CFG_APP_API_SEL is configured for sockets (see section D-13-1 on page 973).

None.

C-14-40 NetSock_RxData() / recv() (TCP)
NetSock_RxDataFrom() / recvfrom() (UDP)

Copy up to a specified number of bytes received from a remote socket into an application memory buffer.

FILES

net_sock.h/net_sock.c
net_bsd.h/net_bsd.c

PROTOTYPES

```
NET_SOCK_RTN_CODE NetSock_RxData(NET_SOCK_ID      sock_id,
                                 void            *pdata_buf,
                                 CPU_INT16U       data_buf_len,
                                 CPU_INT16S       flags,
                                 NET_ERR         *perr);


NET_SOCK_RTN_CODE NetSock_RxDataFrom(NET_SOCK_ID      sock_id,
                                     void            *pdata_buf,
                                     CPU_INT16U       data_buf_len,
                                     CPU_INT16S       flags,
                                     NET_SOCK_ADDR   *paddr_remote,
                                     NET_SOCK_ADDR_  *paddr_len,
                                     void            *pip_opts_buf,
                                     CPU_INT08U       ip_opts_buf_len,
                                     CPU_INT08U      *pip_opts_len,
                                     NET_ERR         *perr);

ssize_t recv(int      sock_id,
             void    *pdata_buf,
             _size_t  data_buf_len,
             int      flags);

ssize_t recvfrom(int              sock_id,
                 void            *pdata_buf,
                 _size_t          data_buf_len,
                 int              flags,
                 struct sockaddr *paddr_remote,
                 socklen_t       *paddr_len);
```

ARGUMENTS

sock_id   This is the socket ID returned by `NetSock_Open()`/`socket()` when the socket was created *or* by `NetSock_Accept()`/`accept()` when a connection was accepted.

pdata_buf   Pointer to the application memory buffer to receive data.

data_buf_len Size of the destination application memory buffer (in bytes).

flags   Flag to select receive options; bit-field flags logically **OR**'d:

NET_SOCK_FLAG_NONE/0	No socket flags selected
NET_SOCK_FLAG_RX_DATA_PEEK/	
MSG_PEEK	Receive socket data without consuming it
NET_SOCK_FLAG_RX_NO_BLOCK/	
MSG_DONTWAIT	Receive socket data without blocking

In most cases, this flag would be set to `NET_SOCK_FLAG_NONE/0`.

paddr_remote Pointer to a socket address structure (see section 8-2 "Socket Interface" on page 212) to return the remote host address that sent the received data.

paddr_len   Pointer to the size of the socket address structure which *must* be passed the size of the socket address structure [e.g., `sizeof(NET_SOCK_ADDR_IP)`]. Returns size of the accepted connection's socket address structure, if no errors; returns 0, otherwise.

pip_opts_buf Pointer to buffer to receive possible IP options.

pip_opts_len Pointer to variable that will receive the return size of any received IP options.

perr   Pointer to variable that will receive the return error code from this function:

```
NET_SOCK_ERR_NONE
NET_SOCK_ERR_NULL_PTR
NET_SOCK_ERR_NULL_SIZE
NET_SOCK_ERR_NOT_USED
NET_SOCK_ERR_CLOSED
```

```
NET_SOCK_ERR_INVALID_SOCK
NET_SOCK_ERR_INVALID_FAMILY
NET_SOCK_ERR_INVALID_PROTOCOL
NET_SOCK_ERR_INVALID_TYPE
NET_SOCK_ERR_INVALID_STATE
NET_SOCK_ERR_INVALID_OP
NET_SOCK_ERR_INVALID_FLAG
NET_SOCK_ERR_INVALID_ADDR_LEN
NET_SOCK_ERR_INVALID_DATA_SIZE
NET_SOCK_ERR_CONN_FAIL
NET_SOCK_ERR_FAULT
NET_SOCK_ERR_RX_Q_EMPTY
NET_SOCK_ERR_RX_Q_CLOSED
NET_ERR_RX
NET_CONN_ERR_NULL_PTR
NET_CONN_ERR_NOT_USED
NET_CONN_ERR_INVALID_CONN
NET_CONN_ERR_INVALID_ADDR_LEN
NET_CONN_ERR_ADDR_NOT_USED
NET_ERR_INIT_INCOMPLETE
NET_OS_ERR_LOCK
```

RETURNED VALUE

Positive number of bytes received, if successful;

`NET_SOCK_BSD_RTN_CODE_CONN_CLOSED/0`, if the socket is closed;

`NET_SOCK_BSD_ERR_RX/-1`, otherwise.

BLOCKING VS NON-BLOCKING

The default setting for μC/TCP-IP is blocking. However, this setting can be changed at compile time by setting the `NET_SOCK_CFG_BLOCK_SEL` (see section D-15-3 on page 977) to one of the following values:

`NET_SOCK_BLOCK_SEL_DFLT` sets blocking mode to the default, or blocking, unless modified by run-time options.

`NET_SOCK_BLOCK_SEL_BLOCK` sets the blocking mode to blocking. This means that a socket receive function will wait forever, until at least one byte of data is available to return or the socket connection is closed, unless a timeout is specified by `NetSock_CfgTimeoutRxQ_Set()` [See section C-14-21 on page 849].

`NET_SOCK_BLOCK_SEL_NO_BLOCK` sets the blocking mode to non-blocking. This means that a socket receive function will *not* wait but immediately return either any available data, socket connection closed, or an error indicating no available data or other possible socket faults. Your application will have to "poll" the socket on a regular basis to receive data.

The current version of μC/TCP-IP selects blocking or non-blocking at compile time for all sockets. A future version may allow the selection of blocking or non-blocking at the individual socket level. However, each socket receive call can pass the `NET_SOCK_FLAG_RX_NO_BLOCK/MSG_DONTWAIT` flag to disable blocking on that call.

REQUIRED CONFIGURATION

`NetSock_RxData()/NetSock_RxDataFrom()` is available only if `NET_CFG_TRANSPORT_LAYER_SEL` is configured for TCP (see section D-12-1 on page 972) and/or `NET_UDP_CFG_APP_API_SEL` is configured for sockets (see section D-13-1 on page 973).

In addition, `recv()/recvfrom()` is available only if `NET_BSD_CFG_API_EN` is enabled (see section D-17-1 on page 983).

NOTES / WARNINGS

TCP sockets typically use `NetSock_RxData()/recv()`, whereas UDP sockets typically use `NetSock_RxDataFrom()/recvfrom()`.

For stream sockets (i.e., TCP), bytes are guaranteed to be received in the same order as they were transmitted, without omissions.

For datagram sockets (i.e., UDP), each receive returns the data from exactly one send but datagram order and delivery is not guaranteed. Also, if the application memory buffer is not big enough to receive an entire datagram, the datagram's data is truncated to the size of the memory buffer and the remaining data is discarded.

Only some receive flag options are implemented. If other flag options are requested, an error is returned so that flag options are *not* silently ignored.

C-14-41 NetSock_Sel() / select() (TCP/UDP)

Check if any sockets are ready for available read or write operations or error conditions.

FILES

net_sock.h/net_sock.c
net_bsd.h/net_bsd.c

PROTOTYPES

```
NET_SOCK_RTN_CODE NetSock_Sel(NET_SOCK_QTY       sock_nbr_max,
                              NET_SOCK_DESC      *psock_desc_rd,
                              NET_SOCK_DESC      *psock_desc_wr,
                              NET_SOCK_DESC      *psock_desc_err,
                              NET_SOCK_TIMEOUT   *ptimeout,
                              NET_ERR            *perr);

int select(int             desc_nbr_max,
           struct fd_set   *pdesc_rd,
           struct fd_set   *pdesc_wr,
           struct fd_set   *pdesc_err,
           struct timeval  *ptimeout);
```

ARGUMENTS

sock_nbr_max   Specifies the maximum number of socket file descriptors in the file descriptor sets.

psock_desc_rd   Pointer to a set of socket file descriptors to:

■ Check for available read operations.

■ Returns the actual socket file descriptors ready for available read operations, if no errors;

   ■ Returns the initial, non-modified set of socket file descriptors, on any errors;

   ■ Returns a null-valued (i.e., zero-cleared) descriptor set, if any timeout expires.

| psock_desc_wr | Pointer to a set of socket file descriptors to: |

- Check for available write operations.

- Returns the actual socket file descriptors ready for available write operations, if no errors;

  - Returns the initial, non-modified set of socket file descriptors, on any errors;

  - Returns a null-valued (i.e., zero-cleared) descriptor set, if any timeout expires.

| psock_desc_err | Pointer to a set of socket file descriptors to: |

- Check for any available socket errors.

- Returns the actual socket file descriptors ready with any pending errors;

  - Returns the initial, non-modified set of socket file descriptors, on any errors;

  - Returns a null-valued (i.e., zero-cleared) descriptor set, if any timeout expires.

| ptimeout | Pointer to a timeout argument. |

| perr | Pointer to variable that will receive the error code from this function: |

```
NET_SOCK_ERR_NONE
NET_SOCK_ERR_TIMEOUT
NET_ERR_INIT_INCOMPLETE
NET_SOCK_ERR_INVALID_DESC
NET_SOCK_ERR_INVALID_TIMEOUT
NET_SOCK_ERR_INVALID_SOCK
NET_SOCK_ERR_INVALID_TYPE
NET_SOCK_ERR_NOT_USED
NET_SOCK_ERR_EVENTS_NBR_MAX
NET_OS_ERR_LOCK
```

RETURNED VALUE

Returns the number of sockets ready with available operations, if successful;

`NET_SOCK_BSD_RTN_CODE_TIMEOUT/0`, upon timeout;

`NET_SOCK_BSD_ERR_SEL/-1`, otherwise.

REQUIRED CONFIGURATION

`NetSock_Sel()` is available only if either `NET_CFG_TRANSPORT_LAYER_SEL` is configured for TCP (see section D-12-1 on page 972) and/or `NET_UDP_CFG_APP_API_SEL` is configured for sockets (see section D-13-1 on page 973) *and* if `NET_SOCK_CFG_SEL_EN` is enabled (see section D-15-4 on page 977).

In addition, `select()` is available only if `NET_BSD_CFG_API_EN` is enabled (see section D-17-1 on page 983).

NOTES / WARNINGS

Supports socket file descriptors *only* (i.e., socket ID numbers).

The descriptor macro's is used to prepare and decode socket file descriptor sets (see section C-14-27 on page 862 through section C-14-31 on page 868).

See "`net_sock.c NetSock_Sel()` Note #3" for more details.

C-14-42 NetSock_TxData() / send() (TCP)
NetSock_TxDataTo() / sendto() (UDP)

Copy bytes from an application memory buffer into a socket to send to a remote socket.

FILES

net_sock.h/net_sock.c
net_bsd.h/net_bsd.c

PROTOTYPES

```
NET_SOCK_RTN_CODE NetSock_TxData(NET_SOCK_ID  sock_id,
                                 void        *p_data,
                                 CPU_INT16U   data_len,
                                 CPU_INT16S   flags,
                                 NET_ERR     *perr);

NET_SOCK_RTN_CODE NetSock_TxDataTo(NET_SOCK_ID        sock_id,
                                   void              *p_data,
                                   CPU_INT16U         data_len,
                                   CPU_INT16S         flags,
                                   NET_SOCK_ADDR     *paddr_remote,
                                   NET_SOCK_ADDR_LEN  addr_len,
                                   NET_ERR           *perr);

ssize_t send (int     sock_id,
              void   *p_data,
              _size_t data_len,
              int     flags);

ssize_t sendto(int              sock_id,
               void            *p_data,
               _size_t          data_len,
               int              flags,
               struct sockaddr *paddr_remote,
               socklen_t        addr_len);
```

ARGUMENTS

sock_id   This is the socket ID returned by **NetSock_Open()/socket()** when the
           socket was created *or* by **NetSock_Accept()/accept()** when a connection
           was accepted.

p_data   Pointer to the application data memory buffer to send.

891

data_len   Size of the application data memory buffer (in bytes).

flags   Flag to select transmit options; bit-field flags logically **OR**'d:

        `NET_SOCK_FLAG_NONE/0`

        `NET_SOCK_FLAG_TX_NO_BLOCK/`   No socket flags selected

        `MSG_DONTWAIT`   Send socket data without blocking

        In most cases, this flag would be set to `NET_SOCK_FLAG_NONE/0`.

paddr_remote Pointer to a socket address structure (see section 8-2 "Socket Interface" on page 212) which contains the remote socket address to send data to.

addr_len   Size of the socket address structure which *must* be passed the size of the socket address structure [e.g., `sizeof(NET_SOCK_ADDR_IP)`].

perr   Pointer to variable that will receive the return error code from this function:

        `NET_SOCK_ERR_NONE`

        `NET_SOCK_ERR_NULL_PTR`

        `NET_SOCK_ERR_NOT_USED`

        `NET_SOCK_ERR_CLOSED`

        `NET_SOCK_ERR_INVALID_SOCK`

        `NET_SOCK_ERR_INVALID_FAMILY`

        `NET_SOCK_ERR_INVALID_PROTOCOL`

        `NET_SOCK_ERR_INVALID_TYPE`

        `NET_SOCK_ERR_INVALID_STATE`

        `NET_SOCK_ERR_INVALID_OP`

        `NET_SOCK_ERR_INVALID_FLAG`

        `NET_SOCK_ERR_INVALID_DATA_SIZE`

        `NET_SOCK_ERR_INVALID_CONN`

        `NET_SOCK_ERR_INVALID_ADDR`

        `NET_SOCK_ERR_INVALID_ADDR_LEN`

        `NET_SOCK_ERR_INVALID_PORT_NBR`

        `NET_SOCK_ERR_ADDR_IN_USE`

        `NET_SOCK_ERR_PORT_NBR_NONE_AVAIL`

        `NET_SOCK_ERR_CONN_FAIL`

        `NET_SOCK_ERR_FAULT`

```
NET_ERR_TX
NET_IF_ERR_INVALID_IF
NET_IP_ERR_ADDR_NONE_AVAIL
NET_IP_ERR_ADDR_CFG_IN_PROGRESS
NET_CONN_ERR_NULL_PTR
NET_CONN_ERR_NOT_USED
NET_CONN_ERR_INVALID_CONN
NET_CONN_ERR_INVALID_FAMILY
NET_CONN_ERR_INVALID_TYPE
NET_CONN_ERR_INVALID_PROTOCOL_IX
NET_CONN_ERR_INVALID_ADDR_LEN
NET_CONN_ERR_ADDR_IN_USE
NET_ERR_INIT_INCOMPLETE
NET_OS_ERR_LOCK
```

RETURNED VALUE

Positive number of bytes (queued to be) sent, if successful;

NET_SOCK_BSD_RTN_CODE_CONN_CLOSED/0, if the socket is closed;

NET_SOCK_BSD_ERR_TX/-1, otherwise.

Note that a positive return value does not mean that the message was successfully delivered to the remote socket, just that it was sent or queued for sending.

BLOCKING VS NON-BLOCKING

The default setting for µC/TCP-IP is blocking. However, this setting can be changed at compile time by setting the NET_SOCK_CFG_BLOCK_SEL (see section D-15-3 on page 977) to one of the following values:

NET_SOCK_BLOCK_SEL_DFLT sets blocking mode to the default, or blocking, unless modified by run-time options.

NET_SOCK_BLOCK_SEL_BLOCK sets the blocking mode to blocking. This means that a socket transmit function will wait forever, until it can send (or queue to send) at least one byte of data or the socket connection is closed, unless a timeout is specified by NetSock_CfgTimeoutTxQ_Set() [See section C-14-24 on page 855].

`NET_SOCK_BLOCK_SEL_NO_BLOCK` sets the blocking mode to non-blocking. This means that a socket transmit function will *not* wait but immediately return as much data sent (or queued to be sent), socket connection closed, or an error indicating no available memory to send (or queue) data or other possible socket faults. The application will have to "poll" the socket on a regular basis to transmit data.

The current version of µC/TCP-IP selects blocking or non-blocking at compile time for all sockets. A future version may allow the selection of blocking or non-blocking at the individual socket level. However, each socket transmit call can pass the `NET_SOCK_FLAG_TX_NO_BLOCK/MSG_DONTWAIT` flag to disable blocking on that call.

Despite these socket-level blocking options, the current version of µC/TCP-IP possibly blocks at the device driver when waiting for the availability of a device's transmitter.

REQUIRED CONFIGURATION

`NetSock_TxData()/NetSock_TxDataTo()` is available only if:

- `NET_CFG_TRANSPORT_LAYER_SEL` is configured for TCP (see section D-12-1 on page 972), and/or

- `NET_UDP_CFG_APP_API_SEL` is configured for sockets (see section D-13-1 on page 973).

In addition, `send()/sendto()` is available only if `NET_BSD_CFG_API_EN` is enabled (see section D-17-1 on page 983).

NOTES / WARNINGS

TCP sockets typically use `NetSock_TxData()/send()`, whereas UDP sockets typically use `NetSock_TxDataTo()/sendto()`.

For datagram sockets (i.e., UDP), each receive returns the data from exactly one send but datagram order and delivery is not guaranteed. Also, if the receive memory buffer is not large enough to receive an entire datagram, the datagram's data is truncated to the size of the memory buffer and the remaining data is discarded.

For datagram sockets (i.e., UDP), all data is sent atomically – i.e., each call to send data *must* be sent in a single, complete datagram. Since µC/TCP-IP does *not* currently support IP transmit fragmentation, if a datagram socket attempts to send data greater than a single datagram, then the socket send is aborted and no socket data is sent.

Only some transmit flag options are implemented. If other flag options are requested, an error is returned so that flag options are *not* silently ignored.

C-15 TCP FUNCTIONS

C-15-1 NetTCP_ConnCfgIdleTimeout()

Configure TCP connection's idle timeout.

FILES

net_tcp.h/net_tcp.c

PROTOTYPE

```
CPU_BOOLEAN NetTCP_ConnCfgIdleTimeout(NET_TCP_CONN_ID     conn_id_tcp,
                                      NET_TCP_TIMEOUT_SEC  timeout_sec,
                                      NET_ERR             *perr);
```

ARGUMENTS

conn_id_tcp TCP connection handle ID to configure connection handle timeout.

timeout_sec Desired value for TCP connection idle timeout (in seconds).

perr Pointer to variable that will receive the return error code from this function:

NET_TCP_ERR_NONE
NET_TCP_ERR_INVALID_ARG
NET_TCP_ERR_INVALID_CONN
NET_TCP_ERR_CONN_NOT_USED
NET_ERR_INIT_INCOMPLETE
NET_OS_ERR_LOCK

RETURNED VALUE

DEF_OK, TCP connection's idle timeout successfully configured.

DEF_FAIL, otherwise.

REQUIRED CONFIGURATION

Available only if **NET_CFG_TRANSPORT_LAYER_SEL** is configured for TCP (see section D-12-1 on page 972).

NOTES / WARNINGS

Configured timeout does not reschedule any current idle timeout in progress but becomes effective the next time a TCP connection sets its idle timeout.

The **conn_id_tcp** argument represents the TCP connection handle – *not* the socket handle. The following code may be used to get the TCP connection handle and configure TCP connection parameters (see also section C-14-32 "NetSock_GetConnTransportID()" on page 869):

```
NET_SOCK_ID      sock_id;
NET_TCP_CONN_ID conn_id_tcp;
NET_ERR          err;

sock_id     = Application's TCP socket ID; /* Get application's TCP socket    ID. */
                                    /* Get socket's      TCP connection ID. */
conn_id_tcp = (NET_TCP_CONN_ID)NetSock_GetConnTransportID(sock_id, &err);

if (err == NET_SOCK_ERR_NONE) {/* If NO errors, ...                                    */
                        /* ... configure TCP connection maximum re-transmit threshold. */
    NetTCP_ConnCfgIdleTimeout(conn_id_tcp, 240u, &err);
}
```

NetTCP_ConnCfgIdleTimeout() is called by application function(s) and *must not* be called with the global network lock already acquired. It *must* block *all* other network protocol tasks by pending on and acquiring the global network lock (see "**net.h** Note #3"). This is required since an application's network protocol suite API function access is asynchronous to other network protocol tasks.

C-15-2 NetTCP_ConnCfgMaxSegSizeLocal()

Configure TCP connection's local maximum segment size.

FILES

net_tcp.h/net_tcp.c

PROTOTYPE

```
CPU_BOOLEAN NetTCP_ConnCfgMaxSegSizeLocal(NET_TCP_CONN_ID    conn_id_tcp,
                                          NET_TCP_SEG_SIZE  max_seg_size,
                                          NET_ERR           *perr);
```

ARGUMENTS

conn_id_tcp TCP connection handle ID to configure local maximum segment size.

max_seg_size Desired maximum segment size.

perr Pointer to variable that will receive the return error code from this function:

> NET_TCP_ERR_NONE
> NET_TCP_ERR_CONN_NOT_USED
> NET_TCP_ERR_INVALID_CONN_STATE
> NET_TCP_ERR_INVALID_CONN_OP
> NET_TCP_ERR_INVALID_CONN_ARG
> NET_TCP_ERR_INVALID_CONN
> NET_TCP_ERR_CONN_NOT_USED
> NET_ERR_INIT_INCOMPLETE
> NET_OS_ERR_LOCK

RETURNED VALUE

DEF_OK, TCP connection's local maximum segment size successfully configured, if no errors.

DEF_FAIL, otherwise.

REQUIRED CONFIGURATION

Available only if **NET_CFG_TRANSPORT_LAYER_SEL** is configured for TCP (see section D-12-1 on page 972).

NOTES / WARNINGS

The **conn_id_tcp** argument represents the TCP connection handle — *not* the socket handle. The following code may be used to get the TCP connection handle and configure TCP connection parameters (see also section C-14-32 "NetSock_GetConnTransportID()" on page 869):

```
NET_SOCK_ID     sock_id;
NET_TCP_CONN_ID conn_id_tcp;
NET_ERR         err;

sock_id     = Application's TCP socket ID; /* Get application's TCP socket    ID. */
                                  /* Get socket's     TCP connection ID. */
conn_id_tcp = (NET_TCP_CONN_ID)NetSock_GetConnTransportID(sock_id, &err);

if (err == NET_SOCK_ERR_NONE) { /* If NO errors, ...                                */
                          /* ... configure TCP connection local maximum segment size. */
    NetTCP_ConnCfgMaxSegSizeLocal(conn_id_tcp, 1360u);
}
```

NetTCP_ConnCfgMaxSegSizeLocal() is called by application function(s) and *must not* be called with the global network lock already acquired. It *must* block *all* other network protocol tasks by pending on and acquiring the global network lock (see "**net.h** Note #3"). This is required since an application's network protocol suite API function access is asynchronous to other network protocol tasks.

C-15-3 NetTCP_ConnCfgReTxMaxTh()

Configure TCP connection's maximum number of same segment retransmissions.

FILES

net_tcp.h/net_tcp.c

PROTOTYPE

```
CPU_BOOLEAN NetTCP_ConnCfgReTxMaxTh(NET_TCP_CONN_ID  conn_id_tcp,
                                    NET_PKT_CTR      nbr_max_re_tx,
                                    NET_ERR          *perr);
```

ARGUMENTS

conn_id_tcp TCP connection handle ID to configure maximum number of same segment retransmissions.

nbr_max_re_tx Desired maximum number of same segment retransmissions.

perr Pointer to variable that will receive the return error code from this function:

> NET_TCP_ERR_NONE
> NET_TCP_ERR_INVALID_ARG
> NET_TCP_ERR_INVALID_CONN
> NET_TCP_ERR_CONN_NOT_USED
> NET_ERR_INIT_INCOMPLETE
> NET_OS_ERR_LOCK

RETURNED VALUE

DEF_OK, TCP connection's maximum number of retransmissions successfully configured, if no errors.

DEF_FAIL, otherwise.

REQUIRED CONFIGURATION

Available only if **NET_CFG_TRANSPORT_LAYER_SEL** is configured for TCP (see section D-12-1 on page 972).

NOTES / WARNINGS

The **conn_id_tcp** argument represents the TCP connection handle – *not* the socket handle. The following code may be used to get the TCP connection handle and configure TCP connection parameters (see also section C-14-32 "NetSock_GetConnTransportID()" on page 869):

```
NET_SOCK_ID      sock_id;
NET_TCP_CONN_ID  conn_id_tcp;
NET_ERR          err;

sock_id     = Application's TCP socket ID; /* Get application's TCP socket    ID. */
                                    /* Get socket's      TCP connection ID. */
conn_id_tcp = (NET_TCP_CONN_ID)NetSock_GetConnTransportID(sock_id, &err);

if (err == NET_SOCK_ERR_NONE) {/* If NO errors, ...                                   */
                      /* ... configure TCP connection maximum re-transmit threshold. */
    NetTCP_ConnCfgReTxMaxTh(conn_id_tcp, 4u, &err);
}
```

NetTCP_ConnCfgReTxMaxTh() is called by application function(s) and *must not* be called with the global network lock already acquired. It *must* block *all* other network protocol tasks by pending on and acquiring the global network lock (see "**net.h** Note #3"). This is required since an application's network protocol suite API function access is asynchronous to other network protocol tasks.

C-15-4 NetTCP_ConnCfgReTxMaxTimeout()

Configure TCP connection's maximum retransmission timeout.

FILES

net_tcp.h/net_tcp.c

PROTOTYPE

```
CPU_BOOLEAN NetTCP_ConnCfgReTxMaxTimeout(NET_TCP_CONN_ID     conn_id_tcp,
                                         NET_TCP_TIMEOUT_SEC timeout_sec,
                                         NET_ERR             *perr);
```

ARGUMENTS

conn_id_tcp   TCP connection handle ID to configure maximum retransmission timeout value.

timeout_sec   Desired value for TCP connection maximum retransmission timeout (in seconds).

perr   Pointer to variable that will receive the return error code from this function:

        NET_TCP_ERR_NONE
        NET_TCP_ERR_INVALID_ARG
        NET_TCP_ERR_INVALID_CONN
        NET_TCP_ERR_CONN_NOT_USED
        NET_ERR_INIT_INCOMPLETE
        NET_OS_ERR_LOCK

RETURNED VALUE

DEF_OK,   TCP connection's maximum retransmission timeout successfully configured, if no errors.

DEF_FAIL,   otherwise.

REQUIRED CONFIGURATION

Available only if **NET_CFG_TRANSPORT_LAYER_SEL** is configured for TCP (see section D-12-1 on page 972).

NOTES / WARNINGS

The conn_id_tcp argument represents the TCP connection handle — *not* the socket handle. The following code may be used to get the TCP connection handle and configure TCP connection parameters (see also section C-14-32 "NetSock_GetConnTransportID()" on page 869):

```
NET_SOCK_ID    sock_id;
NET_TCP_CONN_ID conn_id_tcp;
NET_ERR        err;

sock_id    = Application's TCP socket ID; /* Get application's TCP socket    ID. */
                                   /* Get socket's      TCP connection ID. */
conn_id_tcp = (NET_TCP_CONN_ID)NetSock_GetConnTransportID(sock_id, &err);

if (err == NET_SOCK_ERR_NONE) { /* If NO errors, ...                              */
                          /* ... configure TCP connection maximum re-transmit timeout. */
    NetTCP_ConnCfgReTxMaxTimeout(conn_id_tcp, 30u);
}
```

NetTCP_ConnCfgReTxMaxTimeout() is called by application function(s) and *must not* be called with the global network lock already acquired. It *must* block *all* other network protocol tasks by pending on and acquiring the global network lock (see "**net.h** Note #3"). This is required since an application's network protocol suite API function access is asynchronous to other network protocol tasks.

C-15-5 NetTCP_ConnCfgRxWinSize()

Configure TCP connection's receive window size.

FILES

net_tcp.h/net_tcp.c

PROTOTYPE

```
CPU_BOOLEAN NetTCP_ConnCfgRxWinSize(NET_TCP_CONN_ID  conn_id_tcp,
                                    NET_TCP_WIN_SIZE  win_size,
                                    NET_ERR          *perr);
```

ARGUMENTS

conn_id_tcp TCP connection handle ID to configure receive window size.

win_size   Desired receive window size.

perr   Pointer to variable that will receive the return error code from this function:

> NET_TCP_ERR_NONE
> NET_TCP_ERR_CONN_NOT_USED
> NET_TCP_ERR_INVALID_CONN_STATE
> NET_TCP_ERR_INVALID_CONN_OP
> NET_TCP_ERR_INVALID_ARG
> NET_TCP_ERR_INVALID_CONN
> NET_TCP_ERR_CONN_NOT_USED
> NET_ERR_INIT_INCOMPLETE
> NET_OS_ERR_LOCK

RETURNED VALUE

DEF_OK,   TCP connection's receive window size successfully configured, if no errors.

DEF_FAIL,   otherwise.

REQUIRED CONFIGURATION

Available only if **NET_CFG_TRANSPORT_LAYER_SEL** is configured for TCP (see section D-12-1 on page 972).

NOTES / WARNINGS

The conn_id_tcp argument represents the TCP connection handle – *not* the socket handle. The following code may be used to get the TCP connection handle and configure TCP connection parameters (see also section C-14-32 "NetSock_GetConnTransportID()" on page 869):

```
NET_SOCK_ID     sock_id;
NET_TCP_CONN_ID conn_id_tcp;
NET_ERR         err;

sock_id     = Application's TCP socket ID; /* Get application's TCP socket    ID. */
                                   /* Get socket's      TCP connection ID. */
conn_id_tcp = (NET_TCP_CONN_ID)NetSock_GetConnTransportID(sock_id, &err);

if (err == NET_SOCK_ERR_NONE) { /* If NO errors, ...                          */
                           /* ... configure TCP connection receive window size. */
    NetTCP_ConnCfgRxWinSize(conn_id_tcp, (4u * 1460u));
}
```

NetTCP_ConnCfgRxWindowsSize() is called by application function(s) and *must not* be called with the global network lock already acquired. It *must* block *all* other network protocol tasks by pending on and acquiring the global network lock (see "**net.h** Note #3"). This is required since an application's network protocol suite API function access is asynchronous to other network protocol tasks.

C-15-6 NetTCP_ConnCfgTxWinSize()

Configure TCP connection's transmit window size.

FILES

net_tcp.h/net_tcp.c

PROTOTYPE

```
CPU_BOOLEAN NetTCP_ConnCfgTxWinSize(NET_TCP_CONN_ID   conn_id_tcp,
                                    NET_TCP_WIN_SIZE  win_size,
                                    NET_ERR           *perr);
```

ARGUMENTS

conn_id_tcp TCP connection handle ID to configure transmit window size.

win_size   Desired transmit window size.

perr   Pointer to variable that will receive the return error code from this function:

       NET_TCP_ERR_NONE
       NET_TCP_ERR_CONN_NOT_USED
       NET_TCP_ERR_INVALID_CONN_STATE
       NET_TCP_ERR_INVALID_CONN_OP
       NET_TCP_ERR_INVALID_ARG
       NET_TCP_ERR_INVALID_CONN
       NET_TCP_ERR_CONN_NOT_USED
       NET_ERR_INIT_INCOMPLETE
       NET_OS_ERR_LOCK

RETURNED VALUE

DEF_OK,   TCP connection's transmit window size successfully configured, if no errors.

DEF_FAIL,   otherwise.

REQUIRED CONFIGURATION

Available only if **NET_CFG_TRANSPORT_LAYER_SEL** is configured for TCP (see section D-12-1 on page 972).

NOTES / WARNINGS

The conn_id_tcp argument represents the TCP connection handle – *not* the socket handle. The following code may be used to get the TCP connection handle and configure TCP connection parameters (see also section C-14-32 "NetSock_GetConnTransportID()" on page 869):

```
NET_SOCK_ID      sock_id;
NET_TCP_CONN_ID  conn_id_tcp;
NET_ERR          err;

sock_id     = Application's TCP socket ID; /* Get application's TCP socket    ID. */
                                    /* Get socket's      TCP connection ID. */
conn_id_tcp = (NET_TCP_CONN_ID)NetSock_GetConnTransportID(sock_id, &err);

if (err == NET_SOCK_ERR_NONE) { /* If NO errors, ...                          */
                            /* ... configure TCP connection receive window size. */
    NetTCP_ConnCfgTxWinSize(conn_id_tcp, (4u * 1460u));
}
```

NetTCP_ConnCfgTxWindowsSize() is called by application function(s) and *must not* be called with the global network lock already acquired. It *must* block *all* other network protocol tasks by pending on and acquiring the global network lock (see "**net.h** Note #3"). This is required since an application's network protocol suite API function access is asynchronous to other network protocol tasks.

C-15-7 NetTCP_ConnCfgTxAckImmedRxdPushEn()

Configure TCP connection's transmit immediate acknowledgement for received and pushed TCP segments.

FILES

net_tcp.h/net_tcp.c

PROTOTYPE

```
CPU_BOOLEAN NetTCP_ConnCfgTxAckImmedRxdPushEn(NET_TCP_CONN_ID  conn_id_tcp,
                                              CPU_BOOLEAN      tx_immed_ack_en,
                                              NET_ERR          *perr);
```

ARGUMENTS

conn_id_tcp   TCP connection handle ID to configure transmit immediate acknowledgement for received and pushed TCP segments.

tx_immed_ack_en   Desired value for TCP connection transmit immediate acknowledgement for received and pushed TCP segments:

                              DEF_ENABLED   TCP connection acknowledgements immediately transmitted for any pushed TCP segments received.

                              DEF_DISABLED   TCP connection acknowledgements *not* immediately transmitted for any pushed TCP segments received.

perr   Pointer to variable that will receive the return error code from this function:

                NET_TCP_ERR_NONE
                NET_TCP_ERR_INVALID_ARG
                NET_TCP_ERR_INVALID_CONN
                NET_TCP_ERR_CONN_NOT_USED
                NET_ERR_INIT_INCOMPLETE
                NET_OS_ERR_LOCK

RETURNED VALUE

DEF_OK, TCP connection's transmit immediate acknowledgement for received and pushed TCP segments successfully configured, if no errors.

DEF_FAIL, otherwise.

REQUIRED CONFIGURATION

Available only if **NET_CFG_TRANSPORT_LAYER_SEL** is configured for TCP (see section D-12-1 on page 972).

NOTES / WARNINGS

The **conn_id_tcp** argument represents the TCP connection handle – *not* the socket handle. The following code may be used to get the TCP connection handle and configure TCP connection parameters (see also section C-14-32 on page 869):

```
NET_SOCK_ID      sock_id;
NET_TCP_CONN_ID conn_id_tcp;
NET_ERR          err;

sock_id     = Application's TCP socket ID; /* Get application's TCP socket    ID. */
                                  /* Get socket's       TCP connection ID. */
conn_id_tcp = (NET_TCP_CONN_ID)NetSock_GetConnTransportID(sock_id, &err);

if (err == NET_SOCK_ERR_NONE) {
            /* If NO errors, ...                                           */
            /* ... configure TCP connection transmit immediate ACK for received PUSH. */
    NetTCP_ConnCfgTxAckImmedRxdPushEn(conn_id_tcp, DEF_NO);
}
```

NetTCP_ConnCfgTxAckImmedRxdPushEn() is called by application function(s) and *must not* be called with the global network lock already acquired. It *must* block *all* other network protocol tasks by pending on and acquiring the global network lock (see "**net.h** Note #3"). This is required since an application's network protocol suite API function access is asynchronous to other network protocol tasks.

C-15-8 NetTCP_ConnCfgTxNagleEn()

Configure TCP connection's transmit Nagle algorithm enable.

FILES

net_tcp.h/net_tcp.c

PROTOTYPE

```
CPU_BOOLEAN NetTCP_ConnCfgTxNagleEn(NET_TCP_CONN_ID  conn_id_tcp,
                                    CPU_BOOLEAN      nagle_en,
                                    NET_ERR          *perr);
```

ARGUMENTS

conn_id_tcp Handle identifier of TCP connection to configure transmit Nagle enable.

nagle_en   Desired value for TCP connection transmit Nagle enable :

DEF_ENABLED	TCP connections delay transmitting next data segment(s) until all unacknowledged data is acknowledged **OR** an MSS-sized segment can be transmitted.
DEF_DISABLED	TCP connections transmit all data segment(s) when permitted by local & remote hosts' congestion controls.

perr   Pointer to variable that will receive the return error code from this function:

NET_TCP_ERR_NONE
NET_TCP_ERR_INVALID_ARG
NET_TCP_ERR_INVALID_CONN
NET_TCP_ERR_CONN_NOT_USED
NET_ERR_INIT_INCOMPLETE
NET_OS_ERR_LOCK

RETURNED VALUE

DEF_OK,   TCP connection's transmit Nagle enable successfully configured;

DEF_FAIL,   otherwise.

REQUIRED CONFIGURATION

Available only if **NET_CFG_TRANSPORT_LAYER_SEL** is configured for TCP (see section D-12-1 on page 972).

NOTES / WARNINGS

The **conn_id_tcp** argument represents the TCP connection handle – *not* the socket handle. The following code may be used to get the TCP connection handle and configure TCP connection parameters (see also section C-14-32 "NetSock_GetConnTransportID()" on page 869):

```
NET_SOCK_ID      sock_id;
NET_TCP_CONN_ID  conn_id_tcp;
NET_ERR          err;

sock_id     = Application's TCP socket ID; /* Get application's TCP socket    ID. */
                                    /* Get socket's       TCP connection ID. */
conn_id_tcp = (NET_TCP_CONN_ID)NetSock_GetConnTransportID(sock_id, &err);

if (err == NET_SOCK_ERR_NONE) { /* If NO errors, ...                          */
                        /* ... configure TCP connection Nagle algorithm. */
    NetTCP_ConnCfgTxNagleEn(conn_id_tcp, DEF_DISABLED, &err);
}
```

NetTCP_ConnCfgTxNagleEn() is called by application function(s) and *must not* be called with the global network lock already acquired. It *must* block *all* other network protocol tasks by pending on and acquiring the global network lock (see "**net.h** Note #3"). This is required since an application's network protocol suite API function access is asynchronous to other network protocol tasks.

C-15-9 NetTCP_ConnCfgTxKeepAliveEn()

Configure TCP connection's transmit keep-alive enable.

FILES

net_tcp.h/net_tcp.c

PROTOTYPE

```
CPU_BOOLEAN NetTCP_ConnCfgTxKeepAliveEn(NET_TCP_CONN_ID  conn_id_tcp,
                                        CPU_BOOLEAN      keep_alive_en,
                                        NET_ERR          *perr);
```

ARGUMENTS

conn_id_tcp   Handle identifier of TCP connection to configure transmit
                        keep-alive.

keep_alive_en   Desired value for TCP connection transmit keep-alive enable:

    DEF_ENABLED   TCP connections transmit periodic
                        keep-alive segments if no data segments
                        have been received within the keep-alive
                        timeout.

    DEF_DISABLED   TCP connections transmit a reset segment
                        and close if no data segments have been
                        received within the keep-alive timeout.

perr   Pointer to variable that will receive the return error code from this function:

    NET_TCP_ERR_NONE
    NET_TCP_ERR_INVALID_ARG
    NET_TCP_ERR_INVALID_CONN
    NET_TCP_ERR_CONN_NOT_USED
    NET_ERR_INIT_INCOMPLETE
    NET_OS_ERR_LOCK

RETURNED VALUE

DEF_OK,   TCP connection's transmit keep-alive enable successfully configured;

DEF_FAIL,   otherwise.

REQUIRED CONFIGURATION

Available only if **NET_CFG_TRANSPORT_LAYER_SEL** is configured for TCP (see section D-12-1 on page 972).

NOTES / WARNINGS

The **conn_id_tcp** argument represents the TCP connection handle – *not* the socket handle. The following code may be used to get the TCP connection handle and configure TCP connection parameters (see also section C-14-32 "NetSock_GetConnTransportID()" on page 869):

```
NET_SOCK_ID    sock_id;
NET_TCP_CONN_ID conn_id_tcp;
NET_ERR        err;

sock_id    = Application's TCP socket ID; /* Get application's TCP socket    ID. */
                                   /* Get socket's      TCP connection ID. */
conn_id_tcp = (NET_TCP_CONN_ID)NetSock_GetConnTransportID(sock_id, &err);

if (err == NET_SOCK_ERR_NONE) { /* If NO errors, ...                       */
                          /* ... configure TCP connection Nagle algorithm. */
    NetTCP_ConnCfgTxKeepAliveEn(conn_id_tcp, DEF_ENABLED, &err);
}
```

NetTCP_ConnCfgTxKeepAliveEn() is called by application function(s) and *must not* be called with the global network lock already acquired. It *must* block *all* other network protocol tasks by pending on and acquiring the global network lock (see "**net.h** Note #3"). This is required since an application's network protocol suite API function access is asynchronous to other network protocol tasks.

C-15-10 NetTCP_ConnCfgTxKeepAliveTh()

Configure TCP connection's maximum number of consecutive keep-alives to transmit.

FILES

net_tcp.h/net_tcp.c

PROTOTYPE

```
CPU_BOOLEAN NetTCP_ConnCfgTxKeepAliveTh(NET_TCP_CONN_ID  conn_id_tcp,
                                        NET_PKT_CTR      nbr_max_keep_alive,
                                        NET_ERR          *perr);
```

ARGUMENTS

conn_id_tcp
Handle identifier of TCP connection to configure transmit keep-alive threshold.

keep_alive_en
Desired maximum number of consecutive keep-alives to transmit.

perr
Pointer to variable that will receive the return error code from this function:

> NET_TCP_ERR_NONE
> NET_TCP_ERR_INVALID_ARG
> NET_TCP_ERR_INVALID_CONN
> NET_TCP_ERR_CONN_NOT_USED
> NET_ERR_INIT_INCOMPLETE
> NET_OS_ERR_LOCK

RETURNED VALUE

DEF_OK,
TCP connection's transmit keep-alive enable successfully configured;

DEF_FAIL,
otherwise.

REQUIRED CONFIGURATION

Available only if **NET_CFG_TRANSPORT_LAYER_SEL** is configured for TCP (see section D-12-1 on page 972).

NOTES / WARNINGS

The **conn_id_tcp** argument represents the TCP connection handle – *not* the socket handle. The following code may be used to get the TCP connection handle and configure TCP connection parameters (see also section C-14-32 "NetSock_GetConnTransportID()" on page 869):

```
NET_SOCK_ID      sock_id;
NET_TCP_CONN_ID conn_id_tcp;
NET_ERR          err;

sock_id      = Application's TCP socket ID; /* Get application's TCP socket      ID. */
                                     /* Get socket's      TCP connection ID. */
conn_id_tcp = (NET_TCP_CONN_ID)NetSock_GetConnTransportID(sock_id, &err);

if (err == NET_SOCK_ERR_NONE) { /* If NO errors, ...                          */
                          /* ... configure TCP connection Nagle algorithm. */
    NetTCP_ConnCfgTxKeepAliveTh(conn_id_tcp, 15u, &err);
}
```

NetTCP_ConnCfgTxKeepAliveTh() is called by application function(s) and *must not* be called with the global network lock already acquired. It *must* block *all* other network protocol tasks by pending on and acquiring the global network lock (see "**net.h** Note #3"). This is required since an application's network protocol suite API function access is asynchronous to other network protocol tasks.

915

C-15-11 NetTCP_ConnCfgTxKeepAliveRetryTimeout()

Configure TCP connection's transmit keep-alive retry timeout.

FILES

net_tcp.h/net_tcp.c

PROTOTYPE

```
CPU_BOOLEAN NetTCP_ConnCfgTxKeepAliveRetryTimeout(NET_TCP_CONN_ID    conn_id_tcp,
                                                  NET_TCP_TIMEOUT_SEC timeout_sec,
                                                  NET_ERR             *perr);
```

ARGUMENTS

conn_id_tcp   Handle identifier of TCP connection to configure transmit
                       keep-alive retry timeout.

timeout_sec   Desired value for TCP connection transmit keep-alive retry
                       timeout (in seconds).

perr   Pointer to variable that will receive the return error code from this function:

            NET_TCP_ERR_NONE
            NET_TCP_ERR_INVALID_ARG
            NET_TCP_ERR_INVALID_CONN
            NET_TCP_ERR_CONN_NOT_USED
            NET_ERR_INIT_INCOMPLETE
            NET_OS_ERR_LOCK

RETURNED VALUE

DEF_OK,   TCP connection's transmit keep-alive retry timeout successfully configured;

DEF_FAIL,   otherwise.

REQUIRED CONFIGURATION

Available only if **NET_CFG_TRANSPORT_LAYER_SEL** is configured for TCP (see section D-12-1 on page 972).

NOTES / WARNINGS

The **conn_id_tcp** argument represents the TCP connection handle – *not* the socket handle. The following code may be used to get the TCP connection handle and configure TCP connection parameters (see also section C-14-32 "NetSock_GetConnTransportID()" on page 869):

```
NET_SOCK_ID      sock_id;
NET_TCP_CONN_ID  conn_id_tcp;
NET_ERR          err;

sock_id     = Application's TCP socket ID; /* Get application's TCP socket    ID. */
                                   /* Get socket's      TCP connection ID. */
conn_id_tcp = (NET_TCP_CONN_ID)NetSock_GetConnTransportID(sock_id, &err);

if (err == NET_SOCK_ERR_NONE) { /* If NO errors, ...                       */
                      /* ... configure TCP connection Nagle algorithm. */
    NetTCP_ConnCfgTxKeepAliveRetryTimeout(conn_id_tcp, 20u, &err);
}
```

NetTCP_ConnCfgTxKeepAliveRetryTimeout() is called by application function(s) and *must not* be called with the global network lock already acquired. It *must* block *all* other network protocol tasks by pending on and acquiring the global network lock (see "**net.h** Note #3"). This is required since an application's network protocol suite API function access is asynchronous to other network protocol tasks.

C-15-12 NetTCP_ConnCfgTxAckDlyTimeout()

Configure TCP connection's transmit acknowledgement delay timeout.

FILES

net_tcp.h/net_tcp.c

PROTOTYPE

```
CPU_BOOLEAN NetTCP_ConnCfgTxAckDlyTimeout(NET_TCP_CONN_ID    conn_id_tcp,
                                          NET_TCP_TIMEOUT_MS timeout_ms,
                                          NET_ERR            *perr);
```

ARGUMENTS

conn_id_tcp   Handle identifier of TCP connection to configure transmit acknowledgement delay timeout.

timeout_sec   Desired value for TCP connection transmit acknowledgement delay timeout (in milliseconds).

perr   Pointer to variable that will receive the return error code from this function:

          NET_TCP_ERR_NONE
          NET_TCP_ERR_INVALID_ARG
          NET_TCP_ERR_INVALID_CONN
          NET_TCP_ERR_CONN_NOT_USED
          NET_ERR_INIT_INCOMPLETE
          NET_OS_ERR_LOCK

RETURNED VALUE

DEF_OK,   TCP connection's transmit acknowledgement delay timeout successfully configured;

DEF_FAIL,   otherwise.

REQUIRED CONFIGURATION

Available only if **NET_CFG_TRANSPORT_LAYER_SEL** is configured for TCP (see section D-12-1 on page 972).

NOTES / WARNINGS

The **conn_id_tcp** argument represents the TCP connection handle – *not* the socket handle. The following code may be used to get the TCP connection handle and configure TCP connection parameters (see also section C-14-32 "NetSock_GetConnTransportID()" on page 869):

```
NET_SOCK_ID     sock_id;
NET_TCP_CONN_ID conn_id_tcp;
NET_ERR         err;

sock_id     = Application's TCP socket ID; /* Get application's TCP socket    ID. */
                                     /* Get socket's      TCP connection ID. */
conn_id_tcp = (NET_TCP_CONN_ID)NetSock_GetConnTransportID(sock_id, &err);

if (err == NET_SOCK_ERR_NONE) { /* If NO errors, ...                         */
                           /* ... configure TCP connection Nagle algorithm. */
    NetTCP_ConnCfgTxAckDlyTimeout(conn_id_tcp, 20u, &err);
}
```

NetTCP_ConnCfgTxAckDlyTimeout() is called by application function(s) and *must not* be called with the global network lock already acquired. It *must* block *all* other network protocol tasks by pending on and acquiring the global network lock (see "**net.h** Note #3"). This is required since an application's network protocol suite API function access is asynchronous to other network protocol tasks.

C-15-13 NetTCP_ConnPoolStatGet()

Get TCP connections' statistics pool.

FILES

net_tcp.h/net_tcp.c

PROTOTYPE

```
NET_STAT_POOL NetTCP_ConnPoolStatGet(void);
```

ARGUMENTS

None.

RETURNED VALUE

TCP connections' statistics pool, if no errors.

NULL statistics pool, otherwise.

REQUIRED CONFIGURATION

Available only if NET_CFG_TRANSPORT_LAYER_SEL is configured for TCP (see section D-12-1 on page 972).

NOTES / WARNINGS

None.

C-15-14 NetTCP_ConnPoolStatResetMaxUsed()

Reset TCP connections' statistics pool's maximum number of entries used.

FILES

net_tcp.h/net_tcp.c

PROTOTYPE

```
void NetTCP_ConnPoolStatResetMaxUsed(void);
```

ARGUMENTS

None.

RETURNED VALUE

None.

REQUIRED CONFIGURATION

Available only if **NET_CFG_TRANSPORT_LAYER_SEL** is configured for TCP (see section D-12-1 on page 972).

NOTES / WARNINGS

None.

C-15-15 NetTCP_InitTxSeqNbr()

Application-defined function to initialize TCP's Initial Transmit Sequence Number Counter.

FILES

net_tcp.h/net_bsp.c

PROTOTYPE

```
void NetTCP_InitTxSeqNbr(void);
```

ARGUMENTS

None.

RETURNED VALUE

None.

REQUIRED CONFIGURATION

Available only if **NET_CFG_TRANSPORT_LAYER_SEL** is configured for TCP (see section D-12-1 on page 972).

NOTES / WARNINGS

If TCP module is included, the application is required to initialize TCP's Initial Transmit Sequence Number Counter. Possible initialization methods include:

■ Time-based initialization is one preferred method since it more appropriately provides a pseudo-random initial sequence number.

■ Hardware-generated random number initialization is *not* a preferred method since it tends to produce a discrete set of pseudo-random initial sequence numbers – often the same initial sequence number.

■ Hard-coded initial sequence number is *not* a preferred method since it is *not* random.

C-16 NETWORK TIMER FUNCTIONS

C-16-1 NetTmr_PoolStatGet()

Get Network Timers' statistics pool.

FILES

net_tmr.h/net_tmr.c

PROTOTYPE

```
NET_STAT_POOL NetTmr_PoolStatGet(void);
```

ARGUMENTS

None.

RETURNED VALUE

Network Timers' statistics pool, if no errors.

NULL statistics pool, otherwise.

REQUIRED CONFIGURATION

None.

NOTES / WARNINGS

None.

C-16-2 NetTmr_PoolStatResetMaxUsed()

Reset Network Timers' statistics pool's maximum number of entries used.

FILES

net_tmr.h/net_tmr.c

PROTOTYPE

```
void NetTmr_PoolStatResetMaxUsed(void);
```

ARGUMENTS

None.

RETURNED VALUE

None.

REQUIRED CONFIGURATION

None.

NOTES / WARNINGS

None.

C-17 UDP FUNCTIONS

C-17-1 NetUDP_RxAppData()

Copy up to a specified number of bytes from received UDP packet buffer(s) into an application memory buffer.

FILES

net_udp.h/net_udp.c

PROTOTYPE

```
CPU_INT16U   NetUDP_RxAppData(NET_BUF     *pbuf,
                              void        *pdata_buf,
                              CPU_INT16U  data_buf_len,
                              CPU_INT16U  flags,
                              void        *pip_opts_buf,
                              CPU_INT08U  ip_opts_buf_len,
                              CPU_INT08U  *pip_opts_len,
                              NET_ERR     *perr);
```

ARGUMENTS

pbuf   Pointer to network buffer that received UDP datagram.

pdata_buf   Pointer to application buffer to receive application data.

data_buf_len Size of application receive buffer (in bytes).

flags   Flag to select receive options; bit-field flags logically **OR**'d:

> NET_UDP_FLAG_NONE   No UDP receive flags selected.
>
> NET_UDP_FLAG_RX_DATA_PEEK Receive UDP application data without consuming the data; i.e., do *not* free any UDP receive packet buffer(s).

pip_opts_buf Pointer to buffer to receive possible IP options, if no errors.

`ip_opts_buf_len`	Size of IP options receive buffer (in bytes).
`pip_opts_len`	Pointer to variable that will receive the return size of any received IP options, if no errors.
`perr`	Pointer to variable that will receive the return error code from this function:

> NET_UDP_ERR_NONE
> NET_UDP_ERR_NULL_PTR
> NET_UDP_ERR_INVALID_DATA_SIZE
> NET_UDP_ERR_INVALID_FLAG
> NET_ERR_INIT_INCOMPLETE
> NET_ERR_RX

RETURNED VALUE

Positive number of bytes received, if successful;

0, otherwise.

REQUIRED CONFIGURATION

None.

NOTES / WARNINGS

`NetUDP_RxAppData()` *must* be called with the global network lock already acquired. Expected to be called from application's custom `NetUDP_RxAppDataHandler()` (see section C-17-2 on page 927).

Each UDP receive returns the data from exactly one send but datagram order and delivery is not guaranteed. Also, if the application memory buffer is not large enough to receive an entire datagram, the datagram's data is truncated to the size of the memory buffer and the remaining data is discarded. Therefore, the application memory buffer should be large enough to receive either the maximum UDP datagram size (i.e., 65,507 bytes) *or* the application's expected maximum UDP datagram size.

Only some UDP receive flag options are implemented. If other flag options are requested, an error is returned so that flag options are *not* silently ignored.

C-17-2 NetUDP_RxAppDataHandler()

Application-defined handler to demultiplex and receive UDP packet(s) to application without sockets.

net_udp.h/net_bsp.c

```
void NetUDP_RxAppDataHandler(NET_BUF          *pbuf,
                            NET_IP_ADDR       src_addr,
                            NET_UDP_PORT_NBR  src_port,
                            NET_IP_ADDR       dest_addr,
                            NET_UDP_PORT_NBR  dest_port,
                            NET_ERR          *perr);
```

pbuf   Pointer to network buffer that received UDP datagram.

src_addr   Receive UDP packet's source IP address.

src_port   Receive UDP packet's source UDP port.

dest_addr   Receive UDP packet's destination IP address.

dest_port   Receive UDP packet's destination UDP port.

perr   Pointer to variable that will receive the return error code from this function:

            NET_APP_ERR_NONE
            NET_ERR_RX_DEST
            NET_ERR_RX

None.

REQUIRED CONFIGURATION

Available only if `NET_UDP_CFG_APP_API_SEL` is configured for application demultiplexing (see section D-13-1 on page 973).

NOTES / WARNINGS

`NetUDP_RxAppDataHandler()` *already* called with the global network lock acquired and expects to call NetUDP_RxAppData() to copy data from received UDP packets (see section C-17-1 on page 925).

If `NetUDP_RxAppDataHandler()` services the application data immediately within the handler function, it should do so as quickly as possible since the network's global lock remains acquired for the full duration. Thus, no other network receives or transmits can occur while `NetUDP_RxAppDataHandler()` executes.

`NetUDP_RxAppDataHandler()` may delay servicing the application data but *must* then:

- Acquire the network's global lock *prior* to calling `NetUDP_RxAppData()`

- Release the network's global lock *after* calling `NetUDP_RxAppData()`

If `NetUDP_RxAppDataHandler()` successfully demultiplexes the UDP packets, it should eventually call `NetUDP_RxAppData()` to deframe the UDP packet application data. If `NetUDP_RxAppData()` successfully deframes the UDP packet application data, `NetUDP_RxAppDataHandler()` *must not* call `NetUDP_RxPktFree()` to free the UDP packet's network buffer(s), since `NetUDP_RxAppData()` already frees the network buffer(s). And if the UDP packets were successfully demultiplexed and deframed, `NetUDP_RxAppDataHandler()` must return `NET_APP_ERR_NONE`.

However, if `NetUDP_RxAppDataHandler()` does *not* successfully demultiplex the UDP packets and therefore does *not* call `NetUDP_RxAppData()`, then `NetUDP_RxAppDataHandler()` should return `NET_ERR_RX_DEST` but must *not* free or discard the UDP packet network buffer(s).

But if `NetUDP_RxAppDataHandler()` or `NetUDP_RxAppData()` fails for any other reason, `NetUDP_RxAppDataHandler()` should call `NetUDP_RxPktDiscard()` to discard the UDP packet's network buffer(s) and should return `NET_ERR_RX`.

C-17-3 NetUDP_TxAppData()

Copy bytes from an application memory buffer to send via UDP packet(s).

FILES

net_udp.h/net_udp.c

PROTOTYPE

```
CPU_INT16U
NetUDP_TxAppData(void              *p_data,
                 CPU_INT16U        data_len,
                 NET_IP_ADDR       src_addr,
                 NET_UDP_PORT_NBR  src_port,
                 NET_IP_ADDR       dest_addr,
                 NET_UDP_PORT_NBR  dest_port,
                 NET_IP_TOS        TOS,
                 NET_IP_TTL        TTL,
                 CPU_INT16U        flags_udp,
                 CPU_INT16U        flags_ip,
                 void              *popts_ip,
                 NET_ERR           *perr);
```

ARGUMENTS

p_data   Pointer to application data.

data_len   Length of application data (in bytes).

src_addr   Source IP address.

src_port   Source UDP port.

dest_addr   Destination IP address.

dest_port   Destination UDP port.

TOS   Specific TOS to transmit UDP/IP packet.

TTL   Specific TTL to transmit UDP/IP packet:

`NET_IP_TTL_MIN`	1	minimum	TTL transmit value
`NET_IP_TTL_MAX`	255	maximum	TTL transmit value
`NET_IP_TTL_DFLT`		default	TTL transmit value
`NET_IP_TTL_NONE`	0	replace with default TTL	

flags_udp   Flags to select UDP transmit options; bit-field flags logically **OR**'d:

`NET_UDP_FLAG_NONE`	No UDP transmit flags selected.
`NET_UDP_FLAG_TX_CHK_SUM_DIS`	Disable UDP transmit check-sums.
`NET_UDP_FLAG_TX_BLOCK`	Transmit UDP application data with blocking, if flag set; without blocking, if flag clear.

flags_ip   Flags to select IP transmit options; bit-field flags logically **OR**'d:

`NET_IP_FLAG_NONE`	No IP transmit flags selected.
`NET_IP_FLAG_TX_DONT_FRAG`	Set IP 'Don't Frag' flag.

popts_ip   Pointer to one or more IP options configuration data structures:

`NULL`	No IP transmit options configuration.
`NET_IP_OPT_CFG_ROUTE_TS`	Route and/or Internet Timestamp options configuration.
`NET_IP_OPT_CFG_SECURITY`	Security options configuration.

perr   Pointer to variable that will receive the return error code from this function:

```
NET_UDP_ERR_NONE
NET_UDP_ERR_NULL_PTR
NET_UDP_ERR_INVALID_DATA_SIZE
NET_UDP_ERR_INVALID_LEN_DATA
NET_UDP_ERR_INVALID_PORT_NBR
NET_UDP_ERR_INVALID_FLAG
NET_BUF_ERR_NULL_PTR
NET_BUF_ERR_NONE_AVAIL
```

```
NET_BUF_ERR_INVALID_TYPE
NET_BUF_ERR_INVALID_SIZE
NET_BUF_ERR_INVALID_IX
NET_BUF_ERR_INVALID_LEN
NET_UTIL_ERR_NULL_PTR
NET_UTIL_ERR_NULL_SIZE
NET_UTIL_ERR_INVALID_PROTOCOL
NET_ERR_TX
NET_ERR_INIT_INCOMPLETE
NET_ERR_INVALID_PROTOCOL
NET_OS_ERR_LOCK
```

RETURNED VALUE

Positive number of bytes sent, if successful;

0, otherwise.

REQUIRED CONFIGURATION

None.

NOTES / WARNINGS

Each UDP datagram is sent atomically – i.e., each call to send data *must* be sent in a single, complete datagram. Since µC/TCP-IP does *not* currently support IP transmit fragmentation, if the application attempts to send data greater than a single UDP datagram, then the send is aborted and no data is sent.

Only some UDP transmit flag options are implemented. If other flag options are requested, an error is returned so that flag options are *not* silently ignored.

C-18 GENERAL NETWORK UTILITY FUNCTIONS

C-18-1 NET_UTIL_HOST_TO_NET_16()

Convert 16-bit integer values from CPU host-order to network-order.

FILES

net_util.h

PROTOTYPE

```
NET_UTIL_HOST_TO_NET_16(val);
```

ARGUMENTS

val   16-bit integer data value to convert.

RETURNED VALUE

16-bit integer value in network-order.

REQUIRED CONFIGURATION

None.

NOTES / WARNINGS

For microprocessors that require data access to be aligned to appropriate word boundaries, val and any variable to receive the returned 16-bit integer *must* start on appropriately-aligned CPU addresses. This means that all 16-bit words *must* start on addresses that are multiples of 2 bytes.

C-18-2 NET_UTIL_HOST_TO_NET_32()

Convert 32-bit integer values from CPU host-order to network-order.

FILES

net_util.h

PROTOTYPE

```
NET_UTIL_HOST_TO_NET_32(val);
```

ARGUMENTS

val   32-bit integer data value to convert.

RETURNED VALUE

32-bit integer value in network-order.

REQUIRED CONFIGURATION

None.

NOTES / WARNINGS

For microprocessors that require data access to be aligned to appropriate word boundaries, val and any variable to receive the returned 32-bit integer *must* start on appropriately-aligned CPU addresses. This means that all 32-bit words *must* start on addresses that are multiples of 4 bytes.

C-18-3 NET_UTIL_NET_TO_HOST_16()

Convert 16-bit integer values from network-order to CPU host- order.

FILES

net_util.h

PROTOTYPE

```
NET_UTIL_NET_TO_HOST_16(val);
```

ARGUMENTS

val   16-bit integer data value to convert.

RETURNED VALUE

16-bit integer value in CPU host-order.

REQUIRED CONFIGURATION

None.

NOTES / WARNINGS

For microprocessors that require data access to be aligned to appropriate word boundaries, val and any variable to receive the returned 16-bit integer *must* start on appropriately-aligned CPU addresses. This means that all 16-bit words *must* start on addresses that are multiples of 2 bytes.

C-18-4 NET_UTIL_NET_TO_HOST_32()

Convert 32-bit integer values from network-order to CPU host- order.

FILES

net_util.h

PROTOTYPE

```
NET_UTIL_NET_TO_HOST_32(val);
```

ARGUMENTS

val   32-bit integer data value to convert.

RETURNED VALUE

32-bit integer value in CPU host-order.

REQUIRED CONFIGURATION

None.

NOTES / WARNINGS

For microprocessors that require data access to be aligned to appropriate word boundaries, val and any variable to receive the returned 32-bit integer *must* start on appropriately-aligned CPU addresses. This means that all 32-bit words *must* start on addresses that are multiples of 4 bytes.

C-18-5 NetUtil_TS_Get()

Application-defined function to get the current Internet Timestamp.

FILES

net_util.h/net_bsp.c

PROTOTYPE

```
NET_TS NetUtil_TS_Get (void);
```

ARGUMENTS

None.

RETURNED VALUE

Current Internet Timestamp, if available;

NET_TS_NONE, otherwise.

REQUIRED CONFIGURATION

None.

NOTES / WARNINGS

RFC #791, Section 3.1 'Options: Internet Timestamp' states that "the [Internet] Timestamp is a right-justified, 32-bit timestamp in milliseconds since midnight UT [Universal Time]".

The application is responsible for providing a real-time clock with correct time-zone configuration to implement the Internet Timestamp, if possible. In order to implement this feature, the target hardware must usually include a real-time clock with the correct time zone configuration. However, NetUtil_TS_Get() is not absolutely required and may return NET_TS_NONE if real-time clock hardware is not available.

C-18-6 NetUtil_TS_Get_ms()

Application-defined function to get the current millisecond timestamp.

FILES

net_util.h/net_bsp.c

PROTOTYPE

```
NET_TS_MS NetUtil_TS_Get_ms (void);
```

ARGUMENTS

None.

RETURNED VALUE

Current millisecond timestamp.

REQUIRED CONFIGURATION

None.

NOTES / WARNINGS

The application is responsible for providing a millisecond timestamp clock with adequate resolution and range to satisfy the minimum/maximum TCP RTO values (see 'net_bsp.c NetUtil_TS_Get_ms() Note #1a').

µC/TCP-IP includes µC/OS-II and µC/OS-III implementations which use their OS tick counters as the source for the millisecond timestamp. These implementations can be found in the following directories:

\Micrium\Software\uC-TCPIP-V2\BSP\Template\OS\uCOS-II

\Micrium\Software\uC-TCPIP-V2\BSP\Template\OS\uCOS-III

C-19 BSD FUNCTIONS

C-19-1 accept() (TCP)

Wait for new socket connections on a listening server socket. See section C-14-1 on page 808 for more information.

FILES

net_bsd.h/net_bsd.c

PROTOTYPE

```
int accept(int          sock_id,
        struct sockaddr *paddr_remote,
        socklen_t       *paddr_len);
```

C-19-2 bind() (TCP/UDP)

Assign network addresses to sockets. See section C-14-2 on page 810 for more information.

FILES

net_bsd.h/net_bsd.c

PROTOTYPE

```
int bind(int            sock_id,
        struct sockaddr *paddr_local,
        socklen_t       addr_len);
```

C-19-3 close() (TCP/UDP)

Terminate communication and free a socket. See section C-14-25 on page 857 for more information.

FILES

net_bsd.h/net_bsd.c

PROTOTYPE

```
int close(int sock_id);
```

C-19-4 connect() (TCP/UDP)

Connect a local socket to a remote socket address. See section C-14-26 on page 859 for more information.

FILES

net_bsd.h/net_bsd.c

PROTOTYPE

```
int connect(int           sock_id,
            struct sockaddr *paddr_remote,
            socklen_t       addr_len);
```

C-19-5 FD_CLR() (TCP/UDP)

Remove a socket file descriptor ID as a member of a file descriptor set. See section C-14-27 on page 862 for more information.

FILES

net_bsd.h

PROTOTYPE

```
FD_CLR(fd, fdsetp);
```

REQUIRED CONFIGURATION

Available only if **NET_BSD_CFG_API_EN** is enabled (see section D-17-1 on page 983).

C-19-6 FD_ISSET() (TCP/UDP)

Check if a socket file descriptor ID is a member of a file descriptor set. See section C-14-30 on page 866 for more information.

FILES

net_bsd.h

PROTOTYPE

```
FD_ISSET(fd, fdsetp);
```

REQUIRED CONFIGURATION

Available only if **NET_BSD_CFG_API_EN** is enabled (see section D-17-1 on page 983).

C-19-7 FD_SET() (TCP/UDP)

Add a socket file descriptor ID as a member of a file descriptor set. See section C-14-31 on page 868 for more information.

FILES

net_bsd.h

PROTOTYPE

```
FD_SET(fd, fdsetp);
```

REQUIRED CONFIGURATION

Available only if **NET_BSD_CFG_API_EN** is enabled (see section D-17-1 on page 983).

C-19-8 FD_ZERO() (TCP/UDP)

Initialize/zero-clear a file descriptor set. See section C-14-29 on page 865 for more information.

FILES

net_bsd.h

PROTOTYPE

```
FD_ZERO(fdsetp);
```

REQUIRED CONFIGURATION

Available only if **NET_BSD_CFG_API_EN** is enabled (see section D-17-1 on page 983).

C-19-9 getsockopt() (TCP/UDP)

Get a specific option value on a specific TCP socket. See section C-14-36 on page 878 for more information.

FILES

net_bsd.h/net_bsd.c

PROTOTYPE

```
int getsockopt(int        sock_id,
               int        level,
               int        opt_name,
               void       *popt_val,
               sock_len_t *popt_len);
```

ARGUMENTS

sock_id   This is the socket ID returned by **NetSock_Open()/socket()** when the socket was created *or* by **NetSock_Accept()/accept()** when a connection was accepted.

level   Protocol level from which to retrieve the socket option.

opt_name   Socket option to set the value.

popt_val   Pointer to the socket option value to set.

popt_len   Pointer to the socket option value to get.

RETURNED VALUE

0, if successful;

−1, otherwise.

REQUIRED CONFIGURATION

getsockopt() is available only if either NET_CFG_TRANSPORT_LAYER_SEL is configured for TCP (see section D-12-1 on page 972) and/or NET_UDP_CFG_APP_API_SEL is configured for sockets (see section D-13-1 on page 973), and if NET_BSD_CFG_API_EN is enabled (see section D-17-1 on page 983).

NOTES / WARNINGS

The supported options are:

- Protocol level SOL_SOCKET:

    - SO_TYPE

    - SO_KEEPALIVE

    - SO_ACCEPTCONN

    - SO_SNDBUF / SO_RCVBUF

    - SO_SNDTIMEO / SO_RCVTIMEO

- Protocol level IPPROTO_IP:

    - IP_TOS

    - IP_TTL

    - IP_RECVIF

- Protocol level IPPROTO_TCP:

    - TCP_NODELAY

    - TCP_KEEPCNT

    - TCP_KEEPIDLE

    - TCP_INTVL

C-19-10 htonl()

Convert 32-bit integer values from CPU host-order to network-order. See section C-18-2 on page 933 for more information.

FILES

net_bsd.h

PROTOTYPE

```
htonl(val);
```

REQUIRED CONFIGURATION

Available only if **NET_BSD_CFG_API_EN** is enabled (see section D-17-1 on page 983).

C-19-11 htons()

Convert 16-bit integer values from CPU host-order to network-order. See section C-18-1 on page 932 for more information.

FILES

net_bsd.h

PROTOTYPE

```
htons(val);
```

C-19-12 inet_addr() (IPv4)

Convert a string of an IPv4 address in dotted-decimal notation to an IPv4 address in host-order. See section C-4-3 on page 689 for more information.

FILES

net_bsd.h/net_bsd.c

PROTOTYPE

```
in_addr_t inet_addr(char *paddr);
```

ARGUMENTS

paddr   Pointer to an ASCII string that contains a dotted-decimal IPv4 address.

RETURNED VALUE

Returns the IPv4 address represented by ASCII string in host-order, if no errors.

−1 (i.e., 0xFFFFFFFF), otherwise.

REQUIRED CONFIGURATION

Available only if either NET_CFG_TRANSPORT_LAYER_SEL is configured for TCP (see section D-12-1 on page 972) and/or NET_UDP_CFG_APP_API_SEL is configured for sockets (see section D-13-1 on page 973) *and* if NET_BSD_CFG_API_EN is enabled (see section D-17-1 on page 983).

NOTES / WARNINGS

RFC 1983 states that "dotted decimal notation… refers [to] IP addresses of the form A.B.C.D; where each letter represents, in decimal, one byte of a four byte IP address". In other words, the dotted-decimal notation separates four decimal byte values by the dot, or period, character ('.'). Each decimal value represents one byte of the IP address starting with the most significant byte in network order.

IPv4 Address Examples

DOTTED DECIMAL NOTATION	HEXADECIMAL EQUIVALENT
127.0.0.1	0x7F000001
192.168.1.64	0xC0A80140
255.255.255.0	0xFFFFFF00
MSB .... LSB	MSB .... LSB

MSB   Most Significant Byte in Dotted-Decimal IP Address

LSB   Least Significant Byte in Dotted-Decimal IP Address

The IPv4 dotted-decimal ASCII string *must* include *only* decimal values and the dot, or period, character ('.'); all other characters are trapped as invalid, including any leading or trailing characters. The ASCII string *must* include exactly four decimal values separated by exactly three dot characters. Each decimal value *must not* exceed the maximum byte value (i.e., 255), or exceed the maximum number of digits for each byte (i.e., 3) including any leading zeros.

C-19-13 inet_aton() (IPv4)

Convert an IPv4 address in ASCII dotted-decimal notation to a network protocol IPv4 address in network-order. See section C-4-3 on page 689 for more information.

FILES

net_bsd.h/net_bsd.c

PROTOTYPE

```
int inet_aton(      char    *paddr_in,
            struct in_addr *paddr);
```

ARGUMENTS

paddr_in   Pointer to an ASCII string that contains a dotted-decimal IPv4 address.

paddr   Pointer to an IPv4 address that will receive the converted address.

RETURNED VALUE

1, if no errors.

0, otherwise.

REQUIRED CONFIGURATION

Available only if either NET_CFG_TRANSPORT_LAYER_SEL is configured for TCP (see section D-12-1 on page 972) and/or NET_UDP_CFG_APP_API_SEL is configured for sockets (see section D-13-1 on page 973) *and* if NET_BSD_CFG_API_EN is enabled (see section D-17-1 on page 983).

NOTES / WARNINGS

RFC 1983 states that "dotted decimal notation... refers [to] IP addresses of the form A.B.C.D; where each letter represents, in decimal, one byte of a four-byte IP address". In other words, the dotted-decimal notation separates four decimal byte values by the dot, or period, character ('.'). Each decimal value represents one byte of the IP address starting with the most significant byte in network order.

IPv4 Address Examples

DOTTED DECIMAL NOTATION	HEXADECIMAL EQUIVALENT
127.0.0.1	0x7F000001
192.168.1.64	0xC0A80140
255.255.255.0	0xFFFFFF00
MSB .... LSB	MSB .... LSB

MSB   Most Significant Byte in Dotted-Decimal IP Address

LSB   Least Significant Byte in Dotted-Decimal IP Address

Values specified using IPv4 dotted decimal notation take one of the following forms:

a.b.c.d   When a four parts address is specified, each shall be interpreted as a byte of data and assigned, from left to right, to the four bytes of an internet address.

a.b.c   When three parts address is specified, the last part shall be interpreted as a 16-bit quantity and placed in the rightmost two bytes of the network address. This makes the three part address format convenient for specifying Class B network addresses as "128.net.host".

a.b   When two parts address is specified, the last part shall be interpreted as a 24-bit quantity and placed in the rightmost three bytes of the network address. This makes the two part address format convenient for specifying Class A network addresses as "net.host".

a   When one part address is specified, the value shall be stored directly in the network address without any byte rearrangement.

The dotted-decimal ASCII string MUST:

■ Include only decimal values and the dot, or period, character ("."). All other characters are trapped as invalid, including any leading or trailing characters.

■ Included up to four decimal values, separated bu UP to three dot characters.

■ Ensure that each decimal value does not exceed the maximum value for its form:

■ a.b.c.d - 255.255.255.255

■ a.b.c   - 255.255.255.65535

■ a.b   - 255.16777215

■ a   - 4294967295

■ Ensure that each decimal value does NOT exceed leading zeros.

C-19-14 inet_ntoa() (IPv4)

Convert an IPv4 address in host-order into an IPv4 dotted-decimal notation ASCII string. See section C-4-1 on page 685 for more information.

FILES

net_bsd.h/net_bsd.c

PROTOTYPE

```
char *inet_ntoa(struct in_addr addr);
```

ARGUMENTS

in_addr   IPv4 address (in host-order).

RETURNED VALUE

Pointer to ASCII string of converted IPv4 address (see Notes / Warnings), if no errors.

Pointer to NULL, otherwise.

REQUIRED CONFIGURATION

Available only if either NET_CFG_TRANSPORT_LAYER_SEL is configured for TCP (see section D-12-1 on page 972) and/or NET_UDP_CFG_APP_API_SEL is configured for sockets (see section D-13-1 on page 973) *and* if NET_BSD_CFG_API_EN is enabled (see section D-17-1 on page 983).

RFC 1983 states that "dotted decimal notation... refers [to] IP addresses of the form A.B.C.D; where each letter represents, in decimal, one byte of a four-byte IP address". In other words, the dotted-decimal notation separates four decimal byte values by the dot, or period, character ('.'). Each decimal value represents one byte of the IP address starting with the most significant byte in network order.

IPv4 Address Examples

DOTTED DECIMAL NOTATION	HEXADECIMAL EQUIVALENT
127.0.0.1	0x7F000001
192.168.1.64	0xC0A80140
255.255.255.0	0xFFFFFF00
MSB .... LSB	MSB .... LSB

MSB   Most Significant Byte in Dotted-Decimal IP Address

LSB   Least Significant Byte in Dotted-Decimal IP Address

Since the returned ASCII string is stored in a single, global ASCII string array, this function is *not* reentrant or thread-safe. Therefore, the returned string should be copied as soon as possible before other calls to inet_ntoa() are needed.

C-19-15 listen() (TCP)

Set a socket to accept incoming connections. See section C-14-34 on page 873 for more information.

FILES

net_bsd.h/net_bsd.c

PROTOTYPE

```
int listen(int sock_id,
           int sock_q_size);
```

C-19-16 ntohl()

Convert 32-bit integer values from network-order to CPU host-order. See section C-18-4 on page 935 for more information.

FILES

net_bsd.h

PROTOTYPE

```
ntohl(val);
```

REQUIRED CONFIGURATION

Available only if **NET_BSD_CFG_API_EN** is enabled (see section D-17-1 on page 983).

C-19-17 ntohs()

Convert 16-bit integer values from network-order to CPU host-order. See section C-18-3 on page 934 for more information.

FILES

net_bsd.h

PROTOTYPE

```
ntohs(val);
```

REQUIRED CONFIGURATION

Available only if NET_BSD_CFG_API_EN is enabled (see section D-17-1 on page 983).

C-19-18 recv() / recvfrom() (TCP/UDP)

Copy up to a specified number of bytes received from a remote socket into an application memory buffer. See section C-14-40 on page 884 for more information.

FILES

net_bsd.h/net_bsd.c

PROTOTYPES

```
ssize_t recv(int      sock_id,
             void    *pdata_buf,
            _size_t  data_buf_len,
             int      flags);

ssize_t recvfrom(int                sock_id,
                 void              *pdata_buf,
                _size_t            data_buf_len,
                 int                flags,
                 struct sockaddr  *paddr_remote,
                 socklen_t         *paddr_len);
```

C-19-19 select() (TCP/UDP)

Check if any sockets are ready for available read or write operations or error conditions. See section C-14-41 "NetSock_Sel() / select() (TCP/UDP)" on page 888 for more information.

FILES

net_bsd.h/net_bsd.c

PROTOTYPE

```
int select(int          desc_nbr_max,
           struct fd_set *pdesc_rd,
           struct fd_set *pdesc_wr,
           struct fd_set *pdesc_err,
           struct timeval *ptimeout);
```

C-19-20 send() / sendto() (TCP/UDP)

Copy bytes from an application memory buffer into a socket to send to a remote socket. See section C-14-42 on page 891 for more information.

FILES

net_bsd.h/net_bsd.c

PROTOTYPES

```
ssize_t send (int     sock_id,
              void    *p_data,
              _size_t data_len,
              int     flags);

ssize_t sendto(int              sock_id,
               void             *p_data,
               _size_t          data_len,
               int              flags,
               struct sockaddr *paddr_remote,
               socklen_t        addr_len);
```

C-19-21 setsockopt() (TCP/UDP)

Set a specific option on a specific TCP socket. See section C-14-37 on page 880 for more information.

See section C-14-37 on page 880

FILES

net_bsd.h/net_bsd.c

PROTOTYPE

```
int setsockopt(int        sock_id,
               int        level,
               int        opt_name,
               void       *popt_val,
               sock_len_t opt_len);
```

ARGUMENTS

sock_id   This is the socket ID returned by **NetSock_Open()/socket()** when the socket was created *or* by **NetSock_Accept()/accept()** when a connection was accepted.

level   Protocol level from which to retrieve the socket option.

opt_name   Socket option to set the value.

popt_val   Pointer to the socket option value to set.

opt_len   Option length.

RETURNED VALUE

0, if successful;

−1, otherwise.

REQUIRED CONFIGURATION

setsockopt( ) is available only if either **NET_CFG_TRANSPORT_LAYER_SEL** is configured for TCP (see section D-12-1 on page 972) and/or **NET_UDP_CFG_APP_API_SEL** is configured for sockets (see section D-13-1 on page 973), and if **NET_BSD_CFG_API_EN** is enabled (see section D-17-1 on page 983).

NOTES / WARNINGS

The supported options are:

■ Protocol level **SOL_SOCKET**:

■ SO_KEEPALIVE

■ SO_SNDBUF / SO_RCVBUF

■ SO_SNDTIMEO / SO_RCVTIMEO

■ Protocol level **IPPROTO_IP**:

■ IP_TOS

■ IP_TTL

■ Protocol level **IPPROTO_TCP**:

■ TCP_NODELAY

■ TCP_KEEPCNT

■ TCP_KEEPIDLE

■ TCP_INTVL

C-19-22 socket() (TCP/UDP)

Create a datagram (i.e., UDP) or stream (i.e., TCP) type socket. See section C-14-35 on page 875 for more information.

FILES

net_bsd.h/net_bsd.c

PROTOTYPE

```
int socket(int protocol_family,
           int sock_type,
           int protocol);
```

µC/TCP-IP Configuration and Optimization

µC/TCP-IP is configurable at compile time via approximately 70 **#defines** in an application's **net_cfg.h** and **app_cfg.h** files. µC/TCP-IP uses **#defines** because they allow code and data sizes to be scaled at compile time based on enabled features and the configured number of network objects. This allows the ROM and RAM footprints of µC/TCP-IP to be adjusted based on application requirements.

Most of the **#defines** should be configured with the default configuration values. A handful of values may likely never change because there is currently only one configuration choice available. This leaves approximately a dozen values that should be configured with values that may deviate from the default configuration.

It is recommended that the configuration process begins with the recommended or default configuration values which are shown in **bold**.

Unlike Appendix C on page 649, the sections in this appendix are organized following the order in µC/TCP-IP's template configuration file, **net_cfg.h**.

D-1 NETWORK CONFIGURATION

D-1-1 NET_CFG_INIT_CFG_VALS

NET_CFG_INIT_CFG_VALS is used to determine whether internal TCP/IP parameters are set to default values or are set by the user:

NET_INIT_CFG_VALS_DFLT   μC/TCP-IP initializes all parameters with default values

NET_INIT_CFG_VALS_APP_INIT   Application initializes all μC/TCP-IP parameters with application-specific values

NET_INIT_CFG_VALS_DFLT

Configure μC/TCP-IP's network parameters with default values. The application only needs to call **Net_Init()** to initialize both μC/TCP-IP and its configurable parameters. This configuration is highly recommended since configuring network parameters requires in-depth knowledge of the protocol stack. In fact, most references recommend many of the default values we have selected.

Parameter	Units	Min	Max	Default	Configuration Function
Interface's Network Buffer Low Threshold	% of the Total Number of an Interface's Network Buffers	5%	50%	5%	NetDbg_CfgRsrcBufThLo()
Interface's Network Buffer Low Threshold Hysteresis	% of the Total Number of an Interface's Network Buffers	0%	15%	3%	NetDbg_CfgRsrcBufThLo()
Interface's Large Receive Buffer Low Threshold	% of the Total Number of an Interface's Large Receive Buffers	5%	50%	5%	NetDbg_CfgRsrcBufRxLargeThLo()
Interface's Large Receive Buffer Low Threshold Hysteresis	% of the Total Number of an Interface's Large Receive Buffers	0%	15%	3%	NetDbg_CfgRsrcBufRxLargeThLo()
Interface's Small Transmit Buffer Low Threshold	% of the Total Number of an Interface's Small Transmit Buffers	5%	50%	5%	NetDbg_CfgRsrcBufTxSmallThLo()

Parameter	Units	Min	Max	Default	Configuration Function
Interface's Small Transmit Buffer Low Threshold Hysteresis	% of the Total Number of an Interface's Small Transmit Buffers	0%	15%	3%	`NetDbg_CfgRsrcBufTxSmallThLo()`
Interface's Large Transmit Buffer Low Threshold	% of the Total Number of an Interface's Large Transmit Buffers	5%	50%	5%	`NetDbg_CfgRsrcBufTxLargeThLo()`
Interface's Large Transmit Buffer Low Threshold Hysteresis	% of the Total Number of an Interface's Large Transmit Buffers	0%	15%	3%	`NetDbg_CfgRsrcBufTxLargeThLo()`
Network Timer Low Threshold	% of the Total Number of Network Timers	5%	50%	5%	`NetDbg_CfgRsrcTmrLoTh()`
Network Timer Low Threshold Hysteresis	% of the Total Number of Network Timers	0%	15%	3%	`NetDbg_CfgRsrcTmrLoTh()`
Network Connection Low Threshold	% of the Total Number of Network Connections	5%	50%	5%	`NetDbg_CfgRsrcConnLoTh()`
Network Connection Low Threshold Hysteresis	% of the Total Number of Network Connections	0%	15%	3%	`NetDbg_CfgRsrcConnLoTh()`
ARP Cache Low Threshold	% of the Total Number of ARP Caches	5%	50%	5%	`NetDbg_CfgRsrcARP_CacheLoTh()`
ARP Cache Low Threshold Hysteresis	% of the Total Number of ARP Caches	0%	15%	3%	`NetDbg_CfgRsrcARP_CacheLoTh()`
TCP Connection Low Threshold	% of the Total Number of TCP Connections	5%	50%	5%	`NetDbg_CfgRsrcTCP_ConnLoTh()`
TCP Connection Low Threshold Hysteresis	% of the Total Number of TCP Connections	0%	15%	3%	`NetDbg_CfgRsrcTCP_ConnLoTh()`
Socket Low Threshold	% of the Total Number of Sockets	5%	50%	5%	`NetDbg_CfgRsrcSockLoTh()`
Socket Low Threshold Hysteresis	% of the Total Number of Sockets	0%	15%	3%	`NetDbg_CfgRsrcSockLoTh()`
Resource Monitor Task Time	Seconds	1	600	60	`NetDbg_CfgMonTaskTime()`
Network Connection Accessed Threshold	Number of Network Connections	10	65000	100	`NetConn_CfgAccessTh()`

Parameter	Units	Min	Max	Default	Configuration Function
Network Interface Physical Link Monitor Period	Milliseconds	50	60000	250	`NetIF_CfgPhyLinkPeriod()`
Network Interface Performance Monitor Period	Milliseconds	50	60000	250	`NetIF_CfgPerfMonPeriod()`
ARP Cache Timeout	Seconds	60	600	600	`NetARP_CfgCacheTimeout()`
ARP Cache Accessed Threshold	Number of ARP Caches	100	65000	100	`NetARP_CfgCacheAccessedTh()`
ARP Request Timeout	Seconds	1	10	5	`NetARP_CfgReqTimeout()`
ARP Request Maximum Number of Retries	Maximum Number of Transmitted ARP Request Retries	0	5	3	`NetARP_CfgReqMaxRetries()`
IP Receive Fragments Reassembly Timeout	Seconds	1	15	5	`NetIP_CfgFragReasmTimeout()`
ICMP Transmit Source Quench Threshold	Number of Transmitted ICMP Source Quenches	1	100	5	`NetICMP_CfgTxSrcQuenchTh()`

Table D-1 µC/TCP-IP Internal Configuration Parameters

NET_INIT_CFG_VALS_APP_INIT

It is possible to change the parameters listed in by calling the above configuration functions. These values could be stored in non-volatile memory and recalled at power up (*e.g.*, using EEPROM or battery-backed RAM) by the application. Similarly the values could be hard-coded directly in the application. Regardless of how the application configures the values, if this option is selected, the application must initialize **all** of the above configuration parameters using the configuration functions listed above.

Alternatively, the application could call **Net_InitDflt()** to initialize all of the internal configuration parameters to their default values and then call the configuration functions for only the values to be modified.

D-1-2 **NET_CFG_OPTIMIZE**

Select portions of µC/TCP-IP code may be optimized for better performance or for smallest code size by configuring NET_CFG_OPTIMIZE:

NET_OPTIMIZE_SPD   Optimizes µC/TCP-IP for best speed performance

NET_OPTIMIZE_SIZE   Optimizes µC/TCP-IP for best binary image size

D-1-3 **NET_CFG_OPTIMIZE_ASM_EN**

Select portions of µC/TCP-IP code may even call optimized assembly functions by configuring NET_CFG_OPTIMIZE_ASM_EN:

DEF_DISABLED   No optimized assembly files/functions are included in the µC/TCP-IP build

   or

DEF_ENABLED   Optimized assembly files/functions are included in the µC/TCP-IP build

D-1-4 **NET_CFG_BUILD_LIB_EN**

µC/TCP-IP can be compiled on some toolchains into a linkable library by configuring NET_CFG_BUILD_LIB_EN:

DEF_DISABLED   µC/TCP-IP **not** compiled as a linkable library

   or

DEF_ENABLED   Build µC/TCP-IP as a linkable library

D-2 DEBUG CONFIGURATION

A fair amount of code in µC/TCP-IP has been included to simplify debugging. There are several configuration constants used to aid debugging.

D-2-1 NET_DBG_CFG_INFO_EN

NET_DBG_CFG_INFO_EN is used to enable/disable µC/TCP-IP debug information:

■ Internal constants assigned to global variables

■ Internal variable data sizes calculated and assigned to global variables

NET_DBG_CFG_INFO_EN can be set to either **DEF_DISABLED** or DEF_ENABLED.

D-2-2 NET_DBG_CFG_STATUS_EN

NET_DBG_CFG_STATUS_EN is used to enable/disable µC/TCP-IP run-time status information:

■ Internal resource usage – low or lost resources

■ Internal faults or errors

NET_DBG_CFG_STATUS_EN can be set to either **DEF_DISABLED** or DEF_ENABLED.

D-2-3 NET_DBG_CFG_MEM_CLR_EN

NET_DBG_CFG_MEM_CLR_EN is used to clear internal network data structures when allocated or de-allocated. By clearing, all bytes in internal data structures are set to '0' or to default initialization values. NET_DBG_CFG_MEM_CLR_EN can be set to either **DEF_DISABLED** or DEF_ENABLED. This configuration is typically set it to DEF_DISABLED unless the contents of the internal network data structures need to be examined for debugging purposes. Having the internal network data structures cleared generally helps to differentiate between "proper" data and "pollution".

D-2-4 NET_DBG_CFG_TEST_EN

NET_DBG_CFG_TEST_EN is used internally for testing/debugging purposes and can be set to either **DEF_DISABLED** or DEF_ENABLED.

D-3 ARGUMENT CHECKING CONFIGURATION

Most functions in µC/TCP-IP include code to validate arguments that are passed to it. Specifically, µC/TCP-IP checks to see if passed pointers are **NULL**, if arguments are within valid ranges, etc. The following constants configure additional argument checking.

D-3-1 NET_ERR_CFG_ARG_CHK_EXT_EN

NET_ERR_CFG_ARG_CHK_EXT_EN allows code to be generated to check arguments for functions that can be called by the user and, for functions which are internal but receive arguments from an API that the user can call. Also, enabling this check verifies that µC/TCP-IP is initialized before API tasks and functions perform the desired function.

NET_ERR_CFG_ARG_CHK_EXT_EN can be set to either DEF_DISABLED or **DEF_ENABLED**.

D-3-2 NET_ERR_CFG_ARG_CHK_DBG_EN

NET_ERR_CFG_ARG_CHK_DBG_EN allows code to be generated which checks to make sure that pointers passed to functions are not NULL, and that arguments are within range, etc. NET_ERR_CFG_ARG_CHK_DBG_EN can be set to either **DEF_DISABLED** or DEF_ENABLED.

D-4 NETWORK COUNTER CONFIGURATION

µC/TCP-IP contains code that increments counters to keep track of statistics such as the number of packets received, the number of packets transmitted, etc. Also, µC/TCP-IP contains counters that are incremented when error conditions are detected. The following constants enable or disable network counters.

D-4-1 NET_CTR_CFG_STAT_EN

NET_CTR_CFG_STAT_EN determines whether the code and data space used to keep track of statistics will be included. NET_CTR_CFG_STAT_EN can be set to either **DEF_DISABLED** or **DEF_ENABLED**.

D-4-2 NET_CTR_CFG_ERR_EN

NET_CTR_CFG_ERR_EN determines whether the code and data space used to keep track of errors will be included. NET_CTR_CFG_ERR_EN can be set to either **DEF_DISABLED** or DEF_ENABLED.

D-5 NETWORK TIMER CONFIGURATION

μC/TCP-IP manages software timers used to keep track of timeouts and execute callback functions when needed.

D-5-1 NET_TMR_CFG_NBR_TMR

NET_TMR_CFG_NBR_TMR determines the number of timers that μC/TCP-IP will be managing. Of course, the number of timers affect the amount of RAM required by μC/TCP-IP. Each timer requires 12 bytes plus 4 pointers. Timers are required for:

■ The Network Debug Monitor task   1 total

■ The Network Performance Monitor   1 total

■ The Network Link State Handler   1 total

■ Each ARP cache entry   1 per ARP cache

■ Each IP fragment reassembly   1 per IP fragment chain

■ Each TCP connection   7 per TCP connection

It is recommended to set NET_TMR_CFG_NBR_TMR with at least **12 timers**, but a better starting point may be to allocate the maximum number of timers for all resources.

For instance, if the Network Debug Monitor task is enabled (see section 20-2 "Network Debug Monitor Task" on page 526), 20 ARP caches are configured (NET_ARP_CFG_NBR_CACHE = 20), & 10 TCP connections are configured (NET_TCP_CFG_NBR_CONN = 10); the maximum number of timers for these resources is 1 for the Network Debug Monitor task, 1 for the Network Performance Monitor, 1 for the Link State Handler, (20 * 1) for the ARP caches and, (10 * 7) for TCP connections:

```
# Timers = 1 + 1 + 1 + (20 * 1) + (10 * 7) = 93
```

D-5-2 NET_TMR_CFG_TASK_FREQ

NET_TMR_CFG_TASK_FREQ determines how often (in Hz) network timers are to be updated. This value *must not* be configured as a floating-point number. NET_TMR_CFG_TASK_FREQ is typically set to **10 Hz**.

D-6 NETWORK BUFFER CONFIGURATION

μC/TCP-IP manages Network Buffers to read data to and from network applications and network devices. Network Buffers are specially configured with network devices as described in section 14-1 "Buffer Management" on page 303.

D-7 NETWORK INTERFACE LAYER CONFIGURATION

D-7-1 NET_IF_CFG_MAX_NBR_IF

NET_IF_CFG_MAX_NBR_IF determines the maximum number of network interfaces that µC/TCP-IP may create at run-time. The default value of **1** is for a single network interface.

D-7-2 NET_IF_CFG_LOOPBACK_EN

NET_IF_CFG_LOOPBACK_EN determines whether the code and data space used to support the loopback interface for internal-only communication only will be included. NET_IF_CFG_LOOPBACK_EN can be set to either **DEF_DISABLED** or DEF_ENABLED.

D-7-3 NET_IF_CFG_ETHER_EN

NET_IF_CFG_ETHER_EN determines whether the code and data space used to support Ethernet interfaces and devices will be included. NET_IF_CFG_ETHER_EN can be set to either DEF_DISABLED or **DEF_ENABLED**, but must be enabled if the target expects to communicate over Ethernet networks.

D-7-4 NET_IF_CFG_WIFI_EN

NET_IF_CFG_WIFI_EN determines whether the code and data space used to support wireless interfaces and devices will be included. NET_IF_CFG_WIFI_EN can be set to either DEF_DISABLED or **DEF_ENABLED**, but must be enabled if the target expects to communicate over wireless networks.

D-7-5 NET_IF_CFG_ADDR_FLTR_EN

NET_IF_CFG_ADDR_FLTR_EN determines whether address filtering is enabled or not:

DEF_DISABLED   Addresses are *not* filtered

or

DEF_ENABLED   Addresses are filtered

D-7-6 NET_IF_CFG_TX_SUSPEND_TIMEOUT_MS

NET_IF_CFG_TX_SUSPEND_TIMEOUT_MS configures the network interface transmit suspend timeout value. The value is specified in integer milliseconds. It is recommended to initially set NET_IF_CFG_TX_SUSPEND_TIMEOUT_MS with a value of **1 millisecond**.

D-8 ARP (ADDRESS RESOLUTION PROTOCOL) CONFIGURATION

ARP is only required for some network interfaces such as Ethernet.

D-8-1 NET_ARP_CFG_HW_TYPE

The current version of μC/TCP-IP only supports Ethernet-type networks, and thus NET_ARP_CFG_HW_TYPE should *always* be set to **NET_ARP_HW_TYPE_ETHER**.

D-8-2 NET_ARP_CFG_PROTOCOL_TYPE

The current version of μC/TCP-IP only supports IPv4, and thus NET_ARP_CFG_PROTOCOL_TYPE should *always* be set to **NET_ARP_PROTOCOL_TYPE_IP_V4**.

D-8-3 NET_ARP_CFG_NBR_CACHE

ARP caches the mapping of IP addresses to physical (i.e., MAC) addresses. NET_ARP_CFG_NBR_CACHE configures the number of ARP cache entries. Each cache entry requires approximately 18 bytes of RAM, plus five pointers, plus a hardware address and protocol address (10 bytes assuming Ethernet interfaces and IPv4 addresses).

The number of ARP caches required by the application depends on how many different hosts are expected to communicate. If the application *only* communicates with hosts on remote networks via the local network's default gateway (i.e., router), then only a single ARP cache needs to be configured.

To test µC/TCP-IP with a smaller network, a default number of 3 ARP caches should be sufficient.

D-8-4 NET_ARP_CFG_ADDR_FLTR_EN

NET_ARP_CFG_ADDR_FLTR_EN determines whether to enable address filtering:

DEF_DISABLED   Addresses are *not* filtered

   or

DEF_ENABLED   Addresses are filtered

D-9 IP (INTERNET PROTOCOL) CONFIGURATION

D-9-1 NET_IP_CFG_IF_MAX_NBR_ADDR

NET_IP_CFG_IF_MAX_NBR_ADDR determines the maximum number of IP addresses that may be configured per network interface at run-time. It is recommended to set NET_IP_CFG_IF_MAX_NBR_ADDR to the initial, default value of **1 IP address** per network interface and increased if the µC/TCP-IP target requires more addresses on each interface.

D-9-2 NET_IP_CFG_MULTICAST_SEL

NET_IP_CFG_MULTICAST_SEL is used to determine the IP multicast support level. The allowable values for this parameter are:

NET_IP_MULTICAST_SEL_NONE   No multicasting

NET_IP_MULTICAST_SEL_TX   Transmit multicasting only

NET_IP_MULTICAST_SEL_TX_RX   Transmit and receive multicasting

D-10 ICMP (INTERNET CONTROL MESSAGE PROTOCOL) CONFIGURATION

D-10-1 NET_ICMP_CFG_TX_SRC_QUENCH_EN

ICMP transmits ICMP source quench messages to other hosts when the Network Resources are low (see section 20-2 "Network Debug Monitor Task" on page 526). NET_ICMP_CFG_TX_SRC_QUENCH_EN can be set to either:

DEF_DISABLED   ICMP does not transmit any Source Quenches

or

DEF_ENABLED   ICMP transmits Source Quenches when necessary

D-10-2 NET_ICMP_CFG_TX_SRC_QUENCH_NBR

NET_ICMP_CFG_TX_SRC_QUENCH_NBR configures the number of ICMP transmit source quench entries. Each source quench entry requires approximately **12** bytes of RAM plus two pointers.

The number of entries depends on the number of different hosts to communicate with. It is recommended to set NET_ICMP_CFG_TX_SRC_QUENCH_NBR with an initial value of **5** and adjusted if the µC/TCP-IP target communicates with more or less hosts.

D-11 IGMP (INTERNET GROUP MANAGEMENT PROTOCOL) CONFIGURATION

D-11-1 NET_IGMP_CFG_MAX_NBR_HOST_GRP

`NET_IGMP_CFG_MAX_NBR_HOST_GRP` configures the maximum number of IGMP host groups that may be joined at any one time. Each group entry requires approximately **12** bytes of RAM, plus three pointers, plus a protocol address (**4** bytes assuming IPv4 address).

The number of IGMP host groups required by the application depends on how many host groups are expected to be joined at a given time. Since each configured multicast address requires its own IGMP host group, it is recommended to configure at least one host group per multicast address used by the application, plus one additional host group. Thus for a single multicast address, it is recommended to set `NET_IGMP_CFG_MAX_NBR_HOST_GRP` with an initial value of **2**.

D-12 TRANSPORT LAYER CONFIGURATION

D-12-1 NET_CFG_TRANSPORT_LAYER_SEL

µC/TCP-IP allows you to include code for either UDP alone or for both UDP and TCP. Most application software requires TCP as well as UDP. However, enabling UDP only reduces both the code and data size required by µC/TCP-IP. `NET_CFG_TRANSPORT_LAYER_SEL` can be set to either:

`NET_TRANSPORT_LAYER_SEL_UDP_TCP`   UDP and TCP transport layers included

or

`NET_TRANSPORT_LAYER_SEL_UDP`   Only UDP transport layer included

D-13 UDP (USER DATAGRAM PROTOCOL) CONFIGURATION

D-13-1 NET_UDP_CFG_APP_API_SEL

NET_UDP_CFG_APP_API_SEL is used to determine where to send the de-multiplexed UDP datagram. Specifically, the datagram may be sent to the socket layer, to a function at the application level, or both. NET_UDP_CFG_APP_API_SEL can be set to one of the following values:

NET_UDP_APP_API_SEL_SOCK   De-multiplex receive datagrams to socket layer only

NET_UDP_APP_API_SEL_APP   De-multiplex receive datagrams to the application only

NET_UDP_APP_API_SEL_SOCK_APP   De-multiplex receive datagrams to socket layer first, then to the application

If either NET_UDP_APP_API_SEL_APP or NET_UDP_APP_API_SEL_SOCK_APP is configured, the application must define NetUDP_RxAppDataHandler() to de-multiplex receive datagrams by the application (see section C-17-2 on page 927).

D-13-2 NET_UDP_CFG_RX_CHK_SUM_DISCARD_EN

NET_UDP_CFG_RX_CHK_SUM_DISCARD_EN is used to determine whether received UDP packets without a valid checksum are discarded or are handled and processed. Before a UDP Datagram Check-Sum is validated, it is necessary to check whether the UDP datagram was transmitted with or without a computed Check-Sum (see RFC #768, Section 'Fields: Checksum').

NET_UDP_CFG_RX_CHK_SUM_DISCARD_EN can be set to either:

DEF_DISABLED   UDP Layer processes but flags all UDP datagrams received without a checksum so that "an application may optionally discard datagrams without checksums" (see RFC #1122, Section 4.1.3.4).

or

DEF_ENABLED   All UDP datagrams received without a checksum are discarded.

D-13-3 NET_UDP_CFG_TX_CHK_SUM_EN

NET_UDP_CFG_TX_CHK_SUM_EN is used to determine whether UDP checksums are computed for transmission to other hosts. An application MAY optionally be able to control whether a UDP checksum will be generated (see RFC #1122, Section 4.1.3.4).

NET_UDP_CFG_TX_CHK_SUM_EN can be set to either:

DEF_DISABLED   All UDP datagrams are transmitted without a computed checksum

   or

DEF_ENABLED   All UDP datagrams are transmitted with a computed checksum

D-14 TCP (TRANSPORT CONTROL PROTOCOL) CONFIGURATION

D-14-1 NET_TCP_CFG_NBR_CONN

NET_TCP_CFG_NBR_CONN configures the maximum number of TCP connections that µC/TCP-IP can handle concurrently. This number depends entirely on how many simultaneous TCP connections the application requires. Each TCP connection requires approximately **220** bytes of RAM plus 16 pointers. It is recommended to set NET_TCP_CFG_NBR_CONN with an initial value of **10** and adjust this value if more or less TCP connections are required.

D-14-2 NET_TCP_CFG_RX_WIN_SIZE_OCTET

NET_TCP_CFG_RX_WIN_SIZE_OCTET configures each TCP connection's receive window size. It is recommended to set TCP window sizes to integer multiples of each TCP connection's maximum segment size (MSS). For example, systems with an Ethernet MSS of 1460, a value **5840** (4 * 1460) is probably a better configuration than the default window size of **4096** (4K).

D-14-3 NET_TCP_CFG_TX_WIN_SIZE_OCTET

`NET_TCP_CFG_TX_WIN_SIZE_OCTET` configures each TCP connection's transmit window size. It is recommended to set TCP window sizes to integer multiples of each TCP connection's maximum segment size (MSS). For example, systems with an Ethernet MSS of 1460, a value **5840** (4 * 1460) is probably a better configuration than the default window size of **4096** (4K).

D-14-4 NET_TCP_CFG_TIMEOUT_CONN_MAX_SEG_SEC

`NET_TCP_CFG_TIMEOUT_CONN_MAX_SEG_SEC` configures TCP connections' default maximum segment lifetime timeout (MSL) value, specified in integer seconds. It is recommended to start with a value of **3 seconds**.

If TCP connections are established and closed rapidly, it is possible that this timeout may further delay new TCP connections from becoming available. Thus, an even lower timeout value may be desirable to free TCP connections and make them available as quickly as possible. However, a **0** second timeout prevents µC/TCP-IP from performing the complete TCP connection close sequence and will instead send TCP reset (RST) segments.

D-14-5 NET_TCP_CFG_TIMEOUT_CONN_FIN_WAIT_2_SEC

`NET_TCP_CFG_TIMEOUT_CONN_FIN_WAIT_2_SEC` configures the TCP connection default FIN-WAIT-2 timeout (in seconds *or* no timeout if configured with `NET_TMR_TIME_INFINITE`). On a typical connection close (FIN/ACK/FIN/ACK), this timeout defines the maximum delay between the ACK/FIN packets sent by the remote host. It is recommended to set `NET_TCP_CFG_TIMEOUT_CONN_FIN_WAIT_2_SEC` with a value of 15 seconds.

D-14-6 NET_TCP_CFG_TIMEOUT_CONN_ACK_DLY_MS

`NET_TCP_CFG_TIMEOUT_CONN_ACK_DLY_MS` configures the TCP acknowledgement delay in integer milliseconds. It is recommended to configure the default value of **500 milliseconds** since RFC #2581, Section 4.2 states that "an ACK *must* be generated within 500 ms of the arrival of the first unacknowledged packet".

D-14-7 NET_TCP_CFG_TIMEOUT_CONN_RX_Q_MS

NET_TCP_CFG_TIMEOUT_CONN_RX_Q_MS configures each TCP connection's receive timeout (in milliseconds *or* no timeout if configured with NET_TMR_TIME_INFINITE). It is recommended to start with a value of **3000** milliseconds *or* the no-timeout value of NET_TMR_TIME_INFINITE.

D-14-8 NET_TCP_CFG_TIMEOUT_CONN_TX_Q_MS

NET_TCP_CFG_TIMEOUT_CONN_TX_Q_MS configures each TCP connection's transmit timeout (in milliseconds *or* no timeout if configured with NET_TMR_TIME_INFINITE). It is recommended to start with a value of **3000** milliseconds *or* the no-timeout value of NET_TMR_TIME_INFINITE.

D-15 NETWORK SOCKET CONFIGURATION

µC/TCP-IP supports BSD 4.x sockets and basic socket API for the TCP/UDP/IP protocols.

D-15-1 NET_SOCK_CFG_FAMILY

The current version of µC/TCP-IP only supports IPv4 BSD sockets, and thus NET_SOCK_CFG_FAMILY should *always* be set to **NET_SOCK_FAMILY_IP_V4**.

D-15-2 NET_SOCK_CFG_NBR_SOCK

NET_SOCK_CFG_NBR_SOCK configures the maximum number of sockets that µC/TCP-IP can handle concurrently. This number depends entirely on how many simultaneous socket connections the application requires. Each socket requires approximately **28** bytes of RAM plus three pointers. It is recommended to set NET_SOCK_CFG_NBR_SOCK with an initial value of **10** and adjust this value if more or less sockets are required.

D-15-3 NET_SOCK_CFG_BLOCK_SEL

NET_SOCK_CFG_BLOCK_SEL determines the default blocking (or non-blocking) behavior for sockets:

NET_SOCK_BLOCK_SEL_DFLT   Sockets will be blocking by default, but may be individually configured in a future release

NET_SOCK_BLOCK_SEL_BLOCK   Sockets will be blocking by default

NET_SOCK_BLOCK_SEL_NO_BLOCK   Sockets will be non-blocking by default

If blocking mode is enabled, a timeout can be specified. The amount of time for the timeout is determined by various timeout functions implemented in **net_sock.c**:

NetSock_CfgTimeoutRxQ_Set()   Configure datagram socket receive timeout

NetSock_CfgTimeoutConnReqSet()   Configure socket connection timeout

NetSock_CfgTimeoutConnAcceptSet()   Configure socket accept timeout

NetSock_CfgTimeoutConnClOSset()   Configure socket close timeout

D-15-4 NET_SOCK_CFG_SEL_EN

NET_SOCK_CFG_SEL_EN determines whether or not the code and data space used to support socket **select()** functionality is enabled:

DEF_DISABLED   BSD **select()** API disabled

or

DEF_ENABLED   BSD **select()** API enabled

D-15-5 NET_SOCK_CFG_SEL_NBR_EVENTS_MAX

NET_SOCK_CFG_SEL_NBR_EVENTS_MAX is used to configure the maximum number of socket events/operations that the socket **select()** functionality can wait on. It is recommended to set NET_SOCK_CFG_SEL_NBR_EVENTS_MAX with an initial value of at least **10** and adjust this value if more or less socket **select()** events are required.

D-15-6 NET_SOCK_CFG_CONN_ACCEPT_Q_SIZE_MAX

NET_SOCK_CFG_CONN_ACCEPT_Q_SIZE_MAX is used to configure the absolute maximum queue size of **accept()** connections for stream-type sockets. It is recommended to set NET_SOCK_CFG_CONN_ACCEPT_Q_SIZE_MAX with an initial value of at least **5** and adjust this value if more or less socket connections need to be queued.

D-15-7 NET_SOCK_CFG_PORT_NBR_RANDOM_BASE

NET_SOCK_CFG_PORT_NBR_RANDOM_BASE is used to configure the starting base socket number for "ephemeral" or "random" port numbers. Since two times the number of random ports are required for each socket, the base value for the random port number must be:

```
Random Port Number Base <= 65535 - (2 * NET_SOCK_CFG_NBR_SOCK)
```

The arbitrary default value of **65000** is recommended as a good starting point.

D-15-8 NET_SOCK_CFG_RX_Q_SIZE_OCTET

NET_SOCK_CFG_RX_Q_SIZE_OCTET configures datagram sockets default receive queue buffer size in integer number of octets. According to 4.3BSD, it is recommended to set NET_SOCK_CFG_RX_Q_SIZE_OCTET with a value of 4096 octets. However, systems such as 4.4BSD use larger default buffer sizes, such as 8192 or 16384 bytes. This configuration does not impact TCP default receive windows size.

D-15-9 NET_SOCK_CFG_TX_Q_SIZE_OCTET

NET_SOCK_CFG_TX_Q_SIZE_OCTET configures datagram sockets default transmit queue buffer size in integer number of octets. According to 4.3BSD, it is recommended to set NET_SOCK_CFG_TX_Q_SIZE_OCTET with a value of 4096 octets. However, systems such as 4.4BSD use larger default buffer sizes, such as 8192 or 16384 bytes. This configuration does not impact TCP default transmit windows size.

D-15-10 NET_SOCK_CFG_TIMEOUT_RX_Q_MS

NET_SOCK_CFG_TIMEOUT_RX_Q_MS configures socket timeout value (in milliseconds *or* no timeout if configured with NET_TMR_TIME_INFINITE) for UDP datagram socket recv() operations. It is recommended to set NET_SOCK_CFG_TIMEOUT_RX_Q_MS with a value of 3000 milliseconds *or* the no-timeout value of **NET_TMR_TIME_INFINITE**.

D-15-11 NET_SOCK_CFG_TIMEOUT_CONN_REQ_MS

NET_SOCK_CFG_TIMEOUT_CONN_REQ_MS configures socket timeout value (in milliseconds *or* no timeout if configured with NET_TMR_TIME_INFINITE) for stream socket connect() operations. It is recommended to set NET_SOCK_CFG_TIMEOUT_CONN_REQ_MS with a value of 3000 milliseconds *or* the no-timeout value of **NET_TMR_TIME_INFINITE**.

D-15-12 NET_SOCK_CFG_TIMEOUT_CONN_ACCEPT_MS

NET_SOCK_CFG_TIMEOUT_CONN_ACCEPT_MS configures socket timeout value (in milliseconds *or* no timeout if configured with NET_TMR_TIME_INFINITE) for socket accept() operations. It is recommended to set NET_SOCK_CFG_TIMEOUT_CONN_ACCEPT_MS with a value of 3000 milliseconds *or* the no-timeout value of **NET_TMR_TIME_INFINITE**.

D-15-13 NET_SOCK_CFG_TIMEOUT_CONN_CLOSE_MS

NET_SOCK_CFG_TIMEOUT_CONN_CLOSE_MS configures socket timeout value (in milliseconds *or* no timeout if configured with NET_TMR_TIME_INFINITE) for socket close() operations. It is recommended to set NET_SOCK_CFG_TIMEOUT_CONN_CLOSE_MS with a value of **10000 milliseconds** *or* the no-timeout value of NET_TMR_TIME_INFINITE.

D-16 NETWORK SECURITY MANAGER CONFIGURATION

D-16-1 NET_SECURE_CFG_EN

NET_SECURE_CFG_EN determines whether or not the network security manager is enabled. When the network security manager is enabled, a network security module (e.g., µC/SSL) must be present in the build. **NET_SECURE_CFG_EN** can be set to either:

DEF_DISABLED   Network security manager and security port layer disabled

or

DEF_ENABLED   Network security manager and security port layer enabled

D-16-2 NET_SECURE_CFG_FS_EN

NET_SECURE_CFG_FS_EN determines whether or not file system operations can be used to install keying material. When **NET_SECURE_CFG_FS_EN** is enabled, a file system (e.g., µC/FS) must be present in the build. **NET_SECURE_CFG_FS_EN** can be set to either:

DEF_DISABLED   Keying material cannot be installed from file system

or

DEF_ENABLED   Keying material can be installed from file system

D-16-3 NET_SECURE_CFG_VER

NET_SECURE_CFG_VER determines the default protocol version of the network security layer and can be set to one of the following values:

NET_SECURE_SSL_V2_0   SSL V2.0

NET_SECURE_SSL_V3_0   SSL V3.0

NET_SECURE_TLS_V1_0   TLS V1.0

NET_SECURE_TLS_V1_1   TLS V1.1

NET_SECURE_TLS_V1_2   TLS V1.2

Please refer to the specific network security module (e.g., µC/SSL) to determine which protocol versions are supported.

D-16-4 NET_SECURE_CFG_WORD_SIZE

NET_SECURE_CFG_WORD_SIZE configures an optimized word size for the network security port, if applicable:

CPU_WORD_SIZE_08   8-bit word size

CPU_WORD_SIZE_16   16-bit word size

CPU_WORD_SIZE_32   32-bit word size

CPU_WORD_SIZE_64   64-bit word size

NET_SECURE_CFG_WORD_SIZE should be configured to CPU_WORD_SIZE_64 **only if** 64-bit data types and optimization is available by the specific network security module (e.g., µC/SSL).

D-16-5 NET_SECURE_CFG_CLIENT_DOWNGRADE_EN

NET_SECURE_CFG_CLIENT_DOWNGRADE_EN determines whether or not the client downgrade option is enabled. If client downgrading is enabled, client applications will be allowed to connect on a server that is using a protocol version older than NET_SECURE_CFG_VER. NET_SECURE_CFG_CLIENT_DOWNGRADE_EN can be set to either **DEF_DISABLED** or DEF_ENABLED but it is recommended to disable client downgrading.

D-16-6 NET_SECURE_CFG_SERVER_DOWNGRADE_EN

NET_SECURE_CFG_SERVER_DOWNGRADE_EN determines whether or not the server downgrade option is enabled. If server downgrading is enabled, server will be allowed to accept connection request coming from clients that are using a protocol version older than NET_SECURE_CFG_VER. NET_SECURE_CFG_SERVER_DOWNGRADE_EN can be set to either DEF_DISABLED or **DEF_ENABLED** but it is recommended to enable server downgrading.

D-16-7 NET_SECURE_CFG_MAX_NBR_SOCK

NET_SECURE_CFG_MAX_NBR_SOCK configures the maximum number of sockets that can be secured. If your application is a simple TCP server, you need to have two secure sockets (one listening socket and one accepted socket). If your application is a simple TCP client, you will only need to have one secure socket to connect. It is recommended to set NET_SECURE_CFG_MAX_NBR_SOCK to the initial value of **5 sockets** and adjust this value if more or less sockets are required. However, the maximum number of secure sockets must be less than or equal to NET_SOCK_CFG_NBR_SOCK (see section D-15-2 on page 976).

D-16-8 NET_SECURE_CFG_MAX_NBR_CA

NET_SECURE_CFG_MAX_NBR_CA configures the maximum number of certificate authorities (CAs) that can be installed. If many CAs are installed, they are saved into a linked-list. When the client receives the server public key certificate, it scans the linked-list to see if it is trusted by one of the installed CAs.

D-16-9 NET_SECURE_CFG_MAX_KEY_LEN

NET_SECURE_CFG_MAX_KEY_LEN configures the maximum length (in bytes) of a certificate authority, a public key certificate or a private key. It is recommended to set NET_SECURE_CFG_MAX_KEY_LEN to the default value of **1500** for standard keying material and adjust this value if required. You can find the size of any certificate authority, public key or private key by right clicking on the DER or PEM file on a Windows environment and by choosing 'Properties'. Usually DER encoded keying material is smaller than PEM encoded keying material.

D-16-10 NET_SECURE_CFG_MAX_ISSUER_CN_LEN

`NET_SECURE_CFG_MAX_ISSUER_CN_LEN` configures the maximum length (in bytes) of common names. The common name is chosen during the creation of the certificate. Most of the time, it is the name of the company that is using the certificate (i.e, Micrium, Google, Paypal, etc.). It is recommended to set `NET_SECURE_CFG_MAX_ISSUER_CN_LEN` with an initial value of **20** and adjust this value if longer or shorter common names are required.

D-16-11 NET_SECURE_CFG_MAX_PUBLIC_KEY_LEN

`NET_SECURE_CFG_MAX_PUBLIC_KEY_LEN` configures the maximum length (in bytes) of public key. The public key is part of the public key certificate and is chosen during the creation of the certificate. It is recommended to set `NET_SECURE_CFG_MAX_PUBLIC_KEY_LEN` with an initial value of **256** and adjust this value if longer or shorter public keys are required.

D-17 BSD SOCKETS CONFIGURATION

D-17-1 NET_BSD_CFG_API_EN

`NET_BSD_CFG_API_EN` determines whether or not the standard BSD 4.x socket API is included in the build:

`DEF_DISABLED`   BSD 4.x layer API disabled

or

`DEF_ENABLED`   BSD 4.x layer API enabled

D-18 NETWORK APPLICATION INTERFACE CONFIGURATION

D-18-1 NET_APP_CFG_API_EN

NET_APP_CFG_API_EN determines whether or not a simplified network application programming interface (API) is included in the build:

DEF_DISABLED   Network API layer disabled

or

DEF_ENABLED   Network API layer enabled

D-19 NETWORK CONNECTION MANAGER CONFIGURATION

D-19-1 NET_CONN_CFG_FAMILY

The current version of µC/TCP-IP only supports IPv4 connections, and thus NET_CONN_CFG_FAMILY should *always* be set to **NET_CONN_FAMILY_IP_V4_SOCK**.

D-19-2 NET_CONN_CFG_NBR_CONN

NET_CONN_CFG_NBR_CONN configures the maximum number of connections that µC/TCP-IP can handle concurrently. This number depends entirely on how many simultaneous connections the application requires and *must* be at least greater than the configured number of application (socket) connections and transport layer (TCP) connections. Each connection requires approximately **28** bytes of RAM, plus five pointers, plus two protocol addresses (**8** bytes assuming IPv4 addresses). It is recommended to set NET_CONN_CFG_NBR_CONN with an initial value of **20** and adjust this value if more or less connections are required.

D-20 APPLICATION-SPECIFIC CONFIGURATION

This section defines the configuration constants related to µC/TCP-IP but that are application-specific. Most of these configuration constants relate to the various ports for µC/TCP-IP such as the CPU, OS, device, or network interface ports. Other configuration constants relate to the compiler and standard library ports.

These configuration constants should be defined in an application's **app_cfg.h** file.

D-20-1 OPERATING SYSTEM CONFIGURATION

The following configuration constants relate to the µC/TCP-IP OS port. For many OSs, the µC/TCP-IP task priorities, stack sizes, and other options will need to be explicitly configured for the particular OS (consult the specific OS's documentation for more information).

The priority of µC/TCP-IP tasks is dependent on the network communication requirements of the application. For most applications, the priority for µC/TCP-IP tasks is typically lower than the priority for other application tasks.

For µC/OS-II and µC/OS-III, the following macros must be configured within **app_cfg.h**:

```
NET_OS_CFG_IF_TX_DEALLOC_PRIO          10   (highest priority)
NET_OS_CFG_TMR_TASK_PRIO               51
NET_OS_CFG_IF_RX_TASK_PRIO             52   (lowest  priority)
```

The arbitrary task priorities of **10**, **51**, and **52** are a good starting point for most applications, where the network interface Transmit De-allocation task is assigned a higher priority than all application tasks that use µC/TCP-IP network services but the Network Timer task and network interface Receive task are assigned lower priorities than almost all other application tasks.

```
NET_OS_CFG_IF_TX_DEALLOC_TASK_STK_SIZE  1000
NET_OS_CFG_IF_RX_TASK_STK_SIZE          1000
NET_OS_CFG_TMR_TASK_STK_SIZE            1000
```

The arbitrary stack size of **1000** is a good starting point for most applications.

The only guaranteed method of determining the required task stack sizes is to calculate the maximum stack usage for each task. Obviously, the maximum stack usage for a task is the total stack usage along the task's most-stack-greedy function path plus the (maximum) stack usage for interrupts. Note that the most-stack-greedy function path is not necessarily the longest or deepest function path.

The easiest and best method for calculating the maximum stack usage for any task/function should be performed statically by the compiler or by a static analysis tool since these can calculate function/task maximum stack usage based on the compiler's actual code generation and optimization settings. So for optimal task stack configuration, we recommend to invest in a task stack calculator tool compatible with your build toolchain.

D-20-2 µC/TCP-IP CONFIGURATION

The following configuration constants relate to the µC/TCP-IP OS port. For many OSs, the µC/TCP-IP maximum queue sizes may need to be explicitly configured for the particular OS (consult the specific OS's documentation for more information).

For µC/OS-II and µC/OS-III, the following macros must be configured within **app_cfg.h**:

NET_OS_CFG_IF_RX_Q_SIZE

NET_OS_CFG_IF_TX_DEALLOC_Q_SIZE

The values configured for these macros depend on additional application dependent information such as the number of transmit or receive buffers configured for the total number of interfaces.

The following configuration for the above macros are recommended:

NET_OS_CFG_IF_RX_Q_SIZE should be configured such that it reflects the total number of DMA receive descriptors on all physical interfaces. If DMA is not available, or a combination of DMA and I/O based interfaces are configured then this number reflects the maximum number of packets than can be acknowledged and signaled for during a single receive interrupt event for all interfaces.

For example, if one interface has 10 receive descriptors and another interface is I/O based but is capable of receiving 4 frames within its internal memory and issuing a single interrupt request, then the NET_OS_CFG_IF_RX_Q_SIZE macro should be configured to 14. Defining a number in excess of the maximum number of receivable frames per interrupt across all interfaces would not be harmful, but the additional queue space will not be utilized.

NET_OS_CFG_IF_TX_DEALLOC_Q_SIZE should be defined to be the total number of small and large transmit buffers declared for all interfaces.

D-21 µC/TCP-IP OPTIMIZATION

D-21-1 OPTIMIZING µC/TCP-IP FOR ADDITIONAL PERFORMANCE

There are several configuration combinations that can improve overall µC/TCP-IP performance. The following items can be used as a starting point:

1   Enable the assembly port optimizations, if available in the architecture.

2   Configure the µC/TCP-IP for speed optimization.

3   Configure optimum TCP window sizes for TCP communication. Disable argument checking, statistics and error counters.

ASSEMBLY OPTIMIZATION

First, if using the ARM architecture, or other supported optimized architecture, the files net_util_a.asm and lib_mem_a.asm may be included into the project and the following macros should be defined and enabled:

```
app_cfg.h: #define LIB_MEM_CFG_OPTIMIZE_ASM_EN
net_cfg.h: Set NET_CFG_OPTIMIZE_ASM_EN to DEF_ENABLED
```

These files are generally located in the following directories:

```
\Micrium\Software\uC-LIB\Ports\ARM\IAR\lib_mem_a.asm
\Micrium\Software\uC-TCPIP-V2\Ports\ARM\IAR\net_util_a.asm
```

ENABLE SPEED OPTIMIZATION

Second, you may compile the Network Protocol Stack with speed optimizations enabled.

This can be accomplished by configuring the **net_cfg.h** macro `NET_CFG_OPTIMIZE` to `NET_OPTIMIZE_SPD`.

TCP OPTIMIZATION

Third, the two **net_cfg.h** macros `NET_TCP_CFG_RX_WIN_SIZE_OCTET` and `NET_TCP_CFG_TX_WIN_SIZE_OCTET` should configure each TCP connection's receive and transmit window sizes. It is recommended to set TCP window sizes to integer multiples of each TCP connection's maximum segment size (MSS). For example, systems with an Ethernet MSS of 1460, a value **5840** (4 * 1460) is probably a better configuration than the default window size of **4096** (4K).

DISABLE ARGUMENT CHECKING

Finally, once the application has been validated, argument checking, statistics and error counters may optionally be disabled by configuring the following macros to **DEF_DISABLED**:

```
NET_ERR_CFG_ARG_CHK_EXT_EN
NET_ERR_CFG_ARG_CHK_DBG_EN
NET_CTR_CFG_STAT_EN
NET_CTR_CFG_ERR_EN
```

μC/TCP-IP Error Codes

This appendix provides a brief explanation of μC/TCP-IP error codes defined in **net_err.h**. Any error codes not listed here may be searched in **net_err.h** for both their numerical value and usage.

Each error has a numerical value. The error codes are grouped. The definition of the groups are:

Error code group	Numbering serie
NETWORK-OS LAYER	1000
NETWORK UTILITY LIBRARY	2000
ASCII LIBRARY	3000
NETWORK STATISTIC MANAGEMENT	4000
NETWORK TIMER MANAGEMENT	5000
NETWORK BUFFER MANAGEMENT	6000
NETWORK CONNECTION MANAGEMENT	6000
NETWORK BOARD SUPPORT PACKAGE (BSP)	10000
NETWORK DEVICE	11000
NETWORK PHYSICAL LAYER	12000
NETWORK INTERFACE LAYER	13000
ARP LAYER	15000
NETWORK LAYER MANAGEMENT	20000
IP LAYER	21000
ICMP LAYER	22000
IGMP LAYER	23000
UDP LAYER	30000

Error code group	Numbering serie
TCP LAYER	31000
APPLICATION LAYER	40000
NETWORK SOCKET LAYER	41000
NETWORK SECURITY MANAGER LAYER	50000
NETWORK SECURITY LAYER	51000

E-1 NETWORK ERROR CODES

10	NET_ERR_INIT_INCOMPLETE	Network initialization *not* complete.
20	NET_ERR_INVALID_PROTOCOL	Invalid/unknown network protocol type.
30	NET_ERR_INVALID_TRANSACTION	Invalid/unknown network buffer pool type.
400	NET_ERR_RX	General receive error. Receive data discarded.
450	NET_ERR_RX_DEST	Destination address and/or port -number not available on this host.
500	NET_ERR_TX	General transmit error. No data transmitted. A momentarily delay should be performed to allow additional buffers to be de-allocated before calling send( ), NetSock_TxData( ) or NetSock_TxDataTo( ).

E-2 ARP ERROR CODES

15000	NET_ARP_ERR_NONE	ARP operation completed successfully.
15020	NET_ARP_ERR_NULL_PTR	Argument(s) passed NULL pointer.
15102	NET_ARP_ERR_INVALID_HW_ADDR_LEN	Invalid ARP hardware address length.
15105	NET_ARP_ERR_INVALID_PROTOCOL_LEN	Invalid ARP protocol address length.
15150	NET_ARP_ERR_CACHE_NONE_AVAIL	No ARP cache entry structures available.
15151	NET_ARP_ERR_CACHE_INVALID_TYPE	ARP cache type invalid or unknown.
15155	NET_ARP_ERR_CACHE_NOT_FOUND	ARP cache entry not found.
15156	NET_ARP_ERR_CACHE_PEND	ARP cache resolution pending.

E-3 NETWORK ASCII ERROR CODES

3000	NET_ASCII_ERR_NONE	ASCII operation completed successfully.
3020	NET_ASCII_ERR_NULL_PTR	Argument(s) passed NULL pointer.
3100	NET_ASCII_ERR_INVALID_STR_LEN	Invalid ASCII string length.
3101	NET_ASCII_ERR_INVALID_CHAR_LEN	Invalid ASCII character length.
3102	NET_ASCII_ERR_INVALID_CHAR_VAL	Invalid ASCII character value.
3103	NET_ASCII_ERR_INVALID_CHAR_SEQ	Invalid ASCII character sequence.
3200	NET_ASCII_ERR_INVALID_CHAR	Invalid ASCII character.

E-4 NETWORK BUFFER ERROR CODES

6010	NET_BUF_ERR_NONE_AVAIL	No network buffers of required size available.
6031	NET_BUF_ERR_INVALID_SIZE	Invalid network buffer pool size.
6032	NET_BUF_ERR_INVALID_IX	Invalid buffer index outside data area.
6033	NET_BUF_ERR_INVALID_LEN	Invalid buffer length specified outside of data area.
6040	NET_BUF_ERR_POOL_INIT	Network buffer pool initialization failed.
6050	NET_BUF_ERR_INVALID_POOL_TYPE	Invalid network buffer pool type.
6051	NET_BUF_ERR_INVALID_POOL_ADDR	Invalid network buffer pool address.
6053	NET_BUF_ERR_INVALID_POOL_QTY	Invalid number of pool buffers configured.

E-5 ICMP ERROR CODES

E-6 NETWORK INTERFACE ERROR CODES

13000	`NET_IF_ERR_NONE`	Network interface operation completed successfully.
13010	`NET_IF_ERR_NONE_AVAIL`	No network interfaces available. The value of `NET_IF_CFG_MAX_NBR_IF` should be increased in `net_cfg.h`.
13020	`NET_IF_ERR_NULL_PTR`	Argument(s) passed NULL pointer.
13021	`NET_IF_ERR_NULL_FNCT`	NULL interface API function pointer encountered.
13100	`NET_IF_ERR_INVALID_IF`	Invalid network interface number specified.
13101	`NET_IF_ERR_INVALID_CFG`	Invalid network interface configuration specified.
13110	`NET_IF_ERR_INVALID_STATE`	Invalid network interface state for specified operation.
13120	`NET_IF_ERR_INVALID_IO_CTRL_OPT`	Invalid I/O control option parameter specified.
13200	`NET_IF_ERR_INVALID_MTU`	Invalid hardware MTU specified.
13210	`NET_IF_ERR_INVALID_ADDR`	Invalid hardware address specified.
13211	`NET_IF_ERR_INVALID_ADDR_LEN`	Invalid hardware address length specified.

E-7 IP ERROR CODES

21000	`NET_IP_ERR_NONE`	IP operation completed successfully.
21020	`NET_IP_ERR_NULL_PTR`	Argument(s) passed NULL pointer.
21115	`NET_IP_ERR_INVALID_ADDR_HOST`	Invalid host IP address.
21117	`NET_IP_ERR_INVALID_ADDR_GATEWAY`	Invalid gateway IP address.
21201	`NET_IP_ERR_ADDR_CFG_STATE`	Invalid IP address state for attempted operation.
21202	`NET_IP_ERR_ADDR_CFG_IN_PROGRESS`	Interface address configuration in progress.
21203	`NET_IP_ERR_ADDR_CFG_IN_USE`	Specified IP address currently in use.
21210	`NET_IP_ERR_ADDR_NONE_AVAIL`	No IP addresses configured.
21211	`NET_IP_ERR_ADDR_NOT_FOUND`	IP address not found.
21220	`NET_IP_ERR_ADDR_TBL_SIZE`	Invalid IP address table size argument passed.

21221	NET_IP_ERR_ADDR_TBL_EMPTY	IP address table empty.
21222	NET_IP_ERR_ADDR_TBL_FULL	IP address table full.

E-8 IGMP ERROR CODES

23000	NET_IGMP_ERR_NONE	IGMP operation completed successfully.
23100	NET_IGMP_ERR_INVALID_VER	Invalid IGMP version.
23101	NET_IGMP_ERR_INVALID_TYPE	Invalid IGMP message type.
23102	NET_IGMP_ERR_INVALID_LEN	Invalid IGMP message lenth.
23103	NET_IGMP_ERR_INVALID_CHK_SUM	Invalid IGMP checksum.
23104	NET_IGMP_ERR_INVALID_ADDR_SRC	Invalid IGMP IP source address.
23105	NET_IGMP_ERR_INVALID_ADDR_DEST	Invalid IGMP IP destination address.
23106	NET_IGMP_ERR_INVALID_ADDR_GRP	Invalid IGMP IP host group address
23200	NET_IGMP_ERR_HOST_GRP_NONE_AVAIL	No host group available.
23201	NET_IGMP_ERR_HOST_GRP_INVALID_TYPE	Invalid or unknown IGMP host group type.
23202	NET_IGMP_ERR_HOST_GRP_NOT_FOUND	No IGMP host group found.

E-9 OS ERROR CODES

1010	NET_OS_ERR_LOCK	Network global lock access *not* acquired. OS-implemented lock may be corrupted.

E

E-10 UDP ERROR CODES

30040	NET_UDP_ERR_INVALID_DATA_SIZE	UDP receive or transmit data does not fit into the receive or transmit buffer.In the case of receive, excess data bytes are dropped; for transmit, no data is sent.
30105	NET_UDP_ERR_INVALID_FLAG	Invalid UDP flags specified.
30101	NET_UDP_ERR_INVALID_LEN_DATA	Invalid protocol/data length.
30103	NET_UDP_ERR_INVALID_PORT_NBR	Invalid UDP port number.
30000	NET_UDP_ERR_NONE	UDP operation completed successfully.
30020	NET_UDP_ERR_NULL_PTR	Argument(s) passed NULL pointer.
	NET_UDP_ERR_NULL_SIZE	Argument(s) passed NULL size.

E-11 NETWORK SOCKET ERROR CODES

41072	NET_SOCK_ERR_ADDR_IN_USE	Socket address (IP / port number) already in use.
41020	NET_SOCK_ERR_CLOSED	Socket already/previously closed.
41106	NET_SOCK_ERR_CLOSE_IN_PROGRESS	Socket already closing.
41130	NET_SOCK_ERR_CONN_ACCEPT_Q_NONE _AVAIL	Accept connection handle identifier not available.
41110	NET_SOCK_ERR_CONN_FAIL	Socket operation failed.
41100	NET_SOCK_ERR_CONN_IN_USE	Socket address (IP / port number) already connected.
41122	NET_SOCK_ERR_CONN_SIGNAL_TIMEOUT	Socket operation not signaled before specified timeout.
41091	NET_SOCK_ERR_EVENTS_NBR_MAX	Number of configured socket events is greater than the maximum number of socket events.
41021	NET_SOCK_ERR_FAULT	Fatal socket fault; close socket immediately.
41070	NET_SOCK_ERR_INVALID_ADDR	Invalid socket address specified.
41071	NET_SOCK_ERR_INVALID_ADDR_LEN	Invalid socket address length specified.
41055	NET_SOCK_ERR_INVALID_CONN	Invalid socket connection.
41040	NET_SOCK_ERR_INVALID_DATA_SIZE	Socket receive or transmit data does not fit into the receive or transmit buffer.In the case of receive, excess data bytes are dropped; for transmit, no data is sent.
41054	NET_SOCK_ERR_INVALID_DESC	Invalid socket descriptor number.
41050	NET_SOCK_ERR_INVALID_FAMILY	Invalid socket family; close socket immediately.

41058	NET_SOCK_ERR_INVALID_FLAG	Invalid socket flags specified.
41057	NET_SOCK_ERR_INVALID_OP	Invalid socket operation; e.g., socket not in the correct state for specified socket call.
41080	NET_SOCK_ERR_INVALID_PORT_NBR	Invalid port number specified.
41051	NET_SOCK_ERR_INVALID_PROTOCOL	Invalid socket protocol; close socket immediately.
41053	NET_SOCK_ERR_INVALID_SOCK	Invalid socket number specified.
41056	NET_SOCK_ERR_INVALID_STATE	Invalid socket state; close socket immediately.
41059	NET_SOCK_ERR_INVALID_TIMEOUT	Invalid or no timeout specified.
41052	NET_SOCK_ERR_INVALID_TYPE	Invalid socket type; close socket immediately.
41000	NET_SOCK_ERR_NONE	Socket operation completed successfully.
41010	NET_SOCK_ERR_NONE_AVAIL	No available socket resources to allocate; NET_SOCK_CFG_NBR_SOCK should be increased in net_cfg.h.
41011	NET_SOCK_ERR_NOT_USED	Socket not used; do not close or use the socket for further operations.
41030	NET_SOCK_ERR_NULL_PTR	Argument(s) passed NULL pointer.
41031	NET_SOCK_ERR_NULL_SIZE	Argument(s) passed NULL size.
41085	NET_SOCK_ERR_PORT_NBR_NONE_AVAIL	Random local port number not available.
41400	NET_SOCK_ERR_RX_Q_CLOSED	Socket receive queue closed (received FIN from peer).
41401	NET_SOCK_ERR_RX_Q_EMPTY	Socket receive queue empty.
41022	NET_SOCK_ERR_TIMEOUT	No socket events occurred before timeout expired.

E

E-12 NETWORK SECURITY MANAGER ERROR CODES

50005	NET_SECURE_MGR_ERR_FORMAT	Invalid keying material format.
50002	NET_SECURE_MGR_ERR_INIT	Failed to initialize network security manager.
50000	NET_SECURE_MGR_ERR_NONE	Network security manager operation successful.
50001	NET_SECURE_MGR_ERR_NOT_AVAIL	Network security manager not available.
50003	NET_SECURE_MGR_ERR_NULL_PTR	Argument(s) passed NULL pointer.
50004	NET_SECURE_MGR_ERR_TYPE	Invalid keying material type.

E-13 NETWORK SECURITY ERROR CODES

51011	NET_SECURE_ERR_BLK_FREE	Failed to free block from memory pool.
51010	NET_SECURE_ERR_BLK_GET	Failed to get block from memory pool.
51013	NET_SECURE_ERR_HANDSHAKE	Failed to perform secure handshake.
51002	NET_SECURE_ERR_INIT_POOL	Failed to initialize memory pool.
51020	NET_SECURE_ERR_INSTALL	Failed to install keying material.
51024	NET_SECURE_ERR_INSTALL_CA_SLOT	No more CA slot available.
51023	NET_SECURE_ERR_INSTALL_DATE_CREATION	Keying material creation date is invalid.
51022	NET_SECURE_ERR_INSTALL_DATE_EXPIRATION	Keying material is expired.
51021	NET_SECURE_ERR_INSTALL_NOT_TRUSTED	Keying material is not trusted.
50000	NET_SECURE_ERR_NONE	Network security operation successful.
51001	NET_SECURE_ERR_NOT_AVAIL	Failed to get secure session from memory pool.
51012	NET_SECURE_ERR_NULL_PTR	Argument(s) passed NULL pointer.

µC/TCP-IP Typical Usage

This appendix provides a brief explanation to a variety of common questions regarding how to use µC/TCP-IP.

F-1 µC/TCP-IP CONFIGURATION AND INITIALIZATION

F-1-1 µC/TCP-IP STACK CONFIGURATION

Refer to Appendix D, "µC/TCP-IP Configuration and Optimization" on page 959 for information on this topic.

F-1-2 µC/LIB MEMORY HEAP INITIALIZATION

The µC/LIB memory heap is used for allocation of the following objects:

1   Transmit small buffers

2   Transmit large buffers

3   Receive large buffers

4   Network Buffers (Network Buffer header and pointer to data area)

5   DMA receive descriptors

6   DMA transmit descriptors

7   Interface data area

8   Device driver data area

In the following example, the use of a Network Device Driver with DMA support is assumed. DMA descriptors are included in the analysis. The size of Network Buffer Data Areas (1, 2, 3) vary based on configuration. Refer to Chapter 9, "Buffer Management" on page 277. However, for this example, the following object sizes in bytes are assumed:

- Small transmit buffers: 152

- Large transmit buffers: 1594 for maximum sized TCP packets

- Large receive buffers: 1518

- Size of DMA receive descriptor: 8

- Size of DMA transmit descriptor: 8

- Ethernet interface data area: 7

- Average Ethernet device driver data area: 108

With a 4-byte alignment on all memory pool objects, it results in a worst case disposal of three leading bytes for each object. In practice this is not usually true since the size of most objects tend to be even multiples of four. Therefore, the alignment is preserved after having aligned the start of the pool data area. However, this makes the case for allocating objects with size to the next greatest multiple of four in order to prevent lost space due to misalignment.

The approximate memory heap size may be determined according to the following expressions:

```
nbr buf per interface    = nbr small Tx buf +
                           nbr large Tx buf +
                           nbr large Rx buf

nbr net buf per interface = nbr buf per interface
```

```
nbr objects    =  nbr buf per interface     +
                  nbr net buf per interface +
                  nbr Rx descriptors        +
                  nbr Tx descriptors        +
                  1 Ethernet       data area +
                  1 Device driver data area

interface mem = (nbr small Tx buf       *   152) +
                (nbr large Tx buf       *  1594) +
                (nbr large Rx buf       *  1518) +
                (nbr Rx descriptors     *     8) +
                (nbr Tx descriptors     *     8) +
                (Ethernet IF  data area *     7) +
                (Ethernet Drv data area *   108) +
                (nbr objects            *     3)

total mem required = nbr interfaces * interface mem
```

EXAMPLE

With the following configuration, the memory heap required is:

- 10 small transmit buffers

- 10 large transmit buffers

- 10 large receive buffers

- 6 receive descriptors

- 20 transmit descriptors

- Ethernet interface (interface + device driver data area required)

```
nbr     buf per interface = 10 + 10 + 10                    = 30
nbr net buf per interface = nbr buf per interface           = 30
nbr objects               = (30 + 30 + 6 + 20 + 1 + 1) = 88
interface mem             = (10 *  152) +
                            (10 * 1594) +
                            (10 * 1518) +
                            ( 6 *    8) +
                            (20 *    8) +
                            ( 1 *    7) +
                            ( 1 *  108) +
                            (88 *    3) = 33,227 bytes

total mem required = 33,227 ( + localhost memory, if enabled)
```

The localhost interface, when enabled, requires a similar amount of memory except that it does not require Rx and Tx descriptors, an IF data area, or a device driver data area.

The value determined by these expressions is only an estimate. In some cases, it may be possible to reduce the size of the µC/LIB memory heap by inspecting the variable `Mem_PoolHeap.SegSizeRem` after all interfaces have been successfully initialized and any additional application allocations (if applicable) have been completed.

Excess heap space, if present, may be subtracted from the lib heap size configuration macro, `LIB_MEM_CFG_HEAP_SIZE`, present in `app_cfg.h`.

F-1-3 µC/TCP-IP TASK STACKS

In general, the size of µC/TCP-IP task stacks is dependent on the CPU architecture and compiler used.

On ARM processors, experience has shown that configuring the task stacks to 1024 `OS_STK` entries (4,096 bytes) is sufficient for most applications. Certainly, the stack sizes may be examined and reduced accordingly once the run-time behavior of the device has been analyzed and additional stack space deemed to be unnecessary.

The only guaranteed method of determining the required task stack sizes is to calculate the maximum stack usage for each task. Obviously, the maximum stack usage for a task is the total stack usage along the task's most-stack-greedy function path plus the (maximum) stack usage for interrupts. Note that the most-stack-greedy function path is not necessarily the longest or deepest function path.

The easiest and best method for calculating the maximum stack usage for any task/function should be performed statically by the compiler or by a static analysis tool since these can calculate function/task maximum stack usage based on the compiler's actual code generation and optimization settings. So for optimal task stack configuration, we recommend to invest in a task stack calculator tool compatible with your build toolchain.

See also section D-20-1 "Operating System Configuration" on page 985.

F-1-4 µC/TCP-IP TASK PRIORITIES

We recommend to configure the Network Protocol Stack task priorities as follows:

```
NET_OS_CFG_IF_TX_DEALLOC_TASK_PRIO   (highest priority)
NET_OS_CFG_TMR_TASK_PRIO
NET_OS_CFG_IF_RX_TASK_PRIO            (lowest  priority)
```

We recommend that the µC/TCP-IP Timer task and network interface Receive task be lower priority than almost all other application tasks; but we recommend that the network interface Transmit De-allocation task be higher priority than all application tasks that use µC/TCP-IP network services.

See also section D-20-1 "Operating System Configuration" on page 985.

F-1-5 µC/TCP-IP QUEUE SIZES

Refer to section D-20-2 "µC/TCP-IP Configuration" on page 986.

F-1-6 µC/TCP-IP INITIALIZATION

The following example code demonstrates the initialization of two identical network interface devices via a local, application developer provided function named **AppInit_TCPIP()**. Another example of this method can also be found in section 13-3 "Application Code" on page 295

The first interface is bound to two different sets of network addresses on two separate networks. The second interface is configured to operate on one of the same networks as the first interface, but could easily be plugged into a separate network that happens to use the same address ranges.

```
static void AppInit_TCPIP (void)
{
    NET_IF_NBR    if_nbr;
    NET_IP_ADDR   ip;
    NET_IP_ADDR   msk;
    NET_IP_ADDR   gateway;
    CPU_BOOLEAN   cfg_success;
    NET_ERR       err;

    Mem_Init();                                                              (1)
    err = Net_Init();                                                        (2)
    if (err != NET_ERR_NONE) {
        return;
    }

    if_nbr = NetIF_Add((void    *)&NetIF_API_Ether,                          (3)
                       (void    *)&NetDev_API_FEC,
                       (void    *)&NetDev_BSP_FEC_0,
                       (void    *)&NetDev_Cfg_FEC_0,
                       (void    *)&NetPHY_API_Generic,
                       (void    *)&NetPhy_Cfg_FEC_0,
                       (NET_ERR *)&err);

    if (err == NET_IF_ERR_NONE) {
        ip          = NetASCII_Str_to_IP((CPU_CHAR *)"192.168.1.2",   &err); (4)
        msk         = NetASCII_Str_to_IP((CPU_CHAR *)"255.255.255.0", &err);
        gateway     = NetASCII_Str_to_IP((CPU_CHAR *)"192.168.1.1",   &err);
        cfg_success = NetIP_CfgAddrAdd(if_nbr, ip, msk, gateway, &err);      (5)

        ip          = NetASCII_Str_to_IP((CPU_CHAR *)"10.10.1.2",     &err); (6)
        msk         = NetASCII_Str_to_IP((CPU_CHAR *)"255.255.255.0", &err);
        gateway     = NetASCII_Str_to_IP((CPU_CHAR *)"10.10.1.1",     &err);
        cfg_success = NetIP_CfgAddrAdd(if_nbr, ip, msk, gateway, &err);      (7)

        NetIF_Start(if_nbr, &err);                                          (8)
    }
```

```
if_nbr = NetIF_Add((void    *)&NetIF_API_Ether,                      (9)
                   (void    *)&NetDev_API_FEC,
                   (void    *)&NetDev_BSP_FEC_1,
                   (void    *)&NetDev_Cfg_FEC_1,
                   (void    *)&NetPHY_API_Generic,
                   (void    *)&NetPhy_Cfg_FEC_1,
                   (NET_ERR *)&err);

if (err == NET_IF_ERR_NONE) {
    ip          = NetASCII_Str_to_IP((CPU_CHAR *)"192.168.1.3",    &err);   (10)
    msk         = NetASCII_Str_to_IP((CPU_CHAR *)"255.255.255.0", &err);
    gateway     = NetASCII_Str_to_IP((CPU_CHAR *)"192.168.1.1",  &err);
    cfg_success = NetIP_CfgAddrAdd(if_nbr, ip, msk, gateway, &err);         (11)

    NetIF_Start(if_nbr, &err);                                             (12)
}
}
```

Listing F-1 **Complete Initialization Example**

LF-1(1)   Initialize µC/LIB memory management. Most applications call this function PRIOR to **AppInit_TCPIP()** so that other parts of the application may benefit from memory management functionality prior to initializing µC/TCP-IP.

LF-1(2)   Initialize µC/TCP-IP. This function must only be called once following the call to µC/LIB **Mem_Init()**. The return error code should be checked for **NET_ERR_NONE** before proceeding

LF-1(3)   Add the first network interface to the system. In this case, an Ethernet interface bound to a Freescale FEC hardware device and generic (MII or RMII) compliant physical layer device is being configured. The interface uses a different device configuration structure than the second interface being added in Step 8. Each interface requires a unique device BSP interface and configuration structure. Physical layer device configuration structures however could be re-used if the Physical layer configurations are exactly the same. The return error should be checked before starting the interface.

LF-1(4)   Obtain the hexadecimal equivalents for the first set of Internet addresses to configure on the first added interface.

LF-1(5)   Configure the first added interface with the first set of specified addresses.

LF-1(6)   Obtain the hexadecimal equivalents for the second set of Internet addresses to configure on the first added interface. The same local variables have been used as when the first set of address information was configured. Once the address set is configured to the interface, as in Step 4, the local copies of the configured addresses are no longer necessary and can be overwritten with the next set of addresses to configure.

LF-1(7)   Configure the first added interface with the second set of specified addresses.

LF-1(8)   Start the first interface. The return error code should be checked, but this depends on whether the application will attempt to restart the interface should an error occur. This example assumes that no error occurs when starting the interface. Initialization for the first interface is now complete, and if no further initialization takes place, the first interface will respond to ICMP Echo (ping) requests on either of its configured addresses.

LF-1(9)   Add the second network interface to the system. In this case, an Ethernet interface bound to a Freescale FEC hardware device and generic (MII or RMII) compliant physical layer device is being configured. The interface uses a different device configuration structure than the first interface added in Step 2. Each interface requires a unique device BSP interface and configuration structure. Physical layer device configuration structures, however, could be re-used if the Physical layer configurations are exactly the same. The return error should be checked before starting the interface.

LF-1(10)   Obtain the hexadecimal equivalents for the first and only set of Internet addresses to configure on the second added interface.

LF-1(11)   Configure the second interface with the first and only set of specified addresses.

LF-1(12)   Start the second interface. The return error code should be checked, but this depends on whether the application will attempt to restart the interface should an error occur. This example assumes that no error occurs when starting the interface. Initialization for the second interface is now complete and it will respond to ICMP Echo (ping) requests on its configured address.

F-2 NETWORK INTERFACES, DEVICES, AND BUFFERS

F-2-1 NETWORK INTERFACE CONFIGURATION

ADDING AN INTERFACE

Interfaces may be added to the stack by calling **NetIF_Add()**. Each new interface requires additional BSP. The order of addition is critical to ensure that the interface number assigned to the new interface matches the code defined within **net_bsp.c**. See section 16-1 "Network Interface Configuration" on page 361 for more information on configuring and adding interfaces.

STARTING AN INTERFACE

Interfaces may be started by calling **NetIF_Start()**. See section 16-2-1 "Starting Network Interfaces" on page 366 for more information on starting interfaces.

STOPPING AN INTERFACE

Interfaces may be started by calling **NetIF_Stop()**. See section 16-2-2 "Stopping Network Interfaces" on page 367 for more information on stopping interfaces.

CHECKING FOR ENABLED INTERFACE

The application may check if an interface is enabled by calling **NetIF_IsEn()** or **NetIF_IsEnCfgd()**. See section C-9-10 "NetIF_IsEn()" on page 749 and section C-9-11 "NetIF_IsEnCfgd()" on page 750 for more information.

F

F-2-2 NETWORK AND DEVICE BUFFER CONFIGURATION

LARGE TRANSMIT BUFFERS ARE 1594 BYTES

Refer to the section 9-3 "Network Buffer Sizes" on page 279 for more information.

NUMBER OF RX PR TX BUFFERS TO CONFIGURE

The number of large receive, small transmit and large transmit buffers configured for a specific interface depend on several factors.

1 Desired level of performance.

2 Amount of data to be either transmitted or received.

3 Ability of the target application to either produce or consume transmitted or received data.

4 Average CPU utilization.

5 Average network utilization.

The discussion on the bandwidth-delay product is always valid. In general, the more buffers the better. However, the number of buffers can be tailored based on the application. For example, if an application receives a lot of data but transmits very little, then it may be sufficient to define a number of small transmit buffers for operations such as TCP acknowledgements and allocate the remaining memory to large receive buffers. Similarly, if an application transmits and receives little, then the buffer allocation emphasis should be on defining more transmit buffers. However, there is a caveat:

If the application is written such that the task that consumes receive data runs infrequently or the CPU utilization is high and the receiving application task(s) becomes starved for CPU time, then more receive buffers will be required.

To ensure the highest level of performance possible, it makes sense to define as many buffers as possible and use the interface and pool statistics data in order to refine the number after having run the application for a while. A busy network will require more receive buffers in order to handle the additional broadcast messages that will be received.

In general, at least two large and two small transmit buffers should be configured. This assumes that neither the network or CPU are very busy.

Many applications will receive properly with four or more large receive buffers. However, for TCP applications that move a lot of data between the target and the peer, this number may need to be higher.

Specifying too few transmit or receive buffers may lead to stalls in communication and possibly even dead-lock. Care should be taken when configuring the number of buffers. µC/TCP-IP is often tested with configurations of 10 or more small transmit, large transmit, and large receive buffers.

All device configuration structures and declarations are in the provided files named **net_dev_cfg.c** and **net_dev_cfg.h**. Each configuration structure must be completely initialized in the specified order. The following listing shows where to define the number of buffers per interface as calculated

```
const  NET_DEV_CFG_ETHER  NetDev_Cfg_Processor_0 = {
    ,
    1518,                                        (1)
      10,                                        (2)
      16,
       0,

    NET_IF_MEM_TYPE_MAIN,
    1594,                                        (3)
       5,                                        (4)
     256,                                        (5)
       5,                                        (6)
      16,
       0,

    0x00000000,                              •
            0,

      10,                                        (7)
       5,                                        (8)

    0x40001000,
            0,

     "00:50:C2:25:60:02"
};
```

LF-2(1)   Receive buffer size. This field sets the size of the largest receivable packet and may be set to match the application's requirements.

LF-2(2)   Number of receive buffers. This setting controls the number of receive buffers that will be allocated to the interface. This value *must* be set greater than or equal to one buffer if the interface is receiving *only* UDP. If TCP data is expected to be transferred across the interface, then there *must* be the minimum of receive buffers as calculated by the BDP.

LF-2(3)   Large transmit buffer size. This field controls the size of the large transmit buffers allocated to the device in bytes. This field has no effect if the number of large transmit buffers is configured to zero. Setting the size of the large transmit buffers below 1594, bytes may hinder the stack's ability to transmit full-sized IP datagrams since IP transmit fragmentation is not yet supported. Micrium recommends setting this field to 1594 bytes in order to accommodate µC/TCP-IPs internal packet building mechanisms.

LF-2(4)   Number of large transmit buffers. This field controls the number of large transmit buffers allocated to the device. The developer may set this field to zero to make room for additional small transmit buffers, however, the size of the maximum transmittable UDP packet will depend on the size of the small transmit buffers, (see #5).

LF-2(5)   Small transmit buffer size. For devices with a minimal amount of RAM, it is possible to allocate small transmit buffers as well as large transmit buffers. In general, Micrium recommends 256 byte small transmit buffers, however, the developer may adjust this value according to the application requirements. This field has no effect if the number of small transmit buffers is configured to zero.

LF-2(6)   Number of small transmit buffers. This field controls the number of small transmit buffers allocated to the device. The developer may set this field to zero to make room for additional large transmit buffers if required.

NUMBER OF DMA DESCRIPTORS TO CONFIGURE

If the hardware device is an Ethernet MAC that supports DMA, then the number of configured receive descriptors will play an important role in determining overall performance for the configured interface.

For applications with 10 or less large receive buffers, it is desirable to configure the number of receive descriptors to that of 60% to 70% of the number of configured receive buffers.

In this example, 60% of 10 receive buffers allows for four receive buffers to be available to the stack waiting to be processed by application tasks. While the application is processing data, the hardware may continue to receive additional frames up to the number of configured receive descriptors.

There is, however, a point in which configuring additional receive descriptors no longer greatly impacts performance. For applications with 20 or more buffers, the number of descriptors can be configured to 50% of the number of configured receive buffers. After this point, only the number of buffers remains a significant factor; especially for slower or busy CPUs and networks with higher utilization.

In general, if the CPU is not busy and the µC/TCP-IP Receive task has the opportunity to run often, the ratio of receive descriptors to receive buffers may be reduced further for very high numbers of available receive buffers (e.g., 50 or more).

The number of transmit descriptors should be configured such that it is equal to the number of small plus the number of large transmit buffers.

These numbers only serve as a starting point. The application and the environment that the device will be attached to will ultimately dictate the number of required transmit and receive descriptors necessary for achieving maximum performance.

Specifying too few descriptors can cause communication delays. See Listing F-2 for descriptors configuration.

LF-2(7)   Number of receive descriptors. For DMA-based devices, this value is utilized by the device driver during initialization in order to allocate a fixed-size pool of receive descriptors to be used by the device. The number of descriptors *must* be less than the number of configured receive buffers. Micrium recommends setting this value to approximately 60% to 70%f of the number of receive buffers. Non DMA based devices may configure this value to zero.

LF-2(8)   Number of transmit descriptors. For DMA-based devices, this value is utilized by the device driver during initialization in order to allocate a fixed-size pool of transmit descriptors to be used by the device. For best performance, the number of transmit descriptors should be equal to the number of small, plus the number of large transmit buffers configured for the device. Non DMA based devices may configure this value to zero.

CONFIGURING TCP WINDOW SIZES

Once number and size of the transmit and receive buffers are configured, as explained in the previous section, the last thing that need to be done is to configure the TCP Transmit and Receive Window sizes. These parameters are found in the **net_cfg.h** file in the **TRANSMISSION CONTROL PROTOCOL LAYER CONFIGURATION** section.

```
#define  NET_TCP_CFG_RX_WIN_SIZE_OCTET   4096  /* Configure TCP connection receive  window size.
*/  (1)
#define  NET_TCP_CFG_TX_WIN_SIZE_OCTET   4096  /* Configure TCP connection transmit window size.
*/  (2)
```

Listing F-3 **TCP Transmit and Receive Window Size configuration**

LF-3(1)   This **#define** configures the TCP Receive Window size. It is recommended to set this parameter to the number of receive descriptors in the case of DMA or to the number of receive buffers in the case of non-DMA, multiplied by the MSS. For example, if 4 descriptors or 4 receive buffers are required, the TCP Receive WIndow size is 4 * 1460 = 5840 bytes.

LF-3(2)   This **#define** configures the TCP Transmit Window size. It is recommended to set this parameter to the number of transmit descriptors in the case of DMA or to the number of transmit buffers in the case of non-DMA, multiplied by the MSS. For example, if 2 descriptors or 2 receive buffers are required, the TCP Receive WIndow size is 2 * 1460 = 2920 bytes.

WRITING OR OBTAINING ADDITIONAL DEVICE DRIVERS

Contact Micrium for information regarding obtaining additional device drivers. If a specific driver is not available, Micrium may develop the driver by providing engineering consulting services.

Alternately, a new device driver may be developed by filling in a template driver provided with the µC/TCP-IP source code.

See Chapter 16, "Device Driver Implementation" on page 365 for more information.

F-2-3 ETHERNET MAC ADDRESS

GETTING AN INTERFACE MAC ADDRESS

The application may call `NetIF_AddrHW_Get()` to obtain the MAC address for a specific interface.

CHANGING AN INTERFACE MAC ADDRESS

The application may call `NetIF_AddrHW_Set()` in order to set the MAC address for a specific interface.

GETTING A HOST MAC ADDRESS ON MY NETWORK

In order to determine the MAC address of a host on the network, the Network Protocol Stack must have an ARP cache entry for the specified host protocol address. An application may check to see if an ARP cache entry is present by calling `NetARP_CacheGetAddrHW()`.

If an ARP cache entry is not found, the application may call `NetARP_ProbeAddrOnNet()` to send an ARP request to all hosts on the network. If the target host is present, an ARP reply will be received shortly and the application should wait and then call `NetARP_CacheGetAddrHW()` to determine if the ARP reply has been entered into the ARP cache.

The following example shows how to obtain the Ethernet MAC address of a host on the local area network:

```
void AppGetRemoteHW_Addr (void)
{
  NET_IP_ADDR    addr_ip_local;
  NET_IP_ADDR    addr_ip_remote;
  CPU_CHAR      *paddr_ip_remote;
  CPU_CHAR       addr_hw_str[NET_IF_ETHER_ADDR_SIZE_STR];
  CPU_INT08U     addr_hw[NET_IF_ETHER_ADDR_SIZE];
  NET_ERR        err;


                            /* ------------- PREPARE IP ADDRs ------------- */
  paddr_ip_local = "10.10.1.10";   /* MUST be one of host's configured IP addrs.  */
   addr_ip_local = NetASCII_Str_to_IP((CPU_CHAR *) paddr_ip_local,
                                      (NET_ERR  *)&err);
  if (err != NET_ASCII_ERR_NONE) {
    printf(" Error #%d converting IP address %s", err, paddr_ip_local);
    return;
  }


  paddr_ip_remote = "10.10.1.50";   /* Remote host's IP addr to get hardware addr. */
   addr_ip_remote = NetASCII_Str_to_IP((CPU_CHAR *) paddr_ip_remote,
                                       (NET_ERR  *)&err);
  if (err != NET_ASCII_ERR_NONE) {
    printf(" Error #%d converting IP address %s", err, paddr_ip_remote);
    return;
  }


  addr_ip_local  = NET_UTIL_HOST_TO_NET_32(addr_ip_local);
  addr_ip_remote = NET_UTIL_HOST_TO_NET_32(addr_ip_remote);


                            /* ------------ PROBE ADDR ON NET ------------- */
  NetARP_ProbeAddrOnNet((NET_PROTOCOL_TYPE) NET_PROTOCOL_TYPE_IP_V4,
                        (CPU_INT08U       *)&addr_ip_local,
                        (CPU_INT08U       *)&addr_ip_remote,
                        (NET_ARP_ADDR_LEN ) sizeof(addr_ip_remote),
                        (NET_ERR          *)&err);
  if (err != NET_ARP_ERR_NONE) {
    printf(" Error #%d probing address %s on network", err, addr_ip_remote);
    return;
  }

  OSTimeDly(2);                          /* Delay short time for ARP to probe network.   */
```

```
                              /* ---- QUERY ARP CACHE FOR REMOTE HW ADDR ---- */
(void)NetARP_CacheGetAddrHW((CPU_INT08U    *)&addr_hw[0],
                            (NET_ARP_ADDR_LEN) sizeof(addr_hw_str),
                            (CPU_INT08U    *)&addr_ip_remote,
                            (NET_ARP_ADDR_LEN) sizeof(addr_ip_remote),
                            (NET_ERR       *)&err);
    switch (err) {
      case NET_ARP_ERR_NONE:
        NetASCII_MAC_to_Str((CPU_INT08U *)&addr_hw[0],
                            (CPU_CHAR    *)&addr_hw_str[0],
                            (CPU_BOOLEAN ) DEF_NO,
                            (CPU_BOOLEAN ) DEF_YES,
                            (NET_ERR    *)&err);
        if (err != NET_ASCII_ERR_NONE) {
          printf(" Error #%d converting hardware address", err);
          return;
        }

        printf(" Remote IP Addr %s @ HW Addr %s\n\r", paddr_ip_remote, &addr_hw_str[0]);
        break;


      case NET_ARP_ERR_CACHE_NOT_FOUND:
        printf("  Remote IP Addr %s NOT found on network\n\r", paddr_ip_remote);
        break;


      case NET_ARP_ERR_CACHE_PEND:
        printf("  Remote IP Addr %s NOT YET found on network\n\r", paddr_ip_remote);
        break;


      case NET_ARP_ERR_NULL_PTR:
      case NET_ARP_ERR_INVALID_HW_ADDR_LEN:
      case NET_ARP_ERR_INVALID_PROTOCOL_ADDR_LEN:
      default:
        printf(" Error #%d querying ARP cache", err);
        break;
    }
}
```

Listing F-4 **Obtaining the Ethernet MAC address of a host**

F-2-4 ETHERNET PHY LINK STATE

INCREASING THE RATE OF LINK STATE POLLING

The application may increase the μC/TCP-IP link state polling rate by calling -NetIF_CfgPhyLinkPeriod() (see section C-9-6 on page 740). The default value is 250ms.

GETTING THE CURRENT LINK STATE FOR AN INTERFACE

μC/TCP-IP provides two mechanisms for obtaining interface link state.

1   A function which reads a global variable that is periodically updated.

2   A function which reads the current link state from the hardware.

Method 1 provides the fastest mechanism to obtain link state since it does not require communication with the physical layer device. For most applications, this mechanism is suitable and if necessary, the polling rate can be increased by calling NetIF_CfgPhyLinkPeriod(). In order to utilize Method 1, the application may call NetIF_LinkStateGet() which returns NET_IF_LINK_UP or NET_IF_LINK_DOWN.

The accuracy of Method 1 can be improved by using a physical layer device and driver combination that supports link state change interrupts. In this circumstance, the value of the global variable containing the link state is updated immediately following a link state change. Therefore, the polling rate can be reduced further if desired and a call to NetIF_LinkStateGet() will return the actual link state.

Method 2 requires the application to call NetIF_IO_Ctrl() with the option parameter set to either NET_IF_IO_CTRL_LINK_STATE_GET or NET_IF_IO_CTRL_LINK_STATE_GET_INFO.

■   If the application specifies NET_IF_IO_CTRL_LINK_STATE_GET, then NET_IF_LINK_UP or NET_IF_LINK_DOWN will be returned.

■   Alternatively, if the application specifies NET_IF_IO_CTRL_LINK_STATE_GET_INFO, the link state details such as speed and duplex will be returned.

The advantage to Method 2 is that the link state returned is the actual link state as reported by the hardware at the time of the function call. However, the overhead of communicating with the physical layer device may be high and therefore some cycles may be wasted waiting for the result since the connection bus between the CPU and the physical layer device is often only a couple of MHz.

FORCING AN ETHERNET PHY TO A SPECIFIC LINK STATE

The generic PHY driver that comes with μC/TCP-IP does not provide a mechanism for disabling auto-negotiation and specifying a desired link state. This restriction is required in order to remain MII register block compliant with all (R)MII compliant physical layer devices.

However, μC/TCP-IP does provide a mechanism for coaching the physical layer device into advertising only the desired auto-negotiation states. This may be achieved by adjusting the physical layer device configuration as specified in **net_dev_cfg.c** with alternative link speed and duplex values.

The following is an example physical layer device configuration structure.

```
NET_PHY_CFG_ETHER NetPhy_Cfg_Generic_0 = {
    0,
    NET_PHY_BUS_MODE_MII,
    NET_PHY_TYPE_EXT,
    NET_PHY_SPD_AUTO,
    NET_PHY_DUPLEX_AUTO
};
```

The parameters **NET_PHY_SPD_AUTO** and **NET_PHY_DUPLEX_AUTO** may be changed to match any of the following settings:

```
NET_PHY_SPD_10
NET_PHY_SPD_100
NET_PHY_SPD_1000
NET_PHY_SPD_AUTO
NET_PHY_DUPLEX_HALF
NET_PHY_DUPLEX_FULL
NET_PHY_DUPLEX_AUTO
```

This mechanism is only effective when both the physical layer device attached to the target and the remote link state partner support auto-negotiation.

F-3 IP ADDRESS CONFIGURATION

F-3-1 CONVERTING IP ADDRESSES TO AND FROM THEIR DOTTED DECIMAL REPRESENTATION

µC/TCP-IP contains functions to perform various string operations on IP addresses.

The following example shows how to use the NetASCII module in order to convert IP addresses to and from their dotted-decimal representations:

```
NET_IP_ADDR ip;
CPU_INT08U  ip_str[16];
NET_ERR     err;
ip = NetASCII_Str_to_IP((CPU_CHAR *)"192.168.1.65", &err);
NetASCII_IP_to_Str(ip, &ip_str[0], DEF_NO, &err);
```

F-3-2 ASSIGNING STATIC IP ADDRESSES TO AN INTERFACE

The constant **NET_IP_CFG_IF_MAX_NBR_ADDR** specified in **net_cfg.h** determines the maximum number of IP addresses that may be assigned to an interface. Many IP addresses may be added up to the specified maximum by calling **NetIP_CfgAddrAdd( )**.

Configuring an IP gateway address is not necessary when communicating only within your local network.

```
CPU_BOOLEAN cfg_success;


ip          = NetASCII_Str_to_IP((CPU_CHAR *)"192.168.1.65", perr);
msk         = NetASCII_Str_to_IP((CPU_CHAR *)"255.255.255.0", perr);
gateway     = NetASCII_Str_to_IP((CPU_CHAR *)"192.168.1.1",  perr);
cfg_success = NetIP_CfgAddrAdd(if_nbr, ip, msk, gateway, perr);
```

F-3-3 REMOVING STATICALLY ASSIGNED IP ADDRESSES FROM AN INTERFACE

Statically assigned IP addresses for a specific interface may be removed by calling `NetIP_CfgAddrRemove()`.

Alternatively, the application may call `NetIP_CfgAddrRemoveAll()` to remove all configured static addresses for a specific interface.

F-3-4 GETTING A DYNAMIC IP ADDRESS

µC/DHCPc must be obtained and integrated into the application to dynamically assign an IP address to an interface.

F-3-5 GETTING ALL THE IP ADDRESSES CONFIGURED ON A SPECIFIC INTERFACE

The application may obtain the protocol address information for a specific interface by calling `NetIP_GetAddrHost()`. This function may return one or more configured addresses.

Similarly, the application may call `NetIP_GetAddrSubnetMask()` and `NetIP_GetAddrDfltGateway()` in order to determine the subnet mask and gateway information for a specific interface.

F-4 SOCKET PROGRAMMING

F-4-1 USING µC/TCP-IP SOCKETS

Refer to Chapter 18, "Socket Programming" on page 501 for code examples on this topic.

F-4-2 JOINING AND LEAVING AN IGMP HOST GROUP

µC/TCP-IP supports IP multicasting with IGMP. In order to receive packets addressed to a given IP multicast group address, the stack must have been configured to support multicasting in **net_cfg.h**, and that host group has to be joined.

The following examples show how to join and leave an IP multicast group with µC/TCP-IP:

```
NET_IF_NBR  if_nbr;
NET_IP_ADDR group_ip_addr;
NET_ERR     err;


if_nbr       = NET_IF_NBR_BASE_CFGD;
group_ip_addr = NetASCII_Str_to_IP("233.0.0.1", &err);
if (err != NET_ASCII_ERR_NONE) {
  /* Handle error. */
}
NetIGMP_HostGrpJoin(if_nbr, group_ip_addr, &err);
if (err != NET_IGMP_ERR_NONE) {
  /* Handle error. */
}
[...]
NetIGMP_HostGrpLeave(if_nbr, group_ip_addr, &err);
if (err != NET_IGMP_ERR_NONE) {
  /* Handle error. */
}
```

F-4-3 TRANSMITTING TO A MULTICAST IP GROUP ADDRESS

Transmitting to an IP multicast group is identical to transmitting to a unicast or broadcast address. However, the stack must be configured to enable multicast transmit.

F-4-4 RECEIVING FROM A MULTICAST IP GROUP

An IP multicast group must be joined before packets can be received from it from it (see section F-4-2 "Joining and Leaving an IGMP Host Group" on page 1018 for more information). Once this is done, receiving from a multicast group only requires a socket bound to the **NET_SOCK_ADDR_IP_WILDCARD** address, as shown in the following example:

```
NET_SOCK_ID        sock;
NET_SOCK_ADDR_IP   sock_addr_ip;
NET_SOCK_ADDR      addr_remote;
NET_SOCK_ADDR_LEN  addr_remote_len;
CPU_CHAR           rx_buf[100];
CPU_INT16U         rx_len;
NET_ERR            err;


sock = NetSock_Open((NET_SOCK_PROTOCOL_FAMILY) NET_SOCK_ADDR_FAMILY_IP_V4,
                    (NET_SOCK_TYPE            ) NET_SOCK_TYPE_DATAGRAM,
                    (NET_SOCK_PROTOCOL        ) NET_SOCK_PROTOCOL_UDP,
                    (NET_ERR                 *)&err);
if (err != NET_SOCK_ERR_NONE) {
   /* Handle error. */
}
Mem_Set(&sock_addr_ip, (CPU_CHAR)0, sizeof(sock_addr_ip));
sock_addr_ip.AddrFamily = NET_SOCK_ADDR_FAMILY_IP_V4;
sock_addr_ip.Addr       = NET_UTIL_HOST_TO_NET_32(NET_SOCK_ADDR_IP_WILDCARD);
sock_addr_ip.Port       = NET_UTIL_HOST_TO_NET_16(10000);
NetSock_Bind((NET_SOCK_ID      ) sock,
             (NET_SOCK_ADDR    *)&sock_addr_ip,
             (NET_SOCK_ADDR_LEN) NET_SOCK_ADDR_SIZE,
             (NET_ERR          *)&err);
if (err != NET_SOCK_ERR_NONE) {
   /* Handle error. */
}


rx_len = NetSock_RxDataFrom((NET_SOCK_ID       ) sock,
                            (void             *)&rx_buf [0],
                            (CPU_INT16U        ) BUF_SIZE,
                            (CPU_INT16S        ) NET_SOCK_FLAG_NONE,
                            (NET_SOCK_ADDR     *)&addr_remote,
                            (NET_SOCK_ADDR_LEN *)&addr_remote_len,
                            (void             *) 0,
                            (CPU_INT08U        ) 0,
                            (CPU_INT08U       *) 0,
                            (NET_ERR          *)&err);
```

F-4-5 THE APPLICATION RECEIVE SOCKET ERRORS IMMEDIATELY AFTER REBOOT

Immediately after a network interface is added, the physical layer device is reset and network interface and device initialization begins. However, it may take up to three seconds for the average Ethernet physical layer device to complete auto-negotiation. During this time, the socket layer will return NET_SOCK_ERR_LINK_DOWN for sockets that are bound to the interface in question.

The application should attempt to retry the socket operation with a short delay between attempts until network link has been established.

F-4-6 REDUCING THE NUMBER OF TRANSITORY ERRORS (NET_ERR_TX)

The number of transmit buffer should be increased. Additionally, it may be helpful to add a short delay between successive calls to socket transmit functions.

F-4-7 CONTROLLING SOCKET BLOCKING OPTIONS

Socket blocking options may be configured during compile time by adjusting the net_cfg.h macro NET_SOCK_CFG_BLOCK_SEL to the following values:

NET_SOCK_BLOCK_SEL_DFLT
NET_SOCK_BLOCK_SEL_BLOCK
NET_SOCK_BLOCK_SEL_NO_BLOCK

NET_SOCK_BLOCK_SEL_DFLT selects blocking as the default option, however, allows run-time code to override blocking settings by specifying additional socket.

NET_SOCK_BLOCK_SEL_BLOCK configures all sockets to always block.

NET_SOCK_BLOCK_SEL_NO_BLOCK configures all sockets to non blocking.

See the section C-14-40 on page 884 and section C-14-42 on page 891 for more information about sockets and blocking options.

F-4-8 DETECTING IF A SOCKET IS STILL CONNECTED TO A PEER

Applications may call `NetSock_IsConn()` to determine if a socket is (still) connected to a remote socket (see section C-14-33 on page 871).

Alternatively, applications may make a non-blocking call to `recv()`, `NetSock_RxData()`, or `NetSock_RxDataFrom()` and inspect the return value. If data or a non-fatal, transitory error is returned, then the socket is still connected; otherwise, if '0' or a fatal error is returned, then the socket is disconnected or closed.

F-4-9 RECEIVING -1 INSTEAD OF 0 WHEN CALLING RECV() FOR A CLOSED SOCKET

When a remote peer closes a socket, and the target application calls one of the receive socket functions, µC/TCP-IP will first report that the receive queue is empty and return a -1 for both BSD and µC/TCP-IP socket API functions. The next call to receive will indicate that the socket has been closed by the remote peer.

This is a known issue and will be corrected in subsequent versions of µC/TCP-IP.

F-4-10 DETERMINE THE INTERFACE FOR RECEIVED UDP DATAGRAM

If a UDP socket server is bound to the "any" address, then it is not currently possible to know which interface received the UDP datagram. This is a limitation in the BSD socket API and therefore no solution has been implemented in the µC/TCP-IP socket API.

In order to guarantee which interface a UDP packet was received on, the socket server must bind a specific interface address.

In fact, if a UDP datagram is received on a listening socket bound to the "any" address and the application transmits a response back to the peer using the same socket, then the newly transmitted UDP datagram will be transmitted from the default interface. The default interface may or may not be the interface in which the UDP datagram originated.

F-5 µC/TCP-IP STATISTICS AND DEBUG

F-5-1 PERFORMANCE STATISTICS DURING RUN-TIME

µC/TCP-IP periodically measures and estimates run-time performance on a per interface basis. The performance data is stored in the global µC/TCP-IP statistics data structure, `Net_StatCtrs` which is of type `NET_CTR_STATS`.

Each interface has a performance metric structure which is allocated within a single array of `NET_CTR_IF_STATS`. Each index in the array represents a different interface.

In order to access the performance metrics for a specific interface number, the application may externally access the array by viewing the variable `Net_StatCtrs.NetIF_StatCtrs[if_nbr].field_name`, where `if_nbr` represents the interface number in question, 0 for the loopback interface, and where `field_name` corresponds to one of the fields below.

Possible field names:

```
NetIF_StatRxNbrOctets
NetIF_StatRxNbrOctetsPerSec
NetIF_StatRxNbrOctetsPerSecMax
NetIF_StatRxNbrPktCtr
NetIF_StatRxNbrPktCtrPerSec
NetIF_StatRxNbrPktCtrPerSecMax
NetIF_StatRxNbrPktCtrProcessed
NetIF_StatTxNbrOctets
NetIF_StatTxNbrOctetsPerSec
NetIF_StatTxNbrOctetsPerSecMax
NetIF_StatTxNbrPktCtr
NetIF_StatTxNbrPktCtrPerSec
NetIF_StatTxNbrPktCtrPerSecMax
NetIF_StatTxNbrPktCtrProcessed
```

See Chapter 21, "Statistics and Error Counters" on page 527 for more information.

F-5-2 VIEWING ERROR AND STATISTICS COUNTERS

In order to access the statistics and error counters, the application may externally access the global µC/TCP-IP statistics array by referencing the members of the structure variable **Net_StatCtrs**.

See Chapter 21, "Statistics and Error Counters" on page 527 for more information.

F-5-3 USING NETWORK DEBUG FUNCTIONS TO CHECK NETWORK STATUS CONDITIONS

Example(s) demonstrating how to use the network debug status functions include:

```
NET_DBG_STATUS net_status;
CPU_BOOLEAN    net_fault;
CPU_BOOLEAN    net_fault_conn;
CPU_BOOLEAN    net_rsrc_lost;
CPU_BOOLEAN    net_rsrc_low;

net_status     = NetDbg_ChkStatus();
net_fault      = DEF_BIT_IS_SET(net_status, NET_DBG_STATUS_FAULT);
net_fault_conn = DEF_BIT_IS_SET(net_status, NET_DBG_STATUS_FAULT_CONN);
net_rsrc_lost  = DEF_BIT_IS_SET(net_status, NET_DBG_STATUS_RSRC_LOST);
net_rsrc_lo    = DEF_BIT_IS_SET(net_status, NET_DBG_STATUS_RSRC_LO);
net_status     = NetDbg_ChkStatusTmrs();
```

F-6 USING NETWORK SECURITY MANAGER

The network security manager requires the presence of a network security layer such as µC/SSL. The port layer developed for the network security layer is reponsible of securing the sockets and applying the security strategy over typical socket programming functions. From an application point of view, the usage of µC/TCP-IP network security manager is very simple. It requires two basic step. The application code shipped with µC/TCP-IP includes a project that shows how to use the network security manager.

F-6-1 KEYING MATERIAL INSTALLATION

In order to acheive secure handshake connections, some keying material must be installed before performing any secure socket operation. With µC/SSL, the client side needs to install certificates authorities to validate the identity of the public key certificate sent by the server side. On the opposite, a server needs to install a public key certificare / private key pair to send the the clients that wants to connect. This keying material can be installed using the network security manager APIs decribed in section C-13-1 on page 804 and section C-13-2 on page 806 of µC/TCP-IP user manual. The following example demonstrates how to install a PEM certificate authority from a constant buffer.

```
CPU_SIZE_T  Micrium_Ca_Cert_Pem_Len = 994;
CPU_CHAR    Micrium_Ca_Cert_Pem[] =
"-----BEGIN CERTIFICATE-----\r\n"
"MIICpTCCAg4CCQDNdHgFKaYRWDANBgkqhkiG9w0BAQUFADCBljELMAkGA1UEBhMC\r\n"
"Q0ExDzANBgNVBAgMBlF1ZWJlYzERMA8GA1UEBwwITW9udHJlYWwxFTATBgNVBAoM\r\n"
"DElpY3JpdW0gSW5jLjEZMBcGA1UECwwQRW1iZWRkZWQgU3lzdGVtczEQMA4GA1UE\r\n"
"AwwHTWljcmllbTEfMB0GCSqGSIb3DQEJARYQaW5mb0BtaWNyaXVtLmNvbTAeFw0x\r\n"
"aXVtMR8wHQYJKoZIhvcNAQkBFhBpbmZvQG1pY3JpdW0uY29tMIGfMA0GCSqGSIb3\r\n"
[...]
"CZFtP3vbY0SA6gFrCvCcKjTWRapzQKwSYknMulQorP4mdwZDeCYsikkn8bI5//zn\r\n"
"CInLCmrWdbrCEtj23t0wefw8fyNQxkKi9JdbzLVwxjIQt8wMq1CnTOQRa7aGX5Uw\r\n"
"QQIDAQABMA0GCSqGSIb3DQEBBQUAA4GBACqyJeSDQ3j5KohXIvV+iBOrl5qbI1PS\r\n"
"WAHf4PSyiTX0Spa58VSdhM4sestd/FELBWo/MHKIfBdoLMhg2frDZE5e7m8Ftq1R\r\n"
"1YBKNbTzIJNjwTajkUPz38BjXb5sqLyPK8wRbjadm2pOlw1f7bIFunpbHpV+1XA1\r\n"
"tk3W32BqKfzy\r\n"
"-----END CERTIFICATE-----\r\n";


void  Task (void)
{
    NET_ERR  err;


    NetSecureMgr_InstallBuf((CPU_INT08U *)Micrium_Ca_Cert_Pem,
                                          NET_SECURE_INSTALL_TYPE_CA,
                                          NET_SECURE_INSTALL_FORMAT_PEM,
                                          Micrium_Ca_Cert_Pem_Len,
                                         &err);
    if (err != NET_SECURE_MGR_ERR_NONE) {
        APP_TRACE_INFO(("    uC/TCP-IP:NetSecureMgr_InstallBuf() error %d \n", err));
        return;
    }
}
```

The following example demonstrates how to install a DER certificate authority, PEM public key certificate and a DER private key from the file system.

```
#define  Micrium_Ca_Cert_File_Der            "\\ca-cert.der"
#define  Micrium_Srv_Cert_File_Pem           "\\server-cert.pem"
#define  Micrium_Srv_Key_File_Der            "\\server-key.der"
void  Task (void  *p_arg)
{
    NET_ERR  err;


    NetSecureMgr_InstallFile(Micrium_Ca_Cert_File_Der,
                             NET_SECURE_INSTALL_TYPE_CA,
                             NET_SECURE_INSTALL_FORMAT_DER,
                             &err);
    if (err != NET_SECURE_MGR_ERR_NONE) {
        APP_TRACE_INFO(("    uC/TCP-IP:NetSecureMgr_InstallFile() error %d \n", err));
        return;
    }


    NetSecureMgr_InstallFile(Micrium_Srv_Cert_File_Pem,
                             NET_SECURE_INSTALL_TYPE_CERT,
                             NET_SECURE_INSTALL_FORMAT_PEM,
                             &err);
    if (err != NET_SECURE_MGR_ERR_NONE) {
        APP_TRACE_INFO(("    uC/TCP-IP:NetSecureMgr_InstallFile() error %d \n", err));
        return;
    }


    NetSecureMgr_InstallFile(Micrium_Srv_Key_File_Der,
                             NET_SECURE_INSTALL_TYPE_KEY,
                             NET_SECURE_INSTALL_FORMAT_DER,
                             &err);
    if (err != NET_SECURE_MGR_ERR_NONE) {
        APP_TRACE_INFO(("    uC/TCP-IP:NetSecureMgr_InstallFile() error %d \n", err));
        return;
    }
}
```

F

F-6-2 SECURING A SOCKET

Once the appropriate keying material is installed, a TCP socket can be secured if it has been successfully open. A simple function call is used to setup the secure flag on the socket. This function is documented in section C-14-4 on page 815 of µC/TCP-IP user manual. With this simple API, you can secure your custom TCP client or server application. Pleae note that all Micrium applications running over TCP has already been modified to support secure sockets (µC/HTTPs, µC/TELNETs, µC/FTPs, µC/FTPc, µC/SMTPc, µC/POP3c). The following example demonstrates how to open and secure a TCP socket

```
void  Task (void  *p_arg)
{
    NET_ERR  net_err;
    sock_id = NetSock_Open(NET_SOCK_ADDR_FAMILY_IP_V4,
                           NET_SOCK_TYPE_STREAM,
                           NET_SOCK_PROTOCOL_TCP,
                           &net_err);
    if (net_err == NET_SOCK_ERR_NONE) {

#ifdef  NET_SECURE_MODULE_PRESENT
        (void)NetSock_CfgSecure((NET_SOCK_ID   ) sock_id,
                                (CPU_BOOLEAN   ) DEF_YES,
                                (NET_ERR      *)&net_err);
        if (net_err != NET_SOCK_ERR_NONE) {
            APP_TRACE_INFO(("Open socket failed. No secure socket available.\n"));
            return (DEF_FAIL);
        }
#endif
    }
}
```

F-7 MISCELLANEOUS

F-7-1 SENDING AND RECEIVING ICMP ECHO REQUESTS FROM THE TARGET

From the user application, µC/TCP-IP does not support sending and receiving ICMP Echo Request and Reply messages However, the target is capable of receiving externally generated ICMP Echo Request messages and replying them accordingly. At this time, there are no means to generate an ICMP Echo Request from the target.

F-7-2 TCP KEEP-ALIVES

µC/TCP-IP does not currently support TCP Keep-Alives. If both ends of the connection are running different Network Protocol Stacks, you may attempt to enable TCP Keep-Alives on the remote side. Alternatively, the application will have to send something through the socket to the remote peer in order to ensure that the TCP connection remains open.

F-7-3 USING µC/TCP-IP FOR INTER-PROCESS COMMUNICATION

It is possible for tasks to communicate with sockets via the localhost interface which must be enabled.

Labrosse, Jean J. 2009, *μC/OS-III, The Real-Time Kernel*, Micrium Press, 2009, ISBN 978-0-98223375-3-0.

Douglas E. Comer. 2006, *Internetworking With TCP/IP Volume 1: Principles Protocols, and Architecture, 5th edition*, 2006. (Hardcover - Jul 10, 2005) ISBN 0-13-187671-6.

W. Richard Stevens. 1993, *TCP/IP Illustrated, Volume 1: The Protocols*, Addison-Wesley Professional Computing Series, Published Dec 31, 1993 by Addison-Wesley Professional, Hardcover , ISBN-10: 0-201-63346-9

W. Richard Stevens, Bill Fenner, Andrew M. Rudoff. *Unix Network Programming, Volume 1: The Sockets Networking API (3rd Edition)* (Addison-Wesley Professional Computing Series) (Hardcover), ISBN-10: 0-13-141155-1

IEEE Standard 802.3-1985, *Technical Committee on Computer Communications of the IEEE Computer Society.* (1985), IEEE Standard 802.3-1985, IEEE, pp. 121, ISBN 0-471-82749-5

Request for Comments (RFCs), Internet Engineering Task Force (IETF). The complete list of RFCs can be found at http://www.faqs.org/rfcs/.

Brian "Beej Jorgensen" Hall, 2009, *Beej's Guide to Network Programming, Version 3.0.13,* March 23, 2009, http://beej.us/guide/bgnet/

The Motor Industry Software Reliability Association, *MISRA-C:2004*, Guidelines for the Use of the C Language in Critical Systems, October 2004. www.misra-c.com.

G

µC/TCP-IP Licensing Policy

H-1 µC/TCP-IP LICENSING

H-1-1 µC/OS-III AND µC/TCP-IP LICENSING

This book includes µC/OS-III in source form for free short-term evaluation, for educational use or for peaceful research. We provide ALL the source code for your convenience and to help you experience µC/OS-III. The fact that the source is provided does *not* mean that you can use it commercially without paying a licensing fee. Knowledge of the source code may NOT be used to develop a similar product either.

This book also contains µC/TCP-IP, precompiled in linkable object form. It is not necessary to purchase anything else, as long as the initial purchase is used for educational purposes. Once the code is used to create a commercial project/product for profit, however, it is necessary to purchase a license.

You are required to purchase this license when the decision to use µC/OS-III and/or µC/TCP-IP in a design is made, not when the design is ready to go to production.

If you are unsure about whether you need to obtain a license for your application, please contact Micrium and discuss the intended use with a sales representative.

H-1-2 µC/TCP-IP MAINTENANCE RENEWAL

Licensing µC/TCP-IP provides one year of limited technical support and maintenance and source code updates. Renew the maintenance agreement for continued support and source code updates.Contact sales@Micrium.com for additional information.

H-1-3 µC/TCP-IP SOURCE CODE UPDATES

If you are under maintenance, you will be automatically emailed when source code updates become available. You can then download your available updates from the Micrium FTP server. If you are no longer under maintenance, or forget your Micrium FTP user name or password, please contact sales@Micrium.com.

H-1-4 µC/TCP-IP SUPPORT

Support is available for licensed customers. Please visit the customer support section in www.Micrium.com. If you are not a current user, please register to create your account. A web form will be offered to you to submit your support question,

Licensed customers can also use the following contact:

CONTACT MICRIUM

Micrium
1290 Weston Road, Suite 306
Weston, FL 33326

+1 954 217 2036
+1 954 217 2037 (FAX)

µC/TCP-IP™
The Embedded Protocol Stack

and the
Texas Instruments LM3S9B92

Christian Légaré
and
The Stellaris Team

Micriµm
Press

Weston, FL 33326

Micriµm Press
1290 Weston Road, Suite 306
Weston, FL 33326
USA
www.micrium.com

For bulk orders, please contact Micrium Press at: +1 954 217 2036

Micriµm
Press

ISBN: 978-1-935772-00-2

100-uC-TCPIP-TI-LM3S9B92-001

Foreword

In the almost 30 years that I have been active in the embedded systems industry, I have worked with everything from the smallest 8-bit processor to the latest of five generations of 32-bit processors. I have spent a great deal of time developing embedded processing boards, devices, and ASICs, as well as software tools, libraries, and real-time operating systems (RTOSs). During the first part of my tenure, commercial RTOSs were not widely used because they were very expensive, required royalty payments, were only available in object form, and never had the BSP (HAL) you needed. Most developers wrote their own homegrown RTOS, the functions of which ranged from an event-loop to a simple scheduler to a monstrosity that no one understood anymore (the author left, and his four total comments apparently were not quite enough to decipher it).

In 1992, Jean Labrosse shocked the industry by writing an article in *Embedded Systems Programming* magazine explaining and showing the code to a really nice RTOS that was efficient and easy to understand. This groundbreaking event led to a new generation of RTOS vendors who licensed their products with source code and without royalties—finally making a commercial RTOS a reasonable option for many. It also opened the door to an open-source model for RTOS that has proved to be very successful. His follow-on book, *MicroC/OS-II: The Real-Time Kernel*, accomplished two interesting feats: it allowed users of RTOSs to better understand how they work as well as the trade-offs involved, resulting in better applications and implementations; and it laid bare many of the essentials of RTOS design to a larger number of developers, similar to the "dragon" book for compiler writers (*Principles of Compiler Design*, by Alfred Aho and Jeffrey D. Ullman). Prior to this book, most OS books gave RTOSs short shrift at best and were generally unreadable.

When I worked at ARM designing ARMv7-M (Cortex™-M3/M4), embedded operating systems were very much on my mind. I put a great deal of effort into ensuring that the new processor core would be able to work efficiently with RTOSs, knowing that the processor's system handling was usually the enemy of real-time OSs. I worked with Jean Labrosse as well as a few others to ensure that any instructions and facilities I added would be useful and optimal. µC/OS was quick to exploit most of those features, probably faster and more fully than any other RTOS. From the CLZ instruction (count leading zeros) to find the highest priority ready task, to PendSV/SVC (pended system call/system service call) for scheduling, to knowing that SysTick will be there for the base tick feature, µC/OS was able to immediately gain major advantage in performance and determinism. Micriµm also was quick to take advantage of debug and test facilities to not only optimize the kernel but also allow the developer to optimize the application, including use of the specialized hardware in Cortex-M3.

Texas Instruments' Stellaris® family of microcontrollers, the first Cortex™-M3 implementation, is a natural fit for µC/OS. The StellarisWare® Peripheral Driver Library was leveraged by µC/OS from early on (so avoiding the dreaded BSP/HAL porting problem). Micriµm was quick to support advanced communications capabilities such as Ethernet, greatly increasing the productivity of application developers by providing a stable base for development and allowing them to focus on their actual applications instead of middleware. The fast, deterministic interrupt performance of the Stellaris MCUs ensures that TCP/IP and stacked networking protocols can be used while still meeting hard, real-time system requirements. In addition, Stellaris MCUs are currently the only ARM-based MCUs that integrate the Ethernet PHY, simplifying system design and reducing cost.

As you read this book, I believe you will gain a good understanding of how your application, µC/OS-III and µC/TCP-IP stack work together, how to get the best determinism, how to avoid the pitfalls of high jitter and priority inversion, how to streamline data and task flow, and how to take advantage of the hardware and OS facilities to get the most from your application.

Paul Kimelman
Chief Architect, Stellaris Business Unit
Texas Instruments

Acknowledgements

STELLARIS® TEAM

- Dexter Travis, Alex Bestavros, and Juan Benavides—software examples

- Rebecca Rostetter—board packaging. project planning

- Sue Cozart, Denise Fischer—Part II Stellaris material

- Jonathan Guy—circuit design, *EVALBOT User's Guide*

- David Yanoshak—mechanical design and board layout

Acknowledgements

Introduction

Part II of this book provides an example project that highlights the features of μC/TCP-IP with interactive hardware and software examples, IAR Embedded Workbench tools, and detailed instructions. The EVALBOT project is packaged with this book and contains everything you need to get the project running quickly.

1-1 EVALBOT OVERVIEW

The EVALBOT is a small robotic device that features a board with a Stellaris® LM3S9B92 microcontroller with Ethernet, USB OTG (On-The-Go), and I^{2}S. The kit contains wheels that are easy to attach to the board, a display, batteries, a USB cable, and a CD with the IAR tools, the StellarisWare® software, and all the necessary documentation. Figure 1-1 shows the top-side of the EVALBOT.

Figure 1-1 **Stellaris® EVALBOT Robot**

The board features include:

- Stellaris® LM3S9B92-IQC80 microcontroller
  - 256 KB Flash memory/96 KB SRAM
  - Ethernet
  - USB OTG
  - I^2S

- microSD card support

- I^2S audio codec with speaker

- USB 2.0 Host and Device connectors

- Ethernet 10/100 port with two LED indicators

- OLED graphics display

- Wireless communication expansion port

- On/Reset and Off buttons and power indicator LED

- Two application-defined buttons

- Left and right bump sensors

- Standard ARM® 10-pin JTAG debug connector for use as an In-Circuit Debug Interface (ICDI)

- I/O signal break-out pads for hardware prototyping

- Battery power through 3 AAA batteries or power through USB

The LM3S9B92 features high performance along with industrial connectivity, expanded peripheral interface connectivity, and low-power optimization for battery-backed applications. The LM3S9B92 provides a fully-integrated Ethernet with both MAC and PHY layers, 2 CAN 2.0 A/B controllers, and USB full-speed OTG or Host/Device with integrated PHY. Also included are two separate ADC units along with extended StellarisWare software in ROM, including the Peripheral Driver Library and Boot Loader, AES cryptography tables, and CRC error-detection functionality. The LM3S9B92 includes additional enhancements such as an internal 16-MHz precision oscillator with software trim capability, a second watchdog timer on an independent clock domain, and a uniquely flexible external peripheral interface (EPI), which is a 32-bit dedicated parallel bus for external peripherals that supports SDRAM, SRAM/Flash, and machine-to-machine up to 150 Mbytes/sec usage.

The StellarisWare software included in ROM is an extensive suite of software designed to simplify and speed development of Stellaris-based microcontroller applications and contains:

- Stellaris Peripheral Driver Library for peripheral initialization and control functions

- Stellaris USB Library for USB Device, USB Host, or USB OTG applications

- Stellaris Graphics Library for graphical display support

- Stellaris® Boot Loader and vector table

- Advanced Encryption Standard (AES) cryptography tables

- Cyclic Redundancy Check (CRC) error detection functionality

StellarisWare also includes a wide array of example code and applications and can be used royalty-free on any Stellaris microcontroller.

1-2 CONTENTS OF PART II

Chapter 1, Introduction. This chapter.

Chapter 2, The ARM Cortex-M3 and Stellaris® Microcontrollers. It provides an overview of the Stellaris implementation of the ARM Cortex-M3 CPU.

Chapter 3, Getting Started with the Stellaris® EVALBOT Evaluation Kit. This chapter explains how to connect the board to your PC, how to download the 32 K Kickstart version of IAR Systems Embedded Workbench for ARM, and how to run the example code.

Chapter 4, Stellaris® Robotic Evaluation Board (EVALBOT) User's Manual. This chapter describes the EVALBOT evaluation board.

Chapter 5, Using the EVALBOT Examples. This chapter describes the steps you need to follow to get started with the examples for the EVALBOT. Once you have completed these basic steps, you can then get started with any of the examples that follow.

Chapter 6, Basic Example. This example provides a method to verify the μC/TCP-IP implementation using the ICMP Echo Request (ping). This simple project is designed to familiarize you with the μC/TCP-IP stack and the TI Stellaris LM3S9B92 port of the stack. This example also provides a foundation for the remainder of the examples in this book.

Chapter 7, HTTP Server Example. In this example, you interact with an embedded web server using the EVALBOT with a web browser. It demonstrates the use of μC/TCP-IP and μC/HTTPs to display status and allow control of the EVALBOT using a simple HTML form.

Chapter 8, TCP Sockets Example. This Ethernet client example demonstrates how μC/OS-III and μC/TCP-IP IP can be used in conjunction with the EVALBOT evaluation board to create a TCP socket application gathering data from NOAA's National Weather Service server (http://www.weather.gov) using Simple Object Access Protocol (SOAP).

Appendix A, Ethernet Driver. The driver for the Stellaris Ethernet Controller is presented.

Appendix B, IAR Systems Embedded Workbench for ARM. This appendix provides a description of IAR Systems Embedded Workbench for the ARM architecture (EWARM).

Appendix C, Bibliography

Appendix D, Licensing Policy.

Chapter

2

The ARM Cortex-M3 and Stellaris® Microcontrollers

The ARM Cortex family is a new generation of processor that provides a standard architecture for a wide range of technological demands. Unlike other ARM CPUs, the Cortex family is a complete processor core that provides a standard CPU and system architecture. The Cortex-M3 family is designed for cost-sensitive and microcontroller applications.

This chapter provides a brief summary of the Cortex-M3 architecture. Additional reference material is provided in Appendix C, "Bibliography" on page 1181.

While ARM7 and ARM9 CPUs are successfully integrated into standard microcontrollers, they do show their SoC heritage. Each specific manufacturer has designed an interrupt handling solution. However, the Cortex-M3 provides a standardized microcontroller core, which goes beyond the CPU to provide the complete heart of a microcontroller (including the interrupt system, SysTick timer, debug system and memory map). The 4 Gbyte address space of Cortex-M3 is split into well-defined regions for code, SRAM, peripherals, and system peripherals. Unlike the ARM7, the Cortex-M3 is a Harvard architecture with multiple busses that allow it to perform operations in parallel, boosting overall performance. Unlike earlier ARM architectures, the Cortex family allows unaligned data access. This ensures the most efficient use of the internal SRAM. The Cortex family also supports setting and clearing of bits within two 1Mbyte regions of memory by a method called bit banding. This allows efficient access to peripheral registers and flags located in SRAM memory, without the need for a full Boolean processor.

One of the key components of the Cortex-M3 core is the Nested Vector Interrupt Controller (NVIC). The NVIC provides a standard interrupt structure for all Cortex-based microcontrollers and exceptional interrupt handling. The NVIC provides dedicated interrupt vectors for up to 240 peripheral sources so that each interrupt source can be individually prioritized. In the case of back-to-back interrupts, the NVIC uses a "tail chaining" method that allows successive interrupts to be serviced with minimal overhead. During the interrupt-stacking phase, a high-priority interrupt can preempt a low-priority interrupt without incurring additional CPU cycles. The interrupt structure is also tightly coupled to the low-power modes within the Cortex-M3 core.

Although the Cortex-M3 is designed as a low cost core, it is still a 32-bit CPU with support for two operating modes: Thread mode and Handler mode, which can be configured with their own stacks. This allows more sophisticated software design and support for such real-time kernels as μC/OS-II and μC/OS-III.

The Cortex core also includes a 24-bit auto reload timer that is intended to provide a periodic interrupt for the kernel. While the ARM7 and ARM9 CPUs have two instruction sets (the ARM 32-bit and Thumb 16-bit), the Cortex family is designed to support the ARM Thumb-2 instruction set. This blends both 16-bit and 32-bit instructions to deliver the performance of the ARM 32-bit instruction set with the code density of the Thumb 16-bit instruction set. The Thumb-2 is a rich instruction set designed as a target for C/C++ compilers. This means that a Cortex application can be entirely coded in C.

2-1 THE CORTEX CPU

The Cortex CPU is a 32-bit RISC CPU. This CPU has a simplified version of the ARM7/9 programmer's model, but a richer instruction set with good integer math support, better bit manipulation, and 'harder' real-time performance.

The Cortex CPU executes most instructions in a single cycle, which is achieved with a three-stage pipeline.

The Cortex CPU is a RISC processor featuring a load and store architecture. In order to perform data processing instructions, the operands must be loaded into CPU registers, the data operation must be performed on these registers, and the results saved back to memory. Consequently, all program activity focuses on the CPU registers.

As shown in Figure 2-1, the CPU registers consists of sixteen 32-bit wide registers. Registers R0-R12 can be used to hold variables or addresses. Registers R13-R15 have special functions within the Cortex CPU. Register R13 is used as a stack pointer. This register is banked, which allows the Cortex CPU to have two operating modes, each with their own separate stack space. In the Cortex CPU the two stacks are called the main stack (ISR stack) and the process stack (Task stack). The next register R14 is called the link register, and it is used to store the return address when a call is made to a function. This allows the Cortex CPU to make a fast entry and exit to a function. If the code calls several levels of subroutines, the compiler automatically stores R14 onto the stack. The final register R15 is the program counter. Since R15 is part of the CPU registers it can be read and manipulated like any other register.

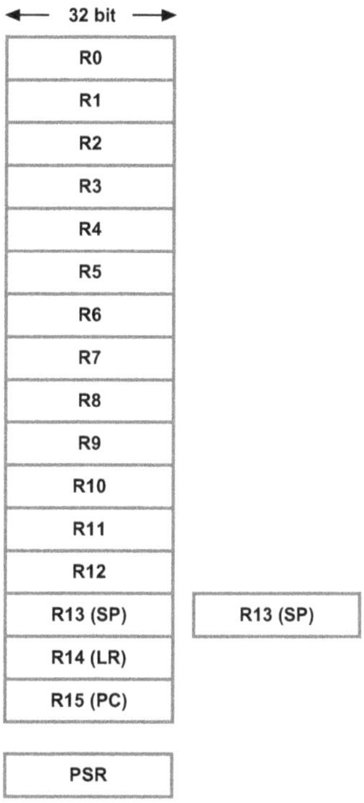

Figure 2-1 **The Cortex-M3 CPU Registers**

2-1-1 THE PROGRAM STATUS REGISTER

In addition to the CPU registers there is a separate register called the Program Status Register (PSR). The PSR is not part of the main CPU registers and is only accessible through two dedicated instructions. The PSR contains a number of fields that influence the execution of the Cortex CPU. Refer to the Cortex-M3 Technical Reference Manual for details.

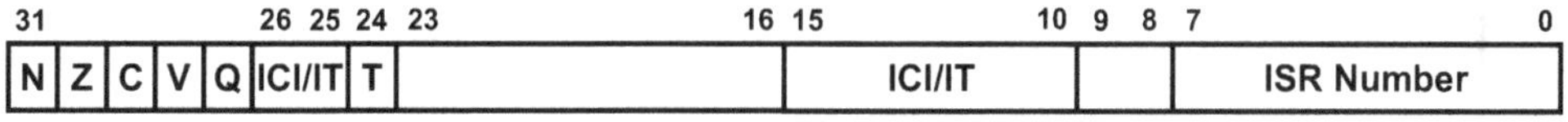

Figure 2-2 **The Cortex-M3 PSR Register**

While most Thumb-2 instructions execute in a single cycle, some (such as load and store instructions) take multiple cycles. To enable the Cortex CPU to have a deterministic interrupt response time, these instructions are interruptible.

2-1-2 STACKING AND INTERRUPTS

Tasks execute in Thread mode using the process stack; interrupts execute in Handler mode using the main stack. The task context is automatically saved on the process stack when an exception occurs, whereupon the processor moves to Handler mode, making the main stack active. On return from the exception, the task context is restored and Thread mode reinstated.

Figure 2-3 shows the stacking order of the CPU registers during an exception or interrupt. The software only needs to save/restore registers R4-R11 (if required by the Interrupt Service Routine); the other registers are saved automatically by hardware upon accepting the interrupt.

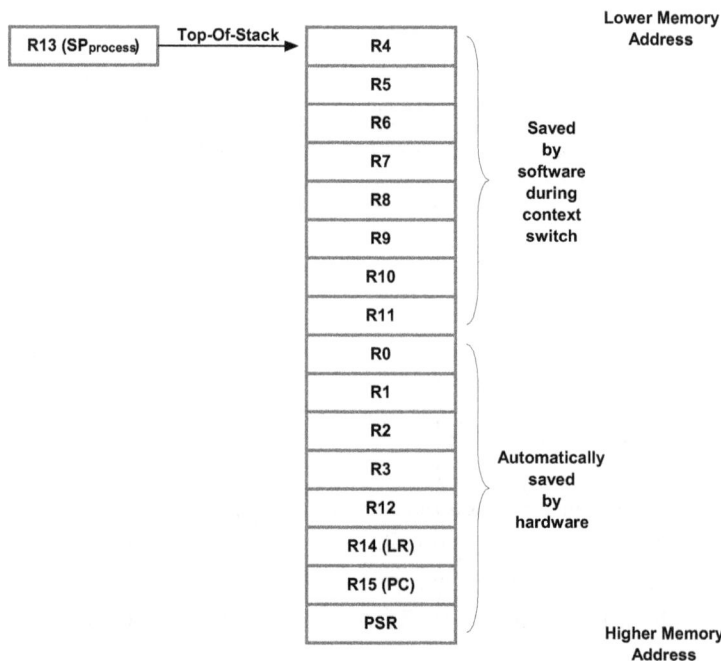

Figure 2-3 **Cortex-M3 Register Stacking Order**

2-2 NESTED VECTOR INTERRUPT CONTROLLER (NVIC)

The Cortex-M3 includes not only the core CPU (ALU, control logic, data interface, instruction decoding, etc.), but also several integrated peripherals. Most important is the Nested Vectored Interrupt Controller (NVIC), designed for low latency, efficiency and configurability.

The NVIC saves half of the processor registers automatically upon interrupt, restoring them upon exit, which allows for efficient interrupt handling. Moreover, back-to-back interrupts are handled without saving/restoring registers (since that is unnecessary). This is called Tail Chaining.

The Stellaris implementation of the NVIC offers 8 priority levels, with dynamic priority assignment. It also is capable of handling between 1 and 240 external interrupt sources.

The NVIC is a standard unit within the Cortex core. This means that all Cortex-based microcontrollers have the same interrupt structure, regardless of the manufacturer. Therefore, application code and operating systems can be easily ported from one microcontroller to another, and the programmer does not need to learn a new set of registers. The NVIC is also designed to have very low interrupt latency. This is both a feature of the NVIC itself and of the Thumb-2 instruction set, which allows such multi-cycle instructions as load and store multiple to be interruptible.

The NVIC peripheral eases the migration between Cortex-M3 processors. This is particularly true for µC/OS-III.

2-3 EXCEPTION VECTOR TABLE

The Cortex vector table starts at the bottom of the address range. However, rather than start at zero, the vector table starts at address 0x00000004 and the first four bytes are used to store the starting address of the stack pointer. The vector table is shown in Table 2-1.

Each of the interrupt vector entries is four bytes wide and holds the start address of each service routine associated with the interrupt. The first 15 entries are for exceptions that occur within the Cortex core. These include the reset vector, non-maskable interrupt, fault and error management, debug exceptions, and the SysTick timer interrupt. The Thumb-2 instruction set also includes system service call instructions which, when executed, generate an exception. The user peripheral interrupts start from entry 16, and will be linked to peripherals as defined for the specific Stellaris microcontroller. In software, the vector table is usually maintained in the startup by locating the service routine addresses at the base of memory.

No.	Type	Priority	Description
1	Reset	-3	Reset
2	NMI	-2	Non-Maskable Interrupts
3	Hard Fault	-1	Default fault if other handler not implemented
4	MemManageFault	programmable	MPU violation
5	Bus Fault	programmable	Fault if AHB error
6	Usage Fault	programmable	Program error exception
7-10	Reserved		
11	SV Call	programmable	System Call Service
12	Debug Monitor	programmable	Breakpoints, watchpoints, external debug
13	Reserved	N/A	
14	PendSV	programmable	Pendable request
15	SysTick	programmable	System tick timer
16	Interrupt #0	programmable	External interrupt #0
:	:	:	:
:	:	:	:
256	Interrupt #240	programmable	External interrupt #240

Table 2-1 **The Cortex-M3 Exception Table**

The PendSV vector is used by µC/OS-III to perform a context switch, while the SysTick vector is used by µC/OS-III for the clock tick interrupt.

2-4 SYSTICK (SYSTEM TICK)

The Cortex core includes a 24-bit down counter with auto reload and end of count interrupt, called the SysTick. The SysTick was designed to be used as an RTOS clock tick interrupt, and it is present in all Cortex implementations.

The SysTick timer has three registers. The current value and reload value should be initialized with the count period. The control and status register contains an ENABLE bit to start the timer running, and a TICKINT bit to enable its interrupt line.

The SysTick peripheral eases the migration between Cortex-M3 processors, which is particularly true for µC/OS-III.

2-5 MEMORY MAP

Unlike most previous ARM processors, the Cortex-M3 has a fixed-memory map as shown in Figure 2-4.

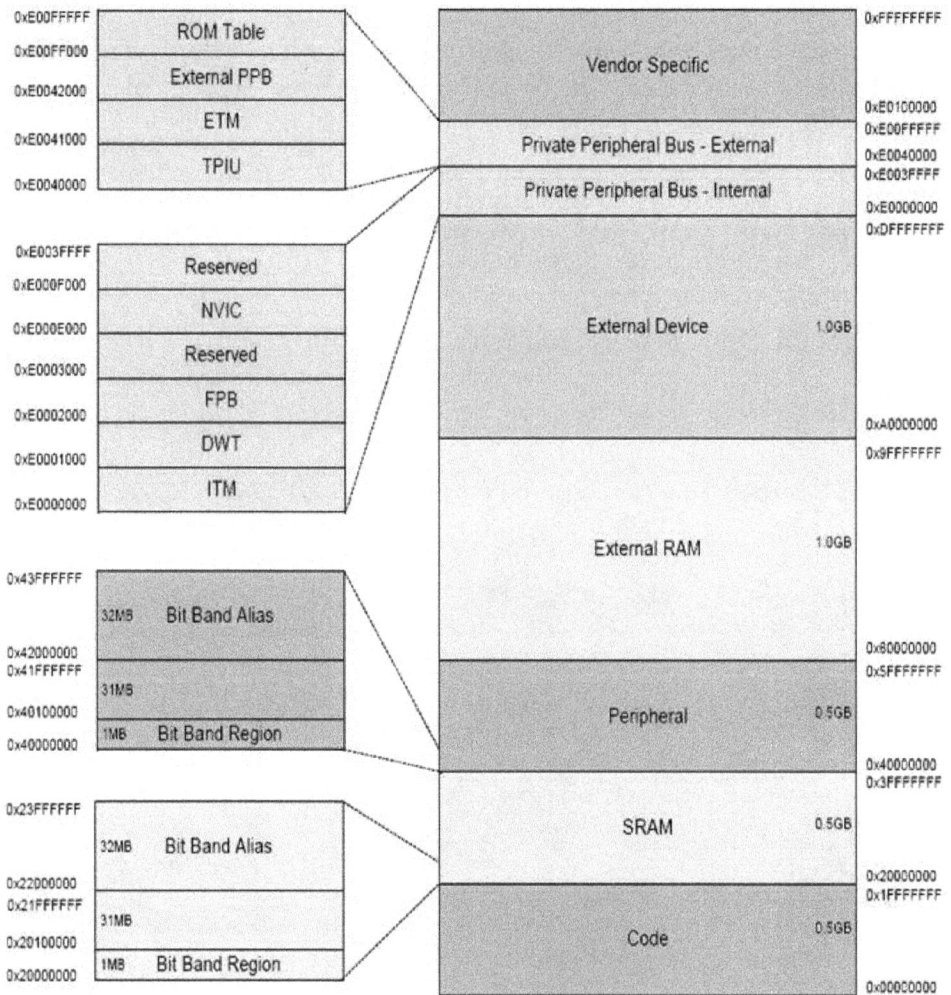

Figure 2-4 **Cortex-M3 Memory Map**

The first 1.0 Gbyte of memory is split evenly between a code region and an SRAM region. Although code can be loaded and executed from the SRAM, instructions would be fetched using the system bus, which incurs an extra wait state. It is likely that code would run slower from SRAM than from on-chip FLASH memory located in the code region.

The next 0.5 Gbyte of memory is the on-chip peripheral region. All user peripherals provided by the microcontroller vendor are located in this region.

The first Mbyte of both the SRAM and Peripheral regions is bit-addressable using a technique called bit banding. Since all SRAM and user peripherals on the processor are located in these regions, every memory location of the processor can be manipulated in a word-wide or bitwise fashion.

The next 2.0 Gbytes of address space is allocated to external memory-mapped SRAM and peripherals.

The final 0.5 Gbyte is allocated to the internal Cortex processor peripherals and a region for future vendor-specific enhancements to the Cortex processor. All Cortex processor registers are at fixed locations for all Cortex-based microcontrollers.

2-6 INSTRUCTION SET

The ARM7 and ARM9 CPUs execute two instruction sets: the ARM 32-bit instruction set and the Thumb 16-bit instruction set. This allows developers to optimize a program by selecting the instruction set used for different procedures: for example, 32-bit instructions for speed, and 16-bit instructions for code compression.

The Cortex CPU is designed to execute the Thumb-2 instruction set, which is a blend of 16-bit and 32-bit instructions. The Thumb-2 instruction set yields a 26% code density improvement over the ARM 32-bit instruction set, and a 25% improvement in performance over the Thumb 16-bit instruction set.

The Thumb-2 instruction set has improved multiply instructions, which can execute in a single cycle, and a hardware divide that takes between 2 – 7 cycles.

Of special interest to μC/OS-III is the Count Leading Zeros (CLZ) instruction, which greatly improves the scheduling algorithm.

2-7 DEBUGGING FEATURES

The Cortex core has a debug system called CoreSight as shown in Figure 2-5. The full CoreSight debug system has a Debug Access Port (DAP), which allows connection to the microcontroller by a JTAG tool. The debug tool can connect using the standard 4-pin JTAG interface or a serial 2-wire interface.

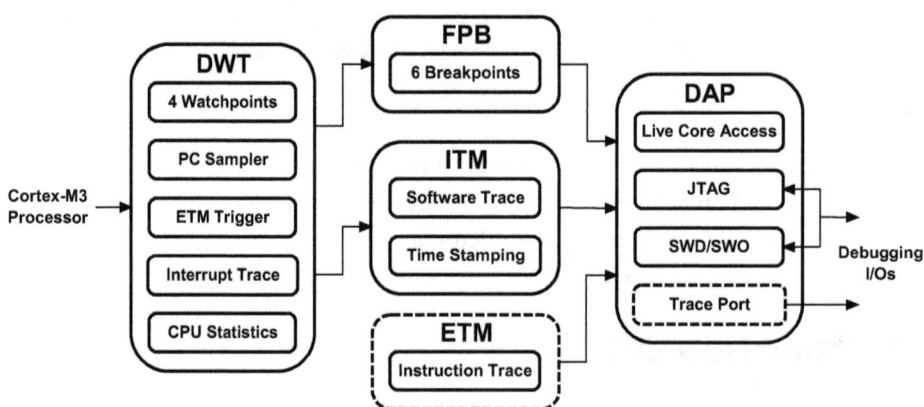

Figure 2-5 **Cortex-M3 CoreSight Debug System**

In addition to the JTAG debug features, the full CoreSight debug system contains a Data Watch Trace (DWT) and an Embedded Trace Macrocell (ETM). For software testing, there is Instrumentation Trace Macrocell (ITM) and Flash Patch Block (FPB). Stellaris microcontrollers implement the CoreSight debug system, but do not include the Embedded Trace Macrocell.

The CoreSight debug system provides six hardware breakpoints which can be non-intrusively set and cleared while the Cortex CPU is running. In addition, the Data Watch Trace allows you to view the contents of memory locations non-intrusively while the Cortex CPU runs. The CoreSight debug system can stay active when the Cortex core enters a low power or sleep mode. This makes a world of difference when debugging a low-power application. Additionally, the Stellaris timers can be halted when the CPU is halted by the CoreSight system. This allows you to single-step the code and keep the timers in synchronization with the instructions executing on the Cortex CPU.

The Data Watch Trace module also contains a 32-bit CPU cycle counter, which can be used to make time measurements. This is particularly interesting for µC/CPU, which can use this cycle counter for time stamping.

2-8 TEXAS INSTRUMENTS' STELLARIS® MICROCONTROLLERS

Stellaris® 32-bit microcontrollers combine sophisticated, flexible, mixed-signal system-on-chip integration with unparalleled real-time multi-tasking capabilities. Complex applications previously impossible with legacy microcontrollers can now be accommodated with ease by powerful, cost-effective, and simple-to-program Stellaris microcontrollers. With entry-level pricing at $1.00, the Stellaris product line allows for standardization that eliminates future architectural upgrades or software tools changes.

With single-cycle access to on-chip flash at speeds up to 50 MHz, Stellaris microcontrollers deliver 1.25 DMIPS/MHz – better than ARM7 and ARM9. In addition, Stellaris micro-controllers provide all the typical peripherals, such as timers, dual ADC modules, CAN 2.0, full speed USB Device/Host/OTG, I^2C, SPI, I^2S, Ethernet, QEI, and PWM modules. But the capabilities of these peripherals are far from typical. For example, Stellaris devices provide an Ethernet controller that has an integrated MAC and PHY, saving design time, board space, and cost. The GPIOs are highly capable with programmable drive strength, bit-addressable access, fast toggle speed (up to $\frac{1}{2}$ the system clock), and various configurations. The External Peripheral Interface (EPI) extends these capabilities, offering efficient communication to off-chip SDRAM, Host-Bus devices, and FPGAs. The ADC modules have highly flexible digital comparators and can be closely linked to the powerful PWM units, enabling sophisticated motor control applications.

For safety-critical industrial and consumer applications, Stellaris microcontrollers offer integrated features such as high-reliability, automotive-grade Flash memory, up to two watchdog timers that take advantage of the non-maskable interrupt (NMI) handler safety feature of the ARM® Cortex™-M3 processor, and deterministic, fast interrupt processing through the nested vectored interrupt controller (NVIC). Some Stellaris family members also offer an integrated precision oscillator to supply an independent time base when periodic safety tests are executed. In addition, select Stellaris microcontrollers include ROM preloaded with a cyclic redundancy check (CRC) function, which is especially useful in verifying the contents of the Stellaris microcontroller's memory.

With Stellaris microcontrollers, all programming can be in C/C++, even interrupt service routines and startup code. StellarisWare® software support makes code development even easier with code and royalty-free libraries for applications support. The Stellaris Peripheral Driver Library provides a royalty-free set of peripheral drivers and can be used as applications examples or directly included in user applications as-is. In addition, all Stellaris microcontrollers ship with either a serial flash loader programmed into flash or a boot loader in ROM, providing maximum flexibility for production programming options. The royalty-free boot loader facilitates in-field updates for end applications, with flexible interface options and program signaling.

With all that is offered by Stellaris microcontrollers based on the Cortex™-M3, you may never have to switch architectures again!

Getting Started with the Stellaris® EVALBOT Evaluation Kit

The Stellaris EVALBOT Evaluation Kit provides a low-cost way to start designing simple robotic applications with Stellaris microcontrollers. The EVALBOT Evaluation Board (EVB) functions as a complete evaluation target that also includes a debugger interface that can be used to program and debug the evaluation board as well as any other external Stellaris device. The included USB cable is all that is needed to provide power and communication to the host PC. Three included AA batteries provide power for mobile applications.

3-1 REQUIREMENTS

■ You have a PC, with a USB interface, running Microsoft® Windows 2000, Windows XP, Windows Vista or Windows 7.

■ You have an Internet connection.

SOFTWARE DOWNLOAD

Before connecting the EVALBOT to your PC, download and install the supporting software and device drivers for the board. These can be found at `http://micrium.com/page/downloads/os-iii_files` listed under "µC/OS-III for TI Stellaris."

After downloading the file `Micrium-Book-uCOS-III-LM3S9B92.exe`, run it and unzip the contents to a directory on your hard disk.

3-2 DOWNLOADING µC/PROBE

µC/Probe is an award-winning Microsoft Windows-based application that allows users to display or change the value (at run time) of virtually any variable or memory location on a connected embedded target. See Appendix B, "Micriµm's µC/Probe" on page 817 for a brief introduction.

µC/Probe is used in all of the examples described in Chapter 3 to gain run-time visibility. There are two versions of µC/Probe:

The *Full Version* of µC/Probe is included with all µC/OS-III licenses. The Full Version supports J-Link, RS-232C, TCP/IP, USB, and other interfaces.

The *Full Version* allows users to display or change an unlimited number of variables.

The Trial Version is not time limited, but only allows users to display or change up to eight application variables. However, the trial version allows users to monitor any µC/OS-III variables because µC/Probe is µC/OS-III aware.

Both versions are available from Micriµm's website. Simply point your favorite browser to:

`www.Micrium.com/Books/Micrium-uCOS-III`

Follow the links to download the desired version (or both). If not already registered on the Micriµm website, you will be asked to do so. Once downloaded, execute the appropriate µC/Probe setup file:

`Micrium-uC-Probe-Setup-Full.exe`
`Micrium-uC-Probe-Setup-Trial.exe`

3-3 DOWNLOADING THE IAR EMBEDDED WORKBENCH FOR ARM

Examples provided with this book were tested using the IAR Embedded Workbench for ARM V5.5. You can download the 32K Kickstart version from the IAR website. This version allows users to create applications up to 32 Kbytes in size (excluding µC/OS-III). The file from IAR is about 400 MBytes. If you have a slow Internet connection or are planning to install a new version of Windows, you might want to consider archiving this file on a CD or even a USB drive.

You can download IAR tools from (case sensitive):

www.iar.com/MicriumuCOSIII

■ Click the Download IAR Embedded Workbench >> link in the middle of the page. This will bring you to the 'Download Evaluation Software' page on the IAR website.

■ Locate the "ARM" processor row and go to the "Kickstart edition" column on that same row and clock on the link for v5.50 (32K) link (or newer version if that's available). A page titled KickStart edition of IAR Embedded Workbench will be displayed.

■ After reading this page, simply click Continue.

■ You will again be required to register. Unfortunately, the information you provided to register with Micrium is not transferred to IAR and vice-versa. Fill out the form and click Submit.

■ Save the file to a convenient location.

■ You should receive a License number and Key for EWARM-KS32 from IAR.

■ Double-click the IAR executable file (EWARM-KS-WEB-5505.exe) (or a similar file if newer) and install the files on the disk drive of your choice, at the root.

You can use the full version of the IAR Embedded Workbench if you are already a licensee.

3-4 BOARD SET-UP

Assuming you followed the assembly instructions you will, by now, have seen the EVALBOT driving around under battery power. The board can also be powered via a USB connection. This configuration would typically be used when downloading or debugging software on the board. To connect the EVALBOT to a PC, use the USB-miniB to USB-A cable supplied in the kit. Connect the miniB (smaller) end of the USB cable to the connector labeled "ICDI." Connect the other end (Type A) to a free USB port on your host PC. The USB is capable of sourcing up to 500 mA for each attached device, which is sufficient for the evaluation board. If connecting the board through a USB hub, it must be a powered hub. Once the board is connected to the PC, press the button marked "ON/RESET" next to the display on the EVALBOT.

(i) The next step explains how to install the FTDI drivers for the board. Some customers with previous installations of the FTDI drivers may experience trouble when installing newer (2.02.04 and later) versions of the driver. The problem only seems to affect users of Windows XP, and not Windows Vista. If you have any problems with the driver installation, go to http://www.ti.com/lm_ftdi_driver for more information.

When you plug in the EVALBOT for the first time, Windows starts the Found New Hardware Wizard and asks if Windows can connect to Windows Update to search for software. Select "No, not this time" and then click Next.

Figure 3-1 **Found New Hardware Wizard**

Next, the Found New Hardware Wizard asks from where to install the software. Select "Install from a list or specific location (Advanced)" and click Next.

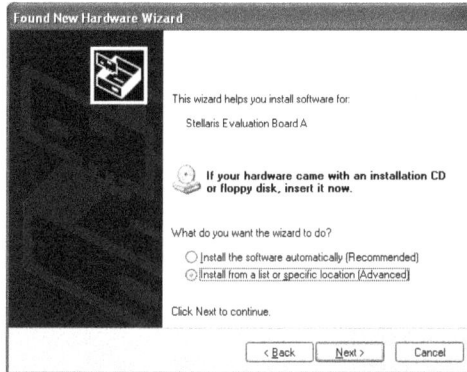

Figure 3-2 **Install from a specific location**

Figure 3-2 **Install from a specific location**

Select "Search for the best driver in these locations," and check the "Include this location in the search" option. Click the Browse button and navigate to the **FTDI-Stellaris** directory that was created when you unzipped the downloaded software package. If you unzipped the software into the root of your C: drive, for example, this would be **C:\Stellaris_FTDI-2_06_00**. Click Next.

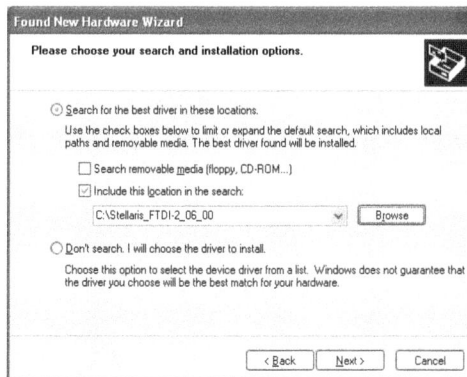

Figure 3-3 **Search the CD-ROM**

Windows finishes installing the drivers for "Stellaris Evaluation Board A." When the driver install is finished, the Found New Hardware Wizard window appears like the one below. Click Finish to close the dialog box.

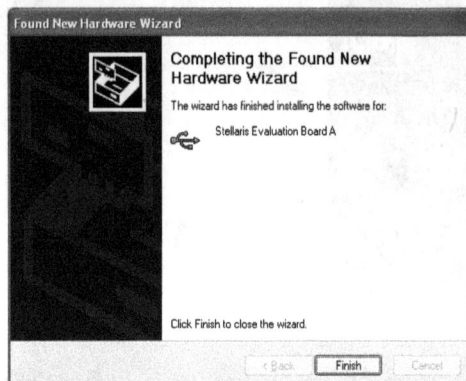

Figure 3-4 **Finished installing**

You have just installed the drivers for "Stellaris Evaluation Board A." The USB device built into the EVALBOT is a composite USB device. After you click Finish, Windows will automatically install a driver for the "Luminary Micro ICDI Stellaris Evaluation Board B" part of the composite USB device. Follow the same instructions as above to install the drivers for this device.

The Found New Hardware Wizard appears one last time. This is to install the drivers for the "Stellaris Virtual COM Port." Again, follow the same instructions to install the drivers for this device.

Now all of the FTDI drivers for the EVALBOT Evaluation Board have been installed. These drivers give the debugger access to the JTAG/SWD interface and the host PC access to the Virtual COM Port.

With the drivers installed, Windows will automatically detect any new Stellaris boards that you attach, and install the drivers for you.

3-5 QUICKSTART APPLICATION

The EVALBOT Evaluation Board comes preprogrammed with a quickstart application. Once you have powered the board by pressing the ON/RESET button, this application runs automatically. Press SWITCH1 to start the robot moving and SWITCH2 to stop the motion. The quickstart application provides autonomous control of the EVALBOT evaluation board using the motors and bump sensors on the board. This project demonstrates how μC/OS-III, in conjunction with the EVALBOT evaluation board, can be used to create an autonomous motor control application. The robot drives forward until either the robot bumps into something or a bounded random time value expires. If either of these events occur, the robot turns in a random direction and then continues driving forward.

The bump sensors on the front of the EVALBOT board are used to detect the robot bumping into something while driving forward. If the left bump sensor is triggered, the robot turns to the right and then continues driving forward. Conversely, if the right bump sensor is triggered, the robot turns to the left and then continues driving forward.

In addition to the bump sensors, a timer expiration event causes the robot to change directions while driving forward. A timer is configured to expire in a bounded random amount of time when the robot begins to drive forward. If the timer expires prior to bumping into something, the robot randomly chooses to turn to the left or right, and then continues driving forward.

For more information on how the application works, see Chapter 9, "Autonomous Control of the EVALBOT" on page 862.

3-6 SOFTWARE DEVELOPMENT TOOLS

The next step is to install and run the software development tools included in the development kit. For more information, see Chapter 5, "Using the EVALBOT Examples" on page 1075. Additional tools may be available through the www.ti.com/stellaris web site.

3-7 REFERENCES

The following references are available for download at www.ti.com/stellaris:

- *StellarisWare® Peripheral Driver Library User's Manual*

- *Stellaris® LM3S9B92 Microcontroller Data Sheet*

Stellaris® Robotic Evaluation Board (EVALBOT) User's Manual

4-1 BOARD OVERVIEW

The Stellaris® Robotic Evaluation Board (EVALBOT) is a robotic evaluation platform for the Stellaris LM3S9B92 microcontroller. The board also uses a range of Texas Instruments analog components for motor drive, power supply, and communications functions. The EVALBOT's electronics arrive ready-to-run. The board's robotics capabilities require less than 30 minutes of mechanical assembly. Figure 4-1 shows a photo of the EVALBOT.

Figure 4-1 **Stellaris® EVALBOT Robot**

When roaming, three AA batteries supply power to the EVALBOT. The EVALBOT automatically selects USB power when tethered to a PC as a USB device or when debugging. Test points are provided to all key EVALBOT signals. Two 20-pin headers enable future wireless communications using standardized Texas Instruments' low-power embedded radio modules (EM boards). Additional uncommitted microcontroller signals are available on break-out pads arranged in rows adjacent to the microcontroller.

The EVALBOT has factory-installed quickstart software resident in on-chip Flash memory. For software debugging and Flash programming, an integrated In-Circuit Debug Interface (ICDI) requires only a single USB cable for debug and serial port functions.

4-1-1 FEATURES

The EVALBOT board includes the following features:

- Evaluation board with robotic capabilities

- Mechanical components assembled by user

- Stellaris® LM3S9B92-IQC80 microcontroller

- MicroSD card connector

- I^2S audio codec with speaker

- USB Host and Device connectors

- RJ45 Ethernet connector

- Bright 96 x 6 Blue OLED display

- On-board In-Circuit Debug Interface (ICDI)

- Battery power (3 AA batteries) or power through USB

- Wireless communication expansion port

- Robot features

  - Two DC gear-motors provide drive and steering

  - Opto-sensors detect wheel rotation with 45° resolution

  - Sensors for "bump" detection

4-1-2 BLOCK DIAGRAM

The EVALBOT evaluation board uses the Stellaris® LM3S9B92 microcontroller and includes a 10/100 Ethernet port and a USB 2.0 full-speed On-the-Go (OTG) port. The EVALBOT combines all mechanical and electrical components on a single circuit board. Figure 4-2 shows a block diagram of the electrical section of the EVALBOT.

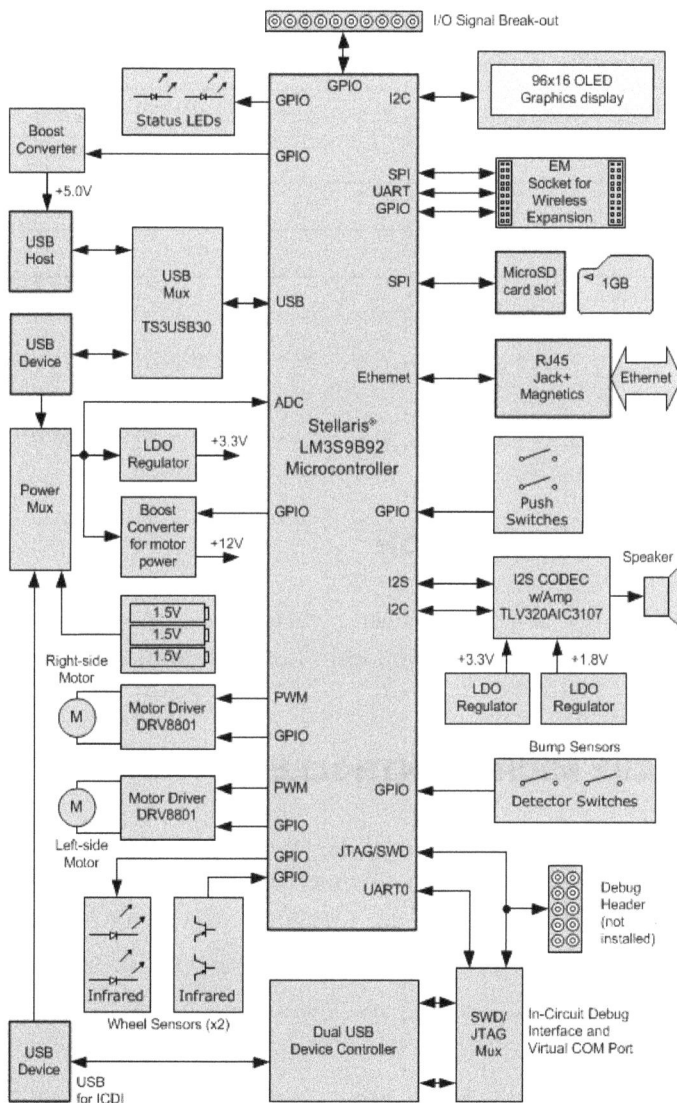

Figure 4-2 **EVALBOT Block Diagram**

4-1-3 SPECIFICATIONS

Table 4-1 shows the specifications for the EVALBOT.

Parameter	Min	Typical	Max
Battery Supply Voltage	3.5 V	4.5 V	5.0 V
USB Supply Voltage	4.0 V	5.0 V	5.25 V
Battery current (typical stationary)	–	100 mA	–
Battery current (typical in motion)	–	200 mA	–
Power down supply current		0.5 uA	
AA Alkaline Battery Capacity	–	2.5 A/Hr*	–
Reverse Battery Protection		No	
Allowable Battery/USB Current			0.5A

* From Energizer E91 data sheet.

Table 4-1 **EVALBOT Specifications**

4-2 HARDWARE DESCRIPTION

The EVALBOT consists of a 4-inch diameter circuit board populated with a Stellaris LM3S9B92 microcontroller and 14 additional Texas Instruments analog and digital semiconductors.

4-2-1 LM3S9B92 MICROCONTROLLER

The Stellaris LM3S9B92 is an ARM® Cortex™-M3-based microcontroller with 256-KB flash memory, 96-KB SRAM, 80-MHz operation, Ethernet MAC/PHY, USB Host/Device/OTG, and a wide range of other peripherals. See the LM3S9B92 microcontroller data sheet (order number DS-LM3S9B92) for complete device details.

Unused microcontroller signals are routed to either the 20-pin EM expansion headers or to 0.1" pitch break-out pads which are labeled with their GPIO reference. An internal multiplexer allows different peripheral functions to be assigned to each of these GPIO pads. When adding external circuitry, consideration should be given to the additional load on the EVALBOT's power rails.

The reference design may include additional components necessary to address silicon errata. For details of those circuit functions, see the LM3S9B92 Errata document.

4-2-2 CLOCKING

The EVALBOT uses a 16.0-MHz crystal (Y3) to complete the LM3S9B92 microcontroller's main internal clock circuit. An internal PLL, configured in software, multiples this clock to higher frequencies for core and peripheral timing.

A 25.0 MHz (Y1) crystal provides an accurate timebase for the Ethernet PHY.

4-2-3 RESET

The RESET signal into the LM3S9B92 microcontroller connects to the Reset/On switch (SW6) and to the ICDI circuit for a debugger-controlled reset.

External reset is asserted (active low) under any one of three conditions:

- Power-on reset (filtered by an R-C network)

- Reset/On push switch SW6 held down

- By the ICDI circuit when instructed by the debugger (this capability is optional, and may not be supported by all debuggers).

The OLED Module and Audio CODEC have special Reset timing requirements requiring a dedicated control line from the microcontroller.

4-2-4 POWER SUPPLIES

The EVALBOT can be powered either from batteries, the ICDI USB cable, or a USB device cable. The power source is determined by a Texas Instruments TPS2113 Auto Switching Power Mux and two Schottky diodes. Battery power is selected automatically when USB power is not present.

Table 4-2 shows the EVALBOT's power supplies. Each supply is generated directly or indirectly from the main power bus, +VS, using either a linear regulator or boost converter.

Name	Voltage	Max Current	Use
+VS	3.5 – 5.0 V	0.5 A	Main power distribution bus to other power rails
+3.3V	+3.3 V	150 mA	Logic power supply for main MCU, digital, and ICDI functions
+3.3VA	+3.3 V	150 mA	Analog and I/O power for audio CODEC
+1.8V	+1.8 V	25 mA	Digital/core power for audio CODEC
+5V_HVBUS	+5.25 V	100 mA	USB Host power supply
+12V	+12 V	100 mA	Motor driver power supply
+10V	+10 V	5 mA	OLED bias power supply

Table 4-2 **EVALBOT Power Supplies**

The board's on/off feature uses two push switches (SW5, SW6) and a simple feedback circuit through the inverter created by MOSFET Q3. An internal 1uA constant current source on the TPS2113's Enable pin (ENn) ensures that the TPS2113 is initially powered on when power is connected. Resistor R47 sets the overcurrent protection to 0.5 A.

4-2-5 ORGANIC LED DISPLAY

The user interface consists of a 96 x 16 OLED display and two push switches. The OLED display has an integrated controller IC with a parallel, SPI, and I^2C interfaces. In this design, the I^2C interface is used. The OLED display is limited to 'write-only' in this mode, so pixel data cannot be read back from the display

4-2-6 microSD CARD

EVALBOT includes a microSD card interface, which interfaces to the MCU using an SPI interface. Because power to the SD card is not controlled, removing or inserting the card while power is applied is not recommended.

4-2-7 AUDIO

A Texas Instruments TLV320AIC3107 CODEC adds a high performance audio stage to the EVALBOT. An integrated mono class-D amplifier drives an on-board speaker, with other audio inputs and outputs available on break-out header pads. An I2S interface carries the output (and input) audio data streams, while an I2C interface configures the CODEC. Most unused audio pins are available on nearby pads (0.05" pitch).

4-2-8 ETHERNET

With its fully integrated 10/100 Ethernet MAC and PHY, the LM3S9B92 requires only a standard Jack with integrated magnetics and a few passive components. The TX and RX signals are routed to the jack as a differential pair. The PHY incorporates MDI/MDI-X cross-over, so the function of the TX and RX pairs can be swapped in software.

4-2-9 USB

The LM3S9B92 microcontroller has Host, Device and OTG USB capabilities. EVALBOT supports USB Host and Device with dedicated connectors and a Texas Instruments T3USB30E high-speed USB multiplexer to select between them.

4-2-10 ROBOTIC FEATURES

Two 12-V gear motors provide locomotion to the EVALBOT. A Texas Instruments' DRV8801 Full-Bridge motor driver IC controls each motor; providing direction control, over-current and short-circuit protection, dead-time insertion and several switching schemes.

Each EVALBOT wheel has two infra-red optical sensors which generate a quadrature signal as the wheel rotates. The IR emitters (D2, D3, D11, and D12) each connect to a GPIO signal so that the MCU can turn off the LEDs for power saving when not in motion. The GPIO outputs should be configured for 8 mA drive-strength to ensure the IR emitters have sufficient intensity.

Left and right bumpers detect collisions using simple detector switches. The GPIO inputs should have internal pull-up resistors enabled and may optionally be configured to generate an interrupt when a collision occurs.

4-2-11 EXPANSION

The EM port on EVALBOT enables RF connectivity using a range of Low-Power RF Evaluation Modules (EM boards) from Texas Instruments. EM boards cover both sub 1-GHz and 2.4 GHz bands and are a supported by several different protocol stacks.

The EM port can also be used for general-purpose expansion. SPI, UART and GPIO signals are available. Table 4-3 lists the connector part numbers. Two identical connectors should be installed on a 1.20" pitch.

Supplier	Part Number	Description	Use
Samtec	TFM-110-02-S-D	SMT Header 20-pos 0.050" pitch	EVALBOT EM port
Samtec	SFM-110-02-S-D	SMT Socket 20-pos 0.050" pitch	EM board

Table 4-3 **Connector Part Numbers**

In additional to the EM port, EVALBOT also has 9 GPIO (PJ0..7, PE7), Power and GND connections on a 0.1" grid.

4-2-12 DEBUGGING

EVALBOT includes an integrated In-Circuit Debug Interface (ICDI) for debugging, serial communication and power over a single USB cable. Based on an FTDI FT2232 USB controller, the ICDI supports all major Cortex-M3 development environments.

Stellaris microcontrollers support programming and debugging using either JTAG or SWD. JTAG uses the signals TCK, TMS, TDI, and TDO. SWD requires fewer signals (SWCLK, SWDIO, and, optionally, SWO for trace). The debugger determines which debug protocol is used.

An external debug interface can be used with EVALBOT if connector J4 is installed by the user.

JTAG/SWD

The FT2232 is factory-configured by Texas Instruments to implement a JTAG/SWD port (synchronous serial) on channel A and a Virtual COM Port (VCP) on channel B. This feature allows two simultaneous communications links between the host computer and the target device using a single USB cable. Separate Windows drivers for each function can be found in the directory created by downloading, unzipping, and running the `Micrium-Book-uCOS-III-LM3S9B92.exe` file, see section 3-1 "Requirements" on page 1055

The In-Circuit Debug Interface USB capabilities are completely independent from the LM3S9B92's on-chip USB functionality.

A small serial EEPROM holds the FT2232 configuration data. The EEPROM is not accessible by the LM3S9B92 microcontroller. For full details on FT2232 operation, go to www.ftdichip.com.

The FT2232 USB device performs JTAG/SWD serial operations under the control of the debugger. A simple logic circuit multiplexes SWD and JTAG functions and, when working in SWD mode, provides direction control for the bidirectional data line.

VIRTUAL COM PORT

The Virtual COM Port (VCP) allows Windows applications (such as HyperTerminal) to communicate with UART0 on the LM3S9B92 over USB. Once the FT2232 VCP driver is installed, Windows assigns a COM port number to the VCP channel.

SERIAL WIRE OUT

EVALBOT also supports the Cortex-M3 Serial-Wire Output (SWO) trace capabilities. Under debugger control, on-board logic can route the SWO data stream to the VCP transmit channel. The debugger software can then decode and interpret the trace information received from the Virtual Com Port. The normal VCP connection to UART0 is interrupted when using SWO. Not all debuggers support SWO.

See the *Stellaris LM3S9B92 Microcontroller Data Sheet* for additional information on the Trace Port Interface Unit (TPIU).

4-3 REFERENCES

In addition to this document, the following references are available for download at www.ti.com/stellaris.

- *Stellaris LM3S9B92 Microcontroller Data Sheet*

- *DMOS Full-Bridge Motor Drivers Data Sheet (DRV8801RTY)*

- *Low-Power Stereo CODEC with Integrated Mono Class-D Amplifier Data Sheet (TLV320AIC3107)*

- *200mA, Low IQ, Low Dropout Regulator for Portables Data Sheet (TLV70018)*

- *200mA, Low IQ, Low Dropout Regulator for Portables Data Sheet (TLV70033)*

- *50mA, 24V, 3.2-μA Supply Current, Low-Dropout Linear Regulator in SC70 Package Data Sheet (TPS71501)*

- *650 kHz/1.2MHz Step-Up DC-DC Converter w/ Forced PWM Mode Data Sheet (TPS61085)*

- *High-Speed USB 2.0 (480 Mbps) 1:2 Multiplexer/Demultiplexer Switch With Single Enable Data Sheet (TS3USB30)*

- *Dual In/Single Out Autoswitching Power MUX Data Sheet (TPS2113)*

- *Adjustable, 600-mA Switch, 90% Efficient PFM/PWM Boost Converter in ThinSOT Data Sheet (TPS61073)*

The following data sheets can be obtained from the manufacturer:

- *P13701 OLED Display Data Sheet from RiT Display Corporation*

- *SSD1300 OLED Controller Data Sheet from Solomon Systech Limited*

4

Using the EVALBOT Examples

This chapter describes the steps you need to follow to get started with the examples for the EVALBOT. Once you have completed these basic steps, you can then get started with any of the following examples:

- Chapter 6, "Basic Example" on page 1083

- Chapter 7, "HTTP Server Example" on page 1095

- Chapter 8, "TCP Sockets Example" on page 1121

5-1 OPENING THE PROJECT

Start the IAR Embedded Workbench for ARM IDE. From the "File" menu, select "Open > Workspace" as shown in Figure 5-1 to open the following workspace:

\Micrium\Software\EvalBoards\TexasInstruments\LM3S9B92-EVALBOT\IAR\uC-TCPIP-LM 3S9B92-EVALBOT.eww

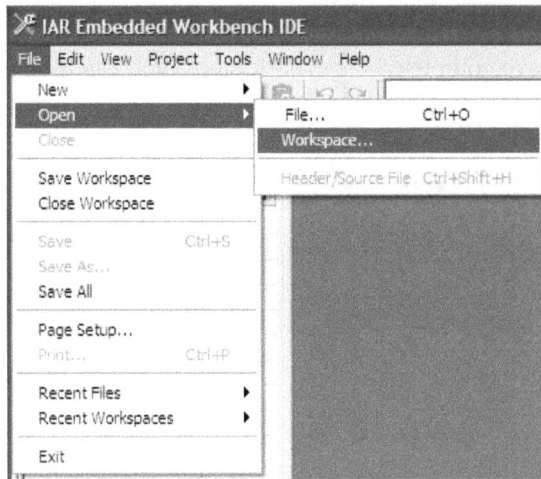

Figure 5-1 **Open the uC-TCPIP-LM3S9B92-EVALBOT.eww Workspace**

In the workspace explorer window, select the tab for the project you want to open. This example shows the uC-TCPIP-Ex4 tab. The workspace window shows all of the files in the corresponding project. The files within the project are sorted into groups represented by folder icons in the workspace window. Figure 5-2 shows the project files for uC-TCPIP-v2-Ex4 in the workspace explorer window.

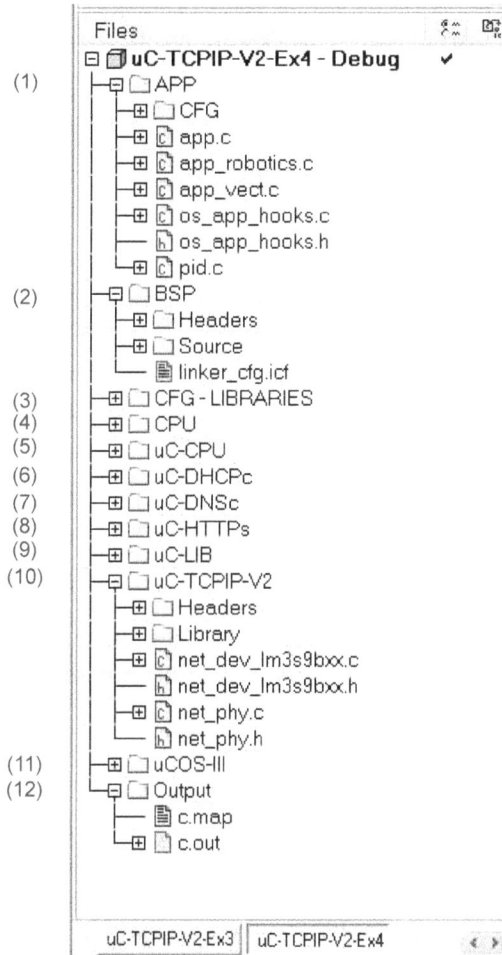

Figure 5-2 **uC-TCPIP-v2-Ex4 Project in Workspace Explorer Window**

F5-2(1)   The **APP** group includes all of the application files for this example. The subgroup **CFG** includes the header files used to configure the application.

F5-2(2)   The **BSP** group contains the files that comprise the board support package. The board support package includes the code used to control the peripherals on the board. For this example, the software to control the LEDs, pushbuttons, bump sensors, and motors will be used.

F5-2(3)   The **CFG – LIBRARIES** group includes the header files used to configure the µC/CPU, µC/LIB, and µC/OS-III libraries included in this project.

F5-2(4)   The **CPU** group includes the Stellaris family's peripheral driver library. The peripheral driver library contains the drivers and header files needed to control all of the peripherals for the Stellaris family of microcontrollers.

F5-2(5)   The **uC/CPU** group contains the µC/CPU precompiled library as well as the header files used to describe the contents of the library.

F5-2(6)   The **uC-DHCPc** group contains the pre-compiled library as well as header files for the Micrium DHCP client interface. This is used to negotiate an IP address for the EVALBOT.

F5-2(7)   The **uC-DNSc** group contains the pre-compiled library as well as header files for the Micrium DNS client interface.

F5-2(8)   The **uC-HTTPs** group contains the pre-compiled library as well as header files for the Micrium HTTP server.

F5-2(9)   The **uC/LIB** group contains the µC/LIB precompiled library as well as the header files used to describe the contents of the library.

F5-2(10)   The **uC-TCPIP-v2** group contains the pre-compiled library as well as header files for the base Micrium TCP/IP stack. It also contains the source for the port layer for the Stellaris LM3S9B92 microcontroller on EVALBOT.

F5-2(11)   The **uC/OS-III** group contains the µCOS-III precompiled library and the header files used to describe the contents of the library. In addition, the `os_cfg_app.c` and `os_dbg.c` files are included in this group to allow certain behavior to be defined at compile time.

F5-2(12)   The **Output** group contains the files generated by the compiler/linker.

5-2 RUNNING THE PROJECT

You can run this project in one of two ways:

■ **Connected to the PC when using the IAR Embedded Workbench debugger**

When doing this, raise the EVALBOT so that the wheels are not touching any surface. Doing so keeps the EVALBOT from moving around while running the project.

■ **Disconnected from the PC**

The EVALBOT must first be connected to the PC to program the example application into the LM3S9B92 microcontroller using IAR Embedded Workbench. After this, the EVALBOT can be disconnected from the PC and placed on the ground so that it can move around freely.

i   To run this project, raise the EVALBOT so that the wheels are not touching any surface. Doing so will keep the EVALBOT from moving, while still testing the functionality of the project.

To run the project using either of the above methods, you must perform the following steps (which are described in more detail on the following pages).

STEP 1: CONNECT THE EVM-EVALBOT TO YOUR PC

Connect the EVALBOT to your PC. Connect the Mini-B end of the USB cable provided in the kit to the ICDI USB connector on the EVALBOT. Connect the other end of the USB cable to a free USB port on your PC.

STEP 2: BUILD THE PROJECT

Select "Make" from the "Project" menu in IAR Embedded Workbench as shown in Figure 5-3.

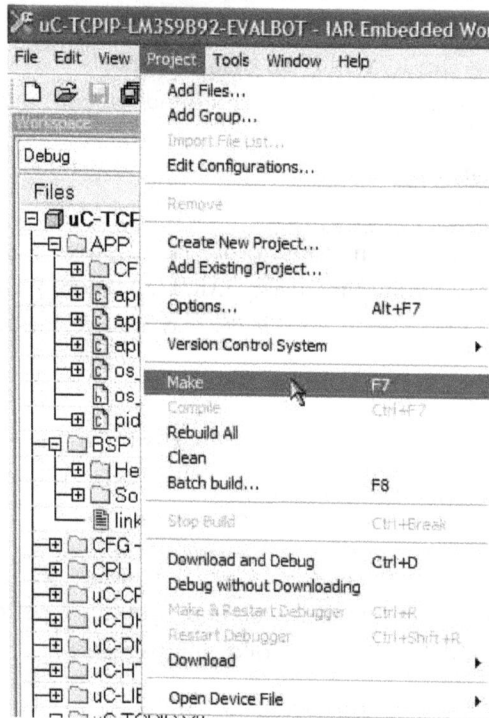

Figure 5-3 **Building the Project**

STEP 3: RUN AND DEBUG THE APPLICATION

Start the debugger by clicking the "Download and Debug" icon as shown in Figure 5-4. The application is programmed to the internal Flash of the LM3S9B92 microcontroller and the debugger starts. The code automatically starts executing and stops at the **main()** function in the **app.c** file.

Download and Debug

Figure 5-4 **Downloading the Application and Starting the Debugger**

If you want to run the EVALBOT while disconnected from the PC, stop the debugger by clicking the "Stop" icon, as shown in Figure 5-5, now that the internal flash has been programmed. You can disconnect the EVALBOT board from the PC and place it on the floor. Press the SWITCH1 pushbutton to start moving the EVALBOT. To learn how the project works, move on to the next section.

If you want to continue using the debugger or µC/Probe, leave the EVALBOT connected to the PC while raised so that the wheels are not touching any surface.

Start the application by clicking the "Go" icon as shown in Figure 5-5. Once the application is running, use the SWITCH1 pushbutton to start running the motors. Push the button again to stop the motors. You can trigger the bump sensors which simulates the EVALBOT bumping into something to test the behavior.

Click the "Stop" icon to stop the application. To reset the application, click the "Reset" icon. See Figure 5-5 and Figure 5-6 for details. The other icons can be used to step through the application.

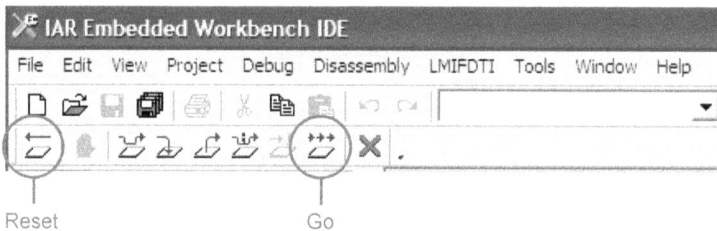

Figure 5-5 **Go and Reset Icons**

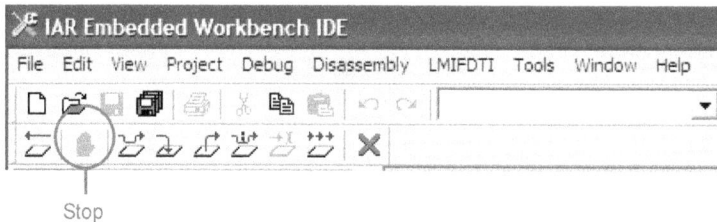

Figure 5-6 **Stop Icon**

5

5-3 SUMMARY

You are now ready to start using the following Stellaris examples:

6

Basic Example

The example described in this chapter provides a method to verify the μC/TCP-IP implementation using the ICMP Echo Request commonly known as "ping." This simple project is designed to familiarize the user with the μC/TCP-IP stack and the TI Stellaris LM3S9B92 port of the stack. This example also provides a foundation for the remainder of the examples in this book.

The ping example uses a single application task to configure the μC/OS-III RTOS and the μC/TCP-IP stack. The application task initializes the stack and establishes a dynamic IP address via DHCP. DHCP can also be disabled by modifying **APP_DHCPc_EN** which is defined near the beginning of **app.c**. Once initialization is complete, the application task toggles the board LEDs while dedicated μC/TCP-IP stack tasks manage network communications.

6-1 HOW THE PROJECT WORKS

Listing 6-1 shows the code for the **main( )** function.

```
void main (void)
{
    OS_ERR err_os;                                                  (1)

    OSInit(&err_os);                                                (2)

    OSTaskCreate((OS_TCB      *)&AppTaskStartTCB,                   (3)
                 (CPU_CHAR    *)"App Task Start",
                 (OS_TASK_PTR ) AppTaskStart,
                 (void        *) 0,
                 (OS_PRIO     ) APP_OS_CFG_START_TASK_PRIO,
                 (CPU_STK     *)&AppStartTaskStk[0],
                 (CPU_STK_SIZE) APP_OS_CFG_START_TASK_STK_SIZE / 10u,
                 (CPU_STK_SIZE) APP_OS_CFG_START_TASK_STK_SIZE,
                 (OS_MSG_QTY  ) 0u,
                 (OS_TICK     ) 0u,
                 (void        *) 0,
                 (OS_OPT      )(OS_OPT_TASK_STK_CHK | OS_OPT_TASK_STK_CLR),
                 (OS_ERR      *)&err_os);
    APP_TEST_FAULT(err_os, OS_ERR_NONE);

    OSStart(&err_os);                                              (4)
    APP_TEST_FAULT(err_os, OS_ERR_NONE);
}
```

Listing 6-1 **main() in app.c**

L6-1(1)   Disables all LM3S9B92 interrupts.

L6-1(2)   Initializes the µC/OS-III operating system prior to creating any tasks or starting multi-tasking.

L6-1(3)   Creates a single start task. This task spawns daughter tasks as needed and serves as an application background task.

L6-1(4)   Starts the µC/OS-III scheduler, causing the start task to be made ready and executed. This function does not return.

Listing 6-2 shows the code for the **App_TaskStart()** task which initializes the board support package (BSP) and the application. After initialization, it executes as a low priority application background task. The background task blinks the EVALBOT's user LEDs to assist in verifying that the application is active.

```
bbstatic void App_TaskStart (void  *p_arg)
{
    CPU_INT32U  cpu_clk_freq;
    CPU_INT32U  cnts;
    OS_ERR      err_os;
    CPU_CHAR    addr_ip_ascii[NET_ASCII_LEN_MAX_ADDR_IP];
    NET_ERR     net_err;
    NET_IF_NBR  if_nbr;
    (void)&p_arg;
    (void)&App_IP_DNS_Srvr;
    BSP_Init();                                             (1)
    CPU_Init();                                             (2)
    cpu_clk_freq = BSP_CPUClkFreq();
    cnts = cpu_clk_freq / (CPU_INT32U)OSCfg_TickRate_Hz;
    OS_CPU_SysTickInit(cnts);
#if (OS_CFG_STAT_TASK_EN > 0u)
    OSStatTaskCPUUsageInit(&err_os);
#endif
#ifdef CPU_CFG_INT_DIS_MEAS_EN
    CPU_IntDisMeasMaxCurReset();
#endif
#if (BSP_SER_COMM_EN == DEF_ENABLED)
    BSP_Ser_Init(19200);                                   (3)
#endif
    Mem_Init();                                            (4)
    App_TCPIP_Init(&if_nbr);                               (5)
    BSP_DisplayClear();                                    (6)
    BSP_DisplayStringDraw("IP ADDRESS", 0, 0);
    NetASCII_IP_to_Str(App_IP_Addrs[if_nbr][0], addr_ip_ascii, 0, &net_err);
    if (net_err != NET_ASCII_ERR_NONE) {
        BSP_DisplayStringDraw("INVALID", 0,1);
    } else {
        BSP_DisplayStringDraw((CPU_INT08S const*) addr_ip_ascii, 0, 1);  (7)
    }
    BSP_LED_Off(0u);
```

```
    while (DEF_ON) {                                              (8)
        BSP_LED_Toggle(0u);
        OSTimeDlyHMSM((CPU_INT16U) 0u,
                      (CPU_INT16U) 0u,
                      (CPU_INT16U) 0u,
                      (CPU_INT16U) 100u,
                      (OS_OPT     ) OS_OPT_TIME_HMSM_STRICT,
                      (OS_ERR    *)&err_os);
    }
}
```

Listing 6-2 **App_TaskStart()** in app.c

L6-2(1)   Initializes the board support package (BSP). This configures the display, button, sensor, and other board interfaces.

L6-2(2)   Performs LM3S9B92-specific initialization. The **CPU_Init()** function is a part of the µC/OS-III and µC/TCP-IP port to this processor.

L6-2(3)   Initializes the serial interface, if enabled. The serial interface is used for various serial debugging functions. See **app_cfg.h** for more information.

L6-2(4)   Initializes the dynamic memory management module. Dynamic memory allocation is used extensively by the µC/TCP-IP stack as it handles incoming and outgoing packets.

L6-2(5)   Initializes the µC/TCP-IP stack.

L6-2(6)   Clears the EVALBOT display.

L6-2(7)   Displays the EVALBOT's IP address. Use this address when connecting to the EVALBOT from a PC or other networked device.

L6-2(8)   An infinite loop toggles the board LEDs at a constant rate. Failure to toggle the LEDs indicates that the system is blocked in a higher priority task. Additional background user application code may be inserted here.

The `App_TCPIP_Init()` function shown in Listing 6-3 sets up the µC/TCP-IP stack.

```
static  void  App_TCPIP_Init (NET_IF_NBR  *if_nbr)
{
    NET_IP_ADDR  msk;
    NET_IP_ADDR  gateway;
    NET_ERR      err_net;


    err_net = Net_Init();                                        (1)
    APP_TEST_FAULT(err_net, NET_ERR_NONE);


    *if_nbr  = NetIF_Add((void    *)&NetIF_API_Ether,            (2)
                         (void    *)&NetDev_API_LM3S9Bxx,
                         (void    *)&NetDev_BSP_LM3S9Bxx,
                         (void    *)&NetDev_Cfg_LM3S9Bxx,
                         (void    *)&NetPhy_API_Generic,
                         (void    *)&NetPhy_Cfg_LM3S9Bxx,
                         (NET_ERR *)&err_net);
    APP_TEST_FAULT(err_net, NET_IF_ERR_NONE);

    NetIF_Start(*if_nbr, &err_net);                              (3)
    APP_TEST_FAULT(err_net, NET_IF_ERR_NONE);

#if (APP_DHCPc_EN == DEF_ENABLED)

    (void)&msk;
    (void)&gateway;
    APP_TRACE_INFO(("\n\r"));

    BSP_DisplayStringDraw("DHCP Enabled...",0,0);                (4)
    BSP_DisplayStringDraw("Waiting for IP", 0,1);
    App_TCPIP_Init_DHCPc(*if_nbr);                               (5)
```

6

```
#else

    App_IP_Addrs[*if_nbr][0] = NetASCII_Str_to_IP(TCP_CLIENT_CFG_ADDR_BIND,
                                                  (NET_ERR  *)&err_net);
    APP_TEST_FAULT(err_net, NET_ASCII_ERR_NONE);

    msk = NetASCII_Str_to_IP((CPU_CHAR *)"255.255.255.0",
                             (NET_ERR  *)&err_net);
    APP_TEST_FAULT(err_net, NET_ASCII_ERR_NONE);


    gateway = NetASCII_Str_to_IP((CPU_CHAR *)"192.168.1.1",
                                 (NET_ERR  *)&err_net);
    APP_TEST_FAULT(err_net, NET_ASCII_ERR_NONE);

    NetIP_CfgAddrAdd(*if_nbr, ip, msk, gateway, &err_net);            (6)
    APP_TEST_FAULT(err_net, NET_IP_ERR_NONE);

#endif //APP_DHCPc_EN

}
```

Listing 6-3 **App_TCPIP_Init()**

L6-3(1) Initializes the stack. The **Net_Init()** function must be called prior to any other µC/TCP-IP function.

L6-3(2) Adds the Ethernet interface to the stack. This function also provides the stack with pointers to the board and processor-specific structures which comprise the port.

L6-3(3) Starts the µC/TCP-IP stack functionality on the Ethernet interface.

L6-3(4) Displays the DHCP message on EVALBOT. Alerts the user that DHCP configuration is underway.

L6-3(5) Initializes the DHCP client interface. If this initialization completes without error, then a dynamic IP address has been set prior to return.

L6-3(6) If not using DHCP, then completes IP address configuration using a default IP address and gateway.

The DHCP client is configured and a dynamic IP address obtained using the
App_TCPIP_Init_DHCPc() function as shown in Listing 6-4.

```
static  void  App_TCPIP_Init_DHCPc (NET_IF_NBR  if_nbr)
{
    DHCPc_OPT_CODE      req_param[DHCPc_CFG_PARAM_REQ_TBL_SIZE];
    CPU_INT08U          req_param_qty;
    CPU_BOOLEAN         cfg_done;
    CPU_BOOLEAN         chk_dly;
    DHCPc_STATUS        dhcp_status;
    DHCPc_ERR           dhcp_err;
    CPU_INT08U          opt_buf[5 * sizeof(NET_IP_ADDR)];
    CPU_INT16U          opt_buf_len;
    NET_IP_ADDRS_QTY    addr_ip_tbl_qty;
    NET_IP_ADDR         addr_ip_tbl[NET_IP_CFG_IF_MAX_NBR_ADDR];
    NET_IP_ADDR         addr_ip;
    CPU_CHAR            addr_ip_str[NET_ASCII_LEN_MAX_ADDR_IP];
    NET_ERR             net_err;
    OS_ERR              os_err;


    dhcp_err = DHCPc_Init();                                        (1)
    APP_TEST_FAULT(dhcp_err, DHCPc_ERR_NONE);


    req_param[0]  = DHCP_OPT_DOMAIN_NAME_SERVER;
    req_param_qty = 1;

    DHCPc_Start((NET_IF_NBR       ) if_nbr,
                (DHCPc_OPT_CODE *)&req_param[0],
                (CPU_INT08U       ) req_param_qty,
                (DHCPc_ERR       *)&dhcp_err);                      (2)
    APP_TEST_FAULT(dhcp_err, DHCPc_ERR_NONE);

    dhcp_status = DHCP_STATUS_NONE;
    cfg_done    = DEF_NO;
    chk_dly     = DEF_NO;

    while (cfg_done != DEF_YES) {                                   (3)
        if (chk_dly == DEF_YES) {
            NetOS_TimeDly_ms(100, &os_err);
            BSP_LED_Toggle(0);
        }
        dhcp_status = DHCPc_ChkStatus(if_nbr, &dhcp_err);           (4)

        switch (dhcp_status) {
            case DHCP_STATUS_CFGD:
                 cfg_done = DEF_YES;
                 break;
```

```
        case DHCP_STATUS_CFGD_NO_TMR:
             cfg_done = DEF_YES;
             break;

        case DHCP_STATUS_CFGD_LOCAL_LINK:
             cfg_done = DEF_YES;
             break;

        case DHCP_STATUS_FAIL:
             cfg_done = DEF_YES;
             break;

        case DHCP_STATUS_CFG_IN_PROGRESS:
        default:
             chk_dly  = DEF_YES;
             break;
    }
}

if (dhcp_status != DHCP_STATUS_FAIL) {
    addr_ip_tbl_qty = sizeof(addr_ip_tbl) / sizeof(NET_IP_ADDR);
    (void)NetIP_GetAddrHost((NET_IF_NBR        ) if_nbr,
                            (NET_IP_ADDR      *)&addr_ip_tbl[0],
                            (NET_IP_ADDRS_QTY *)&addr_ip_tbl_qty,
                            (NET_ERR          *)&net_err);

    switch (net_err) {
        case NET_IP_ERR_NONE:
             addr_ip                = addr_ip_tbl[0];
             App_IP_Addrs[if_nbr][0] =  addr_ip;                    (5)
             break;
        case NET_IF_ERR_INVALID_IF:
        case NET_IP_ERR_NULL_PTR:
        case NET_IP_ERR_ADDR_CFG_IN_PROGRESS:
        case NET_IP_ERR_ADDR_TBL_SIZE:
        case NET_IP_ERR_ADDR_NONE_AVAIL:
        default:
             (void)Str_Copy((CPU_CHAR *)&addr_ip_str[0],
                            (CPU_CHAR *) APP_IP_ADDR_STR_UNKNOWN);
             break;
    }
}
}
```

Listing 6-4 **App_TCPIP_Init_DHCPc()**

6

L6-4(1)   Initializes the DHCP client functionality provided by the µC/TCP-IP stack.

L6-4(2)   Starts the DHCP client functionality.

L6-4(3)   Loops with small delay until the DHCP module has finished the IP address resolution process.

L6-4(4)   Periodically checks the DHCP module status to determine if address resolution is complete.

L6-4(5)   Adds the newly acquired IP address to the application's address table.

L6-4(6)   Adds the discovered DNS server's address to the application's address table.

Figure 6-1 shows the progression of a ping request and reply through the application and the µC/TCP-IP stack. The figure also shows how the tasks interact for this application.

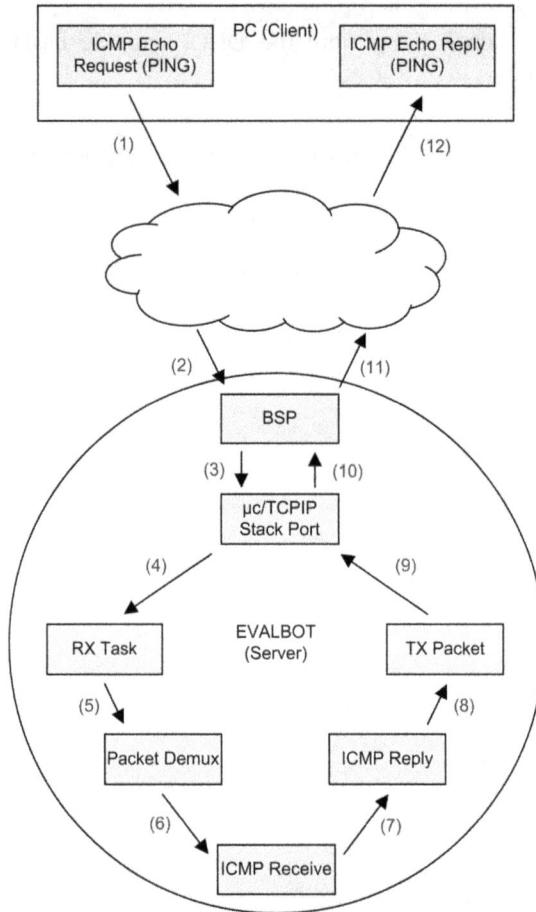

Figure 6-1 **Interaction of application tasks**

F6-1(1)   User issues ping command which transmits an ICMP Echo Request to the EVALBOT.

F6-1(2)   EVALBOT BSP vectors to the LM3S9B92 Ethernet interrupt service routine which configures the µDMA to copy the packet to a local buffer.

F6-1(3)   The interrupt service routine is triggered again to alert the system that the µDMA transfer is complete. The µC/TCP-IP port then signals the stack's receive task that a packet is ready for decoding.

F6-1(4)   The NetOS_IF_RxTask() task function is made ready and validates the packet.

F6-1(5)   The **NetIF_RxTaskHandler()** and **NetIP_RxPktValidate()** functions determine which protocol should handle the new packet.

F6-1(6)   The **NetICMP_Rx()** function determines that the packet is an echo request and starts the echo reply process.

F6-1(7)   The **NetICMP_TxMsgReply()** function formulates the reply packet.

F6-1(8)   **NetIP_Tx()** and other functions bundle the packet and hand it off to the LM3S9B92 µC/TCP-IP port.

F6-1(9)   The µC/TCP-IP port loads the packet into the LM3S9B92 Ethernet hardware using the **NetDev_Tx()** function.

F6-1(10)   The EVALBOT BSP manages interrupts and the completion of the transfer to the physical interface.

F6-1(11)   Echo reply packet is transmitted.

F6-1(12)   Echo reply is received and analyzed by user application.

6-2 SUMMARY

This example serves to verify that network communications are functional with the µC/TCP-IP stack. A simple echo request demonstrates the interaction between the board support package, the LM3S9B92 stack port, and the µC/TCP-IP stack itself. The IP address of the EVALBOT is obtained via DHCP and displayed for easy reference. This example also serves as a foundation for the remainder of examples in this book.

7

HTTP Server Example

The ability of a user to interact with an embedded web server from any location using any device with a web browser has become ubiquitous. The applications for this interaction range from checking the status of a home security system to controlling industrial robotics. This example demonstrates the use of µC/TCP-IP and µC/HTTPs to display status and allow control of the EVALBOT using a simple HTML form.

7-1 HOW THE PROJECT WORKS

This example is divided into two parts: the HTTP server application and robotic control of the EVALBOT.

7-1-1 HTTP SERVER APPLICATION

As explained in previous examples the **main()** function initializes µC/OS-III, creates a single startup task and starts the scheduler which in turn allows the startup task to run. The code for the **App_TaskStart()** has also been shown in previous examples. It remains largely unchanged with the exception of adding subroutine calls to **App_HTTPs_Init()** and **AppRobotTasksCreate()**. The latter function is an application layer routine that creates a series of tasks used for controlling motion of the EVALBOT. It is found in the file **app_robotics.c** and is explained in section 7-1-2 "Robot Control" on page 1104 of this chapter. The **App_HTTPs_Init()** function performs required application level initialization of the µC/HTTPs module and is explained in Listing 7-1 on page 1097.

```
static void App_HTTPs_Init (void)
{
    CPU_BOOLEAN cfg_success;


    cfg_success = HTTPs_Init(DEF_DISABLED);                              (1)
    APP_TEST_FAULT(cfg_success, DEF_OK);


    cfg_success = Apps_FS_Init();                                        (2)
    APP_TEST_FAULT(cfg_success, DEF_OK);


    cfg_success = Apps_FS_AddFile(HTTPs_INDEX_HTML_NAME,                 (3)
                              (void *) data_index_html,
                              sizeof(data_index_html));
    APP_TEST_FAULT(cfg_success, DEF_OK);


    cfg_success = Apps_FS_AddFile((CPU_CHAR *)&HTTPs_LOGO_GIF_NAME,
                              (void *)data_logo_gif,
                              (CPU_INT32U) sizeof(data_logo_gif));
    APP_TEST_FAULT(cfg_success, DEF_OK);


    cfg_success = Apps_FS_AddFile((CPU_CHAR *)&HTTPs_ARROW_F_GIF_NAME,
                              (CPU_CHAR *)&data_arrow_f_gif,
                              (CPU_INT32U) sizeof(data_arrow_f_gif));
    APP_TEST_FAULT(cfg_success, DEF_OK);


    cfg_success = Apps_FS_AddFile((CPU_CHAR *)&HTTPs_ARROW_FL_GIF_NAME,
                              (CPU_CHAR *)&data_arrow_fl_gif,
                              (CPU_INT32U) sizeof(data_arrow_fl_gif));
    APP_TEST_FAULT(cfg_success, DEF_OK);


    cfg_success = Apps_FS_AddFile((CPU_CHAR *)&HTTPs_ARROW_FR_GIF_NAME,
                              (CPU_CHAR *)&data_arrow_fr_gif,
                              (CPU_INT32U) sizeof(data_arrow_fr_gif));
    APP_TEST_FAULT(cfg_success, DEF_OK);


    cfg_success = Apps_FS_AddFile((CPU_CHAR *)&HTTPs_ARROW_B_GIF_NAME,
                              (CPU_CHAR *)&data_arrow_b_gif,
                              (CPU_INT32U) sizeof(data_arrow_b_gif));
    APP_TEST_FAULT(cfg_success, DEF_OK);


    cfg_success = Apps_FS_AddFile((CPU_CHAR *)&HTTPs_ARROW_BL_GIF_NAME,
                              (CPU_CHAR *)&data_arrow_bl_gif,
                              (CPU_INT32U) sizeof(data_arrow_bl_gif));
    APP_TEST_FAULT(cfg_success, DEF_OK);
```

```
    cfg_success = Apps_FS_AddFile((CPU_CHAR *)&HTTPs_ARROW_BR_GIF_NAME,
                                  (CPU_CHAR *)&data_arrow_br_gif,
                                  (CPU_INT32U) sizeof(data_arrow_br_gif));
    APP_TEST_FAULT(cfg_success, DEF_OK);


    cfg_success = Apps_FS_AddFile((CPU_CHAR *)&HTTPs_STOP_GIF_NAME,
                                  (CPU_CHAR *)&data_stop_gif,
                                  (CPU_INT32U) sizeof(data_stop_gif));
    APP_TEST_FAULT(cfg_success, DEF_OK);


    cfg_success = Apps_FS_AddFile((CPU_CHAR *)&HTTPs_EVALBOT_GIF_NAME,
                                  (CPU_CHAR *)&data_evalbot_gif,
                                  (CPU_INT32U) sizeof(data_evalbot_gif));
    APP_TEST_FAULT(cfg_success, DEF_OK);
}
```

Listing 7-1 **App_HTTPs_Init()**

L7-1(1)   Calls the **HTTPs_Init()** function to start the server and its tasks.

L7-1(2)   Uses **Apps_FS_Init()** to initialize the static file system used for this application.

L7-1(3)   Adds each of the files that will be available on the HTTP server to the file system using **Apps_FS_AddFile()**.

The µC/TCP-IP module provides for two callback functions that make interaction between the web browser and the embedded application simple. The **HTTPs_ValReq()** function is called when the µC/HTTPs module encounters a special token in a file that it is sending to a client. The **HTTPs_ValReq()** function replaces the token with the real-time value of an application variable that the token signifies. The **HTTPs_ValRx()** function is called by the µC/HTTPs module to allow the developer to handle POST operations typically generated when a user submits a form in their web browser.

The operation of the **HTTPs_ValReq()** function is explained in Listing 7-2.

7

```
CPU_BOOLEAN HTTPs_ValReq (CPU_CHAR    *p_tok,
                         CPU_CHAR   **p_val)
{
    CPU_CHAR    buf[HTTPs_VAL_REQ_BUF_LEN];
#if   (LIB_VERSION >= 126u)
    CPU_INT32U  ver;
#elif (LIB_STR_CFG_FP_EN == DEF_ENABLED)
    CPU_FP32    ver;
#endif
    OS_TICK     os_time_tick;
    CPU_FP32    os_time_sec;
    OS_ERR      os_err;


   (void)Str_Copy(&buf[0], "%%%%%%%%");
   *p_val = &buf[0];


    if (Str_Cmp(p_tok, "OS_VERSION")               == 0) {                        (1)
#if (LIB_VERSION >= 126u)
#if (OS_VERSION  >  300u)
        ver =  OS_VERSION / 1000;
        (void)Str_FmtNbr_Int32U(ver,   2, DEF_NBR_BASE_DEC, ' ',
                                          DEF_NO, DEF_NO,  &buf[0]);
        buf[2] = '.';

        ver = (OS_VERSION /   10) % 100;
        (void)Str_FmtNbr_Int32U(ver,   2, DEF_NBR_BASE_DEC, '0',
                                          DEF_NO, DEF_NO,  &buf[3]);
        buf[5] = '.';

        ver = (OS_VERSION /    1) %  10;
        (void)Str_FmtNbr_Int32U(ver,   1, DEF_NBR_BASE_DEC, '0',
                                          DEF_NO, DEF_YES, &buf[6]);
        buf[8] = '\0';

#else
        ver =  OS_VERSION /  100;
        (void)Str_FmtNbr_Int32U(ver,   2, DEF_NBR_BASE_DEC, ' ',
                                          DEF_NO, DEF_NO,  &buf[0]);
        buf[2] = '.';

        ver = (OS_VERSION /    1) % 100;
        (void)Str_FmtNbr_Int32U(ver,   2, DEF_NBR_BASE_DEC, '0',
                                          DEF_NO, DEF_YES, &buf[3]);
        buf[5] = '\0';
#endif
```

```
#elif (LIB_STR_CFG_FP_EN == DEF_ENABLED)
#if   (OS_VERSION > 300u)
        ver = (CPU_FP32)OS_VERSION / 1000;
        (void)Str_FmtNbr_32(ver,  2,  2,  ' ',  DEF_NO,  &buf[0]);


        ver = (CPU_FP32)OS_VERSION /   10;
        (void)Str_FmtNbr_32(ver,  0,  1,  '\0', DEF_YES, &buf[6]);

#else
        ver = (CPU_FP32)OS_VERSION / 100;
        (void)Str_FmtNbr_32(ver, 2,  2,  '\0', DEF_YES, &buf[0]);
#endif
#endif


    } else if (Str_Cmp(p_tok, "OS_TIME"        ) == 0) {                    (2)
        os_time_tick = (OS_TICK )OSTimeGet(&os_err);
        os_time_sec  = (CPU_FP32)os_time_tick / OS_CFG_TICK_RATE_HZ;
        (void)Str_FmtNbr_32(os_time_sec, 7u,  3u,  '\0', DEF_YES, &buf[0]);

    } else if (Str_Cmp(p_tok, "NET_VERSION") == 0) {                        (3)
#if (LIB_VERSION >= 126u)
#if (NET_VERSION >  205u)
        ver =  NET_VERSION / 10000;
        (void)Str_FmtNbr_Int32U(ver,  2, DEF_NBR_BASE_DEC, ' ',
                                       DEF_NO, DEF_NO, &buf[0]);
        buf[2] = '.';

        ver = (NET_VERSION /   100) % 100;
        (void)Str_FmtNbr_Int32U(ver,  2, DEF_NBR_BASE_DEC, '0',
                                       DEF_NO, DEF_NO, &buf[3]);
        buf[5] = '.';

        ver = (NET_VERSION /     1) % 100;
        (void)Str_FmtNbr_Int32U(ver,  2, DEF_NBR_BASE_DEC, '0',
                                       DEF_NO, DEF_YES, &buf[6]);
        buf[8] = '\0';

#else
        ver =  NET_VERSION /   100;
        (void)Str_FmtNbr_Int32U(ver,  2, DEF_NBR_BASE_DEC, ' ',
                                       DEF_NO, DEF_NO,  &buf[0]);
        buf[2] = '.';

        ver = (NET_VERSION /     1) % 100;
        (void)Str_FmtNbr_Int32U(ver,  2, DEF_NBR_BASE_DEC, '0',
                                       DEF_NO, DEF_YES, &buf[3]);
        buf[5] = '\0';
#endif
```

```
#elif (LIB_STR_CFG_FP_EN == DEF_ENABLED)
#if   (NET_VERSION > 205u)
        ver = (CPU_FP32)NET_VERSION / 10000;
        (void)Str_FmtNbr_32(ver, 2, 2, ' ', DEF_NO, &buf[0]);


        ver = (CPU_FP32)NET_VERSION /  100;
        (void)Str_FmtNbr_32(ver, 0, 2, '\0', DEF_YES, &buf[6]);

#else
        ver = (CPU_FP32)NET_VERSION /  100;
        (void)Str_FmtNbr_32(ver, 2, 2, '\0', DEF_YES, &buf[0]);
#endif
#endif
    } else if (Str_Cmp(p_tok, "SPEED_L") == 0) {                        (4)
        (void)Str_FmtNbr_Int32S(AppRobotMotorActualSpeedGet(LEFT_SIDE), 3,
                        DEF_NBR_BASE_DEC, '\0', DEF_NO,
                        DEF_YES, &buf[0]);

    } else if (Str_Cmp(p_tok, "SPEED_R") == 0) {                        (5)
        (void)Str_FmtNbr_Int32S(AppRobotMotorActualSpeedGet(RIGHT_SIDE), 3,
                        DEF_NBR_BASE_DEC, '\0', DEF_NO,
                        DEF_YES, &buf[0]);

    } else if (Str_Cmp(p_tok, "BUMP_L") == 0) {                         (6)
        (void)Str_FmtNbr_Int32S(BSP_BumpSensorGetStatus(1), 3,
                        DEF_NBR_BASE_DEC, '\0', DEF_NO,
                        DEF_YES, &buf[0]);

    } else if (Str_Cmp(p_tok, "BUMP_R") == 0) {                         (7)
        (void)Str_FmtNbr_Int32S(BSP_BumpSensorGetStatus(2), 3,
                        DEF_NBR_BASE_DEC, '\0', DEF_NO,
                        DEF_YES, &buf[0]);

    }

    return DEF_OK;
}
```

Listing 7-2 **HTTPs_ValReq()**

L7-2(1)   If the token string is requesting "OS_VERSION," then store the µC/OS-III version number into the return buffer to be inserted into the HTML file.

L7-2(2)   If the token string is requesting "OS_TIME," then store the current time as tracked by µC/OS-III into the return buffer to be inserted into the HTML file.

L7-2(3)   If the token string is requesting "NET_VERSION," then store the µC/OS-III version number into the return buffer to be inserted into the HTML file.

L7-2(4)   Loads the speed of the left EVALBOT motor into the return buffer.

L7-2(5)   Loads the speed of the right EVALBOT motor into the return buffer.

L7-2(6)   Inserts the status of the left bump sensor into the return buffer.

L7-2(7)   Inserts the status of the right bump sensor into the return buffer.

Listing 7-3 explains the use of the **HTTPs_ValRx()** function.

```
CPU_BOOLEAN HTTPs_ValRx(CPU_CHAR *p_var, CPU_CHAR *p_val)
{
    CPU_INT16U   cmp_str;
    CPU_BOOLEAN  ret_val;
    OS_ERR       err;


    cmp_str = Str_Cmp((CPU_CHAR *)p_var,
                      (CPU_CHAR *)HTML_CONTROL_INPUT_NAME);            (1)
    if (cmp_str == 0) {
       cmp_str = Str_Cmp((CPU_CHAR *)p_val,
                         (CPU_CHAR *)HTML_CONTROL_FORWARD);            (2)
       if (cmp_str == 0) {
          OSFlagPost(&AppRobotControlFlagGroup,
                     FLAG_COMMAND_FORWARD,
                     OS_OPT_POST_FLAG_SET,
                     &err);

          ret_val = DEF_OK;
       }

       cmp_str = Str_Cmp((CPU_CHAR *)p_val,
                         (CPU_CHAR *)HTML_CONTROL_FORWARD_LEFT);       (3)
       if (cmp_str == 0) {
          OSFlagPost(&AppRobotControlFlagGroup,
                     FLAG_COMMAND_FORWARD_LEFT,
                     OS_OPT_POST_FLAG_SET,
                     &err);

          ret_val = DEF_OK;
       }
```

```
        cmp_str = Str_Cmp((CPU_CHAR *)p_val,
                          (CPU_CHAR *)HTML_CONTROL_FORWARD_RIGHT);          (4)
        if (cmp_str == 0) {
            OSFlagPost(&AppRobotControlFlagGroup,
                       FLAG_COMMAND_FORWARD_RIGHT,
                       OS_OPT_POST_FLAG_SET,
                       &err);

            ret_val = DEF_OK;
        }


        cmp_str = Str_Cmp((CPU_CHAR *)p_val,
                          (CPU_CHAR *)HTML_CONTROL_REVERSE);                (5)
        if (cmp_str == 0) {
            OSFlagPost(&AppRobotControlFlagGroup,
                       FLAG_COMMAND_REVERSE,
                       OS_OPT_POST_FLAG_SET,
                       &err);
            ret_val = DEF_OK;
        }


        cmp_str = Str_Cmp((CPU_CHAR *)p_val,
                          (CPU_CHAR *)HTML_CONTROL_REVERSE_LEFT);           (6)
        if (cmp_str == 0) {
            OSFlagPost(&AppRobotControlFlagGroup,
                       FLAG_COMMAND_REVERSE_LEFT,
                       OS_OPT_POST_FLAG_SET,
                       &err);
            ret_val = DEF_OK;
        }


        cmp_str = Str_Cmp((CPU_CHAR *)p_val,
                          (CPU_CHAR *)HTML_CONTROL_REVERSE_RIGHT);          (7)
        if (cmp_str == 0) {
            OSFlagPost(&AppRobotControlFlagGroup,
                       FLAG_COMMAND_REVERSE_RIGHT,
                       OS_OPT_POST_FLAG_SET,
                       &err);
            ret_val = DEF_OK;
        }


        cmp_str = Str_Cmp((CPU_CHAR *)p_val,
                          (CPU_CHAR *)HTML_CONTROL_STOP);                   (8)
        if (cmp_str == 0) {
            OSFlagPost(&AppRobotControlFlagGroup,
                       FLAG_COMMAND_STOP,
                       OS_OPT_POST_FLAG_SET,
                       &err);
```

```
            ret_val = DEF_OK;
    }


}

    return (ret_val);
}
```

Listing 7-3 **HTTPs_ValRx()**

L7-3(1)   Verifies the input name. This allows the developer to create multiple forms in HTML by assigning them different names.

L7-3(2)   Determines if the user requested a forward motion. If yes, sends the appropriate flag to the robot control task.

L7-3(3)   Determines if the user requested a forward left turn motion. If yes, sends the appropriate flag to the robot control task.

L7-3(4)   Determines if the user requested a forward right turn motion. If yes, sends the appropriate flag to the robot control task.

L7-3(5)   Determines if the user requested a reverse motion. If yes, sends the appropriate flag to the robot control task.

L7-3(6)   Determines if the user requested a reverse left motion. If yes, sends the appropriate flag to the robot control task.

L7-3(7)   Determines if the user requested a reverse right motion. If yes, sends the appropriate flag to the robot control task.

L7-3(8)   Determines if the user requested the EVALBOT to stop. If yes, sends the appropriate flag to the robot control task.

7-1-2 ROBOT CONTROL

The EVALBOT's motion and inputs are controlled by a collection of six tasks found in the `app_robotics.c` file. These tasks are created when the `App_TaskStart()` function calls the `AppRobotTasksCreate()` function. The robot control tasks created are:

- `AppTaskRobotControl` - the main control task.

- `AppTaskRobotLeftMotorDrive` - the left motor control task.

- `AppTaskRobotRightMotorDrive` - the right motor control task.

- `AppTaskRobotLeftMotorPID` - the left motor PID controller task.

- `AppTaskRobotRightMotorPID` - the right motor PID controller task.

- `AppTaskRobotInputMonitor` - the task to monitor button and bump sensor events.

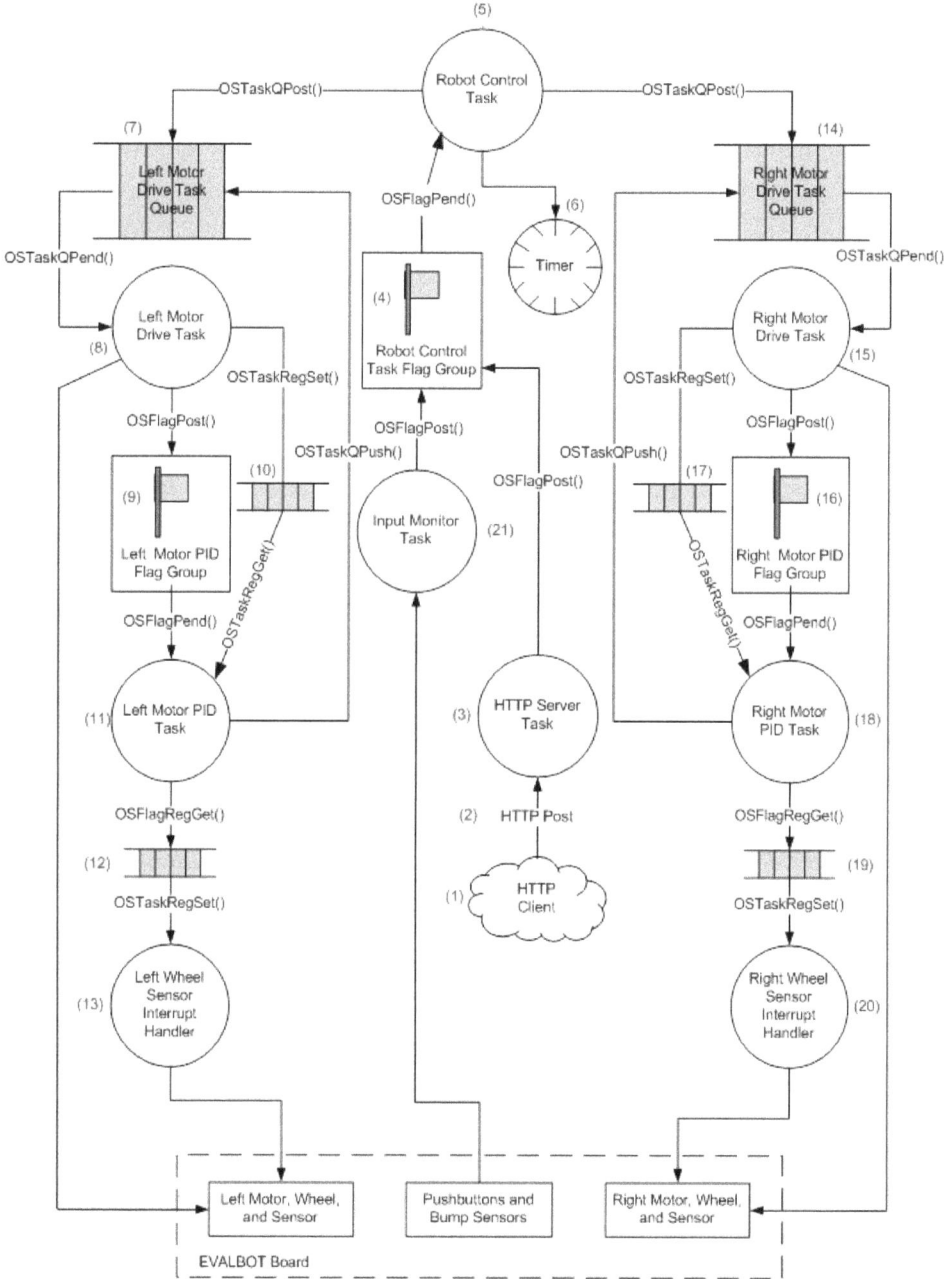

Figure 7-1 **Interaction of Application Tasks**

7

F7-1(1)   User loads HTML pages by typing EVALBOT IP address into the URL field of the browser.

F7-1(2)   User initiates an HTTP post operation by clicking on one of the control icons on the web page served by the EVALBOT.

F7-1(3)   The HTTP Server Task interprets the HTTP post and posts a corresponding flag to the Robot Control Task flag group.

F7-1(4)   The Robot Control Task Flag Group contains four flags for local control and seven flags that represent the commands that come from the HTTP Server Task.

F7-1(5)   The Robot Control Task transitions between states based on flags being posted to its flag group. It will post messages to the Left Motor Task and the Right Motor Task as appropriate.

F7-1(6)   A timer is used for the amount of time that EVALBOT executes the command before returning to the idle state.

F7-1(7)   The Left Motor Drive Task Queue passes messages to the Left Motor Drive Task.

F7-1(8)   The Left Motor Drive Task waits to receive a message. When a message is received, the Left Motor Drive Task drives the left motor accordingly.

F7-1(9)   The Left Motor PID Task Flag Group consists of two flags; one to start the PID controller, and one to stop the PID controller.

F7-1(10)   The Left Motor PID Task Register sets the target speed from the Left Motor Drive Task.

F7-1(11)   The Left Motor PID Task reacts to flags posted from the Left Motor Drive Task as well as its register contents being set by the Left Motor Drive Task and the Left Wheel Sensor Interrupt Handler.

F7-1(12)   The Left Motor PID Task Register sets the actual speed from the Left Wheel Sensor Interrupt Handler.

F7-1(13)   The Left Wheel Sensor Interrupt Handler handles edge interrupts generated by the left wheel sensor and calculates the speed. This speed information is then shared with the Left Motor PID Task.

F7-1(14)   The Right Motor Drive Task Queue passes messages to the Right Motor Drive Task.

F7-1(15)   The Right Motor Drive Task waits to receive a message. When a message has been received, it drives the right motor accordingly.

F7-1(16)   The Right Motor PID Task Flag Group consists of two flags; one to start the PID controller, and one to stop the PID controller.

F7-1(17)   The Right Motor PID Task Register sets the target speed from the Right Motor Drive Task.

F7-1(18)   The Right Motor PID Task reacts to flags posted from the Right Motor Drive Task as well as its register contents being set by the Right Motor Drive Task and the Right Wheel Sensor Interrupt Handler.

F7-1(19)   The Right Motor PID Task Register sets the actual speed from the Right Wheel Sensor Interrupt Handler.

F7-1(20)   The Right Wheel Sensor Interrupt Handler handles edge interrupts generated by the right wheel sensor and calculates the speed. This speed information is then shared with the Right Motor PID Task.

F7-1(21)   The Input Monitor Task monitors the state of the push buttons and bump sensors. A flag is posted to the Robot Control Task Flag Group if the state of the input changes. The flag indicates which input has changed.

The code for the **AppTaskRobotInputMonitor()** is shown in Listing 7-4.

```
static void AppTaskRobotInputMonitor (void *p_arg)
{
    CPU_INT08U  ucData;
    OS_ERR      err;
    CPU_INT08U  ucSwitches;
    CPU_INT08U  ucDelta;
    CPU_INT08U  ucSwitchesClockA;
    CPU_INT08U  ucSwitchesClockB;


    ucSwitches       = 0x0Fu;                                        (1)
    ucSwitchesClockA =    0u;
    ucSwitchesClockB =    0u;


    while (DEF_ON) {                                                 (2)
        OSTimeDlyHMSM(0u, 0u, 0u, 5u,                               (3)
                      OS_OPT_TIME_HMSM_STRICT,
                      &err);

        ucData =  BSP_PushButtonGetStatus(1u)        |              (4)
                 (BSP_PushButtonGetStatus(2u) << 1u) |
                 (BSP_BumpSensorGetStatus(1u) << 2u) |
                 (BSP_BumpSensorGetStatus(2u) << 3u);

        ucDelta = ucData ^ ucSwitches;                              (5)

        ucSwitchesClockA ^=  ucSwitchesClockB;
        ucSwitchesClockB  = ~ucSwitchesClockB;

        ucSwitchesClockA &= ucDelta;
        ucSwitchesClockB &= ucDelta;

        ucSwitches &=    ucSwitchesClockA | ucSwitchesClockB;
        ucSwitches |= (~(ucSwitchesClockA | ucSwitchesClockB)) & ucData;

        ucDelta ^= ucSwitchesClockA | ucSwitchesClockB;

        if ((ucDelta & 0x0Fu) && (~ucSwitches & 0x0Fu)) {          (6)
            RandomAddEntropy(OSTimeGet(&err));                     (7)
            RandomSeed();                                          (8)
        }

        if ((ucDelta & 0x03u) && (~ucSwitches & 0x03u)) {
            OSFlagPost(&AppRobotControlFlagGroup,                  (9)
                       FLAG_PUSH_BUTTON,
                       OS_OPT_POST_FLAG_SET,
                       &err);
        }
```

```
        if ((ucDelta & 0x04u) && (~ucSwitches & 0x04u)) {
            OSFlagPost(&AppRobotControlFlagGroup,                    (10)
                    FLAG_RIGHT_BUMP_SENSOR,
                    OS_OPT_POST_FLAG_SET,
                    &err);
        }

        if ((ucDelta & 0x08u) && (~ucSwitches & 0x08u)) {
            OSFlagPost(&AppRobotControlFlagGroup,                    (11)
                    FLAG_LEFT_BUMP_SENSOR,
                    OS_OPT_POST_FLAG_SET,
                    &err);
        }
    }
}
```

Listing 7-4 **lAppTaskRobotInputMonitor()** in app.c

L7-4(1)   Initializes the variables that require initialization.

L7-4(2)   Sets the infinite loop for this task.

L7-4(3)   The **OSTimeDlyHMSM( )** function delays the task from being ready to run for 5 milliseconds. This delay causes the code within the main task loop to execute approximately every 5 milliseconds.

L7-4(4)   The current state of the pushbuttons and the bump sensors are read and stored to a bit-mapped variable where each bit indicates the state of a single pushbutton or bump sensor.

L7-4(5)   The next eight lines of code handle the debouncing of the pushbuttons and bump sensors.

L7-4(6)   Checks to see if any of the pushbuttons or bump sensors were just pressed.

L7-4(7)   Adds the current time to the random number generator's entropy pool.

L7-4(8)   Seeds the random number generator using the updated entropy pool.

L7-4(9)   Posts the pushbutton flag to the Robot Control Task Flag Group if either pushbutton is pressed.

L7-4(10)   Posts the right bump sensor flag to the Robot Control Task Flag Group if the right bump sensor is pressed.

L7-4(11)   Posts the left bump sensor flag to the Robot Control Task Flag Group if the left bump sensor is pressed.

The code for the **AppTaskRobotControl()** is shown in Listing 7-5.

```
static  void  AppTaskRobotControl (void  *p_arg)
{
    CPU_INT16U         usDriveTimeWindow;
    CPU_INT08U         pucMotorSpeed[2];
    tControlTaskState  eState;
    OS_FLAGS           flags;
    OS_ERR             err;
    CPU_TS             ts;


    OSFlagCreate(&AppRobotControlFlagGroup,                         (1)
                 "Robot Control Task Flag Group",
                 (OS_FLAGS)0,
                 &err);

    eState          = CONTROL_IDLE;                                 (2)
    usDriveTimeWindow = INIT_DRIVE_TIME_WINDOW;                     (3)

    while (DEF_ON) {                                                (4)
        switch (eState) {                                          (5)
            case CONTROL_IDLE:                                     (6)
                OSFlagPend(&AppRobotControlFlagGroup,
                           FLAG_PUSH_BUTTON       +
                           FLAG_LEFT_BUMP_SENSOR +
                           FLAG_RIGHT_BUMP_SENSOR,
                           0u,
                           OS_OPT_PEND_FLAG_SET_ANY + OS_OPT_PEND_FLAG_CONSUME,
                           &ts,
                           &err);
                flags = OSFlagPendGetFlagsRdy(&err);
                if ((flags & FLAG_LEFT_BUMP_SENSOR) ||
                    (flags & FLAG_RIGHT_BUMP_SENSOR)) {
                    break;
                }
                eState = CONTROL_DRIVE_FORWARD;
                break;
```

```
case CONTROL_DRIVE_FORWARD:                                    (7)
    if ((((RandomNumber() >> 16u) * 100u) >> 16u) < 75u) {
        AppRobotDriveForward(65u, 65u);
    } else {
        pucMotorSpeed[0] = (((RandomNumber() >> 16u) * 10u) >> 16u) + 60u;
        pucMotorSpeed[1] = (((RandomNumber() >> 16u) * 10u) >> 16u) + 45u;
        if (RandomNumber() & 0x80000000u) {
            AppRobotDriveForward(pucMotorSpeed[1], pucMotorSpeed[0]);
        } else {
            AppRobotDriveForward(pucMotorSpeed[0], pucMotorSpeed[1]);
        }
    }
    AppRobotDriveTmrInit(usDriveTimeWindow);
    eState = CONTROL_DRIVING_FORWARD;
    break;

case CONTROL_DRIVING_FORWARD:                                  (8)
    OSFlagPend(&AppRobotControlFlagGroup,
               FLAG_PUSH_BUTTON        +
               FLAG_RIGHT_BUMP_SENSOR  +
               FLAG_LEFT_BUMP_SENSOR   +
               FLAG_TIMER_EXPIRATION,
               0u,
               OS_OPT_PEND_FLAG_SET_ANY + OS_OPT_PEND_FLAG_CONSUME,
               &ts,
               &err);
    AppRobotDriveTmrDel();
    AppRobotStop();
    flags = OSFlagPendGetFlagsRdy(&err);
    if (flags & FLAG_PUSH_BUTTON) {
        eState = CONTROL_IDLE;
    } else if (flags & FLAG_TIMER_EXPIRATION) {
        usDriveTimeWindow = INIT_DRIVE_TIME_WINDOW;
        if (RandomNumber() & 0x80000000u) {
            eState = CONTROL_TURN_LEFT;
        } else {
            eState = CONTROL_TURN_RIGHT;
        }
    } else if (flags & FLAG_RIGHT_BUMP_SENSOR) {
        usDriveTimeWindow = (usDriveTimeWindow * 3u) / 4u;
        eState = CONTROL_TURN_LEFT;
    } else if (flags & FLAG_LEFT_BUMP_SENSOR) {
        usDriveTimeWindow = (usDriveTimeWindow * u3) / 4u;
        eState = CONTROL_TURN_RIGHT;
    }
    break;
```

```
        case CONTROL_TURN_LEFT:                                      (9)
            AppRobotTurnLeft();
            AppRobotTurnTmrInit();
            eState = CONTROL_TURNING;
            break;

        case CONTROL_TURN_RIGHT:                                     (10)
            AppRobotTurnRight();
            AppRobotTurnTmrInit();
            eState = CONTROL_TURNING;
            break;

        case CONTROL_TURNING:                                        (11)
            OSFlagPend(&AppRobotControlFlagGroup,
                       FLAG_PUSH_BUTTON        +
                       FLAG_LEFT_BUMP_SENSOR  +
                       FLAG_RIGHT_BUMP_SENSOR +
                       FLAG_TIMER_EXPIRATION,
                       0u,
                       OS_OPT_PEND_FLAG_SET_ANY + OS_OPT_PEND_FLAG_CONSUME,
                       &ts,
                       &err);
            flags = OSFlagPendGetFlagsRdy(&err);
            if ((flags & FLAG_LEFT_BUMP_SENSOR) ||
                (flags & FLAG_RIGHT_BUMP_SENSOR)) {
                break;
            }
            AppRobotTurnTmrDel();
            AppRobotStop();
            if (flags & FLAG_PUSH_BUTTON) {
                eState = CONTROL_IDLE;
            } else if (flags & FLAG_TIMER_EXPIRATION) {
                eState = CONTROL_DRIVE_FORWARD;
            }
            break;
    }
  }
}
```

Listing 7-5 **AppTaskRobotControl()**

L7-5(1)   Sets the state of the Robot Control Task to idle.

L7-5(2)   Configures the drive time window to its initial value. This is the duration of
            time that the EVALBOT executes a command received from the HTTP server
            before returning to the idle state.

L7-5(3)   Sets the infinite loop for this task.

L7-5(4)   Switches the EVALBOT's state based on the current state.

L7-5(5)   Defines the idle state. Gets the flag that caused the task to be ready to run. If one of the bump sensors is triggered, break causes the idle state to be reentered and pended again. This consumes the bump sensor flags while maintaining the idle state. If a command flag was posted by the HTTP server application the state is changed causing the EVALBOT to execute the desired action.

L7-5(6)   Defines the drive forward state. This is a transitional state that sets up EVALBOT to start driving forward. The forward velocity is set. The drive timer is initialized to stop forward motion when it expires. Finally, the state is changed to the driving forward state.

L7-5(7)   Defines the three motion states: driving forward, driving reverse and turning. Pends until a flag is posted. The flags are then processed depending on what flag has been posted and the current state of the robot. If a push button, timer or stop command flag was posted the EVALBOT returns to the idle state. If a bump sensor is triggered and the EVALBOT is driving forward the EVALBOT returns to the idle state. If a flag to turn forward left or reverse right was posted the EVALBOT will move to the turn left state. If a command to turn forward right or reverse left was posted the EVALBOT will move to the turn right state. If a reverse flag was posted the EVALBOT will change to the drive reverse state. Finally, if a forward flag was posted the EVALBOT will change to the drive forward state.

L7-5(8)   Defines the drive reverse state. This is a transitional state that sets up the EVALBOT to start driving straight in reverse. The reverse velocity is set. The drive timer is initialized to stop reverse motion when it expires. Finally, the state is changed to the driving reverse state.

L7-5(9)   Defines the turn left state. This is a transitional state that sets up the EVALBOT to turn to the left. This is a forward turn to the left which in this application is equivalent to a reverse turn to the right. The motor velocities are set to counter-rotate to the left. The drive timer is initialized to stop the turn when the timer expires.

L7-5(10)   Defines the turn right state. This is a transitional state that sets up the EVALBOT to turn to the right. This is a forward right turn which in this application is equivalent to a reverse turn to the left. The motor velocities are set to counter-rotate to the right. The drive timer is initialized to stop the turn when the timer expires.

The Left Motor Drive Task and the Right Motor Drive Task are independent tasks that execute the same function. The code for the **AppTaskRobotMotorDrive()** tasks is shown in Listing 7-6.

```
static  void  AppTaskRobotMotorDrive (void  *p_arg)
{
    CPU_INT08U  *pucMsg;
    OS_MSG_SIZE  msg_size;
    CPU_INT16U   usPercent;
    tSide        eSide;
    OS_ERR       err;
    CPU_TS       ts;


    eSide = *(tSide *)p_arg;                                      (1)

    while (DEF_ON) {                                             (2)
        pucMsg = (CPU_INT08U *)OSTaskQPend(0u,                   (3)
                                 OS_OPT_PEND_BLOCKING,
                                 &msg_size,
                                 &ts,
                                 &err);
        switch (pucMsg[0]) {                                    (4)
            case MSG_TYPE_MOTOR_DRIVE_START:                    (5)
                if (pucMsg[1] == MOTOR_DRIVE_FORWARD) {
                    BSP_MotorDir(eSide, FORWARD);
                } else {
                    BSP_MotorDir(eSide, REVERSE);
                }
                BSP_MotorSpeed(eSide, 0u);
                BSP_MotorRun(eSide);
                AppRobotMotorDriveSensorEnable(eSide);
                AppRobotMotorPIDTaskActualSpeedSet(eSide, 0u);
                AppRobotMotorPIDTaskTargetSpeedSet(eSide, pucMsg[2]);
                AppRobotMotorPIDTaskStart(eSide);
                break;
```

```
                case MSG_TYPE_MOTOR_STOP:                             (6)
                    BSP_MotorStop(eSide);
                    AppRobotMotorDriveSensorDisable(eSide);
                    AppRobotMotorPIDTaskStop(eSide);
                    break;

                case MSG_TYPE_MOTOR_DRIVE:                            (7)
                    usPercent = (pucMsg[1] << 8u) | (pucMsg[2]);
                    BSP_MotorSpeed(eSide, usPercent);
                    break;

                default:
                    break;
            }
        }
    }
```

Listing 7-6 **AppTaskRobotMotorDrive() in app.c**

L7-6(1)   The motor that this task is intended for (left or right) is passed to the function in p_arg. The value of p_arg is defined when the task is created. eSide is initialized with which motor this task is intended for.

L7-6(2)   Sets the infinite loop for this task.

L7-6(3)   Pends until a message is received.

L7-6(4)   Switches based on the message type. The message type is defined by the first byte of the message.

L7-6(5)   Sets the motor drive start message that comes from the Robot Control Task. Gets the drive direction from the second byte of the message and sets the direction of the motor accordingly. Sets the message speed to 0. This is updated by messages sent from the PID task. Enables the motor to run. Resets and enables capturing of the edge detection from the wheel sensor. Clears the actual speed value and sets the desired speed value, both used by the PID task. Finally, starts the PID task.

L7-6(6)   Sets the motor drive stop message that comes from the Robot Control Task. Stops the motor. Disables capturing of the edge detection from the wheel sensor and stops the PID task.

L7-6(7)   Sets the motor drive message that comes from the PID task. The new drive strength to drive the motor with is read from the second and third bytes of the message, and the motor speed is updated according to that value.

The Left and Right Motor PID Tasks are independent tasks that execute the same function. The code for the **AppTaskRobotMotorPID()** tasks is shown in Listing 7-7.

```
static void AppTaskRobotMotorPID (void *p_arg)
{
    CPU_INT32S    lDelta;
    CPU_INT32U    ulPercent;
    CPU_INT08U    ucTargetSpeed;
    CPU_INT08U    ucActualSpeed;
    CPU_INT08U    pucMotorMsg[3];
    tPIDState     sSpeedState;
    tPIDTaskState eState;
    tSide         eSide;
    OS_ERR        err;


    eSide  = *(tSide *)p_arg;                                        (1)
    AppRobotMotorPIDTaskFlagCreate(eSide);                           (2)
    eState = PID_IDLE;                                               (3)
    while (DEF_ON) {                                                 (4)
        switch (eState) {                                           (5)
            case PID_IDLE:                                          (6)
                    AppRobotMotorPIDTaskStartFlagPend(eSide);
                    eState = PID_START;
                    break;

            case PID_START:                                        (7)
                    PIDInitialize(&sSpeedState,
                                 (100u << 16u) / 3277,
                                 0u,
                                 0u,
                                 3277u << 16u,
                                 0u);
                    eState = PID_RUNNING;
                    break;

            case PID_RUNNING:                                      (8)
                    if (AppRobotMotorPIDTaskStopFlagPend(eSide) == OS_ERR_TIMEOUT) {
                        ucTargetSpeed = AppRobotMotorPIDTaskTargetSpeedGet(eSide);
                        ucActualSpeed = AppRobotMotorPIDTaskActualSpeedGet(eSide);
                        lDelta        = ((CPU_INT32S)ucTargetSpeed) -
                                        ((CPU_INT32S)ucActualSpeed);
                        ulPercent     = PIDUpdate(&sSpeedState, lDelta);
```

```
                 if (ulPercent > (100u << 16u)) {
                     ulPercent =  100u << 16u;
                 }

                 pucMotorMsg[0] = MSG_TYPE_MOTOR_DRIVE;
                 pucMotorMsg[1] =   ulPercent >> 16u; // upper byte of 8.8 percentage
                 pucMotorMsg[2] = ((ulPercent & 0xFF00u) >> 8u);
                 OSTaskQPost((eSide == LEFT_SIDE) ?
                              (OS_TCB    *)&AppTaskRobotLeftMotorDriveTCB :
                              (OS_TCB    *)&AppTaskRobotRightMotorDriveTCB,
                              (void      *)&pucMotorMsg[0],
                              (OS_MSG_SIZE) 3u,
                              (OS_OPT    ) OS_OPT_POST_FIFO,
                              (OS_ERR    *)&err);
             } else {
                 eState = PID_IDLE;
             }
             break;

         default:
             break;
         }
     }
 }
```

Listing 7-7 **Left Motor PID Task and Right Motor PID Task in app.c**

L7-7(1)   The motor that this task is intended for (left or right) is passed to the function
            in **p_arg**. The value of **p_arg** is defined when the task is created. eSide is
            initialized with the intended motor.

L7-7(2)   Creates the flag group for this task.

L7-7(3)   Sets the state of the Motor PID Task to idle.

L7-7(4)   Sets the infinite loop for this task.

L7-7(5)   Switches the EVALBOT's state based on the current state.

L7-7(6)   Defines the idle state. Pends until the start flag has been posted. After the start
            flag has been posted, moves to the start state.

L7-7(7)   Defines the start state. Initializes the PID controller with a P of 0, I of 0.05, and D of 0. The P, I, and D parameter values are in 16.16 fixed-point format. Moves to the running state.

L7-7(8)   Defines the running state. Pends until the stop flag is set or the 10 ms timeout occurs. This allows the PID Task to run approximately every 10 ms while also monitoring the stop flag. If the timeout occurs, gets the target and actual speeds, calculates the difference, gets the new motor drive value from the PID controller, and posts the motor drive message to the Motor Drive Task. If the stop flag is posted, then moves to the idle state.

The Left Wheel Sensor Interrupt and the Right Wheel Sensor Interrupt share the same interrupt handler. The code for the **AppRobotWheelSensorIntHandler()** interrupt handler is shown in Listing 7-8.

```
static void AppRobotWheelSensorIntHandler (void)
{
    static CPU_INT32U   ulRightEdgePrevTime;
    static CPU_INT32U   ulLeftEdgePrevTime;
    CPU_INT32U          ulRightEdgeDiff;
    CPU_INT32U          ulLeftEdgeDiff;
    CPU_INT32U          ulRightEdgeTime;
    CPU_INT32U          ulLeftEdgeTime;
    CPU_INT08U          ucRightRPM;
    CPU_INT08U          ucLeftRPM;
    CPU_INT32U          ulStatus;
    OS_ERR              err;


    ulStatus = GPIOPinIntStatus(LEFT_SIDE_SENSOR_PORT, DEF_TRUE);       (1)
    if (ulStatus & LEFT_SIDE_SENSOR_PIN) {
        GPIOPinIntClear(LEFT_SIDE_SENSOR_PORT,                          (2)
                    LEFT_SIDE_SENSOR_PIN);
        if (AppRobotLeftWheelFirstEdge) {
            ulLeftEdgePrevTime = OSTimeGet(&err);                      (3)
            AppRobotLeftWheelFirstEdge = DEF_FALSE;
```

```
        } else {
            ulLeftEdgeTime = OSTimeGet(&err);                      (4)
            if (ulLeftEdgeTime <= ulLeftEdgePrevTime) {
                ulLeftEdgeDiff  = ulLeftEdgeTime +
                                (0xFFFFFFFFu - ulLeftEdgePrevTime) + 1u;
            } else {
                ulLeftEdgeDiff  = ulLeftEdgeTime - ulLeftEdgePrevTime;
            }
            ucLeftRPM = (60u * OSCfg_TickRate_Hz) /
                        (16u * ulLeftEdgeDiff);
            ulLeftEdgePrevTime = ulLeftEdgeTime;
            AppRobotMotorPIDTaskActualSpeedSet(LEFT_SIDE, ucLeftRPM);
        }
    }
    ulStatus = GPIOPinIntStatus(RIGHT_SIDE_SENSOR_PORT, DEF_TRUE);   (5)
    if (ulStatus & RIGHT_SIDE_SENSOR_PIN) {
        GPIOPinIntClear(RIGHT_SIDE_SENSOR_PORT,                      (6)
                        RIGHT_SIDE_SENSOR_PIN);
        if (AppRobotRightWheelFirstEdge) {
            ulRightEdgePrevTime      = OSTimeGet(&err);             (7)
            AppRobotRightWheelFirstEdge = DEF_FALSE;
        } else {
            ulRightEdgeTime = OSTimeGet(&err);                     (8)
            if (ulRightEdgeTime <= ulRightEdgePrevTime) {
                ulRightEdgeDiff  = ulRightEdgeTime +
                                (0xFFFFFFFFu - ulRightEdgePrevTime) + 1u;
            } else {
                ulRightEdgeDiff  = ulRightEdgeTime - ulRightEdgePrevTime;
            }
            ucRightRPM          = (60u * OSCfg_TickRate_Hz) /
                                (16u * ulRightEdgeDiff);
            ulRightEdgePrevTime = ulRightEdgeTime;
            AppRobotMotorPIDTaskActualSpeedSet(RIGHT_SIDE, ucRightRPM);
        }
    }
}
```

Listing 7-8 **Left Wheel and Right Wheel Sensor Interrupt Handler in app.c**

L7-8(1)   Gets the interrupt state for the left-side sensor GPIO port.

L7-8(2)   Clears the left sensor interrupt status flag which was set.

L7-8(3)   If this is the first edge, then speed cannot yet be calculated. Saves the current time to the previous time variable and indicates that we are no longer looking for the first edge.

L7-8(4)   This interrupt was not due to the first edge. Gets the current time. Calculates the difference between the current time and the previous time. Uses the difference in time to calculate the wheel RPM and then copies the current time to the previous time. Gives the actual speed to the Left Motor PID Task.

L7-8(5)   Gets the interrupt state for the right-side sensor GPIO port.

L7-8(6)   Clears the right sensor interrupt status flag which was set.

L7-8(7)   If this is the first edge, then speed cannot yet be calculated. Saves the current time to the previous time variable and indicates that we are no longer looking for the first edge.

L7-8(8)   This interrupt was not due to the first edge. Gets the current time. Calculates the difference between the current time and the previous time. Uses the difference in time to calculate the wheel RPM and then copies the current time to the previous time. Gives the actual speed to the Right Motor PID Task.

7-2 SUMMARY

This example demonstrates the use of µC/TCP-IP and µC/HTTPs to interact with an embedded web server using a simple HTML form to display status. The second part of the example then shows the robot control task relaying the appropriate information to the two motor drive tasks allowing the user to control the EVALBOT.

TCP Sockets Example

The Ethernet Client example demonstrates how the µC/OS-III RTOS and the µC/TCP-IP IP stack can be used in conjunction with the EVM-EVALBOT evaluation board to create a TCP socket application gathering data from NOAA's National Weather Service server (http://www.weather.gov) using Simple Object Access Protocol (SOAP) requests.

The application task initializes the µC/TCP-IP stack and either uses a static IP address or acquires a dynamic IP address via DHCP. Once a valid IP is obtained, the EVALBOT then sends a SOAP request to the NOAA National Weather Service server for a listing of their predefined primary cities. The received response is parsed into memory arrays and displayed on the EVALBOT's OLED display. The user can then scroll through the list of cities using the left and right bump sensors and then press either Switch 1 or Switch 2 to send another SOAP request to the National Weather Service server for the weather of the desired city. The daily high and low temperatures are parsed from the data response and displayed on the EVALBOT's OLED display below the city name.

8

8-1 HOW THE PROJECT WORKS

Listing 8-1 shows the code for the **main()** function.

```
void main (void)
{
    OS_ERR err_os;

    BSP_IntDisAll();                                                      (1)

    OSInit(&err_os);                                                      (2)
    APP_TEST_FAULT(err_os, OS_ERR_NONE);

    OSTaskCreate((OS_TCB     *)&AppTaskStartTCB,                          (3)
                 (CPU_CHAR   *)"App Task Start",
                 (OS_TASK_PTR ) AppTaskStart,
                 (void       *) 0,
                 (OS_PRIO     ) APP_OS_CFG_START_TASK_PRIO,
                 (CPU_STK    *)&AppStartTaskStk[0],
                 (CPU_STK_SIZE) APP_OS_CFG_START_TASK_STK_SIZE / 10u,
                 (CPU_STK_SIZE) APP_OS_CFG_START_TASK_STK_SIZE,
                 (OS_MSG_QTY  ) 0u,
                 (OS_TICK     ) 0u,
                 (void       *) 0,
                 (OS_OPT      )(OS_OPT_TASK_STK_CHK | OS_OPT_TASK_STK_CLR),
                 (OS_ERR     *)&err_os);
    APP_TEST_FAULT(err_os, OS_ERR_NONE);

    OSStart(&err_os);                                                     (4)
    APP_TEST_FAULT(err_os, OS_ERR_NONE);
}
```

Listing 8-1 **main() in app.c**

L8-1(1)   Calls the **BSP_IntDisAll()** function which disables all interrupts to the CPU. The code for this function is located in the **bsp_int.c** file.

L8-1(2)   Initializes the µC/OS-III operating system prior to creating any tasks or multi-tasking.

L8-1(3)   Calls the **OSTaskCreate()** function to create the **App_TaskStart()** task which creates all the tasks in this application.

L8-1(4)   Calls the **OSStart()** function which starts the µC/OS-III scheduler. This function does not return.

Listing 8-2 shows the code for the **App_TaskStart()** task which initializes the board support package (BSP) and the application. After initialization, it executes as a low priority application background task. The background task blinks the EVALBOT's user LEDs to assist in verifying that the application is active.

```
static void App_TaskStart (void *p_arg)
{
    CPU_INT32U  cpu_clk_freq;
    CPU_INT32U  cnts;
    OS_ERR      err_os;

    (void)&p_arg;
    BSP_Init();                                                    (1)
    CPU_Init();                                                    (2)

    cpu_clk_freq = BSP_CPUClkFreq();                               (3)
    cnts = cpu_clk_freq / (CPU_INT32U)OSCfg_TickRate_Hz;
    OS_CPU_SysTickInit(cnts);

#if (OS_CFG_STAT_TASK_EN > 0u)
    OSStatTaskCPUUsageInit(&err_os);                               (4)
#endif

#ifdef CPU_CFG_INT_DIS_MEAS_EN
    CPU_IntDisMeasMaxCurReset();                                   (5)
#endif

#if (BSP_SER_COMM_EN == DEF_ENABLED)
    BSP_Ser_Init(115200);                                         (6)
#endif

    Mem_Init();                                                    (7)
    AppTasksCreate();                                              (8)

    while (DEF_ON) {                                               (9)
        BSP_LED_Toggle(2u);
        OSTimeDlyHMSM((CPU_INT16U) 0u,                            (10)
                     (CPU_INT16U) 0u,
                     (CPU_INT16U) 1u,
                     (CPU_INT16U) 0u,
                     (OS_OPT    ) OS_OPT_TIME_HMSM_STRICT,
                     (OS_ERR   *)&err_os);
    }
}
```

Listing 8-2 **App_TaskStart() in app.c**

8

L8-2(1)   Initializes the board support package (BSP). This configures the display, button, sensor, and other board interfaces.

L8-2(2)   Performs LM3S9B92-specific initialization. The `CPU_Init()` function is a part of the µC/OS-III and µC/TCP-IP port to this processor.

L8-2(3)   Sets up the SysTick timer which is built into the ARM® Cortex™-M3 core. The SysTick timer is used as the system tick timer for the µC/OS-III.

L8-2(4)   Computes the CPU capacity using the `OSStatTaskCPUUsageInit()` function. This is used by the OS's statistic task.

L8-2(5)   Initializes the process of calculating the time that interrupts are disabled using the `CPU_IntDisMeasMaxCurReset()` function.

L8-2(6)   Initializes the USB Virtual COM port interface. The Virtual COM port is used for various serial I/O. See the `app_cfg.h` file for more information

L8-2(7)   Initializes the dynamic memory management module using the `Mem_Init()` function. Dynamic memory allocation is used extensively by the µC/TCP-IP stack as it handles incoming and outgoing Ethernet packets.

L8-2(8)   Initializes the tasks and objects used by the application using the `AppTasksCreate()` function.

L8-2(9)   This infinite `while()` loop defines the main body of the task. This loop toggles the board's LED2 at constant rate. Failure to toggle LED2 indicates the system is blocked in a higher priority task. Additional background user application code may be inserted here.

L8-2(10)   Delays the task for 1 second using the `OSTimeDlyHMSM()` function. This delay causes the code in the main loop to execute once every second.

The `AppTasksCreate()` function creates all of the tasks that make up the application. The following three application tasks are created.

▣ `App_NetworkTask` - the main network task.

▣ `App_DisplayTask` - the OLED display task.

▣ `App_InputMonitorTask` - the task to monitor button and bump sensor events.

In addition, the following flag groups are created:

▣ `AppClientControlFlagGroup` - the flag group used for application control.

▣ `AppClientNetworkFlagGroup` - the flag group used for Ethernet startup and updates.

Figure 8-1 shows the data flow for the Ethernet Client example.

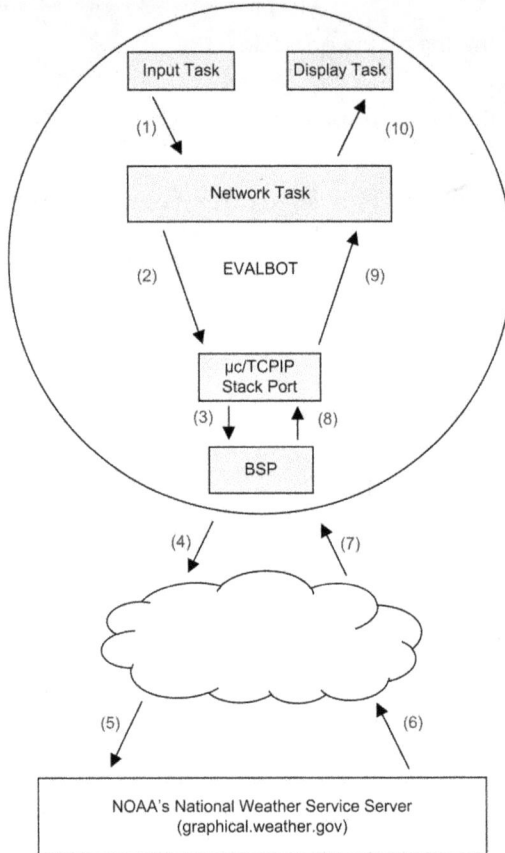

Figure 8-1 **Ethernet Client Example Data Flow**

F8-1(1)   The Input Task sends the user request to the Network Task and builds the SOAP request.

F8-1(2)   The µC/TCP-IP port loads the packet into the LM3S9B92 Ethernet hardware using the `NetSock_TxData()` function.

F8-1(3)   The EVALBOT BSP manages interrupts and the completion of the transfer to the physical interface.

F8-1(4)   The SOAP request is transmitted to the internet.

F8-1(5) ✱   The SOAP request is routed to NOAA's National Weather Service server where the request is interpreted.

F8-1(6)   NOAA's National Weather Service server sends the response which has the requested weather data.

F8-1(7)   The EVALBOT BSP vectors to the LM3S9B92 Ethernet interrupt service routine which configures the μDMA to copy the packet to a local buffer.

F8-1(8)   The interrupt service routine is triggered again to alert the system that the μDMA transfer is complete. The μC/TCP-IP port then signals the stack's receive task that a packet is ready for decoding.

F8-1(9)   The Network Task receives from the stack using the **NetSock_RxData()** function.

F8-1(10)   The parsed weather data is sent to the Display Task and displayed on the EVALBOT's OLED display.

The code for the **App_NetworkTask()** is shown below in Listing 8-3.

```
static void App_NetworkTask (void *p_arg)
{
    OS_ERR              err_os;
    NET_ERR             net_err;
    CPU_TS              ts;
    NET_SOCK_ID         sock_id;
    NET_IP_ADDR         server_ip_addr;
    NET_SOCK_ADDR_IP    server_sock_addr_ip;
    NET_SOCK_RTN_CODE   conn_rtn_code;
    CPU_INT32S          sIRxSize;
    CPU_CHAR            pcRxBuf[RX_BUF_SIZE];


    (void)&p_arg;

    App_TCPIP_Init();                                               (1)

    sock_id = NetSock_Open( NET_SOCK_FAMILY_IP_V4,                  (2)
                            NET_SOCK_TYPE_STREAM,
                            NET_SOCK_PROTOCOL_TCP,
                           &net_err);
    APP_TEST_FAULT(net_err, NET_SOCK_ERR_NONE);

    server_ip_addr = NetASCII_Str_to_IP( SERVER_IP_ADDR,           (3)
                                        &net_err);
    APP_TEST_FAULT(net_err, NET_ASCII_ERR_NONE);

    server_sock_addr_ip.AddrFamily = NET_SOCK_ADDR_FAMILY_IP_V4;   (4)
    server_sock_addr_ip.Addr       = NET_UTIL_HOST_TO_NET_32(server_ip_addr);
    server_sock_addr_ip.Port       = NET_UTIL_HOST_TO_NET_16(SERVER_PORT);

    conn_rtn_code = NetSock_Conn((NET_SOCK_ID)      sock_id,       (5)
                                 (NET_SOCK_ADDR *) &server_sock_addr_ip,
                                 (NET_SOCK_ADDR_LEN)sizeof(server_sock_addr_ip),
                                 (NET_ERR *)        &net_err);
    (void)conn_rtn_code;
    APP_TEST_FAULT(net_err, NET_SOCK_ERR_NONE);

#if (PROXY_SERVER == DEF_ENABLED)
    NetSock_TxData(        sock_id,                                (6)
                   (void *)g_pcServerConnectReq,
                           sizeof(g_pcServerConnectReq) - 1,
                           NET_SOCK_FLAG_NONE,
                          &net_err);
    APP_TEST_FAULT(net_err, NET_SOCK_ERR_NONE);
#endif
```

```
OSFlagPost(&AppClientNetworkFlagGroup,                        (7)
           FLAG_SOAP_SERVER_CON,
           OS_OPT_POST_FLAG_SET,
           &err_os);


NetSock_TxData(        sock_id,                               (8)
               (void *)g_pcSOAPReqLatLong,
                       sizeof(g_pcSOAPReqLatLong) - 1,
                       NET_SOCK_FLAG_NONE,
                       &net_err);
APP_TEST_FAULT(net_err, NET_SOCK_ERR_NONE);


OSFlagPost(&AppClientNetworkFlagGroup,                        (9)
           FLAG_SOAP_REQUEST_SENT,
           OS_OPT_POST_FLAG_SET,
           &err_os);

do {
    sIRxSize = NetSock_RxData( sock_id,                       (10)
                               pcRxBuf,
                               RX_BUF_SIZE,
                               NET_SOCK_FLAG_NONE,
                               &net_err);
    if ((net_err) != (NET_SOCK_ERR_RX_Q_CLOSED)) {           (11)
        APP_TEST_FAULT(net_err, NET_SOCK_ERR_NONE);
    }

    OSTimeDly(DELAY_RX,                                       (12)
              OS_OPT_TIME_DLY,
              &err_os);

    ParseRxDataLatLong(pcRxBuf, sIRxSize);                    (13)
} while (sIRxSize != 0);                                      (14)

 OSFlagPost(&AppClientNetworkFlagGroup,                       (15)
            FLAG_SOAP_RECEIVED,
            OS_OPT_POST_FLAG_SET,
            &err_os);

conn_rtn_code = NetSock_Close( sock_id,                       (16)
                               &net_err);
APP_TEST_FAULT(net_err, NET_SOCK_ERR_NONE);
```

8

```
OSFlagPost(&AppClientNetworkFlagGroup,                              (17)
           FLAG_SOAP_COMPLETE,
           OS_OPT_POST_FLAG_SET,
           &err_os);

while (DEF_ON) {
    OSFlagPend(&AppClientControlFlagGroup,                          (18)
               FLAG_READY_FOR_UPDATE,
               0u,
               OS_OPT_PEND_FLAG_SET_ANY | OS_OPT_PEND_FLAG_CONSUME,
               &ts,
               &err_os);

    BSP_LED_On(1u);                                                 (19)

    BuildWeatherSOAPReq();                                          (20)

    sock_id = NetSock_Open( NET_SOCK_FAMILY_IP_V4,
                            NET_SOCK_TYPE_STREAM,
                            NET_SOCK_PROTOCOL_TCP,
                           &net_err);
    APP_TEST_FAULT(net_err, NET_SOCK_ERR_NONE);

    server_ip_addr = NetASCII_Str_to_IP( SERVER_IP_ADDR,
                                        &net_err);
    APP_TEST_FAULT(net_err, NET_ASCII_ERR_NONE);

    server_sock_addr_ip.AddrFamily = NET_SOCK_ADDR_FAMILY_IP_V4;
    server_sock_addr_ip.Addr       = NET_UTIL_HOST_TO_NET_32(server_ip_addr);
    server_sock_addr_ip.Port       = NET_UTIL_HOST_TO_NET_16(SERVER_PORT);

    conn_rtn_code = NetSock_Conn((NET_SOCK_ID)      sock_id,
                                 (NET_SOCK_ADDR *) &server_sock_addr_ip,
                                 (NET_SOCK_ADDR_LEN)sizeof(server_sock_addr_ip),
                                 (NET_ERR *)       &net_err);
    APP_TEST_FAULT(net_err, NET_SOCK_ERR_NONE);

#if (PROXY_SERVER == DEF_ENABLED)
    NetSock_TxData(        sock_id,
                  (void *)g_pcServerConnectReq,
                          sizeof(g_pcServerConnectReq) - 1,
                          NET_SOCK_FLAG_NONE,
                         &net_err);
    APP_TEST_FAULT(net_err, NET_SOCK_ERR_NONE);
#endif
```

```
    NetSock_TxData(        sock_id,                              (21)
                    (void *)g_pcSOAPReqWeather,
                        sizeof(g_pcSOAPReqWeather) - 1,
                        NET_SOCK_FLAG_NONE,
                        &net_err);
    APP_TEST_FAULT(net_err, NET_SOCK_ERR_NONE);


    g_cState = 0;                                               (22)


    do {
        sIRxSize = NetSock_RxData( sock_id,
                                   pcRxBuf,
                                   RX_BUF_SIZE,
                                   NET_SOCK_FLAG_NONE,
                                   &net_err);
        if((net_err) != (NET_SOCK_ERR_RX_Q_CLOSED)) {
            APP_TEST_FAULT(net_err, NET_SOCK_ERR_NONE);
        }

        OSTimeDly( DELAY_RX,
                   OS_OPT_TIME_DLY,
                   &err_os);

        ParseRxDataWeather(pcRxBuf, sIRxSize);                  (23)
    } while (sIRxSize != 0);


    conn_rtn_code = NetSock_Close( sock_id,
                                   &net_err);
    APP_TEST_FAULT(net_err, NET_SOCK_ERR_NONE);


    OSFlagPost(&AppClientNetworkFlagGroup,                      (24)
               FLAG_SOAP_UPDATE,
               OS_OPT_POST_FLAG_SET,
               &err_os);


        BSP_LED_Off(1u);                                        (25)
    OSTimeDlyHMSM((CPU_INT16U) 0u,
                  (CPU_INT16U) 0u,
                  (CPU_INT16U) 0u,
                  (CPU_INT16U) 100u,
                  (OS_OPT    ) OS_OPT_TIME_HMSM_STRICT,
                  (OS_ERR   *)&err_os);
    }
}
```

Listing 8-3 **App_NetworkTask()**

8

L8-3(1) Calls the **App_TCPIP_Init()** function to set up the µC/TCP-IP stack. The **App_TCPIP_Init()** function is described in Listing 6-3 on page 1088. The difference when it is called in this task is that the code to display the IP address on the EVALBOT's OLED display has been moved into the Display Task. If the **APP_DHCPc_EN** function is set to **DEF_ENABLED,** this function also calls the **App_TCPIP_Init_DHCPc()** function which is described in detail in Listing 6-4 on page 1090. The **App_TCPIP_Init_DHCPc()** task starts DHCP and obtains a dynamic IP address, otherwise, the stack is assigned a default IP address and gateway.

L8-3(2) Calls the **NetSock_Open()** function to create a stream (TCP) socket using IPv4.

L8-3(3) Sets up the server (or proxy) address in the correct format for the µC/TCP-IP stack.

L8-3(4) Sets up the server IP socket structure in the correct format.

L8-3(5) Calls the **NetSock_Conn()** function to connect the local socket to the server (or proxy) address.

L8-3(6) When there is a proxy present, then the PROXY_SERVER macro must be set to **DEF_ENABLED** at compile time. This configuration sends a HTTP CONNECT request which instructs the proxy to establish a connection with NOAA's National Weather Service. When there is no proxy present, the code in (5) establishes the connection to NOAA's National Weather Service.

L8-3(7) Posts a flag in the **AppClientNetworkFlagGroup** indicating that a connect to the NOAA National Weather Service server is in place.

L8-3(8) Uses the **NetSock_TxData()** function to send a Simple Object Access Protocol (SOAP) request to the NOAA's National Weather Service server. This request asks the server for the list of predefined primary cities and their corresponding latitude and longitude values. The latitude and longitude values are used later when requesting the weather for a city.

L8-3(9) Posts a flag in the **AppClientNetworkFlagGroup** indicating that the SOAP request has been sent successfully.

L8-3(10)   Calls the **NetSock_RxData()** function to receive the data, in blocks of 100 bytes, from the server. This call is a blocking function that returns when there is data available or if an error occurs.

L8-3(11)   Checks for errors. The only acceptable error is **NET_SOCK_ERR_RX_Q_CLOSED**, which means that NOAA's National Weather Service has closed the connection (received FIN from peer). This error occurs once NOAA's National Weather Service has fulfilled the request and all the data has been sent.

L8-3(12)   Delays 1 ms to allow for the data to process.

L8-3(13)   Sends the received data to the **ParseRxDataLatLong()** parsing function to look for the primary city names and latitude and longitude values. This function also puts the information into predefined SRAM arrays.

L8-3(14)   Continues to receive data until there is no data left to process.

L8-3(15)   Posts a flag in the **AppClientNetworkFlagGroup** indicating that the data has been successfully received from NOAA's National Weather Service.

L8-3(16)   Calls the **NetSock_Close()** to terminate the communication and free up the TCP socket.

L8-3(17)   Posts a flag in the **AppClientNetworkFlagGroup** indicating that the SOAP communication with the server is complete.

L8-3(18)   Pends a flag in the **AppClientNetworkFlagGroup** waiting for the user to request the weather and indicating that the application is ready to receive the request.

L8-3(19)   Turns on LED1 to indicate the TCP communication process has started.

L8-3(20)   Calls the **BuildWeatherSOAPReq()** to modify the weather SOAP request with the latitude and longitude values associated with the selected city.

L8-3(21)   Uses the **NetSock_TxData()** function to send a SOAP request to NOAA's National Weather Service server. This request asks the server for the daily weather of an area specified by the latitude and longitude.

L8-3(22)   Restarts the state machine. This state machine is used to parse the SOAP response from NOAA's National Weather Service server.

L8-3(23)   Sends the received data to the **ParseRxDataLatLong()** parsing function to search for daily low and daily high weather values. This function also puts the information into an array which is used to display the values on the EVALBOT's OLED display.

L8-3(24)   Posts a flag in the **AppClientNetworkFlagGroup** indicating that the weather data is received and ready to be displayed.

L8-3(25)   Turns off LED1 to indicate the TCP communication process has completed.

The code for the **App_DisplayTask()** is shown in Listing 8-4.

```c
static void App_DisplayTask (void *p_arg)
{
    OS_ERR      err_os;
    NET_ERR     net_err;
    CPU_CHAR    addr_ip_ascii[NET_ASCII_LEN_MAX_ADDR_IP];
    CPU_TS      ts;
    OS_FLAGS    flags;
    CPU_INT32U  ulIndex;

    (void)&p_arg;

    BSP_DisplayStringDraw("  SOAP Client  ", 0, LCD_TOP_ROW);        (1)
    BSP_DisplayStringDraw("    Example    ", 0, LCD_BOT_ROW);

    OSTimeDly( 2000u,                                                (2)
               OS_OPT_TIME_DLY,
               &err_os);

    OSFlagPend(&AppClientNetworkFlagGroup,                          (3)
               FLAG_TCPIP_INIT,
               0u,
               OS_OPT_PEND_FLAG_SET_ANY | OS_OPT_PEND_FLAG_CONSUME,
               &ts,
               &err_os);

    #if (APP_DHCPc_EN == DEF_ENABLED)
    BSP_DisplayStringDraw("DHCP Started.  ", 0, LCD_TOP_ROW);
    #else
    BSP_DisplayStringDraw("TCPIP Init.    ", 0, LCD_TOP_ROW);
```

```
#endif //DEF_ENABLED
    BSP_DisplayStringDraw("Waiting for IP.", 0, LCD_BOT_ROW);
    OSFlagPend(&AppClientNetworkFlagGroup,                              (4)
            FLAG_IP_ASSIGNED,
            0u,
            OS_OPT_PEND_FLAG_SET_ANY | OS_OPT_PEND_FLAG_CONSUME,
            &ts,
            &err_os);


    BSP_DisplayClear();                                                 (5)


    NetASCII_IP_to_Str( App_IP_Addrs[if_nbr][0],                        (6)
                    addr_ip_ascii,
                    0,
                    &net_err);


    if (net_err != NET_ASCII_ERR_NONE) {                                (7)
        BSP_DisplayStringDraw("Error:", 0, LCD_TOP_ROW);
        BSP_DisplayStringDraw("  INVALID IP", 0, LCD_BOT_ROW);
    } else {
        BSP_DisplayStringDraw("IP Address:", 0, LCD_TOP_ROW);
        BSP_DisplayStringDraw((CPU_INT08S const*) addr_ip_ascii, 0,
                    LCD_BOT_ROW);
    }
    OSTimeDly( 2000u,                                                   (8)
            OS_OPT_TIME_DLY,
            &err_os);


    BSP_DisplayStringDraw("Connecting. . .", 0, LCD_TOP_ROW);


    OSFlagPend(&AppClientNetworkFlagGroup,                              (9)
            FLAG_SOAP_SERVER_CON,
            0u,
            OS_OPT_PEND_FLAG_SET_ANY | OS_OPT_PEND_FLAG_CONSUME,
            &ts,
            &err_os);


    BSP_DisplayStringDraw("Connected.     ", 0, LCD_TOP_ROW);


    OSFlagPend(&AppClientNetworkFlagGroup,                              (10)
            FLAG_SOAP_REQUEST_SENT,
            0u,
            OS_OPT_PEND_FLAG_SET_ANY | OS_OPT_PEND_FLAG_CONSUME,
            &ts,
            &err_os);


    BSP_DisplayStringDraw("Sent SOAP Req. ", 0, LCD_TOP_ROW);
```

```
OSFlagPend(&AppClientNetworkFlagGroup,                              (11)
        FLAG_SOAP_RECEIVED,
        0u,
        OS_OPT_PEND_FLAG_SET_ANY | OS_OPT_PEND_FLAG_CONSUME,
        &ts,
        &err_os);

BSP_DisplayStringDraw("Data received. ", 0, LCD_TOP_ROW);

OSFlagPend(&AppClientNetworkFlagGroup,                              (12)
        FLAG_SOAP_COMPLETE,
        0u,
        OS_OPT_PEND_FLAG_SET_ANY | OS_OPT_PEND_FLAG_CONSUME,
        &ts,
        &err_os);

OSTimeDly( 1000u,
        OS_OPT_TIME_DLY,
        &err_os);

BSP_DisplayStringDraw("Press Bumpers  ", 0, LCD_TOP_ROW);           (13)
BSP_DisplayStringDraw("to scroll.     ", 0, LCD_BOT_ROW);

OSFlagPend(&AppClientControlFlagGroup,                             (14)
        FLAG_RIGHT_BUMP_SENSOR | FLAG_LEFT_BUMP_SENSOR,
        0u,
        OS_OPT_PEND_FLAG_SET_ANY,
        &ts,
        &err_os);

while (DEF_ON) {

    OSFlagPend(&AppClientControlFlagGroup,                         (15)
            FLAG_RIGHT_BUMP_SENSOR | FLAG_LEFT_BUMP_SENSOR |
            FLAG_PUSH_BUTTON,
            0u,
            OS_OPT_PEND_FLAG_SET_ANY | OS_OPT_PEND_FLAG_CONSUME,
            &ts,
            &err_os);

    flags = OSFlagPendGetFlagsRdy(&err_os);                       (16)

    if ((flags & FLAG_RIGHT_BUMP_SENSOR) == FLAG_RIGHT_BUMP_SENSOR) {  (17)
        g_ulCitySelectionIndex++;
        if (g_ulCitySelectionIndex > PRIMARY_CITIES_BOUNDRY_TOP) {
            g_ulCitySelectionIndex = PRIMARY_CITIES_BOUNDRY_BOT;
        }
```

```
      BSP_DisplayStringDraw("                ", 0, LCD_TOP_ROW);
      BSP_DisplayStringDraw("                ", 0, LCD_BOT_ROW);
      BSP_DisplayStringDraw((CPU_INT08S const *)
                            g_pcCityNames[g_ulCitySelectionIndex],
                            0, LCD_TOP_ROW);
      BSP_DisplayStringDraw("Push SW for temp", 0, LCD_BOT_ROW);
  } else if ((flags & FLAG_LEFT_BUMP_SENSOR) == FLAG_LEFT_BUMP_SENSOR) {      (18)
      g_ulCitySelectionIndex--;
      if (g_ulCitySelectionIndex > PRIMARY_CITIES_BOUNDRY_TOP) {
          g_ulCitySelectionIndex = PRIMARY_CITIES_BOUNDRY_TOP;
      }

      BSP_DisplayStringDraw("                ", 0, LCD_TOP_ROW);
      BSP_DisplayStringDraw("                ", 0, LCD_BOT_ROW);
      BSP_DisplayStringDraw((CPU_INT08S const *)
                            g_pcCityNames[g_ulCitySelectionIndex],
                            0, LCD_TOP_ROW);
      BSP_DisplayStringDraw("Push SW for temp", 0, LCD_BOT_ROW);
  } else if ((flags & FLAG_PUSH_BUTTON) == FLAG_PUSH_BUTTON) {                (19)
      OSFlagPost(&AppClientControlFlagGroup,
                 FLAG_READY_FOR_UPDATE,
                 OS_OPT_POST_FLAG_SET,
                 &err_os);

      BSP_DisplayStringDraw("Working. . .    ", 0, LCD_BOT_ROW);

      OSFlagPend(&AppClientNetworkFlagGroup,                                 (20)
                 FLAG_SOAP_UPDATE,
                 0u,
                 OS_OPT_PEND_FLAG_SET_ANY | OS_OPT_PEND_FLAG_CONSUME,
                 &ts,
                 &err_os);

      BSP_DisplayStringDraw((CPU_INT08S const *)g_pcWeatherData, 0,          (21)
                            LCD_BOT_ROW);
      for (ulIndex = 0; ulIndex < (sizeof(g_pcWeatherData) - 1); ulIndex++) { (22)
          g_pcWeatherData[ulIndex] = ' ';
      }
      g_pcWeatherData[0] = 'L';
      g_pcWeatherData[1] = ':';
      g_pcWeatherData[8] = 'H';
      g_pcWeatherData[9] = ':';
      OS_FlagClr(&AppClientControlFlagGroup);                               (23)
  }
```

```
        OSTimeDlyHMSM((CPU_INT16U) 0u,
                      (CPU_INT16U) 0u,
                      (CPU_INT16U) 0u,
                      (CPU_INT16U) 100u,
                      (OS_OPT     ) OS_OPT_TIME_HMSM_STRICT,
                      (OS_ERR   *)&err_os);
    }
}
```

Listing 8-4 **App_DisplayTask()**

L8-4(1)   Displays the example name on EVALBOT's OLED display.

L8-4(2)   Adds a two-second delay to allow enough time for the user to read the
             message.

L8-4(3)   Pends a flag in the **AppClientNetworkFlagGroup** waiting for the TCP/IP to
             initialize.

L8-4(4)   Pends a flag in the **AppClientNetworkFlagGroup** waiting for an IP to be
             assigned via DHCP or statically.

L8-4(5)   Calls the **BSP_DisplayClear()** function to clear EVALBOT's OLED display.

L8-4(6)   Converts the IP address to a string format so it can be displayed on EVALBOT's
             OLED display.

L8-4(7)   Confirms there was no error with the conversion of the IP address and then
             displays the address on EVALBOT's OLED display.

L8-4(8)   Adds a two-second delay to allow enough time for the user to read the IP
             address.

L8-4(9)   Pends a flag in **AppClientNetworkFlagGroup** to wait for the connection to
             NOAA's National Weather Service server.

L8-4(10)   Pends a flag in **AppClientNetworkFlagGroup** to wait for the SOAP request to
             be successfully sent.

L8-4(11)   Pends a flag in **AppClientNetworkFlagGroup** to wait for the data to be successfully received data from the NOAA's National Weather Service.

L8-4(12)   Pends a flag in **AppClientNetworkFlagGroup** to wait for the SOAP communication with the server to complete.

L8-4(13)   Displays a message on the EVALBOT's OLED display indicating to use the bumpers to scroll through the primary cities from NOAA's National Weather Service.

L8-4(14)   Pends a flag in **AppClientControlFlagGroup** indicating that the bumpers have been pressed at least once which prevents a weather request being made with Switch 1 or Switch 2 before the user has selected a city.

L8-4(15)   Pends a flag in **AppClientControlFlagGroup** to wait for any user input.

L8-4(16)   Calls the **OSFlagPendGetFlagsRdy()** function to get the set flag(s).

L8-4(17)   Scrolls up through the list of cities if the right bump sensor is pressed. Displays the newly selected city name on EVALBOT's OLED display.

L8-4(18)   Scrolls down through the list of cities if the left bump sensor is pressed. Displays the newly selected city name on EVALBOT's OLED display.

L8-4(19)   Posts a flag in **AppClientControlFlagGroup** if Switch 1 or Switch 2 is pressed that indicates that the user requested the weather and the Display Task is ready to receive the request.

L8-4(20)   Pends a flag in **AppClientNetworkFlagGroup** to wait for the weather data to be received and is ready to be displayed.

L8-4(21)   Displays the weather data on the bottom row of the EVALBOT's OLED display.

L8-4(22)   Resets and formats the array used to store the weather data for the next request.

L8-4(23)   Clears any input that was received during the weather update.

The code for the **AppTaskRobotInputMonitor()** is shown below in Listing 8-5.

```
static void AppTaskRobotInputMonitor(void *p_arg)
{
    CPU_INT08U  ucData;
    CPU_INT08U  ucSwitches;
    CPU_INT08U  ucDelta;
    CPU_INT08U  ucSwitchesClockA;
    CPU_INT08U  ucSwitchesClockB;
    OS_ERR      err;


    ucSwitches      = 0x0F;                                          (1)
    ucSwitchesClockA = 0;
    ucSwitchesClockB = 0;

    while (DEF_TRUE) {                                               (2)
        OSTimeDlyHMSM( 0, 0, 0, 5,                                   (3)
                       OS_OPT_TIME_HMSM_STRICT,
                       &err);

        ucData =  BSP_PushButtonGetStatus(1) |                      (4)
                 (BSP_PushButtonGetStatus(2) << 1) |
                 (BSP_BumpSensorGetStatus(1) << 2) |
                 (BSP_BumpSensorGetStatus(2) << 3);

        ucDelta = ucData ^   ucSwitches;                            (5)
        ucSwitchesClockA ^= ucSwitchesClockB;
        ucSwitchesClockB  = ~ucSwitchesClockB;
        ucSwitchesClockA &= ucDelta;
        ucSwitchesClockB &= ucDelta;
        ucSwitches &= ucSwitchesClockA | ucSwitchesClockB;
        ucSwitches |= (~(ucSwitchesClockA | ucSwitchesClockB)) & ucData;
        ucDelta ^= (ucSwitchesClockA | ucSwitchesClockB);

        if ((ucDelta & 0x0F) && (~ucSwitches & 0x0F)) {            (6)
            RandomAddEntropy(OSTimeGet(&err));                     (7)
            RandomSeed();                                          (8)
        }
```

```
        if ((ucDelta & 0x03) && (~ucSwitches & 0x03)) {
            OSFlagPost(&AppClientControlFlagGroup,                    (9)
                    FLAG_PUSH_BUTTON,
                    OS_OPT_POST_FLAG_SET,
                    &err);
        }

        if ((ucDelta & 0x04) && (~ucSwitches & 0x04)) {
            OSFlagPost(&AppClientControlFlagGroup,                    (10)
                    FLAG_RIGHT_BUMP_SENSOR,
                    OS_OPT_POST_FLAG_SET,
                    &err);
        }

        if ((ucDelta & 0x08) && (~ucSwitches & 0x08)) {
            OSFlagPost(&AppClientControlFlagGroup,                    (11)
                    FLAG_LEFT_BUMP_SENSOR,
                    OS_OPT_POST_FLAG_SET,
                    &err);
        }
    }
}
```

Listing 8-5 **AppTaskRobotInputMonitor()**

L8-5(1)   Starts the initialization variables.

L8-5(2)   Identifies the infinite loop for this task.

L8-5(3)   Delays the task from being ready run for 5 milliseconds by using the **OSTimeDlyHMSM()** function. This delay causes the code within the main task loop to execute approximately every 5 milliseconds.

L8-5(4)   Reads and stores the current state of the push buttons and the bump sensors to a bit-mapped variable where each bit indicates the state of a single push button or bump sensor.

L8-5(5)   Handles the push buttons and bump sensors debouncing.

L8-5(6)   Checks to see if any of the push buttons or bump sensors were just pressed.

L8-5(7)   Adds the current time to the random number generator's entropy pool.

L8-5(8)   Seeds the random number generator using the updated entropy pool.

L8-5(9)   Posts the push button flag to the `AppClientControlFlagGroup` if either push button was just pressed.

L8-5(10)   Posts the right bump sensor flag to the `AppClientControlFlagGroup` if the right bump sensor was just pressed.

L8-5(11)   Posts the left bump sensor flag to the `AppClientControlFlagGroup` if the left bump sensor was just pressed.

8-2 SUMMARY

This example demonstrates the client capabilities of the µC/TCP-IP stack. Using the EVALBOT evaluation board, we were able to create a TCP socket application that requested data from NOAA's National Weather Service (http://www.weather.gov) using Simple Object Access Protocol (SOAP) requests. This example also demonstrates how to use tasks to control different aspects of the software flow including monitoring the input, displaying data on the OLED display, and managing the TCP data. The µC/OS-III RTOS built-in flag mechanism passes information among the tasks.

Appendix

A

Ethernet Driver

Chapter 2, "Introduction to Networking" on page 45 of Part I of this book showed that the internet protocol suite can be described as a set of layers. Each layer solves a set of requirements involving the transmission of data and provides a well defined service to upper layer protocols. The table below shows how the combination of Texas Instruments hardware and Micrium software delivers the full implementation of each layer in Part II of this book.

Layer	Function	Implemented by
Layer 7, 6 and 5 Application	Interfaces with the API of Micrium's µC/TCP-IP stack.	Micrium's Examples with IP connectivity.
Layer 4 Transport	Isolates the three upper application layers from the complexities of layers 1 through 3 by providing the functions necessary to ensure the reliability of point-to-point data communications.	Micrium's µC/TCP-IP code at $\Micrium\Software\uC-TCP-IP-V2\Source\net_*.*
Layer 3 Network	Establishes, maintains and terminates network connections by handling the routing of packets from one piece of equipment to another.	Micrium's µC/TCP-IP code at $\Micrium\Software\uC-TCP-IP-V2\Source\net_*.*
Layer 2 Data Link	Handles the packaging of bits into frames and their transmission or reception over physical circuits. It is at this layer that most error detection and correction is performed.	Texas Instruments' LM3S9B92 MCU integrated ethernet controller and Micrium's device driver code at $\Micrium\Software\uC-TCPIP-V2\Dev\Ether\LM3S9Bxx\net_dev_lm3s9bxx.*
Layer 1 Physical	Handles the transmission of bits over physical circuits. It is best described by its physical parameters such as the amount of signal voltage swing and the duration of voltages among others.	Generic PHY built on chip and Micrium's driver code at $\Micrium\Software\uC-TCPIP-V2\Dev\Ether\PHY\Generic\net_phy.*

Table A-1 **TCP/IP model layers**

Layers 3 and 4 are implemented by Micrium's µC/TCP-IP stack, which is discussed in great detail in Part I of this book.

Layer 2 is implemented by the Ethernet controller built-in the Texas Instruments LM3S9B92 MCU.

Layer 1 is implemented by the generic PHY built on the LM3S9B92 chip.

This appendix will cover the details behind the DMA-based µC/TCP-IP driver for the Texas Instruments LM3S9B92. It starts by describing some of the main features of the Ethernet Controller. The appendix proceeds at explaining a few details about the Stellaris® EVALBOT before describing the driver code.

For the examples provided with this book, the LM3S9B92 Ethernet driver is delivered in object code only. To access source code, a license must be obtained from Micrium (see Appendix H, "µC/TCP-IP Licensing Policy" on page 1031).

Micrium provides a Network Device Driver API and data type naming conventions. By following these naming conventions, as well as standard Micrium conventions and software development patterns, the process of device driver debugging and testing is simplified, allowing developers to become familiar with device drivers authored by others.

It is important to develop a driver to be re-entrant, as µC/TCP-IP supports multiple interfaces of the same type. By avoiding global macros and variables (e.g., using the device data area, and defining macros within the driver **.c** file), driver developers ensure that projects containing multiple device driver files are able to compile.

Chapter 16, "Device Driver Implementation" on page 365 provides the guidelines for the architecture of a Network Device Driver. Micrium also provides Network Driver templates that are located in the following directory:

```
$\Micrium\Software\uC-TCPIP-V2\Dev\Ether\Template
```

A-1 LM3S9B92 ON-CHIP ETHERNET CONTROLLER

The Stellaris® Ethernet Controller consists of a fully integrated media access controller (MAC) and network physical (PHY) interface. The Ethernet Controller conforms to IEEE 802.3 specifications and fully supports 10BASE-T and 100BASE-TX standards.

As shown in Figure A-1, the Ethernet Controller is functionally divided into two layers: the Media Access Controller (MAC) layer and the Network Physical (PHY) layer. These layers correspond to the OSI model layers 2 and 1, respectively. The CPU accesses the Ethernet Controller via the MAC layer. The MAC layer provides transmit and receive processing for Ethernet frames. The MAC layer also provides the interface to the PHY layer via an internal Media Independent Interface (MII). The PHY layer communicates with the Ethernet bus.

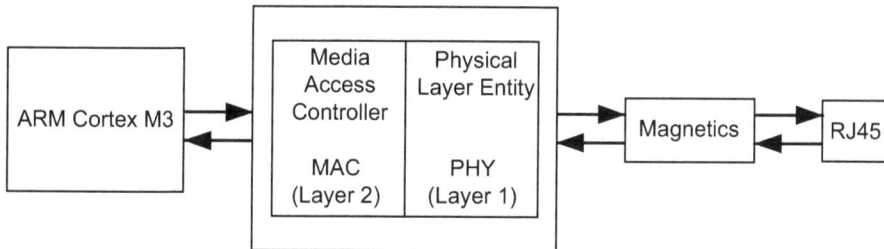

Figure A-1 **Ethernet Controller**

A-1-1 ETHERNET CONTROLLER SPECIFICATIONS

- Conforms to the IEEE 802.3-2002 specification:

  - 10BASE-T/100BASE-TX IEEE-802.3 compliant. Requires only a dual 1:1 isolation transformer interface to the line.

  - 10BASE-T/100BASE-TX ENDEC, 100BASE-TX scrambler/descrambler

  - Full-featured auto-negotiation

- Multiple operational modes:

  - Full- and half-duplex 100 Mbps

  - Full- and half-duplex 10 Mbps

  - Power-saving and power-down modes

- Highly configurable:

  - Programmable MAC address

  - LED activity selection

  - Promiscuous mode support

  - CRC error-rejection control

  - User-configurable interrupts

- Physical media manipulation:

  - MDI/MDI-X cross-over support through software assist

  - Register-programmable transmit amplitude

  - Automatic polarity correction and 10BASE-T signal reception

- Efficient transfers using Micro Direct Memory Access Controller (µDMA):

  - Separate channels for transmit and receive

  - Receive channel request asserted on packet receipt

  - Transmit channel request asserted on empty transmit FIFO

The following sections provide the implementation of a driver for the LM3S9B92 integrated Ethernet controller based on the driver template in:

`$\Micrium\Software\uC-TCPIP-V2\Dev\Ether\Template`

Any changes from the template are identified.

A-2 DEVICE DRIVER CONVENTIONS

All Ethernet device drivers are named **net_dev_<controller>.c** and **.h**, where **<controller>** represents the name of the device. The names for the purposes of this book are **net_dev_lm3s9bxx.c** and **net_dev_lm3s9bxx.h** and are located in the following directory:

$\Micrium\Software\uC-TCP-IP-V2\Dev\Ether\LM3S9Bxx\

A-3 DMA-BASED DEVICE DRIVER FOR THE LM3S9B92

The µC/TCP-IP device driver memory map comprises the LM3S9B92 Ethernet MAC module memory map (device registers), the LM3S9B92 MII Management module (MACMCTL) memory map, the LM3S9B92 µDMA register map, and the different data structures allocated by the driver developer.

DMA-based device drivers such as the one presented in this book allocate memory from the µC/LIB memory module for descriptors, data buffers, pointers and other variables. By using the µC/LIB memory module instead of declaring arrays, the driver developer can easily align descriptors to any required boundary and benefit from the run-time flexibility of the device configuration structure.

A-3-1 DEVICE REGISTER STRUCTURE NAME

Each device driver contains a structure **NET_DEV** with typically one or more **CPU_REG32** data types, which represent each device register present in the device address space.

Some of the most important device registers are illustrated in Figure A-2, which shows the internal structure of the Ethernet Controller and how the register set relates to various functions.

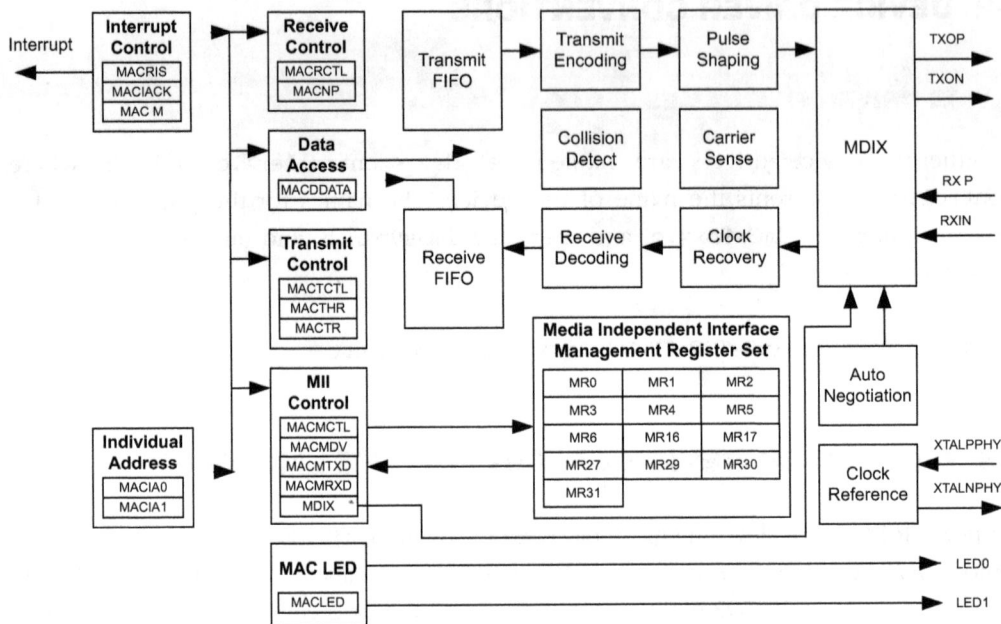

Figure A-2 **Ethernet Controller Block Diagram**

Each structure member must be named in accordance with the documented register name provided within the device documentation. All register names within the **NET_DEV** structure are capitalized.

The device register definition structure must take into account appropriate register offsets and apply reserved space as required. The registers listed within the register definition structure must reflect the exact ordering and data sizes illustrated in the LM3S9B92 data sheet.

The device register definition structure is mapped over the register memory map which is composed of the Ethernet MAC and MII Management registers. The MAC register addresses given are relative to the Ethernet base address of 0x40048000. The MII Management registers are accessed using the MACMCTL register.

Reserved bits should be written with 0 and ignored on read to allow future extension. Unused registers read zero and a write has no effect.

An example of the device registers defined in **net_dev_lm3s9bxx.c** is provided in Listing A-1.

```
typedef struct net_dev {
    CPU_REG32 MACIS;        /* Ethernet MAC Raw Interrupt Status/Acknowledge.  */
    CPU_REG32 MACIM;        /* Ethernet MAC Interrupt Mask.                    */
    CPU_REG32 MACRCTL;      /* Ethernet MAC Receive Control.                   */
    CPU_REG32 MACTCTL;      /* Ethernet MAC Transmit Control.                  */
    CPU_REG32 MACDATA;      /* Ethernet MAC Data.                              */
    CPU_REG32 MACIA0;       /* Ethernet MAC Individual Address 0.              */
    CPU_REG32 MACIA1;       /* Ethernet MAC Individual Address 1.              */
    CPU_REG32 MACTHR;       /* Ethernet MAC Threshold.                         */
    CPU_REG32 MACMCTL;      /* Ethernet MAC Management Control.                */
    CPU_REG32 MACMDV;       /* Ethernet MAC Management Divider.                */
    CPU_REG32 Reserved0;    /* [Reserved].                                     */
    CPU_REG32 MACMTXD;      /* Ethernet MAC Management Transmit Data.          */
    CPU_REG32 MACMRXD;      /* Ethernet MAC Management Receive Data.           */
    CPU_REG32 MACNP;        /* Ethernet MAC Number of Packets.                 */
    CPU_REG32 MACTR;        /* Ethernet MAC Transmission Request.              */
    CPU_REG32 Reserved1;    /* [Reserved].                                     */
    CPU_REG32 MACLED;       /* Ethernet MAC LED Encoding.                      */
    CPU_REG32 MACIX;        /* Ethernet PHY MDIX.                              */
} NET_DEV;
```

Listing A-1 **Register Definitions in net_dev_lm3s9bxx.c**

A-3-2 DMA

The 10/100-Mbps Ethernet MAC on the LM3S9B92 features a dedicated DMA controller known as µDMA, responsible for updating the Transmit and Receive Buffer Descriptors every time a frame has been transmitted or received.

The Ethernet peripheral provides request signals to the µDMA controller and has a dedicated channel for transmit and one for receive. The request is a single type for both channels. Burst requests are not supported. The Rx channel request is asserted when a packet is received while the Tx channel request is asserted when the transmit FIFO becomes empty.

No special configuration is needed to enable the Ethernet peripheral for use with the µDMA controller.

Because the size of a received packet is not known until the header is examined, it is best to set up the initial µDMA transfer to copy the first 4 words including the packet length plus the Ethernet header from the Rx FIFO when the Rx request occurs. The µDMA causes an interrupt when this transfer is complete. Upon entering the interrupt handler, the packet length in the FIFO and the Ethernet header are in a buffer and can be examined. Once the packet length is known, then another µDMA transfer can be set up to transfer the remaining received packet payload from the FIFO into a buffer. This transfer should be initiated by software. Another interrupt occurs when this transfer is done.

Even though the Tx channel generates a Tx empty request, the recommended way to handle µDMA transfers for transmitting packets is to set up the transfer from the buffer containing the packet to the transmit FIFO, and then to initiate the transfer with a software request. An interrupt occurs when this transfer is complete. For both channels, the "auto-request" transfer mode should be used. See the LM3S9B92 data sheet section "Micro Direct Memory Access (µDMA)" on page 344 for more details about programming the µDMA controller.

DMA-based device drivers like the one described in this book contain one or more data types for the device descriptors. When possible, for devices with one descriptor format, the name of the descriptor data type should be **DEV_DESC**. Variations of this name may exist for devices with more than one type of descriptor. Listing A-2 shows an example of the Rx and Tx descriptors for the LM3S9B92:

```
typedef struct dev_desc {
    CPU_REG32   Status;      /* DMA status register.            */
    CPU_REG32   Len;         /* DMA buffer size.                */
    CPU_INT08U  *Addr;       /* DMA buffer pointer              */
    DEV_DESC    *Next;       /* DMA next descriptor pointer.    */
} DEV_DESC;
```

Listing A-2 **Descriptor Data Type Structure DEV_DESC defined in net_dev_lm3s9bxx.c**

DMA device drivers will allocate memory for descriptors (when applicable) and a device data area. The data area structure typically includes error counters and variables used to track the state of the device as shown in Code Listing A-3:

```
                                    /* -------------- DEVICE INSTANCE DATA -------------- */
typedef struct net_dev_data {
    CPU_INT08U  *TxBufCompPtr;      /* Tx buffer pointer.                                 */
    CPU_BOOLEAN TxDMA_En;           /* Tx DMA enable flag.                                */
    CPU_INT32U  *RxBufCompPtr;      /* Rx buffer pointer.                                 */
    CPU_INT32U  RxPktLen;           /* Rx Packet Length.                                  */
    CPU_BOOLEAN RxDMA_En;           /* Rx DMA enable flag.                                */
#ifdef NET_MULTICAST_PRESENT
    CPU_INT32U  RxMulticastCtr;     /* Rx Multicast enable counter.                       */
#endif
} NET_DEV_DATA;
```

Listing A-3 **Device Data Area Data Type Structure NET_DEV_DATA defined in net_dev_lm3s9bxx.c**

The driver developer basically starts by allocating two memory pools large enough to store the receive and transmit descriptors and the receive and transmit data buffers; this is performed via calls to the µC/LIB memory module.

The number of descriptors and the size and number of data buffers become an optimization problem where you want to maximize performance by increasing the number of descriptors and the size and number of data buffers, but at the same time you want to keep your data footprint to the minimum. A minimum of two descriptors for the reception of Ethernet frames should be configured, because while the controller is transferring a recently received Ethernet frame, it must have an available descriptor in order to receive the next incoming Ethernet frame.

The following section describes in detail all the API functions that support the initialization of the DMA engine, allocation and initialization of the Device Data Area and Descriptors, ISRs and functions to interface with the PHY.

A-4 API

All device drivers contain an API structure named in accordance to the following rule: **NetDev_API_<controller>**, where controller represents the name of the device being abstracted by the driver, for example **NetDev_API_LM3Sxxxx**.

Device driver API structures are used by the application during the call to **NetIF_Add( )**. This API structure allows higher layers to call specific device driver functions via function pointer instead of by name. This enables the network protocol suite to compile and operate with multiple device drivers.

Device driver function names may be arbitrarily chosen. However, it is recommended that device functions be named using the names provided below. All driver function prototypes should be located within the driver C source file (**net_dev_lm3s9bxx.c**) and be declared as static functions to prevent name clashes with other network protocol suite device drivers.

In most cases, the API structure provided below should suffice for most device drivers exactly as is, with the exception that the API structure's name *must* be unique and clearly identify the device being implemented. The API structure is also externally declared in the device driver header file (**net_dev_lm3s9bxx.h**) with the exact same name and type.

```c
const  NET_DEV_API_ETHER  NetDev_API_RX_EtherC = { NetDev_Init,
                                                   NetDev_Start,
                                                   NetDev_Stop,
                                                   NetDev_Rx,
                                                   NetDev_Tx,
#if  (NET_VERSION >= 20600u)
                                                   NetDev_AddrMulticastAdd,
                                                   NetDev_AddrMulticastRemove,
#endif
                                                   NetDev_ISR_Handler,
                                                   NetDev_IO_Ctrl,
#if ((NET_VERSION <  20600u) && \
     (NET_VERSION >= 205u))
                                                   NetDev_AddrMulticastAdd,
                                                   NetDev_AddrMulticastRemove,
#endif
                                                   NetDev_MII_Rd,
                                                   NetDev_MII_Wr
                                                 };
```

Listing A-4 **LM3S9B92 Ethernet interface API**

It is the device driver developer's responsibility to ensure that all of the functions listed within the API are properly implemented, and that the order of the functions within the API structure is correct.

Device driver API function names are not unique amongst Micriµm drivers. Name clashes between device drivers are avoided by never globally prototyping device driver functions and ensuring that all references to functions within the driver are obtained by pointers within the API structure. The developer may arbitrarily name the functions within the source file so long as the API structure is properly declared. The user application should never need to call API functions by name. Unless special care is taken, calling device driver functions by name may lead to unpredictable results due to reentrancy.

All functions that require device register access must obtain reference to the device hardware register space *prior* to attempting to access any registers. Register definitions should not be absolute and should use the provided base address within the device configuration structure, and the device register definition structure, to properly resolve register addresses during run-time.

DMA-based ethernet drivers such as the driver for the LM3S9B92 require three additional functions for initializing Rx and Tx descriptors, and for incrementing a pointer to the current Rx descriptor.

The functions common to DMA-based drivers are:

- `NetDev_RxDescInit()`

- `NetDev_RxDescPtrCurInc()`

- `NetDev_TxDescInit()`

- `NetDev_RxDescFreeAll()`

The API structure shown in Listing A-4 is defined in **net_dev_lm3s9bxx.c** and the following sections describe the API functions.

A-5 NetDev_Init()

The function **NetDev_Init()** is defined in **net_dev_lm3s9bxx.c**. The function initializes the Network Driver Layer and its prototype is shown below:

```
static  void  NetDev_Init (NET_IF   *pif,
                           NET_ERR  *perr)
{
                    /* Initializes the required clock sources.               */
                    /* Initializes the external interrupt controller.        */
                    /* Initializes the external GPIO controller.             */
                    /* Initializes the driver state variables.               */
                    /* Allocates memory for device DMA descriptors.          */
                    /* Initializes the additional device registers in modes: */
                    /* (R)MII mode / PHY bus type.                           */
                    /* Disables device interrupts.                           */
                    /* Disables device receiver and transmitter.             */
                    /* Any other necessary device initialization.            */
}
```

The arguments are:

▧ **pif**: Pointer to the interface requiring service.

▧ **perr**: Pointer to return error code.

A-6 NetDev_Start()

The function NetDev_Start() is defined in net_dev_lm3s9bxx.c. The function starts network interface hardware and its prototype is shown below:

```
static   void   NetDev_Start (NET_IF   *pif,
                              NET_ERR  *perr)
{
                              /* Initializes the transmit semaphore count.       */
                              /* Initializes the hardware address registers.     */
                              /* Initializes the receive and transmit descriptors. */
                              /* Clears all pending interrupt sources.           */
                              /* Enables the supported interrupts.               */
                              /* Enables the transmitter and receiver.           */
                              /* Starts / Enables DMA.                           */
}
```

The arguments are:

- **pif**: Pointer to the interface requiring service.

- **perr**: Pointer to return error code.

A-7 NetDev_Stop()

The function **NetDev_Stop()** is defined in **net_dev_lm3s9bxx.c**. The function shuts down the network interface hardware and its prototype is shown below:

```
static  void  NetDev_Stop (NET_IF   *pif,
                           NET_ERR  *perr)
{
                     /* Disables the receiver and transmitter.              */
                     /* Disables receive and transmit interrupts.           */
                     /* Clears pending interrupt requests.                  */
                     /* Flushes FIFOs, if applicable.                       */
                     /* Frees all receive descriptors (Returns ownership to hw). */
                     /* Deallocates all transmit buffers.                   */
}
```

The arguments are:

- **pif**: Pointer to the interface requiring service.

- **perr**: Pointer to return error code.

A-8 NetDev_Rx()

The function NetDev_Rx() is defined in net_dev_lm3s9bxx.c. The function returns a pointer to the received data to the caller:

```
static   void  NetDev_Rx (NET_IF       *pif,
                          CPU_INT08U  **p_data,
                          CPU_INT16U   *size,
                          NET_ERR       *perr)
{
                  /* Determine which receive descriptor caused the interrupt.   */
                  /* Obtain pointer in data area to replace existing data area. */
                  /* Reconfigure descriptor with pointer to new data area.      */
                  /* Set return values. Pointer to received data area and size. */
                  /* Update current receive descriptor pointer.                 */
                  /* Increment counters.                                        */
}
```

The arguments are:

- **pif**: Pointer to the interface requiring service.

- **p_data**: Pointer to pointer to received DMA data area. The received data area address should be returned to the stack by dereferencing p_data as *p_data = (address of receive data area).

- **size**: Pointer to size. The number of bytes received should be returned to the stack by dereferencing size as *size = (number of bytes).

- **perr**: Pointer to return error code.

A-9 NetDev_Tx()

The function `NetDev_Tx()` is defined in **net_dev_lm3s9bxx.c**. The function transmits the specified data and its prototype is shown below:

```
static  void  NetDev_Tx (NET_IF      *pif,
                         CPU_INT08U  **p_data,
                         CPU_INT16U  *size,
                         NET_ERR     *perr)
{
                         /* Check if the transmitter is ready.                      */
                         /* Configure the next transmit descriptor for pointer to data */
                         /* and data size.                                         */
                         /* Issue the transmit command.                            */
                         /* Increment pointer to next transmit descriptor.         */
}
```

The arguments are:

- **pif**: Pointer to the interface requiring service.

- **p_data**: Pointer to pointer to transmitted DMA data area. The transmitted data area address should be returned to the stack by dereferencing p_data as *p_data = (address of transmit data area).

- **size**: Pointer to size. The number of bytes transmitted should be returned to the stack by dereferencing size as *size = (number of bytes).

- **perr**: Pointer to return error code.

A-10 NetDev_RxDescFreeAll()

The function **NetDev_RxDescFreeAll()** is defined in **net_dev_lm3s9bxx.c**. The function returns the descriptor memory block and descriptor data area memory blocks back to their respective memory pools and its prototype is shown below:

```
static  void  NetDev_RxDescFreeAll (NET_IF   *pif,
                                    NET_ERR  *perr)
{
                            /* Free Rx descriptor data areas.                */
                            /* Return data area to Rx data area pool.        */
                            /* Free Rx descriptor memory block.              */
                            /* Free Rx descriptor block to Rx descriptor pool. */
}
```

The arguments are:

▧   **pif**: Pointer to the interface requiring service.

▧   **perr**: Pointer to return error code.

A-11 NetDev_RxDescInit()

The function `NetDev_RxDescInit()` is defined in **net_dev_lm3s9bxx.c**. The function initializes the Rx descriptor list for the specified interface and its prototype is shown below:

```
static void NetDev_RxDescInit (NET_IF   *pif,
                               NET_ERR  *perr)
{
                            /* Obtain reference to the Rx descriptor(s) memory block.*/
                            /* Initialize Rx descriptor pointers.                    */
                            /* Obtain Rx descriptor data areas.                      */
                            /* Initialize hardware registers by configuring the DMA  */
                            /* engine with the Rx descriptor start address, by       */
                            /* setting the maximum receive buffer size and by        */
                            /* configuring the DMA descriptor ring start address.    */
}
```

The arguments are:

- **pif**: Pointer to the interface requiring service.

- **perr**: Pointer to return error code.

Memory allocation for the descriptors and receive buffers *must* be performed *before* calling this function. This ensures that multiple calls to this function do *not* allocate additional memory to the interface and that the Rx descriptors may be safely re-initialized by calling this function.

A-12 NetDev_RxDescPtrCurInc()

The function **NetDev_RxDescPtrCurInc()** is defined in **net_dev_lm3s9bxx.c**. The function increments the current descriptor pointer to the next receive descriptor and its prototype is shown below:

```
static  void  NetDev_RxDescPtrCurInc (NET_IF *pif)
{
                    /* Return ownership of current descriptor back to DMA.      */
                    /* Point to the next descriptor.                            */
}
```

The only argument is:

- **pif**: Pointer to the interface requiring service.

A-13 NetDev_TxDescInit()

The function **NetDev_TxDescInit()** is defined in **net_dev_lm3s9bxx.c**. The function initializes the Tx descriptor list for the specified interface and its prototype is shown below:

```
static  void  NetDev_TxDescInit (NET_IF   *pif,
                                 NET_ERR  *perr)
{
                    /* Obtain reference to the Tx descriptor(s) memory block. */
                    /* Initialize Tx descriptor pointers.                     */
                    /* Obtain Tx descriptor data areas.                       */
                    /* Initialize hardware registers.                         */
}
```

The arguments are:

- **pif**: Pointer to the interface requiring service.

- **perr**: Pointer to return error code.

A-14 NetDev_ISR_Handler()

The Ethernet Controller can generate an interrupt for one or more of the following conditions:

- A frame has been received into an empty Rx FIFO

- A frame transmission error has occurred

- A frame has been transmitted successfully

- A frame has been received with inadequate room in the Rx FIFO (overrun)

- A frame has been received with one or more error conditions (for example, FCS failed)

- An MII management transaction between the MAC and PHY layers has completed

- One or more of the following PHY layer conditions occurs:

  - Auto-Negotiate Complete

  - Remote Fault

  - Link Partner Acknowledge

  - Parallel Detect Fault

  - Page Received

As we previously discussed in section A-3-2 "DMA" on page 1149, the DMA engine is responsible for updating the Tx and Rx Buffer Descriptors every time a frame has been transmitted or received.

In the case of receptions, the Stellaris Ethernet Controller' MAC generates a Packet Received interrupt (RXINT). This indicates that at least one packet has been received. Software can use the MACNP register to determine if more than one packet is present in the receive FIFO.

In the case of transmissions, the MAC generates a FIFO empty interrupt (TXEMP) that indicates the transmit packet was transmitted and the FIFO is ready for the next packet.

The function **NetDev_ISR_Handler()** handles such interrupts. The function is defined in **net_dev_lm3s9bxx.c** and its prototype is shown below:

```
static  void  NetDev_ISR_Handler (NET_IF           *pif,
                                  NET_DEV_ISR_TYPE  type)
{
                                /* Handle Reception Interrupts.                */
    if (EDMAC_EESR[FR]) {
                                /* Signal the network interface (IF) receive task of a */
                                /* received packet.                            */
                                /* Clear the interrupt.                        */
    }

                                /* Handle Transmission Interrupts.             */
    if (EDMAC_EESR[TC]) {
                                /* Post each descriptor data area address to the  */
                                /* transmit deallocation task.                 */
                                /* Signal the network interface (IF) that the device  */
                                /* transmit is ready.                          */
                                /* Point to the next buffer descriptor and wrap around */
                                /* the end of the descriptors list if necessary.  */
                                /* Clear the interrupt.                        */
    }
}
```

The arguments are:

- **pif**: Pointer to the interface requiring service.

- **type**: Network Interface defined argument representing the type of ISR in progress. Codes for Rx, Tx, Overrun, Jabber, etc... are defined within net_if.h and are passed into this function by the corresponding Net BSP ISR handler function. The Net BSP ISR handler function may be called by a specific ISR vector and therefore know which ISR type code to pass. Otherwise, the Net BSP may pass **NET_DEV_ISR_TYPE_UNKNOWN** and the device driver MAY ignore the parameter when the ISR type can be deduced by reading an available interrupt status register.

The **NetDev_ISR_Handler()** function is called by name from the context of an ISR. This ISR handler must service and clear all necessary and enabled interrupt events for the device.

In the case of an interrupt occurring prior to Network Protocol Stack initialization, the device driver should ensure that the interrupt source is cleared in order to prevent the potential for an infinite interrupt loop during system initialization.

Many DMA devices generate only one interrupt event for several ready receive descriptors. In order to accommodate this, it is recommended that all DMA based drivers count the number of ready receive descriptors during the receive event and signal the receive task for ONLY newly received descriptors which have not yet been signaled for during the last receive interrupt event.

Many DMA devices generate only one interrupt event for several transmit complete descriptors. In this case, the driver MUST determine which descriptors have completed transmission and post each descriptor data area address to the transmit deallocation task.

A-15 NetDev_IO_Ctrl()

The **NetDev_IO_Ctrl()** function is defined in **net_dev_lm3s9bxx.c**. Its prototype is below:

```
static  void  NetDev_IO_Ctrl (NET_IF      *pif,
                              CPU_INT08U   opt,
                              void        *p_data,
                              NET_ERR     *perr)
{
    .
    .
    .
}
```

The arguments are:

- **pif**: Pointer to the interface requiring service.

- **opt**: Option code representing desired function to perform.

- **data**: Pointer to optional data for either sending or receiving additional function arguments or return data.

- **perr**: Pointer to return error code.

The `NetDev_IO_Ctrl()` function provides a mechanism for the PHY driver to update the MAC link and duplex settings, as well as a method for the application and link state timer to obtain the current link status. Additional user specified driver functionality may be added, if necessary. Micrium provides an IO control function template since most of the code is re-usable.

This function's most important task is to execute the code within the `NET_IF_IO_CTRL_LINK_STATE_UPDATE` switch block. This particular IO control functionality is exercised whenever a link state change is detected either via interrupt or `NetTmr` task polling. Some MACs require software to set registers indicating the current PHY link speed and duplex. This information is used by the MAC to compute critical network access timing.

If link state update functionality is not properly implemented, erratic network behavior will likely result when operating at various combinations of link speed and duplex.

A-16 NetDev_AddrMultiCastAdd()

The `NetDev_AddrMultiCastAdd()` function is defined in `net_dev_lm3s9bxx.c` and its prototype is shown below:

```
static  void  NetDev_AddrMulticastAdd (NET_IF      *pif,
                                       CPU_INT08U  *paddr_hw,
                                       CPU_INT08U   addr_hw_len,
                                       NET_ERR     *perr)
{
    .
    .
    .
}
```

The arguments are:

▨ **pif**: Pointer to the interface requiring service.

▨ **paddr_hw**: Pointer to hardware address.

▨ **addr_hw_len**: Length of hardware address.

▨ **perr**: Pointer to return error code.

The **NetDev_AddrMultiCastAdd()** function configures the hardware address filtering to accept a specified hardware address.

The following code snippet may be added to **app.c** after network initialization to generate a call to **NetDev_AddrMulticastAdd()**:

```
NET_ERR       err;
NET_IP_ADDR   ip;
NET_IF_NBR    if_nbr;
...
if_nbr = 1;
ip = NetASCII_Str_to_IP("224.0.0.1", &err);
ip = NET_UTIL_HOST_TO_NET_32(ip);
NetIF_AddrMulticastAdd(if_nbr,
                      (CPU_INT08U *)&ip,
                      (CPU_SIZE_T )sizeof(ip),
                       NET_PROTOCOL_TYPE_IP_V4,
                      &err);
```

The Ethernet device driver for the Texas Instruments LM3S9B92 is capable of the following multicast address filtering techniques:

- Perfect filtering of ONE multicast address.

- Imperfect hash filtering of 64 multicast addresses.

- Promiscuous non-filtering. Disable filtering of all received frames.

This function for the LM3S9B92 implements the imperfect hash filtering of 64 multicast addresses mechanism.

A-17 NetDev_AddrMultiCastRemove()

The NetDev_AddrMultiCastRemove() function is defined in net_dev_lm3s9bxx.c and its prototype is shown below:

```
static  void  NetDev_AddrMulticastRemove (NET_IF      *pif,
                                          CPU_INT08U  *paddr_hw,
                                          CPU_INT08U   addr_hw_len,
                                          NET_ERR     *perr)
{
    .
    .
    .
}
```

The arguments are:

■ **pif**: Pointer to the interface requiring service.

■ **paddr_hw**: Pointer to hardware address.

■ **addr_hw_len**: Length of hardware address.

■ **perr**: Pointer to return error code.

The NetDev_AddrMultiCastRemove() function configures hardware address filtering to reject a specified hardware address. See NetDev_AddrMulticastAdd(). Once NetDev_AddrMulticastAdd() has been verified, the code used to compute the hash may be reproduced for NetDev_AddrMulticastRemove(). The only difference between the functions is that NetDev_AddrMulticastRemove() decrements the hash bit reference counters and clears the hash filter register bits.

A-18 NetDev_MII_Rd()

The `NetDev_MII_Rd()` function is defined in `net_dev_lm3s9bxx.c` and its prototype is shown below:

```
static  void  NetDev_MII_Rd (NET_IF      *pif,
                             CPU_INT08U  phy_addr,
                             CPU_INT08U  reg_addr,
                             CPU_INT16U  *p_data,
                             NET_ERR     *perr)
{
    .
    .
    .
}
```

The arguments are:

■ **pif**: Pointer to the interface requiring service.

■ **phy_addr**: (R)MII bus address of the PHY requiring service.

■ **reg_addr**: PHY register number to read from.

■ **p_data**: Pointer to variable to store returned register data.

■ **perr**: Pointer to return error code.

The function `NetDev_MII_Rd()` is called by the PHY layer to configure physical layer device registers. This function may be copied from a template but will require changes to adapt it to your specific MAC device. The only recommendation for this function is to ensure that PHY operations are performed without a time-out and that an error is returned if a time-out occurs. A time-out may be implemented in the form of a simple loop that counts from 0 to `PHY_RD_TO`.

Should a timeout occur, software should return `NET_PHY_ERR_TIMEOUT_REG_RD`, otherwise `NET_PHY_ERR_NONE`.

A-19 NetDev_MII_Wr()

The NetDev_MII_Wr() function is defined in **net_dev_lm3s9bxx.c** and its prototype is shown below:

```
static  void  NetDev_MII_Wr (NET_IF       *pif,
                             CPU_INT08U   phy_addr,
                             CPU_INT08U   reg_addr,
                             CPU_INT16U   data,
                             NET_ERR      *perr)
{
    .
    .
    .
}
```

The arguments are:

- **pif**: Pointer to the interface requiring service.

- **phy_addr**: (R)MII bus address of the PHY requiring service.

- **reg_addr**: PHY register number to write to.

- **data**: Data to write to the specified PHY register.

- **perr**: Pointer to return error code.

The function **NetDev_MII_Wr()** is called by the PHY layer to configure physical layer device registers. This function may be copied from a template but will require changes to adapt it to your specific MAC device. The only recommendation for this function is to ensure that PHY operations are performed without a time-out and that an error is returned if a time-out occurs. A time-out may be implemented in the form of a simple loop that counts from 0 to **PHY_WR_TO**.

Should a time-out occur, software should return **NET_PHY_ERR_TIMEOUT_REG_WR**, otherwise **NET_PHY_ERR_NONE**.

B

IAR Systems IAR Embedded Workbench for ARM

IAR Embedded Workbench is a set of highly sophisticated and easy-to-use development tools for embedded applications. It integrates the IAR C/C++ Compiler™, assembler, linker, librarian, text editor, project manager and C-SPY® Debugger in an integrated development environment (IDE).

With its built-in chip-specific code optimizer, IAR Embedded Workbench generates very efficient and reliable FLASH/ROMable code for ARM devices. In addition to this solid technology, the IAR Systems also provides professional world-wide technical support.

The KickStart™ edition of IAR Embedded Workbench is free of charge and you may use it for as long as you want. KickStart tools are ideal for creating small applications, or for getting started fast on a new project. The only requirement is that you register to obtain a license key.

The KickStart edition is code-size limited, but a fully functional integrated development environment that includes a project manager, editor, compiler, assembler, linker, librarian, and debugger tools. A complete set of user guides is included in PDF format.

The KickStart edition corresponds to the latest release of the full edition of IAR Embedded Workbench, with the following exceptions:

- It has a code size limitation (32 Kbytes).

- It does not include source code for runtime libraries.

- It does not include support for MISRA C.

- There is limited technical support.

The KickStart edition of IAR Embedded Workbench allows you to run all of the examples provided in this book.

B-1 IAR EMBEDDED WORKBENCH FOR ARM – HIGHLIGHTS

The full version of the IAR Embedded Workbench for ARM offers the following features.

- Support for:

  - ARM7™

  - ARM9™

  - ARM9E™

  - ARM10™

  - ARM11

  - SecurCore

  - Cortex-M0

  - Cortex-M1

  - Cortex-M

  - Cortex-R4

  - Intel® XScale™

- Most compact and efficient code

- ARM Embedded Application Binary Interface (EABI)

- Extensive support for hardware and RTOS-aware debugging

- Total solutions for ARM

- New Cortex-M3 debug features

- Function profiler

- Interrupt graph window

- Data log window

- MISRA C:2004 support

- Extensive device support

- Over 1400 example projects

- µC/OS-II Kernel Awareness built-into the C-Spy debugger

Figure B-1 shows a block diagram of the major EWARM components.

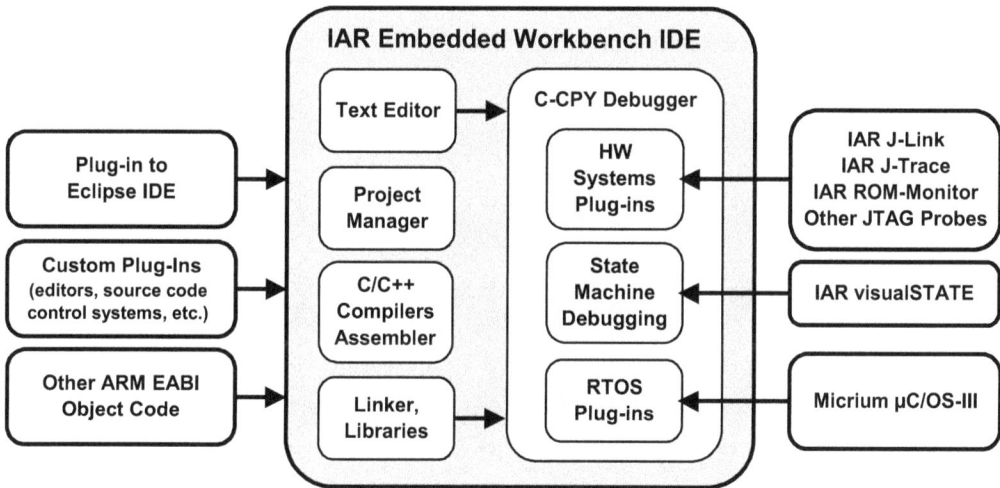

Figure B-1 **IAR Embedded Workbench**

B-2 MODULAR AND EXTENSIBLE IDE

- A seamlessly Integrated Development Environment (IDE) for building and debugging embedded applications

- Powerful project management allowing multiple projects in one workspace

- Build integration with IAR visualSTATE

- Hierarchical project representation

- Dockable and floating windows management

- Smart source browser

- Tool options configurable globally, on groups of source files, or individual source files

- Multi-file compilation support for even better code optimization

- Flexible project building via batch build, pre/post-build or custom build with access to external tools in the build process.

- Integration with source code control systems

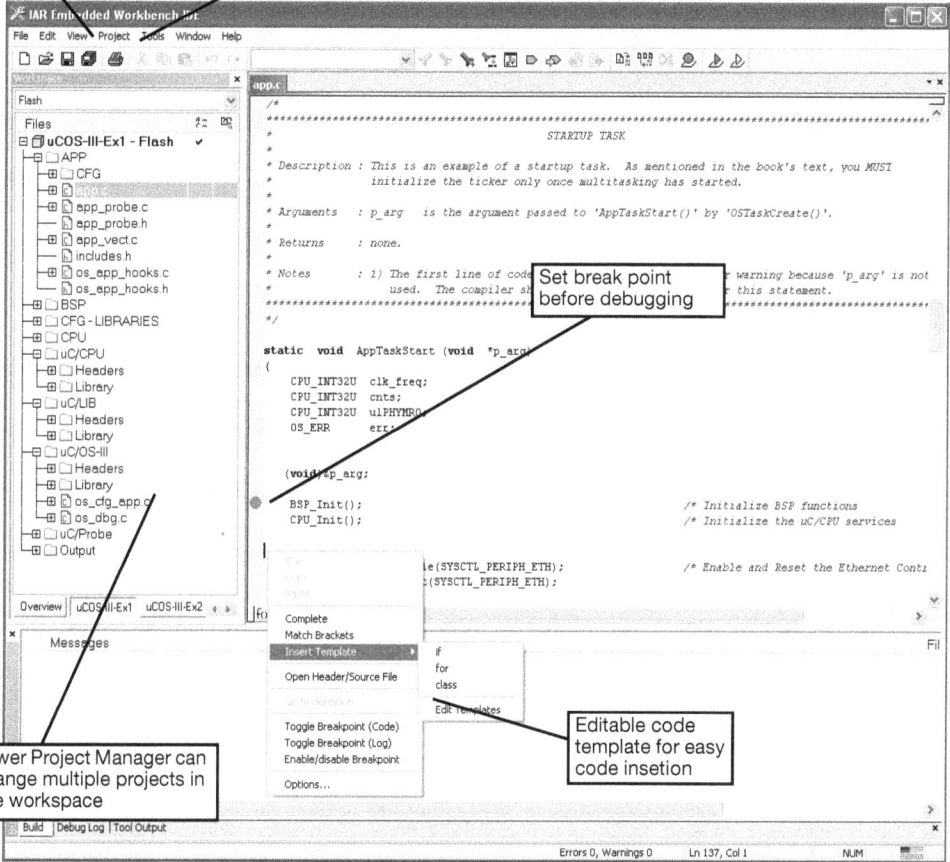

Figure B-2 **IAR Embedded Workbench IDE**

B-3 HIGHLY OPTIMIZING C/C++ COMPILER

■ Support for C, EC++ and extended EC++ including templates, namespace, standard template library (STL) etc.

■ ARM Embedded Application Binary Interface (EABI) and ARM Cortex Microcontroller Software Interface Standard (CMSIS) compliant

■ Interoperability and binary compatibility with other EABI compliant tools

1175

■ Automatic checking of MISRA C rules

■ Support for ARM, Thumb1 and Thumb2 processor modes

■ Support for 4 Gbyte applications in all processor modes

■ Support for 64-bit long

■ Reentrant code

■ 32- and 64-bit floating-point types in standard IEEE format

■ Multiple levels of optimizations on code size and execution speed allowing different transformations enabled, such as function inlining, loop unrolling etc.

■ Advanced global and target-specific optimizer generating the most compact and stable code

■ Compressed initializers

■ Support for ARM7, ARM7E, ARM9, ARM9E, ARM10E, ARM11, Cortex-M0, Cortex-M1, Cortex-M3, Cortex-R4 and Intel XScale

■ Support for ARM, Thumb1 and Thumb2 processor modes

■ Generates code for ARM VFP series of floating-point coprocessors

■ Little/big endian mode

B-4 DEVICE SUPPORT

Device support on five levels:

■ Core support - instruction set, debugger interface (for all supported devices)

■ Header/DDF files - peripheral register names in C/asm source and debugger (for all supported devices)

- Flash loader for on-chip flash or off-chip EVB flash (for most of our supported devices)

- Project examples - varies from simple to fairly complex applications (for most of our supported devices)

- Detailed device support list at www.iar.com/ewarm

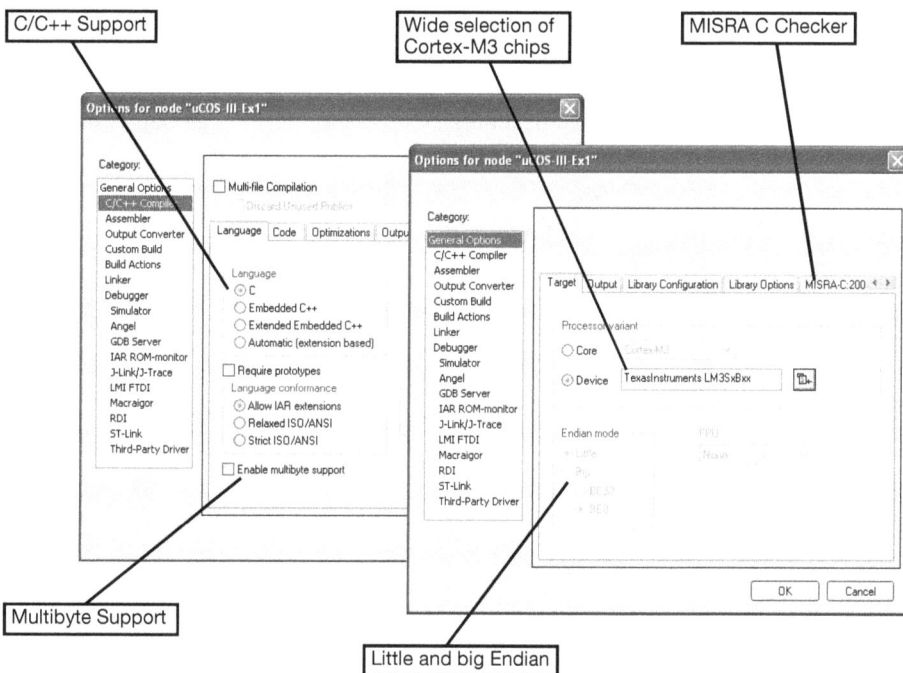

Figure B-3 **Device Support**

B-5 STATE-OF-THE-ART C-SPY® DEBUGGER

- Cortex-M3 SWV/SWO debugger support

- Complex code and data breakpoints

- User selectable breakpoint types (hardware/software)

- Unlimited number of breakpoints in flash via optional license for J-Link

■ Runtime stack analysis - stack window to monitor the memory consumption and integrity of the stack

■ Complete support for stack unwinding even at high optimization levels

■ Profiling and code coverage performance analysis tools

■ Trace utility with expressions, such as variables and register values, to examine execution history

■ Versatile monitoring of registers, structures, call chain, locals, global variables and peripheral registers

■ Smart STL container display in Watch window

■ Symbolic memory window and static watch window

■ I/O and interrupt simulation

■ True editing-while-debugging

■ Drag and drop model

■ Target access to host file system via file I/O

■ Built-in µC/OS-II Kernel Awareness

B-6 C-SPY DEBUGGER AND TARGET SYSTEM SUPPORT

The C-SPY Debugger for the ARM core is available with drivers for the following target systems:

■ Simulator

■ Emulator (JTAG/SWD)

■ IAR J-Link probe, JTAG and SWD support, connection via USB or TCP/IP server

- RDI (Remote Debug Interface), such as Abatron BDI1000 & BDI2000, EPI Majic, Ashling Opella, Aiji OpenICE, Signum JTAGjet, ARM Multi-ICE

- Macraigor JTAG interfaces: Macraigor Raven, Wiggler, mpDemon, usbDemon, usb2Demon and usb2Sprite

- ST ST-LINK JTAG debug probe

B-7 IAR ASSEMBLER

- A powerful relocating macro assembler with a versatile set of directives and operators

- Built-in C language preprocessor, accepting all C macro definitions

B-8 IAR J-LINK LINKER

- Complete linking, relocation and format generation to produce FLASH/PROMable code

- Flexible commands allowing detailed control of code and data placement

- Optimized linking removing unused code and data

- Direct linking of raw binary images, for instance multimedia files

- Comprehensive cross-reference and dependency memory maps

- Link compatibility with object files and libraries generated by other EABI compliant tools

B-9 IAR LIBRARY AND LIBRARY TOOLS

- All required ISO/ANSI C and C++ libraries and source included

- All low-level routines such as **writechar()** and **readchar()** provided in full source code

- Lightweight runtime library, user-configurable to match the needs of the application; full source included

- Library tools for creating and maintaining library projects, libraries and library modules

- Listings of entry points and symbolic information

B-10 COMPREHENSIVE DOCUMENTATION

- Efficient coding hints for embedded application

- Extensive step-by-step tutorials

- Context sensitive help and hypertext versions of the user documentation available online

B-11 FIRST CLASS TECHNICAL SUPPORT

IAR Systems has a global organization with local presence through branch offices and a worldwide distributor network. Extended, customized technical services are available.

Appendix

C

Bibliography

- *ARM® CoreSight Technical Reference Manual*

- *ARM® Cortex™M3 Technical Reference Manual*

- *Stellaris® LM3S9B92 Microcontroller Data Sheet*

- *Stellaris® LM3S9B92 Errata*

- *ARM® Cortex™-M3 Errata*

- *ARM® v7-M Architecture Application Level Reference Manual*

- *Stellaris® Boot Loader User's Guide*

- *Stellaris® Peripheral Driver Library User's Guide*

- *Stellaris® ROM User' Guide*

- *Stellaris® LM3S9B92 Microcontroller Data Sheet*

- *DRV8801RTY Data Sheet*, Literature Number SLVA322
  Full bridge motor driver

- *TLV320AIC3107 Data Sheet*, Literature Number SLOS545
  Low-power Stereo Codec with Integrated Mono Class-D Speaker Amplifier

- *TLV70018 Data Sheet*, Literature Number SLVSA00
  200-mA, Low-I_Q, Low-Dropout Regulator for Portable Devices

- *TLV70033 Data Sheet*, Literature Number SLVSA00
  200-mA, Low-IQ, Low-Dropout Regulator for Portable Devices

- *TPS71501 Data Sheet*, Literature Number SLVS338
  50mA, 24V, 3.2-μA Supply Current, Low-Dropout Linear Regulator in SC70 Package

- *TPS61085 Data Sheet*, Literature Number SLVS859
  18.5V, 2A, 650kHz, 1.2MHz Step-Up DC-DC Converter with Forced PWM Mode

- *TS3USB30 Data Sheet*, Literature Number SCDS237
  High-Speed USB 2.0 (480 Mbps) 1:2 Multiplexer/Demultiplexer Switch With Single Enable

- *TPS2113 Data Sheet*, Literature Number SLVS446
  Dual In/Single Out Autoswitching Power MUX

- *TPS61073 Data Sheet*, Literature Number SLVS510
  Adjustable, 600-mA Switch, 90% Efficient PFM/PWM Boost Converter in ThinSOT-23

The following data sheets can be obtained from the manufacturer:

- *P13701 OLED Display Data Sheet* from RiT Display Corporation

- *SSD1300 OLED Controller Data Sheet* from Solomon Systech Limited

µC/OS-III and µC/TCP-IP Licensing Policy

D-1 µC/OS-III AND µC/TCP-IP LICENSING

This book includes µC/OS-III in source form for free short-term evaluation, for educational use or for peaceful research. We provide ALL the source code for your convenience and to help you experience µC/OS-III. The fact that the source is provided does NOT mean that you can use it commercially without paying a licensing fee. Knowledge of the source code may NOT be used to develop a similar product either. The book also includes µC/TCP-IP precompiled in linkable object form.

The reader can purchase the Texas Instruments Stellaris® EVALBOT separately from TI and may use µC/OS-III and µC/TCP-IP with the Stellaris® EVALBOT. It is not necessary to purchase anything else, as long as the initial purchase is used for educational purposes. Once the code is used to create a commercial project/product for profit, however, it is necessary to purchase a license.

It is necessary to purchase this license when the decision to use µC/OS-III and/or µC/TCP-IP in a design is made, not when the design is ready to go to production.

If you are unsure about whether you need to obtain a license for your application, please contact Micriµm and discuss the intended use with a sales representative.

D-2 µC/TCP-IP MAINTENANCE RENEWAL

Licensing µC/TCP-IP provides one year of limited technical support and maintenance and source code updates. Renew the maintenance agreement for continued support and source code updates. Contact sales@Micrium.com for additional information.

D-3 µC/TCP-IP SOURCE CODE UPDATES

If you are under maintenance, you will be automatically emailed when source code updates become available. You can then download your available updates from the Micriµm FTP server. If you are no longer under maintenance, or forget your Micriµm FTP username or password, please contact sales@Micrium.com.

D-4 µC/TCP-IP SUPPORT

Support is available for licensed customers. Please visit the customer support section in www.Micrium.com. If you are not a current user, please register to create your account. A web form will be offered to you to submit your support question,

Licensed customers can also use the following contact:

CONTACT MICRIUM

Micriµm
1290 Weston Road, Suite 306
Weston, FL 33326

+1 954 217 2036
+1 954 217 2037 (FAX)

E-Mail: sales@Micriµm.com
Website: www.Micriµm.com

Index

Z

Micrium

Index

Stellaris®

Connected. Versatile. Cost-effective.

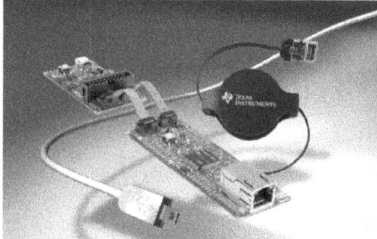

**Stellaris LM3S9B90
Ethernet Evaluation Kit**

featuring USB, Ethernet
and CAN

$99

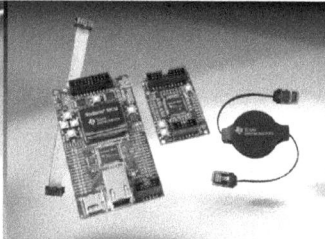

**Stellaris LM3S8962
Evaluation Kit**

featuring integrated Ethernet
and CAN

$89

**Stellaris LM3S3748
Evaluation Kit**

featuring USB Host/Device

$109

Stellaris® Means:

- Deterministic ARM® Cortex™-M3 cores
- Real-time multi-tasking MCUs
- Advanced interrupt-driven software with Stellarisware® software

**Stellaris LM3S6965
Ethernet Evaluation Kit**

demonstrating an embedded
web server out-of-the-box

$69

**Stellaris LM3S811
Evaluation Kit**

featuring basic embedded
control

$49

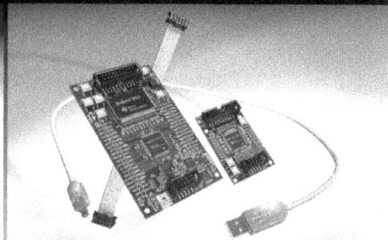

**Stellaris LM3S2965 CAN
Evaluation Kit**

demonstrating a CAN network
out-of-the-box

$79

TEXAS INSTRUMENTS

1197